Fear, Avoidance and Phobias

A Fundamental Analysis

Fear, Avoidance, and Phobias

A Fundamental Analysis

Edited by
M. Ray Denny
Michigan State University

LEA
1991

LAWRENCE ERLBAUM ASSOCIATES, PUBLISHERS
Hillsdale, New Jersey   Hove and London

Lawrence Erlbaum Associates, Inc., Publishers
365 Broadway
Hillsdale, New Jersey 07642

Library of Congress Cataloging-in-Publication Data

Fear, avoidance, and phobias : a fundamental analysis / edited by M.
Ray Denny.
   p. cm.
   Includes bibliographical references and indexes.
   ISBN 0-8058-0316-5 (cloth).—ISBN 0-8058-0317-3 (pbk.)
   1. Fear. 2. Avoidance (Psychology) 3. Aversive stimuli.
4. Phobias. 5. Neurophysiology. I. Denny, M. Ray (Maurice Ray).
BF575.F2F39   1990
152.4'6—dc20
                                        90-43393
                                            CIP

Printed in the United States of America
10 9 8 7 6 5 4 3 2 1

To all my former students, however it might apply.

Contents

Preface

There has not been a comprehensive coverage of the field of aversive events and behavior since the publication of F. R. Brush's edited book *Aversive Conditioning and Learning* in 1971, with a dozen contributors, and Campbell and Church's edited book *Punishment and Aversive Behavior*, 1969. This large, complex, interesting, and important area has been brought up to date and expanded in the present volume. Here, new phenomena, like conditioned analgesia, are wrestled with theoretically; and old phenomena that have remained fairly intransigent, even after many more data have accrued, are reanalyzed.

The field is especially important because it provides basic data and theory for potentially solving many of the behavior problems that beset human beings. Much of clinical psychology (anxiety, phobias, neuroses, etc.), and much that related to aggression and conflict resolution have their roots in the topics of this book. And at least 2 of the chapters deal with direct applications of the basic material to problems that torment humans. The remaining 10 chapters constitute a broad coverage of a critical area by a group of competent, recognized investigators.

This coverage includes an original and extensive neurophysiological theory of fear; an analysis of avoidance learning by means of a computer-based model that shows considerable analytical promise; relatively new and convincing interpretations of learned helplessness and self-punitive behavior; several rebuttals of the notion that avoidance can occur without fear, which in one case sheds new light on the concept of conditioned inhibition; a critical review of the memory of aversive events; plus a good deal more.

M. Ray Denny
East Lansing, Michigan

Contributors

Bruce Abbott, Department of Psychological Sciences, Indiana University/ Purdue University at Fort Wayne.

Loring Crepeau, Department of Psychology, Bowling Green State University.

Helen B. Daly, Department of Psychology, State University of New York at Oswego.

John T. Daly, Department of Psychology, State University of New York at Oswego.

Sanford Dean, Psychology Department, Northern Illinois University.

Dennis Delprato, Department of Psychology, Eastern Michigan University.

M. Ray Denny, Department of Psychology, Michigan State University.

Nancy K. Dess, Department of Psychology, Occidental College.

Paul L. DeVito, Department of Psychology, St. Joseph's University.

Michael S. Fanselow, Department of Psychology, University of California at Los Angeles.

Harry Fowler, Department of Psychology, University of Pittsburgh.

Donald J. Levis, Department of Psychology, State University of New York at Binghamton.

Donald T. Lysle, Department of Psychology, University of Pittsburgh.

Dorothy E. McAllister, Department of Psychology, Northern Illinois University.

Wallace R. McAllister, Department of Psychology, Northern Illinois University.

Thomas R. Minor, Psychology Department, University of California at Los Angeles.

J. Bruce Overmier, Department of Psychology, University of Minnesota.

Jaak Panksepp, Department of Psychology, Bowling Green State University.

Catherine M. Pittman, Department of Psychology, Saint Mary's College.

David C. Riccio, Department of Psychology, Kent State University.

Kenneth W. Rusiniak, Department of Psychology, Eastern Michigan University.

David S. Sacks, Department of Psychology, Bowling Green State University.

Norman E. Spear, Department of Psychology, State University of New York at Binghamton.

Thomas G. Stampfl, Department of Psychology, University of Wisconsin at Milwaukee.

PROLEGOMENON: On the Study of Aversively Motivated Behavior

J. Bruce Overmier
University of Minnesota

In 1898, the comparative psychologist E. L. Thorndike enunciated the Laws of Effect, specifying the conditions under which learning of instrumental acts would take place. According to these laws, acts followed by "satisfyers" would become strengthened and those followed by "annoyers" would be weakened. That the removal or presentation of aversive events can control behavior of animals and humans can hardly be claimed as a new discovery by psychologists. Indeed, hedonistic principles were formally incorporated into natural philosophy as early as 300 B.C. by Epicurus and have been reiterated intermittently since then. Moreover, throughout history these principles have been used informally in the handling and training of our beasts of burden, the raising of our children ("spare the rod and spoil the child"), and indeed, the regulation of our fellow citizens (e.g., Woffenstein, 1953).

Why then is there a need to study the aversive control of behavior formally? Because pleasing events also have long been used informally in the same settings, we could similarly ask "Why is there a need to study the appetitive control of behavior formally?"—but we rarely do ask that question. There is a need to study both to come to understand the laws according to which and the mechanisms by which such control over behavior is exerted (e.g., Rachlin & Herrnstein, 1969). We both want and need to know how much of the behavior is (a) attributable to the eliciting, motivational, and associative learning properties of these events, (b) the relative efficacy of such events in these aspects of behavior control, and (c) the collateral consequences of using such events in learning paradigms.

1

Hundreds of volumes of study have in fact been devoted to the study of "satisfyers," appetitive events, and rewards. Although we now know a great deal, we are still discovering new principles (e.g. Sidman, Kirk, & Willson–Morris, 1985; Trapold, 1970) of both theoretical and applied importance (e.g., Dube et al., 1987). Due to the natural sensitivities of experimental psychologists (and wide promulgation of a few unsubstantiated myths about the ineffectiveness of punishment for learning, e.g., Skinner, 1938; Thorndike, 1931) very much less research—perhaps 80% less—has addressed the functional properties of "annoyers," aversive events, and punishers (Overmier & Archer, 1989). Hence, we still have much more to learn.

This general failure to study aversively based learning fully is especially surprising, given that much of the emotional and behavioral dysfunction (e.g., neuroses, phobias, depression) we see in the world around us has been attributed either to the occurence of aversively based learning (e.g. Marks, 1969; Masserman, 1943; Liddell, 1956) or to failure to learn in aversive contexts (Engel & Schmale, 1972; Seligman, 1975). Even disease resistance and susceptibility are attributed to such learning or failures to learn (Ader, 1981; Eysenck, 1987). Moreover, the studies of aversively based learning which model human dysfunction have in fact provided bases for substantial therapies (e.g. Levis, 1970; Wolpe, 1962) and raised important new questions about both psychological functioning (Kamin, 1968; Miller, 1969; Mineka & Kihlstrom, 1978) and its relation to physiological functioning (Fanselow, 1985; Gray, 1981; Liebeskind & Paul, 1977; Maier, Laudenslager, & Ryan, 1985).

It is exactly because of these successes—and others—that there is now increasing scientific interest in the study of aversive learning in animals. The hope is both to increase our basic understanding *and* to develop animal models of psychobiological function and dysfunction (Keehn, 1979; Maser & Seligman, 1977; Mineka, 1985; Overmier & Hellhammer, 1988; Serban & Kling, 1976). The efforts to develop animal models of human dysfunction have been roundly criticized by groups opposing research with animals (Kuker–Reines, 1982; Pratt, 1980) claiming "irrelevance" or "nongeneralizability" beyond the particular animal species studied. Unfortunately, these widely read popular criticisms fail to grasp fully the nature and functions of the modeling process (Calabrese, 1983; Fox, 1986; Henn, Johnson, Edwards, & Anderson, 1985; Overmier & Patterson, 1988; Rowan, 1984; Willner, 1986).

Nonetheless, these antiresearch criticisms are having chilling effects (Verhetsel, 1986) and are counterproductively limiting research through legislation (Rogers, 1986). These critics seek to *abolish* by legislation physical and psychological pain as an object of research. Moreover, these critics argue (e.g., Regan, 1983, p. 388) that humans have no basic right *not* to be harmed by "natural diseases." But we DO have the right to defend ourselves to the best of our scientific abilities against diseases and disorders that impair our physical and cognitive functioning. Such self-defense is part of the continuing struggle for existence that is the prime natural law of all life (Dawkins, 1976; McCabe, 1986; Spencer, 1897) and justifies our experiments with animals (Bernard, 1957/1865). And, it is now apparent that research on aversively motivated behavior is yielding scientific insights into psychobiological processes of applied value in helping those who must cope with stress and pain (e.g., Weiss, Herd, & Fox, 1981).

Most commonly, laboratory studies of aversively motivated behavior use electrocutaneous stimuli, which are referred to as "shocks" in the vernacular.

The electrocutaneous stimuli used in most behavioral experiments activate primarily the fast A fibers. At accepted values, then, these cutaneous electrical shocks fool the animal into responding *as if* it were in immanent danger of tissue damage with the consequent activation of appropriate behavioral and emotional systems to respond to this threat. It is the ability to elicit *these* responses to physical threat, but *without* any genuine *danger* of tissue damage that has led to the widespread use of electrical shocks in the study of pain and its behavioral, physiological, and psychological consequences.

It is sometimes argued that electrical shocks are so "unnatural" as to be useful only to the merely curious. Those making such a claim have never touched an electric ray (as described by Aristotle in *Historia Animalium*) or other electric fish or eels; electrical shocks do occur in nature! Although not "natural," we also commonly use electrical fences and devices to control livestock on farms.

In that rural context, there also occurs another phenomenon, attributable to the many motors used on modern farms: "stray voltage" shocks. This so-called "stray voltage" produces accidental shocks to animals as they enter barns, drink from water troughs, and so on; these shocks cause significant reductions in animal productivity (Norell, Gustafson, Appleman, & Overmier, 1983; Obst, 1982).

Importantly, we might consider whether electrical shocks mimic in function the effects of "natural" pain stimulations. When a strange rat intrudes into the warren of a colony of other rats, it is attacked and bitten, presumably eliciting pain along with squealing and flight; re-entries may be attempted with the usual consequence of defeat. Such defeated rats when subsequently tested show reduced open-field behavior and impaired FR-2 shuttle-box escape learning—a pattern of consequences that is exactly duplicated by giving a rat a series of relatively brief uncontrollable electric shocks rather than the natural bites (Williams & Lierle, 1988). So, electric shocks do mimic some natural sources of pain and do so without the risk of tissue damage and permanent injury inherent in such natural events.

Most importantly, we must note that the principles and processes discovered in research on aversively motivated behaviors using electric shock appear to be of great generality and apply to human function and learning motivated by other kinds of aversive events. Discussions and illustrations of this generalizability are provided in reviews by Arvey and Ivancevch (1980), Gray (1981), Mineka (1985), Seligman (1975), and Turkkan (1989), among others. Indeed, today's most common therapy for phobias that has provided relief for so many hundred thousands of patients is based upon exactly such animal research using electric shocks (Wolpe, 1962). Even so, we still have much more progress ahead of us as we discover the extensions of the newly emerging basic research findings.

The use of electric shocks in the study of aversively motivated behavior with animals provides a safe and effective way to model phenomena of psychological importance and to gain insight into the cognitive and emotional processes of animals and humans.

ACKNOWLEDGMENT

From a presentation at NIMH–NIDA Methods in Neuroscience Workshop December, 1987. Supported in part by grants to the Center for Research in Learning, Perception, and Cognition from N.I.C.H.D. and the Colleges of the University of Minnesota.

REFERENCES

Ader, R. (1981). *Psychoneuroimmunology*. New York: Academic Press.

Arvey, R. D., & Ivancevch, J. M. (1980). Punishment in organizations: A review, propositions and research suggestions. *Academy of Management Review, 5*, 123–132.

Bernard, C. (1957). *An introduction to the study of experimental medicine*. New York: Dover. (Translated from the original, 1865, by H. C. Greene)

Calabrese, E. J. (1983). *Principles of animal extrapolation*. New York: Wiley.

Dawkins, R. (1976). *The selfish gene*. New York: Oxford University Press.

Dube, W. V., McIlvance, W. J., Mackay, H. A., & Stoddard, L. T. (1987). Stimulus class membership established via stimulus-reinforcer relations (in mentally retarded adults). *Journal of the Experimental Analysis of Behavior, 47*, 159–175.

Engel, G. L., & Schmale, A. H. (1972). Conservation-withdrawal: A primary regulatory process for organismic homeostasis. In *Physiology, Emotions, and Psychosomatic Illness*, Ciba Foundation Symposium, No. 8. Amsterdam: Elsevier, pp. 57–85.

Eysenck, H. J. (1987). Anxiety, learned helplessness, and cancer: a causal theory. *Journal of Anxiety Disorders, 1*, 87–104.

Fanselow, M. S. (1985). Odors released by stressed rats produce opioid analygesia in unstressed rats. *Behavioral Neuroscience*, *99*, 589–592.

Fox, M. A. (1986). *The case for animal experimentation: An evolutionary and ethical perspective*. Berkeley: University of California Press.

Gray J. A. (1981). *The neuropsychology of anxiety*. Oxford, England: Oxford University Press.

Henn, F. A., Johnson, J. Edwards, E., & Anderson, D. (1985). Melancholia in rodents: Neurobiology and pharmacology. *Psychopharmacology Bulletin*, *21*, 443–446.

Kamin, L. (1968). Attention-like processes in classical conditioning. In M. R. Jones (Ed.), *Miami symposium on the prediction of behavior: Aversive stimulation*. Coral Gables, FL: University of Miami Press, pp. 9–31.

Keehn, J. D. (1979). *Psychopathology in animals*. New York: Academic Press.

Kuker–Reines, B. (1982). *Psychology experiments on animals*. Boston: New England Antivivisectionalist Society.

Levis, D. J. (1970). *Learning approaches to therapeutic behavior change*. Chicago: Aldine.

Liddell, H. S. (1956). *Emotional hazards in animals and man*. Springfield, IL: C. A. Thomas.

Liebeskind, J., & Paul, I. (1977). Psychological and physiological mechanisms of pain. *Annual Review of Psychology*, *28*, 41–60.

Maier, S. F., Laudenslager, M. L., & Ryan, S. M. (1985). Stressor controllability, immune function, and endogenous opiates. In F. R. Brush & J. B. Overmier (Eds.), *Affect, conditioning, and cognition*. Hillsdale, NJ: Lawrence Erlbaum Associates, pp. 183–210.

Marks, I. M. (1969). *Fears and phobias*. New York: Academic Press.

Maser, J. D., & Seligman, M. E. P. (1977). *Psychopathology: Experimental models*. San Francisco: Freeman.

Masserman, J. H. (1943). *Behaviour and neurosis*. Chicago: University of Chicago Press.

McCabe, K. (1986, August). Who will live, who will die. *Washingtonian Magazine*, p. 118.

Miller, N. E. (1969). Learning of visceral and glandular responses. *Science (NY)*, *163*, 434–445.

Mineka, S. (1985). Animal models of anxiety-based disorders: Their usefulness and limitations. In A. H. Tuma & J. D. Maser (Eds.). *Anxiety and the anxiety disorders*. Hillsdale, NJ: Lawrence Erlbaum Associates, pp. 199–259.

Mineka, S., & Kihlstrom, J. (1978). Unpredictable and uncontrollable aversive events. *Journal of Abnormal Psychology*, *87*, 256–271.

Norell, R. J., Gustafson, R. J., Appleman, R. D., & Overmier, J. B. (1983). Behavioral studies of dairy cattle sensitivity to electrical currents. *Transactions of the American Society of Agricultural Engineers*, *26*, 1506–1511.

Obst, L. R. (1982). Tracking down the shocking truth. *Minnesota Science*, *37*(2–3), 11–13.

Overmier, J. B., & Archer, T. (1989). Historical perspectives on the study of aversively motivated behavior: History and a new look. In T. Archer & L. G. Nilsson (Eds.), *Aversion, avoidance, and anxiety: Perspectives on aversively motivated behavior*, (pp. 3–39). Hillsdale, NJ: Lawrence Erlbaum Associates.

Overmier, J. B., & Hellhammer, D. (1988). The learned helplessness model of human depression. In P. Soubrie et al. (Eds.), *Animal models in psychiatric disorders: 2. An inquiry into schizophrenia and depression* (pp. 177–202). Basel, Switzerland: Karger.

Overmier, J. B., & Patterson, J. (1988). Animal models of human psychopathology. In P. Soubrie et al. (Eds.), *Animal models in psychiatric disorders: 1. Selected models of anxiety, depression and psychosis* (pp. 1–35). Basel, Switzerland: Karger.

Pratt, D. (1980). *Alternatives to pain in experiments on animals*. New York: Argus Archives.

Rachlin, H., & Herrnstein, R. J. (1969). Hedonism revisited: On the negative law of effect. In B. A. Campbell & R. M. Church (Eds.), *Punishment and aversive behavior*. New York: Appleton–Century–Crofts, pp. 83–109.

Regan, T. (1983). *The case for animal rights*. Berkeley: University of California Press.

Rogers, C. L. (1986). *Effects of regulation on the use of animals in biomedical research.* Washington, DC: National Press Club (sponsored by American Association for the Advancement of Science, American Association of Universities, & S.I.P.I.)

Rowan, A. N. (1984). *Of mice, models, and men.* Albany, NY: SUNY Press.

Seligman, M. E. P. (1975). *Helplessness: On depression development and death.* San Francisco: Freeman.

Serban, G., & Kling, A. (1976). *Animal models in human psychobiology.* New York: Plenum.

Sidman, M., Kirk, B., & Willson–Morris, M. (1985). Six member stimulus classes generated by conditioned discrimination procedures. *Journal of the Experimental Analysis of Behavior, 43,* 21–42.

Skinner, B. F. (1938). *Behavior of organisms.* New York: Appleton–Century.

Spencer, H. (1897). *Principles of biology.* New York: Appleton.

Thorndike, E. C. (1898). Animal intelligence: An experimental study of the associative processes in animals. *Psychological Review, Monographs Supplement, 2* (4, whole No. 8).

Thorndike, R. L. (1931). *Human learning.* New York: Appleton–Century.

Trapold, M. A. (1970). Are expectancies based upon different positive reinforcing events discriminably different? *Learning and Motivation, 1,* 129–140.

Turkkan, J. (1989). Classical conditioning: The new hegemony. *Behavioral and Brain Sciences, 12,* 121–136.

Verhetsel, E. (1986). *They threaten your health.* Tucson, AZ: People for Ethical Animal Research.

Weiss, S. M., Herd, J. A., & Fox, B. H. (1981). Perspectives on behavioral medicine. New York: Academic Press.

Williams, J. L., & Lierle, D. M. (1988). Effects of repeated defeat by a dominant conspecific on subsequent pain sensitivity, open-field activity, and escape learning. *Animal Learning and Behavior, 16,* 477–485.

Willner, P. (1986). Validation criteria for animal models of human mental disorder: Learned helplessness as a paradigm case. *Progress in Neuropsychopharmacology and Biological Psychiatry, 10,* 677–690.

Woffenstein, M. (1953). Trends in infant care. *American Journal of Orthopsychiatry, 23,* 120–130.

Wolpe, J. (1962). Experimental foundations of some new psychotherapeutic methods. In A. J. Bachrach (Ed.), *Experimental foundations of clinical psychology.* New York: Basic Books.

1 The Psycho- and Neurobiology of Fear Systems in the Brain

Jaak Panksepp, David S. Sacks, Loring J. Crepeau
Bowling Green State University, Ohio

Bruce B. Abbott
Indiana–Purdue University at Fort Wayne

THEORETICAL PERSPECTIVES

The study of the emotion of fear in psychology has a long and checkered history. Long before the field of psychology was conceived, the power of fear to alter human behavior was widely recognized. Likewise, detection of fear in animals confronted by threatening situations did not require an ethologically tutored eye. Thus it was not surprising that, when scientific investigation of fear in animals began around the turn of the century, stereotypical and apparently innate behavioral responses to fear-provoking situations were among the first to be noted. Yet the emerging antipathy toward the use of instinctual/internal concepts and the development of accounts of fear based on conditioning soon deflected attention from these behaviors as researchers formulated a variety of conceptions of how conditioned anxiety emerges from the pairing of pain and environmental contingencies. Thus, relatively little effort was devoted to unraveling the innate, *unconditional* nature of fear, nor was much attention given to extensively analyzing the neurobiological basis of the most obvious behavioral indexes of fear, such as flight, freezing, shivering, and threat-induced squealing.

Although behavioral analyses have shown how previously neutral stimuli can acquire the ability to produce fear and channel learned behaviors appropriate to a threatening situation, a strictly behavioral analysis will never yield a fundamental (reductionistic) explanation of fear. That must come from an understanding of the underlying brain processes.

In the present chapter, we will argue that specific systems of the brain,

7

situated largely in subcortical areas, unconditionally generate a variety of somatic, behavioral, visceral, hormonal and psychic changes that characterize fear. Presumably, such emotive systems evolved because the behavioral and bodily changes controlled by certain neural patterns were especially effective, during the long course of brain evolution, in warding off threats of bodily destruction. The neural mechanisms that provide executive control over the various bodily expressions of fear, subjectively felt, may constitute the affective concept of fear. We assume that such neural systems can be accessed directly by a variety of environmental events (e.g., sudden pain or startling stimuli) and perceptions (e.g., angry threat or loss of bodily support). Such emotive systems appear to be designed to come under the conditional control of various neutral stimuli in the environment via Pavlovian learning mechanisms. In highly cerebrated species, the primal emotional systems can presumably influence higher-level perceptions, cognitions and fantasies. The basic neural ground plans for such emotional "operating" systems appear to be remarkably similar (homologous) in the brains of all surviving mammalian species because of the substantial part of the evolutionary journey they have shared (Bronson, 1968; Panksepp, 1989a, 1989b, 1990).

It seems that a "command system" for fear is a basic reality of brain organization. As first documented by Hess (for English summary see his 1957 monograph), a very intense pattern of fear-like behavior, with appropriate autonomic changes, can be elicited by electrical stimulation of the brain (ESB) along what seems to be a subcortical neural continuum coursing from the amygdala to the region of the mesencephalic central gray (CG), via the anterior and ventromedial strata of the hypothalamus. Historically, there has been a reticence to consider such circuitry as the fundamental substrate of fear, largely because we cannot directly evaluate the affective experiences of other animals. Also, several early investigators advocated the apparently mistaken perspective that the traumatic emotive motor displays produced by ESB were *pseudoaffective* responses, not accompanied by truly fearful emotional experiences. Psychologists interested in anxiety and avoidance behaviors tended to neglect the study of these circuits, because it was generally assumed that fear was best conceptualized and routinely measured as a learned response to painful stimuli. There is now sufficient indirect evidence from neuropharmacological, brain lesion, and brain stimulation studies to indicate the existence of a basic fear circuit, but the facts remain to be gathered, milled, and leavened into a general theoretical perspective on fear. This chapter and a related one (Panksepp, 1990) are designed to help fill that void.

Several current behavioral perspectives have also shared the conclusion that animals may possess a coherently operating "defense motivational" system that mediates avoidance behaviors (Bolles, 1970; Bolles & Fanselow, 1980; Masterson & Crawford, 1982). Although pharmacological work on those systems has been initiated, the behavioral perspectives remain to be interfaced with the type of synthesis envisioned here. This chapter hopes to provide a psycho–neuro–behavioral synthesis that will promote the needed interdisciplinary research on the basic neural mechanisms for fear which exist in the brain.

Historically, *psychobiological* analyses of fear systems have proceeded along four major trajectories: (1) Via the study of higher brain mechanisms that may be involved in elaborating the cognitive/perceptual components of fear-motivated behaviors (e.g., see Gray, 1982, 1987); (2) Via the study of brain mechanisms that mediate species-typical, "instinctual" processes, such as flight and freezing, which may reflect the executive organization of fear (e.g., as summarized in Adams, 1979; Blanchard & Blanchard, 1984; Panksepp, 1982, 1985, 1990); (3) Via the study of antianxiety drugs that appear to modulate brain mechanisms which mediate punishment (e.g., see Shephard, 1986, for a summary); and (4) Via analysis of peripheral psychophysiological changes that accompany fearful affect (e.g., Lang, Levin, Miller, & Kozak, 1983). The focus of the present chapter will be largely on the second approach, with only modest attention to the others. However, we will also try to relate the knowledge concerning the brain circuits to the ethological analysis of spontaneous fear behaviors and traditional animal models that have been used to study fear.

In summary, we provisionally define the concept of fear in reductionistic neural terms: *Fear* is the central state that arises from the activity of a specific transdiencephalic emotional circuit which is recruited when body safety is threatened. This circuit provides executive synchronization to the various brain and bodily processes (from behavioral to automatic changes) which are recruited to fend off imminent threat unconditionally. Activity in this circuit, affectively felt, is the primal neural source of words such as "fear" in human languages. We would further re-emphasize that the full refinement of this definition can only be accomplished via the intensive study of the underlying neurobiological processes and the specification of how those systems interact with environmental events and learning mechanisms of the brain. We would emphasize at this point, however, that there seem to be several innate trepidation systems in the brain, which can yield considerable semantic confusion when problematical concepts such as fear and anxiety are used to discuss animal behavior.

Existing psychobiological data suggest that brain systems which respond to direct threats to survival are capable of being distinguished from those which respond to the need of social animals (especially the young) to sustain social cohesion. At present, there is more biological knowledge concerning the separation-distress system than the fear system. Since that work has been summarized elsewhere (Panksepp, 1981; Panksepp, Herman, Vilberg, Bishop, & DeEskinazi, 1980; Panksepp, Normansell, Herman, Bishop, & Crepeau, 1988; Panksepp, Siviy, & Normansell, 1985), we will not incorporate that material into the present coverage. Also, several recent monographs have been devoted to summarizing existing knowledge concerning the biological effects of social separation (Reite & Fields, 1985) and brain control of social vocalizations (Newman, 1988).

Ethological Evidence for an Innate Fear System

Any general outline of innate fear-induced responses must be tempered by the recognition that selective pressures acting on different species may have operated to produce different behavioral adaptations to threat. Although the specific motor adaptations may be produced by somewhat different "wiring" in the brain, the central executive structures which synchronize the diversity of specific fear responses appear to have been conserved in a remarkably similar manner in all mammals. The conservation of function at a deep executive level highlights the fact that at an appropriate level of neural abstraction, a predator is a predator (whether lion or ferret) and escape is escape (whether effected by hopping into a burrow or outdistancing the opposition). Because the functional role of fear remains the same (and the primal neural response to being threatened was solved early in vertebrate brain evolution), more recent selective pressures may have acted primarily on stimulus triggers and specific behavioral responses while leaving the phylogenetically older executive systems for emotional orchestration relatively unchanged. It would thus be expected that threatening situations would induce similar emotional states across animals with similarly organized emotive command circuits. In addition, predatory strategies, such as the surprise attack, that hold good in widely varying situations and are used with good effect by a variety of predators, have common stimulus properties (sudden, rapid approach, etc.). Evolutionary pressures may thus have promoted the retention of very similar environmental features as releasing stimuli for fear across a variety of species.

Behavioral responses to various threats have been cataloged in a fairly wide range of species (Adams, 1980). The present descriptions will center around those of mammals and especially the rat, because this is the species most often used in physiological and psychological research on fear-related behavior. At the outset, however, it must be emphasized that the behavioral indicators of defense may often be capable of being dissociated from the central state of fear. For instance, it is easy to envision that flight behaviors could occur with no internal experience of dread. Likewise, a behavior that may be a good indicator of fear, such as frozen immobility, may in fact be used as a behavioral strategy in service of a totally different motivational system. For example, cranes fishing on the shoreline commonly freeze for long periods of time as they stalk their prey. By remaining immobile as they focus on their strike-range, they optimize their opportunity to attack prey which are designed to move swiftly out of reach. Thus, freezing may be an excellent behavioral measure of fear in certain situations, but a poor one in others. Although such problems of measurement and interpretation abound in the study of animal behavior, they are difficult to resolve without hedonic preference tests—an issue which will receive some attention later in this chapter.

Abundant behavioral evidence supports the position that the mammalian brain contains executive circuitry "tailored" by evolutionary selection to prepare the animal for threats to body integrity. Perhaps the earliest systematically gathered evidence supporting the existence and evolution of brain emotive circuits was provided by Darwin (1872) in *The Expression of the Emotions in Man and Animals*. In that contribution, Darwin pieced together observations on species ranging from dogs and cats to chimpanzees and humans, and concluded that each species displayed stereotyped behavioral patterns which had evolved to communicate the emotional state of the animal. Darwin noted that fear-provoking situations often produced characteristic physiological changes, common across a wide variety of species, which included blanching of color in the face, trembling, urination and defecation, and (in humans) sweating. Although Darwin could not identify the physiological source of these changes, many are now recognized as the consequences of sympathetic nervous system activation. Cannon (1936) characterized these changes in detail, and proposed that they function to prepare the organism for "fight or flight."

In addition to these physiological "preparatory" responses, situations that elicit fear promote a variety of adaptive behavioral responses to threat, which vary with the nature of the threat, the environmental support for the different behavioral options, and the specific selective forces that have acted on the species during its more recent evolutionary history. Some of the earliest evidence for the existence of innate unconditional responses to danger stimuli was provided by Small (1889) in a study involving 22 day-old rat pups. Loud noises were shown to produce a "reflex recoil," which included crouching and huddling together at the rear of their cages, and occasionally "whining." A subsequent, more systematic examination (Griffith, 1920) revealed a stereotyped immobility response, which Griffith called "freezing." This was often accompanied by signs of visceral disturbance. Curti (1935) provided a description of the time course of freezing and "thawing," noting that rats may freeze in a variety of motionless postures, with shallow respiration, for periods up to several minutes, punctuated by brief, limited movement.

Early reports examining the unconditional aspects of fear have often employed conditional fear paradigms and focused upon the induction of freezing in experimental animals. For instance, Hunt and Brady (1951), using a "conditional emotional response" (CER) paradigm, noted the "crouching" response of rats during CS presentation, and suggested that the response might be learned. However, in a later paper (Hunt, Jernberg, & Brady, 1952), crouching was described as an "unlearned side-effect" of the conditioned fear.

Recent work in laboratory rats demonstrates that the innate response tendency of freezing is readily conditioned to contextual cues associated with foot shock (e.g., Blanchard & Blanchard, 1969; Bolles & Collier, 1976), and is not simply a prolonged aftereffect of shock itself (Fanselow, 1980). In addition, freezing is readily elicited by exposure to a variety of natural rat predators, including cats (Blanchard & Blanchard, 1971; Blanchard, Fukunaga, & Blanchard, 1976; Curti, 1935; Griffith, 1919; 1920; Lester & Fanselow, 1985), dogs (Curti, 1935, but see Griffith, 1920), ferrets (Cameron & Blampied, 1980) and, in wild, unhandled rats, humans (Blanchard, Flannelly, & Blanchard, 1986). However, there is some disagreement concerning the effective components of these complex stimuli. Although Griffith (1920) reported that cat odor alone was a releasing stimulus for freezing, others report this stimulus fails to induce freezing (Blanchard, Mast & Blanchard, 1975; Curti, 1935). The most effective releasing stimulus provided by a cat and other predators may consist of certain types of movement, especially toward the target rat (Blanchard et al., 1975; Curti, 1935). Freezing has also been reported to occur following sudden unexpected sounds (Brown, Kalish, & Farber, 1951; Curti, 1935; Small, 1889), or during exposure to novel stimuli such as an unfamiliar "open field" (Bronson, 1968; Hall, 1934).

The adaptive utility of freezing to such stimuli in the natural environment has been noted by many investigators (e.g., Hediger, 1955; Myer, 1971). When a predator approaches from a distance, an animal may escape detection by holding still and thus not drawing attention to itself. Freezing is not likely to be adaptive, however, if the predator has sighted the prey and is within the prey's "flight distance," the minimum distance from which the prey is likely to be able to escape the predator (Hediger, 1955). Once within this zone, the predator triggers flight in the prey, especially if the environment provides an evident avenue of escape. Flight is generally directed away from the source of threat, and toward areas likely to provide cover and safety from the predator. Rats tend to follow the walls ("thigmotaxis") and squeeze into any small, dark area that may provide safety. In more natural surroundings, the rat will seek shelter within its own burrow if that is within reach.

If escape proves impossible, many animals will face the predator and engage in threat behavior, which may include vocalizations, piloerection, and display of defensive weapons such as teeth or claws. In rats as well as many other mammals, these displays may include squealing or hissing (Blanchard et al., 1986), defensive upright or lateral postures, and teeth-chattering, but not piloerection, which is seen only in offense (Adams, 1980). If these threats fail to discourage the predator from attacking, defensive fighting, combined with attempts to flee, follow the attack. Defensive fighting in rats includes vocalization, upright "boxing" posture, and attempts to bite the opponent using the "lunge and bite attack" (Adams, 1980) or "jump-attack" (Blanchard et al., 1986) directed at the opponent's face. If this defensive strategy succeeds in opening an avenue of escape, the rat will then flee. This behavior is used when the rat has been cornered by a predator and is not often seen in conspecific encounters (Adams, 1980).

Attempts to capture a frightened and cornered rat elicits running, squealing, struggling, and biting. Dorsal contacts in a confined space produce an exaggerated startle and jumping, whereas struggling, vocalization, and biting occur during attempts to pick it up (Blanchard et al., 1986).

Many of the defensive behaviors described herein are seen not only in predatory encounters, but also in defensive encounters with unfamiliar conspecifics, although they may be modified to some extent. Indeed, Adams (1980) suggests that defense against conspecifics probably evolved from predatory defenses. The defensive boxing posture, for example, appears to be effective in limiting the offensive rat's access to the defender's back and flank, the apparent offensive target for bites (Adams, 1980; Blanchard & Blanchard, 1977). Biting attacks by the defensive animal, which are likely to occur against predators, are rarely seen in conspecific encounters except in response to being bitten by the offensive animal (Blanchard & Blanchard, 1977). In these encounters, the defensive animal was always an intruder of the resident's home cage.

Ratner (1967) suggested that the elicitation of freezing versus active defensive behaviors depends on the distance of the predator, a view that was recently confirmed by Blanchard et al. (1986) and theoretically amplified by Fanselow and Lester (1988). Blanchard and colleagues tested the responses of both wild and laboratory rats to an approaching predator (the experimentor) in an oval runway. Initially, the dominant response of both wild and laboratory rats to the approaching experimenter was freezing. In wild rats, freezing was replaced by fleeing at closer distances. When wild rats were cornered at the end of a hallway, they tended to freeze at distances greater than 1 to 5 meters. Threat behaviors, including screaming and display of teeth, began at about 2 meters and became more intense as distance decreased. Approach within half a meter tended to produce the lunge and bite attack.

If captured, many animals will become immobile, a strategy thought to promote survival by minimizing struggling, which triggers tighter grasping by the predator. As the predator relaxes its grip, the prey may suddenly "come to life" and flee. Whether the tonic immobility of "animal hypnosis," which has been extensively studied in chickens (Gallup, 1974), is governed by the types of brain circuits that produce the tense crouching characteristic of rodent freezing remains entirely uncertain at present.

As this brief synopsis suggests, the rat possesses a number of defensive responses to threat whose innate character is firmly indicated by their highly stereotyped appearance and by the fact that they can be elicited in naïve animals by characteristic stimuli apparently on the animals' first exposure to them. In addition to the behaviors that have already been described, several others have been extensively studied, such as defensive burying (Treit, 1985) and potentiated startle (Davis, 1986). In addition, fearful animals exhibit characteristic autonomic responses, including cardiovascular, respiratory, and gastrointestinal/urogenital changes. Whether these diverse responses to threat share a common neurophysiological triggering influence in the fear command system envisioned here is an important issue that cannot be settled by a purely functional (i.e., observational) approach. The answer to this problem must come from an appreciation of the underlying neural circuitry and its interconnections which, once conceptually outlined, can guide the mechanistic analysis of the details of the underlying processes.

A Preliminary Model of the Proposed Fear-Executive System

In order to provide an overall framework for the following discussions, we have sketched a preliminary functional model of the fear-executive system, highlighting its major presumed neural inputs and outputs (see Fig. 1.1). Under this model, information-processing systems discriminate innate (unconditional) or learned (conditioned) danger stimuli that may appear in the animal's perceptual environment. These stimuli can engage central state control mechanisms, which probably include both a septohippocamal/frontothalamic "alarm" system and an amygdalo-hypothalmo-central gray "fear" system. The two systems are assumed to engage response output mechanisms in a mutually inhibitory fashion. The response output systems organize passive and active defense responses, which include both innate and learned motor patterns. The septohippocampal component of the system is largely based on the theoretical view espoused by Gray (1987), and will not be covered here in detail. In addition, it seems that a thalamic-frontal cortical influence on alerting and orienting an animal to fearful stimuli (Irisawa & Iwasaki, 1986) will deserve equal attention for a comprehensive understanding of the perceptual processes that instigate fear in the nervous system.

The "alarm" system presumably consists of inhibitory circuits that block

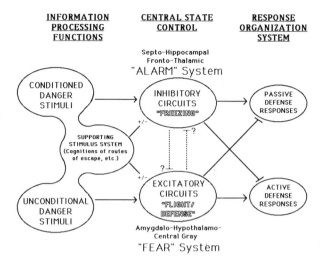

FIG. 1.1. A provisional schematization of the type of information flow that is envisioned to elaborate fear in the brain. Arrows indicate the presumed flow of excitatory information, while T-bars indicate inhibitory information. Overall, the central processing of fear appears to revolve around two distinct type of circuits: those that promote active defense responses (e.g., flight) and those that elaborate passive defense responses (e.g., freezing). Although this summary suggests that the executive circuits for these functions may be anatomically quite distant from each other along the neuro-axis, it should be noted that we have provisional data that induction of freezing may, to some extent, be a function of circuits which course through the Amygdalo–Hypothalamo–Central Gray trajectory (e.g., see Fig. 1.6).

ongoing behaviors induced by other motivational systems, including those motivated by the "fear" system, and enhance passive defense responses such as hiding and freezing. Although in the present context we have designated this as the "alarm" system, we will only tangentially touch on issues pertinent to understanding that system in the present coverage (for a more extensive coverage of those issues from the present theoretical vantage, see Panksepp, 1990). On the other hand, the "fear" system, as conceptualized here, consists of excitatory circuits that promote active defensive behaviors such as flight, and suppress passive defense responses. It is also possible that direct, mutually-inhibitory connections operate between these two central mechanisms (dotted lines). The extent to which these central functions can be ascribed to the anatomical designations specified herein remains to be firmly determined, and there will surely be some surprises. For instance, as discussed in subsequent sections we presently have preliminary evidence that the amygdalo-hypothalamo-central gray system may also mediate inhibitory freezing behaviors. In the present model, supporting stimulus conditions (i.e., those which lead to cognitive appraisal) help shape the selection of active versus passive response mechanisms, and their subsequent expression. For example, the same danger stimulus may activate flight if a place of safety is nearby, or defensive freezing if there is no avenue of escape. In neurologically simplified animals whose perceptual abilities have been compromised, such as decorticates, we predict that passive defense strategies will be diminished markedly while active ones may actually be increased, which would suggest primacy for the active mechanism in brain evolution, and hence probably also in the affective attributes of fear.

Although this preliminary model lacks detail and leaves out many important processes (e.g., interactions with other motivational/emotional systems), it does serve to highlight the importance of stimulus conditions for response selection in the intact animal. The same physiological manipulation may have very different behavioral results, depending on the presence or absence of an appropriate fear-eliciting stimulus, the nature of that stimulus, and the presence or absence of stimulus support for the various behavioral response options. However, the fact that many of the response strategies engaged by these stimuli appear to be innate, and organized at a rather low level of the neuroaxis, provides better opportunities for identifying those brain mechanisms activated or inhibited by a particular physiological manipulation. Because pain (usually foot shock) has typically been used to engage these innate fear response mechanisms, a discussion of the relationship between the distinct but interactive neural mechanisms that generate fear and pain is also offered.

The Relations Between Fear and Pain

Is the mere perception of pain sufficient to mediate conditioned anxiety? Does pain directly cause the autonomic and behavioral changes characteristic of fear, without any mediation by intervening emotional systems? If that were exclusively the case, one could easily posit that fear is merely a social construction, rather than an intrinsic function of the nervous system.

That viewpoint is certainly logical and parsimonious, but in our opinion it is not correct. The evidence suggests that pain typically activates a distinct emotional system that spontaneously facilitates escape from threatening events. Aversive painful stimulation applied to the body surface of an animal yields vigorous escape behaviors resembling flight, whereas stimulation of classic pain systems within the brain does not. Activation of thalamic pain system by ESB in rats produces only a grimacing withdrawal reaction subjectively suggesting pain (Sacks & Panksepp, unpublished observations), and not flight. Human studies typically report various forms of mild discomfort (burning, tingling, dull aching, sharp pin-prick) elicited by ESB of various sites in the thalamic pain system (Halliday & Logue

1971; Tasker, Organ, Rowe, & Hawrylyshyn, 1976), but to our knowledge, such patients have never reported subjective feelings resembling fear. Apparently, focal ESB of thalamic pain systems only activates a small part of the pain system normally activated by peripheral stimulation, and may not activate the fear system at all.

Only at lower levels of the brain stem, where pain systems diverge into reticular fields, does ESB begin to yield flight behaviors. Also, at practically all ESB sites from which flight behavior is obtained, one needs to employ much higher levels of electrical energy before unambiguous behavioral indicators of pain, such as squealing, are activated. It is noteworthy that fearful animals also squeal or hiss when merely threatened, indicating that this response system can be activated independently of actual pain. In order to aid possible comparisons between pain and fear circuits, we have included a brief synopsis of the organization of the pain systems in the brain as an appendix at the end of this chapter.

The present viewpoint is that the systems of fear and pain may interact in the reticular formation (RF). Nociceptive information traveling upstream passes through the reticular core, which provides input into nonspecific arousal mechanisms, and to more specific circuits that govern behavioral/psychological effects such as fear. In other words, as pain fibers project onto the CG, medial zones of the hypothalamus, and perhaps as far rostrally as the amygdala, the sensation of pain comes to instigate the emotion of fear. Although it is clear that neural impulses instigated by nociceptive stimulation do reach the CG and hypothalamus (e.g., Ono, Nakamura, Nishijo, & Fukuda, 1986), we assume that these interactions serve to arouse fear motivation circuits, rather than to mediate the perception of pain. Indeed, lesion data suggest that the areas of the brain that herein are considered to constitute the core of the fear system are not very important for the perception of pain. For instance, although relatively small lesions restricted to the CG can attenuate pain responsivity somewhat, merely increasing the size of the lesion can restore pain sensitivity to normal levels (Melzack, Stotler, & Livingston, 1958). Other studies have reported that lesions restricted to the dorsal central gray, where the most intense fear-like behaviors are elicited, do not decrease pain sensitivity at all (Liebman, Mayer, & Liebeskind, 1970; Mayer & Liebeskind, 1974). Likewise, lesions of the ventral central gray reduce only fearfulness, leaving pain sensitivity unaffected (Edwards & Adams, 1974; Kinscheck, Watkins, & Mayer, 1984). At the hypothalamic level, lesions in areas thought to contain a high density of fear fibers can actually produce hyperalgesia, with the largest increases in pain sensitivity found with medial hypothalamic lesions (Vidal & Jacobs, 1980). Additionally, medial hypothalamic ESB produces analgesia to focal facial heating (Carstens, 1986; Cunningham, Goldsmith, & Hellon, 1986), and suppresses arousal of nociceptive spinal dorsal horn neurons (Culhane & Carstens, 1988).

In short, although there is no doubt that brain systems for pain and fear interact strongly, it seems reasonable to conceptualize fear and pain as substantially independent systems. However, their extensive interaction permits the pain system to activate the fear command circuit, which would then recruit psychological, behavioral, and multiple bodily resources to cope with the imminent threat. Conversely, the fear system can also modulate the pain system, so as to allow animals to focus on external events during threatening situations (Bolles & Fanselow, 1980). We assume the fear system generates motor patterns of flight/escape via activation of pre-programmed motor subroutines, some of which may be situated at levels as high as the basal ganglia, but many of which are probably wired at lower brain stem, cerebellar, and even spinal levels (as suggested by the flight-like hind-leg thrusting which is typically seen in a decapitated animal). Conversely, activation of the fear circuit also presumably modulates downstream pain inhibition (emotion-induced analgesia) systems of the central gray and mesencephalic RF (which will be discussed more thoroughly in subsequent sections).

Accordingly, there are abundant data which affirm that fear and pain systems can be dissociated, and the rest of this chapter will share the perspective that the subcortical circuitry from which flight behavior can be elicited during localized application of ESB highlights the trajectory of the brain circuits whose unconditional function is the mediation of fear. This system is envisioned to mediate the experience of feeling scared, as well as the concurrent activation of spontaneous fear behaviors such as flight as well as the many bodily changes that characterize fear. It may also establish brain conditions for the expression of passive fear tendencies such as freezing, and may also indirectly promote the arousal of cognitive mechanisms necessary for coping with the devilishly complex aversive contingencies often employed in the laboratory. Alternatively, one could envision circumstances where excessive fear tendencies could compromise the acquisition of certain avoidance behaviors (Bolles, 1970). Flight behaviors that are too rapidly engaged, or freezing behaviors that are too persistently sustained could prevent an animal from focusing on the contingencies of the environment.

THE 'FEAR COMMAND SYSTEM' OF THE BRAIN

It remains uncertain how the brain organizes emotions. One recent suggestion is that the basic emotions including fear are organized around genetically hard-wired executive circuits. Such a coordinating or "command circuit" for fear (Panksepp, 1981, 1982, 1986) is thought to actively inhibit competing behavior patterns (such as feeding, reproduction and "pain" responsivity) so that the relevant species-typical defense behaviors can be exhibited. At the same time, memory systems are concurrently engaged to promote the learning of stimulus characteristics that predict threat, which can help the organisms avoid dangers in the future. ESB work suggests that a basic fear/flight circuit courses through the amygdala/anterior lateral hypothalamic/central gray axis, and that it elaborates the unconditional attributes of fear. The anatomy of this system is such that a great amount of sensory and behavioral information could be integrated by a single executive circuit. At a higher perceptual level, integration involves the development of knowledge about which world events should be considered dangerous. Neurophysiologically, this function seems to be mediated by the higher levels of the circuit within specific subareas of the temporal lobe, including especially the central and lateral amygdaloid nuclei, which also help initiate various autonomic responses that characterize fear. On a lower level of integration, the anterior lateral hypothalamus may mediate the various hormonal, viscera, and somatic fear responses, thereby further linking psychic activity functions with the bodily changes that must be effected for adaptive behavior. This level of activity may be especially important not only for certain types of physiological arousal, but also for the affective intensity of the emotion. At an even lower level of integration within this command circuit, such as at the level of the central gray, species-typical motor patterns of defense (flight, freezing, squealing) may become activated, and various competing perceptual (pain, hunger, and thirst) and motor tendencies (recuperative behaviors, feeding, and drinking) may be inhibited.

Five lines of evidence support the claim that the anterior lateral hypothalamic area (AHA), amygdala, and central gray play a critical part in the control of this emotion: (1) Behavioral studies indicate that ESB of these areas evokes fear-like behaviors, induces avoidance learning, and mediates the acquisition of avoidance learning to fear-inducing stimuli. (2) As determined by modern neuroanatomical and neurophysiological techniques, strong linkages exist between these brain areas where ESB elicits flight. (3) Lesions of these areas disrupt some learned behaviors which are presumably indicative of the central state of fear. (4) Endogenous pain inhibition is modulated by fear and the circuits that have been described appear to mediate pain regulatory functions. (5) Finally, pharmacological manipulations of the amygdala/anterior lateral hypothalamus/central gray axis with antianxiety agents modify the behavioral manifestations of fear.

ESB-Evoked Fear

The initial evidence for a harmoniously operating emotional circuit for fear arose from brain-stimulation studies (Hess, 1957). Animals show characteristic and easily repeatable fear-like behavior patterns (with many out-

TABLE 1.1
Representative Studies that have found Unconditional Flight and Escape Behaviors during ESB

Task	Species	*Site	Reference
Unconditional Responses:			
Flight only	cat	AHA,CG	Skultety (1963)
	rat	MH	Sandner et al. (1982)
	cat	AHA	Fuchs & Siegel (1984)
Flight and de-fensive attack	cat	LH,CG,AM	de Molina & Hunsperger (1962)
	cat	AHA,VMH	Fuchs et al. (1985a)
	cat	AHA,VMH	Fuchs et al. (1985b)
Conditional Escape:			
Lever press to escape stimu-lation	rat	LH	Nakao (1958)
	rat	LH,CG	Olds & Olds (1962)
	rat	LH,CG	Olds & Olds (1963)
	rat	CG,Med.Lem	Olds et al. (1964)
	rat	AHA	Panksepp et al. (1970)
	cat	LH	Wada & Matsuda (1970)
	rat	LH,MH	Schmitt & Karli (1984)
	rat	CG	Moriyama et al. (1984)
	rat	CG,MH	Moreau et al. (1986)
	rat	CG	Sandner et al. (1985)
	mouse	CG	Cazala & Schmitt (1987)
Flight to escape stimulation	cat	DMT	Roberts (1962)
	rat	MH	Sandner et al. (1982)
	rat	CG	Bovier et al. (1983)
Shuttle-box side to es-cape stimula-tion	rat	MH	Schmitt and Karli (1984)

*Abbreviations as in Table 1.2.

ward indicators suggesting they are experiencing a highly negative fear-like affective state) when stimulated along a specific neural continuum that courses between the amygdala and the central gray of the mesencephalon. The general anatomy of this system, as determined by many stimulation studies (see Table 1.1), is schematized in Fig. 1.2.

The behaviors observed are dramatic and highly replicable. For instance, rats confined in a small test chamber and stimulated at low current levels exhibit an initial alerting, and then begin to move rapidly around the test

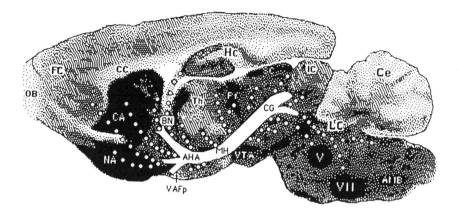

FIG. 1.2.   A general summary of the anatomical trajectory of the brain
system which mediates active defense behaviors, and presumably provides synchronized control over the many cognitive, affective, behavioral, physiological and hormonal changes which characterize fear (the
depicition is on a parasaggital summary of acetylcholine-esterase
staining, as adapted from a map constructed by Paxinos & Watson,
1982). This command circuit is envisioned to be a two-way avenue of
communication between various nuclei of the amygdala, especially
the central nucleus, and the mesencephalic central gray via anterior
and medial hypothalamic areas. There are multiple entry and exit points
to this circuit (as depicted by "o o o"s). Although the system can be
dissected into multiple subfunctions, it is conceived of as operating as
a coherent whole, to provide synchronization to the many brain functions that characterize fear. Anatomical Index: OB–Olfactory bulbs;
FC–Frontal cortex; CC–Corpus callosum; CA–Caudate nucleus; NA–
Nucleus Accumbens; BN–Bed nucleus of the stria terminalis; AHA–
Anterior hypothalamic area; VAFp–Ventral amygdalo-fugal pathway;
VTA–Ventral tegmental area; SC–Superior colliculus; IC–Inferior col-
liculus; CG–Central Gray; Ce–Cerebellum; LC–Locus Coeruleus; V–
Motor Nucleus of the trigemminal; VII–Nucleus of the Facial nerve;
AMB–Nucleus Ambiguus.

chamber, typically stopping at corners, where they quickly move up and
down as if seeking an avenue of exit. At slightly higher current levels, the
overall behavior pattern becomes markedly intensified. Interspersed with
the horizontally directed flight, animals exhibit vigorous leaps as if trying
to escape from the situation. During this artificially induced motivation,
they are able to jump out of boxes with walls several feet high. However,
only at much higher current levels is any squealing evoked. Because squealing is typically observed in rats even when quite mild external pain is
applied, it appears that the flight-producing stimulation is not simply evoking pain. The animals also exhibit marked autonomic arousal, and these
changes have been extensively characterized (Mancia & Zanchetti, 1981).
Many of the behavioral and autonomic indexes can even be elicited in

anesthetized animals. For instance, we routinely monitor the types of ESB-induced behavioral changes as we implant electrodes into the brain. When stimulation of the AHA in pentobarbital-anesthetized animals induces deep thoracic breathing and occasional hind leg thrusting and thrashing, we can be certain that stimulation in the waking state will induce aversive-flight behaviors at much lower current levels. When stimulation is applied at the apparent center of this system, one routinely gets a deep, gasp-like inhibition of breathing in rats, with sustained thoracic contraction, whereas nearby electrodes yield only invigorated breathing.

The motivational characteristics of this type of brain stimulation have been extensively studied. There is general agreement that flight-provoking stimulation is highly aversive, because it can effectively sustain instrumental escape behaviors (Delgado, Roberts, & Miller, 1954). Escape from such stimulation has been observed in all mammalian species studied (key reference sources are summarized in Table 1.1). Stimulation of the amygdala can also elicit species-typical defense reactions indicative of fear in animals (Gloor, 1960; MacLean & Delgado, 1953; Ursin, Jellestad, & Gabrera, 1981), and feelings of fear in humans (Gloor, Olivier, & Quesney, 1981). These reactions are also elicited following stimulation of various regions of the hypothalamus, especially anterior and medial zones (Grossman, 1970; Panksepp, 1971; Sandner, Schmitt & Karli, 1982) and from many sites within and adjacent to the central gray of the mesencephalon (Bovier, Broekkamp, & Lloyd, 1982; Cazala & Schmitt, 1987; Moreau, Schmitt, & Karli, 1986; Sandner, Schmitt & Karli, 1985). At an impressionistic level, the evoked behaviors are remarkably similar from all structures, even though as one descends the neuroaxis, the behaviors are typically more intense and stereotyped, and the thresholds for behavior are generally lower. Although comprehensive ethological studies of the evoked behavioral changes remain to be done, the apparent behavioral communalities suggest that all these brain structures are connected and concurrently involved in the elaboration of a functionally homogeneous affective tendency.

The issue of whether this type of brain stimulation can motivate anticipatory avoidance behavior has been more troublesome (the available results are summarized in Table 1.2). One of the earliest investigators in the field, Masserman (1941) strongly advocated the position that hypothalamic ESB had no real emotional meaning for the seemingly horrified animals because they exhibited no anticipatory trepidation to stimuli that predicted forthcoming stimulation. To our knowledge, Masserman never provided adequate histology of the brain areas he stimulated, and his behavioral descriptions suggest that he may have been activating rage rather than fear processes in the cats he studied. Whether the conditioned properties of rage systems should resemble those of the fear system is an unresolved issue, and it is possible that Masserman's early data were irrelevant to the

TABLE 1.2
Table of Studies Using Avoidance Tasks

Task	Species	*Site	Outcome	Reference
One-way avoidance	cat	AHA,LH,MH	+	Cohen et al. (1957)
	cat	CG,Med.Lem.	+	Delgado et al. (1955)
	rat	LH	±	Mogenson (1962)
	rat	CG	+	Stein (1965)
	rat	CG	±	Cox (1967)
	cat	LH	−	Wada & Matsuda (1970)
Conditional T-maze avoidance	rat	LH	−	Bower & Miller (1958)
	cat	MT(alarm)	+	Roberts (1958a&b)
		MH (flight)	−	
	cat	DMT	+	Roberts (1962)
Conditional leverl press/push avoidance	cat	CG,Med.Lem.	−	Delgado et al. (1954)
	cat	LH	−	Wada & Matsuda (1970)
	cat	LH	−	Wada & Matsuda (1970)
Conditional emotional response		LH	+	Nakao (1958)
	cat			
	cat	LH	+	Thomas & Basbaum (1972)
	rat	CG	+	DiScala et al. (1987)
Place avoidance	rat	AHA	+	Sacks & Panksepp (1988)
	rat	CG	−	Sacks (1987)
	rat	CG	+	Roberts & Cox (1987)
	cat	LH	+	Nakao (1958)
Food dish avoidance	cat	CG,Med.Lem.	+	Delgado et al. (1955)
	cat	LH	+	Nakao (1958)

*Abbreviations: PVG = periventricular gray; Med. Lem. = medial lemniscus; AHA = anterior lateral hypothalamic area; VMH = ventral medial hypothalamus; VT = ventral medial tegmentum; MH = medial hypothalamus; CG = central gray; DMT = dorsal medial thalamus; MT = medial thalamus; AM = amygdala.

issue of how fear is organized via the hypothalamic circuit envisioned here. In any case, several early studies indicated that aversive flight-producing ESB can sustain several types of avoidance behaviors (Delgado et al., 1954; Delgado, Rosvold, & Looney, 1956; Nakao, 1958), but an equally remarkable number of studies reported little tendency of animals to avoid predictable ESB to comparable brain sites (Bower & Miller, 1958; Roberts,

1958a; Wada & Matsuda, 1970). Mixed results have also been reported, with avoidance obtained at some electrode locations but not others (Delgado et al., 1954; Roberts, 1958a, 1958b). In general, everyone seems to agree that animals exhibit more difficulty in acquiring traditional active avoidance responses when ESB rather than foot shock is used to motivate learning. Mogenson's (1962) experience is typical. Of three rats, two acquired one-way shuttle avoidance in an average of 141 trials, and the third animal failed to reach the criterion of 10 consecutive avoidances. Animals tested with grid shock learned the task in about 68 trials. Thus, animals do take longer to learn to avoid aversive ESB than foot shock, and the degree to which this type of ESB is producing a central state which can be associated with external events has remained controversial until recently.

Three recent reports have all affirmed that such stimulation can support the development of conditional anxieties (DiScala, Mana, Jacobs, & Phillips, 1987; Roberts & Cox, 1987; Sacks & Panksepp, 1987, 1988). DiScala et al. (1987) found that the pairing of fear producing ESB to the central gray with neutral tones yielded CER patterns of response inhibition when the tones were subsequently presented during appetitive behaviors. Roberts and Cox (1987) found that similar mesencephalic stimulation could mediate development of a conditioned place avoidance. Sacks and Panksepp (1987) demonstrated that animals exhibit marked freezing in environments where they had been subjected to ESB of fear sites in the AHA. Furthermore, such ESB could motivate subsequent behavioral choices, as indicated by the tendency of animals to avoid environments in which the ESB had been administered (Sacks & Panksepp, 1988). Taken together, these "hedonic" studies suggest that ESB-induced flight behavior is accompanied by an aversive internal state which can be associated with environmental cues. Earlier studies may have failed to observe clear conditioning effects because of a host of situational variables. For instance, it is common in avoidance research to use discrete cures, and perhaps the emotional state evoked by ESB is so intense that it reduces the tendency of animals to focus on minor environmental changes. The animals may be so "flooded" with fearful affect that certain experimentally imposed demand characteristics are not sufficiently salient or ecologically meaningful to channel development of anticipatory flight behaviors. Also, it is possible that conditioned freezing in such situations tends to retard the behavioral flexibility that is essential for active avoidance responding. In this context, it is worth noting that, following certain brain lesions situated outside the primal fear circuitry postulated herein, animals appear unable to exhibit effective avoidance responses, even though they appear to anticipate that shock is forthcoming. For instance, following dorsomedial thalamic lesions, rats never acquire the final component of one-way avoidance, even though they approach and orient to the exit route. Before crossing over, they freeze at the "exit-gate" and jump through only after footshock comes on (Vanderwolf, 1971). Parenthetically, electrical stimulation of that brain area does not produce flight, even though the affect generated is sufficiently aversive for the animals to acquire a relatively slow escape responding (Panksepp, unpublished observations, 1969). The possibility that thalamic stimulation evokes an emotional response, such as "alarm," which alerts the animal to potential dangers, and which is distinct from fear/flight deserves further experimental attention (Roberts, 1958a, 1962).

At present it seems that flight-producing ESB can sustain conditioned fear behaviors when measures of simple behavioral inhibition or place aversion are used, but does not readily sustain conditioned avoidance consistently in more complex anticipatory flight situations. To shed further light on this issue, we tested a small group of animals in one of the more complex avoidance paradigms that is currently available, namely the tendency of animals to choose signaled over unsignaled aversive events. With grid shock as the source of motivation, rats readily acquire a strong preference for signaled pain, even though that in no way changes the actual shock density to which they are subjected (Abbott & Badia, 1979; see Badia, Harsh, & Abbott, 1979, for a review). In our experience with three animals, such a choice tendency does not develop readily with aversive stimulation of the AHA. Even when the animals had been trained to exhibit a preference for signaled foot shock, they did not readily transfer that preference to signaled AHA stimulation. However, following protracted training, two out of three animals did eventually exhibit a clear preference for the signaled brain stimulation (see best animal in Fig. 1.3). Although the progression toward a preference was comparatively slow and arduous, the ability of the brain stimulation eventually to sustain this type of complex avoidance indicates that the aversive AHA–ESB is not simply producing a pseudoaffective response, but has true emotional meaning for the animal.

Still, these data clearly indicate that the motivational properties of flight-producing ESB and foot shock are distinct, and there is presently no empirically established explanation for the disparity. Perhaps the ESB produces a relatively pure but diffuse fear which has motivational properties different from those produced by well-localized peripheral pain. Fear that can be referred to clear external events may be more capable of being elaborated at higher cognitive levels of cerebral processing that mediate complex behavioral strategies. In this vein, it is noteworthy that, in our experience, decorticate animals also exhibit no preference for signaled foot shock even though it is clear from their behaviors that they can exhibit simple conditioned fears (Abbott & Panksepp, unpublished observations, 1986). Parenthetically, it should be noted that rats also find it much more difficult to avoid actively shock that is applied to the top of their heads than to the skin on their feet (Gardner & Malmo, 1969), and the difficult nature of ESB-avoidance could be as simple as that.

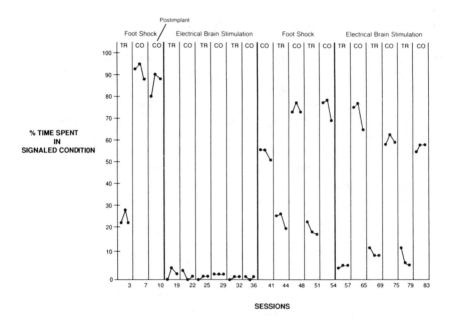

FIG. 1.3. The summary of the training (TR) and testing history of an animal which exhibited the best changeover behavior (CO) to signaled ESB of the AHA (Abbott, 1987, unpublished data). The details of experimental procedures are summarized in Abbott and Badia (1979). Briefly, TR consisted of periods where animals were exposed to the experimental contingencies (alternating periods of signaled and unsignaled shock) with no operant being available, even though amount of lever pressing (and potential consequences) were recorded. The signaled condition was identified by the house light being turned on, and the signaled condition by the light being turned off. During CO, each lever press shifted the animal from the unsignaled condition to the signaled condition for 1 min, after which the unsignaled shock condition was re-established. (It should be noted that the density of shock was the same under both signaled and unsignaled conditions.) The animal was initially trained to exhibit almost maximal changeover behavior to foot shock (1 ma, 0.5 sec), following which the AHA electrode was implanted at a site which yielded clear flight behavior. CO behavior was not disrupted by the surgery. When tested with AHA stimulation (0.5 ma, 0.5 sec), the animal exhibited no changeover behavior (through 3 cycles of training, even though it still exhibited strong changeover when tested with foot shock). When placed back into the ESB condition once more, the animal started to exhibit reliable changeover behavior to the signaled condition.

At least to the extent that simple conditioned fear behaviors can be taken as indicative of such internal states, the above data suggest that flight-producing ESB has affective meaning for the animal. Moreover, the data also affirm that the animal has difficulty dealing "adaptively" in response to the activation of such a state when relatively complex avoidance demands are made. Thus, although the ESB evoked experience does not have the basic characteristics of an aversive state resembling fear, it may be free of certain perceptual attributes, such as externally referred pain (at appropriate body locations), which may be essential for animals to learn complex ways to avoid. In short, the brain may be designed in such a way that animals can readily learn to avoid stimuli that predict the onset of normal environmentally evoked fears, but the underlying circuits may not be designed to avoid fear that arises independently of the environment. If true, this could have implications for the clinical treatment of free-floating anxieties.

Anatomical, Electrophysiological, and Neurochemical Issues

The second line of evidence supporting the claim that the amygdala/anterior lateral hypothalamus/central gray axis mediates the experience of fear involves anatomical evidence derived from the analysis of the underlying brain circuits with modern histological techniques (metabolic, antereograde, and retrograde tracing). These procedures have produced a relatively fine-grained neuroanatomical map of the potential structures involved with ESB-induced fear behaviors. Fuchs and Siegel (1984) and Fuchs, Edinger, and Siegel (1985a) have extensively studied the anatomy of this system in cats. Using both [^{3}H]leucine placed into hypothalamic flight sites for antereograde tracing and [^{14}C]2-deoxyglucose as a functional tracer during ventromedial hypothalamic stimulation, these investigators have provided anatomical support for the claim that cell groups in the anterior hypothalamic nucleus, medial preoptic region, and the dorsomedial hypothalamus are important in the mediation of ESB-induced defensive tendencies.

The evidence gathered by Fuchs et al. (1984, 1985b) shows that hypothalamic fear/defense zones connect rostrally to the bed nucleus of the stria terminalis, the diagonal band, and the amygdala, while sending descending projections to the centrum medianum-parafascicular complex and the midbrain central gray region. In recent years, the higher reaches of this system in the amygdala have attracted considerable attention (Ben–Ari, 1981). Behavioral studies have indicated that the central and lateral amygdaloid areas are especially influential in mediating externally-referenced, non-social fear-related processes (for review, see Panksepp, 1989), whereas social-defensive fears may be more integrally linked to corticomedial amygdalar function (Bolhuis, Fitzgerald, Dijk, & Koolhaas, 1984; Luiten, Kool-haas, deBoer, & Koopmans, 1985). These amygdalar areas have anatomical connections that highlight the trajectory of the fear system as generated by the aforementioned anatomical and ESB studies (Fig. 1.2). Hopkins and Holstege (1978) were the fist to demonstrate a long-axoned pathway that descends from central amygdala down to autonomic control centers of the lower brain stem. In fact, the neurons that contribute to this system appear to be situated in a broad "bed nucleus" which may be confluent with the descending axonal trajectories, at least down to the AHA level. Also, there are abundant descending and ascending reciprocal influences within the trajectory of this circuit (Otterson & Ben–Ari, 1978; Voshart & Van der Kooy, 1981). In short, an intrinsic brain organ system for fear appears to be constituted of specific circuits that course between the amyg-dala (largely via the ventral amygdalo-fugal pathway; see Hilton & Zbro-zyna, 1963) and lower brain stem areas (via periventricular fiber systems) along an anatomical trajectory whose outlines were first established with the rather primitive approach of localized ESB (Fig. 1.2). Although the precise connections of this system remain ambiguous (because available neuroanatomical techniques do not simply highlight a single system), we can be fairly certain from such work that the fear system can collect an enormous amount of information from a great number of other areas of the brain, and can also transmit information to an equally large number of neural targets. The detailed analysis of the neural properties of this circuit is, we believe, the single most important experimental undertaking for a scientific understanding of the nature of fear. At present, our knowl-edge in this area remains quite limited, but still it is much greater than the psychological community probably realizes.

For instance, some of the interactions within this system have been clarified using electrophysiological procedures. The effect of concurrently manipulating different points along this system supports a strong functional relationship between the central gray and the hypothalamus. Specific pop-ulations of central gray neurons are activated by electrical stimulation of the medial hypothalamus (Sanders, Klein, Mayes, Heym, & Handwerker, 1980), suggesting that hypothalamic "fear" influences may impinge on mesencephalic "fear" zones. Conversely, flight/escape induced by hypo-thalamic ESB can be facilitated by ventral CG stimulation, whereas dorsal CG stimulation can also attenuate hypothalamic ESB induced flight/escape (Brutus, Shaikh, & Siegel, 1985), presumably by activating brain-stem analgesic systems. Thus, the fear system may contain reciprocal facilitatory and inhibitory components within relatively nearby subcircuits. In any event, these results show that the aversive effects of electrical stimulation of the central gray depend, at least in part, on descending influences from the lateral hypothalamus, and that upstream influences from the central gray modulate the function of higher areas. In addition, there are local hypothalamic hierarchical control influences, with the AHA having primacy over other hypothalamic areas. When the AHA is lesioned, defensive responses normally elicited from ventromedial hypothalamic sites are attenuated (Fuchs et al., 1985b).

Although the principal neurotransmitters within this command system remain to be identified, a number of candidates are indicated by anatomical criteria from immunocytochemical studies, and on the basis of behavioral criteria from pharmacological studies. For instance, a host of peptide transmitters are concentrated in the central nucleus of the amygdala (ACE) and the bed nucleus of the stria terminalis (BNST), including gallanin, met-enkephalin, Substance P, neurotensin, somatostatin, & dynorphin (Gray & Magnuson, 1987). If one would seek to identify which neurochemical system(s) constitute the fear system, there are now a large number of ascending and descending candidates that have the appropriate geography (Nieuwenhuys, 1985). On the basis of both anatomical and behavioral considerations, the Diazepam Binding Inhibitor (DBI), Corticotrophin Releasing Factor (CRF), Adrenocorticotrophic Hormone (ACTH) and alpha-Melanoctye Stimulating Hormone (a-MSH) peptide systems stand out as potential key contributors to various aspects of fear. DBI injected into the brain has proanxiety effects (Ferrero, Santi, Conti–Tronconi, Costa, & Guidotti, 1986), CRF can arouse and agitate animals, facilitate freezing and other distress behaviors (Koob & Bloom, 1985; Sutton, Koob, LeMoal, Rivier, & Vale, 1982), and a-MSH yields behavior patterns which resemble fearful crouching (Abbott & Panksepp, 1988). More recently, we have found that ACTH 1–24 induces a similar type of freezing behavior in domestic chicks. Also, it should be noted that administration of curare into the brain can evoke a powerful fear-like flight/agitation pattern (Desci & Varszegi, 1969; Panksepp, et al., 1983), suggesting that certain cholinergic systems, perhaps those which bind alpha-bungarotoxin (Clarke, Schwartz, Paul, Pert, & Pert, 1985), may have a key function within the system. Also, administration of the glutamate receptor stimulants N–methyl–D–aspartate (NMDA) and kainic acid (KA) can provoke fear-like behavior patterns (Bandler, DePaulis, & Vergnes, 1985; Normansell, Zeisloft, & Panksepp, 1988), which indicates the need for further analysis of gluatmatergic systems in the genesis of the active components of fear (also see Sun & Guyenet, 1986).

Lesion Studies of the Fear Circuit and Behavioral Measures of Anxiety

We have recently conducted a series of acute ESB studies of the fear circuit in pentobarbital anesthetized guinea pigs. The behavioral end-points analyzed were ESB-induced increases in respiration (Figs. 1.4 and 1.5) and ESB-induced hind-leg thrusting (which is presumably an indicator of flight

FIG. 1.4. A summary of
respiratory activity for three
guinea pigs stimulated at
various depths (at 200 uA sine-
wave current administered
continuously for 15 sec) with
an unipolar electrode passed
through the AHA. Points are
plotted as distance from the
ventral surface of the brain. All
animals exhibited a zone of
about 4 mm where breathing
was increased 250–500%,
Throughout this area, flight
behaviors are observed when
ESB is administered to awake
animals.

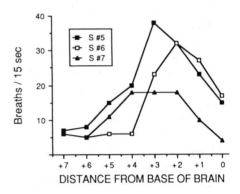

tendencies). The responses seem to be capable of being elicited equally
well on both sides of the brain. In one series of ablation studies we attempted to determine whether the responses could be attenuated by aspiration of areas rostral to the stimulation sites. We found that we could
aspirate all CNS tissue rostral to all stimulation sites without eliminating
the ESB-induced behaviors. One could continue to aspirate all of the
nervous system down to the level of the mesencephalon, and if stimulation
was applied to the face of the remaining brain stem, one could continue
to obtain the foregoing behavioral indicators essentially intact.

The respiratory response was largely unaffected by complete midsaggital
transections down through the pontine level (although one animal, S4,
showed some attenutation). In agreement with the aspiration studies, total
frontal cuts rostral to the stimulation sites have no effect on the ESB
responses, whereas bilateral cuts caudal to the electrode sites essentially
abolished the stimulation-induced behaviors, indicating that descending
neural circuits, rather than humoral pathways, are triggering the observed
behaviors. With unilateral brain-stem transections at the mesencephalic
level, cuts contralateral to the electrode (S3 and S4) had no effect on
breathing rate and hind-leg thrusting, suggesting the behavioral changes
do not require crossed pathways. Ipsilateral cuts (S1 and S2) attenuated
each behavior markedly (see Fig. 1.5). However, some of the ESB-induced
breathing effect did survive such ipsilateral cuts, suggesting that there may
be some crossed or humoral influence that can sustain the behavior. Although this last issue deserves further experimental attention (especially
with smaller lesions placed in mesencephalic areas), these data suggest that
primal fear circuitry is constituted largely of bilaterally symmetrical circuits
whose influences remain largely restricted to each side of the brain. It is

especially noteworthy that the unconditional indicators of fear remain relatively intact as one descends the neuroaxis, even when higher areas from which the responses could be elicited are totally eliminated. Because the higher areas are not needed for eliciting the gross behavioral indicators that can be activated in anesthetized animals, it seems reasonable to suppose that those areas provide a variety of higher modulatory influences, regulating the basic behavioral expressions which are preorganized at lower levels.

The experiments described herein indicate that many of the behavioral attributes of the fear system can be studied in anesthetized animals, an approach that has been effectively pursued with autonomic measures (e.g., Hilton & Redfern, 1986; Yardley & Hilton, 1986). However, the extent to which this circuit participates in normal fearful behaviors can only be evaluated in awake animals. If most of the innate attributes of fear are orchestrated by the circuit described, and if various species typical defensive behaviors response to threats operate via the auspices of this system, then it would be predicted that restricted lesions along its trajectory would seriously compromise the animals' ability to acquire fearful responses to new environmental contingencies. We will herein summarize pertinent work

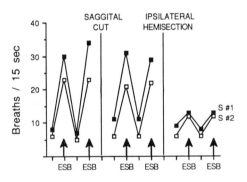

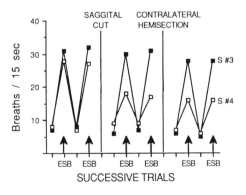

FIG. 1.5. Respiratory patterns of guinea pigs during 15-sec periods of AHA–ESB interspersed with comparable no-stimulation periods (with at least 30-sec intertrial intervals). Saggital cuts consisted of passing a spatula at the midline (down to the base of the brain) from the genu of the corpus callosum rostrally through the level of the pons caudally. The hemisections consisted of passing a spatula to the ventral surface of the brain from the midline through the lateral extent of the brain stem. It is noteworthy that similar cuts 1–2 mm anterior to the site of stimulation had no effect on the evoked breathing patterns.

at each of the three major hierarchical levels of this circuit (mesencephalic, diencephalic, & telencephalic).

The Central Gray.   The importance of the central gray in the behavioral manifestations of "fear" is not only supported by data showing that electrical stimulation of ventral central gray sites produces flight/escape behaviors, but also by the fact that damage to this area compromises shock avoidance. Lesions in the central gray reduced general emotionality in open-field performance, decrease the effects of punishment on food-seeking behavior, decrease foot-shock-induced defensive boxing and produce deficits in active and passive active avoidance learning (Edwards & Adams, 1974; Liebman et al., 1970; Roberts & Cox, 1987) and, as mentioned before, decrease flight behaviors evoked by hypothalamic stimulation (Schmitt, Paunovic, & Karli, 1979; Skultety, 1963). Conversely, lesions of the medial hypothalamus have also been shown to reduce the aversiveness of central gray stimulation, with lateral hypothalamic lesions at the same level having little effect (Sandner et al., 1985), which again affirms reciprocal influences among the various levels of control within this circuit.

The Level of the Hypothalamus.   The importance of the hypothalamic fiber tracts in the mediation of fear behaviors is supported by the finding that surgical damage to specific hypothalamic subareas can markedly alter avoidance responding. The effects on behavior of hypothalamic nuclei disconnection seem to vary according to the nuclei involved. Anterior hypothalamic disconnection has little effect on shuttle-box avoidance (Grossman & Grossman, 1970), whereas posterior and medial hypothalamic disconnection from the lateral hypothalamus disrupts it (Grossman, 1970; Grossman & Grossman, 1970), perhaps by reducing the fear associated with the aversive stimulus. Such effects are generally consistent with the present conceptualization of fear circuitry (Fig. 1.2).

Although localized medial hypothalamic lesions produce an increase in the affective response associated with rage (Grossman, 1966, 1970), which also appears as excessive affective responsivity in fear-provoking situations (because these animals respond very aggressively to threats), in fact these animals appear to be *less* fearful when evaluated by formal behavioral tests. Such animals exhibit marked reductions in various avoidance behaviors (Colpaert, 1975; Colpaert & Wiepkema, 1976), but the avoidance effects do vary substantially as a function of the intensity of threat. If the task is a "low-drive escape avoidance situation" (Grossman, 1966), such as a shuttle-box avoidance task, escape performance is often improved (Grossman, 1966; Levine & Soliday, 1960). However, if the task is a "high-drive avoidance situation" (Grossman, 1966), where "fear" would presumably be sustained at a higher level, performance is usually reduced (Olds & Frey, 1971; Sandner et al., 1985).

Although much work has been done with hypothalamic lesions and fear-motivated tasks, there seems to be one noteworthy omission. To our knowledge, no one has produced bilateral lesions at behaviorally verified AHA locations where flight can be produced with ESB, and observed the behavior of animals in various fear situations. Such studies are presently being conducted in our laboratory, and the preliminary results indicate that freezing, but not threat-induced flight or learned two-way avoidance, is diminished markedly by such damage (Sacks & Panksepp, 1988, unpublished work).

Amygdaloid Lesions.   The first component in the fear command circuit, the amygdala, receives both corticolimbic and thalamolimbic sensory inputs (LeDoux, Ruggiero, & Reis, 1985; Turner, Mishkin, & Knapp, 1980), as well as direct olfactory inputs from the main and accessory olfactory bulbs (Luiten et al., 1985). The amygdala receives projections from areas mediating all sensory systems (deOlmos, Alheid, & Beltramino, 1985; LeDoux et al., 1985; Turner, Mishkin, & Knapp, 1980; Van Hoesen, 1981), and it responds to all forms of sensory stimuli (Le Gal La Salle & Ben–Ari, 1981; Pascoe & Kapp, 1985). Iwata, LeDoux, Meeley, Arneric, and Reis (1986) propose that thalamolimbic inputs might elaborate "fast" sensory input processing, which is important for initial orientation, as well as immediate autonomic arousal. Conversely, the corticolimbic inputs provide less immediate, more refined sensory information. Gloor (1978) proposes that the amygdala provides the "affective tone" or "mood" for the animal, depending on the information available to it at the time. Subsequently, amygdalar output can direct emotional behaviors, especially those related to fear (Kapp, Pascoe, & Bixler, 1984).

The reduction in apparent fearfulness produced by amygdaloid lesions extends to the realm of noxious social stimuli, since lesioning the corticomedial amygdaloid (CMA) nucleus produces a deficit in an animal's ability to learn species-typical submission behavior in response to the dominant animal in the social group (Bolhuis et al., 1984; Luiten et al., 1985), and attenuates defensive behaviors, such as reactions to a cat, a shock prod, or an approaching investigator, in laboratory-raised and wild rats (Blanchard & Blanchard, 1972a; Kemble, Blanchard, Blanchard, & Takushi, 1984). In view of such effects, it is not surprising that wild rats can be tamed by amygdala damage (Blanchard, Blanchard, et al., 1981; Kemble et al., 1984). In addition to reducing fearfulness directly, amygdala lesions have also been shown to attenuate the fear induced by hypothalamic stimulation, indicating that upstream influences from the amygdala can modulate hypothalamic activity (Maeda & Nakao, 1986).

The role of the amygdala in providing affective coloring to memory is coming to be widely recognized (Aggleton & Mishkin, 1986; Gallagher & Kapp, 1981; Sarter & Markowitsch, 1985), and the contribution of the amygdala in the elaboration of fear has now been extensively explored using traditional learning-based measures of anxiety. Amygdaloid lesions have been shown to reduce both active (Coover, Ursin, & Levine, 1973; Eclander & Karli, 1980; Horvath, 1963; McIntyre & Stein, 1973; Riolobos, 1986; Ursin, 1965; Werka, Skar, & Ursin, 1978) and passive avoidance learning (Coover et al., 1973; Grossman, Grossman, & Walsh, 1975; McIntyre & Stein, 1973; Pellegrino, 1968; Ursin, 1965; Werka et al., 1978). These deficits seem to be due to a reduction in fearfulness (Spevack, Campbell, & Drake, 1975; Werka et al., 1978) and not simply to memory deficits because retention of tasks acquired prior to lesion placements is not affected (Horvath, 1963). CER acquisition can also be hampered by amygdaloid lesions (Kellicut & Schwartzbaum, 1963; Spevack et al., 1975), and this manipulation also increases exploration in open field tests (Ursin et al., 1981; Werka et al., 1978). Stria terminalis or medial amygdala lesions have been reported to disinhibit food-cup approach in cats (Ursin, 1965). CMA lesions in rats have been reported to elevate rates of punished lever pressing for food (Poplawsky & McVeigh, 1981), drinking from an electified sipper tube (Pellegrino, 1986), and to impair the development of CER (Thompson & Schwartzbaum, 1964).

Endogenous 'Pain' Inhibition Pathways

Another line of evidence consistent with the claim that the amygdala/anterior lateral hypothalamic/central gray axis mediates the experience of fear includes studies that implicate the central gray in the modulation of pain perception. On the basis of evidence suggesting that fear can produce analgesia, Bolles and Fanselow (1980) have developed a line of thinking suggesting that opioid-based psychoneural interactions would allow an animal to suppress the sensation of pain during a fear-induced struggle for survival, because any immediate attempt to deal with the pain might reduce the animal's ability to escape. The apparent role of the central gray in elaborating both fear and pain provides a clear anatomical substrate whereby the fear systems of the brain could interact with those that control noiciceptive inputs to perceptual/awareness systems of the brain (see Appendix). There is now an abundant literature that implicates centromedial areas of the mesencephalon in the transmission of pain (vide supra) and modulation of pain intensity (for reviews, see Behbehani & Fields, 1979; Cannon, Liebeskind, & Frenk, 1978; Millan, 1986). In addition to producing analgesia following ESB, central gray neurons respond maximally to noxious peripheral stimulation (Sanders et al., 1980). Whether such increases in neural firing reflect the role of the central CG in pain transmission or pain inhibition is not known.

However, it is clear that CG of the mesencephalon is a major locus for the inhibition of noxious sensory stimulation. CG lesions generally do not abolish pain responsivity (Brutus, Kelly, Glusman, & Bodnar, 1974; Liebman et al., 1970; Mayer & Liebeskind, 1974), whereas ESB applied to this area generally has that effect. This inhibitory influence does not work simply by disrupting sensory information from primary pain conducting fiber tracts passing through the CG, but by postsynaptically inhibiting higher-order transmission of noxious information. The active CG inhibition of pain can originate from a number of levels within the central nervous system (Basbaum & Fields, 1984; Mohrland, 1982). Downstream inhibition may be instigated directly by higher influences, such as hypothalamic fear circuits, or perhaps by behavior inhibiting "alarm" circuits that may project onto enkephalinergic interneurons of the CG, which activate secondary interneurons projecting to descending analgesia circuits outlined by Basbaum and Fields (1984).

Pharmacological Manipulations and Fear

The last class of evidence that supports the contention that the amygdala/anterior lateral hypothalamus/central gray generates the emotion of fear is the use of drugs to reduce levels of fearful responding in animals. At the level of amygdala, drug administration to discrete regions of the amygdala can reduce fearful behaviors. The amygdala contains a high density of benzodiazepine (BZ) and opioid receptors (Goodman, Snyder, Kuhar, & Young, 1980; Niehoff & Kuhar, 1983), and amygdalar injections of BZs can exert anticonflict effects (Nagy, Zambo, & Decsi, 1979; Scheel–Krüger, & Petersen, 1982; Shibata, Kataoka, Yamashita, & Ueki, 1986), and can also reverse CER-induced operant suppression (Thomas, Lewis, & Iversen, 1985), without producing nonspecific sedation or analgesia. Opioid injections into the central nucleus of the amygdala (ACE) reduce anxiety as measured by the social interaction test (File & Rodgers, 1979), and such injections can also attenuate bradycardiac fear CRs in rabbits (Gallagher, Kapp, McNall, & Pascoe, 1981).

Anxiolytic drugs also attenuate flight/escape responses associated with electrical stimulation of the fear system. Pharmacological manipulations that have reliably reduced such ESB-induced behaviors have generally been agents that involve the inhibitory neurotransmitter gamma–amniobutyric acid (GABA). Panksepp, Gandelman, and Trowill (1970) found that AHA stimulation that produces flight/escape behavior can be attenuated by benzodiazepines, the class of antianxiety agents that was eventually found to operate, at least in part, via facilitation of GABA transmission (Tallman & Gallagher, 1985). This class of drugs has also been shown to reduce AHA ESB-induced "affective defensive reaction" in cats (Malick, 1970) and to attenuate the aversive qualities of stimulation of the dorsomedial midbrain/central gray region (Moriyama, Ichimaru, & Gomita, 1984; Olds,

Hogberg, & Olds, 1964). Other researchers have found that GABA receptor stimulators, such as chlordiazepoxide and pentobarbital, reduced flight/escape behaviors evoked by central gray stimulation, whereas the injection of the GABA receptor antagonists, bicuculline and picrotoxin, induce flight/escape behaviors (Brandao, de Aguilar, & Graeff, 1982). Ethyl alcohol, another GABA transmission stimulator, has been shown to decrease the aversive nature of periaqueductal gray (PAG) stimulation (Bovier et al., 1982). It has also been shown that blocking the action of GABA with drugs that interfere with glutamic acid decarboxylase (the enzyme responsible for GABA synthesis) produces flight/escape behavior following injections into either the hypothalamus or the central gray (Brandao, DiScala, Bouchet, & Schmitt, 1986).

In conclusion, all five classes of evidence strongly support the position that a primal fear circuit courses through an amygdaloid, anterior-medial hypothalamic, central-gray continuum. Although alternative psychobiological conceptions of fear have been advanced (e.g., a septohippocampal behavioral inhibition system (Gray, 1987), a locus coeruleus noradrenergic hypothesis (Redmond, 1979), a medial raphe serotonin hypothesis (see Graeff, Quintero, & Gray, 1980; Wise, Berger, & Stein, 1972), we do not believe they have the explanatory power of the theoretical approach outlined here. Whether all these lines of thought can be synthesized into a single perspective remains to be seen (also see Panksepp, 1989).

ANIMAL MODELS OF ANXIETY AND 'THE FEAR SYSTEM'

Clearly, ESB studies provide the most comprehensive information about the trajectory of the fear circuit in the brain, and hence we deem that approach to be an excellent neurological model of fear. In addition, a great number of behavioral models of anxiety have been extensively employed, most often in the context of evaluating pharmacological agents. Presumably, their validity and the validity of the present conception could be cross-checked by evaluating the predictions that emerge from their concurrent consideration. To facilitate cross-talk between these areas of inquiry (which heretofore have proceeded independently), we will summarize that area of behavioral research and speculate upon some potential linkages with the present perspective.

Animal models commonly evaluate the effectiveness of anxiolytic agents on how well they can resurrect previously attenuated, operantly reinforced behavior. In the CER paradigm, reinforced operant responding is suppressed by a stimulus that has been previously paired with inescapable foot shock. Operant behavior can also be suppressed by punishing a reinforced response in the presence of a discriminative stimulus, as in the Geller–Seifter conflict test (Geller & Seifter, 1960) and the Vogel test (Vogel, Beer, & Clody, 1971). Both CER and punished responding have been employed to predict how well benzodiazepine (BZ) will alleviate anxiety in humans. It appears that acute BZ administration effectively reduces the magnitude of the CER, although chronic administration is ineffective (Millenson & Leslie, 1974). In the Geller–Seifter and Vogel procedures, BZs can also increase punished rates of responding (i.e., they reduce conflict). Further, the clinical efficacy of different BZs in human populations is closely correlated with their ability to release punished responding. However, the information such models provides has been described as "strictly correlational" (Treit, 1985).

Interpreting what it means when responses are disinhibited following BZ administration remains problematic, because putative changes in central states of anxiety cannot readily be divorced from nonspecific BZ effects, in particular BZ-induced consummatory behaviors. These agents increase food and water intake in situations in which an animal might be considered anxious and thus ingesting less (e.g., when operantly reinforced behaviors are concurrently punished, in novel situations, and in cases in which food or water is provided in a novel container); but an animal receiving BZs will also consume more in situations in which the food or water is untainted and familiar and the animal is well habituated to the test situation. Whether BZs decrease the negative aspects of the situation (i.e., reduce anxiety by altering neuronal activity in the circuitry mediating fear), increase the positive aspects of the consummatory behavior (i.e., food or water palatability), or simply ressurect ongoing behaviors through nonspecific behavioral disinhibition remains unclear.

Lal and Emmett–Oglesby (1983) developed another animal model of anxiety, the pentylenetetrazol (PTZ) discrimination test. In this test, animals are first trained to lever-press for food, and subsequently to press one of two levers to indicate whether or not they had been injected with subconvulsant dose of PTZ. These authors argue that this test involves the animals' use of "interoceptive cues" that are present following PTZ administration (Schuster & Brady, 1971). BZs appear to interfere with the perception of these cues, as indicated by poor performance in discriminative lever pressing. Although humans commonly report feeling substantial anxiety after receiving subconvulsant doses of PTZ (Rodin & Calhoun, 1970), we do not know whether PTZ-induced interoceptive stimuli in other animals reflect a feeling akin to our own experience of anxiety. It would be of interest to determine whether damage to the fear system postulated herein will attenuate the discriminability of PTZ-induced interoceptive cues. In view of such problems, Pellow, Chopin, File, and Briley (1985) argue that validation of most animal models of anxiety has not been adequately demonstrated, and that the behavioral changes employed need to be scrutinized more closely.

Other animal models of anxiety, such as avoidance paradigms, use behavioral measures that appear similar to what humans commonly exhibit when feeling anxious. However, reports that employ avoidance paradigms provide a confusing array of findings (see Soubrie, 1986, for a review). For example, although BZs impair passive avoidance, they also facilitate two-way active avoidance and fail to influence one-way active avoidance. Consequently, the validity of all such tests as measures of a unidimensional aspect of experimentally-induced anxiety may be questioned.

All these models require the animal to learn an association before behavioral tests can be performed. Also, the behaviors frequently tested are contrived (e.g., lever pressing). It might be more elegant to measure species-specific, unlearned behaviors in animals exposed to threatening events (i.e., behaviors such as those described earlier in this chapter). Also, if associative learning is to be employed, it would be advantageous to make the threat source more distinctive than traditional stimuli, such as foot shock. Threats the animal encounters in the wild may be most informative, as they would be expected to elicit most directly activity in the brain fear-circuit complex.

One model that clearly satisfies the first requirement is the social interaction test (File, 1984, 1985; File, Hyde, & Pool, 1976), which evaluates the ability of pharmacological agents to reverse the attenuation of ongoing, unlearned social behaviors. Two adult male rats are placed together in a neutral test arena, and "anxiety" is produced in the animals by bright illumination and unfamiliarity with the test chamber. How much the animals engage in "social interaction" is recorded during a 10-minute trial. An animal less likely to engage in social interaction is considered to be more anxious. These investigators have shown that BZ administration increases levels of social interaction under these test conditions. However, only the cumulative time that the animals spend "socially engaged" is measured, and the frequency of each of the behaviors considered to be elements of social interaction—sniffing, following, grooming, mounting, nipping, boxing, wrestling, jumping on and over the partner are simply lumped together. These BZ-induced increases in the amount of time animals spend socially engaged might actually be due to changes in levels of only one or two of the behaviors measured. Indeed, in an earlier study File et al. (1976) conceded that the myriad of behaviors considered to be elements of social interaction include some activities not directly affected by anxiety. More recently Treit (1985) also noted his trouble validating some of these behaviors as measures of anxiety. Nonetheless, all the original behaviors are still employed as an index of anxiety among rats in more recent studies (e.g., File, 1985). Therefore, to argue convincingly that this model is indeed valid would require the analysis of BZ affects after removing from the list those behaviors which remain unaffected by clearly established anxiety manipulations. For instance, we have found that specific measures of play behavior in juvenile rats can serve as a strong spontaneous behavioral baseline for analysis of the disrupting influence of threatening stimuli (Crepeau & Panksepp, 1987).

More recently, Pellow et al. (1985) evaluated another animal model for testing anxiolytic agents, the elevated plus-maze test (Montgomery, 1958). The test apparatus consists of four 50-$\times$-10-cm arms arranged in a plus sign elevated 50 cm above the floor. One pair of opposing arms is open, whereas the sides and ends of the other two arms are enclosed by 40-cm walls (the ceiling is open). The animal is placed at the center of the plus, alternately facing an open arm or a closed arm, and the first arm that the animal enters is recorded, as well as the total number of entries onto open/ closed arms, and the total time the animal spends on each arm. Acute BZ administration increases the number of entries onto, as well as total time spent on the open arms, whereas nonanxiolytic agents fail to affect open arm exploration. Pellow et al. argue that increased open arm exploration indicates an immediate anxiolytic effect of BZs, which provides an advantage over those models that require pretraining the animals in operant tasks and pretreating them with BZs for several days in order to eliminate drug-induced sedation. However, although acute BZ administration reliably increased open arm exploration, there were evident problems. The "anxiolytic" drug effects disappeared when the animals were tested following 5 days of BZ pretreatment.

Human patients rarely exhibit tolerance to the anxiolytic efficacy of BZs, even following months of taking a standard dose of the drug on a daily basis. However, one shortcoming that appears common to several animal models of anxiety is that tolerance to the anxiolytic effects of BZs develops rapidly. For example, tolerance has been reported in rats receiving injections of BZ after (1) Five days, using elevated-plus maze (Pellow et al., 1985); (2) Twenty-five days, using the social interaction test (Vellucci & File, 1979); (3) Ten days, using the defensive burying paradigm (Treit, 1985), and (4) Nine days in mice, using a four-plate test (Stephens & Schneider, 1985).

As has been discussed, many of the behaviors indexed in traditional animal models of anxiety require further validation. Most current models measure changes in levels of behaviors following some associative learning by the animal. The behavioral measures are often unnatural to the organism and for purposes of measurement, contrived. Also, the learning situation often includes competing behavioral tendencies that can make it impossible or very difficult for the animal to learn. Instead of using such tasks, we argue for using species-typical reactions to some ethologically valid aversive event, such as confrontations with an aggressive conspecific or a natural predator. Some of the behaviors that could be studied in this way include flight, freezing, defecation, and urination, defensive fighting, defensive burying, and potentiated startle. The last two have recently come into relatively common use.

The potentiated startle paradigm (Brown et al., 1951; Davis & Astrachan, 1978), another model which has been recently advocated, employs presentation of a classically conditioned CS with a sudden-onset loud sound, and the heightened amplitude of the reflexive startle response is measured. The enhanced startle amplitude is taken to indicate that anxiety has been induced by the CS, and systemic BZ administration selectively attenuates the CS-induced potentiated startle (Davis, 1986).

Treit (1985) argues that the "conditioned defensive burying" paradigm (Pinel & Treit, 1978) offers a robust analogue to human anxiety. Animals being tested receive a shock from a prod mounted on one end of the test chamber. Subsequently (as long as 20 days later), the animal will work to bury the prod with bedding. Treit maintains that "burying appears to be a complex, species-typical defensive response of rodents to a variety of naturally occurring aversive stimuli . . ." (p. 213), and it therefore provides a valuable model for studying anxiolytic agents. The analysis of other naturalistic behaviors may be equally valuable.

The Psychobiology of Naturalistic Behavioral Changes that Reflect Fear, with a Specific Focus on Freezing

Only a modest amount of evidence concerning brain systems that control behavioral output in traditional models of fear is presently available. Somewhat more effort has been devoted to analyzing changes in spontaneous fearful tendencies following direct manipulations of the CNS, with a substantial amount of work having been devoted to the analysis of potentiated startle, some for freezing, a more modest amount for flight, and next to nothing for other relevant behaviors discussed in earlier sections (e.g., flight).

Changes in freezing behavior have been fairly extensively documented following damage to higher reaches of the fear circuit, especially to the septohippocampal behavioral inhibition system (Gray, 1987). Hippocampal lesions can reduce conditioned freezing behaviors (Blanchard & Blanchard, 1972b), whereas damage to other higher areas of the brain thought to mediate fear or anxiety, such as the cingulate cortex, have relatively little effect (Divac, Mogenson, Blanchard, & Blanchard, 1984). Amygdaloid damage, on the other hand, also reduces shock-induced freezing and conflict behaviors (Pellegrino, 1968; Shibata et al., 1986; Spevack et al., 1975), as well as defeat-induced freezing and related defense behaviors that occur in agonistic situations (Bolhuis et al., 1984; Luiten et al., 1985). The antifear effects of amygdaloid lesions generalize to other spontaneous fear tendencies, such as potentiated startle (Hitchcock & Davis, 1986, 1987), and the tendency of chronic stress to cause ulceration (Henke, 1988). In addition, amygdalar lesions and damage to nearby basal ganglia and lower mesencephalic areas can tame wild rats (Blanchard, Blanchard, Lee, & Nakamura, 1979; Blanchard, Blanchard, Lee, & Williams, 1981; Blanchard, Williams, Lee, & Blanchard, 1981; Kemble et al., 1984, Woods, 1956).

There is relatively little work on the effects of lesions within the lower reaches of fear circuitry on freezing behavior, but recent work from our lab does indicate that lesions of the AHA can markedly reduce footshock induced freezing (Sacks & Panksepp, 1988, unpublished data). Other recent work indicates that cerebellar vermal lesions can attenuate both freezing and neophobic responses (Supple, Leaton, & Fanselow, 1987), which confirms the rather unexpected role of the cerebellum in the mediation of emotional behavior (Heath, 1986). To our knowledge, no one has yet thoroughly analyzed the effects of mesencephalic central gray lesions on freezing tendencies, but there is abundant work in both mammals (e.g., Skultety, 1963) and birds (Andrew & de Lanerolle, 1974) indicating that animals with such brain damage exhibit markedly diminished flight tendencies. Also, Graeff and colleagues have found that freezing can be promoted unconditionally by application of ESB to nearby areas of the median raphe (Graeff et al., 1980). In sum, abundant data with naturalistic fear behaviors suggest that some type of harmoniously operating emotive circuit running from the amygdala to the central gray mediates the affective tendency called fear. It also seems that activity in this "active fear" system can establish a central state whereby future awareness of contiguously presented stimuli can activate "passive fear" tendencies, such as crouching, freeezing, and hiding, which may be organized around a separate behavioral inhibition circuit in the brain.

Although much of our coverage has been premised on the notion that the behavioral inhibition/freezing system in the brain may be rather distinct from the flight system, to our knowledge no concurrent empirical analysis of brain control of flight and freezing has yet been conducted. In fact, both responses could emerge from a common system. For instance, from a circuit interaction perspective, it would be attractive if both active and passive fear responses were organized in nearby circuits of the brain. It would theoretically simplify matters if a low level of activity within a basic fear circuit promoted freezing, whereas high level of activity within the same system promoted flight. That would make it easier to envision how the contextual cues paired with stimuli that trigger flight would on subsequent occasions promote freezing. Thus, we have initiated studies to determine

FIG. 1.6. Analysis of ESB-
evoked behavior patterns in an
animal being stimulated with
ascending 5 uA steps in the
AHA fear zone for the fist
time (sine-wave current
administered through biopolar
electrodes). Proper positioning
of the electrode in a flight area
had been verified during
surgery by the induction of
respiratory changes. At the
three lowest current levels, the
stimulation increased freezing.
Rearing behavior was
invigorated at the current step
prior to evocation of flight.
Eight other animals tested in
the same way have yielded the
same behavior patterns (Sacks
& Pansepp, 1988).

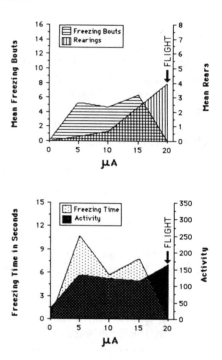

whether activation of brain loci that can invoke flight might not also produce freezing at lower current levels. That, in fact, has proved to be the
case (Fig. 1.6). ESB applied to the AHA at subflight current levels can
markedly increase freezing during the very first stimulation session. Whether
both the ESB-induced freezing and flight are due to differential levels of
activation within a single circuit, or to activation of separate nearby circuits,
remains unknown. We suspect that the former option is more likely, since
we have now observed the pattern summarized in Fig. 1.6 from a series
of widely distributed flight sites. It is most remarkable that from all sites,
freezing appeared at lower current levels than flight, suggesting the operation of a single system.

Psychopharmacology of Freezing

To date only a few studies have addressed the effects of pharmacological
agents on freezing. Krieckhause, Miller, and Zimmerman (1965) found
that d–amphetamine (2 mg/kg) reduced freezing to a CS associated with
foot shock. A series of studies by Fanselow (1984) have shown that the
opiate blockers, naloxone and naltrexone, increase freezing to shock-
associated contextual cues, but only if these agents are present during
conditioning. Fanselow ascribes this effect to the blocking of an opiate

analgesic system that is normally activated by fear-eliciting stimuli, rather than to any direct effect on the psychological and physiological mechanisms mediating fear. Lester and Fanselow (1985) reported that naloxone had no effect on freezing in female laboratory rats exposed to a cat.

The effects of the benzodiazepines midazolam (MDZ), chlordiazepoxide (CDP), and diazepam (DZP) on freezing were tested by Fanselow and Helmstetter (1988). MDZ and DZP reduced freezing to chamber cues associated with shock, whether the drugs were present during shock conditioning, or during behavioral testing conducted 24 hours later. CDP use also reduced freezing slightly, but the change was not reliable. We have also (Abbott, unpublished data, 1988) tested 5, 10, and 20 mg/kg CDP in a paradigm almost identical to that used by Fanselow and Helmstetter (1988) and obtained a different outcome. CDP had little effect on freezing at 5 mg/kg, but at the higher doses, freezing was potentiated by the drug. This effect does not appear to be due entirely to motor sedation. The preshock incidence of paw withdrawal from the grid induced by injection of formalin into the paw (recuperative behavior) was not affected by the 10 mg/kg dose and was increased by the 20 mg/kg dose. This effect cannot be ascribed to drug-induced sedation, because drug injections intended to habituate the subjects to the motor-suppressive effect of CDP had no effect on the outcome of the experiment. A similar effect of CDP on freezing was noted by Cameron and Blampied (1980) in rats exposed to a predator (ferret).

An effect similar to that produced by CDP was also noted recently by Blanchard, Blanchard, Flannelly, and Hori (1986), following treatment with ethanol. In a naturalistic setting, control rats tended to freeze when the experimenter approached within 1–4 ms, but freezing gave way to active defensive behaviors at a distance of 0.5 ms. Ethanol had no effect on freezing at the greater distances, but blocked the suppression of freezing seen at 0.5 m in a dose-dependent manner. It may be that both ethanol and CDP increase freezing by suppressing tendencies toward active defense.

As data with benzodiazepines and ethanol suggest, the effects of pharmacological manipulations on freezing are likely to be complex, depending on the specific defensive response tendencies affected and the test situation. Fig. 1.7 shows the results of a recent experiment conducted in our laboratory that highlight problems associated with pharmacological manipulations and assessment of the fear behaviors assumed to be indicative of underlying affect. Freezing to chamber cues was assessed for five 1-minute epochs prior to delivery of shock in the chamber (baseline), immediately postshock, and 24 hours postshock. Morphine, (2 mg/kg, a dosage that essentially eliminates separation induced distress vocalizations (DVs) in dogs, monkeys, guinea pigs, rats and chicks) and produces modest anal-

FIG. 1.7. Comparison of freezing time and bouts indicated by foot shock (1 sec at 0.6 mA) in rats administered morphine (2 mg/kg), scopolamine (1 mg/kg), clonidine (5μg/kg) and vehicle (1 cc/kg). Freezing levels were assessed during 5 single minute epochs before, immediately postshock and 24-hr postshock. Morphine and vehicle animals froze similarly during postshock and 24 hr later, whereas scopolamine treated animals were unable to freeze due to apparent motor activation during the postshock phase, and perhaps due to amnesia 24 hr later. Clonidine treated animals exhibited high levels of sedation (which could have obscured a true freezing response) and prevented memorial integration of the experience for the test given 24 hr later.

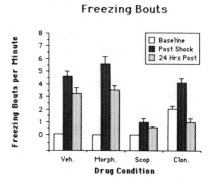

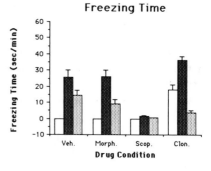

gesia, had little effect on freezing. The fact that morphine, which has such powerful effects on other forms of trepidation (such as separation distress), had little effect on freezing suggests that the opiate system may not act primarily on fear systems, but on related affective processes which can occasionally modify measures of fear. Additionally, scopolamine (1 mg/kg, which has been reported to produce a fear-like state in humans) actually decreased freezing both immediately after the shock and 24 hours later. The reduction of freezing immediately postshock was presumably due to a high level of motoric activation that interfered with the maintenance of the freezing response. In addition, because of the important role of cholinergic systems in memory, the animals may have exhibited no freezing 24 hours later because of drug-induced amnesia. In other words, the changes in freeezing may have had little to do with fear. Clonidine (50 μg/kg) however, produced a high degree of motoric inactivation, which could be scored as increased freezing, but which may have actually obscured the true freezing response during the post shock periods. The reduction of freezing 24 hours later may have actually reflected the relaxation/sedation present during the training session (which was mistakenly scored as increased freezing). In short, the side-effects associated with various pharmacological manipulations may prevent the accurate assessment of fear-induced behaviors. All this highlights the many difficulties in evaluating changes in the central affective states of animals other than humans—a problem that has hampered progress in our understanding of animal behavior since the inception of experimental psychology.

CONCLUDING REMARKS

Historically, the study of "fear" in psychology has been an exercise in cataloging external stimuli and correlating them with behavioral responses or else the phenomenological appraisal of these external stimuli. The correlational path, which has been pursued with the aid of animal models, has helped elucidate the external conditions that promote fear. In general, the study of fear has relied upon identifying the external stimuli and the stimulus characteristics that generate the emotion, and rarely upon the experience of the emotion itself, which may be psychologically irreducible. From our viewpoint, to understand the sources of fear, one has to go to a deeper, neural level of analysis.

Of course, the ability of animals to deal with threatening events is complex and multifaceted. There is no doubt that a multifactor theory (Fig. 1.1) is needed to account for the ability of animals to defend themselves and to avoid the dangers of their worlds. Thus, a relatively unidimensional theory such as the one summarized here, encompassing a central neural command system for a relatively homogeneous emotive impulse, may seem unrealistic. We would submit, however, that it is not unrealistic from an affective perspective. We believe that the basic systems that elaborate the affective/behavioral aspects of fear were an early solution for dealing with threatening events, and that higher neural evolution only increased the behavioral repertoire and overall flexibility of creatures, without changing basic affective tendencies. Thus, in various complex situations, animals may actually learn to avoid threats faster when they are less, rather than more, emotionally aroused. In many avoidance situations, the aroused emotional circuits may add little to the behavioral strategies that emerge, providing only the background "value system" which dictates the general trajectory of behavioral output. Accordingly, our position is that primal fear circuits are more directly involved in generating affect, and related instinctual tendencies, rather than behavioral/cognitive strategies in a situation. Only through the construction of more subtle behavioral tests may the influence of these background values be brought to the foreground of behavior. In general, it would seem that the background affective tone of animals, and the ancient behavioral dictates of the underlying emotional systems, can be observed more clearly through physiological/autonomic changes and the direct observation of the spontaneous behavioral tendencies of animals rather than through the analysis of operant behaviors. We believe that the solution to the puzzle of fear will emerge from a close neurobiological study of the circuitry sketched in this chapter.

Although our conception of a harmoniously operating fear system is a simple one, we would emphasize that the true neurobiological complexity of the system is surely staggering. We are far from an adequate reductionistic understanding of its operating principles. At best, we presently have a bare outline to help guide work on the details of the system. It is certain that the fear system can be dissected into subfunctions. For instance, the autonomic and behavioral expressions of conditioned fear appear to diverge, within the fiber systems that descend from the central nucleus of the amygdala (LeDoux, Iwata, Cicchetti, & Reis, 1988), but this is quite a separate issue than the question of whether the system is designed in such a way that the subsystems operate as a well-orchestrated, harmonious whole, as opposed to independently operating functions. The present view maintains that the circuitry is designed to operate synchronously because of executive influences that permeate the whole system. Fortunately, the biological complexity of such basic neuropsychological processes can now be incisively addressed, and the prospects of such knowledge beckons our discipline to pursue reductionistic approaches with a vigor that has not been a characteristic of our scientific past.

APPENDIX: NEURAL MECHANISMS OF PAIN PERCEPTION

The fact that pain can commonly generate fear underscores the theoretical need for the command system of fear to interact with the pain system at some level of the neuroaxis. For this reason, we have decided to include a brief synopsis of how pain is organized in the brain. The available evidence of the underlying circuitry is schematized in Fig. 1.8.

Cutaneous pain perception is initiated by the stimulation of nociceptors on the body surface and is transmitted via thin, slow-conducting, and unmyelinated C fibers and via thicker, faster conducting and myelinated A–delta fibers to the dorsal horns of the spinal cord, where there is considerable preprocessing of pain information and subsequent gating of the noxious stimulation prior to further processing by the brain (Dennis & Melzack, 1977).

Two aspects of pain perception involve the discriminative aspects of the sensations and motivational and affective aspects of the sensations. According to Casey (1978), the discriminative aspects of pain appear to be mediated by the direct axonal projections of the spinothalamic tract as they directly ascend to the ventrobasal thalamic nuclei, the ventral posterior

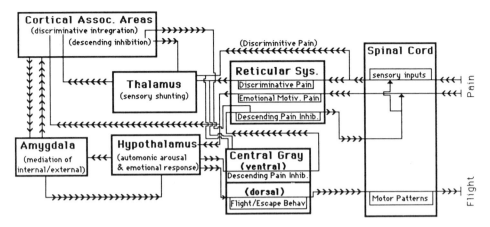

FIG. 1.8. A general flow diagram of the in-flow of nociceptive information through the CNS and the out-flow of active defense behaviors such as flight. This diagram highlights the functional connectivity of the pain and fear system.

lateral (VPL), the ventral posterior medial (VPM) and the parafascicular nuclei of the thalamus. Activation of these inputs may help instigate an "alarm" state in the nervous system. The posterior group of thalamic nucleic may have contributed to discriminative aspects of pain perception. However, some of the axons of ascending pain systems first project to the reticular formation (RF), perhaps shunting information to emotional systems, and then on to the thalamus. Once pain information has reached various thalamic nuclei it is then shunted to the somatosensory cortex where spatiotemporal discriminative analysis and integration of this information with other sensory systems can occur.

The motivational and affective components of pain perception appear to be mediated largely by the axonal projections of more ancient spino-reticular pathways which follow a more diffuse, polysynaptic pathway to the RF. Axons of these systems also send information onward to hypothalamic and limbic forebrain cell groups mediating autonomic arousal and emotional states. Additionally, both motivational and discriminative aspects of pain sensation are influenced by descending activity from the forebrain. This descending activity can exert active inhibition of the noxious sensations ascending in the spinal cord.

The importance of the RF in the perception of pain is twofold. First, the RF is a diffuse, interconnected network of neurons that incorporates a high degree of polysensory convergence. This convergence of the axons of multiple sensory systems including the axons associated with pain perception allows for the possibility of sensory integration across the various somatic sense modalities. Second, it is strategically situated in the brainstem as a relay juncture. The major ascending target areas of the RF include sensory and motor areas of cerebral cortex, the thalamus and hypothalamus, whereas the major efferent pathways include descending spinal pathways which can gate, inhibit or amplify incoming information (Basbaum & Fields, 1984).

Interestingly, the role of the mesencephalic RF of the higher brain stem in the transmission of nociceptive information may be somewhat different than that of the medullary RF of the lower brain stem, since the rostral RF has more functional connections to the thalamus and the somatosensory cortex (Molinari, Bentivoglio, Minciacchi, Granato, & Macchi, 1986). Also, this tissue may play a role in central analgesic mechanisms because of its responsiveness to opiate drugs, the presence of endogenous opioid-binding sites, and the identification of many opioid-secreting terminals among these cell groups (Basbaum & Fields, 1984).

The functional relationship among the many afferent and efferent pathways of the RF complex, as well as the interconnected nature of its neuronal population, raises the possibility of its involvement as the key anatomical junction between the systems of pain and fear. Since the trajectory of the pain system passes through the RF, it is likely that afferent ascending influences are routed to the hypothalamus and limbic system where emotional and motivated activity is governed. The interaction between the systems of pain and fear would allow noxious cutaneous information to motivate an organism to escape and reduce the risk of further bodily damage, while producing consequences needed for the formation of associations about salient environmental cues predicting threat. In short, pain is nature's way of teaching animals to avoid destruction, while fear is nature's way of teaching animals to avoid pain.

REFERENCES

Abbott B., & Badia, P. (1979). Choice for signaled over unsignaled shock as a function of signal length. *Journal of the Experimental Analysis of Behavior, 32,* 409–417.

Abbott, B., & Panksepp, J. (1988). Alpha-MSH effects on separation induced distress vocalizations. *Abstracts for the Society of Neuroscience, 14,* 287.

Adams, D. B. (1979). Brain mechanisms for offense, defense, and submission. *Behavioral and Brain Sciences, 2,* 201–241.

Adams, D. B. (1980). Motivational systems of agonistic behavior in muroid rodents: A comparative review and neural model. *Aggressive Behavior, 6,* 295–346.

Aggleton, J. P., & Mishkin, M. (1986). The amygdala: Gateway to the emotions. In R. Plutchik & H. Kellerman (Eds.), *Emotion: Theory, research and experience.* Orlando, FL: Academic Press, pp. 218–299.

Andrew, R. J., & de Lanerolle, N. (1974). The effects of muting lesions on emotional behaviour and behaviour normally associated with calling. *Brain Behavior and Evolution, 10,* 377–399.

Badia, P., Harsh, J., & Abbott, B. (1979). Predictable and unpredictable aversive events: Data and theory. *Psychological Bulletin, 86,* 1107–1131.

Bandler, R., DePaulis, A., & Vergnes, M. (1985). Identification of midbrain neurones mediating defensive behaviour in the rat by microinjections of excitatory amino acids. *Behavioural Brain Research, 15,* 107–119.

Basbaum, A. I., & Fields, H. L. (1984). Endogenous pain control systems: Brainstem spinal pathways and endorphine circuitry. *Annual Review of Neuroscience, 7,* 309–338.

Behbehani, M. M., & Fields, H. L. (1979). Evidence that an excitatory connection between the periaqueductal gray and nucleus raphe magnus mediates stimulation produced analgesia. *Brain Research, 170,* 85–93.

Ben-Ari, Y., (Ed.). (1981). *The amygdaloid complex.* Amsterdam: Elsevier/North-Holland Biomedical Press.

Blanchard, R. J., & Blanchard, D. C. (1969). Crouching as an index of fear. *Journal of Comparative and Physiological Psychology, 67,* 370–375.

Blanchard, R. J., & Blanchard, D. C. (1971). Defensive reactions in the albino rat. *Learning and Motivation, 2,* 351–362.

Blanchard, D. C., & Blanchard, R. J. (1972a). Innate and conditioned reactions to threat in rats with amygdaloid lesions. *Journal of Comparative and Physiological Psychology, 81,* 281–290.

Blanchard, R. J., & Blanchard, D. C. (1972b). Effects of hippocampal lesions on the rat's reaction to a cat. *Journal of Comparative and Physiological Psychology, 48,* 77–82.

Blanchard, R. J., & Blanchard, D. C. (1977). Aggressive behavior in the rat. *Behavioral Biology, 21,* 197–224.

Blanchard, D. C., & Blanchard, R. J. (1984). Inadequacy of the pain-aggression hypothesis revealed in naturalistic settings. *Aggressive Behavior, 10,* 33–46.

Blanchard, R. J., Blanchard, D. C., Flannelly, K. J., & Hori, K. (1986). Ethanol changes patterns of defensive behavior in wild rats. *Physiology and Behavior, 38,* 645–650.

Blanchard, D. C., Blanchard, R. J., Lee, E. M. C., & Nakamura, S. (1979). Defensive behaviors in rats following septal and septal-amygdala lesions. *Journal of Comparative and Physiological Psychology, 93,* 378–390.

Blanchard, D. C., Blanchard, R. C., Lee, E. M. C., & Williams, G. (1981). Taming in the wild Norway rat following lesions in the basal ganglia. *Physiology and Behavior, 27,* 995–1000.

Blanchard, R. J., Flannelly, K. J., & Blanchard, D. C. (1986). Defensive behavior of laboratory and wild Rattus norvegicus. *Journal of Comparative Psychology, 100,* 101–107.

Blanchard, R. J., Fukunaga, K. K., & Blanchard, D. C. (1976). Environmental control of defense reactions to footshock. *Bulletin of the Psychonomic Society 8,* 129–130.

Blanchard, R. J., Mast, M., & Blanchard, D. C. (1975). Stimulus control of defensive reactions in the albino rat. *Journal of Comparative and Physiological Psychology, 88,* 81–88.

Blanchard, D. C., Williams, G., Lee, E. M. C., & Blanchard, R. J. (1981). Taming of wild *Rattus norvegicus* by lesions of the mesencephalic central gray. *Physiological Psychology, 9,* 157–161.

Bolhuis, J. J., Fitzgerald, R. E., Dijk, D. J., & Koolhaas, M. (1984). The corticomedial amygdala and learning in an agonistic situation in the rat. *Physiology and Behavior, 32,* 575–579.

Bolles, R. C. (1970). Species-specific defense reactions and avoidance learning. *Psychological Review, 77,* 32–48.

Bolles, R. C., & Collier, A. C. (1976). The effect of predictive cues on freezing in rats. *Animal Learning and Behavior, 4,* 6–8.

Bolles, R. C., & Fanselow, M. S. (1980). A perceptual-defensive-recuperative model of fear and pain. *Behavioral and Brain Sciences, 3,* 291–323.

Bovier, M. E., Broekkamp, C. L., & Lloyd, K. G. (1982). Ethyl alcohol effect on escape from electrical periaqueductal gray stimulation in rats. *Pharmacology, Biochemistry and Behavior, 21,* 353–356.

Bower, G. H., & Miller, N. E. (1958). Rewarding and punishing effects from stimulating the same place in the rat's brain. *Journal of Comparative and Physiological Psychology, 51,* 669–678.

Brandao, M. L., de Aguilar, J. C., & Graeff, F. G. (1982). GABA mediation of the antiaversive action of minor tranquilizers. *Pharmacology, Biochemistry and Behavior, 16,* 397–402.

Brandao, M. L., DiScala, G., Bouchet, M. J., & Schmitt, P. (1986). Escape behavior produced by the blockade of glutamic acid decarboxylase (GAD) in the mesencephalic central gray or medial hypothalamus. *Pharmacology, Biochemistry and Behavior, 24,* 497–501.

Bronson, G. W. (1968). The fear of novelty. *Psychological Bulletin, 69,* 350–358.

Brown, J. S., Kalish, H. I., & Farber, I. E. (1951). Conditioned fear as revealed by magnitude of startle response to an auditory stimulus. *Journal of Experimental Psychology, 41,* 317–328.

Brutus, M., Kelly, D. D., Glusman, M., & Bodnar, R. J. (1974). PAG lesions and nonnarcotic nociception. *Neuroscience Abstracts, 5,* 2056.

Brutus, M. Shaikh, M. B., & Siegel, A. (1985). Differential control of hypothamically elicited flight behavior by the midbrain periaqueductal gray in the cat. *Behavioral Brain Research, 17,* 235–244.

Cameron, D. B., & Blampied, N. M. (1980). Rats' reactions to a predator: Modification by chlordiazepoxide. *New Zealand Psycholgist, 9,* 9–13.

Cannon, W. B. (1936). *Bodily changes in pain, hunger, fear and rage* (3rd ed.). New York: Appleton–Century.

Cannon, T. J., Liebeskind, J. C., & Frenk, H. (1978). Neural and neurochemical mechanisms of pain inhibition. In R. A. Sternback (Ed.), *The psychology of pain.* New York: Raven Press, pp. 27–48.

Carstens, E. (1986). Hypothalamic inhibition of rat dorsal horn neuronal responses to noxious skin heating. *Pain, 25,* 95–107.

Casey, K. L. (1978). Neural mechanisms of pain. In E. C. Carterette & M. P. Friedman (Eds.), *Handbook of perception* (Vol. VIB). New York: Academic Press, pp. 183–230.

Cazala, P., & Schmitt, P. (1987). Dorso-ventral variation in the attenuating effect of lateral hypothalamic stimulation on the switch-off response elicited from the mesencephalic central gray area. *Physiology and Behavior, 40,* 625–629.

Clarke, P. B. S., Schwartz, R. D., Paul, S. M., Pert, C. B., & Pert, A. (1985). Nicotinic binding in rat brain autoradiographic comparison of [³H]acetylcholine, [³H]nicotine, and [¹²⁵I]-a-bungarotoxin. *Journal of Neuroscience, 5,* 1307–1315.

Cohen, B. D., Brown, G. W., & Brown, M. L. (1957). Avoidance learning motivated by electrical stimulation of the brain. *American Journal of Physiology, 179,* 587–593.

Colpaert, F. C. (1975). The ventromedial hypothalamus and the control of avoidance behavior and aggression: Fear hypothesis versus response-suppression theory of limbic system function. *Behavioral Biology, 15,* 27–44.

Colpaert, F. C., & Wiepkema, P. R. (1976). The ventromedial hypothalamus: Fear conditioning and passive avoidance in rats. *Physiology and Behavior, 16,* 91–96.

Coover, G., Ursin, H., & Levine, S. (1973). Corticosterone and avoidance in rats with basolateral amygdaloid lesions. *Journal of Comparative and Physiological Psychology, 85,* 111–122.

Cox, V. C. (1967). Avoidance conditioning with central and peripheral aversive stimulation. *Canadian Journal of Psychology, 21,* 425–435.

Crepeau, L., & Panksepp, J. (1987). Effects of chlordiazepoxide and morphine on CER-attenuated juvenile rat play. *Neuroscience Abstracts, 13,* 1323.

Culhane, E. S., & Carstens, E. (1988). Medial hypothalamic stimulation suppresses nociceptive spinal dorsal horn neurons but not the tail flick reflex in the rat. *Brain Research, 438,* 137–144.

Cunningham, P. M., Goldsmith, G. E., & Hellon, R. F. (1986). Medial hypothalamic stimulation produces analgesia to facial heating in unrestrained rats. *Neuroscience Letters, 68,* 107–111.

Curti, M. W. (1935). Native fear responses of white rats in the presence of cats. *Psychological Monographs, 46,* 76–98.

Darwin, C. (1872). *The expression of the emotions in man and animals.* London: John Murray.

Davis, M. (1986). Pharmacological and anatomical analysis of fear conditioning using the fear-potentiated startle paradigm. *Behavioral Neuroscience, 100,* 314–824.

Davis, M., & Astrachan, D. I. (1978). Conditioned fear and startle magnitude: Effects of different footshock or backshock intensities used in training. *Journal of Experimental Psychology: Animal Behavior Processes, 4,* 95–103.

Delgado, J. M. R., Roberts, W. W., & Miller, N. E. (1954). Learning motivated by electrical stimulation of the brain. *American Journal of Physiology, 179,* 587–593.

Delgado, J. M. R., Rosvold, H. E., & Looney, E. (1956). Evoking conditioned fear by electrical stimulation of subcortical structures in the monkey brain. *Journal of Comparative and Physiological Psychology, 49,* 373–380.

deOlmos, J., Alheid, G. F., & Beltramino, C. A. (1985). Amygdala. In G. Paxinos (Ed.), *The rat nervous system, I. Forebrain and midbrain.* Sydney: Academic Press, 223–234.

Dennis, S. G., & Melzack, R. (1977). Pain-signalling systems in dorsal and ventral spinal cord. *Pain, 4,* 97–132.

Desci, L., & Varszegi, M. K. (1969). Fear and escape reactions evoked by the intrahypothalamic injection of d-tubocurarine in unrestrained cats. *Acta Physiologica Academiae Scientiarum Hungaricae, 36,* 95–104.

de Molina, A. F., & Hunsperger, R. W. (1962). Organization of the subcortical system governing defense and flight reactions in the cat. *Journal of Physiology (London), 160,* 200–213.

Di Scala, G., Mana, M. J., Jacobs, W. J., & Phillips, A. G. (1987). Evidence of pavlovian conditioned fear following electrical stimulation of the periaqueductal grey in the rat. *Physiology and Behavior, 40,* 55–63.

Divac, I., Mogensen, J., Blanchard, R. J., & Blanchard, D. C. (1984). Mesial cortical lesions and fear behavior in the wild rat. *Physiological Psychology, 12,* 271–274.

Eclander, F., & Karli, P. (1980). Effects of infant and adult amygdaloid lesions upon acquisition of two-way active avoidance by the adult rat: Influence of rearing conditions. *Physiology and Behavior, 42,* 887–893.

Edwards, M. A., & Adams, D. B. (1974). Role of midbrain central gray in pain-induced defensive boxing in rats. *Physiology and Behavior, 13,* 113–121.

Fanselow, M. S. (1980). Conditional and unconditional components of post-shock freezing. *Pavlovian Journal of Biological Science, 15,* 177–182.

Fanselow, M. S. (1984). What is conditioned fear? *Trends in Neuroscience, 7,* 460–462.

Fanselow, M. S., & Helmstetter, F. J. (1988). Conditional analgesia, defensive freezing, and benzodiazepines. *Behavioral Neuroscience, 102,* 233–243.

Fanselow, M. S., & Lester, L. S. (1988). A functional behavioristic approach to aversively motivated behavior: Predatory imminence as a determinant of the topography of defensive behavior. In R. C. Bolles & M. D. Beecher (Eds.), *Evolution and learning.* Hillsdale, N.J.: Lawrence Erlbaum Associates, pp. 185–212.

Ferrero, P., Santi, M. R., Conti–Tronconi, B., Costa, E., & Guidotti, A. (1986). Study of an octadecaneuropeptide derived from diazepam binding inhibitor (DBI): Biological activity and presence in rat brain. *Proceedings of the National Academy of Sciences, USA, 83,* 827–831.

File, S. E. (1984). Behavioral pharmacology of benzodiazepines. *Progress in Neuropsychology and Biological Psychiatry, 8*, 19–31.

File, S. E., (1985). Tolerance to the behavioral actions of benzodiazepines. *Neuroscience and Biobehavioral Review, 9*, 113–121.

File, S. E., Hyde, J. R. G., & Pool, M. (1976). Effects of ethanol and chlordiazepoxide on social interaction in rats. *British Journal of Pharmacology, 58*, 465P.

File, S. E., & Rodgers, R. J. (1979). Partial anxiolytic action of morphine sulfate following microinjection into the central nucleus of the amygdala in rats. *Pharmacology, Biochemistry and Behavior, 11*, 313–318.

Fuchs, S. A. G., Edinger, H. M., & Siegel, A. (1985a). The organization of the hypothalamic pathway mediating affective defense behavior in the cat. *Brain Research, 330*, 77–92.

Fuchs, S. A. G., Edinger, H. M., & Siegel, A. (1985b). The role of the anterior hypothalamus in affective defense behavior elicited from the ventromedial hypothalamus of the cat. *Brain Research, 330*, 93–107.

Fuchs, S. A. G., & Siegel, A. (1984). Neural pathways mediating hypothalamically elicited flight behavior in the cat. *Brain Research, 306*, 263–281.

Gallagher, M. & Kapp, B. S. (1981). Influence of amygdala opiate-sensitive mechanisms, fear motivated responses, and memory processes for aversive experiences. In J. L. Martinez, Jr., R. S. Jensen, R. B. Messing, H. Righter, & J. L. McGaugh, (Eds.), *Endogenous peptides and learning and memory processes*. New York: Academic Press, pp. 445–461.

Gallagher, M., Kapp, B. S., McNall, C. L., & Pascoe, J. P. (1981). Opiate effects in the amygdala central nucleus on heart rate conditioning in rabbits. *Pharmacology, Biochemistry and Behavior, 14*, 497–505.

Gallup, G. G., Jr. (1974). Animal hypnosis: Factual status of a fictional concept. *Psychological Bulletin, 81*, 836–853.

Gardner, L., & Malmo, R. B. (1969). Effects of low-level septal stimulation on escape: Significance for limbic-midbrain interaction in pain. *Journal of Comparative and Physiological Psychology, 68*, 65–73.

Geller, I., & Seifter, J. (1960). The effects of meprobamate, barbiturates, d-amphetamine and promazine on experimentally induced conflict in the rat. *Psychopharmacologia, 1*, 482–492.

Gloor, P. (1960). Amygdala. In J. Field (Ed.), *Handbook of physiology* (Vol. 2). Washington, DC: American Physiological Society, pp. 1395–1420.

Gloor, P. (1978). Inputs and outputs of the amygdala: What the amygdala is trying to tell the rest of the brain. In K. E. Livingstone & A. H. Kieivicz (Eds.), *Limbic mechanisms*. New York: Plenum Press, pp. 189–207.

Gloor, P., Olivier, A. & Quesney, L. F. (1981). The role of the amygdala in the expression of psychic phenomena in temproal lobe seizures. In Y. Ben–Ari (Ed.), *The amygdaloid complex*. New York: Elsevier/North-Holland Press, pp. 489–498.

Goodman, R. R., Snyder, S. H., Kuhar, M. J., & Young, W. S., III (1980). Differentiation of delta and mu opiate receptor localizations by light microscopic autoradiography. *Proceedings of the National Academy of Science, 77*, 6239–6243.

Graeff, F. G., Quintero, S., & Gray, J. A. (1980). Median raphe stimulation, hippocampal theta rhythm and threat-induced behavioral inhibition. *Physiology and Behavior, 25*, 253–261.

Gray, J. A. (1982). *The neuropsychology of anxiety: An enquiry into the function of the septo-hippocampal system*. Oxford, England: Oxford University Press.

Gray, J. A. (1987). *The psychology of fear and stress*. Cambridge, England: Cambridge University Press.

Gray, T. S., & Magnuson, D. J. (1987). Neuropeptide neuronal efferents from the bed nucleus of the stria terminalis and central amygdaloid nucleus to the dorsal vagal comples in the rat. *Journal of Comparative Neurology, 262*, 365–374.

Griffith, C. R. (1919). A possible case of instinctive behavior in the white rat. *Science, 50*, 166–167.
Griffith, C. R. (1920). The behavior of white rats in the presence of cats. *Psychobiology, 2*, 19–28.
Grossman, S. P. (1966). The VMH: a center for affective reactions, satiety, or both? *Physiology and Behavior, 1*, 1–10.
Grossman, S. P. (1970). Avoidance behavior and aggression in rats with transections of the lateral connections of the medial or lateral hypothalamus. *Physiology and Behavior, 5*, 1103–1108.
Grossman, S. P., & Grossman, L. (1970). Surgical interruption of the anterior or posterior connections of the hypothalamus: Effects on aggression and avoidance behavior. *Physiology and Behavior, 5*, 1313–1317.
Grossman, S. P., Grossman, R. L., & Walsh, S. (1975). Functional organization of the rat amygdala with respect to avoidance behavior. *Journal of Comparative and Physiological Psychology, 88*, 829–850.
Hall, C. S. (1934). Emotional behavior in the rat: I. Defecation and urination as measures of individual differences in emotionality. *Journal of Comparative Psychology, 18*, 385–403.
Halliday, A. M., & Logue, V. (1971). Painful sensations evoked by electrical stimulation in the thalamus. In C. G. Somjen (Ed.), *International Symposium on Neurophysiology in Man*. Amsterdam: Excerpta Medica, pp. 221–230.
Hediger, H. (1955). *Studies of the psychology and behavior of captive animals in zoos and circuses*. London: Butterworths.
Henke, P. G. (1988). Electrophysiological activity in the central nucleus of the amygdala: Emotionality and stress ulcers in rats. *Behavioral Neuroscience, 102*, 77–83.
Hess, W. R. (1957). *The functional organization of the diencephalon*. New York: Grune & Stratton.
Hilton, S. M., & Redfern, W. S. (1986). A search for brain stem cell group integrating the defence reaction in the rat. *Journal of Physiology (London), 378*, 213–228.
Hilton, S. M., & Zbrozyna, A. W. (1963). Amygdaloid region for defence reactions and its efferent pathway to the brain stem. *Journal of Physiology, 165*, 160–173.
Hitchcock, J., & Davis, M. (1986). Lesions of the amygdala, but not of the cerebellum or red nucleus, block conditioned fear as measured with the potentiated startle paradigm. *Behavioral Neuroscience, 100*, 11–22.
Hitchcock, J., & Davis, M. (1987). Fear-potentiated startle using an auditory conditioned stimulus: Effect of lesions of the amygdala. *Physiology and Behavior, 39*, 403–408.
Hopkins, D. A., & Holstege, G. (1978). Amygdaloid projections to the mesencephalon, pons and medulla oblongata in the cat. *Experimental Brain Research, 32*, 529–547.
Horvath, F. E. (1963). Effects of basolateral amygdalectomy on three types of avoidance behavior in cats. *Journal of Comparative and Physiological Psychology, 56*, 380–389.
Hunt, H. F., & Brady, J. V. (1951). Some effects of electro-convulsive shock on a conditioned emotional response ("anxiety"). *Journal of Comparative and Physiological Psychology, 44*, 88–98.
Hunt, H. F., Jernberg, P., & Brady, J. V. (1952). The effect of electroconvulsive shock (ECS) on a conditioned emotional response: The effect of post-ECS extinction on the reappearance of the response. *Journal of Comparative and Physiological Psychology, 45*, 589–599.
Irisawa, N., & Iwasaki, T. (1986). Aversive CS-specific alterations of evoked potentials in limbic and related areas of rats. *Physiology and Behavior, 37*, 61–67.
Iwata, J., LeDoux, J. E., Meeley, M. P., Arneric, S., & Reis, D. J. (1986). Intrinsic neurons in the amygdaloid field projected to by the medial geniculate body mediate emotional responses conditioned to acoustic stimuli. *Brain Research, 383*, 195–214.

Kapp, B. S., Pascoe, J. P., & Bixler, M. A. (1984). The amygdala: A neuroanatomical systems approach to its contribution to aversive conditioning. In N. Butters & L. Squire (Eds.), *The neuropsychology of memory*. New York: Guilford Press, pp. 473–488.

Kellicut, M. H., & Schwartzbaum, J. S. (1963). Formation of a conditional emotional response (CER) following lesions of the amygdaloid complex in rats. *Psychological Reports, 12*, 351–358.

Kemble, E. D., Blanchard, D. C., Blanchard, R. J., & Takushi, R. (1984). Taming in wild rats following medial amygdaloid lesions. *Physiology and Behavior, 32*, 131–134.

Kinscheck, I. B., Watkins, L. R., & Mayer, D. J. (1984). Fear is not critical to classically conditioned analgesia: The effects of periaqueductal gray lesions and administration of chlordiazepoxide. *Brain Research, 298*, 33–44.

Koob, G. F., & Bloom, F. E. (1985). Corticotropin releasing factor and behavior. *Federation Proceedings, 44*, 259–263.

Krieckhause, E. E., Miller, N. E., & Zimmerman, P. (1965). Reduction of freezing behavior and improvement of shock avoidance by d-amphetamine. *Journal of Comparative and Physiological Psychology, 60*, 36–40.

Lal, H., & Emmett–Oglesby, M. W. (1983). Behavioral analogues of anxiety. *Neuropharmacology, 22*, 1423–1441.

Lang, P. J., Levin, D. N., Miller, G. A., & Kozak, M. J. (1983). Fear behavior, fear imagery, and the psychophysiology of emotion: The problem of affective response integration. *Journal of Abnormal Psychology, 92*, 276–306.

LeDoux, J. E., Iwata, J., Cicchetti, P., & Reis, D. J. (1988). Different projections of the central amygdaloid nucleus mediate autonomic and behavioral correlates of conditioned fear. *Journal of Neuroscience, 8*, 2517–2529.

LeDoux, J. E., Ruggiero, D. A., & Reis, D. J. (1985). Projections to the subcortical forebrain from anatomically defined regions of the medial geniculate body of the rat. *Journal of Comparative Neurology, 242*, 182–213.

Le Gal La Salle, G., & Ben–Ari, Y. (1981). Unit activity in the amygdaloid complex: A review. In Y. Ben–Ari (Ed.), *The Amygdaloid Complex*. New York: Elsevier/North-Holland Press, pp. 227–237.

Lester, L. S., & Fanselow, M. S. (1985). Exposure to a cat produces opiod analgesia in rats. *Behavioral Neuroscience, 99*, 756–759.

Levine, S., & Soliday, S. (1960). The effects of hypothalamic lesions on conditioned avoidance learning. *Journal of Comparative and Physiological Psychology, 53*, 497–501.

Liebman, J. M., Mayer, D. J., & Liebeskind, J. C. (1970). Mesencephalic central gray in rats. *Journal of Comparative and Physiological Psychology, 74*, 426–433.

Luiten, P. G. M., Koolhaas, J. M., deBoer, S., & Koopmans, J. (1985). The cortico-medial amygdala in the central nervous system organization of agonistic behavior. *Brain Research, 332*, 283–297.

MacLean, P. D., & Delgado, J. M. R. (1953). Electrical and chemical stimulation of frontotemproal portion of limbic system in waking animal. *EEG and Clinical Neurophysiology, 5*, 91–100.

Maeda, H., & Nakao, H. (1986). Delayed reinforcement of switch-off behavior and amygdaloid lesion in cats. *Physiology and Behavior, 36*, 339–342.

Malick, J. B. (1970). Effects of selected drugs on stimulus-bound emotional behavior elicited by hypothalamic stimulation in the cat. *Archives of International Pharmodynamics, 186*, 137–141.

Mancia, G., & Zanchetti, A. (1981). Hypothalamic control of autonomic functions. in P. J. Morgane & J. Panksepp (Eds.), *Behavioral studies of the hypothalamus* (Vol. 3). New York: Marcel Dekker.

Masserman, J. H. (1941). Is the hypothalamus a center of emotion? *Psychosomatic Medicine, 3*, 3–25.

Masterson, F. A., & Crawford, M. (1982). The defense motivation system: A theory of avoidance behavior. *Behavioral and Brain Sciences, 5*, 661–696.

Mayer, D. J., & Liebeskind, J. C. (1974). Pain reduction by focal electrical stimulation of the brain: An anatomical and behavioral analysis. *Brain Research, 68*, 73–93.

McIntyre, M., & Stein, D. G. (1973). Differential effects of one-vs two stage amygdaloid lesions on activity, exploratory, and avoidance behavior in the albino rat. *Behavioral Biology, 9*, 451–465.

Melzack, R., Stotler, W. A., & Livingston, W. K. (1958). Effects of discrete brainstem lesions in cats on perception of noxious stimulation. *Journal of Neurophysiology, 21*, 353–367.

Millan, M. J. (1986). Multiple opioid systems and pain. *Pain, 27*, 303–347.

Millenson, J. R., & Leslie, J. (1974). The conditioned emotional response (CER) as a baseline for the study of anti-anxiety drugs. *Neuropharmacology, 13*, 1–9.

Mogenson, G. J. (1962). Avoidance learning to aversive brain stimulation. *Psychological Reports, 10*, 558.

Mohrland, J.S. (1982). Pain pathways: potential sites for analgetic action. In D. Lednicer (Ed.), *Central analgetics.* New York: Wiley, pp. 1–51.

Molinari, M., Bentivoglio, M., Minciacchi, D., Granato, A., & Macchi, G. (1986). Spinal afferents and cortical efferents of the anterior intralaminar nuclei: an anterograde-retrograde tracing study. *Neuroscience Letters, 72*, 258–264.

Montgomery, K. C. (1958). The relation between fear induced by novel stimulation and exploratory behavior. *Journal of Comparative and Physiological Psychology, 48*, 254–260.

Moreau, J. L., Schmitt, P., & Karli, P. (1986). Ventral tegmental stimulation modulates centrally induced escape responding. *Physiology and Behavior, 36*, 9–15.

Moriyama, M., Ichimaru, Y., & Gomita, Y. (1984). Behavioral suppression using intracranial reward and punishment: Effects of benzodiazepines. *Pharmacology Biochemistry & Behavior, 21*, 773–778.

Myer, J.S. (1971). Some effects of noncontingent aversive stimulation. *Aversive conditioning and learning.* New York: Academic Press, pp. 469–536.

Nagy, J., Zambo, K., & Decsi, L. (1979). Anti-anxiety action of diazepam after intra-amygdaloid application in the rat. *Neuropharmacology, 18*, 573–576.

Nakao, H. (1958). Emotional behavior produced by hypothalamic stimulation. *American Journal of Physiology, 194*, 411–418.

Niehoff, D. L., & Kuhar, M. J. (1983). Benzodiazepine receptors: Localization in rat amygdala. *Journal of Neuroscience, 3*, 2091–2097.

Newman, J. D. (Ed.). (1988). *The physiological control of mammalian vocalizations.* New York: Plenum Press.

Niehoff, D. L., & Kuhar, M. J. (1983). Benzodiazepine receptors: Localization in rat amygdala. *Journal of Neuroscience, 3*, 2091–2097.

Nieuwenhuys, R. (1985). *Chemoarchitecture of the brain.* Berlin: Springer–Verlag.

Normansell, L., Zeisloft, D., & Panksepp, J. (1988). Effects of kainic acid on emotional and sensorimotor behavior in domestic chicks. *Neuroscience Abstracts, 14*, 1105.

Olds, M. E., & Frey, J. H. (1971). Effects of hypothalamic lesions on escape behavior produced by midbrain electric stimulation. *American Journal of Psychology, 221*, 8–18.

Olds, M. E., Hogberg, D., & Olds, J. (1964). Tranquilizer action on thalamic and midbrain escape behavior. *American Journal of Physiology, 206*, 515–520.

Olds, M. E., & Olds, J. (1962). Approach-escape interactions in rat brian. *American Journal of Physiology, 203*, 803–810.

Olds, M. E., & Olds, J. (1963). Approach-avoidance analysis of rat diencephalon. *Journal of Comparative Neurology, 120*, 259–295.

Ono, T., Nakamura, K., Nishijo, H., & Fukuda, M. (1986). Hypothalamic neuron involvement in integration of reward, aversion, and cue signals. *Journal of Neuroscience, 56*, 63–79.

Otterson, O. P., & Ben–Ari, Y. (1978). Pontine and mesencephalic afferents to the central nucleus of the amygdala of the rat. *Neuroscience Letters, 8*, 329–334.

Panksepp, J. (1971). Aggression elicited by electrical stimulation of the hypothalamus in albino rats. *Physiology and Behavior, 6*, 321–329.

Panksepp, J. (1981). Hypothalamic integration of behavior: Rewards, punishments and related psychological processes. In P. J. Morgane & J. Panksepp (Eds.), *Handbook of the hypothalamus*, New York, Marcel Dekker, pp. 289–431.

Panksepp, J. (1982). Toward a general psychobiological theory of emotions. *Behavioral and Brain Sciences, 5*, 407–468.

Panksepp, J. (1985). Mood changes. In P. J. Vinken, G. W. Bruyn, & H. L. Klawans (Eds.), *Handbook of clinical neurology* (Vol. 1). Amsterdam: Elsevier Science Publishers, pp. 271–285.

Panksepp, J. (1986). The anatomy of emotions. In R. Plutchik & H. Kellerman (Eds.), *Emotion: Theory, research and experience*. New York: Academic Press, pp. 91–124.

Panksepp, J. (1989a). The psychobiology of emotions: The animal side of human feelings. In G. Gainotti & C. Caltagirane (Eds.), *Experimental brain research, Series 18, Emotions and the dual brain*, (pp. 31–55). Heidelberg: Springer-Verlag.

Panksepp, J. (1989b). The neurobiology of emotions: Of animal brains and human feelings. In H. Wagner & A. Manstead (Eds.), *Handbook of social psychophysiology*, (pp. 5–26). Chichester, England: Wiley.

Panksepp, J. (1990). The psychoneurology of fear: Evolutionary perspectives and the role of animal models in understanding human anxiety. In *Handbook of anxiety*. (Vol. 3, pp. 3–58) Amsterdam: Elsevier/North-Holland Biomedical Press.

Panksepp, J., Gandelman, R., & Trowill, J. (1970). Modulation of hypothalamic self-stimulation and escape behavior by chlordiazepoxide. *Physiology and Behavior, 5*, 965–969.

Panksepp, J., Herman, B. H., Vilberg, T., Bishop, P., & DeEskinazi, F. G. (1980). Endogenous opioids and social behavior. *Neuroscience and Biobehavioral Reviews, 4*, 473–487.

Panksepp, J., Normansell, L., Siviy, S., Buchanan, A., Zolovick, A., Rossi, J., & Conner, R. (1983). A cholinergic command circuit for separation distress? *Neuroscience Abstracts, 9*, 979.

Panksepp J., Normansell, L., Herman, B., Bishop, P., & Crepeau, L. (1988). Neural and neurochemical control of the separation distress call. In J. D. Newman (Ed.), *The physiological control of mammalian vocalization* (pp. 263–299). New York: Plenum.

Panksepp, J., Siviy, S., & Normansell, L. (1985). Brain opioids and social emotions: In M. Reite & T. Fields (Eds.), *The psychobiology of attachment and separation*. New York: Academic Press, pp. 3–49.

Pascoe, J. P., & Kapp, B. S. (1985). Electrophysiological characteristics of amygdaloid central nucleus neurons in the awake rabbit. *Brain Research Bulletin, 14*, 331–338.

Paxinos, G., & Watson, C. (1982). *The rat brain in stereotaxic coordinates*. New York: Academic Press.

Pellegrino, L. (1968). Amygdaloid lesions and behavioral inhibition in the rat. *Journal of Comparative and Physiological Psychology, 65*, 483–491.

Pellow, S., Chopin, P., File, S. E., & Briley, M. (1985). Validation of open:closed arm entries in an elevated plus-maze as a measure of anxiety in the rat. *Journal of Neuroscience Methods, 14*, 149–167.

Pinel, J. P. J., & Treit, D. (1978). Burying as a defensive response in rats. *Journal of Comparative and Physiological Psychology, 92*, 708–712.

Poplawsky, A., & McVeigh, J. S. (1981). The effects of differential lesions of the amygdala on response suppression. *Physiology and Behavior, 26*, 617–621.

Ratner, S. C. (1967). Comparative aspects of hypnosis. In J. E. Gordon (Ed.), *Handbook of clinical and experimental hypnosis*. New York: Macmillan, pp. 550–587.

Redmond, D. E., Jr. (1979). New and old evidence for the involvement of a brain norepinephrine system in anxiety. In W. G. Fann, I. Karacan, A. D. Pokorny, & R. L. Williams (Eds.), *Phenomenology and treatment of anxiety*. New York: Spectrum, pp. 153–203.

Reite, M., & Fields, T. (Eds.). (1985). *The psychobiology and attachment and separation*. New York: Academic Press.

Riolobos, A. S. (1986). Differential effects of chemical and electrocoagulation of the central amygdaloid nucleus on active avoidance responses. *Physiology and Behavior, 36*, 441–444.

Roberts, W. W. (1958a). Rapid escape learning without avoidance learning motivated by hypothalamic stimulation in cats. *Journal of Comparative Physiological Psychology, 51*, 391–399.

Roberts, W. W. (1958b). Both rewarding and punishing effects from stimulation of posterior hypothalamus of cat with same electrode at same intensity. *Journal of Comparative Physiological Psychology, 51*, 400–407.

Roberts, W. W. (1962). Fear-like behaviors elicited from dorsomedial thalamus of cat. *Journal of Comparative and Physiological Psychology, 55*, 191–197.

Roberts, V. J., & Cox, V. C. (1987). Active avoidance conditioning with dorsal central gray stimulation in a place preference paradigm. *Psychobiology, 15*, 167–170.

Rodin, E. A., & Calhoun, H. D. (1970). Metrazol tolerance in a "normal" volunteer population. *Journal of Nervous and Mental Disease, 150*, 438–450.

Rosen, J. B., & Davis, M. (1988). enhancement of acoustic startle by electrical stimulation of the amygdala. *Behavioral Neuroscience, 102*, 195–202.

Sacks, D. S., & Panksepp, J. (1987). Electrical stimulation of the lateral hypothalamic fear/flight sites in rats produces conditional freezing. *Neuroscience Abstracts, 13*, 452.

Sacks, D. S., & Panksepp, J. (1988). ESB of lateral hypothalamic fear/flight sites in rats produces conditional plave avoidance. *Neuroscience Abstracts, 14*, 1104.

Sanders, K. H., Klein, C. E., Mayes, J. E., Heym, C. H., & Handwerker, H. O. (1980). Differential effects of noxious and non-noxious input on nuerones according to location in ventral periaqueductal gray or dorsal raphe. *Brain Research 186*, 83–97.

Sandner, G., Schmitt, P., & Karli, P. (1982). Effect of medial hypothalamic stimulation inducing both escape and approach on unit activity in rat mesencephalon. *Physiology and Behavior, 29*, 269–274.

Sandner, G., Schmitt, P., & Karli, P. (1985). Effects of hypothalamic lesions on central gray stimulation induced escape behavior and on withdrawal reactions in the rat. *Physiology and Behavior, 34*, 291–297.

Sarter, M., & Markowitsch, H. J. (1985). Involvement of the amygdala in learning and memory: A critical review with emphasis on anatomical relations. *Behavioral Neuroscience, 99*, 342–380.

Scheel-Krüger, J., & Petersen, E. N. (1982). Anticonflict effect of the benzodiazepines mediated by a GABAeric mechanisms in the amygdala. *European Journal of Pharmacology, 82*, 115–116.

Schmitt, P., & Karli, P. (1984). Interactions between aversive and rewarding effects of hypothalamic stimulations. *Physiology & Behavior, 32*, 617–627.

Schmitt, P., Paunovic, V. R., & Karli, P. (1979). Effects of mesencephalic central gray and raphe nuclei lesions on hypothalamically induced escape. *Physiology and Behavior, 23*, 85–95.

Schuster, C. R., & Brady, J. V. (1971). The discriminative control of a food-reinforced operant by interoceptive stimulation. In T. Thompson & R. Pickens (Eds.), *Stimulus properties of drugs*. New York: Appleton–Century–Crofts, pp. 133–148.

Shephard, R. A. (1986). Neurotransmitters, anxiety and benzodiazepines: A behavioral review. *Neuroscience and Biobehavioral Reviews, 10*, 449–461.

Shibata, K., Kataoka, Y., Yamashita, K., & Ueki, S. (1986). An important role of the central amygdaloid nucleus and mammillary body in the mediation of conflict behavior in rats. *Brain Research, 372*, 159–162.

Skultety, F. M. (1963). Stimulation of periaqueductal gray and hypothalamus. *Archives of Neurology, 8*, 608–620.

Small, W. S. (1889). Notes on the psychic development of the young white rat. *American Journal of Psychology, 11*, 80–100.

Soubrie, P. (1986). Reconciling the role of central serotonin neurons in human and animal behavior. *Behavioral and Brain Sciences, 9*, 319–364.

Spevack, A. A., Campbell, C. T., & Drake, L. (1975). Effect of amygdalectomy on habituation and CER in rats. *Physiology and Behavior, 15*, 199–207.

Stein, L. (1965). Facilitation of avoidance behavior by positive brain stimulation. *Journal of Comparative and Physiological Psychology, 60*, 9–19.

Stephens, D. N., & Schneider, H. H. (1985). Tolerance to the benzodiazepam in an animal model of anxiolytic activity. *Psychopharmacologia, 87*, 322–327.

Sun, M. K., & Guyenet, P. G. (1986). Hypothalamic glutaminergic input to medullary sympathoexcitatory neurons in rat. *American Journal of Physiology, 251*, 798–810.

Supple, W. F., Leaton, R. N., & Fanselow, M. S. (1987). Effects of cerebellar vermal lesions on species-specific fear responses, neophobia, and taste-aversion learning in rats. *Physiology and Behavior, 39*, 579–586.

Sutton, R. E., Koob, G. F., LeMoal, M., Rivier, J., & Vale, W. (1982). Corticotropin releasing factor produces behavioral activation in rats. *Nature, 297*, 331–333.

Tallman, J. F., & Gallagher, D. W. (1985). The GABA-ergic system: A locus of benzodiazepine action. *Annual Review of Neuroscience, 8*, 21–44.

Tasker, R. R., Organ, L. W., Rowe, I. H., & Hawrylyshyn, P. (1976). Human spinothalamic tract-stimulation mapping in the spinal cord and brainstem. In J. J. Bonica & D. Able-Fessard (Eds.), *Advances in brain research and therapy*. New York: Raven Press, pp. 251–257.

Thomas, E., & Basbaum, C. (1972). Excitatory and inhibitory processes in hypothalamic conditioning in cats: Role of the history of the negative stimulus. *Journal of Comparative and Physiological Psychology, 79*, 419–424.

Thomas, S. R., Lewis, M. E., & Iversen, S. D. (1985). Correlation of [^{3}H]diazepam binding density with anxiolytic locus in the amygdaloid complex in the rat. *Brain Research, 342*, 85–90.

Thompson, J. B., & Schwartzbaum, J. S. (1964). Discrimination behavior and conditioned suppression (CER) following localized lesions in the amygdala and putamen. *Psychological Reports, 15*, 587–606.

Treit, D. (1985). Animal models for the study of anti-anxiety agents: A review. *Neuroscience and Biobehavioral Reviews, 9*, 203–222.

Turner, B. H., Mishkin, M., & Knapp, M. (1980). Organization of amygdalopetal projections from modality-specific association areas in the monkey. *Journal of Comparative Neurology, 191*, 515–543.

Ursin, H. (1965). The effort of amygdaloid lesions on flight and defense behavior in cats. *Experimental Neurology, 11*, 61–79.

Ursin, H., Jellestad, R., & Gabrera, I. G. (1981). The amygdala, exploration and fear. In Y. Ben-Ari (Ed.), *The amygdaloid complex*. Amsterdam: Elsevier/North-Holland Biomedical Press, pp. 317–329.

Vanderwolf, C. H. (1971). Limbic-diencephalic mechanism of voluntary movement. *Psychological Review, 78*, 83–113.

Van Hoesen, G. W. (1981). The differential distribution, diversity and sprouting of cortical projections to the amygdala in the rhesus monkey. In Y. Ben–Ari (Ed.), *The amygdaloid complex*. Amsterdam: Elsevier/North-Holland Biomedical Press, pp. 77–90.

Vellucci, S. V., & File, S. E. (1979). Chlordiazepoxide loses its anxiolytic action with long-term treatment. *Psychopharmacologia, 62*, 61–65.

Vidal, C., & Jacobs, J. (1980). The effect of medial hypothalamic lesions on pain control. *Brain Research, 199*, 89–100.

Vogel, J. R., Beer, B., & Clody, D. E. (1971). A simple and reliable conflict procedure for testing anti-anxiety agents. *Psychopharmacologia, 21*, 1–7.

Voshart, K., & Van der Kooy, D. (1981). The organization of the efferent projections of the parabrachial nucleus to the forebrain in the rat: A retrograde fluorescent double labelling study. *Brain Research, 212*, 271–286.

Wada, J. A., & Matsuda, M. (1970). Can hypothalamically induced escape behavior be conditioned? *Experimental Neurology, 28*, 507–512.

Werka, T., Skar, J., & Ursin, H. (1978). Exploration and avoidance in rats with lesions in amygdala and piriform cortex. *Journal of Comparative and Physiological Psychology, 92*, 672–681.

Wise, C.D., Berger, B. D., & Stein, L. (1972). Anxiety-reducing activity by reduction of serotonin turnover in the brain. *Science, 117*, 180–183.

Woods, J. W. (1956). Taming of the wild norway rat by rhinencephalic lesions. *Nature, 178*, 869.

Yardley, C. P., & Hilton, S. M. (1986). The hypothalamic and brain-stem areas form which the cardiovascular and behavioral components of the defence reaction are elicited in the rat. *Journal of the Autonomic Nervous System, 15*, 227–244.

2 Analgesia as a Response to Aversive Pavlovian Conditional Stimuli: Cognitive and Emotional Mediators

Michael S. Fanselow
University of California at Los Angeles

A Vietnam veteran diagnosed with Posttraumatic Stress Disorder (PTSD) syndrome enters the Veterans Administration Medical Center in Manchester, N.H., to participate in an experiment. Following the viewing of an ambush scene from the movie "Platoon," a painful heat stimulus delivered to his forearm feels less intense and less unpleasant than it does following viewing of the "Life Cycle of the Oystercatcher" (Pitman, Orr, van der Kolk, & de Jong, submitted). Vietnam veterans not diagnosed with PTSD do not show this analgesia. This reduction in pain in the PTSD patient is decreased by the opiate antagonist naloxone, suggesting mediation by endogenous opioids. In a similar vein, a 35-year-old woman with a severe snake phobia showed an elevation in plasma β-Endorphin levels following presentation of a snake (Thyer & Matthews, 1986). When human volunteers without psychological disturbance are presented with a warning signal indicating that they are about to receive very painful electric shock, they become analgesic. The analgesia is reversed by treatment with naloxone (Willer & Ernst, 1986). In several anecdotal reports, soldiers barely noticed severe wounds while involved in combat (Beecher, 1956; Wall, 1979); and this phenomenon has not escaped the notice of fiction writers (e.g., Conan Doyle, 1897).

Well-controlled laboratory studies indicate that fear-provoking situations have similar effects in rodents. For example, rats placed in a chamber in which they have received electric shock in the past, display reduced reactions to an injury produced by injecting a formalin solution into a paw. Endogenous opiates are involved, as this analgesia is blocked by systemic administration of the opioid antagonists naloxone (Fanselow, 1984a) and naltrexone (Fanselow & Baackes, 1982). Several findings indicate that this analgesia results from Pavlovian conditioning. Analgesia requires the presence of previously neutral stimuli that were present at the time of shock delivery (Fanselow, 1984a; Fanselow & Baackes, 1982); that is, it depends on the presence of a conditional stimulus (CS). Equivalent analgesia is produced upon re-exposure to the CS regardless of how long ago the unconditional stimulus (US) was presented (Fanselow, 1984a). It is subject to extinction (Fanselow, 1984a; Ross & Randich, 1985), external inhibition (Grau, 1987) and Pavlovian blocking (Ross, 1985). Because of these features, I will refer to the phenomenon as conditional analgesia. An important point to consider is that the analgesia can be produced by certain stimuli that are not themselves painful. "Platoon" is not a primary painful sensory event to PTSD patients, and the confines of an observation chamber are not painful to a rat. The analgesia can be produced in a manner temporally discontiguous from primary painful stimuli. Rather, stimulus conditions that either produce an expectancy or memory of a painful event or that trigger an emotional state, such as fear, are responsible for this conditional analgesia.

The problem of how analgesia is mediated is the focus of the present chapter. The question raised is, what is the psychological root of conditional analgesia. Is a cognitive mediator, such as an expectancy or memory of a previously received painful event directly responsible for the analgesia? Or is an emotional state, such as fear, the underlying basis? Separation of these factors may be of heuristic value. The central thesis behind this chapter is that experimental strategies are available that may make it possible to attempt such a separation. However, first it is necessary to dispense with a different question and determine if the changes in responding produced by CSs are really due to a modification in the experience of pain, or if something less interesting, such as response interference, is all that is going on.

RULING OUT RESPONSE COMPETITION AND ATTENTIONAL ACCOUNTS

In labeling this reduction in pain-related behavior *conditional analgesia* the implication is that the subject experiences a moderation in the sensory impact of a painful stimulus. Physiological mechanisms capable of producing such a change in sensory experience have been described in detail (e.g., Basbaum & Fields, 1984) and it is this machinery that is assumed to mediate conditional analgesia. However, previously neutral stimuli that have been paired with electric shock produce pronounced overt behavioral changes. It is plausible that these overt behavioral changes interfere with the behavioral index of pain sensitivity.

One approach to militate against such a peripheralistic explanation is to demonstrate that conditional analgesia is found over a wide variety of index responses. This has been done. Conditional analgesia is easily demonstrated with three commonly used assays for narcotic analgesia in rats. These assays are: (1) The formalin test, in which a dilute formaldehyde solution is given subcutaneously to a paw and behavioral responses directed at the injury are measured (e.g., Fanselow & Baackes, 1982), (2) The hot plate test, where a rat is placed on a moderately hot surface (e.g., 48–55°C) and the latency to paw lick or jump from the heated surface is taken, (e.g., MacLennan, Jackson, & Maier, 1980; Ross & Randich, 1985), and (3) The tail flick test, where the latency for a reflexive withdrawal response from radiant heat is timed (MacLennan, Jackson, & Maier, 1980; Watkins, Cobelli & Mayer, 1982). Additionally, analgesia in the PTSD patients was detected via unpleasantness ratings made on a visual analogue scale, a measure that would not be expected to be influenced by motor interference. This multiplicity of measures that reflect conditional analgesia seems to diminish the plausibility of the motor artifact explanation.

Another way to obtain multiple response measures of pain sensitivity makes use of the biphasic reaction rats have to brief electric foot shock. Immediately upon shock delivery, rats show an initial burst of vigorous activity that is gradually replaced by a suppression of overt movements. The former is termed the activity burst, the latter freezing (Fanselow, 1982). More painful shocks increase both of these responses; the activity burst is lengthened but eventually it is replaced by an even more pronounced freezing response. In frightened rats, naloxone enhances both of these reactions in a manner that exactly parallels increases in the intensity of shock (Fanselow, 1984b). Since these responses are defined in a topographically opposite manner, accounting for the effect of naloxone by any sort of peripheral mediation is difficult.

A second line of evidence against the peripheral motor alternative comes from the use of opioid antagonists. These drugs reverse the analgesia (Fanselow, 1984a; Fanselow & Baackes, 1982; Fanselow & Bolles, 1979; Matzel & Miller, 1987; Watkins et al., 1982). This pharmacological effect is consistent with what is known about the physiological mechanisms known to mediate pain inhibition. Additionally, while opiate antagonists restore reactions to painful stimuli in frightened rats, they do not otherwise influence the overt behavior of these subjects (Fanselow, 1984a; Helmstetter & Fanselow, 1987). Taking the opiate antagonist data in combination with the multiple behavioral measures that indicate analgesia, it seems that conditional analgesia can not be ascribed to motor interference.

Another possible alternative is that rather than being analgesic the frightened rat is just less attentive. However, frightened rats are not generally less attentive for they show enhanced startle reactions to nonnociceptive stimuli (Brown, Kalish, & Farber, 1951; Leaton & Borazcz, 1985). Indeed, while naloxone enhances the activity burst to a painful shock, it reduces a similar activity burst generated by an auditory/visual/vibratory stimulus (Fanselow, 1984b). This finding is reminiscent of the observation that morphine, if injected into the periaqueductal gray, causes decreased reactivity to painful stimulation but enhanced reactivity to nonpainful stimuli (Criswell, 1975; Jacquet & Lajtha, 1974; Liebeskind, Guilbaud, Besson, & Oliveras, 1973; Sharpe, Garnett, & Cicero, 1974). The periaqueductal gray is a brain structure involved in the aforementioned physiological machinery that modulates pain perception (Mayer, Wolfe, Akil, Carder, & Liebeskind, 1971). On the other hand, if this attention deficit is taken to mean one selective to painful stimuli then there is no argument, because such an attention deficit is exactly what is implied by the term analgesia.

NOMENCLATURE FOR EMOTIONAL AND COGNITIVE MEDIATION

Given that an animal experiences a conditioning procedure consisting of pairing a CS with a shock US, what are the contents of learning that result in the CS's ability to generate a conditional response (CR). The learning that follows the pairing of two stimulus events has been described as the formation of an expectancy (e.g., Bolles, 1972); when presented with a CS the animal expects the US. The classic work of Rescorla (1973a, 1974) indicates that following such procedures animals encode aspects of the reinforcer into memory and that conditional performance occurs because the CS has acquired the ability to activate these memories. Rescorla developed procedures that allowed modification of the US independently from associative strength. Support for his interpretation of conditioning derives from the finding that changes in the memory of the US alter conditional responding to the CS.

Thus following conditioning, the CS has the ability to activate an expectancy or memorial representation of the US. It is not the purpose of this chapter to differentiate between these two hypothetical constructs (expectancy or representation). Rather, we will explore the contribution of such a cognitive mediator to conditional analgesia. In general terms, a cognitive mediator (M_c) is a mediator activated by a CS and encodes relatively specific information about the US. It may refer to an expectancy of the US (Bolles, 1972), or a memorial representation of the US (Rescorla, 1973a, 1974).

A CS that has been paired with shock results in a constellation of responses. Pronounced changes in respiration and cardiovascular functioning occur (de Toledo & Black, 1966; LeDoux, Sakaguchi, & Reis, 1983; Obrist, Sutterer, & Howard, 1972; Wolfe & Soltysik, 1981). Startle reflexes are potentiated (Brown et al., 1951; Davis, 1987). Aversively motivated behaviors, particularly species specific defensive responses (SSDRs), are enhanced (Bolles, 1970; Rescorla & Solomon, 1967). On the other hand, appetitively motivated behaviors such as feeding and drinking are suppressed (Annau & Kamin, 1961; Rescorla & Solomon, 1967). This pattern of behavioral changes suggests that, rather than eliciting a reflex, the CS changes the state of the organism. This state has been referred to as an emotional or motivational state. It has been labeled fear or anxiety because it is thought that it corresponds to the subjective state of humans placed in threatening situations. This state may reflect the activation of the neurophysiological mechanisms that evolved in many species to protect individuals of the species against predation (Adams, 1979; Bolles & Fanselow, 1980). Again, the purpose here is not to discuss the various views on this emotional/motivational state. Rather, it is to determine what contributions this emotional mediator (M_c) makes to the conditional analgesic response.

While M_c is most strongly tied to its antecedent stimulus conditions (CS and US), M_c is most strongly tied to its consequent behavioral manifestations. A commonly used index of M_c in rats is the freezing response, which, for this species, appears to be the dominant fear related defensive behavior (Fanselow & Lester, 1988). The remainder of this chapter will focus on the following question: Given that a CS for a nociceptive US such as shock can activate two different mediators, M_c and M_c, which is responsible for the conditional analgesic response? The idea is that these two different conceptualizations are experimentally distinguishable and therefore the psychogenic mediators of conditional analgesia can be determined.

THE PERCEPTUAL–DEFENSIVE–RECUPERATIVE MODEL

The first statement concerning the psychological mediation of conditional analgesia was the Perceptual–Defensive–Recuperative (PDR) model described by Bolles and me (Bolles & Fanselow, 1980; Fanselow & Bolles, 1979). In its original form, we suggested that if a rat was exposed to a procedure in which a CS is correlated with a nociceptive US the CS acquires the ability to produce an expectancy of that US. This expectancy was not the inevitable consequence of CS presentation, rather the activation of the expectancy by a CS may depend on its being given in an appropriate context. This context may correspond to Pavlovian occasion setters (Bouton & Swartzentruber, 1986; Holland, 1983; Rescorla, 1985). One reason we suggested that such a cognitive mediator was necessary was to account for situations in which the CS–US association was not the sole determinant of conditional responding.

Once the expectancy was activated, it in turn switched on the animal's defensive motivational system. The defensive system was labelled fear. Fear was not activated only by an expectancy of a nociceptive event; innately recognized danger stimuli such as predators (Hirsch & Bolles, 1980) also served as adequate antecedent conditions. On the consequent side, fear was defined by the occurrence of SSDRs, such as freezing. The PDR model assumed that analgesia was an SSDR. Conditional analgesia functioned to prevent pain-related behaviors, such as unconditional reflexes and recuperative responses, from interfering with SSDRs when the animal was in a situation that necessitated defense. Thus, according to the model analgesia functions much like the cardiopulmonary changes that occur in dangerous situations (e.g., Hofer, 1970, LeDoux et al., 1983; Wolfe & Soltysik, 1981). Both play a supportive role to the more behaviorally obvious SSDRs, such as freezing, fighting, or flight.

In applying the mediational nomenclature provided herein to the PDR model, M_c corresponds to the CS produced expectancy of the US and M_e corresponds to fear (i.e, activation of the defensive motivational system). The mediational framework of the original PDR model is one in which the CS activates M_c, which in turn activates M_e. M_e is responsible for both the overt fear response (SSDRs such as freezing), cardiopulmonary changes (e.g., respiratory acceleration), and conditional analgesia. This sequence is diagrammed in Fig. 2.1.

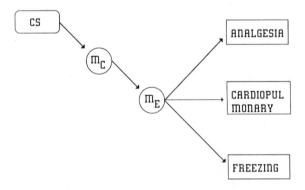

EMOTIONAL MEDIATION OF CONDITIONAL ANALGESIA

FIG. 2.1. The emotional mediational account, where conditional analgesia is mediated in the same manner as other species-specific defense reactions. The original Perceptual–Defensive–Recuperative model was of this form.

To test this model, procedures that allow for the simultaneous observation of freezing and pain sensitivity were needed. The most common procedures for testing analgesia, hot plate, and tail flick were too behaviorally restrictive to observe freezing. However, the formalin test developed in Melzack's laboratory at McGill seemed ideal in that it examined freely moving rats and was very sensitive to narcotic analgesics (Abbott, Franklin, Ludwick, Melzack, 1981; Dennis, Choiniere, & Melzack, 1980; Dubuisson & Dennis, 1977). Using a modification of the formalin test that allowed for the concurrent measurement of freezing, we found that conditioning manipulations designed to influence conditional freezing influenced formalin-elicited behavior in a parallel manner. Freezing and an opioid form of analgesia covaried (Fanselow, 1984a; Fanselow & Baackes, 1982).

MODIFICATIONS OF THE PDR MODEL

Subsequent to the original findings of a relationship between freezing and analgesia, a few investigators have suggested that fear and analgesia may not covary perfectly (Kinscheck, Watkins, & Mayer, 1984; Ross, 1986; Ross & Randich, 1985). For example, Kinscheck et al. found that librium, a drug that might be expected to attenuate fear, did not invariably antagonize conditional analgesia. Ross and Randich (1985) found conditional freezing after a single light–shock pairing but analgesia required two pairings. Unfortunately, none of these experiments employed concurrent measurement of fear and analgesia. The Kinscheck et al. experiments contained no formal observations of fear related behavior. Ross's experiments (Ross, 1986; Ross & Randich, 1985) evaluated freezing but it was measured at times separate from the measurement of pain sensitivity. The design of Ross's experiments allowed a conditioning treatment to intervene between the measurement of freezing and analgesia (e.g., an extinction trial, a conditioning trial, etc). So perfect correlations might not be expected under such situations. Nevertheless, Ross (Ross, 1986; Ross & Randich, 1985) proposed an interesting modification of the original PDR model that would deal better with disassociations of fear and analgesia. This was, "an account that emphasizes the mediation of conditioned analgesia by an acquired expectancy or representation of the US" (Ross & Randich, 1985, p. 430). According to this view, rather than fear being responsible, "the representation of the forthcoming US would directly activate pain-inhibition systems" (Ross & Randich, 1985, p. 430). This suggestion, in which M_c activates analgesia, is diagrammed in Fig. 2.2.

A model of conditional analgesia utilizing Wagner's (1981) SOP model, proposed by Grau (1987), is similar to that of Ross in that certain memorial states are assumed to be responsible for conditional analgesia. In Wagner's

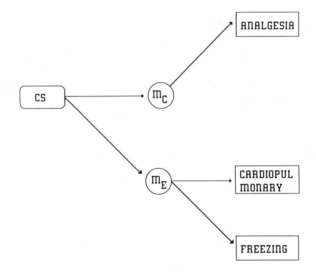

COGNITVE MEDIATION OF CONDITIONAL ANALGESIA

FIG. 2.2. The cognitive mediational accounts, where conditional analgesia is mediated by an expectancy or memorial representation that is distinct from the emotional mediator responsible for fear-related behavior.

model, memorial representations are stored as a node that can be in one of three states of activity: activation into the focus of working memory, activation into the peripheral portion of working memory, or inactive. A fundamental assumption in this theory is that a CS can only activate elements of a memorial node into the peripheral portion of working memory. Therefore, Grau links conditional opioid analgesia to this peripheral state of memorial activation. In terms of the present distinction, this state of memorial activation corresponds most closely to M_c. Again, Grau points out that the "crucial difference between this proposal and the original PDR model is that fear is not required to activate analgesia" (Grau, 1987, p. 284). Therefore, for the present level of analysis the conceptualizations of both Ross and Grau are summarized by Fig. 2.2 and can be contrasted to that presented in Fig. 2.1.

Ross's theoretical suggestion was based on his findings with postconditioning devaluation of the US in a second-order conditional analgesia preparation (Ross, 1986). Following second-order conditioning to a light CS, he devalued the memory of the shock US by subjecting a rat to unsignaled shock while rendered analgesic by morphine. Ross included controls for the possibility of cross-tolerance between morphine and conditional analgesia. This devaluation procedure reduced conditional analgesia. Since, both the models presented in Figs. 2.1 and 2.2 predict such an effect with postconditioning manipulations, this does not provide a test of the two alternatives. A finding that the postconditioning memory devaluation eliminated analgesia but did not affect freezing would favor a cognitive mediation model but Ross did not measure freezing following his postconditioning manipulation. Therefore, Ross's data are not inconsistent with either alternative.

TESTS OF M_c VERSUS M_e AS THE MEDIATOR OF CONDITIONAL ANALGESIA

Three general strategies provide tests of cognitive versus emotional mediation of analgesia: (1) Activate M_c while preventing activation of M_e. (2) Activate M_e in a manner that circumvents concurrent activation of M_c. (3) Attempt a postconditioning manipulation that alters only M_c or M_e but not both and then determine if this engenders a change in indexes of analgesia and/or fear. Thus it is possible to provide a distinction between the alternatives depicted in Figs. 2.1 and 2.2 on empirical grounds.

Anxiolysis

The fist strategy is to activate the cognitive mediator while conducting a manipulation that prevents activation of the emotional mediator. Treatments designed to attenuate anxiety, (i.e., anxiolytic treatments) would serve such a role. If an animal presented with a CS for a nociceptive US has its emotional reactivity attenuated by an anxiolytic treatment but showed an unabated analgesic response, the cognitive mediational account would be supported (Fig. 2.2). On the other hand, if the anxiolytic treatment attenuated both fear and analgesia, an explanation in terms of emotional mediation would be favored (Fig. 2.1). First, I will describe some pharmacological anxiolytic treatments and then a converging line of evidence from some anatomical manipulations.

The classic pharmacological agents utilized for the attentuation of anxiety are the benzodiazepines. In the laboratory experiment that examined changes in pain sensitivity caused by the anticipation of pain in humans as described earlier, Willer and Ernst (1986) found that valium attenuated both analgesia and autonomic signs of fear. Parallel results in rats following administration of either valium or midazolam using freezing as an index of fear have been found in my laboratory (Fanselow & Helmstetter, 1988). To summarize those findings, rats presented with a CS that was previously paired with shock tended to freeze less and were less analgesic if treated with these benzodiazepines. Similar results were found when the drug was just given prior to training, testing or both (Fanselow & Helmstetter, 1988). In a similar vein, Doi and Sawa (1980) found that, in mice, the analgesia that followed electric tail shock was attenuated by a wide range of benzodiazepines. This antianalgesic action was quite selective, as muscle-relaxant drugs did not produce these effects.

It should be noted that there have been reports of undiminished conditional analgesia following benzodiazepine treatment (Chance, White, Krynock, & Rosecrans, 1979; Hayes, Bennett, Newlon, & Mayer, 1978); Kinscheck et al., 1984). However, these studies can be criticized on several grounds (see Fanselow & Helmstetter, 1988) not the least of which is that they did not employ any assessment of fear-related behavior. Without an independent assessment of fear, all those studies offer is a null result, and we have no way of knowing if the anxiolytic treatment was successful (i.e., was activation of M_c prevented). Concurrent validation of anxiolytic action is especially important with benzodiazepines because there have been occasional reports of failure to find antianxiety effects with these substances (e.g., Scobie & Garski, 1970). All the published studies that successfully demonstrated a reduction in an independent index of anxiety by benzodiazepines, also found a reduction in analgesia.

Lesions of the amygdala reduce a number of fear-related behaviors including freezing. Helmstetter, Leaton, Fanselow, and Calcagnetti (1988) examined animals with relatively small bilateral electrolytic lesions of the amygdala that included some damage to the central nucleus and lateral regions of the amygdala. When put through our standard conditional analgesia procedures these rats showed reduced freezing, corroborating reports of earlier investigators (Blanchard & Blanchard, 1972). Additionally, these animals showed a loss of conditional analgesia. Fig. 2.3 displays the results of one of the Helmstetter et al. studies. The design of that experiment was a 2×2 factorial, where rats with amygdala lesions (or sham surgery controls) were observed for freezing and formalin-induced recuperative behavior in a chamber in which they had received shock (or were no shock controls) 24 hours earlier. Amygdala lesions attenuated freezing and eliminated analgesia in the shock animals but had no appreciable effect on no-shock controls. The amygdala is an area rich in GABA/Benzodiazepine receptors (Niehoff & Kuhar, 1983). Therefore, Helmstetter et al. went on to test the hypothesis that the benzodiazepine-induced attenuation of freezing and analgesia we observed earlier was mediated at the amygdala. We implanted rats with bilateral cannula aimed at the amygdala and found that indeed intra-amygdaloid application of valium produced the same pattern of results obtained with both systemic benzodiazepines or electrolytic amygdaloid lesions.

In conclusion, when a CS that has been paired with shock is presented to an animal that has its emotional reactivity suppressed by an anxiolytic treatment, the animal shows a reduction in conditional analgesia. I am assuming here that the CS still activates M_c but activation of M_c is prevented

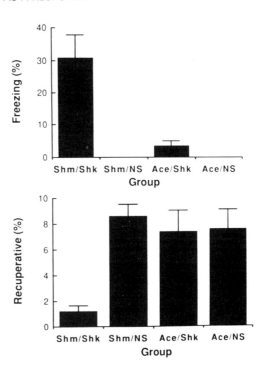

FIG. 2.3. Rats with lesions targeted at the amygdala (Ace) or sham surgery controls (Shm) were observed for freezing and formalin-induced recuperative behavior. The test occurred in a chamber where the rats were either shocked (Shk) or not (NS) the day before. Freezing was observed in the previously shocked animals (Shm/Shk) but not in the nonshocked controls (Shm/NS). Analgesia is indicated by the suppression of recuperative behavior in unoperated rats that were previously shocked (Shm/Shk). Amygdala lesions attenuate both freezing and analgesia (Ace/Shk) (based on Helmstetter et al., 1988).

by the experimental treatment. Therefore, the loss of analgesia supports an interpretation of analgesia as a product of the emotional mediator (i.e., the model presented in Fig. 2.1).

Anxiogenesis

The next line of testing to distinguish between emotional and cognitive mediational accounts would be to activate M_e but not M_c. This would be accomplished by any treatment that produces fear in the absence of conditioning. An adequate test differentiating between these models would not use nociceptive stimuli nor would it use stimuli associated with a nociceptive event. If such an anxiogenic treatment produces analgesia, concurrently with other behavioral signs of fear, the emotional mediational model (Fig. 2.1) would be supported. Alternatively, if such treatments produce signs of fear but not analgesia the cognitive mediational model (Fig. 2.2) would be supported.

Bidirectional modulation of anxiety at the benzodiazepine receptor is possible (Martin, 1987). While benzodiazepine receptor agonists such as valium reduce anxiety, benzodiazepine receptor *inverse* agonists can generate anxiety (Cooper, 1986; Dorow, Horowski, Paschelke, Amin, &

Braestrup, 1983; Huttunen & Myers, 1986; Stephens & Kehr, 1985; Stephens, Kehr, Duka, 1986). Thus benzodiazepine inverse agonists provide a pharmacological anxiogenic manipulation. In rats, we found that the most potent of the inverse agonists, dimethoxy–β–carboline (DMCM), produced three signs of fear quite similar to those we find with conditional fear stimuli, increased defecation, thigmotaxis, and freezing (Fanselow, Helmstetter, & Calcagnetti, in press). This substance also produced analgesia as indicated by a suppression of formalin-induced behavior. In one of our studies, formalin-treated rats were injected with one of several doses of DMCM intraperitoneally (ip) and observed a few min later for freezing and formalin-induced recuperative behavior with a time sampling procedure. The percentages of samples scored as freezing or recuperation are presented in Fig. 2.4. In a dose-dependent manner, DMCM caused both fear and analgesia, as indicated by increased freezing and decreased recuperative behavior, respectively. In another experiment we found that intracerebroventricular administration of DMCM produced analgesia as indicated by an elevation in latency to lick a paw on the hot plate test. This analgesia had an opioid component as it was attenuated by systemic injection of the opioid antagonist naltrexone. All the behavioral effects we observed with DMCM were reversed by the benzodiazepine receptor antagonist, RO15–1788, indicating that DMCM produced its effects at the benzodiazepine receptor (Fanselow, et al., in press). The pattern of results obtained with inverse agonists, is the mirror image of that obtained with benzodiazepine agonists. Even prior to our findings, Rodgers and Randall (1987) reported similar results. Using the radiant heat-elicited tail flick test, they found that both DMCM and another inverse agonist, FG7142, produced analgesia in mice. Both the benzodiazepine antagonist RO15–1788 and the benzodiazepine agonist librium reversed this analgesic action. Note that there is no reason to think that these benzodiazepine inverse agonists trigger an expectancy or memory of a nociceptive event, especially in an animal that never received shock. Rather, it seems more plausible that this pharmacological manipulation gives us direct access to the emotional mediator (M_c). That such treatment produces analgesia supports the emotional mediational model.

The PDR model predicts an alternative method for activating M_c in the absence of activation of M_c. Since that model defines fear as activation of the animal's antipredator defensive system any stimulus that has the ability to activate defensive behavior should suffice. An important class of stimuli that has the power to activate the defensive motivational system is innately recognized predators. Rodents recognize several of their predators even if they have had no prior experience with the predator. For rats and mice this recognition is displayed in the form of freezing (Blanchard & Blanchard, 1971; Hirsch & Bolles , 1980). Lester and I (Lester & Fanselow, 1985) placed rats in an observation chamber that was itself placed in a

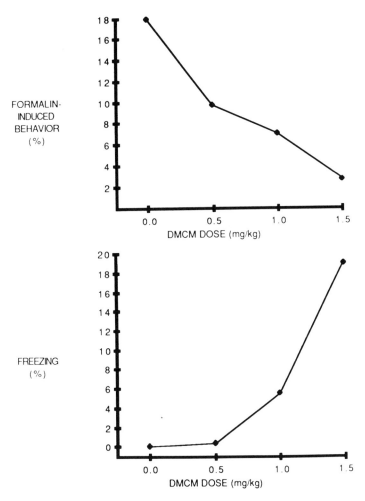

FIG. 2.4.   Rats were given one of three doses of DMCM or its vehicle ip and then observed for formalin-induced recuperative behavior and freezing 10 min later. DMCM appears to produce both freezing and analgesia (suppression of formalin-induced responding) dose dependently (from Fanselow et al., in press).

larger enclosure holding a cat (see Fig. 2.5). The rat could see, hear and smell the cat; the cat could approach but not physically contact the rat. As shown previously by other investigators (Blanchard & Blanchard, 1971; Bronstein & Hirsch, 1976, Satinder, 1976), this sort of exposure to a cat results in freezing. More importantly for the present context, is that the mere presence of a cat produces a suppression of formalin-related behavior. This analgesia was far greater than that produced by simple novelty. Recently, a converging line of evidence was provided with another index of

FIG. 2.5. "If you were in my shoes you would be analgesic too."

pain. Aron Lichtman found that the presence of a cat elevates the threshold value of electrical current needed to elicit a reflexive tail flick response (Lichtman & Fanselow, 1988). Fig. 2.6 contains the results of one of Lichtman's experiments. In this experiment, rats received three series of shocks. Each successive shock of a series was of a higher amperage until a tail-flick response was elicited. Mean threshold amperage for groups of eight rats tested in the presence or absence of a cat are presented. All three determinations were higher in the presence of a cat.

Perhaps the most exquisite documentation for innate recognition of predators by rodents has been done in deermice (*Peromyscus maniculatus*). Several different subspecies of *Peromyscus maniculatus* can be found in different ecological regions, each of which support unique predators. Laboratory-reared *Peromyscus* selectively show defensive behaviors in the presence of predators from the ecological/geographical region of their derivation as opposed to other regions (Hirsch & Bolles, 1980). Recently, Kavaliers (1988) examined hot plate responses of white-footed mice (*Peromyscus leucopus noveboracensis*) in the presence of a natural predator, the short-tail weasel (*Mustela erminea*). Indeed, the weasel used for this study was caught because it entered a mouse trap in pursuit of trapped mice (Kavaliers, personal communication, November, 1987). Analgesia

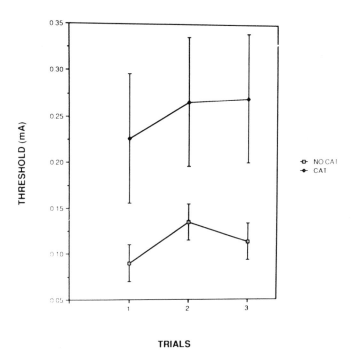

TRIALS

FIG. 2.6. Rats were given three ascending shock titration trials to determine the current necessary to elicit a tail-flick response. The elevated threshold in the rats tested in the presence of a cat indicates analgesia (based on Lichtman & Fanselow, 1988).

was found in response to the weasel but not a control stimulus (a rabbit, *Oryctolagus cuniculus*).

Note that while an innately recognized predator would be expected to activate the defensive motivational system and cause an emotional reaction in an animal, there is no reason to assume that it would activate an expectancy of a nociceptive event in animals that had no prior experience with predators. Thus an innately recognized predator should activate M_e but not M_c. That innately recognized predators produce analgesia suggests that activation of M_e produces analgesia. This conclusion is further supported by Kavaliers (1988) finding that valium reverses the weasel-induced analgesia found in the white-footed mice. There are other innately recognized danger stimuli for rats. Two of them, odors of stressed conspecifics and anterior dorsal tactile stimulation have been examined in my laboratory and both appear to produce an opioid-mediated analgesia (Fanselow, 1985; Fanselow & Sigmundi, 1986).

Thus a number of converging lines of evidence indicate that activation of M_c in the absence of activation of M_c can produce analgesia (the anxiogenesis test). However, when M_c is activated without concurrent activation of M_e, no analgesia is found (the anxiolysis test). It appears that the expectancy of an aversive event is neither necessary nor sufficient for the production of an analgesic response. While it may be possible to produce analgesia in the absence of either a cognitive or an emotional response (Terman, Shavit, Lewis, Cannon, & Liebeskind, 1984), activation of M_c is clearly a sufficient condition for the production of analgesia.

Post-conditioning Changes in the Mediator

There are some procedures available that may allow changes in M_c following conditioning. If these changes in the mediator had a similar effect on an index of fear such as freezing and analgesia, it would support an explanation in terms of emotional mediation. There are limited data available using this strategy, but what there are, seems consistent with an emotional mediation view.

One strategy for changing M_c in Pavlovian conditioning is the devaluation and inflation techniques described by Rescorla (1973a; 1974). The second-order conditioning experiment conducted by Ross (1986) that was described earlier is an example of this approach applied to conditional analgesia. While it was found that devaluation reduced conditional analgesia, Ross did not provide a concurrent measure of fear during the analgesic test. Therefore, his experiment alone does not distinguish between cognitive and emotional mediation. Possibly a change in Mc affected analgesia directly as Ross suggested, but it is equally possible that the change in Mc affected analgesia indirectly through a diminished capacity to activate Me as described in Fig. 2.1. To ascertain which of these two possibilities accounts for the diminution of conditional analgesia, concurrent measurement of fear is necessary.

The mediation of second-order conditioning is greatly affected by the particular conditioning parameters used (Holland & Rescorla, 1975; Rescorla, 1973b, 1979, 1980, 1982; Rescorla & Cunningham, 1979). Certain sets of parameters appear to endow the CS with abilities to activate a cognitive process (i.e., M_c) but more often second-order conditioning procedures produce a CS that directly activates an emotional response (M_c). Apparently, Ross's procedures were of the former type. Recently, Helmstetter and I (Helmstetter & Fanselow, 1989) examined both freezing and analgesia in response to a contextual stimulus that had received a second-order conditioning treatment. This was accomplished by presenting a tone or a light that had previously undergone first-order CS−Shock pairings in a discriminable context. While the rat had never received a shock in this context, after a few context–CS pairings, it evidenced both freezing and analgesia in this situation, compared with appropriate control conditions. Helmstetter and I attempted to change the potential cognitive mediators in the situation by either pairing the first-order CS with a stronger shock or extinguishing it. None of these manipulations altered second-order conditional freezing or second-order conditional analgesia as indexed by the formalin test. This sort of finding is usually taken to mean that second-order responding is mediated by an emotional response (Rizley & Rescorla, 1973). Thus with our procedures second-order responding was not cognitively mediated but with Ross's procedures it was. Despite these differences in mediation, which were probably caused by procedural variations, in both cases analgesia was a component of second-order conditional responding. Therefore, when taken together, these two sets of second-order conditional analgesia studies, suggest that analgesia can be produced by a second-order CS regardless of whether the procedures are those that bestow the CS with the ability to directly activate M_c or M_e. While this data set is limited, the results can be accommodated by the emotional mediation approach described in Fig. 2.1. Ross's procedures may have resulted in a second-order CS that directly activated M_c but produced analgesia via M_c's activation of M_e. Our procedures may have produced analgesia because the second-order CS directly aroused M_e. While these issues are far from settled, it seems that second-order conditioning may provide a powerful tool for further analyses of these mediational issues.

Another manipulation that seems to affect M_c and M_e differentially is the passage of time. Shortly after conditioning, rats seem to have both an emotional response to the CS and a fairly specific representation of the particular US the CS predicts. However, if a long delay intervenes between training and testing, the CS still produces the emotional response but the rat appears to forget the specifics of what the CS predicts (Hendersen, Patterson, & Jackson, 1980). Hendersen et al. suggest that a temporal delay degrades M_c but not M_e. In applying this logic to conditional analgesia, Davis and Hendersen (1985) paired a tone with shock and then tested the animals with the postshock freezing test (Fanselow & Bolles, 1979) either 1 or 90 days later. Time did not affect the freezing elicited by the tone or the tone's ability to trigger a naloxone enhancement of postshock freezing. Most importantly, naloxone enhanced the freezing that followed a single signaled shock equivalently, regardless of the amount of time that passed between training of the signal and testing. The temporal manipulation should have allowed M_c to decay over the 90-day retention interval, while M_e should have remained intact. Since, the delay between training and testing did not affect freezing or analgesia, the data obtained by Davis and Hendersen are consistent with an explanation in terms of emotional mediation by M_c. Again, this data set is too limited to be conclusive by itself. However, the techniques employed seem to provide useful tools for the dissection of these psychological issues.[1]

THE LEARNING PROCESS: OPERANT AND PAVLOVIAN CONSIDERATIONS

An aspect of conditional analgesia that makes it a particularly important CR to aversive conditioners is that the response is defined as one that diminishes the impact of nociceptive stimuli. Since the US typically used is a nociceptive one, shock, the CR has the ability to diminish the impact of the US and therefore is likely to affect further conditioning. One question that stems from this consideration is whether conditional analgesia is a preparatory CR acquired via an operant learning process (Perkins, 1968), or is it an anticipatory CR learned via a Pavlovian process? According to a preparatory account, conditional analgesia is acquired because the analgesic response is reinforced by the reduction it causes in the impact of the shock US (Perkins, 1968). On the other hand, according to an anticipatory view, the correlation of CS and US is sufficient to account for the acquisition of the analgesic CR. However, such a view could acknowledge that the diminution in the effectiveness of the US would be likely to impact negatively on any further conditioning (e.g., Fanselow, 1981). Indeed, my original interest in endogenous opioids was stirred by the possibility that their release might serve as the type of preparatory response that has often been hypothesized to mediate preference for signaled shock (Fanselow, 1979; Fanselow & Bolles, 1977). To test between the anticipatory and preparatory alternatives, Helmstetter and I (Helmstetter & Fanselow, 1987), gave context–shock pairings following either naltrexone (a potent, long-lasting opiate antagonist) or placebo pretreatment. The next day the rats were tested for conditional analgesia in the absence of naltrexone. The administration of naltrexone during context–shock pairings should dimin-

---

[1]As this experiment was based on naloxone's enhancement of postshock freezing it should be remembered that this test most likely reflects a naloxone blockade of a conditional analgesic process (Fanselow, 1984b; Lester & Fanselow, 1987). Davis and Hendersen (1985) also attempted to assess analgesia using the radiant heat tail flick test. Rather than a CS produced analgesia, they detected hyperalgesia. This result may be due to the fact that the tail-flick test was conducted following CS termination in an apparatus different than the original conditioning apparatus. (Presumably, in such a situation, fear reduction or relaxation/relief would be operative; see chapters by Denny and the McAllisters, this volume, Ed.)

ish the ability of the analgesic CR to attenuate the aversiveness of the US. The logic here is the same as that used for omission procedures in distinguishing between operant and Pavlovian approaches of learning (Gormezano & Coleman, 1973). We found that rats showed equivalent analgesia regardless of naltrexone treatment during CS–shock pairings. If naltrexone was given during analgesic *testing* it reversed the analgesia. This indicates that our naltrexone administration procedure was effective in reducing the analgesic CR. Therefore, it appears that analgesia is not acquired because it is reinforcing; conditional analgesia is best thought of as a Pavlovian anticipatory CR not an instrumental preparatory response.

As an anticipatory CR, conditional analgesia may serve an important role in conditioning. During the course of conditioning, as the analgesic response strengthens, it should gradually diminish the impact of the US it precedes. In this way, analgesia may act as a negative feedback loop that regulates conditioning (Fanselow, 1986; Fanselow & Sigmundi, 1987). Conditional analgesia may be partly responsible for situations in which a signaled US loses its impact, such as blocking (Kamin, 1968), the US pre-exposure effect (Randich & LoLordo, 1979) preference for signaled shock (Fanselow, 1980b), and when conditioning is at its asymptote (Rescorla & Wagner, 1972). Support for this interpretation is provided by studies that show that naloxone can cause unblocking (Fanselow & Bolles, 1979; Schull, 1979), reduce the US pre-exposure effect (Matzel, Hallam, & Miller, 1988), reverse preference for signaled shock (Fanselow 1979), and raise the asymptote of fear conditioning (Fanselow, 1981). Some theoreticians have gone so far as to suggest that conditional analgesia may be the mechanism that underlies the basic conditioning process described by the Rescorla and Wagner (1972) model (e.g., Fanselow, 1981, 1986; Fanselow & Sigmundi, 1987; Schull, 1979). According to such views, conditional analgesia regulates conditioning to a level appropriate for the particular US and situation. Conditioning will proceed as long as the impact of the US is great enough to overcome the analgesia. Conditioning stops when the analgesic CR is strong enough to neutralize the US. In this regulatory manner, conditional analgesia's impact on conditioning serves an adaptive role. A stronger US would require more analgesia to be neutralized and therefore would support greater conditioning. If a particular US is already signaled, the analgesic CR will prevent the US from supporting further conditioning. Through such a negative feedback arrangement, conditional analgesia may serve an important information processing function for the animal. The diminution in the effectiveness of a signaled US is often interpreted in cognitive terms (e.g., Terry, 1976). However, it seems likely that in some cases emotional factors (i.e., M_c) may play a role and further, that conditional analgesia may be one underlying mechanism.

SUMMARY

In this chapter, three converging strategies for testing between cognitive and emotional mediation explanations of conditional analgesia were examined. Each strategy was represented by several different methodologies and several different laboratories. I have attempted to examine evidence derived from pharmacological, physiological, ethological, and associative techniques. In each case the results are consistent with an account in terms of emotional mediation. Analgesia appears to be most closely related to the value of M_e not M_c. (This result is consistent with major findings described in several other chapters in this volume, Ed.). It seems that the analgesia produced by aversive Pavlovian conditioning procedures is organized in a manner similar to that of other fear related behaviors. This pattern of findings is quite consistent with the suggestion of the original PDR model that conditional analgesia is a component of the animal's defensive motivational system. However, alternative mediational networks are conceivable and further research should be directed at testing their viability. For example, a CS might activate both M_e and M_c via parallel pathways. If this was the case, it would be possible for each mediator to lead to a different form of analgesia (Grau, 1987; Watkins & Mayer, 1982). All that can be said presently is that there seems to be a strong relationship between opioid analgesia and the emotional state that also leads to innate defensive behaviors.

While I am relating conditional analgesia to the emotional response elicited by the CS, it should be made clear that this emotional response (M_e) is different from the emotional response produced by the shock US. For example, while shock readily conditions freezing it does not itself unconditionally elicit freezing (e.g., Fanselow & Lester, 1988). This pattern, where the CR differs from the unconditional response (UR), is also apparent with analgesia (e.g., Fanselow, 1984a). There appears to be multiple endogenous pain control systems, some mediated by opioids and some that appear nonopioid (Fanselow, 1984a; Terman et al., 1984). Shock parameters that unconditionally produce a nonopioid analgesia appear to condition an opioid form of analgesia (Watkins et al., 1982) indicating again that the CR and the UR may take a different form. Indeed, both Grau (1987) and Watkins et al. have suggested that regardless of the type of endogenous analgesia (opioid or nonopioid) unconditionally produced by the US, conditional analgesia is always mediated by an opioid mechanism. Therefore, this approach in terms of emotional mediation should not be confused with an explanation in terms of traditional S–R associations. An S–R interpretation has severe problems accounting for the great differences between the CR and UR found in fear conditioning. Rather, the approach provided by the PDR model is that a nociceptive stimulus unconditionally activates a motivational state that predisposes an animal to recuperate from injurious stimulation. However, the same unconditional stimulus supports conditioning of a defensive motivational system to previously neutral stimuli correlated with it. Conditional analgesia is one behavioral consequence of activation of this defensive system.

Since analgesia is a consequence of activation of the defensive motivational system, this CR is acquired, like other conditional defensive responses as a Pavlovian response. However, this Pavlovian response can in turn modulate subsequent aversive conditioning because of its ability to modulate the impact of any further signaled USs. Thus conditional analgesia serves two functions. One is to regulate the amount of conditioning possible. The other is to prevent pain-related responses from interfering with the animals' defensive efforts.

ACKNOWLEDGMENTS

The research described herein and the preparation of this chapter was supported by NSF grant No. 86–06787. I thank R. C. Bolles, F. J. Helmstetter, and M. E. Bouton for comments on an earlier version. I wish to thank the following for their generous donations of pharmacological agents: Drs. P. F. Sorter, W. Haefely, M. Da Prada, and R. Eigenmann of Hoffman–La Roche for diazepam, midazolam, and RO15–1788; Dr. D. N. Stephens of Schering for DMCM; Dr. N. C. Birkhead of Endo Laboratories for naloxone; and the National Institute on Drug Abuse for naltrexone.

REFERENCES

Abbott, F. V., Franklin, K. B. J., Ludwick, R. J., & Melzack, R. (1981). Apparent lack of tolerance in the formalin test suggests different mechanisms for morphine analgesia in different types of pain. *Pharmacology Biochemistry and Behavior, 15*, 637–640.

Adams, D. B. (1979). Brain mechanisms for offense, defense and submission. *Behavioral and Brain Sciences, 2*, 201, 241.

Annau, Z, & Kamin, L. J. (1961). The conditioned emotional response as a function of intensity of the US. *Journal of Comparative and Physiological Psychology, 54*, 428–432.

Basbaum, A. I., & Fields, H. L. (1984). Endogenous pain control systems: Brainstem, spinal pathways, and endorphin circuitry. *Annual Review of Neuroscience, 7*, 309–328.

Beecher, H. K. (1956). Relationship and significance of wound to the pain experienced. *Journal of the American Medical Association, 161*, 1609–1613.

Blanchard, R. J., & Blanchard, D. C. (1971). Defensive reactions in the albino rat. *Learning and Motivation, 2*, 351–362.

Blanchard, D. C., & Blanchard, R. J. (1972). Innate and conditioned reactions to threat in rats with amygdaloid lesions. *Journal of Comparative and Physiological Psychology, 81*, 281–290.

Bolles, R. C. (1970). Species-specific defense reactions and avoidance learning. *Psychological Review, 77,* 32–48.

Bolles, R. C. (1972). Reinforcement, expectancy, and learning. *Psychological Review, 79,* 394–409.

Bolles, R. C., & Fanselow, M. S. (1980). A perceptual-defensive-recuperative model of fear and pain. *Behavioral and Brain Sciences, 3,* 291–301.

Bouton, M. E., & Swartzentruber, D. (1986). Analysis of the associative and occasion-setting properties of contexts participating in a pavlovian discrimination. *Journal of Experimental Psychology: Animal Behavior Processes, 12,* 333–350.

Bronstein, P. M., & Hirsch, S. M. (1976). The ontogeny of defensive reactions in Norway rats. *Journal of Comparative and Physiological Psychology, 90,* 620–628.

Brown, J.S., Kalish, H. I., & Farber, I. E. (1951). Conditioned fear as revealed by magnitude of startle response to an auditory stimulus. *Journal of Experimental Psychology, 41,* 317–328.

Chance, W. T., White, A. C., Krynock, G. M., & Rosecrans, J. A. (1979). Autoanalgesia: Acquisition, blockade, and relationship to opiate binding. *European Journal of Pharmacology, 58,* 461–468.

Conan Doyle, A. (1897). The tragedy of the korosko. *Strand Magazine, 14,* 363–371.

Cooper, S. J. (1986). B-Carbolines characterized as benzodiazepine receptor agonists and inverse agonists produce bi-directional changes in palatable food consumption. *Brain Research Bulletin, 17,* 627–637.

Criswell, H. E. (1975). Analgesia and hyperreactivity following morphine microinjection into mouse brain. *Pharmacology Biochemistry and Behavior, 4,* 23–26.

Davis, M. (1987). Pharmacological and anatomical analysis of fear conditioning using the fear-potentiated startle paradigm. *Behavioral Neuroscience, 100,* 814–824.

Davis, H. D., & Hendersen, R. W. (1985). Effects of conditioned fear on responsiveness to pain: Long-term retention and reversibility by naloxone. *Behavioral Neuroscience, 99,* 277–289.

de Toledo, L., & Black, A. H. (1966). Heart rate: Changes during conditioned suppression in rats. *Science, 152,* 1404–1406.

Dennis, S. G., Choiniere, M., & Melzack, R. (1980). Simulation-produced analgesia in rats: Assessment by two pain tests and correlation with self-stimulation. *Experimental Neurology, 68,* 295–309.

Doi, T., & Sawa, N. (1980). Antagonistic effects of psycholeptic drugs on stress-induced analgesia. *Archives Internationales De Pharmacodynamie, 247,* 264–274.

Dorow, R., Horowski, R., Paschelke, G., Amin, M., & Braestrup, C. (1983). Severe anxiety induced by FG 7142, A B–Carboline Ligand for benzodiazepine receptors. *Lancet,* 98–99.

Dubuisson, D., & Dennis, S. G. (1977). The formalin test: A quantitative study of the analgesic effects of morphine meperidine, and brain stimulation in rats and cats. *Pain, 4,* 161–174.

Fanselow, M. S. (1979). Naloxone attenuates rat's preference for signaled shock. *Physiological Psychology, 7,* 70–74.

Fanselow, M. S. (1980). Safety signals and preference for signaled shock. *Journal of Experimental Psychology: Animal Behavior Processes, 6,* 65–80.

Fanselow, M. S. (1981). Naloxone and Pavlovian fear conditioning. *Learning and Motivation, 12,* 398–419.

Fanselow, M. S. (1982). the post-shock activity burst. *Animal Learning and Behavior, 10,* 448–454.

Fanselow, M. S. (1984a). Shock-induced analgesia on the Formalin Test: Effects of shock severity, naloxone, hypophysectomy and associative variables. *Behavioral Neuroscience, 98,* 79–95.

Fanselow, M. S. (1984b). Opiate modulation of the active and inactive components of the postshock reaction: Parallels between naloxone pretreatment and shock intensity, *Behavioral Neuroscience*, *98*, 269–277.

Fanselow, M. S. (1985). Odors released by stressed rats produce opioid analgesia in unstressed rats. *Behavioral Neuroscience*, *99*, 589–592.

Fanselow, M. S. (1986). Conditioned fear-induced opiate analgesia: A competing motivational state theory of stress-analgesia. *Annals of the New York Academy of Sciences*, *467*, 40–54.

Fanselow, M. S., & Baackes, M. P. (1982). Conditioned fear-induced opiate analgesia on the formalin test: Evidence for two aversive motivational systems. *Learning and Motivation*, *13*, 200–221.

Fanselow, M. S., & Bolles, R. C. (1977). Naloxone attenuates rats' preference for signaled shock. *Bulletin of the Psychonomic Society*, *10*, 246.

Fanselow, M. S., & Bolles, R. C. (1979). Triggering of the endorphin analgesic reaction by a cue previously associated with shock: Reversal by naloxone. *Bulletin of the Psychonomic Society*, *14*, 88–190.

Fanselow, M. S., & Helmstetter, F. J., (1988). Conditional analgesia defensive freezing and benzodiazepines, *Behavioral Neuroscience*, *102*, 233–243.

Fanselow, M. S., Helmstetter, F. J., & Calcagnetti, D. J. (in press). Parallels between the behavioral effects of Dimethoxy–β–Carboline (DMCM) and conditional fear stimuli. In L. Dachowski & C. F. Flaherty (Eds.), *Current topics in animal learning: Brain, emotion, and cognition*. Hillsdale, NJ: Lawrence Erlbaum Associates.

Fanselow, M. S., & Lester, L. S. (1988). A functional behavioristic approach to aversively motivated behavior: Predatory imminence as a determinant of the topography of defensive behavior. In R. C. Bolles & M. D. Beecher (Eds.), *Evolution and Learning* (pp. 185–212). Hillsdale, NJ: Lawrence Erlbaum Associates.

Fanselow, M. S., & Sigmundi, R. A. (1986). Species specific danger signals, endogenous opioid analgesia, and defensive behavior. *Journal of Experimental Psychology: Animal Behavior Processes*, *12*, 301–309.

Gormezano, I. & Coleman, S. R. (1973). The law of effect and CR contingent modification of the UCS. *Conditioned Reflex*, *8*, 41–56.

Grau, J. W. (1987). The central representation of an aversive event maintains the opioid and nonopioid forms of analgesia. *Behavioral Neuroscience*, *101*, 272–288.

Hayes, R. L., Bennett, G. J., Newlon, P. G., & Mayer, D. J. (1978). Behavioral and physiological studies of non-narcotic analgesia in the rat elicited by certain environmental stimuli, *Brain Research*, *155*, 69–90.

Helmstetter, F. J., & Fanselow, M. S. (1987). Effects of naltrexone on learning and performance of conditional fear-induced freezing and opioid analgesia. *Physiology Behavior*, *39*, 501–505.

Helmstetter, F. J., & Fanselow, M. S. (in press). Differential second-order aversive conditioning using contextual stimuli. *Animal Learning and Behavior*.

Helmstetter, F. J., Leaton, R. N., Fanselow, M. S., & Calcagnetti, D. J. (1988). *The amygdala is involved in the expression of conditional analgesia*. Paper presented at the meeting of the Society for Neuroscience in New Orleans.

Hendersen, R. W., Patterson, J. M., & Jackson, R. L. (1980). Acquisition and retention of control of instrumental behavior by a cue-signaling airblast: How specific are conditioned anticipations? *Learning and Motivation*, *11*, 407–426.

Hirsch, S. M., & Bolles, R. C. (1980). On the ability of prey to recognize predators. *Zeitschrift für Tierpsychologie*, *54*, 71–84.

Hofer, M. A. (1970). Cardiac and respiratory function during sudden prolonged immobility in wild rodents. *Psychosomatic Medicine*, *32*, 633–647.

Holland, P. C. (1983). Occasion setting in Pavlovian feature positive discriminations. In

M. L. Commons, R. J. Herrnstein, & A. R. Wagner (Eds.), *Quantitative analyses of behavior: Discrimination processes* (Vol. 4, pp. 183–206). Cambridge, MA: Ballinger.

Holland, P. C., & Rescorla, R. A. (1975). Second-order conditioning with food unconditioned stimulus. *Journal of Comparative and Physiological Psychology, 88*, 459–467.

Huttunen, P., & Myers, R. D. (1986). Tetrahydro-B-Carboline micro-injected into the hippocampus induces an anxiety-like state in the rat, *Pharmacology Biochemistry and Behavior, 24*, 1733–1738.

Jacquet, Y. F., & Lajtha, A. (1974). Paradoxical effects after microinjection of morphine in the periaqueductal gray matter in the rat. *Science, 185*, 1055–1057.

Kamin, L. J. (1969). Predictability, surprise attention, and conditioning. In B. A. Campbell & R. M. Church (Eds.), *Punishment and aversive behavior.* New York: Appleton–Century–Crofts.

Kavaliers, M. (1988). Brief exposure to a natural predator, the short-tail weasel, induces benzodiazepine sensitive analgesia in white-footed mice, *Physiology and Behavior, 43*, 187–193.

Kinscheck, I. B., Watkins, L. R., & Mayer, D. J. (1984). Fear is not critical to classically conditioned analgesia: The effects of periaqueductal gray lesions and administration of chlordiazepoxide. *Brain Research, 298*, 33–34.

Leaton, R. N., & Borszcz, G. S. (1985). Potentiated startle: Its relation to freezing and shock intensity in rats. *Journal of Experimental Psychology, Animal Behavior Processes, 11*, 421–428.

LeDoux, J. E., Sakaguchi, A., & Reis, D. J. (1983). Alpha-methylDOPA dissociates hypertension, cardiovascular reactivity and emotional behavior in spontaneously hypertensive rats. *Brain Research, 259*, 69–76.

Lester, L. S., & Fanselow, M. S. (1986). Naloxone's enhancement of freezing: Modulation of perceived intensity or memory processes? *Physiological Psychology, 14*, 5–10.

Lichtman, A. H., & Fanselow, M. S. (1988). *Presentation of a cat produces increased tail flick thresholds in rats.* Paper presented at the meeting of the Society for Neuroscience in New Orleans.

Liebeskind, J. C., Guilbaud, G., Besson, J. M., & Oliveras, J. L. (1973). Analgesia from electrical stimulation of the periaqueductal gray matter in the cat: Behavioral observations and inhibitory effects on spinal cord interneurons. *Brain Research, 50*, 441–446.

MacLennan, A. J., Jackson, R. L., & Maier, S. F. (1980). Conditioned analgesia in the rat. *Bulletin of the Psychonomic Society, 15*, 387–390.

Martin, I. L. (1987). The benzodiazepines and their receptors: 25 years of progress. *Neuropharmacology, 26*, 957–970.

Matzel, L. D., Hallam, S., & Miller, R. R. (1988). Contribution of conditioned analgesia to the shock-induced US-preexposure deficit. *Animal Learning and Behavior, 16*, 486–492.

Matzel, L. D., & Miller, R. R. (1987). Recruitment time of conditioned opioid analgesia. *Physiology and Behavior, 39*, 135–140.

Mayer, D. J., Wolfe, T. L., Akil, H., Carder, B., & Liebeskind, J. C. (1971). Analgesia from electrical stimulation in the brainstem of the rat. *Science, 174*, 1351–1354.

Niehoff, D., & Kuhar, M. J. (1983). Benzodiazepine receptors: localization in rat amygdala. *Journal of Neuroscience, 3*, 2091–2097.

Obrist, P. A., Sutterer, J. R., & Howard, J. L. (1972). Preparatory cardiac changes: A psychobiological approach. In A. H. Black & W. F. Prokasy (Eds.), *Classical Conditioning: II. Current research and theory* (pp. 312–340). New York: Appleton–Century–Crofts.

Perkins, C. C. (1968). An analysis of the concept of reinforcement, *Psychological Review, 75*, 155–172.

Pitman, R. K., Orr, S. P., van der Kolk, B. A., de Jong, J. B., & Greenberg, M. S. Opioid-mediated stress-induced analgesia in Post-traumatic stress disorder. Manuscript submitted for publication.

Randich, R. A., & LoLordo, V. M. (1979). Associative and nonassociative theories of the UCS preexposure effect: Implications for Pavlovian conditioning. *Psychological Bulletin, 86*, 523–548.

Rescorla, R. A. (1973a). Effect of US habituation following conditioning, *Journal of Comparative Physiological Psychology, 82*, 137–143.

Rescorla, R. A. (1973b). Second-order conditioning: Implications for theories of learning. In F. J. McGuigan & D. Lumsden (Eds.), *Contemporary approaches to learning and conditioning.* New York: Winston.

Rescorla, R. A. (1974). Effect of inflation of the unconditioned stimulus value following conditioning, *Journal of Comparative and Physiological Psychology, 86*, 101–106.

Rescorla, R. A. (1979). Aspects of the reinforcer learned in second-order Pavlovian conditioning. *Journal of Experimental Psychology: Animal Behavior Processes, 5*, 79–95.

Rescorla, R. A. (1980). *Pavlovian second-order conditioning* Hillsdale, NJ: Lawrence Erlbaum Associates.

Rescorla, R. A. (1982). Simultaneous second-order conditioning produces S–S learning in conditioned suppression. *Journal of Experimental Psychology: Animal Behavior Processes, 8*, 23–32.

Rescorla, R. A. (1985). Inhibition and facilitation. In R. R. Miller & N. E. Spear (Eds.), *Information processing in animals: Conditioned Inhibition* (pp. 299–326) Hillsdale, NJ: Lawrence Erlbaum Associates.

Rescorla, R. A., & Cunningham, C. L. (1979). Spatial contiguity facilitates Pavlovian second-order conditioning. *Journal of Experimental Psychology: Animal Behavior Processes, 5*, 152–161.

Rescorla, R. A., & Solomon, R. L. (1967). Two-process learning theory: Relationships between Pavlovian conditioning and instrumental learning. *Psychological Review, 74*, 151–182.

Rescorla, R. A., & Wagner, A. R. (1972). A theory of Pavlovian conditioning: Variations in the effectiveness of reinforcement and nonreinforcement. In A. H. Black & W. F. Prokasy (Eds.), *Classical Conditioning: II. Current Research and Theory* (pp. 64–99). New York: Appleton–Century–Crofts.

Rizley, R. C., & Rescorla, R. A. (1972). Associations in second-order conditioning and sensory preconditioning. *Journal of Comparative and Physiological Psychology, 81*, 1–11.

Rodgers, R. J. & Randall, J. I. (1987). Benzodiazepine ligands nociception and "defeat" analgesia. *Psychopharmacology, 91*, 305–315.

Ross, R. T. (1985). Blocking and unblocking of conditioned analgesia. *Learning and Motivation, 16*, 173–189.

Ross, R. T. (1986). Pavlovian second-order conditioned analgesia. *Journal of Experimental Psychology: Animal Behavior Processes, 12*, 32–39.

Ross, R. T., & Randich, A. (1985). Associative aspects of conditioned analgesia evoked by a discrete CS. *Animal Learning and Behavior, 13*, 419–431.

Satinder, K. P. (1976). Reactions of selectively bred strains of rats to a cat. *Animal Learning and Behavior, 4*, 172–176.

Schull, J. (1979). A conditioned opponent theory of Pavlovian conditioning and habituation. In G. Bower (Ed.), *The psychology of learning and motivation, 13*, 57–90. New York: Academic Press.

Scobie, S. R., & Garske, G. (1970). Chlordiazepoxide and conditioned suppression. *Psychopharmacologia, 16*, 272–280.

Sharpe, L. G., Garnett, J.E ., & Cicero, T. J. (1974). Analgesia and hyperreactivity produced by intracranial microinjections of morphine into the peri-aqueductal gray matter of the rat, *Behavioral Biology, 11*, 303–313.

Stephens, D. N., & Kehr, W. (1985). β-Carbolines can enhance or antagonize the effects of punishment in mice, *Psychopharmacology, 85*, 143–147.

Stephens, D. N., Kehr, W., & Duka, T. (1986). Anxiolytic and anxiogenic B-carbolines: Tools for the study of anxiety mechanism. In G. Biggio & E. Costa (Eds.), *GABAergic transmission and anxiety*. New York: Raven Press.

Terman, G. W., Shavit, Y., Lewis, J. W., Cannon, J. T., & Liebeskind, J. C. (1984). Intrinsic mechanisms of pain inhibition: Activation by stress. *Science, 226*, 1270–1277.

Terry, W. S. (1976). The effects of priming US representation in short-term memory on Pavlovian conditioning. *Journal of Experimental Psychology: Animal Behavior Processes, 2*, 354–370.

Thyer, B. A., & Matthews, J. (1986). The effect of phobic anxiety on plasma B-endorphin: A single-subject experiment. *Behavior Research Therapy, 24*, 237–241.

Wagner, A. R. (1981). SOP: A model of automatic memory processing in animal behavior. In N. E. Spear & R. R. Miller (Eds.), *Information processing in animals: Memory mechanisms* (pp. 5–47). Hillsdale, NJ: Lawrence Erlbaum Associates.

Wall, P. D. (1979). On the relation of injury to pain. *Pain, 6*, 253–264.

Watkins, L. R., Cobelli, D. A., & Mayer, D. J. (1982). Classical conditioning of front paw and hind paw footshock induced analgesia (FSIA): Naloxone reversibility and descending pathways. *Brain Research, 243*, 119–132.

Watkins, L. R., & Mayer, D. J. (1982). Organization of endogenous opiate and nonopiate pain control systems. *Science, 216*, 1185–1192.

Willer, J. C., & Ernst, M. (1986). Somatovegetative changes in stress-induced analgesia in man: An electrophysiological and pharmacological study. *Annals of the New York Academy of Sciences, 467*, 256–272.

Wolfe, G. E., & Soltysik, S. S. (1981). Instrumentation and techniques: An apparatus for behavioral and physiological study of aversive conditioning in cats and kittens. *Behavior Research Methods and Instrumentation, 13*, 637–642.

3

Inverting the Traditional View of "Learned Helplessness"

Thomas R. Minor
University of California, Los Angeles

Nancy K. Dess
Occidental College

J. Bruce Overmier
University of Minnesota

I. INTRODUCTION

This chapter reviews recent work on the prediction and control of stressors and offers an alternative interpretation for the so-called "learned helplessness" effect. This research problem grew out of a series of experiments conducted in the mid- to late 1960s in Richard Solomon's laboratory at the University of Pennsylvania. Overmier and Leaf (1965) initially noted that avoidance learning was enhanced in dogs given Pavlovian training in a different apparatus 24 hr earlier and speculated that this facilitation resulted from retarded escape learning. The possibility of an escape deficit was systematically confirmed in a later study by Overmier and Seligman (1967), who coined the term "learned helplessness" to characterize a syndrome consisting of associative, motivational, and emotional deficits. Further analysis (Seligman & Maier, 1967) indicated that escape performance was not impaired when dogs received equivalent pretreatment with escapable shock. Finally, in an important historical development, Maier and Seligman (1976; Maier, Seligman, & Solomon, 1969; Seligman, Maier, & Solomon, 1971) concluded that helplessness results from exposure to uncontrollable aversive events and offered a theoretical framework to accommodate the conclusion (i.e., the learned helplessness hypothesis).

The study of learned helplessness and stressor controllability recently entered its third decade. The paradigm is now considered a leading animal model of depression (Overmier & Hellhammer, 1988; Seligman, 1975; Willner, 1984) and is used increasingly to study the somatic consequences of stress. However, the popularity of this paradigm is not entirely well

87

deserved: We are little closer to understanding how the dimension of control impacts upon an organism than we were at the outset, more than 20 years ago.

This chapter offers alternative strategic and theoretical approaches to the study of helplessness with the intent of stimulating research on its nature and determinants. The immense popularity of the learned helplessness concept has blocked the development of alternative analyses. One aid in circumventing this block is to recognize that the focus on the uncontrollability of aversive events in the seminal experiments was arbitrary—several other features of the induction operation (e.g., stressor severity, cyclicity, or unpredictability) could and should have received equal weight. Given the difficulty we have had in reaching a consensus on any aspect of the phenomenon, it seems a timely occasion to rethink the tenets of the theory.

A. The Helplessness Paradigm

Most of the research discussed in this chapter was conducted with rats. Our standard procedure is similar to the one used in the original dog experiments, with the apparatus physically scaled to the rat. In the pretreatment phase, sets of three rats (a triad) are restrained in small wheel-turn chambers. The first rat in each triad is exposed to 100 unsignaled, shock-escape trials on a variable time 60-sec schedule. Shock (1.0 mA) is delivered through fixed tail electrodes. Wheel-turn responses by this Escape rat are ineffective during the first 0.8 sec of a trial, but thereafter, a complete rotation of the wheel terminates shock. The Escape rat's behavior determines shock duration on each trial for a second, Yoked rat. Shock is inescapable for the Yoked rat because wheel-turn responses have no effect on shock onset or termination. Thus physical stress is equated between Escape and Yoked conditions, but the two groups differ in the extent to which they can exert behavioral control over the stressor. The third member of the triad is restrained in the chamber and provides a nonshocked baseline from which any differential effects of stressor escapability can be assessed during later testing.

The timing and nature of the test vary with the specific interests of the experimenter. However, the *learned helplessness effect* traditionally is defined by the disruption of shuttle-escape performance 24 hr after inescapable shock (Maier, Albin, & Testa, 1973). The shuttle-escape test begins with five FR–1 trials in which shock (0.6 mA) is terminated by a single shuttle response, followed by 25 trials in which the escape contingency is increased to an FR–2 requirement. Shock terminates automatically if the appropriate response requirement is not met within 40 sec of shock onset. The typical outcome of this procedure is that Yoked rats show near-maximum escape latencies during the FR–2 trials. By contrast, Escape and

Restrained rats have similar FR–2 escape latencies, averaging about 13 sec.

B. Learned Helplessness Hypothesis

1. Tenets of the Hypothesis

The learned helplessness hypothesis accounts for this pattern of results by assuming that subjects learn the contingency to which they are exposed during pretreatment and respond accordingly during testing. Specifically, unpredictable, uncontrollable shock is assumed to represent the area in an instrumental contingency space which corresponds to response–reinforcer independence (Maier et al., 1969). Subjects learn the independence between responding and shock termination during exposure to inescapable shock and develop an expectation that future events will be similarly uncontrollable. This expectation of helplessness works in two ways to impair later escape performance. First, learning that responding and outcomes are independent proactively interferes with the learning of the positive escape contingency that exists during testing. Second, the expectation that responding will be ineffective in modifying test shocks reduces the motivation to engage in the type of instrumental behavior that would increase contact with the escape contingency. Thus, the expectation of helplessness serves as a cognitive mediator of later associative and motivational deficits.

2. Critique

Learned helplessness theory made an important contribution to the study of stress effects in several ways. Differential pathology following experience with an aversive event was tied directly to a definable experimental contingency. The explanation for performance deficits was simple and internally consistent. Moreover, Seligman's (1975) elaboration on the emotional impact of uncontrollable aversive events served to stimulate research on the environmental causes of depression and related pathology.

Despite these positive points, some of the assumptions of the learned helplessness hypothesis did not have a strong empirical basis. The hypothesis stemmed directly from the characterization of pretreatment shocks as operationally uncontrollable. Maier et al. (1969) claimed that pretreatment with inescapable shock, "either unsignaled or preceded by a CS" (p. 319), interfered with later escape performance. However, in the seminal reports on helplessness (Overmier & Seligman, 1967; Seligman & Maier, 1967) pretreatment shocks were unpredictable as well as uncontrollable. Stressor predictability was rejected as a causal factor on the basis of one experiment in which only 50% of the shock trials were preceded by a warning signal

(Overmier & Seligman, 1967, Experiment 3), certainly a less than optimal condition for assessing the effects of predictability, Thus, the attribution of helplessness solely to the uncontrollability of pretreatment shock, and the decision to emphasize instrumental operations (rather than Pavlovian ones) in later research, was arbitrary.

Nevertheless, manipulation of stressor controllability rapidly became the standard means of studying helplessness. Indeed, Maier and Seligman (1976) stated, "Learned helplessness is defined as an effect resulting from the uncontrollability of aversive events" (p. 33). Thus, helplessness was defined in terms of only one feature of the operation that produced it. Impaired performance in Yoked (but not Escape) subjects constituted learned helplessness; conversely, equivalent deficits in both groups was not helplessness and was deemed irrelevant. This definition seriously constrained attempts to determine whether stressor controllability is uniquely causal to helplessness: In essence, controllability was an axiom rather than a testable premise of the theory.

The impact of these unfortunate aspects of the learned helplessness hypothesis has been substantial. Until recently, the study of stressor prediction and control has been conducted largely independently. The notion that the uncontrollability of aversive events is *the* essential ingredient of helplessness has gone unassailed. However, recent data suggest that predictability may be as important to understanding helplessness effects as is controllability; in fact, there is now reason to question whether the effects of control can be studied independently of prediction.

C. An Alternative Strategy

Overmier (1988) recently proposed a strategy for the study of stress effects that treats the comparison between groups in terms of the complexity of the underlying operations. The approach is based on the premise that the stressfulness of an event is best measured by the presentation of the event alone, unencumbered by additional experimental contingencies. More complex procedures potentially modulate (either augment or attenuate) the baseline reaction. Fig. 3.1 illustrates the types of operations that might serve as modulator variables. The intersection between the dimensions of type of stressor, potential modulator operations, and psychobiological indices of stress creates a matrix, the cells of which represent the domain of possible observations related to stress.

Analyzing the helplessness phenomenon within this "modulator" framework produces a subtle, but important, shift in perspective. The simplest stressful operation in the triadic design is exposure to a series of unpredictable, uncontrollable (i.e., unsignaled, inescapable, and unavoidable) shocks. As an alternative to treating uncontrollability as an indivisible component of the stressor, the modulator analysis attributes any effect of

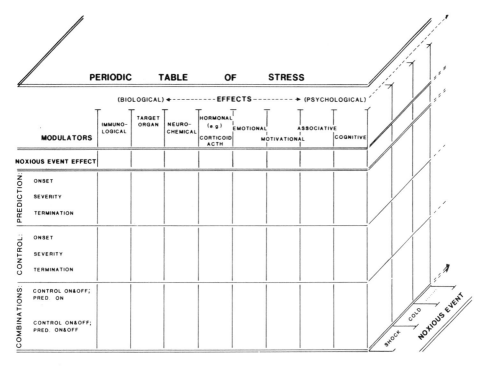

FIG. 3.1. Table illustrates the potential interaction between noxious events, modulator variables, and several psychobiological indexes of stress. Filling in the cells of the matrix should yield a basis for an empirical definition of coping at various system levels and the conditions under which it occurs (after Overmier, 1988).

the procedure to shock per se. Stressor controllability is analyzed only by *adding* the appropriate contingency to the baseline procedure and comparing the two conditions. If the procedures produce differential outcomes, then the added contingency is assumed to generate a psychological context that modulates the baseline reaction to the stressor. From this view, the triadic design is more appropriately regarded as a procedure for studying coping processes than it is for analyzing the impact of uncontrollable stresses. The central issue becomes how an escape contingency prevents the deleterious effects of traumatic shock.

The modulator analysis also places the study of helplessness in a broader context by increasing the number of observations that are potentially relevant to the phenomenon. No *a priori* assumptions are made about the ability of an operation to modulate the effects of a stressor. Thus variables such as stressor predictability, cyclicity, severity, and so on, are given equal status with controllability. Moreover, whereas the learned helplessness hypothesis directs us to look primarily for behavioral indexes of cognitive and motivational dysfunction, the modulator approach again makes no assumptions concerning the nature of the disorder and recognizes that an operation might have different effects on different stress measures. Thus researchers are not constrained by the particulars of a theory and are encouraged to look at multiple indexes.

There are shortcomings to this type of inductive analysis, however. The modulator space illustrated in Fig. 3.1 is quite large, perhaps infinitely so; yet, it provides no means of prioritizing a search among the cells of the matrix. Thus, the framework is useful primarily as a heuristic in specifying the magnitude of the task ahead of us. Theory, on the other hand, normally serves to limit the number of observations that are presumed relevant to a phenomenon. Unfortunately, this immediate advantage to theory also is its long-term weakness. By defining *the* domain of relevant observations for a phenomenon, a theory necessarily ignores other potentially important variables and provides no mechanism for identifying extradomain factors or assessing their contribution (Kuhn, 1962).

The strongest analysis seems to emerge when inductive and deductive approaches are combined. Overmier's modulator framework removes the "conceptual blinders" associated with theorizing. The matrix in Fig. 3.1 provides the broader context that is often missing in deductive analysis— variables falling outside the domain of a theory should be easily identified and their effects occasionally tested. Theory can be regarded as simply a means of prioritizing the search among cells of the matrix.

Overmier's modulator analysis is used to present an alternative interpretation for the helplessness effect, the anxiety hypothesis, in the remainder of this chapter. We will view exposure to unpredictable, uncontrollable shock as the baseline procedure in the triadic design and more complex operations as potential modulators of the baseline. In addition, theoretical assumption are made concerning the critical features of the stress reaction that cause helplessness and how modulator operations act to prevent impairment.

II. THE ANXIETY HYPOTHESIS

Anxiety interpretations of helplessness are based on the premise that escapable and inescapable shock are differentially fear inducing. The concept can be traced to Mowrer and Viek's (1948) seminal study of shock controllability in which they argued that inescapable shock elicits pain plus fear, whereas escapable shock elicits only pain. Greater distress during inescapable shock was attributed to uncertainty about the maximum duration of shock on a trial. Fear was absent during escapable shock because the response and its symbolic representation were connected with relief following termination shock.

Several recent observations have rekindled interest in the role of fear in stressor controllability effects (e.g., Gray, 1982; Mineka, Cook, & Miller, 1984; Minor & LoLordo, 1984; Rosellini, DeCola, & Warren, 1986; Volpicelli, Ulm, Altenor, 1984; Weiss et al., 1982). The combined outcome of these experiments provides a plausible foundation for an anxiety-based explanation, one version of which will be outlined.

The helplessness paradigm is viewed as a protocol for experimentally inducing anxiety. Anxiety is assumed to be engendered and modified by Pavlovian operations and principles. As discussed in detail later, this postulate creates special problems for the analysis of escapable shock; however, it serves to operationalize an otherwise ill-defined construct, and also constrains the type of explanations that can be proposed for various aspects of helplessness. The differential effects of escapable and inescapable shock are attributed to the characteristics of the anxiety response associated with each event. Whereas inescapable shock is assumed to engender intense, chronic anxiety, the fear elicited by escapable shock is moderate and acute. Given these assumptions, analyzing the determinants of helplessness reduces to two broad categories of questions: (1) Why does chronic fear during inescapable shock cause later performance deficits; and (2) How does an escape response reduce chronic fear to eliminate performance deficits?

A. Inescapable Shock as the Stress Baseline

1. Development of Chronic Fear

Overmier (1988) has argued that an analysis of stress effects should begin with a description of the baseline reaction to the simplest procedure. Within the current theoretical context, the initial problem is to describe the baseline anxiety or fear reaction to unsignaled, inescapable shock. Our baseline for inescapable shock should include a description of the fear reaction, the variables controlling that reaction, and its immediate consequences that contribute to later performance deficits. In the ideal case, this description would identify the causal factors in helplessness.

Seligman (1968; Seligman & Binik, 1977) argued that unsignaled, inescapable shock engenders chronic fear (also see Mowrer & Viek, 1948). The term "chronic" in this context referred to the temporal pattern of fear during the intertrial interval (ITI). The absence of temporal fluctuations in fear was attributed to an inability to discriminate between periods of relative danger and safety. Essentially, inescapable shock was viewed as a low-information condition that yielded neither explicit warning nor safety signals, and therefore, subjects remained chronically afraid.

Other investigators, however, have argued that shock termination elicits unconditional after-reactions that are antagonistic to fear (Denny, 1971; Solomon & Corbit, 1974). For instance, Denny defined *relief* as an immediate autonomic reaction to shock termination and *relaxation* as a musculoskeletal response that emerges at longer postshock times. Both reactions can be conditioned to stimuli presented at the appropriate postshock interval and could serve to reduce the chronicity of fear during shock pretreatment.

Although these after-reactions will play an important role in our analysis of escape and other modulator operations, they probably do not alter fear during inescapable shock. Relaxation presumably emerges 25 to 40 sec after a trial and peaks roughly 150 sec into the ITI (Denny, 1971). Under our standard pretreatment procedure, the average (60 sec) and minimum ITI (20 sec) are too short for peak relaxation to occur or to be conditioned to ambient stimuli (also see Maier, Rapaport, & Wheatley, 1976). Under these parameters, relaxation is also frequently punished by the next shock, just as it emerges in reaction to the preceding shock. Denny and his colleagues (e.g., Denny, 1971, 1976; Denny & Dmitruk, 1967) have argued that relaxation-produced stimuli become fear provoking under these conditions due to repeated pairings with shock, resulting in pervasive or "free-floating" anxiety. Thus, the onset of relaxation and related stimuli could augment rather than attenuate fear during inescapable shock.

According to Denny (1971), relief emerges a few seconds after shock and dissipates 10 or 15 sec later, and hence, should not be subject to the same punishment effects as is relaxation, at least in our procedure. Nonetheless, the available data suggest that relief does not play an important fear-reducing role in the helplessness paradigm, *unless* an explicit (or implicit) safety stimulus is presented in the postshock interval (Jackson & Minor, 1988; Mineka et al., 1984; Rosellini et al., 1986). Such safety cues are not available during exposure to unsignaled, inescapable shock (Seligman & Binik, 1977); hence, subjects should remain chronically afraid throughout the ITI.

2. Consequences of Chronic Fear

Exposure to unsignaled, inescapable shock can be regarded as a simple Pavlovian procedure in which fear is conditioned to apparatus cues. As will be discussed in more detail, the conditioning of fear to the pretreatment context provides an important basis for associative transfer when similar cues are present in the test apparatus (Bersh, Whitehouse, Blustein, & Alloy, 1986; Coen, 1985; Minor & LoLordo, 1984; Williams, 1987). However, asymptotic fear conditioning occurs rapidly in this procedure, probably within 20 trials (King, Pfister, & DiGuisto, 1975), too few shocks to produce a helplessness effect (Anisman & Zacharko, 1986; Looney & Cohen, 1972; Minor, Pelleymounter, & Maier, 1988). Moreover, although conditioned aversive associations usually are retained over a long interval (Hoffman, Fleshler, & Jensen, 1963; Minor, 1990a), many of the effects of inescapable shock dissipate within 72 hr of the original stress session (Overmier & Seligman, 1967; Seligman, Rosellini, & Kozak, 1975). Thus simple fear conditioning is unlikely to be solely responsible for helplessness.

The focus on the chronicity of fear is intended as a logical means of accommodating the nonassociative effects of inescapable shock (Gray, 1982; Minor & LoLordo, 1984; Weiss et al., 1981). The helplessness paradigm is an atypical conditioning procedure in that behavioral impairment emerges only after exposure to a large number of intense inescapable shocks (Looney & Cohen, 1972; Minor et al., 1988). If inescapable shock engenders chronic fear, then the neural substrates of fear or anxiety should undergo intense, chronic activation over an extended period of time. Apparently, fear-related pathways are incapable of this type of prolonged activity. Inescapable shock results in a number of neuroanatomical abnormalities, including alterations in the pituitary–adrenal axis (Dess, Linwick, Patterson, Overmier, & Levine, 1983; Haracz, Minor, Wilkins, & Zimmermann, 1988), and catecholaminergic (e.g., Weiss et al., 1981), serotonergic (Hellhammer, Bell, Ludwig, & Rea, 1983), GABAergic (Petty & Sherman, 1981), cholinergic (Anisman & Zacharko, 1986) and opioidergic neurotransmission (Maier, 1986). There is convincing evidence that several of these changes are critically involved in the learned helplessness effect and related disorders (see Anisman & Zacharko, 1986; Gray, 1982; Weiss & Simson, 1985, for reviews). It is beyond the scope of this chapter to assess the relevant hypotheses and related data extensively, and we will treat the neural imbalance suggested by the foregoing studies as a logical consequence of chronically activating fear-related pathways.

3. Transsituational Transfer

The initial effects of inescapable shock transfer across physically different environments, responses, and reinforcers to impair performance in a wide variety of test tasks (Maier & Seligman, 1976). At the same time, this interference effect often is limited to a relatively brief interval (24 to 72 hr) after the pretreatment session. At longer retention intervals, inescapably shocked rats perform as well as restrained controls (Seligman et al., 1975). Any successful explanation of helplessness must account for both aspects of transfer.

Weiss et al. (1981) suggested that the broad transfer and time-dependent variations in helplessness resulted from the interaction of associative and nonassociative factors at the time of testing. According to this account, subjects eventually recover from the nonassociative effects of inescapable shock, but remain vulnerable to subsequent stresses for 24 to 72 hr (see Weiss & Simson, 1985, for an extensive discussion of the processes involved in recovery from neural imbalance). The conditioning of fear to apparatus cues presumably is more permanent. Exposure to similar stimuli at the time of testing results in maximum reactivation of fear-related neural pathways. If the test is conducted shortly after pretreatment (e.g., 24 hr later), such conditioned stimuli serve to reinstate the imbalance among critical neurotransmitters and performance deficits ensue. Initial exposure to escapable shock is assumed to have less of an impact on test performance because it is less fear inducing. Less fear is conditioned to apparatus cues as a result, and the nonassociative effects of excessive fear on neurotransmission are prevented. Behavioral data relevant to these assumptions are reviewed herein.

a. Associative Transfer.   The extent to which learning in one context influences performance in another traditionally has been assumed to be a direct function of the similarity between the two situations. Weiss et al.'s (1981) proposal concerning the conditioning and later elicitation of fear by similar apparatus cues is certainly within this tradition. Of course, the difficulty for an explanation based on stimulus generalization is that pretreatment and test apparatus are often quite different. For instance, our wheel-turn chambers and shuttleboxes differ in their physical dimensions, background lighting and auditory cues, and mode of shock delivery. Such physical dissimilarities should minimize generalization between phases; yet, inescapably shocked rats reliably show retarded shuttle-escape performance in our procedure. Associative transfer seems less likely considering that inescapable shock disrupts performance in such a wide variety of tasks. However, Minor and LoLordo (1984) identified one apparatus cue that might have provided an undetected source of stimulus generalization in several studies of helplessness in rats.

Rats exude a unique odor during experience with powerful stressors (MacKay–Sim & Laing, 1980; Valenta & Rigby, 1968). These stress odors tend to overshadow other features of a conditioning context, leading to a strong odor–shock association, and become critical retrieval cues in later tests for aversive learning as a result (Coen, 1985; King, 1969; King et al., 1975; Minor & LoLordo, 1984; Thomas, Riccio, & Myer, 1977; Williams, 1987). Because apparatus usually is not cleaned frequently or thoroughly, stress odors tend to accumulate wherever rats encounter threatening stimuli. Thus, broad associative transfer of helplessness could occur because this strongly conditioned element of the pretreatment context also is a ubiquitous feature of test environments.

This hypothesis was strongly supported by the finding that similar odors had to be present in the pretreatment and test apparatus for deficits in escape performance to occur 24 hr after inescapable shock (Minor & LoLordo, 1984). If odors were mismatched across phases, deficits in lever-press and shuttle-escape test performance were eliminated in inescapably shocked rats. This outcome was obtained regardless of whether the pretreatment odor was biological (stress odorants) or artificial (peppermint). Subsequent work has shown that contextual odors also contribute to the diminished pain sensitivity (Coen, 1985) and defensive burying (Williams & Lierle, 1987) shown by inescapably shocked rats.

Although these studies clearly establish a role of associative transfer in the helplessness paradigm, they do not indicate whether odors associated with inescapable shock are differentially fear inducing. Here we review more recent work on the conditioning and odor-mediated transfer of fear following inescapable shock (Minor 1990a). These experiments were based on the finding that helplessness effects can be conditioned to an artificial odor (Coen, 1985; Minor & LoLordo, 1984). The basic procedure consisted of exposing thirsty rats to escapable shock (E), yoked inescapable shock (Y), or restraint (R) in wheel-turn chambers odorized by peppermint extract. Rats were then given 30-min access to water in a novel apparatus 22 and 48 hr later. The pretreatment odor occurred as a static cue in the test chamber for half of the rats in each pretreatment condition (EO, YO, & RO), but was absent for the remaining subjects (ENO, YNO, & RNO). The suppression of drinking in the presence of the odor was taken as a measure of conditioned fear. Fig. 3.2 shows the results of three experiments using this basic procedure. Each plot is the average lick rate in each group based on the entire 30 min of each test session.

The data in the top panel of Fig. 3.2 indicate that differences in the level of fear conditioned during pretreatment with escapable and inescapable shock (e.g., Mineka et al., 1984) transfer to a test conducted in a different apparatus. Rats tested in the no-odor condition (ENO, YNO, RNO) had similar overall lick rates in Test 1 and Test 2. By contrast, drinking was differentially suppressed among groups tested in the presence of the pretreatment odor. Restrained rats (RO) drank only slightly less than did no-odor groups. Escape rats (EO) showed some suppression on Test 1 relative to RO rats, but the groups had similar lick rates during Test 2. Most importantly, Group YO showed greater suppression than did Groups EO and RO throughout testing. Thus, an odor associated with inescapable shock elicited greater fear and was more resistant to extinction.

The same general procedure was used to assess the retention of an odor–shock association and the role of forgetting in recovery from helplessness. Although conditioned aversive associations usually are retained over intervals far longer than 72 hr, forgetting could provide a simple explanation for the dissipation of helplessness over time. The pretreatment odor might

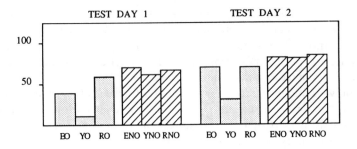

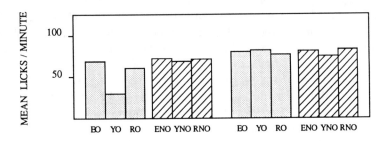

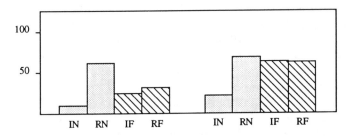

FIG. 3.2. Mean lick rates during each of two test sessions for the various groups in three experiments. Top panel: Thirsty rats were exposed to escapable shock (E), yoked inescapable shock (Y), or restraint (R) in chambers odorized by peppermint. All rats were given the opportunity to drink in a novel chamber 22 and 48 hr later either in the presence of (EO, YO, RO) or the absence of (ENO, YNO, RNO) the pretreatment odor. Middle panel: Following triadic pretreatment in a chamber containing conspecific stress odors, rats were given the opportunity to drink in a novel chamber that either contained (EO, YO, RO) or did not contain (ENO, YNO, RNO) novel peppermint odor to test for enhanced neophobia following inescapable shock. Bottom panel: Following exposure to inescapable shock (I) or restraint (R) in the presence of peppermint odor, rats were given the opportunity to drink in either a familiar (IF, RF) or a novel (IN, RN) chamber that was odorized by peppermint.

not be an effective retrieval cue for inescapable shock when a test is conducted in a different apparatus 72 hr later. A test under these conditions would be functionally equivalent to testing in the absence of the pretreatment odor, a condition which does not produce behavioral impairment (Coen, 1985; Minor & LoLordo, 1984; Williams & Lierle, 1987).

The appropriate experiment provided no evidence of forgetting. Rats exposed to inescapable shock in odorized tubes showed equivalent lick suppression in the presence of the odor at 22- and 72-hr retention intervals. Thus an inability of the cue to elicit fear during testing cannot be responsible for time-dependent variations in helplessness.

It appears, then, that an odor associated with inescapable shock must be present in a test conducted 24 hr later for helplessness effects to occur. However, the pretreatment odor continues to elicit fear in a transsituational test at a retention interval when helplessness effects do not occur. Two conclusions seem possible given this pattern of data: (1) The amount of fear elicited by situational cues at the time of testing is not causally related to helplessness and some other aspect of the odor–shock relation accounts for associative transfer; or (2) Conditioned fear is a necessary, but not a sufficient, condition for impaired test performance. The latter possibility is perfectly consistent with Weiss et al.'s (1981) suggestion that helplessness results from an interaction of associative and nonassociative factors. If both conditions are necessary, then the dissipation of helplessness over time could be explained by the recovery from the nonassociative effects of inescapable shock.

b. Nonassociative Transfer. The experiments that have been described also provided evidence of a nonassociative effect of inescapable shock. Although the Yoked rats tested in the no-odor condition had overall drinking rates similar to control levels, local drinking varied across conditions. Specifically, inescapably shocked rats were slow to initiate drinking during the first test session. One possible explanation for this effect is that neophobia, the fear of novel places, was enhanced as a nonassociative consequence of inescapable shock pretreatment. A neophobic reaction to the unfamiliar test chamber would have decreased exploration early in the session, delaying the initiation of drinking relative to restrained controls. An attempt was made to enhance neophobia during testing to assess this possibility.

Rats initially received standard triadic pretreatments in wheel-turn chambers containing the odors of stressed conspecifics. Lick suppression tests were administered 22 and 48 hr later. If the transient suppression of drinking in inescapably shocked rats resulted from initial neophobia of the test context, then that reaction should be enhanced and prolonged by adding novel features to the test context. Thus *novel* peppermint odor was presented during testing for Groups EO, YO, and RO. As shown in the middle panel of Fig. 3.2, drinking was suppressed in YO rats during Test 1 relative to groups EO and RO. This novelty-enhanced suppression was short-lived, however, and completely absent on Test 2.

Importantly, a separate experiment indicated that the ability of a novel odor to suppress drinking in inescapably shocked rats diminished within 72 hr, more quickly than did conditioned suppression. This recovery time course for enhanced neophobia is similar to that for the nonassociative, neurochemical effects of inescapable shock (Weiss et al., 1981), and in fact, may be related to the depletion of brain catecholamine concentrations (Britton, Ksir, Thatcher–Britton, Young & Koob, 1984). Thus exposure to inescapable shock appears to have associative and nonassociative effects, both of which contribute to the suppression of test drinking 24 hr (but not 72 hr) after pretreatment.

c. Interaction of Factors.   A final question was how these two sources of fear combined to suppress test drinking. Neophobia was a small and transient source of suppression and if it simply summated with conditioned suppression, its contribution to overall fear during testing would have been minimal. On the other hand, these processes could have acted synergistically. The pretreatment odor may be an ambiguous cue when tested outside the original context. Some initial neophobia to the test environment may be needed for the odor's conditioned aversive properties to be expressed. In turn, the presence of a potential danger signal in an unfamiliar environment could serve to enhance and maintain initial wariness of the situation. From this view, a much weaker overall fear response would be expected if the odor were presented in a familiar, but otherwise hedonically neutral, context.

The contribution of neophobia was assessed by comparing conditioned suppression to the pretreatment odor when testing occurred in a familiar or a novel apparatus. Access to the water spout was blocked, and two groups (F: familiar context) initially were familiarized with the drinking chambers over five consecutive daily sessions. Two other groups (N: novel test context) were placed in holding cages on these days. One group from each condition was exposed to inescapable shock (Groups IF and IN) and the other groups were restrained (Groups FN and RN) in tubes odorized by peppermint. Lick suppression tests were administered on the following 2 days. The pretreatment odor was present for all groups.

Overall lick rates in the four groups are shown in the lower panel of Fig. 3.2. When the test context was novel (Groups IN and RN), the odor differentially and substantially suppressed licking in preshocked rats on both test days. Familiarity with the chambers dramatically altered fear of the odor. Drinking was equivalent in Groups IF and RF on both test days, but somewhat suppressed relative to Group RN on Test 1. However, clear differences in fear between IN and IF rats were evident on Test 2: Whereas the odor failed to suppress licking in Group IF, IN rats showed greatly reduced drinking relative to all other groups. These data suggest that neophobia plays a central role in determining the level of fear experienced during a transsituational test. Some neophobia of the test context apparently is necessary for the associative properties of the pretreatment odor to be fully expressed.

4. Summary

In this section it was argued that subjects are unable to discriminate between dangerous and safe periods during exposure to unsignaled, inescapable shock and remain chronically afraid throughout the pretreatment session as a result (Seligman, 1968; Seligman & Binik, 1977). Chronic fear has two immediate effects that contribute to later performance deficits. First, odors in the pretreatment environment become strongly associated with inescapable shock and serve as critical retrieval cues during later testing. Second, excess time in fear has nonassociative effects, as exemplified by enhanced neophobia. These factors interact when testing is conducted 24 hr after pretreatment; both factors appear to be necessary, neither is sufficient to impair performance. We have not identified specific mechanisms (e.g., response competition, cognitive dysfunction, etc.) by which fear acts to disrupt performance. This issue is addressed in the final section of the chapter.

B. Modulation of Anxiety

The ability to escape shock during the pretreatment session usually prevents the otherwise deleterious effects of shock exposure (Maier & Seligman, 1976). This section is concerned with the psychological context that is generated by adding an escape contingency (or other modulator operation) to the baseline schedule of shock delivery. Before treating this issue in detail, however, we need to correct a shortcoming in, and offer a modest expansion of, the concept of a modulator.

Overmier (1988) defined modulator variables as experimental operations that alter the reaction to the baseline stress procedure. The relevant experiment consists of exposing one group to the baseline procedure, and a second to the baseline operation in conjunction with a potential modulator operation of interest. An implicit assumption of this analysis is that each operation yields a unimodal distribution of reactions. The condition is not always met: For instance, the effect of inescapable shock on later shuttle-escape performance in rats has been characterized as an "all-or-none" phenomenon (Maier et al., 1973). Whereas the majority of rats show the maximum possible deficit, some subjects show no impairment at all; hence, the distribution of reactions to inescapable shock frequently is bimodal. Which mode represents the true baseline in such cases? Of course, the problem usually is finessed by computing a group mean, despite its inaccuracy as a measure of central tendency.

As an alternative to masking individual differences, the modulator framework can be expanded to include two categories: (1) *Extrinsic* modulators or experimental operations; and (2) *Intrinsic* modulators or subject variables. The effects of an extrinsic modulator are determined by addition of an experimental contingency to the basic stressor operation and assessing any difference in outcomes between conditions. Intrinsic modulation, on the other hand, is observed as variance about the typical baseline response to inescapable shock. Something in a subject's genetic makeup, learning history, or their interaction prior to entering the experiment alters the typical effect of inescapable shock. Intrinsic modulation is assumed to occur as a proactive effect of some undisclosed variable. Importantly, this reformulation yields a conceptual framework that allows us to account for all the variance in an experiment: That is, extrinsic and intrinsic modulators represent, respectively, between- and within-group variance.

Unfortunately, there is no table of organismic factors to guide the study of intrinsic modulators that is comparable to the extrinsic variables shown in Fig. 3.1. Nonetheless, the concept of intrinsic modulation is useful when a stress reaction is thought to covary with some complex "trait" (e.g., emotionality, dominance, attributional style) which is not easily linked to a specific learning history, either for lack of adequate theory or because it emerges from a gene–environment interaction. Potential intrinsic modulators can be assessed by characterizing subjects with respect to the trait prior to assessing reactions to the baseline operation. If variations in the typical baseline reaction are predicted by the pretest, then the trait would be indicated as an intrinsic modulator. Because the exact nature and origin of such traits are not known, the problem should then shift to analyzing the trait. Thus, whereas an analysis of extrinsic modulators fosters an inductive (bottom–up) approach, the study of intrinsic variables suggests a deductive (top–down) analysis.

The following discussion of coping mechanisms in the helplessness paradigm is organized around this distinction between extrinsic and intrinsic modulators. Here we will be concerned not only with whether a modulator variable is effective in altering the baseline stress reaction, but also with the mechanisms involved.

1. Extrinsic Modulators

This section is concerned with the effects of adding an escape contingency to the baseline schedule of shock delivery. If chronic fear causes helplessness as we argued above, then the well-established ability of an escape response to prevent helplessness must occur because fear is reduced during the pretreatment session. However, because fear is engendered and modified by Pavlovian operations and principles, fear cannot be reduced as a direct consequence of learning the instrumental escape contingency; instead, it must occur as an emergent (Pavlovian) consequence of the acquisition process. Thus, whereas learned helplessness theorists (e.g., Seligman et al., 1971) essentially elevated exposure to inescapable shock to a form of instrumental contingency learning, the anxiety hypothesis is forced to interpret escape learning in Pavlovian terms. Three hypotheses are outlined below that are consistent this approach.

a. Signal Features of an Escape Response. Weiss (1971) argued that the level of protection afforded by a coping response was related to the amount of "relevant feedback" it provided. Relevant feedback was defined as response-produced stimuli correlated with the absence of the stressor. This class of events presumably includes proprioceptive feedback and response-produced changes in the environment. If these stimuli acquire signal value during conditioning, then some of the benefits of control could stem from enhanced prediction.

There has been a resurgence of interest in the concept of relevant feedback and its application to helplessness, largely due to the work of Mineka and her colleagues (Mineka et al., 1984; Starr & Mineka, 1977). Mineka et al. provided convincing evidence that greater fear is conditioned to situational and discrete stimuli during inescapable shock than during escapable shock. More importantly, the fear-inducing properties of inescapable shock were markedly reduced when a brief "feedback" stimulus was presented immediately after each shock trial. Recent extensions of this work also have shown that stimulus feedback alleviates the effects of inescapable shock on hypoalgesia (Maier & Keith, 1987), later escape learning (Volpicelli et al., 1984), and ulcer formation during subsequent restraint stress (Overmier, Murison, Skoglund, & Ursin, 1985).

These data and related findings provide a solid basis for questioning whether controllability is central to helplessness. Although operational controllability is not altered by the addition of stimulus feedback, many of the stressor's effects are eliminated. The similarity between stimulus feedback and the theoretical concept of relevant feedback suggests that the former operation is stress reducing because it models a critical predictive feature of an escape response (but see Maier & Keith, 1987, for an alternative explanation).

Seligman's safety signal hypothesis (Seligman, 1968; Seligman & Binik, 1977) suggests that feedback stimuli should work directly to reduce the chronicity of fear during pretreatment with inescapable shock. According to this view, when shock is preceded by a warning stimulus, the absence of that signal predicts the absence of shock. Thus signaling shock onset reduces the impact of a stressor by indirectly generating safety signals. Such implied safety cues or explicit feedback stimuli should acquire the ability to elicit relief and relaxation responses due to their association with a shock-free period.

Escape responses should be similarly fear reducing if the interoceptive stimuli generated by the act of escaping acquire predictive value in the manner of discrete external events. Escape-produced stimuli and external feedback stimuli presumably have similar temporal and contingent relations with shock, and therefore, should work in a similar manner to reduce the total amount of time spent in fear during the ITI. Less fear should be conditioned to the pretreatment context as a consequence, and fear-related neural pathways should not undergo the continuous activation produced by inescapable shock. Thus escape responses could exert their modulatory effect through a Pavlovian rather than an instrumental process.

Two lines of research are suggested by this modified relevant feedback hypothesis. First, if chronic fear causes helplessness, then any manipulation that reduces the total amount of time spent in fear should serve as an effective modulator. For instance, if Seligman's safety-signal hypothesis is correct, then signaling the onset of inescapable shock should be roughly equivalent to signaling periods of safety. Both operations should work to reduce the total amount of time spent in fear and the level of fear conditioned to the pretreatment context. Second, it should be possible to model the benefits of an escape response by presenting exteroceptive stimuli in various contingent relations with inescapable shock. When all of the relevant signal features of response-generated stimuli are represented by explicit stimuli, the dimension of controllability should not contribute to the immediate or proactive effects of shock.

Two recent studies from our laboratories (Jackson & Minor, 1988; Overmier & Murison, 1989) demonstrated symmetrical effects of forward and backward Pavlovian conditioning on measures of fear and helplessness. Overmier and Murison (1989) found similar effects of forward and backward signal–shock pairings in a study of the ulcerogenic effects of "resting" in the conditioning context following immersion in cold water. The study was particularly elegant in that all rats had similar conditioning histories. Three groups of rats received shock in either a forward, backward, or a random relation with a signal in one context. Each group later received additional exposure to signals and shocks in other contexts so that their conditioning histories were operationally equivalent. Following conditioning, all rats were immersed in cold water and then allowed to "rest" in the original conditioning context. Forward and backward signal–shock relations were equally effective in reducing ulcerations relative to the random control.

Jackson and Minor (1988) exposed rats to forward (FOR), backward (BACK), or random (RAN) presentations of a signal and inescapable shock during pretreatment. The nature of the signal (houselight onset: Groups FORON, BACKON, RANON; or houselight termination: FOR-OFF, BACKOFF, RANOFF) also was manipulated in an attempt to influence the course of conditioning in each signal–shock condition. Twenty-four hr later rats from each pretreatment condition were tested either for shuttle-escape performance or for fear of the pretreatment context via a lick suppression test. If the foregoing hypothesis is correct, the efficacy of a particular signal–shock relation in preventing later deficits in escape performance should be inversely related to the level of fear elicited and conditioned during pretreatment.

The left panel in Fig. 3.3 shows escape latencies in blocks of five trials in each signal-shock condition. Random signal-shock presentations (RANON; RANOFF) were ineffective in altering the deleterious effects of unsignaled, inescapable shock (Group S) on FR–2 escape performance. The protection afforded by forward and backward relations varied with the nature of the signal. Relative to restrained controls (Group R), a backward relation prevented later escape deficits when a decrease in illumination served as the signal (BACKOFF), but offered no protection when the signal was light onset (BACKON). Conversely, shuttle-escape deficits were eliminated by forward signal–shock pairing when light (FORON), but not darkness (FOROFF), served as the signal.

The right panel in Fig 3.3 provides a measure of the level of fear conditioned to the pretreatment context. Thirsty rats (Jackson & Minor, 1988, Experiment 3) were trained to drink from a water spout in the pretreatment context prior to conditioning with unsignaled inescapable shock, or forward or backward signal-shock presentations. All rats received 15-min access to water in the pretreatment context on the following day. This session was conducted in constant illumination (NOSIG-ON, FOR-OFF, & BAK-OFF) or constant darkness (NOSIG-OFF, FOR-ON, BAK-ON), depending on which condition had served as the background for the signal during pretreatment. The strength of contextual fear is reflected in the suppression of drinking.

The efficacy of each condition in preventing deficits in escape performance (left panel) was inversely related to the level of fear conditioned to the pretreatment apparatus (right panel). Forward darkness–shock and backward light–shock presentations failed to prevent later escape deficits and conditioned as much fear to the pretreatment context as did unsignaled shock. By contrast, forward light-shock and backward darkness-shock re-

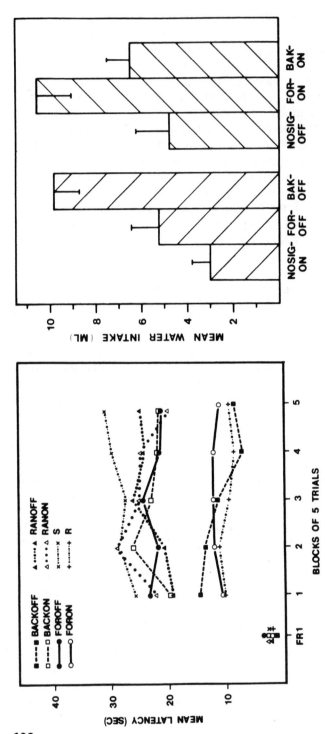

FIG. 3.3. Left panel: Shuttle-escape latencies for groups exposed to forward (FORON, FOROFF), backward (BACK-ON, BACKOFF), or random (RANON, RANOFF) presentations of a signal and inescapable shock 24 hr earlier. The signal was either an increase (ON) or a decrease (OFF) in illumination. These groups are compared to rats receiving inescapable shock (S) or restraint (R) in the absence of a signal. Right panel: Mean water intake in the pretreatment context for thirsty rats receiving forward (FOR-ON, FOR-OFF) or backward (BAK-ON, BAK-OFF) pairings of a signal and inescapable shock, or inescapable shock in the absence of a signal (NOSIG-ON, NOSIG-OFF) 24 hr earlier.

lations prevented later escape deficits and markedly reduced fear of the pretreatment context.[1] These data and those of Overmier and Murison (1989) provide convergent evidence that when danger and safety signals are equally effective in reducing fear to the pretreatment context, they have similar modulatory effects on test measures of stress pathology.

Signaling shock onset during pretreatment apparently reduces contextual fear conditioning and the amount of time spent in fear. However, because a forward CS becomes fear provoking itself, any advantage of signaling shock during pretreatment may be compromised when the CS occurs in the test. Indeed, signaling the onset of inescapable shock impairs later escape/avoidance performance when the CS is presented as a warning signal for test trials (Weiss, Krieckhaus, & Conte, 1968) or occurs as a static cue in the test context (Bersh et al., 1986), perhaps by eliciting responses that directly interfere with test performance.

Even though the ability to predict safe intervals during the pretreatment session does modulate helplessness, there is compelling evidence that a safety signal and an escape contingency are not equivalent operations. For instance, the inclusion of short minimum ITIs in the schedule of shock delivery eliminates the ability of feedback stimuli to reduce fear to the pretreatment context (Rosellini et al., 1986) or prevent later deficits in escape performance (Anderson, Hantual, Crowell, & Tohman, 1987; Minor, Trauner, Lee, & Dess, 1990). Because backward inhibitory fear conditioning also is retarded by the use of short minimum ITIs (Moscovitch & LoLordo, 1968), these data suggest that the modulatory action of feedback stimuli derives from a reliable correlation with long, shock-free periods. However, escape responses retain their prophylactic action regardless of the distribution of ITIs (Rosellini et al., 1986). Rosellini, DeCola,

---

[1]The asymmetrical effects of forward and backward relations under the different illumination conditions of this study may indicate that light and darkness are differentially associable with periods of danger and safety. Whereas darkness may have rapidly acquired safety-signal properties during backward signal–shock pairings, it may have become only a weak danger signal in the forward condition. Conversely, light onset may have rapidly become a danger signal in the forward condition, but only weakly associated with safety in the backward condition. If so, forward light–shock and backward darkness–shock pairings would have been more effective in competing with fear conditioning to situational cues during pretreatment than were other conditions (see Jackson & Minor, 1988, for a thorough discussion). This possibility also might account for the occasional finding that a random relation between darkness and inescapable shock can prevent the shuttle-escape deficits (Jackson & Minor, unpublished data, 1983) and analgesia (Maier & Keith, 1987) typically observed 24 hr after shock pretreatment—i.e., fortuitous backward pairings during random presentations of darkness and shock may have resulted in faster acquisition of inhibitory strength than did excitation from occasional forward pairing. From the present perspective, net inhibitory strength in a random cue would have reduced the total amount of time spent in fear during pretreatment, thereby eliminating later performance deficits.

and Warren (1987) also have shown that escape responses inhibit fear earlier in the pretreatment session than do safety signals, an effect which was not easily attributed to differential salience of response-generated and exteroceptive feedback stimuli. These data identify important differences between the two operations. However, they represent a serious challenge to the feedback hypothesis only to the extent that presenting a stimulus immediately after inescapable shock models all the relevant signal features of an escape response—it does not.

Perhaps the most important feature of escape-generated stimuli is that they *predict* shock termination. Mowrer (1960) suggested that a signal for the cessation of shock should elicit a relief reaction and acquire secondary-reinforcing properties. Moskovitch (1972, reported in LoLordo & Fairless, 1985) provided some evidence for the proposal by demonstrating the fear-inhibiting properties of a cessation signal. Importantly, unlike backward conditioning (Moscovitch & LoLordo, 1968), cessation conditioning was not dramatically affected by shortening the minimum ITI.

We recently provided direct evidence for a role of cessation conditioning in the helplessness paradigm (Minor et al., 1990). Rats initially were exposed to inescapable tail shock (I), inescapable shock with a cessation signal (C), inescapable shock followed by a feedback signal (F), or simple restraint (R) in tubes. Highly variable shock durations were used to increase the signal value of the cessation stimulus, which occurred 3 sec prior to the termination of shock on each trial. The signal was presented for 3 sec immediately after each trial in the feedback conditions. One cessation and one feedback group (Groups C–AS and F–AS) received additional fixed-duration (1-sec) shocks 5 sec after a randomly selected 15% of the trials. These brief added shocks allowed us to assess the effects of the minimum ITI on cessation and backward (feedback) conditioning without dramatically altering the severity of the pretreatment session. All six groups were tested for shuttle-escape performance 24 hr later.

As shown in Fig. 3.4, the ability to predict shock termination (Group C) or the ability to predict shock-free periods (Group F) during pretreatment eliminated later deficits in FR–2 shuttle escape (Group I). Shortening the minimum ITI by presenting brief shocks shortly after some trials eliminated the benefits of a feedback signal (Group F–AS), but did not significantly affect the ability of a cessation signal to protect against escape deficits (Group C–AS).

Cessation signals appear to have the properties of an escape response that are not represented by a safety signal. Cessation conditioning yields a potent inhibitor that is resistant to manipulation of the ITI. Although we have not systematically assessed the acquisition of inhibitory strength during the pretreatment session, preliminary data indicate that a combination of cessation and safety signals during inescapable shock has a very powerful prophylactic action, more so than either relation alone. Thus the

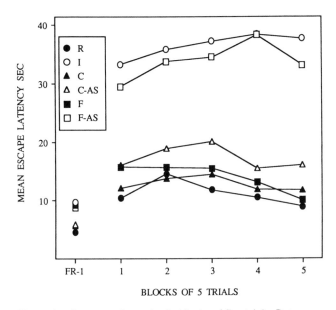

FIG. 3.4. Mean shuttle-escape latencies in blocks of five trials. Rats were exposed to either variable-duration inescapable shocks (I), inescapable shock in conjunction with a cessation signal (C), inescapable shock followed by a feedback signal (backward conditioning: F), or restraint (R) in tubes. One cessation- (C-AS) and one feedback-signal group (F-AS) received brief additional shocks 5 sec after a randomly selected 15% of the pretreatment trials. All rats were tested for shuttle-escape performance 24 hr later.

ability of an escape response to inhibit fear very early in training (Rosellini et al., 1987) could occur because response-generated stimuli have both cessation and safety-signal properties.

Cessation and safety signals may work in fundamentally different ways to reduce fear during shock pretreatment. Because cessation conditioning is not influenced by short minimum ITIs, the acquisition of inhibitory strength probably does not depend on the ability to predict a shock-free period (see Moskovitch & LoLordo, 1968), and as such, probably does not directly alter the chronicity of fear during the ITI. This could cause problems for the anxiety hypothesis. However, cessation signals may exert their modulatory effect by directly altering the effectiveness of the unconditioned stimulus. If cessation conditioning reduces the perceived intensity of shock, the conditioned response (fear) would be diminished as well (e.g., Mackintosh, 1975). Reducing the magnitude of fear via cessation conditioning may be equivalent to reducing the amount of time spent in fear by signaling safe intervals.

Overall, this review of recent data suggests that stressor predictability was dismissed far too early as a potential modulator of the helplessness effect (Maier & Seligman, 1976; Maier et al., 1969). The ability to predict periods of danger, safety, or the termination of shock most certainly does alter the impact of traumatic shock (Anderson et al., 1987; Jackson & Minor, 1988; Maier & Keith, 1987; Mineka et al., 1984; Minor et al., 1990; Overmier & Murison, 1989; Overmier, Murison, Skoglund, & Ursin, 1985; Rosellini et al., 1986; Rosellini et al., 1987). These modulatory effects can be as potent as those accruing from control, and appear to be related to the level of fear-reduction accomplished during pretreatment. As yet, there are not enough data to conclude that the benefits of control simply reduce to enhanced prediction; however, there is good reason to continue to question whether controllability represents an independent modulatory dimension.

b. Attentional Effects of an Escape Contingency.   The addition of an escape contingency to the baseline shock condition may introduce variables that are not directly related to prediction or control. Here we consider the possibility that attention deployment is altered as an emergent consequence of escape training, thereby reducing the capacity to process nociceptive and fear-related stimuli. A variety of data suggest that pain thresholds increase, and aversion ratings decrease, when human subjects engage in some task that is not directly related to the processing of a physical stressor (e.g., Berger & Kanfer, 1975; Greenstein, 1984; Grim & Kanfer, 1976; Maltzman, 1988). For instance, Maltzman (1988) recently demonstrated that the effectiveness of visual distractors in enhancing pain tolerance in a cold-pressor test increased with the complexity and uniqueness of the visual array. These data suggest that processing painful, and perhaps all affective, stimuli requires some allocation of limited attentional resources. As a consequence, the direction of attention away from a source of distress is often an effective strategy for "blunting" (Miller, 1979) the emotional impact of an adverse situation.

Analogous competition for processing resources may occur during the acquisition of an escape response (Goodson & Marx, 1953). The escape manipulandum is likely to become an increasingly salient feature of the pretreatment environment as the contingency between responding and shock termination is learned. Attention to the manipulandum may reduce the capacity to process pain and fear-related stimuli. Any amelioration of nociception should produce a functional reduction in shock intensity, and therefore, a lower overall level of fear. Support for this position is provided by the finding that human subjects show lower pain ratings and arousal indexes when shock is controllable (Bowers, 1968; Staub, Tursky, & Schwartz; 1971). The presence of a salient distractor (e.g., a conspecific) during exposure to shock also attenuates gastric pathology in rats (Weiss, Pohorecky, Salman, & Gruenthal, 1976) and can increase pain tolerance in humans (Craig & Weiss, 1971).

The manipulandum cannot accrue similar associative value when shock is uncontrollable. A random relation between events—such as wheel-turn responding and shock termination—should eliminate any attentional demands of the manipulandum (Mackintosh, 1973). Thus, in the absence of an escape contingency, the rat is deprived not only of behavioral control and enhanced prediction, but also of a potential source of distraction. Perhaps as a consequence, subjects in each condition develop different physical orientations with respect to the locus of shock. Whereas escapably shocked rats orient toward the manipulandum and away from shock, inescapably shocked rats usually end up on their backs (a defensive posture) facing the rear of the chamber and the source of pain. This difference in the direction of attention may allow escapably shocked rats to "blunt" the physical and emotional impact of shock relative to inescapably shocked rats.

c. Proactive Effects of Escape. Experience with escapable shock prior to exposure to inescapable shock prevents later deficits in escape performance (Seligman et al., 1975; Williams & Maier, 1977). This proactive effect of escape training has been termed "immunization" and is conceptually problematical for an anxiety-based interpretation. Relevant feedback or the attentional effects of an added escape contingency in the first training phase would have to work proactively to alter fear during inescapable shock in the second phase to prevent performance deficits in the test phase. As yet, there are not enough data to come to strong conclusions concerning the combined proactive effect of these mechanisms. However, Maier and Warren (1988) have shown that initial experience with stimulus feedback following inescapable shock does not immunize against the effects of subsequent unsignaled, inescapable shock on later escape performance. Thus, even though escape responses and feedback stimuli reduce fear during shock exposure (Mineka et al., 1984), they do not have equivalent proactive effects. Nonetheless, we have argued above that the feedback manipulation does not model all the relevant signal features of an escape response; it is conceivable that initial cessation conditioning could serve as an effective immunizer, particularly if it alters the unconditioned reaction to shock. If so, then the immunization effect can be incorporated into the anxiety framework.

An alternative explanation for immunization is suggested by the most obvious effect of adding an escape contingency to the baseline shock schedule. Specifically, the instrumental contingency trains a stable, active response to shock. This direct behavioral effect of the contingency cannot be modeled by exteroceptive stimulus presentations during inescapable shock. To the extent that training an active response, rather than stress or fear reduction, is responsible for the immunization effect (cf. Anisman, Irwin, Beauchamp, & Zacharko, 1983), stimulus feedback of any form should not contribute to the phenomenon.

Data relevant to this possibility have been obtained in a related procedure—the "learned mastery" paradigm. Volpicelli, Ulm, Altenor, and Seligman (1983) interpreted the passivity of inescapably shocked rats during testing as evidence of their expectation that responding would be futile. Initial immunization training was assumed to protect the subject from this passivity by establishing a cognition of mastery that proactively interfered with the perception of helplessness during exposure to inescapable shock. They argued that this mastery cognition should be directly observable as persistent responding (or attempts to escape) during a test in which shocks were inescapable. Indeed, rats initially exposed to escapable grid shock showed greater response persistence during inescapable grid shock than did inescapably shocked rats or restrained controls.

More recent work suggests a different interpretation of the mastery effect (Minor, 1990b). Rats were exposed to escapable tail shock, inescapable tail shock, inescapable tail shock followed by stimulus feedback, or restraint in wheel-turn chambers and then tested for the number of unconditioned responses to inescapable grid shocks in a shuttlebox 24 hr later. No evidence of enhanced responding by escape rats (i.e., a mastery effect) was obtained in five experiments when the locus of shock delivery (tail or grid) differed across phases. In general, escape, yoked-signal, and restrained rats had similar response rates, regardless of the other aspects of the test. Inescapably shocked rats showed marked suppression of responding relative to all other groups.

As shown in Fig. 3.5, escape (E) rats did show greater response persistence during testing than did all other groups when grid shock was used in both experimental phases. Responding in rats pretreated with yoked inescapable grid shock followed by stimulus feedback (Group YS) was similar to that in restrained controls (Group R) and initially higher (Test 1 and 2) than in rats receiving inescapable shock alone (Group Y).

These data are consistent with Maier and Warren's (1988) findings concerning immunization insofar as they indicate that stimulus feedback and escape training are not identical operations. Although the feedback manipulation eliminated the suppressive effects of inescapable shock on responding in the mastery paradigm, Group YS did not show the level of persistence seen in Group E. However, it is unclear that this outcome points to a critical difference in the modulatory (i.e., anxiety-reducing) effect of escape and feedback operations.

The failure to find equivalence between tail shock and grid shock pretreatments is inconsistent with the type of generalized cognition of control implied by the mastery concept. The results suggest that escapable tail shock conditioned a less active response pattern than did escapable grid shock, or it conditioned equally active responding that failed to transfer because of the difference in mode of shock delivery across experimental phases (Barbaree & Weisman, 1975). As has been argued, this direct effect of an escape contingency on behavior cannot be modeled with inescapable

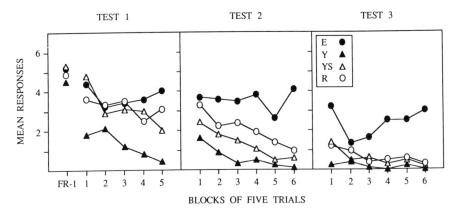

FIG. 3.5. Mean shuttle responses to fixed-duration inescapable shocks in blocks of five trials and over 3 consecutive test days. Rats were pre-exposed to escapable grid shock (E), yoked inescapable shock (Y), yoked inescapable shock followed by a feedback stimulus (Y-FB), or restraint (R) 24 hr prior to Test 1.

shock, regardless of the presence of stimulus feedback. From this view, the mastery effect is actually irrelevant to the stress-reducing capacity of escapable shock and falls outside of the realm of the anxiety hypothesis.

The use of the term "learned mastery" for response persistence in this procedure seems to be a misnomer, given that is there nothing to master in the test. Indeed, following escapable shock with inescapable shock is technically a "loss-of-control" experiment and might be conceived of as detrimental (Hanson, Larson, & Snowdon, 1976). The phenomenon also resembles self-punitive behavior in which increased resistance to extinction results from the punishment of prepotent avoidance or escape responses (e.g., Brown, 1969; also see Dean and Pittman, this volume). Analysis of the mastery effect might be enhanced by considering this older, but fairly extensive literature.

2. Intrinsic Modulators

Impaired performance is not an invariant outcome of exposure to an inescapable shock. Approximately 37% of the dogs pretreated with ines-capable shock in the original helplessness experiments (cf. Maier et al., 1969) failed to show impaired escape-avoidance performance 24 hr later. Individual differences also were evident within (Maier et al., 1973) and across strains of rats (Braud, Wepmann, & Russo, 1969) in the initial attempts to produce the phenomenon. Moreover, the percentage of "resis-tant" rats in a sample usually decreases as the severity of inescapable shock is increased (Anisman & Zacharko, 1986; Looney & Cohen, 1972; Minor et al., 1988), suggesting that individual subjects may range along a continuum from highly vulnerable to highly resistant to stressors.

We have already proposed that individual differences in helplessness result from intrinsic modulation of the baseline stress response. The animal's developmental history, genetic makeup, or the interaction between experience and genotype prior to entering the experiment alters the typical baseline response. We will discuss two intrinsic variables which modulate the reaction to shock and outline some implications of these findings for theories of helplessness.

a. Genetic Modulation of Avoidance Learning and Emotionality.   Brush and his colleagues (see Brush, 1985) have selectively bred Syracuse strains of Long–Evans rats for more than 20 generations on a criterion of high (SHA) or low (SLA) shuttle-avoidance performance. Recent work suggests that these strains differ in emotional reactivity. For instance, SLA animals show greater thigmotaxis and defecation, faster acquisition of passive avoidance and conditioned suppression, and greater stress-induced hypoalgesia than do their SHA counterparts. Although differential susceptibility of the strains to helplessness effects has not been fully examined, they differ on measures of stress-induced finickiness (Brush et al., 1988) and social dominance (Brush, Blanchard, & Blanchard, 1989), both of which are affected by pretreatment with inescapable shock (Dess, Chapman, & Minor, 1988; Williams, 1987).

This line of research provides an ideal example of intrinsic modulation. A potential problem with analyzing an intrinsic modulator arises when subjects are pretested on a trait before the covariance of the trait and the dependent measure of interest is assessed. It is always possible that the process of pretesting, and not the trait per se, accounts for individual variations in test performance (see Overmier, 1988, for a discussion). However, in the work of Brush and his colleagues avoidance was used as a criterion for selective breeding and did not precede the foregoing tests for emotionality—thus the performance of individual subjects was not confounded with the process of pretesting. This research also has included an analysis of the specific components of avoidance behavior that differ between strains (Brush, 1985) and, by the very nature of selective breeding, has established that the differences have a genetic basis.

b. Social Dominance and a SAP Hypothesis.   The research and theory in this section were generated by viewing the helplessness paradigm from an ethological perspective and searching for a natural analog of inescapable shock (Minor, 1983; Minor & LoLordo, 1984; Minor & Williams, 1988). In this regard, exposure to inescapable shock bears a marked resemblance to defeat by a conspecific.

In a typical helplessness experiment, rats are exposed to inescapable shock in a chamber that smells of previously shocked and restrained conspecifics. Shock is delivered through fixed tail electrodes (e.g., Maier et al., 1973) or a pin electrode implanted in the dorsal neck (Seligman & Beagley, 1975). These are the same locations at which a dominant (alpha) male directs biting attacks during a dominance conflict or territorial defense (e.g., Calhoun, 1962; Barnett, 1963). Because of these similarities to an agonistic encounter, inescapably shocked rats may represent the pretreatment session as an attack by a highly aggressive conspecific, resulting in an increase in submissiveness. This possibility is supported by the similar behavioral consequences of defeat and inescapable shock. Both events result in profound hypoalgesia (Maier, 1986; Miczek, Thompson, & Shuster, 1986), reduced social rank (Seward, 1945) and territorial defense (Barnett, 1963; Williams, 1982), and an increased likelihood of species-typical submissive behavior (Calhoun, 1962; Seligman & Beagley, 1975; Williams, 1987).

The proposal that submissiveness is an important component of helplessness is consistent with the current focus on anxiety. Mehrabian (1980) argued that three dimensions are necessary to characterize the subjective feeling of anxiety in human subjects: arousal, displeasure, and submissiveness. In this regard, the "feeling" of submissiveness associated with anxiety in humans may be expressed as species-typical submissive behavior in other social species. Indeed, Bolles (1971) argued that fear stimuli elicit species-specific defensive reactions (SSDRs) and identified fleeing, freezing, and fighting as SSDRs of the rat. In some circumstances the list also might be expanded to include defensive behavior (e.g., defensive boxing, back-lying, ultrasonic vocalizations) that is specifically related to intra-species defense. Thus, if Mehrabian's (1980) analysis holds across species, the behavior of highly anxious animals should be characterized by an increase in submissiveness.

This logic suggests that the helplessness effect may result in part from response competition. Specifically, stimuli associated with inescapable shock may elicit a submissive action pattern (SAP), characterized by timidity, neophobia, and with the appropriate supporting stimuli, specific submissive postures (Minor, 1983). Overall impairment of escape performance in inescapably shocked animals should depend on the extent to which a test procedure provides releasing stimuli for specific submissive behavior that is incompatible with the escape response. From this view, the helplessness effect is properly regarded as an instance of "misbehavior" (Breland & Breland, 1961), the emergence of innately organized behavior that competes with ongoing instrumental performance.

Helplessness is more robust in dogs than it is in rats (Lawry et al., 1978). This species difference may result from a greater probability of eliciting submissive behavior in the shuttle test in dogs. Canine species are highly social, and domestication has increased their readiness to display filial behavior toward humans. Indeed, the behavior of helpless dogs (crouched, tail between legs and ears laid back; see Maier & Seligman, 1976; Seligman, 1975) seems to correspond closely to the type of species-typical display that is shown by a submissive dog toward a dominant member of the pack. A human observer, their odors or those of conspecifics, in conjunction with high levels of fear, could elicit such behavior to compete with barrier jumping, resulting in the helplessness effect.

This account also suggests an alternative to Maier and Seligman's (1976) explanation for the apparent immunity of some dogs to the effects of inescapable shock. Dogs were obtained from a local pound in the original studies (Overmier & Seligman, 1967; Seligman & Maier, 1967). Maier and Seligman (1976) suggested that some of these dogs—that is, the "Philadelphia street-wise" variety—had a long history of controlling everyday events, which proactively interfered with the learning of response-reinforcer independence during inescapable shock, thereby immunizing them against later escape deficits (also see Seligman, Maier, & Geer, 1968). Another possibility is that some of these dogs were unsocialized and less responsive to the cues that release submissive behavior in the shuttle box (Scott & Fuller, 1965). In the absence of competition from specific submissive behavior, the escape performance of these dogs would have improved accordingly.

The evidence for competition from submissive behavior in studies of helplessness in rats is equivocal. Minor and LoLordo (1984; unpublished observations from Experiments 2 and 3) videotaped the shuttle-escape performance of inescapably shocked rats to assess the frequency of competing submissive behavior. Unfortunately, we were unable to characterize clearly any behavior as submissive. Evidence of specific submissive postures has been obtained in other studies, however. Seligman and Beagley (1975) delivered inescapable shock through a pin electrode implanted in the rat's upper back (also the target of a biting attack by a dominant rat). Inescapably shocked rats consistently rolled onto their backs under these conditions. As Blanchard and Blanchard (1988) recently argued, back-lying is uniquely associated with conspecific defense in rats; the posture is adopted by a submissive animal to protect against back bites from a dominant rat. Thus, the predominance of this behavior in inescapably, and not escapably, shocked rats in the Seligman and Beagley study supports a link between submission and helplessness.

One way to reconcile the different behavioral patterns seen in the Minor and LoLordo (1984) and Seligman and Beagley (1975) studies is to assume that inescapable shock engenders a "submissive state," which serves to organize specific submissive postures only in the presence of an appropriate target object. Whereas the delivery of grid shock in a shuttlebox did not yield sufficient environmental support for specific submissive postures (Minor & LoLordo, 1984), the delivery of a painful stimulus to a rat's neck did (Seligman & Beagley, 1975).

This notion of a "submissive state" suggested a further test of the SAP hypothesis. The probability that inescapable shock produces this state should depend on a rat's relative dominance at the time of pretreatment. Male members of a colony establish a rough dominance hierarchy consisting of alpha (dominant) and beta (submissive) individuals (e.g., Barnett, 1963; Calhoun, 1962). If inescapable shock increases submissiveness, then dominant rats should be resistant to developing helplessness, whereas submissive animals might be at increased risk. As such, social dominance may be an important intrinsic modulator of the baseline stress reaction.

As a test of this possibility, rats were sorted into dominance categories on the basis of a food-competition test and aggression toward a colony intruder (Minor & Williams, 1990). Rats meeting the criteria of both tests for dominance (Alpha) or submissiveness (Beta) were then exposed to sixty 5–sec inescapable tail shocks (I) or restraint (R) in a factorial design to create four groups (I–Alpha; R–Alpha; I–Beta; R–Beta). A smaller number of inescapable shocks was used than is typical in our laboratory to increase the probability of identifying individual differences. All rats were tested for shuttle-escape performance 24 hr later.

The escape latencies shown in Fig. 3.6 provide clear evidence that social dominance is an intrinsic modulator of the reaction to inescapable shock.

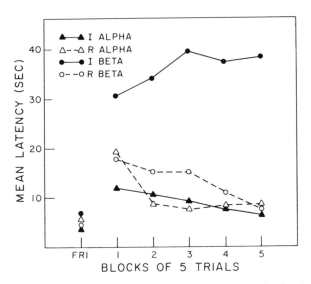

FIG. 3.6.   Shuttle-escape latencies in blocks of five trials for dominant (Alpha) and submissive (Beta) rats that were pre-exposed to inescapable shock (I) or restraint (R) 24 hr earlier.

Beta rats pretreated with inescapable shock (Group I–Beta) showed a large deficit in escape performance relative to restrained controls (Group R–Beta). By contrast, inescapable shock did not impair later escape performance in I–Alpha rats relative to either restrained group. Thus these data suggest that a rat's relative social rank may contribute to individual differences in the helplessness paradigm.

Weiss and his associates independently identified one molecular correlate of dominance that may be crucial to understanding its modulation of helplessness. Dominant rats had higher basal levels of tyrosine hydroxylase, the rate-limiting enzyme in norepinephrine synthesis, than did other rats (Weiss et al., 1982). A higher concentration of this enzyme could prevent, or facilitate recovery from, the norepinephrine-depleting effects of inescapable shock, thereby attenuating later norepinephrine-dependent impairments.

3. Summary

This section has been concerned with the modulation of the baseline stress reaction. Overmier's (1988) concept of a modulator was expanded to include two categories, thus allowing us to account for all of the variance in a typical helplessness experiment. Extrinsic variables are environmental conditions imposed at the time of pretreatment that generate a psychological context which modulates the effects of shock. Intrinsic variables are subject characteristics that account for differences among individuals treated alike.

The discussion of extrinsic modulation primarily addressed the effects of adding an escape contingency to the baseline schedule of shock delivery. This apparently simple manipulation alters the baseline operation in a number of conceptually distinct ways. Three such effects were identified. First, stimuli generated by the act of escaping may become signals for shock termination and a shock-free period. Because cessation and backward conditioning yield effective conditioned inhibitors, these predictive properties of escape-generated stimuli should work to reduce fear during the pretreatment session. Second, the attentional demands of escape responding may reduce the capacity to process affective and nociceptive stimuli, allowing subjects to blunt the emotional impact of shock exposure. Finally, an escape contingency selectively reinforces an active response pattern, which may contribute to immunization and mastery phenomena.

Intrinsic modulators were discussed in the context of individual differences in resistance to helplessness. The work of Brush and his colleagues suggests that emotionality has a genetic basis. Individual differences in avoidance behavior and social dominance are correlated with at least some measures of helplessness. The magnitude of the emotional reaction to inescapable shock may determine the extent to which submissive behavior is elicited and contributes to shuttle-escape deficits.

III. THE DISTRESS SYNDROME

The discussion thus far has centered mainly on the role of fear in the learned helplessness effect, the deficit in escape performance following inescapable shock. However, the effects of inescapable shock are not limited to this test task; debilitation also is implied by other behavioral measures, including choice learning (Jackson, Alexander, & Maier, 1980; Overmier & Wielkiewicz, 1983; Rosellini, DeCola, & Shapiro, 1982), acquisition of an appetitive operant (Rosellini, 1978), feeding (Dess, Minor, & Brewer, 1989), taste aversions (Dess, Minor, & Brewer, 1989; Dess, Raizer, Chapman, & Garcia, 1988) and social interactions (Williams, 1982). These disorders reflect a general stress-induced impairment, which we will term the *distress syndrome*. Understanding the nature of this syndrome has important implications not only for the ultimate causes of the learned helplessness effect, but also the validity of the paradigm as an animal model of depression, anxiety, or other forms of psychopathology. This section outlines a general strategy for characterizing the distress syndrome.

A. A System X Level Analysis

Although the helplessness paradigm has proved useful in identifying a number of outcomes that have important implications for psychopathology, the process of selecting dependent measures for study has been largely unsystematic. There undoubtedly are many potentially important outcomes which have yet to be studied. Furthermore, the relationship between many known outcomes is unclear. A strategy is required with enough breadth to allow identification of new outcomes but with enough structure to organize the relationships among outcomes.

   The dimension of psychobiological indexes shown in Overmier's (1988) modulator space (see Fig. 3.1) represents the breadth that is needed to analyze the distress syndrome. It does not, however, allow the categorization of disorders into meaningful clusters. Furthermore, the ordering of measures from biological to psychological confuses level of analysis with the process under study. It is unclear, for instance, how measures of noradrenergic activity differ from behavioral indexes of cognition, motivation, and so on. Collecting data on this molecular-to-molar continuum does not allow us to discern complementary descriptions of a phenomenon at different levels of analysis.

   As an alternative, a stressor could be assessed for its effects on functional systems. As will be discussed, the available data support a framework based on three such systems, termed cognitive, vegetative, and motor (see Lang, 1968, for a similar approach). Cognition consists of various aspects of information acquisition and processing; vegetative processes include arousal, motivation, and homeostasis; and motor processes control the production of behavioral output.

This distinction has implications for the selection of tasks and the interpretation of the performance of previously shocked animals in a task. If, for instance, the goal is to study the effects of shock on cognitive processes, then a task that involves cognition obviously should be used. However, the systems that have been identified interact extensively, which is fortunate for the animal but a problem for the scientist. Thus, debilitation in the task should not be attributed automatically to cognitive impairment. The contribution of each system to task performance must be addressed through the use of measures differentially sensitive to the systems. The problem is to analyze the percentage of variance in the task attributable to cognitive, vegetative, and motoric processes.

Any of the three systems can be studied at several levels of analysis. This organization suggests a matrix of distress indexes, with cognitive, vegetative, and motor categories crossed with observations ordered from molecular to molar. For example, the effects of shock on ingestion (a vegetative process) can be described in terms of physiological (hypothalamic neurochemistry, basal metabolic rate, etc.), behavioral (diet selection, meal patterning, etc.), or ethological correlates (foraging, comparative analyses, etc.).

B. Application of the Systems Strategy

What follows is not an exhaustive review of the effects of shock. Rather, a few cognitive, vegetative, and motor effects of shock, and their modulation by pretreatment variables are discussed to illustrate the utility of the strategy we have proposed.

1. Cognition

Choice tasks allow an independent assessment of the cognitive and performance effects of a manipulation (Logan, 1968; Spear, 1978; Spear & Spitzer, 1966). The rationale is that variables affecting performance (e.g., motivational or motoric effects) should be reflected in response speed, whereas effects on cognition should be reflected in choice accuracy. Jackson et al. (1980) used a choice task to test a prediction of the learned helplessness hypothesis concerning the effects of inescapable shock on cognition. If exposure to uncontrollable shock results in an inability to associate responses with outcomes, then subjects should have particular difficulty acquiring response-based choice performance (e.g., turning left to terminate shock). Alternatively, if inescapable shock simply impairs motor performance, then any deficit in the test task should be confined to response speed. The experiment provided clear evidence of a cognitive deficit. Inescapably shocked rats made more errors and required more trials to acquire correct choice responses than did restrained controls; control over pretreatment shock eliminated the choice deficit. Although inescapably shocked rats were slower to respond than either escapably shocked or restrained rats, response speed and choice accuracy on any given trial were not correlated.

The use of choice learning in this manner is an excellent example of the strategy that has been outlined. The paradigm allowed the authors to test an hypothesis about the specific nature of the cognitive deficit produced by inescapable shock. Multiple dependent measures were used to separate the cognitive component of the task from vegetative and motor dysfunction, both logically and empirically.

More recent evidence, however, questions their interpretation of the cognitive deficit (Minor, Jackson, & Maier, 1984; Minor et al., 1988). A detailed analysis of choice performance in this task indicated that the results of the seminal study was strongly influenced by two inadvertent test variables; specifically, choice accuracy deficits occurred in inescapably shocked rats only when shock termination was delayed following correct responses and salient task-irrelevant cues were presented on choice trials. Thus, while learned helplessness theory predicts that exposure to inescapable shock should interfere with the formation of response–outcome associations, the actual difficulty appeared to arise at an earlier stage of information processing, perhaps at an attentional level.

A deficit in stimulus selection or filtering is readily accommodated by the anxiety hypothesis. Selective attention is particularly vulnerable to anxiety; overanxious subjects perform poorly in cognitive tasks requiring them to ignore irrelevant information (Easterbrook, 1959; Hamilton, Hockey, & Rejman, 1977; Walley & Weiden, 1973, 1974). According to the anxiety hypothesis, inescapably shocked rats begin the choice task more anxious than do escapably shocked rats or restrained controls, and thus, would be expected to perform poorly in tasks requiring selective attention. Behavioral measures of anxiety and attention appear to be strongly related to forebrain noradrenergic activity (Aston–Jones, 1985; Gray, 1982; Mason & Fibiger, 1979; Redmond, 1979), which is substantially altered by inescapable shock pretreatment (Minor et al., 1988; Weiss et al., 1981).

Although these studies demonstrate cognitive impairment at multiple levels of analysis as predicted by the anxiety hypothesis, considerably more work is needed on the potential cognitive effects of inescapable shock.

However, it is unlikely that the cognitive impairment is limited to an attentional disorder. A broad view of the distress syndrome suggests that studies of perception, memory, and other cognitive processes also may be worthwhile (Eysenck, 1979).

2. Vegetative Regulation

a. Ingestion.   We have argued that when a test task is chosen to reveal the effects of a stressor on a particular system, then the potential influence of other systems also should be determined. Tasks yielding a single dependent measure do not allow the separate influence of each system to be assessed. Before reaching strong conclusions under such circumstances, variables controlling the putatively extraneous systems should be manipulated to assess their contribution to group differences.

For example, Rosellini and his colleagues (Rosellini, 1978; Rosellini & DeCola, 1982; Rosellini, DeCola, Plonsky, Warren, & Stilman, 1984; Rosellini et al., 1982) have used a variety of appetitive tasks to analyze the cognitive effects of inescapable shock. Presumably, changing the nature of the reinforcer from pretreatment to testing reduces the motivational effects of prior shock (e.g., analgesia) and provides a purer index of the cognitive consequences of inescapable shock. If these assumptions are taken at face value, the combined outcome of these studies suggests that helpless rats have difficulty associating responses with positive outcomes, and are more sensitive to instances of response-reinforcer independence. When appetitive test tasks are used, however, it is important to determine whether vegetative processes, specifically ingestion, contribute to the deficits observed. A recent series of studies suggests cautions in attributing impaired appetitive performance solely to cognitive processes.

Dess, Minor, and Brewer (1989) examined food consumption in home cages and body weight in rats pre-exposed to inescapable shock or restraint. Inescapably shocked rats ate less and lost more weight than did restrained controls. This pattern was augmented by quinine adulteration and exposure to brief reinstating shocks on the days following the pretreatment session.

This enhanced finickiness also suppresses drinking of quinine-adulterated water (Dess, Chapman, & Minor, 1988). Inescapably shocked rats drank significantly less bitter water than did controls 1 hr and 24 hr after the stress session. This effect was not attributable to general fluid suppression or an inability of the restrained controls to detect the quinine. However, it is as yet unclear whether the effect was the result of a change in primary sensation or the affective response to the bitter taste. Interestingly, preliminary work in a clinical population indicated that depressed patients uniquely show enhanced sensitivity to bitter tastes (Kappeler, personal communication), suggesting an additional parallel between the distress syndrome and clinical depression.

Finally, shock can support a conditioned taste aversion to a normally preferred substance (Dess et al., 1988). Thirsty rats drank saccharin solution in their home cages and were exposed 15 min later to inescapable shock, escapable shock, or restraint in a novel apparatus. Both shocked groups showed a conditioned aversion to saccharin relative to restrained controls when tested 2 days later in their home cages. Although the precise mechanism of this effect is unknown, the data suggest that shock produces visceral upset (also see Garrick, Minor, Bauck, Weiner, & Guth, 1989).

These studies clearly indicate that ingestion is altered following inescapable shock. Because many of these studies used quinine-adulteration or reinstatement procedures to examine ingestion following shock, it could be argued that the data bear only tangentially on performance in instrumental appetitive tasks. On the other hand, such procedures provided very sensitive measures of ingestive function. Having determined that ingestive function is altered, the question is whether the change contributes to group differences in appetitive instrumental behavior. Of particular concern is whether some aspect of the task results in the type of amplification of ingestive dysfunction that was produced by quinine adulteration or reinstatement. For instance, the degree of effort required in an instrumental task does influence the expression of hunger and the perceived palatability of food (Ettinger & Staddon, 1983) and could contribute to appetitive deficits in inescapably shocked rats (e.g., Rosellini, 1978; Rosellini et al., 1984). The extent of that contribution is indicated by the resistance of differences among groups to a manipulation of effort or similar variables.

b. Hypothalamic, Pituitary–Adrenal Axis. Distinguishing among major systems is especially meaningful if they are differentially sensitive to modulator variables. The well-established ability of control and feedback to modulate cognitive and motor impairment are not consistently observed with vegetative measures. For instance, ingestive (Dess, Chapman, & Minor, 1988; Dess et al., 1989; Dess, Raizer et al., 1988) and hypothalamic, pituitary-adrenal (HPA) activity (Maier, Ryan, Barksdale, & Kalin, 1986; Tsuda & Tanaka, 1985; Weiss, 1971), a classic vegetative index of distress (Selye, 1956), are often affected weakly by these operations. Unfortunately, determining whether vegetative processes are relatively immune to extrinsic modulation is complicated by measurement issues. The data to be presented suggest that the observation of extrinsic modulation of HPA activity depends in part on when and how the functioning of the system is assessed.

Dess et al. (1983) examined the ability of prediction and control to modulate HPA activity. Dogs were exposed to escapable or inescapable shocks that were either signaled or unsignaled by a warning stimulus in a factorial design. Plasma cortisol was measured after pretreatment and after exposure to reinstating shocks in a novel environment 24 hr later. During pretreatment, the ability to escape shock reduced cortisol responses; signaling shock onset had no immediate effect. The opposite pattern was obtained upon reinstatement: Signaling pretreatment shocks reduced HPA reactivity to these milder shocks, whereas prior escape had little effect. If only immediate distress had been assessed, no effect of predictability would have been observed; if only proactive effects had been assessed, no effect of control would have been observed. Because both types of assessments were made, however, it was clear that HPA activity was influenced by prediction as well as control, but at different times and under different conditions.

More recent data suggest that an immediate effect of prediction or a proactive effect of control in the Dess et al. (1983) study may have been masked by ceiling levels of HPA activity (Haracz et al., 1988; Minor, Insel, Wilkins, & Haracz, 1987). Dexamethasone (DEX) is a synthetic glucocorticoid that normally suppresses plasma levels of corticosteroids by mimicking their action in the negative feedback loop of the HPA axis. Rats were injected with either DEX or saline prior to exposure to escapable, yoked inescapable, or no shock in an attempt to reduce the endocrine response to shock and assess HPA dysregulation. Although plasma corticosterone levels immediately after the stress session were similar in saline-treated escapably and inescapably shocked rats, differences were evident among the DEX-treated groups. Corticosterone was significantly less suppressed following inescapable shock than after escapable shock or restraint. A similar pattern among groups was obtained when DEX was administered prior to brief, reinstating shocks 24 hr later. Thus, the administration of DEX provided a more sensitive test of HPA regulation than did simply measuring plasma corticosteroid levels.

Even if sampled in a timely and sensitive fashion, measures of HPA activity often vary so much among subjects treated alike that it is virtually impossible to observe an effect of an extrinsic operation. For example, Weiss (1971) manipulated the predictability and controllability of shock and Natelson et al. (1988) manipulated the severity of restraint stress; both studies yielded dramatic individual differences in corticosterone responses that obscured any potential differences among groups. However, Weiss (1971) did find a significant positive correlation between corticosterone responses and gastric ulceration which differed among groups. And when Natelson et al. (1988) split experimental groups based on the subjects' initial response to the stressor, "high-responders" and low-responders" showed significantly different patterns of habituation to the stressor. Thus, in each study the effects of a putative extrinsic modulator were overwhelmed by within-group variability.

The modulation of ingestion and HPA regulation by extrinsic variables, then, may be more apparent when statistical techniques are used to control for individual differences. However, the very usefulness of these techniques is informative: It seems to reflect the substantial role of intrinsic modulation of many aspects of vegetative distress, perhaps a greater role than for cognitive or motor systems. Analyzing the nature of individual differences in vegetative function after stress may ultimately be more important than the question of extrinsic modulation.

3. Motor Function

Anisman and his colleagues have distinguished general locomotion, motor response initiation, and motor response maintenance processes. Based on observations of the initial burst and persistence of shock-elicited activity (Anisman, deCantanzaro, & Remington, 1978) and escape performance as a function of minimum shock duration (e.g., Anisman, Remington, & Sklar, 1979), they concluded that inescapable shock impairs both the initiation and maintenance of motor activity in mice. Of the two types of deficits, impaired response maintenance accounted better for poor escape performance (e.g., Anisman, Grimmer, Irwin, Remington, & Sklar, 1979). This analysis of a test task in terms of its constituent motor processes is a good example of how characterizing the motor aspect of the distress syndrome could proceed.

Conclusions regarding the motor component of the distress syndrome, however, depend on the context in which behavior is observed. Anisman and Zacharko (1986) recently offered a more elaborate proposal based on their work on stress-induced changes in choice performance. The panic or anxiety engendered by inescapable shock may cause the organism to perseverate on well-learned or highly prepared (e.g., SSDRs) motor programs, thus restricting their defensive repertoire. Furthermore, whether the animal is debilitated in a test task may depend on the compatibility of available motor strategies and the demands of a test task. When the task requires fairly simple or rudimentary response tendencies, the distressed animal may actually benefit from a restricted behavioral repertoire. Conversely, the subject may be ill prepared to deal with novel insults, particularly when the task demands are complex.

A somewhat different conclusion is suggested when inescapably shocked rats are observed in more natural settings (Minor & Williams, 1988; Williams 1982; Williams & Lierle, 1987). Here inescapably shocked rats are more prone to engage in defensive behavior, suggesting that the hierarchy of species-typical agonistic behaviors is shifted toward submissiveness. For instance, rats show less aggression toward intruders and are more rapidly defeated by dominant males following exposure to inescapable shock.

These conclusions are by no means mutually exclusive. Unfortunately, there is no integrative framework that subsumes all the possibilities. Future work may benefit from adopting the recent elaborations of behavioral systems analyses (e.g., Fanselow & Lester, 1988; Timberlake & Lucas, 1988), which provide a detailed view of functional motor modules.

IV. OVERVIEW

Learned helplessness theory provided an important impetus to the study of environmental determinants of stress effects. By emphasizing the causal role of the uncontrollability of shock in helplessness, however, the theory generated an unnecessarily narrow view of the variables that influence the impact of shock and of the types of outcomes to be examined in the paradigm.

Overmier's (1988) modulator perspective provides an alternative analysis that inverts the traditional view of the helplessness paradigm. According to this view, the stressfulness of an event is best measured when the event is presented alone, unencumbered by additional experimental contingencies. More complex procedures are treated as potential modulators of the reaction to the baseline procedure.

The modulator analysis was used as a general framework to organize an alternative interpretation, the anxiety hypothesis, for the nature and determinants of helplessness. Exposure to inescapable shock was assumed to engender intense, chronic fear to cause later performance deficits. Rather than treating controllability as a unitary, global construct, the effects of adding an escape contingency to the baseline shock schedule were analyzed in terms of emergent processes that reduce fear or otherwise account for helplessness effects. Three such processes were identified: (1) Stimuli generated by the act of escaping become signals for shock termination (cessation conditioning) and a shock-free period (backward conditioning) to reduce the intensity and the amount of time spent in fear during the pretreatment session; (2) The attentional demands of the escape task may allow the subject to blunt the affective impact of shock; and (3) An active response topography is strengthened, which contributes to immunization and mastery effects.

Overmier's (1988) concept of a modulator was expanded to include two categories: (1) extrinsic modulators or experimental operations; and (2) intrinsic modulators or subject variables. Intrinsic modulators are "traits" (e.g., emotionality, dominance, attributional style) that either augment or attenuate the typical response to the baseline procedure. Together, the concepts of extrinsic and intrinsic modulation should allow us to account for all the variance in the helplessness experiment.

Finally, the concept of the distress syndrome was introduced to accommodate the broad consequences of a stressor. A system-by-level strategy was outlined to aid the analysis of the nature of the syndrome. Three major systems were distinguished (cognitive, vegetative, and motor), based on the known consequences of inescapable shock. The sensitivity of these systems to stressors and their susceptibility to extrinsic and intrinsic modulation are central issues. The effects of stress on individual systems can be examined by selecting tasks that are more sensitive to the action of one system over another. Nonetheless, because these systems work in an integrated fashion, the contribution of each system to any behavioral outcome must be assessed.

REFERENCES

Anderson, D. C., Hantual, D., Crowell, C. R., & Tohman, K. (1987). *Feedback interpolated shock, and bivalent alteration of inescapable shock treatment effects.* Psychonomic Society meeting, Seattle.

Anisman, H., deCatanzaro, D., & Remington, G. (1978). Escape performance deficits following exposure to inescapable shock: Deficits in motor response maintenance. *Journal of Experimental Psychology: Animal Behavior Processes, 4,* 197–218.

Anisman, H., Grimmer, L., Irwin, J., Remington, G., & Sklar, L. S. (1979). Escape performance following inescapable shock in selectively bred lines of mice. *Journal of Comparative and Physiological Psychology, 93,* 229–241.

Anisman, H., Irwin, J., Beauchamp, C., & Zacharko, R. (1983). Cross-stressor immunization against the behavioral deficit introduced by uncontrollable shock. *Behavioral Neuroscience, 97,* 452–461.

Anisman, H., Remington, G., & Sklar, L. S. (1979). Effects of inescapable shock on subsequent escape performance: Catecholaminergic and cholinergic mediation of response initiation and maintenance. *Psychopharmacology, 61,* 107–124.

Anisman, H., & Zacharko, R. M. (1986). Behavioral and neurochemical consequences associated with stressors. In D. D. Kelly (Ed.), *Stress-induced analgesia* Annals of the New York Academy of Sciences, *467,* 205–225.

Aston-Jones, G. (1985). Behavioral function of the locus coeruleus derived from cellular attributes. *Physiological Psychology, 13,* 118–126.

Barbaree, H. E., & Weisman, R. G. (1975). On the failure of transfer of control from separately conducted Pavlovian conditioning to free-operant avoidance conditioning in rats. *Learning and Motivation, 6,* 498–511.

Barnett, S. A. (1963). *The rat: A study in behavior.* Chicago: Aldine.

Berger, S., & Kanfer, F. H. (1975). Self control: Effects of training and presentation delays on competing responses on tolerance of noxious stimulation. *Psychological Reports, 37,* 1312–1314.

Bersh, P. J., Whitehouse, W. G., Blustein, J. E., & Alloy, L. B. (1986). Interaction of Pavlovian conditioning with a zero operant contingency: Chronic exposure to signaled inescapable shock maintains the learned helplessness effect. *Journal of Experimental Psychology: Animal Behavior Processes, 12,* 277–290.

Blanchard, D. C., & Blanchard, R. J. (1988). Ethoexperimental approaches to the biology of emotion. *Annual Review of Psychology, 39,* 43–68.

Bolles, R. C. (1971). Species-specific defense reactions. In F. R. Brush (Ed.), *Aversive conditioning and learning.* New York: Academic Press.

Bowers, K. S. (1968). Pain, anxiety, and perceived control. *Journal of Consulting and Clinical Psychology, 32,* 596–602.

Braud, W., Wepmann, B., & Russo, D. (1969). Task and species generality of the learned helplessness phenomenon. *Psychonomic Science, 16,* 154–155.

Breland, K., & Breland, M. (1961). The misbehavior of organisms. *American Psychologist, 16,* 661–664.

Britton, D. R., Ksir, C., Thatcher–Britton, K., Young, D., & Koob, G. F. (1984). Brain norepinephrine depleting lesions selectively enhance behavioral responsiveness to novelty. *Physiology and Behavior, 33,* 473–478.

Brown, J. S. (1969). Factors affecting self-punitive locomotor behavior. In B. A. Campbell & R. M. Church (Eds.), *Punishment and aversive behavior* (pp. 467–516). New York: Appleton–Century–Crofts.

Brush, F. R. (1985). Genetic determinants of avoidance learning: Mediation by emotionality? In F. R. Brush & J. B. Overmier (Eds.), *Affect, conditioning, and cognition: Essays on the determinants of behavior.* (pp. 27–42). Hillsdale, NJ: Lawrence Erlbaum Associates.

Brush, F. R., Blanchard, R. J., & Blanchard, D. C. (1989). Social dominance and response to a natural predator by rats selectively bred for differences in shuttle-box avoidance behavior. In R. J. Blanchard, P. F. Brain, D. C. Blanchard, C. S. Parmigiani (Ed.), *Ethoexperimental approaches to the study of behavior.* Dordrecht: Kluwer Academic.

Brush, F. R., Del Paine, S. N., Pelligrino, L. J., Rykaszewski, I. M., Dess, N. K., & Collins, P. Y. (1988). CER suppression, passive avoidance learning, and stress-induced suppression of drinking in the Syracuse high (SHA) and low (SLA) strains of rats (Rattus norvegicus). *Journal of Comparative Psychology, 102,* 337–349.

Calhoun, J. B. (1962). *The ecology and sociology of the Norway rat.* Bethesda, MD: Public Health Services.

Coen, D. J. (1985). *Context and pain perception: Stress-induced analgesia as a function of similarity of odor and apparatus cues between stress analgesia assessment environments.* Unpublished master's thesis, University of Alberta, Canada.

Craig, K. D., & Weiss, S. M. (1971). Vicarious influences on pain-threshold determinations. *Journal of Personality and Social Psychology, 19,* 53–59.

Denny, M. R. (1971). Relaxation theory and experiments. In F. R. Brush (Ed.), *Aversive conditioning and learning.* New York: Academic Press.

Denny, M. R. (1976). Post-aversive relief and relaxation and their implications for behavior therapy. *Journal of Behavior Therapy and Experimental Psychiatry, 7,* 315–321.

Denny, M. R., & Dmitruk, V. M. (1967). Effects of punishing a single failure to avoid. *Journal of Comparative and Physiological Psychology, 63,* 277–281.

Dess, N. K., Chapman, C. D., & Minor, T. R. (1988). Inescapable shock increases finickiness about drinking quinine-adulterated water in rats. *Learning and Motivation, 19,* 408–424.

Dess, N. K., Linwick, D., Patterson, J., Overmier, J. B., & Levine, S. (1983). Immediate and proactive effects of controllability and predictability on plasma cortisol responses to shocks in dogs. *Behavioral Neuroscience, 97,* 1005–1016.

Dess, N. K., Minor, T. R., & Brewer, J. C. (1989). Suppression of feeding and body weight by inescapable shock is modulated by quinine adulteration, stress reinstatement, and controllability. *Physiology and Behavior, 45,* 975–983.

Dess, N. K., Raizer, J., Chapman, C. D., & Garcia, J. (1988). Stressors in the learned helplessness paradigm: Effects on body weight and conditioned taste aversions in rats. *Physiology and Behavior, 44,* 483–490.

Easterbrook, J. A. (1959). The effects of emotion on cue utilization and the organization of behavior. *Psychological Review, 66,* 183–201.

Ettinger, R. H., & Staddon, J. E. R. (1983). Operant regulation of feeding: A static analysis. *Behavioral Neuroscience, 97,* 639–653.

Eysenck, M. W. (1979). Anxiety, learning and memory: A reconceptualization. *Journal of Research in Personality, 13,* 363–385.

Fanselow, M. S., & Lester, L. S. (1988). A functional behavioristic approach to aversively motivated behavior: Predatory imminence as a determinant of the topography of defensive behavior. In R. C. Bolles & M. D. Beecher (Eds.), *Evolution and learning.* (pp. 185–212). Hillsdale, NJ: Lawrence Erlbaum Associates.

Garrick, T., Minor, T. R., Bauck, S., Weiner, H., & Guth, P. (1989). Predictable and unpredictable shock stimulates gastric contractility and causes mucosal injury in rats. *Behavioral Neuroscience, 103,* 124–130.

Goodson, F. E., & Marx, M. H. (1953). Increased resistance to autogenic seizures in rats trained on an instrumental wheel-turning response. *Journal of Comparative and Physiological Psychology, 46,* 255–260.

Gray, J. A. (1982), *The neuropsychology of anxiety.* Oxford, England: Oxford University Press.

Greenstein, S. M. (1984). Pleasant and unpleasant slides: Their effects on pain tolerance. *Cognitive Therapy and Research, 8,* 201–210.

Grim, L., & Kanfer, F. H. (1976). Tolerance of aversive stimulation. *Behavior Therapy, 7,* 593–601.

Hamilton, P., Hockey, G. R., & Rejman, M. (1977). The place of the concept of activation in human information processing: An integrative approach. In S. Dornic (Ed.), *Attention and performance* (Vol. 6, pp. 121–145). Hillsdale, NJ: Lawrence Erlbaum Associates.

Hanson, J. P., Larson, M. E., & Snowdon, C. T. (1976). The effects of control over high intensity noise on plasma cortisol levels in rhesus monkeys. *Behavioral Biology, 16,* 333–340.

Haracz, J. L., Minor, T. R., Wilkins, J. N., & Zimmermann, E. G. (1988). Learned helplessness: An experimental model of the DST in rats. *Biological Psychiatry, 23,* 388–396.

Hellhammer, D. H., Bell, M., Ludwig, M., & Rea, M. A. (1983). Learned helplessness: Effects on brain monoamines. *Society for Neuroscience Abstracts, 9,* 555.

Hoffman, H. S., Fleshler, M., & Jensen, P. (1963). Stimulus aspects of aversive controls: The retention of conditioned suppression. *Journal of the Experimental Analysis of Behavior, 6,* 575–583.

Jackson, R. L., Alexander, J. H., & Maier, S. F. (1980). Learned helplessness, inactivity, and associative deficits: Effects of inescapable shock on response choice escape learning. *Journal of Experimental Psychology: Animal Behavior Processes, 6,* 1–20.

Jackson, R. L., & Minor, T. R. (1988). Effects of signaling inescapable shock on subsequent escape learning: Implications for theories of coping and "learned helplessness." *Journal of Experimental Psychology: Animal Behavior Processes, 14,* 390–400.

King, M. G. (1969). Stimulus generalization of conditioned fear in rats over time. *Journal of Comparative and Physiological Psychology, 69,* 590–600.

King, M. G., Pfister, H. P., & DiGiusto, E. L. (1975). Differential preference for and activation by the odoriferous compartment of a shuttlebox in fear-conditioned and naive rats. *Behavioral Biology, 13,* 175–181.

Kuhn, T. S. (1962). *The structure of scientific revolutions.* Chicago: University of Chicago Press.

Lang, P. J. (1968). Fear reduction and fear behavior: Problems in treating a construct. In J. M. Shlien (Ed.), *Research in psychotherapy* (pp. 115–191). New York: Springer–Verlag.

Lawry, J. A., Lupo, V., Overmier, J. B., Kochevar, J., Hollis, K. L., & Anderson, D. C. (1978). Interference with avoidance behavior as a function of the qualitative properties of inescapable shock. *Animal Learning and Behavior, 6,* 147–154.

Logan, F. A. (1968). Incentive theory in changes in reward. In K. W. Spence & J. T. Spence (Eds.), *The psychology of learning and motivation* (Vol. 2, pp. 1–28). New York: Academic Press.

LoLordo, V. M., & Fairless, J. L. (1985). Pavlovian conditioned inhibition: The literature since 1969. In R. R. Miller & N. Spear (Eds.), *Information processing in animals: Conditioned inhibition* (pp. 1–49) Hillsdale, NJ: Lawrence Erlbaum Associates.

Looney, T. A., & Cohen, P. S. (1972). Retardation of a jump-up escape response in rats pretreated with different frequencies of shock. *Journal of Comparative and Physiological Psychology, 78,* 317–322.

Mackintosh, N. J. (1973). Stimulus selection: Learning to ignore stimuli that predict no change in reinforcement. In R. A. Hinde & J. S. Hinde (Eds.), *Constraints on learning: Limitations and predispositions* (pp. 121–146). Cambridge, England: Academic Press.

Mackintosh. N. J. (1975). *The psychology of animal learning.* New York: Academic Press.

MacKay–Sim, A., & Laing, D. L. (1980). Discrimination of odors of stressed rats by non-stressed rats. *Physiology and Behavior, 13,* 699–704.

Maier, S. F. (1986). Stressor controllability and stress-induced analgesia. In D. D. Kelley (Ed.), *Stress-induced analgesia.* Annals of the New York Academy of Sciences, *467,* 55–72.

Maier, S. F., Albin, R. W., & Testa, T. J. (1973). Failure to learn to escape in rats previously expose to inescapable shock depends on the nature of the escape response. *Journal of Comparative and Physiological Psychology, 85,* 581–592.

Maier, S. F., & Keith, J. (1987). Shock signals and the development of stress-induced analgesia. *Journal of Experimental Psychology: Animal Behavior Processes, 13,* 226–238.

Maier, S. F., Rapaport, P., & Wheatley, K. L. (1976). Conditioned inhibition and the UCS-CS interval. *Animal Learning & Behavior, 4,* 217–220.

Maier, S. F., Ryan, S. M., Barksdale, C. M., & Kalin, N. H. (1986). Stressor controllability and the pituitary-adrenal system. *Behavioral Neuroscience, 100,* 669–674.

Maier, S. F., & Seligman, M. E. P. (1976). Learned helplessness: Theory and evidence. *Journal of Experimental Psychology: General, 105,* 3–46.

Maier, S. F., Seligman, M. E. P., & Solomon, R. L. (1969). Pavlovian fear conditioning and learned helplessness. In B. A. Campbell & R. M. Church (Eds.), *Punishment and aversive behavior.* New York: Appleton–Century–Crofts.

Maier, S. F., & Warren, D. A. (1988). Controllability and safety signals exert dissimilar proactive effects on nociception and escape performance. *Journal of Experimental Psychology: Animal Behavior Processes, 14,* 18–25.

Maltzman, S. (1988). Visual stimuli in distraction strategies for increasing and pain tolerance: The confounding of affect with other stimulus characteristics. *Pavlovian Journal of Biological Science, 23,* 67–74.

Mason, S. T., & Fibiger, H. C. (1979). Noradrenaline and selective attention. *Life Sciences, 25,* 1949–1956.

Mehrabian, A. (1980). *Basic dimensions of general psychological theory; Implications for personality, social, environmental, and developmental studies.* Cambridge, England: Oelgeshlager, Gunn, & Hain.

Miczek, K. A., Thompson, M. L., Shuster, L. (1986). Analgesia following defeat in an aggressive encounter: Development of tolerance and changes in opioid receptors. In D. D. Kelley (Ed.), *Stress-induced analgesia.* Annals of the New York Academy of Sciences, *467,* 14–29.

Miller, S. M. (1979). Controllability and human stress: Method, evidence and theory. *Behaviour Research and Therapy, 17,* 287–364.

Mineka, S., Cook, M., & Miller, S. (1984). Fear conditioned with escapable and inescapable shock: Effects of a feedback stimulus. *Journal of Experimental Psychology: Animal Behavior Processes, 10,* 307–324.

Minor, T. R. (1983). *Submission and uncontrollable shock: Is learned helplessness a case of misbehavior?* Paper presented at the winter conference on Animal Learning. Winter Park, CO.

Minor, T. R. (1990a). Conditioned fear and neophobia following inescapable shock. *Animal Learning and Behavior, 18,* 212–226.

Minor, T. R. (1990b). *Response persistence following escapable shock and inescapable shock followed by stimulus feedback: Some constraint on and an alternative to "learned mastery."* Manuscript in preparation.

Minor, T. R., Insel, T., Wilkins, J. N., & Haracz, J. L. (1987). *Pituitary-adrenal activity following inescapable shock: Effects of dexamethasone.* Psychonomic Society, Seattle.

Minor, T. R., Jackson, R. L., & Maier, S. F. (1984). Effects of task-irrelevant cues and reinforcement delay on choice escape learning following inescapable shock: Evidence for a deficit in selective attention. *Journal of Experimental Psychology: Animal Behavior Processes, 10,* 543–556.

Minor, T. R., Trauner, M. A., Lee, C. Y., & Dess, N. K. (1990). *Modeling the signal features of an escape response: Effects of cessation conditioning in the "learned helplessness" paradigm. Journal of Experimental Psychology: Animal Behavior Processes, 16,* 123–136.

Minor, T. R., & LoLordo, V. M. (1984). Escape deficits following inescapable shock: The role of contextual odor. *Journal of Experimental Psychology: Animal Behavior Processes, 10,* 168–181.

Minor, T. R., Pelleymounter, M. A., & Maier, S. F. (1988). Uncontrollable shock, forebrain norepinephrine, and stimulus selection during choice escape learning. *Psychobiology, 16,* 135–145.

Minor, T. R., & Williams, J. L. (1990). *Social stress, social dominance, and learned helplessness: A SAP hypothesis.* Manuscript in preparation.

Moscovitch, A. (1972). *Pavlovian cessation conditioning.* Unpublished doctoral dissertation, University of Pennsylvania.

Moscovitch, A., & LoLordo, V. M. (1968). Role of safety in the pavlovian backward conditioning procedure. *Journal of Comparative and Physiological Psychology, 66,* 673–678.

Mowrer, O. H. (1960). *Learning theory and behavior,* New York: Wiley.

Mowrer, O. H., & Viek, P. (1948). An experimental analogue of fear from a sense of helplessness. *Journal of Abnormal and Social Psychology, 43,* 193–200.

Natelson, B. H., Ottenweller, J. E., Cook, J. A., Pitman, D., McCarthy, R., & Tapp, W. N. (1988). Effects of stressor intensity on habituation of the adrenocortical stress response. *Physiology and Behavior, 43,* 41–46.

Overmier, J. B. (1988). Psychological determinants of when stressors stress. In D. Hellhammer, I. Florin, & H. Weiner (Eds.), *Neurobiological approaches to human disease* (pp. 236–259). Toronto: Hans Huber.

Overmier, J. B., & Hellhammer, D. H. (1988). The learned helplessness model of human depression. *Animal Models of Psychiatric Disorder, 2,* 177–202.

Overmier, J. B., & Leaf, R. C. (1965). Effects of discriminative Pavlovian fear conditioning upon previously or subsequently acquired avoidance responding. *Journal of Comparative and Physiological Psychology, 60,* 213–217.

Overmier, J. B., & Murison, R. (1989). Post-stress effects of danger and safety signals on gastric ulcerations. *Behavioral Neuroscience, 103,* 1296–1301.

Overmier, J. B., Murison, R., Skoglund, E., & Ursin, H. (1985). Safety signals can mimic responses in reducing the ulcerogenic effects of prior shock. *Physiological Psychology, 13,* 243–247.

Overmier, J. B., & Seligman, M. E. P. (1967). Effects of inescapable shock upon subsequent escape and avoidance responding. *Journal of Comparative and Physiological Psychology, 63,* 28–33.

Overmier, J. B., & Wielkiewicz, R. M. (1983). On predictability as a causal factor in "learned helplessness." *Learning and Motivation, 14,* 324–337.

Petty, F., & Sherman, A. D. (1981). GABAergic modulation of learned helplessness. *Pharmacology, Biochemistry and Behavior, 15,* 576–570.

Redmond, D. E. (1979). New and old evidence for the involvement of a brain norepinephrine in anxiety. In W. G. Fann, I. Karacan, A. D. Pokorny, & R. L. Williams (Eds.), *Phenomenology and treatment of anxiety* (pp. 153–203). New York: Spectrum.

Rosellini, R. A. (1978). Inescapable shock interferes with the acquisition of an appetitive operant. *Animal Learning and Behavior, 6,* 155–159.

Rosellini, R. A., & DeCola, J. P. (1982). Inescapable shock interferes with the acquisition of a low-activity response in an appetitive context. *Animal Learning and Behavior, 9,* 487–490.

Rosellini, R. A., DeCola, J. P., Plonsky, M., Warren, D. A., & Stilman, A. J. (1984). Uncontrollable shock proactively increases sensitivity to response-reinforcer independence in rats. *Journal of Experimental Psychology: Animal; Behavior Processes, 10,* 346–359.

Rosellini, R. A., DeCola, J. P., & Shapiro, N. R. (1982). Cross motivational effects of inescapable shock are associative in nature. *Journal of Experimental Psychology: Animal Behavior Processes, 8,* 376–388.

Rosellini, R. A., DeCola, J. P., & Warren, D. A. (1986). The effects of feedback on contextual fear depends upon the minimum intertrial interval. *Learning and Motivation, 17,* 229–242.

Rosellini, R. A., DeCola, J. P., & Warren, D. A. (1987). Predictability and controllability: Differential effects upon contextual fear. *Learning and Motivation, 18,* 392–420.

Scott, J. P., & Fuller, J. (1965). *Genetics and social behavior in the dog.* Chicago: University of Chicago Press.

Seligman, M. E. P. (1968). Chronic fear produced by unpredictable electric shock. *Journal of Experimental Psychology, 72,* 546–550.

Seligman, M. E. P. (1975). *Helplessness: On depression development and death.* New York: W. H. Freeman.

Seligman, M. E. P., & Beagley, G. (1975). Learned helplessness in the rat. *Journal of Comparative and Physiological Psychology, 88,* 534–541.

Seligman, M. E. P., & Binik, Y. (1977). The safety signal hypothesis. In H. Davis & H. M. B. Hurwitz (Eds), *Operant-Pavlovian interactions* (pp. 165–188). Hillsdale, NJ: Lawrence Erlbaum Associates.

Seligman, M. E. P., & Maier, S. F. (1967). Failure to escape traumatic shock. *Journal of Experimental Psychology, 74,* 1–9.

Seligman, M. E. P., Maier, S. F., & Geer, J. (1968). The alleviation of learned helplessness in the dog. *Journal of Abnormal Psychology, 73,* 256–262.

Seligman, M. E. P., Maier, S. F., & Solomon, R. L. (1971). Unpredictable and uncontrollable aversive events. In F. R. Brush (Ed.), *Aversive conditioning and learning* (pp. 347–400). New York: Academic Press.

Seligman, M. E. P., Rosellini, R. A., & Kozak, M. J. (1975). Learned helplessness in the rat: Time course, immunization and reversibility. *Journal of Comparative and Physiological Psychology, 88,* 542–547.

Selye, H. (1956). *The stress of life.* New York: McGraw–Hill.

Seward, J. P. (1945). Aggressive behavior in the rat: An attempt to establish a dominance hierarchy. *Journal of Comparative Psychology, 38,* 175–197.

Solomon, R. L., & Corbit, J. D. (1974). An opponent-process theory of motivation: I. temporal dynamics of affect. *Psychological Review, 81,* 119–145.

Spear, N. E. (1978). *The processing of memories: Forgetting and retention.* Hillsdale, NJ: Lawrence Erlbaum Associates.

Spear, N. E., & Spitzer, J. H. (1966). Simultaneous and successive contrast effects of reward magnitude and selective learning. *Psychological Monographs, 80*(10, Whole No. 618).

Starr, M. D., & Mineka, S. (1977). Determinants of fear over the course of avoidance learning. *Learning and Motivation, 8,* 332–350.

Staub, E., Tursky, B., & Schwartz, G. E. (1971). Self control and predictability: Their effects on reactions to aversive stimulation. *Journal of Personality and Social Psychology, 18,* 157–162.

Thomas, D. A., Riccio, D. C., & Myer, J. S. (1977). Age of stress-produced odorants and the Kamin effect. *Behavioral Biology, 20,* 433–440.

Timberlake, W., & Lucas, G. A. (1988). Behavioral systems and learning: From misbehavior to general principles. In S. B. Klein & R. R. Mowrer (Eds.), *Contemporary learning theories* (pp. 237–276). Hillsdale, NJ: Lawrence Erlbaum Associates.

Tsuda, A., & Tanaka, M. (1985). Differential changes in noradrenaline turnover in specific regions of rat brain produced by controllable and uncontrollable shocks. *Behavioral Neuroscience, 99,* 802–817.

Valenta, J. G., & Rigby, M. K. (1968). Discrimination of the odor of stressed rats. *Science, 161,* 599–601.

Volpicelli, J. R., Ulm, R. R., & Altenor, A. (1984). Feedback during exposure to inescapable shock and subsequent shock-escape performance. *Learning and Motivation, 15,* 279–286.

Volpicelli, J. R., Ulm, R. R., Altenor, A., & Seligman, M. E. P. (1983). Learned mastery in the rat. *Learning and Motivation, 14,* 204–222.

Walley, R. E., & Weiden, T. D. (1973). Latent inhibition and cognitive masking: A neuropsychological theory of attention. *Psychological Review, 80,* 540–542.

Walley, R. E., & Weiden, T. D. (1974). Giving flesh to a "straw man": A reply to Feeney, Pittman, and Wagner. *Psychological Review, 81,* 540–542.

Weiss, J. M. (1971). Effects of coping behavior with and without a feedback signal on stress pathology in the rat. *Journal of Comparative and Physiological Psychology, 77,* 22–30.

Weiss, J. M., Bailey, W. H., Goodman, P. A., Hoffman, L. J., Ambrose, M. J., Salman, S., & Charry, J. M. (1982). A model for the neurochemical study of depression. In M. Y. Spiegeistein & A. Levy (Eds.), *Behavioral models and the analysis of drug action.* (pp. 195–223). Amsterdam: Elsevier.

Weiss, J. M., Krieckhaus, E. E., & Conte, R. (1968). Effects of fear conditioning on subsequent avoidance behavior. *Journal of Comparative and Physiological Psychology, 65,* 413–421.

Weiss, J. A., Pohorecky, L. A., Salman, S., & Gruenthal, M. (1976). Attenuation of gastric lesions by psychological aspects of aggression in rats. *Journal of Comparative and Physiological Psychology, 90,* 252–259.

Weiss, J. M., & Simson, P. G. (1985). Neurochemical mechanisms underlying stress-induced depression. In T. Field, P. McCabe, & N. Schneiderman (Eds.), *Stress and Coping* (pp. 93–116). Hillsdale, NJ: Lawrence Erlbaum Associates.

Weiss, J. M., Goodman, P. A., Losito, B. G., Corrigan, S., Charry, J. M., & Bailey, W. H. (1981). Behavioral depression produced by an uncontrollable stressor: Relationship to norepinephrine, dopamine, and serotonin levels in various regions of rat brain. *Brain Research Reviews, 3,* 167–205.

Williams, J. L. (1982). Influence of shock controllability by dominant rats on subsequent attack and defensive behaviors toward colony intruders. *Animal Learning and Behavior, 10,* 305–313.

Williams, J. L. (1987). Influence of conspecific stress odors and shock controllability on conditioned defensive burying. *Animal Learning and Behavior, 15,* 333–341.

Williams, J. L., & Lierle, D. M. (1987). Effects of stress controllability, immunization and therapy on subsequent defeat of colony intruders. *Animal Learning and Behavior, 14,* 305–314.

Williams, J. L., & Maier, S. F. (1977). Transituational immunization and therapy of learned helplessness in the rat. *Journal of Experimental Psychology: Animal Behavior Processes, 3,* 240–253.

Willner, P. (1984). The validity of animal models of depression. *Psychopharmacology, 83,* 1–22.

4 Fear Theory and Aversively Motivated Behavior: Some Controversial Issues

Dorothy E. McAllister and Wallace R. McAllister
Northern Illinois University

Classically conditioned fear has played a pivotal role in explaining many diverse types of behavior. In their theoretical treatments, Mowrer (1939) and Miller (1948, 1951) made several assumptions about the properties of learned fear that permit these explanations. They assumed that conditioned fear has drive properties; thus, it can motivate behavior and its reduction can reinforce the learning of instrumental behavior. It was also assumed that fear functions as a response and, therefore, produces stimuli to which other responses may be learned or which may elicit innately associated responses (e.g., freezing or fleeing). See W. R. McAllister and McAllister (1971) for further discussion.

It is important to recognize that fear theory is embedded in general learning theory. Consequently, the laws of classical conditioning, such as those dealing with acquisition, extinction, spontaneous recovery, and so on, should apply to fear just as they do to any other classically conditioned response. Likewise, the laws of instrumental learning, such as those dealing with the number of reinforced trials, the magnitude of reward, the effects of shifts in reward, and so on, should apply to the learning of instrumental responses based on fear just as they do when other sources of motivation and reinforcement are involved.

In the literature, when reference is simply to the conjoint involvement of classical conditioning and instrumental learning, fear theory is frequently called two-process or two-factor theory. However, those terms, when introduced by Mowrer in 1947, had much wider connotations. Specifically, he held that classically conditioned responses, including fear, are learned on the basis of contiguity, whereas instrumentally learned responses are

135

learned on the basis of reinforcement (drive reduction). He further argued that only involuntary, emotional (visceral and vascular) responses, mediated by the autonomic nervous system, can be classically conditioned and that only voluntary, skeletal responses, mediated by the central nervous system, can be learned instrumentally. Because all of these added assumptions about classical and instrumental conditioning are an integral part of Mowrer's two-process theory, we will restrict our use of this term to those instances when the entire theory is under consideration or when others are being quoted. When the interest is only in evaluating the effect of classically conditioned fear on other behavior, the term fear theory will be used.

Although the Mowrer–Miller fear theory has been highly successful over the years in accounting for and in integrating a large amount of empirical data, it has not escaped criticism. Several of the negative critiques of the theory (e.g., Bolles, 1970; Herrnstein, 1969; Seligman & Johnston, 1973) have gained acceptance to such an extent that there is a danger that the criticisms they contain may come to represent the conventional wisdom. The reasons for this acceptance seem to be twofold. In the first place, there is a frequency factor. References to these critiques proliferate, especially among textbook writers, and as has recently been said, "Repetition is the mother of acceptance . . ." (Thomson, 1988). Or, as put by the Bellman in Lewis Carroll's *The Hunting of the Snark*, "What I tell you three times is true." In the second place, there have been only a few attempts to examine the cogency of the arguments that have been presented against fear theory (e.g., Levis, 1979, 1989; Mackintosh, 1974). The present commentary is an attempt to offset this imbalance. It will be restricted to the principal criticisms of the theory. These relate to the lack of parallelism between fear of the conditioned stimulus (CS) and avoidance performance, the purported absence of fear when avoidance responding is well learned, and the finding that the termination of the CS is not a necessary condition for the reinforcement of a signaled avoidance response. Although for convenience these issues will be discussed separately, it should be understood that they are interrelated.

LACK OF PARALLELISM BETWEEN FEAR AND AVOIDANCE PERFORMANCE

The observed lack of parallelism between levels of fear of the CS and of avoidance performance is probably the most frequently cited criticism of fear theory and is erroneously maintained by many writers to be a serious problem for the theory. For example, it has been contended that ". . . a lack of concordance between the momentary strength of the putative avoidance mediator [fear] and other measures of conditioned aversion . . . has rendered [two-process theory] suspect" (Mellitz, Hineline, Whitehouse, & Laurence, 1983, p. 58). In a recent textbook on learning, Domjan and Burkhard (1986, p. 222) claimed that "if two-process theory is correct . . . then the conditioning of fear and of instrumental avoidance responding should proceed together. Contrary to this prediction, conditioned fear and avoidance responding are not always highly correlated." In discussing the results of their research, Mineka and Gino (1980, p. 500) state that "clearly a two-process theorist should expect to see a much closer relationship than we have seen in our experiments between levels of classically conditioned fear of the CS and instrumental avoidance response strength."

Numerous other instances of this viewpoint could be cited. Presumably because of the frequent repetition of such comments, the conclusion that fear theory is embarrassed by this lack of parallelism seems to have been accepted uncritically. The findings are not in dispute, but the conclusion is questionable.

It should be noted that the lack of parallelism typically cited is that between fear of the discrete CS and the number of two-way avoidance responses. As an example, Kamin, Brimer, and Black (1963) found that after 27 consecutive two-way avoidance responses there was less fear of the CS, as measured by the suppression of an appetitively reinforced instrumental response, than there was after 9 consecutive avoidance responses.

Kamin et al. (1963, p. 501), noting this lack of parallelism between fear and avoidance performance, commented that these data "encourage speculation that variables other than fear of the CS are largely responsible for the maintenance of avoidance behavior." This statement is probably the origin of the notion that fear theory requires that there be a high correlation between the amount of fear of the CS and the level of avoidance performance. However, to the best of our knowledge, fear theory, whether expressed by Mowrer or Miller, would not expect such a parallelism in the Kamin et al. and other similar studies (e.g., Mineka & Gino, 1980; Starr & Mineka, 1977).

The acceptance of the parallelism argument probably stems in part from a failure to be sensitive to the distinction between learning and performance. Fear of the CS would be expected to extinguish gradually on avoidance (nonshock) trials[1] and, therefore, to provide diminishing amounts of

---

[1] That nonreinforcement of a learned response results in its extinction is a widely accepted principle. Nevertheless, it has been hypothesized by Starr and Mineka (1977) and Cook, Mineka, and Trumble (1987) that CS-only (nonshock) trials play no role in determining the attenuation of fear of the CS that occurs with extended two-way avoidance training. Rather, they argue that the weakening of fear requires the presence of a feedback stimulus that has its effect only on CS-shock trials. A discussion of the basis for this position and an evaluation of it will be included in the last section of this chapter and in Footnote 2.

motivation and of reinforcement from CS termination as the learning of the avoidance response progresses. At the same time, however, the associative strength of the instrumental avoidance response would be expected to increase with each trial even in the face of lesser, but still sufficient, amounts of reinforcement. The findings of Brush (1957) are consistent with the contention that an instrumental response can increase in strength when performed during an extended series of nonshock (extinction) trials. Such an increase in associative strength could offset the effect of a decrease in motivation and reinforcement and thereby maintain performance. Therefore, it does not follow that more fear of the CS is required to support a long sequence of avoidance responses (e.g., 27) than a short one (e.g., 9). This logic holds for an all-or-none response measure such as frequency, used by Kamin et al., and also for continuous response measures such as latency, used by Mineka and Gino (1980). It should be noted, however, that with an all-or-none (frequency) measure of performance, avoidance responding could continue undiminished even if both the associative strength of the instrumental response and fear decreased as long as minimal, above threshold, levels of each were maintained.

Stated in Hullian terms, performance is a multiplicative function of habit and drive. As applied to the Kamin et al. data, the difference in avoidance performance between the 27- and the 9-criterion groups can be attributed to a greater habit (associative) strength for making the instrumental response in the former group more than compensating for the greater decrease in drive resulting from the extinction of fear of the CS on nonshock trials. The stronger habit strength in the 27-criterion group may be attributed to differences occurring during training in the number and the pattern of reinforced trials from either shock termination or from fear reduction.

That an instrumental response can be acquired and can increase in associative strength while fear is presumably decreasing has been convincingly demonstrated in a large number of acquired-drive studies. A typical procedure used in these studies is first to condition fear classically (CS paired with shock) in one side of an apparatus consisting of two compartments separated by a guillotine door resting on a hurdle. Then, in the absence of shock, subjects are allowed to escape the fear-eliciting CS and situational cues in the shock compartment by jumping the hurdle to the adjacent safe compartment. The rate of learning the hurdle-jumping escape-from-fear (EFF) response and the level of performance reached serve as indexes of fear. A number of studies providing relevant data are cited in D. E. McAllister, McAllister, Hampton, and Scoles (1980); some other studies are those of Spear, Hamberg, and Bryan (1980), Grelle and James (1981), W. R. McAllister, McAllister, and Benton (1983), Quartermain and Judge (1983), and Callen, McAllister, and McAllister (1984).

Some illustrative data from a study by W. R. McAllister, McAllister, Scoles, and Hampton (1986) are shown in Fig. 4.1.

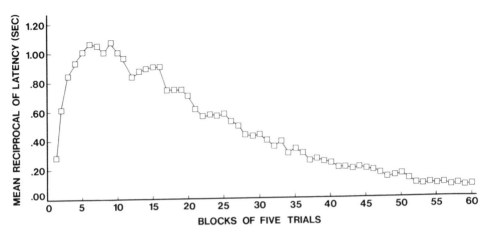

FIG. 4.1.   Mean speed of hurdle jumping over 60 blocks of five trials.
From McAllister, McAllister, Scoles, and Hampton (1986). Reprinted by
permission of the American Psychological Association.

Subjects in this study ($N = 18$) received 25 fear-conditioning trials (light
paired with shock) and subsequently were given hurdle-jumping trials until
responding failed to occur within 60 seconds on 10 consecutive trials. As
can be seen in the figure, speed of hurdle jumping increased for a number
of trials before a gradual decrease occurred. Because no shock was administered during this EFF training, it can be assumed that the unreinforced
presentation of the CS and the situational cues on each trial constituted a
fear-extinction trial for those stimuli. Despite this extinction of fear, speed
of hurdle jumping increased for about 50 trials, indicating a growth in
associative strength for the instrumental response. Presumably, sufficient
response-contingent fear reduction occurred on these trails to provide reinforcement. (The basis for the subsequent decline in performance will be
discussed later). The same argument may be applied to avoidance learning
such as in the Kamin et al. study. During a long series of consecutive
avoidances, the processes described for the EFF task (extinction of fear,
coupled with growth of instrumental associative strength) would be expected to occur because for fear theory an avoidance response is an escape-
from-fear response.

   The foregoing discussion provides one basis for responding to the speculation of Kamin et al. that "variables other than fear of the CS are largely
responsible for the maintenance of avoidance behavior." Specifically, it
seems reasonable to assume that one such variable is the associative strength
of the instrumental avoidance response. Another such variable, fear of the
situational cues, has been almost universally ignored in discussions of the
parallelism issue. This source of fear is, however, an important determinant
of the amount of reinforcement in avoidance learning. The failure to rec-

ognize its relevance has probably contributed to the acceptance of the parallelism argument.

An extension of the reinforcement (fear-reduction) hypothesis of fear theory that specifically includes the role played by fear of situational cues in determining the reinforcement for an instrumental response was first proposed by W. R. McAllister, McAllister, and Douglass (1971). This modification, called Effective Reinforcement Theory (ERT), holds that the effective reinforcement for an avoidance response is related positively to the amount of fear reduction occurring with the response and negatively to the amount of fear present following the response. In addition, as the total amount of fear increases, it is assumed that the amount of fear present following the response becomes relatively more important than the amount of fear reduction in determining effective reinforcement.

One of the predictions of ERT is that in a two-way avoidance task, effective reinforcement, and therefore performance, will increase when fear of the situational cues following a response is minimized while fear of the CS is held constant. Support for this prediction comes from studies in which fear of the situational cues is *decreased* by latent inhibition resulting from preexposure procedures (e.g., Dieter, 1977; Hampton, 1980/1981; W. R. McAllister, McAllister, Dieter, & James, 1979, Experiment 2; Scoles, 1982/1983) or by removing visual and/or tactual fear-eliciting situational cues (e.g., Boyd & Levis, 1979; Kruger, Galvani, & Brown, 1969; D. E. McAllister, McAllister, & Dieter, 1976; W. R. McAllister et al., 1979, Experiment 1; Modaresi, 1975). Conversely, it is predicted that effective reinforcement, and therefore performance, will decrease when fear of the situational cues is augmented. This prediction has been upheld by studies in which such fear has been *increased* by shock-alone trials (Bloom & Campbell, 1966; Mowrer, 1940; Scoles, 1982/1983).

A further prediction from ERT is that, with fear of the situational cues held constant, *increases* in fear of the CS will improve two-way avoidance performance. Confirmatory evidence has been reported (Callen, 1986; W. R. McAllister, McAllister, Scoles, & James, 1978). The opposite prediction, that *decreases* in fear of the CS will degrade two-way avoidance performance when fear of the situational cues is held constant, has also been supported (Feldman, 1977; Hampton, 1980/1981).

In the typical two-way avoidance task, fear of the discrete CS and of the situational cues is present before the response, and fear of the situational cues alone is present after the response. During the course of learning, the amount of fear of these two sources would be expected to change as a result of the formation of a discrimination, based on differential reinforcement, between the CS plus situational cues and the situational cues alone (Mowrer, 1947, p. 110; Mowrer & Lamoreaux, 1951). Because on escape trials shock accompanies the compound stimulus (CS plus situational cues), the compound would continue to elicit fear. However, because the situational cues alone are never paired with shock, fear of these cues should extinguish. As a consequence, the amount of effective reinforcement would be modified.

Such changes in the amount of fear elicited by these two sources have been demonstrated experimentally in a study by W. R. McAllister et al. (1983). Specifically, groups were administered two-way avoidance training to a criterion of either 2, 10, or 20 consecutive avoidance responses. Following achievement of the avoidance criterion, subjects were allowed, in the absence of shock, to escape from one compartment of the shuttlebox to an adjacent, highly distinctive, safe box. The amount of fear of the discrete CS plus the situational cues or of the situational cues alone was measured by the rate and level of learning attained in escaping from these stimuli.

The results from the EFF task are shown in Fig. 4.2 where the number in the legend indicates the avoidance learning criterion, and CS or NCS refers to the presence or absence, respectively, of the discrete CS during the hurdle-jumping trials. The two sources of fear, fear of the discrete CS and fear of the situational cues, have been shown to combine additively to determine performance in this EFF task (W. R. McAllister & McAllister, 1962, 1971, pp. 132–134). Inasmuch as the three CS groups performed alike, it can be assumed that the total amount of fear available to motivate and reinforce instrumental responding was approximately the same for each. However, it is not necessary that these similar performances reflect the same amounts of fear from the two sources. In fact, the results obtained under the NCS condition indicate that fear of the situational cues differed for the several groups. Both the 10- and 20-criterion groups showed little

FIG. 4.2. Mean speed of escaping the CS plus situational cues (CS) or situational cues alone (NCS) as a function of blocks of five trials for groups that had previously attained a criterion of either 2, 10, or 20 consecutive two-way avoidance responses. From McAllister, McAllister, and Benton (1983). Reprinted by permission of Academic Press.

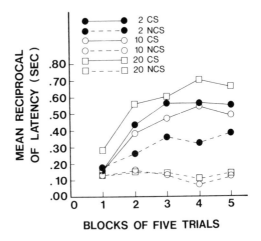

fear of the situational cues, whereas the 2-criterion group showed a considerable amount of such fear. Therefore, it can be concluded that the performance of the 2-CS group reflected fear of both the CS and the situational cues. On the other hand, the performance of the 10- and 20-CS groups can be attributed primarily to fear of the CS.

These results demonstrate that as frequency of avoidance responses increases in a standard two-way avoidance task fear of the situational cues decreases. Although fear of the discrete CS did not show a similar decrease in this study, such a decline in fear would be expected, consistent with previous studies (e.g., Kamin et al., 1963; Starr & Mineka, 1977), if a more stringent avoidance criterion had been used. With respect to the problem of parallelism, and given the notion of effective reinforcement, these findings suggest circumstances whereby the amount of reinforcement for the avoidance response could remain the same or increase even though fear of the CS decreases. That is, if fear of the situational cues decreases at the same rate as fear of the CS, effective reinforcement could remain at the same level, whereas if fear of the situational cues decreases at a faster rate than fear of the CS, effective reinforcement could actually increase. Because of the maintenance or the increase in effective reinforcement, in neither of these cases would a decrease in avoidance performance be expected despite the loss of fear of the CS.

From the point of view of ERT, little can be said about the reinforcement of an avoidance response without knowledge about the relative amounts of fear of the CS and of the situational cues. Because in the study of Kamin et al. (1963), as well as in other similar studies (e.g., Mineka & Gino, 1980; Starr & Mineka, 1977), fear of the situational cues was not measured, there is no way of determining the relative amount of reinforcement that the avoidance response was receiving in their separate groups.

A lack of parallelism between levels of fear and avoidance performance has also been observed in studies that manipulate shock intensity in two-way or bar-press avoidance tasks. In these situations, an inverse relationship between avoidance performance and intensity of shock is a highly reliable finding (see references in W. R. McAllister et al., 1979). The inverse relationship has been taken to be embarrassing to fear theory because the amount of fear conditioned is directly related to shock intensity, and the assumption is that the level of avoidance performance should be directly related to the amount of fear (e.g., D'Amato, 1970, pp. 366–367). Actually, however, the inverse relationship poses a problem for most theories of avoidance learning. Indeed, theoretical treatments of this phenomenon have been infrequent, as has been pointed out by W. R. McAllister et al. (1979, pp. 172–173). Because ERT, unlike other avoidance learning theories, recognizes the importance of fear of the situational cues as well as fear of the CS, it is able to account for the inverse relationship. Specifically, the positive effect of a greater amount of fear reduction from CS termination when shock is strong than when it is weak would be more than offset by the negative effect of a greater amount of fear of the situational cues present after the response. Therefore, effective reinforcement would be less under the strong-shock condition, and performance would be inferior to that obtained with weak shock.

Consistent with the foregoing analysis, an independent measurement of fear has demonstrated that greater fear of situational cues is associated with the inferior two-way avoidance performance observed when shock is strong (W. R. McAllister et al., 1971). Other tests of the ERT interpretation of the inverse relationship have also supported the theory. For example, minimizing fear of the situational cues with preexposure procedures (latent inhibition) has been shown to eliminate the inverse relationship between shock intensity and two-way avoidance performance (Dieter, 1977) or to reverse it (W. R. McAllister et al., 1979). Furthermore, a direct relationship has been obtained when fear of situational cues has been held constant by manipulating shock intensity within subjects (Callen, 1986).

The conclusion to be drawn from this discussion seems to be self-evident: A lack of parallelism between the amount of fear of the CS and the level of avoidance performance is often to be expected. Therefore, the parallelism criticism has little bearing on the adequacy of fear theory, and for this reason, it should be put to rest.

FEAR AND ASYMPTOTIC AVOIDANCE PERFORMANCE

Another assertion made by critics of fear theory is that well-learned avoidance responses can occur in the *absence* of fear. This idea was propagated in large part by the writings of Seligman and Johnston (1973) and Gray (1971, 1975). Although Seligman and Johnston responded cogently to many of the criticisms of fear theory that had been made over the years, they nevertheless concluded that the theory was inadequate because subjects showed no evidence of fear during asymptotic avoidance responding. In their chapter, they repeated this assertion frequently—at least three times! Perhaps the widespread acceptance of this claim indicates that Lewis Carroll's Bellman formulated a powerful law.

Some examples of the proliferation of this assertion follow. In a recent textbook, it is contended that ". . . there are a number of different lines of evidence to suggest that fear is not present in avoidance situations, at least not after avoidance responding has been fully learned and is being sustained" (Schwartz, 1989, p. 206). Also, Rachman and Hodgson (1974, p. 314) stated, "It is a fact . . . that once it is well-established, avoidance behaviour can persist for protracted periods with no decrease in strength, even in the absence of fear." It has also been claimed that "a large body of evidence disputes the notion that anticipatory fear regulates avoidant action. . . .avoidance can persist long after fear of threats has been eliminated" (Bandura, 1986, p. 1389).

The presumed problem for fear theory alluded to in the quotations given is more apparent than real; there seems to be no compelling evidence for the claim. The data that are almost always cited as the basis for the contention that avoidance responding is maintained in the absence of fear come from the studies of Kamin et al. (1963) and Solomon, Kamin, and Wynne (1953). Neither of these studies provides such evidence.

Actually, in the Kamin et al. study, the group that made 27 consecutive avoidance responses exhibited a sizeable amount of fear of the CS. This was indicated by the degree of suppression of bar pressing to the avoidance CS at the outset of the test trials. Suppression at that point provides, of course, the best estimate of the amount of fear present at the end of avoidance training. Even the transformed measure, which is usually reported, does not show an absence of fear, despite the fact that it was based on a larger number of unreinforced test trials during which fear would have extinguished.

In the Solomon et al. study (1953), following the acquisition of a two-way avoidance response, subjects continued to respond for 200 extinction trials with latencies which, during acquisition, would have been classified as avoidance responses. During these trials, observational data were obtained concerning overt behaviors, such as vocalizing, excreting, salivating, trembling, and so on. These behaviors were taken to reflect fear. When this study is cited, it is frequently reported that these putative signs of fear decreased during the extinction trials and eventually ceased to be made. Therefore, it is claimed that avoidance responding occurred in the absence of fear. Probably the basis for this claim is the statement made by Solomon and Wynne in their theoretical paper (1954, p. 359) that "overt signs of anxiety rapidly disappeared" during the extinction trials. This statement is most unfortunate, because it is not in accord with the data reported in the original experimental paper (Solomon et al., 1953, p. 293). There it is stated

> The types of emotional signs which usually disappeared during the course of ordinary extinction were defecation, urination, yelping and shrieking. . . . Whining, barking, and drooling tended to decrease in magnitude but often persisted throughout the 200 trials. Panting tended to persist relatively undiminished if it occurred during the early trials.

Although they also reported that "some dogs showed no overt emotional signs during the latter part of ordinary extinction," it is clear that the data as a whole do not support the blanket assertion that overt signs of fear were not present when avoidance responding was at asymptote. It should be pointed out that other studies in this series (Brush, Brush, & Solomon, 1955; Kamin, 1954) reported that some emotional behavior persisted through a large number (100 or 200) of extinction trials.

Using these overt responses to indicate the presence or absence of fear implies that fear is being defined in terms of these behaviors. If, on the other hand, fear is conceptualized as a central state (Rescorla & Solomon, 1967) or is defined in terms of the prior classical conditioning procedure, that is, the appropriate pairing of neutral and noxious stimuli (W. R. McAllister & McAllister, 1971), such changes in behavior as did occur in the Solomon et al. study are not crucial in evaluating fear theory. Indeed, in 1953, Solomon and Wynne (p. 14) pointed out with respect to these overt signs of emotion that "clearly, such observations give us little information about the events taking place in the nervous system or details about the animal's motivational state."

On the basis of these comments, it would seem that the time is long past due to stop citing the Kamin et al. (1963) and the Solomon et al. (1953) studies as indicating that avoidance responding takes place in the absence of fear. It would be more appropriate to cite other studies, such as those of Levis and Boyd (1979), W. R. McAllister et al. (1983), Mineka and Gino (1980), Morris (1974), and Starr and Mineka (1977), which show that when an avoidance response is well learned a sizable amount of fear of the CS is present.

Gray (1971, 1975), writing before these latter experiments were available, accepted the proposition that avoidance responding can continue in the absence of fear. In order to rescue fear theory from the dilemma posed by this purported result, he proposed a theory which held that well-learned avoidance responses were reinforced, not by the reduction of fear, but rather by the receipt of a safety signal. Although he later concluded (Gray, 1987) that some fear was present when avoidance responding was asymptotic, he retained his safety-signal view of reinforcement. An appraisal of his views will be made in the next section.

THE REINFORCEMENT MECHANISM IN AVERSIVE LEARNING

Another common criticism of fear theory stems from studies showing that avoidance learning can take place when the CS is not immediately terminated by the response. The conclusion that such findings are contrary to fear theory is based on the erroneous belief that according to the theory CS termination is a necessary condition for reinforcement. Thus, for example, it has been stated that for "some theorists . . . termination of the CS is assumed to lead to a reduction of fear which is reinforcing. . . . [and such termination] is held to be an essential ingredient in avoidance learning" (Bolles, 1970, p. 39). It has also been contended that "reduction of Pavlovian conditioned fear by termination of the [CS is] the reinforcer of avoidance behaviour, as traditional two-process theory insists. . . ." (Weisman & Litner, 1972, p. 254). Additionally, it has been claimed that for avoidance responding the CS "may function as a discriminative stimulus for the avoidance response, rather than as a stimulus whose removal is inherently reinforcing, as two-factor theory requires" (Herrnstein, 1969, p. 49). In view of these quotations, it is somewhat ironic that a discrete CS was not used in the classic study of Miller (1948), which has served as a bulwark for fear theory.

Actually, according to fear theory, the reinforcement for an instrumental response comes from fear reduction (Miller & Dollard, 1941; Mowrer, 1939), and the basis for such reduction is irrelevant. All that is required is that less fear be present following the response than preceding it and that the differential in fear be of sufficient magnitude. Because fear can be conditioned to a variety of stimuli, there are many potential sources of stimulus change that can occur following the response and lead to fear reduction. Such stimulus change could involve an external discrete stimulus, such as the termination of a CS, or some change in the situational cues. It could also involve the introduction, with the response, of new stimuli into the stimulus complex thereby producing a decrease in fear through a stimulus generalization decrement or external inhibition. Such stimuli could be internal, generated by the instrumental response, or external. Dolan, Shishimi, and Wagner (1985) provide convincing evidence for this generalization decrement process.

Clearly, the source of fear reduction is not restricted to the termination of a CS. Nevertheless, studies (e.g., Bower, Starr, & Lazarovitz, 1965) showing that two-way avoidance learning can occur even though the CS is not terminated immediately after the response, provided that the response is followed by another stimulus (e.g., a feedback stimulus such as a tone or a light), have been taken as a refutation of fear theory (e.g., Bolles, 1970). The reasoning seems to be that because the neutral feedback stimulus can compensate for the absence of immediate CS termination, the reinforcement mechanism must be something other than fear reduction. This conclusion, however, does not necessarily follow. According to fear theory, the introduction of the neutral feedback stimulus would alter the fear-eliciting stimulus complex present after the response and thereby produce a stimulus generalization decrement of fear.

The reinforcing mechanism of fear theory may be further elucidated. Whenever fear or pain is reduced, it is assumed that a response of relaxation or relief occurs (e.g., Denny, 1971; Denny & Adelman, 1955; Miller, 1951;

Mowrer, 1960). Therefore, the assertion that fear reduction has taken place is tantamount to asserting that a relaxation response has occurred. That is, relaxation may be considered to be fear reduction conceptualized as having the functional properties of a response. As such, relaxation (fear reduction) is conditionable and with trials would be expected to become conditioned to the feedback stimulus. Because relaxation is an antagonist of fear, the feedback stimulus would thereby be endowed with fear-reducing (secondary-reinforcing) properties. It should be clear that internal stimuli produced by the instrumental response can function as feedback stimuli in the same manner as external stimuli. The speed with which the conditioning of relaxation develops to any stimulus would presumably depend on the degree to which the experimental conditions permit relaxation to occur.

These same processes can also endow a neutral stimulus with secondary-reinforcing properties when its presentation is not contingent on a response (e.g., Morris, 1975; Zerbolio, 1968). The procedures typically used for this purpose are congruent with those specified for establishing a stimulus as a Pavlovian conditioned inhibitor of fear (e.g., Rescorla & LoLordo, 1965). As usually stated, all that is required for the conditioning of inhibition is that the stimulus precedes periods free of aversive stimulation in a situation in which aversive stimulation is being administered. This latter requirement, that conditioning take place in an aversive (fearful) situation, is unnecessary if it is assumed that the conditioning of relaxation is the mechanism underlying conditioned inhibition, as has been proposed (LoLordo, 1969, p. 202; W. R. McAllister & McAllister, 1971, p. 120). Evidence supporting this view has been reported by Grelle and James (1981). They found that a neutral stimulus could acquire reinforcing properties in a nonaversive situation as long as it was paired with the occurrence of a relaxation response (fear reduction). This explanation of conditioned inhibition in terms of relaxation is parsimonious in that only one conditioning process need be invoked; all conditioning is excitatory. In addition, it provides a symmetry in that the antagonist of the fear response is another response, relaxation. When a previously neutral stimulus acquires secondary-reinforcing properties, either response contingently (as with a feedback stimulus) or noncontingently, it is generally called a safety signal. (See also the chapter by Denny, this volume, Ed.)

There is precedence for these views. In 1941, Miller and Dollard (pp. 60–61, Footnote 7) proposed that cues produced by "successful escape" responses become rewarding because of their association with relaxation (fear reduction). Also, they identified the response-produced stimuli that elicit relaxation as Pavlovian conditioned inhibitors of fear. In addition, in reiterating the identity of relaxation and fear reduction, Miller (1985, p. 263) referred to the conditioning of fear reduction.

Some critics of fear theory maintain, however, that avoidance responding occurs not as an escape from fear, reinforced by fear reduction or relaxation, but rather as an approach to a positive goal, the safety signal (e.g., Bolles, 1970, 1972a, 1972b, 1975; Gray, 1971, 1975, 1987; Weisman & Litner, 1972). The advocates of this position differ with respect to the mechanism underlying the effectiveness of the safety signal. For Gray, it acts as a secondary reward, the effects of which are "relatively independent of the degree of fear aroused in the situation" (Gray, 1987, p. 220). According to Weisman and Litner, the crucial reinforcing factor for the learning of the avoidance response is the receipt of a positive reward, the safety signal, which acts as an inhibitor of fear of the background cues. Aside from the terminological preference for considering an avoidance response to be an approach rather than an escape response, it is difficult to distinguish this latter position from one espousing fear reduction as reinforcement.

Bolles has offered several theoretical accounts of avoidance performance, each of which employs the notion of a safety signal in one way or another. Although it might seem reasonable to discuss only the latest theory, his earlier versions are cited frequently in the current literature and, therefore, warrant inclusion. His original theory (1970, 1972a) proposed that when an animal (rat) has received aversive stimulation and becomes frightened of the stimuli present, its response repertoire is limited to a few innate species-specific defense responses (SSDRs—fleeing, freezing, or fighting). One of these SSDRs would be emitted, and if effective in functionally getting the animal out of the situation, it would quickly come to be made as an avoidance response. This rapid increase in performance would occur because competing, ineffective SSDRs would be suppressed by punishment. Inasmuch as SSDRs are innate behaviors, avoidance performance, according to this position, requires neither learning nor reinforcement of the instrumental response. Fear theory also posits that an innate hierarchy of responses (e.g., freezing, fleeing) exists initially in an aversive situation (Miller, 1951, p. 441; 1985, p. 265; Miller & Dollard, 1941, pp. 24–28). However, for fear theory such a response increases in probability (is learned) in an avoidance task on the basis of reinforcement (fear reduction).

According to Bolles, there are certain conditions under which other responses which are not SSDRs (e.g., bar pressing) may be learned, albeit slowly, in an avoidance task. Such learning (Bolles, 1970, p. 46) requires that an SSDR that is compatible with the avoidance response occur initially and be partly effective in minimizing the aversiveness of the situation (e.g., freezing on the bar in a bar-press avoidance task and then responding reflexively to shock so as to minimize its duration). As aversiveness decreases, responses other than SSDRs, such as bar pressing, become available. It is assumed that these non-SSDR avoidance responses are reinforced by stimuli (including CS termination) that have previously preceded shock-free periods. As a result, these stimuli, safety signals, come to provide information, or to predict, that shock is not going to occur (Bolles, 1970, pp. 40, 44; 1972a, p. 137). In regard to the role of safety signals, Bolles (1972a, p. 137) stated that "because we seem to have discovered a new reinforcement mechanism, it is not necessary to maintain the untenable argument that animals can learn only SSDR's as avoidance responses." As indicated earlier, for fear theory safety signals are also reinforcing, but their effect is based on the occurrence of relaxation/fear reduction following the response. It is of interest to note that Bolles (1972a, pp. 133–134) likened his theory to that of Denny (1971) and later (p. 137) stated that a safety signal "releases relaxation and produces an abatement of species-specific and learned defensive behaviors." This apparent rapprochement with either fear theory or Denny's theory has not, however, been pursued.

Subsequently, Bolles (1972b) offered a cognitive theory in which he postulated that two expectancies were involved in an avoidance task. One of the expectancies, that the stimuli in the situation are followed by shock, is learned. As a result, these stimuli become danger signals. The other expectancy is that a certain response will lead to safety. Initially, this expectancy would be an SSDR, which is regarded as an unlearned expectancy that certain responses (e.g., fleeing or freezing) predict safety. According to this theory, SSDRs are modifiable, "both by the cues in the situation and by their outcomes" (p. 407). Thus, if an SSDR, for example, the expectancy that running away leads to safety, is disconfirmed by being punished by shock, it will be replaced by the expectancy that running leads to shock. Under this circumstance, the next strongest SSDR will be made. If none of the SSDRs is successful in achieving safety, an expectancy that some arbitrary response (e.g., bar pressing) leads to safety may be learned provided that the contingency between this response and safety is discriminable. This theory differs from the previous ones by considering an SSDR to be an innate expectancy rather than simply an innate behavior and by assuming that an SSDR expectancy is modifiable.

In 1975, Bolles (p. 360) rescinded the aspect of his 1970 SSDR hypothesis that posited different mechanisms for avoidance responses that developed rapidly (selection among SSDRs) from those that are learned slowly (reinforcement by safety signals). In so doing, he argued that "no response learning occurs in the avoidance learning situation! . . . *All* [italics added] avoidance behavior [is] respondent" (p. 364). He then restated his SSDR hypothesis "in a new and much stronger form" as follows:

> The animal's behavior [in an aversive situation] consists *entirely* [italics added] of SSDRs, the topography of which is determined in part by the animal's expectancies of danger and safety and in part by the structure of environmental supporting stimuli. (p. 364)

These expectancies, which develop on the basis of the experimental contingencies, constitute the only learning that takes place in an avoidance learning situation. Avoidance behavior is motivated, but because all such behaviors are innate SSDRs, reinforcement is not required. However, "to the extent that the animal can direct its innate defensive behavior to a specific safety signal . . . such a cue will appear to have a reinforcing effect" (p. 365). This cognitive theory, which considers an SSDR to be an *innate behavior* that is immutable, differs from the previous cognitive theory (Bolles, 1972b) which considered an SSDR to be an *innate expectancy* that is modifiable. There is a further difference between the two theories. The strong stand taken by the 1975 theory, that all aversively motivated behavior is innate, rejects the possibility that non-SSDR responses can be learned as avoidance responses. This assertion was not, however, reconciled with the further statement that an occasional animal may learn a non-SSDR avoidance response such as bar pressing (Bolles, 1975, p. 366). In contrast, the previous theory (Bolles, 1972b) argued explicitly that, under certain conditions, a non-SSDR expectancy that some arbitrary response (e.g., bar pressing) leads to safety can be learned.

In summary, Bolles's various views of avoidance performance have been consistent in assuming that avoidance responses that are SSDRs are unaffected by reinforcement. In his early versions, however, it was assumed that non-SSDR responses could be learned as avoidance responses and that the basis for such learning was the reinforcement provided by safety signals. In his last version, where all avoidance responses are SSDRs, reinforcement plays no role; avoidance performance consists simply of withdrawal from danger cues or approaches to safety cues.

Denny (1971) also considers an avoidance response to be an approach response. According to his theory, a relaxation/approach response occurs following the termination of an aversive event and becomes conditioned to the stimuli present. Through higher-order conditioning, the approach component would come with training to be elicited by the stimuli preceding those to which relaxation is conditioned, and avoidance responding would occur. (For further details, see the chapter by Denny, this volume, Ed.)

Considering the avoidance response to be an approach to safety or to relaxation-eliciting stimuli rather than a response that escapes fear is problematical. It is, of course, inherently difficult to determine empirically whether a response of a subject that changes its location (or condition) is made as an approach to the one location (or condition) or as an escape from the other. However, when an approach response leads to the information that the situation has been changed from dangerous to safe (Bolles, 1970, 1972a) or leads to a stimulus that inhibits fear (Weisman & Litner, 1972) or elicits relaxation that is antagonistic to fear (Denny, 1971), it follows that less fear would be present after the response than before. On this basis, it would appear that, regardless of the terminology employed, a reduction in fear is an intrinsic aspect of instrumental aversive learning. As such, a reinforcement mechanism (fear reduction) is automatically provided whether or not a theorist chooses to acknowledge it.

Gray's safety-signal theory (1971, 1975, 1987) also views an avoidance response as an approach to a positive goal but differs from other such theories with respect to the role played by fear in the maintenance of avoidance responding. In his theorizing, he attempted to cope with the presumed problem that the persistence of avoidance responding is incompatible with fear theory. He argued that, according to fear theory, with increasing numbers of consecutive avoidance responses, fear of the CS would extinguish quickly, reinforcement from fear reduction would thereby decrease, and avoidance responding would cease. Gray noted, however, that even though fear of the CS declines, avoidance responding is maintained (e.g., Kamin et al., 1963). This problem was discussed in the previous section on parallelism in this chapter. The various factors explicated there which seem to resolve the problem (i.e., associative strength of the instrumental avoidance response, the role of fear of situational cues as stated by effective reinforcement theory, and the implications of the all-or-none nature of the avoidance response) were not recognized by Gray in his theorizing. Rather, in his early writings (1971, 1975), Gray held that avoidance responding was maintained in the absence of fear by secondary reinforcement from safety signals. Later, when data suggested that the reinforcing effect of safety signals depended on the presence of fear, Gray (1987) argued that the safety signal played a dual role: protecting fear of the CS from complete extinction (Soltysik, Wolfe, Nicholas, Wilson, & Garcia–Sanchez, 1983) and providing reinforcement for the avoidance response.

It is important for both versions of Gray's theory that the effectiveness of safety signals be independent of the level of fear. This lack of relationship is necessary so that the persistence of avoidance responding in the face of decreased fear is understandable. Gray depended largely on a study by Lawler (1965) as support for this view. In this study, subjects first learned to escape shock by running to a safe box. They were then, in the absence of shock, given test trials in which a choice was allowed between the original safe box and a distinctive new box. For one group, the Neutral group, the start box as well as the runway between the start box and the choice boxes were presumed not to be fear arousing during the test because the floor and walls were changed, and the discrete CS was eliminated. For another group, the Fearful group, the stimulus situation during the test remained as it had been during training. It was found that both groups chose the original safe box more than the new box, but the Neutral group chose it significantly more often than the Fearful group. From this latter result,

Gray concluded that the amount of fear and the secondary-reinforcing properties of safety signals were relatively independent.

There are several reasons to question this conclusion. The fewer choices of the original safe box by the Fearful group is probably artifactual. Five of the eight subjects in that group adopted a position habit which, because the placement of the boxes was alternated randomly, limited the choice of each box to 50%. Furthermore, for two reasons, it is likely that fear was present in the Neutral group. The lid of the apparatus was transparent, thus permitting fear to become conditioned to extra-apparatus cues during the original training. It has been demonstrated that fear of such cues can affect instrumental learning (W. R. McAllister & McAllister, 1965). In addition, because the stimuli of the start box and runway during test were novel, it can be assumed that they were fear arousing to some extent (D. E. McAllister, McAllister, & Zellner, 1966). Thus, it is highly probable that fear was present in both of Lawler's groups, but because of its stronger fear, the position habit occurred only in the Fearful group. On the basis of the foregoing arguments, Lawler's study does not provide evidence for Gray's contention that the effectiveness of safety signals is independent of the level of fear. A further problem, pointed out by LoLordo (1969), is that the task used by Lawler was not appropriate for determining whether the stimuli in the safe box were reinforcing because it did not involve the learning of a new response.

The results of studies from our laboratory, which did measure performance by the learning of a new response, suggest a positive relationship between the level of fear and the reinforcing effect of safety signals. These studies investigated the effect of feedback stimuli (safety signals) when the amount of fear of situational cues present after the response was manipulated (Callen, McAllister, & McAllister, 1983). An acquired drive paradigm, analogous to that described for the experiment whose data are depicted in Fig. 4.1, was used. In one study, fear was first conditioned to a white noise CS and to the situational cues in a white grid compartment. Subsequently, in the absence of shock, the CS was presented, and the subjects were allowed to escape the fear-eliciting stimuli of the conditioning box by jumping a hurdle to an adjacent, identical "safe" box. Prior to the hurdle-jumping training, half of the subjects were placed in the safe box for 1 hour in order to extinguish fear of the situational cues, while the remaining subjects spent the hour in a neutral box and thus did not receive an extinction treatment. There were three no-extinction (NE) and three extinction (E) groups. For all groups, the termination of the CS was delayed (DEL) for 10 seconds after a hurdle-jumping response. Within each extinction condition, two groups received a 10-second feedback stimulus immediately following a response. For one of the groups, the feedback stimulus was a flashing light, F(FL); for the other, it was the termination of

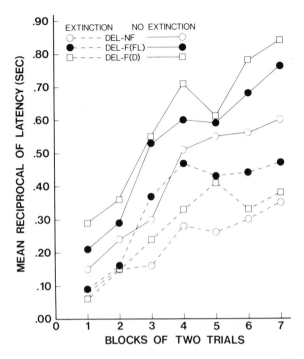

FIG. 4.3. Mean speed of hurdle jumping in blocks of two trials following Extinction or No Extinction of fear of situational cues for groups receiving delayed CS termination (DEL) accompanied by either a flashing light, F(FL), darkness, F(D), or nothing, NF, as a feedback stimulus.

the house light (darkness), F(D). The third group received no feedback stimulus, NF.

The mean speed of hurdle jumping in blocks of two trials for each group is shown in Fig. 4.3. Each E group performed significantly poorer than its corresponding NE group. Apparently, the extinction manipulation was successful in diminishing the amount of fear of the situational cues in the apparatus. As a result, less fear would be available in the E than in the NE groups to motivate instrumental responding. The effectiveness of the feedback stimuli was differential for the two extinction conditions. It should be noted that, because the termination of the CS was delayed, fear from this source was present after the response for all groups. Under the E condition, where fear of the situational cues was minimized by the extinction treatment, the presentation of a feedback stimulus (FL or D) tended to improve performance, compared with the NF condition, but not significantly so. Apparently, there was an insufficient disparity in the amount of fear reduction between the feedback and no-feedback conditions. On the other hand, under the NE condition, where fear of the situational cues had not been extinguished, the presentation of a feedback stimulus following a response did facilitate performance. Specifically, with darkness as a feedback stimulus, performance was improved, compared with the NF group, and this effect was significant by the second single trial. With the flashing light as a feedback stimulus, performance over trials was superior to that of the NF group, but the groups differed reliably only on Trial Block 3. The F(D) group was consistently superior to the F(FL) group over trials, but the difference between the groups was not significant. However, in another study, which replicated the conditions of the three no-extinction groups but with a less intense CS and fewer fear-conditioning trials, performance under the darkness condition was reliably superior to that under both the flashing light and the NF conditions. This effect was manifest by the third single trial. The FL group was consistently superior to the NF group over trials but not significantly so.

Taken as a whole, the results of these studies suggest that, under the circumstance in which feedback stimuli were effective (the no-extinction condition), darkness is superior to a flashing light. (See also the chapter by Minor, Dess, and Overmier, this volume, Ed.) In common with other feedback stimuli, darkness can be expected to reduce fear by altering the stimulus complex to which fear had been conditioned and thereby to produce a stimulus generalization decrement. Its superiority to other feedback stimuli may be attributed to an additional unique reinforcing (fear-reducing) role that it possesses. The special role arises because darkness, of necessity, removes visual situational cues and thereby prevents the elicitation of fear by those cues. It will be recalled that when fear of the situational cues, including the visual cues, was extinguished, darkness was not superior to the flashing light. Because of its added capacity to reduce fear following a response, darkness as a feedback stimulus has been used as a large reward in studies manipulating reward magnitude (D. E. McAllister et al., 1976; W. R. McAllister et al., 1979).

The implication from these studies is that the effectiveness of a feedback stimulus is importantly determined by the amount of fear present following a response. As such, the findings are at odds with Gray's contention that the level of fear and the reinforcing effect of feedback stimuli (safety signals) are relatively independent. In adopting this position, Gray is able to account for the persistence of avoidance responding under standard conditions in the face of diminishing amounts of fear. In so doing, however, his theory encounters a problem in explaining the extinction of such behavior when it does occur.

This explanatory problem may be illustrated with the data shown in Fig. 4.1. As described earlier, those data represent hurdle-jumping EFF performance based upon 25 fear-conditioning trials. Following acquisition of the hurdle-jumping response, the gradual decrease in speed and the eventual cessation of responding is attributable by fear theory to the gradual extinction of fear to a subthreshold level. That a loss of fear, and not a loss in the associative strength of the instrumental response, was responsible for the decline in performance is indicated by a subsequent part of this experiment. Immediately after responding had ceased, a single fear-conditioning trial was given to some of the subjects. This one reconditioning trial resulted in an immediate increase in speed of hurdle jumping to a high level before any relearning of the hurdle-jumping response could have occurred, implying that the associative strength of the instrumental response had not been lost. This recovery in performance was followed by a gradual decline until responding ceased again. Fuller details are given in W. R. McAllister et al. (1986). That the group data both before and after the reconditioning trial are representative of the behavior of the individual subjects is demonstrated in W. R. McAllister and McAllister (1988).

The gradual decline in performance that eventually occurred after the initial conditioning and again after the single reconditioning trial would not be expected by either version of Gray's theory. In both instances, the response-produced cues from making a hurdle-jumping response and the cues of the safe box would become safety signals. Consequently, every response would inevitably be followed by positive reinforcement, the safety signals, and there would be no reason for the response ever to extinguish.

It should be noted that Seligman and Johnston's cognitive (expectancy) theory (1973) has a difficulty similar to that of Gray's safety-signal theory in accounting for extinction data such as those shown in Fig. 4.1. To accommodate such data, provision would have to be made in Gray's theory for a gradual loss of the reinforcing properties of safety signals when there is no apparent change in the experimental contingencies and by Seligman and Johnston's cognitive theory for a gradual loss of the expectancy that responding leads to no shock while it continues to be confirmed.

Of the other theories, only Denny (1971) has explicitly addressed the problem of extinction. With respect to the extinction data under consideration, he would argue that the relaxation response, which is assumed to occur following the instrumental response, would with training chain back through higher-order conditioning and come to be elicited by the stimuli in the start box. Consequently, fear elicited by those stimuli would be counterconditioned by the antagonistic relaxation response. As fear diminishes, the instrumental hurdle-jumping response would gradually cease to be made. This explanation is consistent with fear theory (Miller, 1951).

Such a counterconditioning mechanism can also be used to account for the attenuation of fear of the CS reported by Cook, Mineka, and Trumble (1987). They found a decrease in fear of the CS as the number of training trials increased from 50 to 200. This decrease occurred in master groups that learned a two-way avoidance task as well as in other groups yoked to the master groups with respect to stimulus presentations. In one of the yoked conditions (Y), subjects received a sequence of CS-shock and CS-only trials corresponding to the stimuli received by the master subjects on escape and avoidance trials, respectively. In the other yoked condition (YFC), subjects received only the CS-shock trials corresponding to the escape trials of the master subjects. In the yoked conditions, the attenuation of fear was found only when an exteroceptive feedback stimulus (3 seconds of darkness) was presented appropriately to the Y and the YFC subjects at the time the master subjects responded. This circumstance may be understood by making the reasonable assumption that the yoked subjects were trained in the presence of a sizable amount of fear of the situational cues. As a result, without a feedback stimulus to produce a stimulus generalization decrement of fear, the relaxation response may not have been of sufficient magnitude to allow for its conditioning to the stimuli present (situational cues or stimulus traces of the CS). Thus, the possibility of counterconditioning fear of the CS would be precluded.[2]

In the discussions thus far, performance in aversively motivated instrumental learning has been accounted for simply in terms of fear as the motivator and fear reduction/relaxation as the reinforcement mechanism. There are findings, however, that require a more elaborate theory. These come from studies concerned with the successive negative contrast effect (D. E. McAllister, McAllister, Brooks, & Goldman, 1972; Woods, 1967), the partial reinforcement extinction effect (W. R. McAllister & McAllister,

---

[2]It was further argued by Cook, Mineka, and Trumble (1987) that the feedback stimulus attenuated fear on CS-shock trials but not on CS-only trials. This conclusion rests on their finding that even though CS-only trials did not occur in the YFC condition the observed decrease in fear of the CS with extended trials was the same for that condition as for the Y condition where such trials did occur. One can question this logic. A similar outcome with respect to fear of the CS in the two yoked conditions does not necessarily imply that the same processes were operating. In fact, because of differences in the experimental treatments under which fear of the CS was conditioned and under which such fear could extinguish, it is quite likely that the equal levels of fear in the Y and the YFC conditions were not attained in the same manner. For the Y treatment, the chain of events during the yoked trials consisted of conditioning, extinction (CS-only), and reconditioning trials, whereas for the YFC treatment, only conditioning trials were presented. The deleterious effect of the extinction trials occurring in the Y, but not in the YFC, condition could be compensated for because reconditioning has been shown to be more rapid than original conditioning (e.g., W. R. McAllister, McAllister, Scoles, & Hampton, 1986). Furthermore, the greater number of CS presentations in the Y, compared with the YFC, treatment would provide a greater number of opportunities for the conditioning of relaxation and the eventual counterconditioning of fear of the CS. However, such enhancement in the conditioning of relaxation in the Y treatment could be balanced in the YFC treatment because its longer intertrial intervals would be more propitious for conditioning. Based on these considerations, an interpretation of the Cook et al. data does not demand the conclusion either that CS-only trials play no role in the attenuation of fear of the CS or that a feedback stimulus has fear-attenuating effects only on CS-shock trials.

1971, pp. 130–132, 152–153; Newmark & Capaldi, 1972), and the combination of drive and reward (W. R. McAllister & McAllister, 1967).

To illustrate, consider the negative contrast effect which was obtained in an escape-from-fear task when reward was changed from a high to a low value (D. E. McAllister et al., 1972, Experiment 3). Subjects received 35 fear-conditioning trials (light–shock pairings) in a white, grid-floored side of a two-compartment apparatus. Subsequently, they learned to jump a hurdle, in the absence of shock, from the conditioning box to an adjacent safe box. During these trials, the reward magnitude (amount of fear reduction) was manipulated by varying the similarity of the stimuli in the conditioning and the safe boxes. In the small-reward condition, the safe box was identical to the conditioning box, whereas in the large-reward condition, it was gray with a solid floor. Also, after a jump, the CS was terminated for the large-reward condition, but it was presented in the safe box for the small-reward condition. On Trial 12, the value of the reward was shifted to the opposite magnitude for half of the subjects in each reward condition. The groups were designated in terms of the reward magnitude received before and after the shift. Thus, there was a large-large (L-L), large-small (L-S), small-small (S-S), and a small-large (S-L) group. The results are shown in Fig. 4.4. It is clear that the manipulation of the reward magnitude was effective: Superior performance occurred with large, compared with small, reward. The ensuing shift of reward from a large to a small value (L-S) resulted in a substantial negative contrast effect; that is, performance was degraded below the level of the unshifted control group

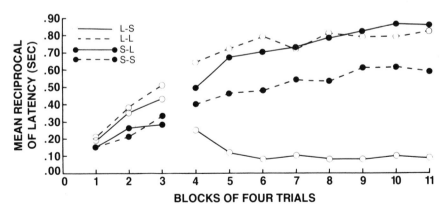

FIG. 4.4.   Mean speed of hurdle jumping in blocks of four trials for control groups with a large (L-L) or small (S-S) reward magnitude throughout massed practice and for groups with reward magnitude shifted (L-S or S-L) at the end of Trial Block 3. From McAllister, McAllister, Brooks, and Goldman (1972). Reprinted by permission of the American Psychological Association.

(S-S). The results of this study in general form have been simulated by Daly and Daly (1987) with their mathematical model, DMOD, that incorporates frustration theory into the Rescorla–Wagner model. (For additional information, see the chapter by Daly and Daly, this volume, Ed.)

The superiority of hurdle-jumping performance with the large, compared with the small, reward can be explained adequately in terms of the greater amount of reinforcement (fear reduction/relaxation) which occurred following the instrumental response in the former condition. However, an explanation of the negative contrast effect requires an elaboration of fear theory (D. E. McAllister et al., 1972, pp. 499–500). To this end, it is postulated that during the hurdle-jumping trials the relaxation response would become conditioned to the stimuli in the safe box. Through stimulus generalization, fractional components of this response (anticipatory relaxation) would come to be elicited by the stimuli in the start compartment and would increase motivation. The strength of the anticipation of relaxation (incentive motivation) would be directly related to reward magnitude and therefore to the speed of hurdle jumping.

Following Amsel (1958), when the expectation of the relaxation acquired under the large-reward condition was disconfirmed by the receipt of a small reward, a primary frustration response would occur and become conditioned to the stimuli in the safe compartment. Through stimulus generalization, fractional anticipatory components of the frustration response would come to be elicited by the stimuli in the start compartment. It is assumed that stimuli produced by anticipatory frustration would elicit responses (e.g., biting the grids) that would be incompatible with the hurdle-jumping response. (A compatible response such as locomoting away from frustration would not be adopted in this situation because escaping frustration in the start box would lead to the receipt of frustration in the safe box.) In addition, because the presence of stimuli from frustration would change the stimulus complex to which the instrumental hurdle-jumping response had been learned, a stimulus generalization decrement would occur. The degradation of performance resulting from these two effects of frustration in the group shifted from large to small reward would be expected to yield the negative contrast effect.

Shifts in reward magnitude in appetitively motivated tasks have effects that are analogous to those that have been described herein for the aversive case. This suggestion of a communality of underlying processes gains support in that the theoretical mechanisms proposed are parallel to those used to explain the results in the appetitive case (Bower, 1961; Daly, 1969).

Some comment seems required regarding the similarity of the elaborated fear theory to the safety-signal theories described previously. The theories proposed by Bolles, Gray, and Weisman and Litner regard the instrumental response as an approach to a positive goal rather than as an escape from fear. The goal object, a safety signal, is received after the response, and no specific mechanism relating to reward value is held to occur before the response. For the elaborated fear theory, responding involves an escape from fear. In addition, however, an approach component is provided by the anticipation of relaxation, and this incentive motivation mechanism occurs prior to the response. It is this aspect of the theory that permits an explanation of more complex phenomena, such as the negative contrast effect, observed in aversively motivated situations. Theories that lack an anticipatory mechanism seem unable to provide an account of such findings.

SUMMARY

A discussion and evaluation of several current criticisms of fear theory led to the conclusion that none had a substantive basis. The criticism pertaining to the observed lack of parallelism between levels of fear of the CS and avoidance performance fails to consider that fear theory ascribes an important role to variables other than fear of the CS in determining performance, namely, the associative strength of the instrumental response and fear of situational cues. In addition, this criticism neglects to consider the implications of the all-or-none nature of the avoidance response. The emphasis placed on the contribution of fear of the situational cues in determining reinforcement, as specified by Effective Reinforcement Theory, is entirely in the spirit of the Mowrer–Miller position.

Another criticism of fear theory, that avoidance responding at asymptote occurs in the absence of fear, was judged to lack empirical support. A further criticism, based on the assertion that termination of the CS is a necessary condition for reinforcement, involves an erroneous interpretation of fear theory. Because fear reduction (relaxation) is the reinforcement mechanism, all that is demanded by fear theory is that a sufficiently lesser amount of fear be present following the response than preceding it. This state of affairs can be achieved by the termination of fear-eliciting stimuli or by the introduction of new stimuli, such as feedback stimuli or safety signals, following the response. It should be recognized that even when theorists characterize reinforcement in aversive instrumental learning as the attainment of a safety signal, a reduction of fear is inevitably implicated.

To account for certain complex phenomena obtained in aversively motivated learning situations, such as the negative contrast effect, some elaboration of fear theory that includes the anticipation of reinforcement (fear reduction/relaxation) is required. Therefore, it was proposed that the concepts of incentive motivation and frustration be employed in the aversive case in a manner analogous to their use in the appetitive case.

ACKNOWLEDGMENT

The authors thank Edward J. Callen for helpful comments on an earlier draft of this manuscript.

REFERENCES

Amsel, A. (1958). The role of frustrative nonreward in noncontinuous reward situations. *Psychological Bulletin, 55,* 102–119.

Bandura, A. (1986). Fearful expectations and avoidant actions as coeffects of perceived self-inefficacy. *American Psychologist, 41,* 1389–1391.

Bloom, J. M., & Campbell, B. A. (1966). Effects of CS omission following avoidance learning. *Journal of Experimental Psychology, 72,* 36–39.

Bolles, R. C. (1970). Species-specific defense reactions and avoidance learning. *Psychological Review, 77,* 32–48.

Bolles, R. C. (1972a). The avoidance learning problem. In G. H. Bower (Ed.), *The psychology of learning and motivation* (Vol. 6, pp. 97–145). New York: Academic Press.

Bolles, R. C. (1972b). Reinforcement, expectancy, and learning. *Psychological Review, 79,* 394–409.

Bolles, R. C. (1975). *Theory of motivation* (2nd ed.). New York: Harper & Row.

Bower, G. H. (1961). A contrast effect in differential conditioning. *Journal of Experimental Psychology, 62,* 196–199.

Bower, G., Starr, R., & Lazarovitz, L. (1965). Amount of response-produced change in the CS and avoidance learning. *Journal of Comparative and Physiological Psychology, 59,* 13–17.

Boyd, T. L., & Levis, D. J. (1979). The interactive effects of shuttlebox situational cues and shock intensity. *American Journal of Psychology, 92,* 125–132.

Brush, F. R. (1957). The effects of shock intensity on the acquisition and extinction of an avoidance response in dogs. *Journal of Comparative and Physiological Psychology, 50,* 547–552.

Brush, F. R., Brush, E. S., & Solomon, R. L. (1955). Traumatic avoidance learning: The effects of CS–US interval with a delayed-conditioning procedure. *Journal of Comparative and Physiological Psychology, 48,* 285–293.

Callen, E. J. (1986). Fear of the CS and of the context in two-way avoidance learning: Between- and within-subjects manipulations. *Animal Learning & Behavior, 14,* 80–89.

Callen, E. J., McAllister, W. R., & McAllister, D. E. (1983, May). *Fear of contextual cues determines the effects of feedback stimuli.* Paper presented at the meeting of the Midwestern Psychological Association, Chicago.

Callen, E. J., McAllister, W. R., & McAllister, D. E. (1984). Investigations of the reinstatement of extinguished fear. *Learning and Motivation, 15,* 302–320.

Cook, M., Mineka, S., & Trumble, D. (1987). The role of response-produced and exteroceptive feedback in the attenuation of fear over the course of avoidance learning. *Journal of Experimental Psychology: Animal Behavior Processes, 13,* 239–249.

Daly, H. B. (1969). Learning of a hurdle-jump response to escape cues paired with reduced reward or frustrative nonreward. *Journal of Experimental Psychology, 79,* 146–157.

Daly, H. B., & Daly, J. T. (1987). A computer simulation/mathematical model of learning: Extension of DMOD from appetitive to aversive situations. *Behavior Research Methods, Instruments, & Computers, 19,* 108–112.

D'Amato, M. R. (1970). *Experimental psychology: Methodology, psychophysics, and learning.* New York: McGraw–Hill.

Denny, M. R. (1971). Relaxation theory and experiments. In F. R. Brush (Ed.), *Aversive conditioning and learning* (pp. 235–295). New York: Academic Press.

Denny, M. R., & Adelman, H. M. (1955). Elicitation theory: I. An analysis of two typical learning situations. *Psychological Review, 62*, 290–296.

Dieter, S. E. (1977). Preexposure to situational cues and shock intensity in two-way avoidance learning. *Animal Learning & Behavior, 5*, 403–406.

Dolan, J. C., Shishimi, A., & Wagner, A. R. (1985). The effects of signaling the US in backward conditioning: A shift from excitatory to inhibitory learning. *Animal Learning & Behavior, 13*, 209–214.

Domjan, M., & Burkhard, B. (1986). *The principles of learning & behavior* (2nd ed.). Monterey, CA: Brooks/Cole.

Feldman, M. A. (1977). The effects of preexposure to a warning or a safety signal on the acquisition of a two-way avoidance response in rats. *Animal Learning & Behavior, 5*, 21–24.

Gray, J. A. (1971). *The psychology of fear and stress*. New York: McGraw–Hill.

Gray, J. A. (1975). *Elements of a two-process theory of learning*. New York: Academic Press.

Gray, J. A. (1987). *The psychology of fear and stress* (2nd ed.). New York: Cambridge University Press.

Grelle, M. J., & James, J. H. (1981). Conditioned inhibition of fear: Evidence for a competing response mechanism. *Learning and Motivation, 12*, 300–320.

Hampton, S. R. (1981). Relationship between preexposure treatments and shock intensity in two-way avoidance learning (Doctoral dissertation, Northern Illinois University, 1980). *Dissertation Abstracts International, 41*, 4718B.

Herrnstein, R. J. (1969). Method and theory in the study of avoidance. *Psychological Review, 76*, 49–69.

Kamin, L. J. (1954). Traumatic avoidance learning: The effects of CS–US interval with a trace-conditioning procedure. *Journal of Comparative and Physiological Psychology, 47*, 65–72.

Kamin, L. J., Brimer, C. J., & Black, A. H. (1963). Conditioned suppression as a monitor of fear of the CS in the course of avoidance training. *Journal of Comparative and Physiological Psychology, 56*, 497–501.

Kruger, B. M., Galvani, P. F., & Brown, J. S. (1969). A comparison of simulated one-way and shuttle avoidance in an automated apparatus. *Behavior Research Methods and Instrumentation, 1*, 143–147.

Lawler, E. E., III. (1965). Secondary reinforcement value of stimuli associated with shock reduction. *Quarterly Journal of Experimental Psychology, 17*, 57–62.

Levis, D. J. (1979). The infrahuman avoidance model of symptom maintenance and implosive therapy. In J. D. Keehn (Ed.), *Psychopathology in animals: Research and clinical implications* (pp. 257–277). New York: Academic Press.

Levis, D. J. (1989). The case for a return to a two-factor theory of avoidance: The failure of non-fear interpretations. In S. B. Klein & R. R. Mowrer (Eds.), *Contemporary learning theories: Pavlovian conditioning and the status of traditional learning theory* (pp. 227–277). Hillsdale, NJ: Lawrence Erlbaum Associates.

Levis, D. J., & Boyd, T. L. (1979). Symptom maintenance: An infrahuman analysis and extension of the conservation of anxiety principle. *Journal of Abnormal Psychology, 88*, 107–120.

LoLordo, V. M. (1969). Positive conditioned reinforcement from aversive situations. *Psychological Bulletin, 72*, 193–203.

Mackintosh, N. J. (1974). *The psychology of animal learning*. New York: Academic Press.

McAllister, D. E., McAllister, W. R., Brooks, C. I., & Goldman, J. A. (1972). Magnitude and shift of reward in instrumental aversive learning in rats. *Journal of Comparative and Physiological Psychology, 80*, 490–501.

McAllister, D. E., McAllister, W. R., & Dieter, S. E. (1976). Reward magnitude and shock variables (continuity and intensity) in shuttlebox-avoidance learning. *Animal Learning & Behavior, 4,* 204–209.

McAllister, D. E., McAllister, W. R., Hampton, S. R., & Scoles, M. T. (1980). Escape-from-fear performance as affected by handling method and an additional CS-shock treatment. *Animal Learning & Behavior, 8,* 417–423.

McAllister, D. E., McAllister, W. R., & Zellner, D. K. (1966). Preference for familiar stimuli in the rat. *Psychological Reports, 19,* 868–870.

McAllister, W. R., & McAllister, D. E. (1962). Role of the CS and of apparatus cues in the measurement of acquired fear. *Psychological Reports, 11,* 749–756.

McAllister, W. R., & McAllister, D. E. (1965). Variables influencing the conditioning and the measurement of acquired fear. In W. F. Prokasy (Ed.), *Classical conditioning: A symposium* (pp. 172–191). New York: Appleton–Century–Crofts.

McAllister, W. R., & McAllister, D. E. (1967). Drive and reward in aversive learning. *American Journal of Psychology, 80,* 377–383.

McAllister, W. R., & McAllister, D. E. (1971). Behavioral measurement of conditioned fear. In F. R. Brush (Ed.), *Aversive conditioning and learning* (pp. 105–179). New York: Academic Press.

McAllister, W. R., & McAllister, D. E. (1988). Reconditioning of extinguished fear after a one-year delay. *Bulletin of the Psychonomic Society, 26,* 463–466.

McAllister, W. R., McAllister, D. E., & Benton, M. M. (1983). Measurement of fear of the conditioned stimulus and of situational cues at several stages of two-way avoidance learning. *Learning and Motivation, 14,* 92–106.

McAllister, W. R., McAllister, D. E., Dieter, S. E., & James, J. H. (1979). Preexposure to situational cues produces a direct relationship between two-way avoidance learning and shock intensity. *Animal Learning & Behavior, 7,* 165–173.

McAllister, W. R., McAllister, D. E., & Douglass, W. K. (1971). The inverse relationship between shock intensity and shuttle-box avoidance learning in rats: A reinforcement explanation. *Journal of Comparative and Physiological Psychology, 74,* 426–433.

McAllister, W. R., McAllister, D. E., Scoles, M. T., & Hampton, S. R. (1986). Persistence of fear-reducing behavior: Relevance for the conditioning theory of neurosis. *Journal of Abnormal Psychology, 95,* 365–372.

McAllister, W. R., McAllister, D. E., Scoles, M. T., & James, J. H. (1978, November). *The influence of prior fear conditioning on avoidance performance.* Paper presented at the meeting of the Psychonomic Society, San Antonio, TX.

Mellitz, M., Hineline, P. N., Whitehouse, W. G., & Laurence, M. T. (1983). Duration-reduction of avoidance sessions as negative reinforcement. *Journal of the Experimental Analysis of Behavior, 40,* 57–67.

Miller, N. E. (1948). Studies of fear as an acquirable drive: I. Fear as motivation and fear-reduction as reinforcement in the learning of new responses. *Journal of Experimental Psychology, 38,* 89–101.

Miller, N. E. (1951). Learnable drives and rewards. In S. S. Stevens (Ed.), *Handbook of experimental psychology* (pp. 435–472). New York: Wiley.

Miller, N. E. (1985). Theoretical models relating animal experiments on fear to clinical phenomena. In A. H. Tuma & J. Maser (Eds.), *Anxiety and the anxiety disorders* (pp. 261–272). Hillsdale, NJ: Lawrence Erlbaum Associates.

Miller, N. E., & Dollard, J. (1941). *Social learning and imitation.* New Haven, CT: Yale University Press.

Mineka, S., & Gino, A. (1980). Dissociation between conditioned emotional response and extended avoidance performance. *Learning and Motivation, 11,* 476–502.

Modaresi, H. A. (1975). One-way characteristic performance of rats under two-way signaled avoidance conditions. *Learning and Motivation, 6,* 484–497.

Morris, R. G. M. (1974). Pavlovian conditioned inhibition of fear during shuttlebox avoidance behavior. *Learning and Motivation, 5,* 424–447.

Morris, R. G. M. (1975). Preconditioning of reinforcing properties to an exteroceptive feedback stimulus. *Learning and Motivation, 6,* 289–298.

Mowrer, O. H. (1939). A stimulus-response analysis of anxiety and its role as a reinforcing agent. *Psychological Review, 46,* 553–565.

Mowrer, O. H. (1940). Anxiety-reduction and learning. *Journal of Experimental Psychology, 27,* 497–516.

Mowrer, O. H. (1947). On the dual nature of learning—A re-interpretation of "conditioning" and "problem-solving." *Harvard Educational Review, 17,* 102–148.

Mowrer, O. H. (1960). *Learning theory and behavior.* New York: Wiley.

Mowrer, O. H., & Lamoreaux, R. R. (1951). Conditioning and conditionality (discrimination). *Psychological Review, 58,* 196–212.

Newmark, J. A., & Capaldi, E. J. (1972, May). *Reward schedule effects in the extinction of an escape from fear reaction.* Paper presented at the meeting of the Midwestern Psychological Association, Cleveland.

Quartermain, D., & Judge, M. E. (1983). Retrieval enhancement in mice by pretest amphetamine injection after a long retention interval. *Physiological Psychology, 11,* 166–172.

Rachman, S., & Hodgson, R. (1974). I. Synchrony and desynchrony in fear and avoidance. *Behavior Research and Therapy, 12,* 311–318.

Rescorla, R. A., & LoLordo, V. M. (1965). Inhibition of avoidance behavior. *Journal of Comparative and Physiological Psychology, 59,* 406–412.

Rescorla, R. A., & Solomon, R. L. (1967). Two-process learning theory: Relationships between Pavlovian conditioning and instrumental learning. *Psychological Review, 74,* 151–182.

Schwartz, B. (1989). *Psychology of learning and behavior* (3rd ed.). New York: Norton.

Scoles, M. T. (1983). An extension of effective reinforcement theory to unsignaled two-way avoidance (Doctoral dissertation, Northern Illinois University, 1982). *Dissertation Abstracts International, 44,* 349B.

Seligman, M. E. P., & Johnston, J. C. (1973). A cognitive theory of avoidance learning. In F. J. McGuigan & D. B. Lumsden (Eds.), *Contemporary approaches to conditioning and learning* (pp. 69–110). New York: Wiley.

Solomon, R. L., Kamin, L. J., & Wynne, L. C. (1953). Traumatic avoidance learning: The outcomes of several extinction procedures with dogs. *Journal of Abnormal and Social Psychology, 48,* 291–302.

Solomon, R. L., & Wynne, L. C. (1953). Traumatic avoidance learning: Acquisition in normal dogs. *Psychological Monographs: General and Applied, 67* (4, Whole No. 354).

Solomon, R. L., & Wynne, L. C. (1954). Traumatic avoidance learning: The principles of anxiety conservation and partial irreversibility. *Psychological Review, 61,* 353–385.

Soltysik, S. S., Wolfe, G. E., Nicholas, T., Wilson, W. J., & Garcia–Sanchez, J. L. (1983). Blocking of inhibitory conditioning within a serial conditioned stimulus-conditioned inhibitor compound: Maintenance of acquired behavior without an unconditioned stimulus. *Learning and Motivation, 14,* 1–29.

Spear, N. E., Hamberg, J. M., & Bryan, R. (1980). Forgetting of recently acquired or recently reactivated memories. *Learning and Motivation, 11,* 456–475.

Starr, M. D., & Mineka, S. (1977). Determinants of fear over the course of avoidance learning. *Learning and Motivation, 8,* 332–350.

Thomson, K. S. (1988). Anatomy of the extinction debate. *American Scientist, 76,* 59–61.

Weisman, R. G., & Litner, J. S. (1972). The role of Pavlovian events in avoidance training. In R. A. Boakes & M. S. Halliday (Eds.), *Inhibition and learning* (pp. 253–270). New York: Academic Press.

Woods, P. J. (1967). Performance changes in escape conditioning following shifts in the magnitude of reinforcement. *Journal of Experimental Psychology, 75,* 487–491.

Zerbolio, D. J., Jr. (1968). Escape and approach responses in avoidance learning. *Canadian Journal of Psychology, 22,* 60–71.

5 Value of Mathematical Modeling of Appetitive and Aversive Learning: Review and Extensions of DMOD

Helen B. Daly and John T. Daly
State University of New York College at Oswego

> "*The information-processing approach and its partial successors in artificial intelligence have made increasingly heavy demands on psychological theory to become more precise, less ambiguous, and better testable. The computational paradigm has forced us to say what we mean exactly"*
> —*(Mandler, 1980, p. 242)*

There are many theories of appetitive learning and many theories of aversive learning, but far fewer theories that try to account for the similarities and differences of both appetitive and aversive learning situations. There are also many verbal theories of learning, but far fewer mathematical or computer simulation models. Does the complexity of most current learning theories require modeling? We believe yes, and will review a mathematical model of both appetitive and aversive learning. It is called DMOD (Daly Modification of the Rescorla and Wagner model; Daly & Daly, 1982, 1984, 1987), and it incorporates many of the assumptions of earlier verbal and mathematical theories. One basic assumption is made: learning is incremental. The same equation is used to calculate the strength of approach and avoidance behavior. What makes DMOD more successful than its predecessors (e.g., Bush & Mosteller, 1955; Rescorla & Wagner, 1972) is that the important goal events are not only the presence of the event (e.g., food or electric shock), but also their subsequent absence and reintroduction. Even though the model is simple because it assumes that learning of each goal event is linear, its implementation with varying goal events gives it some of the power of a nonlinear model.

The title of this book is *Fear, Avoidance, and Phobias*. Is it proper to discuss appetitive learning in a book on aversive events? Research will be reviewed that demonstrates that organisms react to the unexpected omission of a positive reward in the same way they react to painful shock. There also appear to be positive events in aversive learning. The aversive/appetitive distinction seems to refer more to the original goal event that took place, rather than to what happens when they are omitted. DMOD is able to integrate all these results by assuming there are both positive and negative events in both appetitive and aversive learning.

VALUE OF COMPUTER SIMULATION AND MATHEMATICAL MODELS

Computer simulation and mathematical models serve the same function as verbal theories: integration of existing data and prediction of new results. There are, however, those who feel that "if an explanation cannot be framed in a formal way, then it is not clear" (Staddon, 1983, p. 322). As disciplines mature, and develop a large data base, they turn from verbal to mathematical and computer simulation models, because of the advantages implied in the opening quotation. We will review some of them. (1) *Computer simulation models force specification of all assumptions*, because a computer program will not execute if the programmer has failed to incorporate explicitly even the smallest detail. Implicit assumptions are frequently revealed when converting a verbal into a mathematical or computer simulation model. (2) *Computer simulation models allow one to test the importance of assumptions*, because one can easily change an assumption by modifying the input to the program and seeing the effect of the outcome. (3) *Computer simulation models prevent one from overlooking assumptions* when deriving predictions from the model, because all the assumptions are explicitly coded in the computer program. It is therefore easier to use the models correctly and consistently. (4) *Computer simulation models allow one, without mathematical sophistication, to make predictions easily*. One only has to learn how to provide the input to the program. (5) *Computer simulation models aid in logical deduction and allow one to make complex and counterintuitive predictions*, because one does not have to rely on one's logic, reasoning ability, and intuition. This is especially important when a theory has many interacting processes, or when there are several steps in the derivation of a prediction. Interaction effects can also be predicted by simulating several levels of different variables. (6) *Computer simulations give an understanding of the interplay among elements of the model*. One can determine which elements in the model are the primary bases for a prediction. As we watch the growth of appetitive and aversive learning, the active interplay between them can be seen, and elements in DMOD appear to come alive. (7) *Computer simulation models are archives for collected knowledge*, when they are able to simulate a large number of behavioral phenomena. The program can be used to pass on the knowledge of which variables influence which phenomena. They can be used as teaching tools for high school and college students (see Steinhauer's, 1986, application of DMOD), as well as for scientists from related fields. (8) *Mathematical and computer simulation models avoid disagreements over language*, since predictions are independent of the verbal labels one may assign the parameters and variables. (9) *Mathematical models make it easier to communicate with and transfer knowledge to other fields*, because mathematics is considered a universal language and many other fields use mathematical models and computer simulation techniques. (10) *Mathematical models can show similarity between verbal theories*, in cases where they appear to be extremely different. Even if they are mathematically different, they can make many similar predictions. For example, the linear operator and all-or-none models are based on different verbal assumptions, yet mathematical derivations show that they make many similar predictions (Atkinson, Bower, & Crothers, 1965). Herrnstein (1979) put the matching law on a discrete-trial basis, which makes it possible to determine more easily the similarities and differences between it and the linear-operator model of Rescorla and Wagner (1972).

We believe that the area of appetitive and aversive learning is ready to return to mathematical models and develop further computer simulation models. The field now has a huge data base. There is also easy access to sophisticated computers that were not available to learning theorists when they began mathematical modeling in the 1940s and 1950s.

SOME ISSUES IN MATHEMATICAL AND COMPUTER SIMULATION MODELING

The Delta Rule

The delta rule assumes that learning is driven by differences between amount learned and the value of the goal event. This rule has been applied in different forms to different types and levels of learning.

Starting with the assumption that behavior is probability based, Bush and Mosteller (1951) formulated the delta rule as the change in the probability p (delta p) of a response during conditioning and extinction: $\Delta p = a(1 - p) - bp$ (the gain-loss form). This form emphasizes the change in p as a difference between 1 and p when p increments on rewarded trials, $a(1 - p)$. The smaller the p value, the greater the change in p. On nonrewarded trials p decrements. To preserve the probability interpretation, a and b are constrained to lie between 0 and 1. Predictions are derived by using techniques from the calculus, and are evaluated by comparing the mathematically derived predictions for expected values of various random variables with their statistical analogues calculated directly from the experimental data.

Rescorla and Wagner (1972) use the delta rule in a deterministic model. They replaced response probability, p, with V, the strength of the association: $\Delta V = \alpha\beta(\lambda - \overline{V})$. Asymptote is not fixed at 1, as in the Bush and Mosteller probability-based model, but can be any value, and is called lambda (λ). The larger the difference between λ and $\overline{V}$, the greater the change in V. The probability constraints on the coefficients are replaced by constraints needed to have convergent asymptotic solutions, namely, $0 \leq \alpha, \beta \leq 1$. They also assume that delta V is calculated for each cue by the difference between λ and the associative strength to *all* cues present on that trial ($\overline{V} = Va + Vx$, if cues a and x are present), and different cues can have different saliences (the alpha, α, level). V values are also allowed to become negative. Different beta (β) values (learning rates) are used for rewarded and nonrewarded trials, with the beta value used on rewarded trials assumed to be greater than the beta value on nonrewarded trials.

The introduction of the Rescorla and Wagner model coincided with the general availability of high-speed computers. Implemented as part of a computer program, trial-by-trial and asymptotic predictions in complex experimental designs involving multiple cues, changes in the number of cues present, and shifts from rewarded to nonrewarded trials, can be tested against experimental results.

The least-means-square (LMS) or Widrow–Hoff version of the delta rule (which is essentially equivalent to the Rescorla and Wagner form; see Sutton & Barto, 1981), is currently being incorporated into adaptive network or "connectionist" models, as a simple learning mechanism. The LMS rule is often used as a benchmark mechanism in contrast to other rules, and is done in both one-layer networks (e.g., Gluck & Bower, 1988), and in more complicated multilayer networks (see Rumelhart & Mc-Clelland, 1986). These network models are being applied to account for complex human learning, and for behavior at the neural substrate level (Gluck & Thompson, 1987). See also the special edition of the series, The Psychology of Learning and Motivation, called *Computational Models of Learning in Simple Neural Systems* (Hawkins & Bower, 1989).

Computer Simulations

At the simplest level, the computer provides a flexible and powerful calculating device which permits formula-based models to be extended numerically to complex psychological situations. At a more sophisticated level their ability to manipulate symbolic information and abstract data structures is increasingly being exploited.

Ordinal Predictions

The goal of a mathematical model is to make precise predictions about behavior. To be able to do this each parameter must be scaled to actual values used in a given experiment, e.g., grams of food and the λ value. Parameter values can be estimated from the data. For example, in the one-element model, one parameter was estimated from the total number of errors, and all other predictions used this value (Atkinson et al., 1965). Another approach is to use data from simple experimental situations to scale each parameter in the equation, and then use these fixed values when simulating all other simple and complex experimental situations run under identical conditions (e.g., same reward value, cue salience, drive level). The scaling work has not yet been done for many models, and they are therefore restricted to making ordinal predictions: They predict the ordering of the groups rather than precise differences between the groups. The success of these models is most readily seen by predicting the correct ordering of groups, groups by trials interaction effects, and within-groups reversals in performance across trials. Their success is not measured by curve-fitting techniques. This type of model has been called quasi-quantitative, as opposed to specific-quantitative (Hilgard & Bower, 1975), and is used to "explain correct general trends of the empirical function" (p. 377).

Although eventually all models should make precise predictions about behavior, many times the fit between a simulation and the data is not high because the data are unreliable: Too few subjects may have been run, or there may not have been enough control over extraneous variables. Specific-quantitative models may be premature, because few psychological laboratories have developed enough control over the experimental situation to be able to repeat between experiments the exact values of groups run under "identical" conditions, although the relative ordering of the groups is replicated.

Breadth and Depth

Any type of theory can attempt integration and prediction in one small area of research, or attempt breadth to encompass as many different learning phenomena as possible. Historically the field of animal learning has had both types. Models with breadth, however, help integrate and preserve access to our large data base; disparate facts tend to get lost. Other areas of psychology, such as behavior modification and neuropsychology, need to draw on this integrated data base. We believe it is time to combine into one model the best of all existing models in the area of appetitive and aversive learning, with the flexibility to modify it as new results require.

We will review DMOD, a model that we developed to account for and predict trial-by-trial changes in behavior and asymptotic performance in discrete-trial appetitive learning paradigms. We subsequently extended DMOD to aversive learning paradigms, as well as learning in simple free-operant appetitive experiments. A summary of the phenomena successfully simulated appears in the Appendix. This model is based on the Rescorla and Wagner (1972) version of the linear-operator model, Amsel's frustration theory (1958, 1962) in the appetitive case, McAllister's version of fear theory (effective reinforcement theory, McAllister, McAllister, & Douglass, 1971), and Denny's relaxation theory (e.g., Denny, 1971), in the aversive case. These are successful and highly referenced theories, with ever-widening application.[1] DMOD's similarity with other theories will also be recognized by those familiar with theories of learning.

REVIEW OF DMOD

Basic Assumptions

If you wanted to know how far a football would be kicked you would have to know about the strength of the leg doing the kicking, the wind speed, the wind direction, and so forth. You would also have to know how these input variables combine to determine the distance. If you wanted to know how fast one can learn, you would have to know the size of the goal event, the rate of learning, the intensity of the stimuli, and how these imput variables combine to determine learning. We believe that there is substantial psychological and physiological evidence to conclude that simple learning is an incremental process, and we use the Rescorla–Wagner version of the linear-operator model to calculate amount of learning in both appetitive and aversive learning situations:

$$\Delta V = \alpha\beta(\lambda - \overline{V}).$$

ΔV is the change in associative strength on a given trial, and $\overline{V}$ is the total associative strength conditioned to all stimuli present. The three parameters are: alpha (α), the salience of the stimulus; beta (β), the learning rate parameter; and lambda (λ), the size of the goal event, which differs for

---

[1] The Rescorla and Wagner model is being used successfully in both cognitive psychology (Gluck & Bower, 1988), and neuropsychology (Gluck & Thompson, 1987). Frustration theory is currently used to account for the ontogeny of reward effects and effects of hippocampal lesions and fetal alcohol in rat pups (Amsel, 1986).

each type of goal event. We assume that three important goal events are possible in the appetitive case: (1) food, which conditions approach (Vap), (2) omission of food when Vap is conditioned, which conditions avoidance (Vav), and (3) reintroduction of food when Vav is conditioned, which results in counterconditioning (Vcc). We likewise assume that three important goal events are possible in the aversive case: (1) shock, which conditions avoidance (Vav*), (2) omission of shock when Vav* is conditioned, which conditions approach (Vap*), and (3) reintroduction of shock when Vap* is conditioned, which results in "reverse" counterconditioning (Vcc*).

In simple appetitive experiments only Vap is conditioned, in simple aversive experiments only Vav* is conditioned, and DMOD is essentially equivalent to the Rescorla and Wagner (1972) model. A huge body of literature can be accounted for by these two V values (see Rescorla & Wagner, 1972; Wagner & Rescorla, 1972). Where the Rescorla–Wagner model fails is where DMOD has achieved success, and is typically when the goal event is unexpectedly omitted. This unexpected omission is when Vav or Vap* are conditioned. These V values allow the model to account for an even larger range of results without losing the ability to simulate any of the phenomena the Rescorla and Wagner model can (Daly & Daly, 1982, 1987). The model only gains further complexity if the goal event is reintroduced, and Vcc or Vcc* are conditioned. In the appetitive case there can be three V values: Vap (+), Vav (−), and Vcc (+), and in the aversive case there can also be three V values: Vav* (−), Vap* (+), and Vcc* (−). An * is used to differentiate the appetitively-based V gradients from the aversively based V gradients.

There are both similarities and differences between the appetitive and aversive versions of DMOD. They are similar because they both use the same learning equation and assume three possible goal events: the presence, subsequent absence, and reintroduction of the original goal event. The big difference is in the number of positive and negative V values. In the appetitive case there are two positive (+) values and one negative (−) value, and in the aversive case there are two negative values and one positive value. (For those who prefer symmetrical models, note that the complete version of the model has three positive and three negative values.)

A few additional assumptions are needed to implement the model:

1. Lambda Formulas.   The lambda (λ) values differ for each of the six V gradients. They are summarized in Table 5.1. In the appetitive case, the λ value for Vap is determined by the magnitude of the food reward. The λ value for Vav is determined by the discrepancy between the obtained goal event (usually its absence or 0) and the size of the expected goal event ($\overline{V}$ap), which is $(0 - \overline{V}\text{ap})$. Vav is therefore a negative number, and the larger the negative number the greater the amount of conditioned aver-

TABLE 5.1
λ Values for the 6 Goal Events

Goal Event:	Present	Omitted	Reintroduced
Appetitive Learning	Vap (+) e.g., grams of food	Vav (−) 2(0-$\overline{\text{V}}$ap)	Vcc (+) (0-$\overline{\text{V}}$av)
Aversive Learning	Vav* (−) e.g., intensity/dura- tion of shock	Vap* (+) (0-$\overline{\text{V}}$av*)	Vcc* (−) 2(0-$\overline{\text{V}}$ap*)

siveness. Since research has shown that a loss is more important to an individual than an equivalent gain (see Kahneman & Tversky, 1982), we assume that the λ value for Vav is larger than the simple discrepancy between the expected and obtained values (currently multiplied by 2). By inserting this λ value into the basic ΔV formula, the formula to calculate conditioning of Vav is: ΔVav $= \alpha\beta[2(0 - \overline{\text{V}}\text{ap}) - \overline{\text{V}}\text{av}]$. The λ value for Vcc is the discrepancy between the obtained and expected values for $\overline{\text{V}}$av, which is $(0 - \overline{\text{V}}\text{av})$. The first term is 0, because on a rewarded trial no aversiveness is aroused. In the aversive case, the λ value for Vav* is the magnitude of the shock. The discrepancy between the obtained goal event and the size of the expected goal event determine the λ values for Vap* and Vcc*, which are therefore $(0 - \overline{\text{V}}\text{av*})$ for Vap*, and $(0 - \overline{\text{V}}\text{ap*})$ for Vcc*. In keeping with the assumption that aversive events are more important, the λ value for Vcc* is also multiplied by 2. The λ value is 0 when the goal event for any of the V values is absent, and the V value declines in absolute value (e.g., Vap declines when food is absent, ΔVap $= \alpha\beta[0 - \overline{\text{V}}\text{ap}]$). The exact equations can be found in Daly and Daly (1987).

2. λ Value: Secondary Reinforcement (Second-order Conditioning). Stimuli paired with a primary reinforcer (food or shock) can be used to retard extinction or learn new behaviors, and are called secondary reinforcers. To simulate this type of experiment we use the same equation to condition V values, except the λ value is the V value of the secondary reinforcing cue. For example, if Vn is a white noise, and Vc is a click, and the noise was originally paired with food and now the click precedes the presentation of the noise, ΔVc $= \alpha\beta(\text{Vn} - \text{Vc})$. See Daly and Daly (1982, p. 465) for additional details.

3. Incremental versus Decremental Learning Rates. It is assumed that the rate of learning is higher than the rate of unlearning (see Rescorla & Wagner, 1972). Therefore, whenever V values are incremented in absolute value, an increment beta is used (β_I), and whenever V values are decremented, a decrement beta is used (β_D), and $\beta_I > \beta_D$. The increment beta is assumed to reflect the vigor of the goal event, and is therefore determined by the hunger drive level in experiments where a food reward is given, and by the shock intensity in experiments where shocks are given. Certain drugs are assumed to influence β_1 for Vav and Vav*, the learning rate parameter for aversive V values (e.g., alcohol).

4. Total V Value.   Behavior is assumed to be determined by the sum or total value (Vt) of all the V values conditioned:

$$Vt = \overline{V}ap + \overline{V}av + \overline{V}cc \text{ and } Vt^* = \overline{V}av^* + \overline{V}ap^* + \overline{V}cc^*.$$

These are the values used when the organism is close to the goal. Due to previous research (Brown, 1948), a spatial generalization decrement is assumed for aversive gradients only, and Vav, Vav*, and Vcc* are decremented as a function of the distance from the goal (e.g., in a 5-foot runway Vav is at half strength at the start measure, at three-quarters strength in the runway section, and at full strength at the goal). Vav and Vcc* must reach a threshold value (.12) to influence Vt and Vt*. When both food rewards and shocks are given in the same experiment, the simplest assumption possible to predict total (Vtt) behavior is currently being made: Vtt = Vt + Vt*.

5. Inhibition ($-Vap$) and Vav.   Under certain experimental conditions the approach V values can become negative, and the avoidance values (which are normally negative numbers) can become positive. These values are assumed to reflect inhibition within the framework of the Rescorla and Wagner model (Wagner & Rescorla, 1972). We assume that this type of inhibition is what has been called passive inhibition (Terrace, 1972), and that a negative Vap value ($-Vap$) passively inhibits an approach response by subtracting from $+Vap$ conditioned to other stimuli. Its value can only be measured indirectly through summation and retardation tests (e.g., Hearst, 1972; Rescorla, 1969).[2] Vav, which is also a negative number, is not passive inhibition. Vav is an excitatory tendency with a negative value (Amsel, 1972), and makes the organism actively escape from the stimuli (Daly, 1969a, 1969b, 1969c, 1974). Empirical evidence supports DMOD simulations that show that $-Vap$ is maximum after extended discrimination training, but Vav is conditioned and then decreases (becomes less negative) with continued extended discrimination training (Daly & Daly, 1982, p. 461).

---

[2] $-Vap$ is dependent on the prior conditioning of $+Vap$, and therefore it is not surprising that the elimination of $-Vap$ is also dependent on the presence of $+Vap$ (see Zimmer–Hart & Rescorla, 1974: Rescorla, 1987). $-Vap$ is larger than $+Vap$ in absolute magnitude under restricted conditions, and does not occur in the experimental paradigms we have simulated with DMOD

6. Toward versus Away from Goal.   When extending DMOD to the aversive case (Daly & Daly, 1987), we assumed that all learning involves approach to a goal, and V values determine the strength of behavior toward that goal. In appetitive situations, the Vt value determines speed of approaching the goal. In punishment situations, Vt* and Vt values are added. In simple shock escape/avoidance experiments, subjects must also learn to approach a goal, the goal now being a place with less aversiveness. For example, if rats must learn to jump from the shock box to a safe box to either avoid or escape a shock, the cues associated with shock in the shock box have Vav* conditioned to them. The reduction in aversiveness experienced when the subject reaches the safe box is assumed to be the λ value to condition Vap*. On the first trial, the subject probably makes numerous types of responses, probably in some hierarchy of species-specific defense reactions and behavior learned in similar situations. As soon as a response is successful in reaching a less aversive place, approach (Vap*) is conditioned. On subsequent trials, the Vap* value determines the speed of approach to the safe box.

7. Scaling of Parameters.   Scaling of the parameters has not been done, and therefore DMOD is restricted to making ordinal predictions, as are all similar models (e.g., Rescorla & Wagner, 1972; SOP, Wagner, 1981). We, however, use *fixed values* for all simulations. Typically, $\alpha = 1$ for all cues, effectively removing this parameter from the equation, except for configural cues, where $\alpha = .2$; $\beta_I = .15$ if the rats are deprived to 80–85% of their ad lib. weight, $\beta_D = .05$; and λ for food is 1.0 for 12–15 Noyes pellets (.037–.045 mg each), .5 for 5 pellets, and .1 for 1 pellet.

Mapping of Vt (learning) into response strength (performance) has also not been done, and there is every reason to believe that it will be different for each experimental situation (see Rescorla & Wagner, 1972, p. 77).

An "Everyday" Example

The following example may help understand the type of situations we are attempting to simulate with DMOD. Pretend you are learning to use a candy machine. With repeated experiences of putting in money, pulling the lever, and obtaining the candy bar, Vap (approach) is conditioned. Once Vap is fairly large and you pull the lever and no candy appears (the candy machine is broken, a most unpleasant event), you have an aversive reaction that becomes conditioned (Vav, avoidance). You are then in a state of conflict, because both Vap and Vav are conditioned. Repeated nonreward trials increase Vav. If the candy machine suddenly works again, Vcc is conditioned (counterconditioning), and you approach and use the candy machine.

Now pretend that the candy machine always delivers candy, but also gives you an occasional electric shock (the candy machine is not properly grounded). On shock trials Vav* (avoidance) is conditioned, but if the shock does not occur once you expected to get shocked, Vap* (approach) is conditioned. You are now in a state of conflict. If you resolve the conflict and pull the lever expecting not to get a shock but you are shocked, Vcc* is conditioned ("reverse" counterconditioning), and you avoid the candy machine.

Naming V Values Gives Them No Additional Meaning

Application of DMOD to appetitive and aversive learning is simply in terms of the conditioned V values based on different goal events, and they are used to predict the strength of approach and avoidance responses. We have found, however, that it is sometimes easier to understand a mathematical model if the V values are given everyday common names. This is especially true if these names are similar to ones used in the psychological literature. We therefore frequently use the following words to communicate what the V values may refer to. In appetitive learning, when the reward (e.g., food) is given, Vap is conditioned, which may index reward expectancy or hope. When food is expected and does not occur, Vav is conditioned, which may index frustration or disappointment. If food suddenly occurs after repeated experiences of nonreward, Vcc is conditioned, and may index courage to approach aversive nonreward. In aversive learning, when a painful event occurs (e.g., shock), Vav* is conditioned, which may index fear or shock expectancy. When expectancy of shock is conditioned and does not occur, Vap* is conditioned, which may index relief, relaxation, or safety. If shock suddenly occurs after repeated nonshock experiences, Vcc* is conditioned, which may index cowardice. See any theories of learning text for theories that have used these terms (e.g., Amsel, Denny, Hull, McAllisters, Mowrer, Seligman, Spence).

Some people find these labels help their understanding of the model. *Naming V values does not give them extra meaning*, since predictions of the model are based entirely on the V values calculated when simulations are run on a computer. They should only be used if they help to understand the model. It is also possible to give them new names, especially if they enhance understanding of the model. These V values can take on new or old names, depending on the Zeitgeist (cognitive or conditioned expectancy, CS–US representation, neural trace, change in learning or information processed, surprise of the goal event, memory for a goal event, relief, relaxation, or safety value, etc.). In the spirit of radical behaviorism one would not name them. *Forget all names* if you find that they detract from your appreciation of DMOD.

Integration vs. Prediction: Selection of Phenomena to be Simulated

The first test of a model is to see how well it integrates existing data. Therefore, DMOD simulations were first done on well-established behavioral phenomena in appetitive and aversive learning. It is dangerous to develop a new model based on recently discovered phenomena, because the boundary conditions under which they can be obtained and the variables influencing them are unknown. Once a model integrates data successfully, then its predictions must be tested. We tested the predictive power of DMOD in complex learning situations; we tested variables which DMOD predicted should result in a preference for unpredictable rewards, and the effects of ingestion of Lake Ontario salmon (see later sections).

Type of Mathematical/Computer Simulation Model

The discrete-trial version of DMOD is a deterministic (nonprobability based model), numerical, computer simulation, model. Basic learning is assumed to be linear. There are, however, three linear difference equations in the appetitive case, one to calculate Vap, another to calculate Vav, and a third to calculate Vcc. There are also three in the aversive case, for Vav*, Vap*, and Vcc*. Because Vav is based on Vap, and Vcc is based on Vav, and behavior in appetitive learning is assumed to be the sum of the three V values, implementation of the model gives it the power to predict reversals in behavior across trials. DMOD is mathematically simple, involving simple difference equations, all based on the Rescorla–Wagner version of the delta rule. The requirement to do calculations for each cue present, and sum over all cues present, requires it to be implemented as a computer-based model. As implemented, the program does no hidden processing, either numerical or symbolic, on the input, and output is numerical. Because the model is not probabilistic, every simulation run, using identical inputs, results in the same output.

Computer Program Available

An easy to use, menu-based program, with an instruction manual, is available on request from the authors.[3] A series of questions must be answered: Do you want to simulate an appetitive or aversive discrete-trial or free-operant experiment, number of λ values, number of cues, number of trial types, the α, β_I, and β_D, and λ value, which cues are present on which

---

[3]The computer program, with an instruction manual, is available from the authors. It is written in C and will run on UNIX-based micro- and minicomputers, including VAXs and the AT&T UNIX PC, and under DOS (IBM PC/XT/AT) (to obtain a copy send $5.00, to cover disk and postage charges, to the authors, and specify machine type).

trial, and which λ value should be used. One can also simulate higher-order conditioning or secondary reinforcement. The individual V values, as well as their sum, are printed out for each cue on each trial. Since the Vap values in the appetitive case (Vav* in the aversive case) are the V values of the Rescorla–Wagner model (RWMOD), one can determine the differences in the predictions between DMOD and RWMOD.

APPLICATIONS OF DMOD

More than 60 basic learning phenomena have been simulated using DMOD. The primary ones are listed in the Appendix. Before reviewing several additional applications of the model, we will review evidence for aversiveness of nonreward in appetitive learning. All phenomena described have been successfully simulated by DMOD, and reports of the simulations have been published.

Aversiveness (Vav) in Appetitive Learning

Have you ever failed to obtain a candy bar from a candy machine? Was this a neutral experience? The last time I (first author) saw that happen to someone he kicked and then violently shook the machine. Have you ever had a manuscript turned down? Have you ever had a grant application approved with the promise of funding, but money unexpectedly ran out before they funded your grant? People report that these experiences are aversive.

How does one measure aversiveness? Researchers have given rats shocks, and measured different behaviors to determine how aversive the shock was. They measured how much the rats slow down in approach to the place where they were shocked (passive avoidance task), how fast they escape from the shock (escape and avoidance task), how much they suppress responding for food when the stimulus paired with shock is presented (conditioned emotional response, CER, task), and how quickly they learn to escape from the stimuli present during a prior shock phase (escape-from-fear task). The more intense the shock the greater the reaction in all these behavioral tasks (see textbooks in animal learning for references).

The same tasks have been used to measure the aversiveness of omission of a food reward, and all results indicate unpredictable nonreward is aversive. There are countless studies that show that rats rapidly decrease their speed in a runway in approach to a goal box where there is no longer a large food reward (extinction). Variables that enhance acquisition do not slow down extinction as one might expect, but speed it up (called paradoxical reward effects). These results are not paradoxical if one assumes that aversiveness of nonreward is greater, the larger the expectation for food, and that the greater aversiveness causes more avoidance of the goal (e.g., Amsel, 1958, 1962). For example, extinction is faster the larger the food reward in acquisition (magnitude of reward extinction effect). Extinction is also faster the larger the number of acquisition trials (overtraining extinction effect). The larger the number of discrimination acquisition trials (up to a point) the faster the reversal of the discrimination (overlearning reversal effect). An unexpected increase in the delay of reward also results in a rapid decrease in approach to the delayed reward. Shifting from a large to a small reward is also aversive, because subjects reduce their approach to the goal very quickly and run more slowly than a control group that had always been given the small reward (depression or successive negative contrast effect). The larger the difference between the large and small reward the bigger the depression effect. Subjects begin to run more quickly again after extended training with the small reward, indicating that once they have learned to adjust their expectancy to the new small reward, it is no longer aversive. Subjects given discrimination training between a large, versus small, reward run more slowly to the small reward than a control group given only the small reward (simultaneous negative contrast). If a drug known to decrease responses to aversive events is given (e.g., amobarbitol sodium), the depression effect does not occur (Rosen, Glass, & Ison, 1967; see textbooks in animal learning for references).

If rats are given rewards in both goal boxes of a double runway (a second runway is attached to the goal box of the first one), they will run more quickly away from the first goal box when rewards are omitted than a control group that never was given a reward in the first goal box (frustration effect, e.g., Amsel & Roussel, 1952; Daly, 1968; Wagner, 1959). This effect occurs if rewards were given on a continuous, partial reinforcement, or discrimination schedule. If a stimulus that had been paired with nonreward in the goal box during partial reinforcement training is presented earlier in the runway, rats will slow their approach to the goal, especially if large rewards were given (Amsel & Surridge, 1964). This is similar to CER experiments. Pigeons show withdrawal responses from a signal correlated with the absence of food (e.g., Hearst & Franklin, 1977), and rats jump out of the goal box of a runway during extinction training (e.g., Adelman & Maatsch, 1955). Subjects also show a number of "emotional" responses when reward is unexpectedly omitted: Rats urinate and bite the experimenter (personal experience), pigeons flap their wings (Terrace, 1972), and humans kick the candy machine.

Rats will also learn a new response to escape from the stimuli associated with aversive nonreward (escape-from-frustration task, patterned on the escape-from-fear hurdle-jump task, McAllister & McAllister, 1971). Subjects are given runway acquisition training, and a large reward is received in the goal box. Rewards are then omitted, and aversiveness of unexpected nonrewards is conditioned to the stimuli present in the goal box. Subjects are then placed directly into the nonreinforced goal box, a door over a hurdle is opened, and they are allowed to jump over the hurdle into a novel empty box. If the goal box of the runway is aversive, they should learn to jump quickly to the empty box to escape the aversiveness of the goal box where they had been given food rewards. Rats will learn to jump when nonreward was given after continuous reinforcement acquisition (Daly, 1969c), partial reinforcement acquisition (Daly, 1969a), or discrimination learning (Daly, 1971, 1972). The larger the reward in acquisition, the faster they jump from the nonreinforced goal box. Hurdle jumping is also acquired when they are given a small reward after experiencing a large reward on a continuous reinforcement schedule (Daly, 1969c), or on a varied reinforcement schedule (Daly, 1969a). They will also jump out (Daly, 1969b), or press a bar to be lifted out of a box (Daly & McCroskery, 1973), when an instrumental response to obtain food in the first phase was not required (see Daly, 1974, for a review).

The parallels between the results obtained with shock and nonreward are striking, which supports the conclusion that unexpected nonreward is aversive. The two sources of aversiveness also combine to increase the behavioral effects. In the appetitive situation, if rats are given extinction training (food is omitted) and are shocked in the goal box, they stop running more quickly than rats given only extinction training (Daly & Rosenberg, 1973). If a tone previously paired with shock is presented during escape-from-frustration training, they jump more quickly than if the tone and shock had been randomly paired (Daly, 1970). Aggression between two rats given shock is increased if they are also experiencing aversiveness due to nonreward during extinction (Tondat & Daly, 1972).

Reward must be expected and nonreward must be unpredictable for nonreward to be aversive. For example, rats never given a food reward during runway acquisition do not learn to jump to the novel box in the escape-from-frustration task (Daly, 1969c). The most striking instance of the unpredictability factor, however, occurs after extended discrimination training (Daly, 1974). Rats were given 60 runway discrimination trials (DR): 30 trials in a black runway and 30 trials in a white runway in random order, with a 15-pellet food reward in the goal box of one runway only. They then were placed into the goal box which had never contained food, and they learned to jump the hurdle to escape from that goal box to a neutral box, but rats given 240 runway discrimination trials did not show acquisition of the escape response (see earlier description of escape-from-frustration task). The speed of jumping the hurdle is shown in Fig. 5.1. This result was not due to additional experiences with nonreward, because rats given 240 runway trials on a partial reinforcement (PR) schedule (food present in both the black and white goal boxes on a random half of the trials) did acquire the escape response. These data, combined with several other results (see Daly & Daly, 1982, pp. 460–461), lend support to the

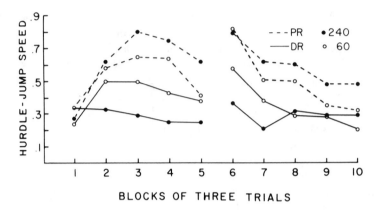

FIG. 5.1. Mean hurdle-jump speeds (1/seconds) to escape from the nonreinforced goal box of a runway to a neutral box, in blocks of three trials, for groups previously given runway discrimination (DR) or partial reinforcement (PR) training for either 60 or 240 trials (reprinted from Daly, 1974).

conclusion that following extended discrimination training, when nonreward is expected, it loses its aversiveness. Following extended partial reinforcement training, where nonreward is not predictable, nonreward remains aversive.

Based on the interpretation of the effects of extended discrimination and partial reinforcement training, one would expect subjects to choose the arm of a maze where reward and nonreward are predictable (a discrimination situation), rather than the arm of a maze where reward and nonreward are unpredictable (a partial reinforcement situation), because nonreward is less aversive on the predictable side. These types of experiments are called "observing response" experiments (e.g., Wyckoff, 1969), because under many conditions subjects make a response to observe the stimuli associated with reward and nonreward: they choose the discrimination side of the maze. If this choice is due to the aversiveness associated with nonreward on the unpredictable reward side and the lack of aversiveness on the predictable reward side, one should be able to measure the level of aversiveness, using the escape-from-frustration hurdle-jump task. Results showed that there is aversiveness only on the unpredictable reward side. Rats were given 240 training trials in a maze in the shape of an E. A choice to one side resulted in a black insert on a random half of the trials and a white insert on the other trials, and one color was associated with reward in the goal box, the other with nonreward (discrimination). The colors were not visible until after the choice was made, and a door closed behind the subject to prevent retracing. A choice to the other side resulted in the same black and white inserts, but they were both followed by reinforcement on half of the trials (partial reinforcement). The floor on the one side of the maze was made of wire mesh, and the floor on the other side was made of smooth metal. The discrimination side and reinforced color were counterbalanced across subjects.

All subjects acquired a strong preference for the predictable reward side. They were then placed into the E maze following the choice point, on either the mesh or smooth floor. The black and white inserts were not visible, and the goal box was blocked off. A door to a novel empty box was opened, and subjects could escape from the choice-point stimuli to the novel box by jumping over the hurdle. The results appear in Fig. 5.2. Only subjects placed in the presence of the floor texture associated with the unpredictable reward side (NON-OBS) learned to jump the hurdle to the novel box. Those given hurdle-jump training from the predictable reward side (OBS), and the control group that was never given food reward on any E maze trial, did not show increases in hurdle-jump speed. Speeds were clearly under the control of the floor texture, because switching the experimental subjects to the other floor texture reversed speeds. These results indicate that preference for the predictable reward side in the E maze is due to the aversiveness of the unpredictable side.

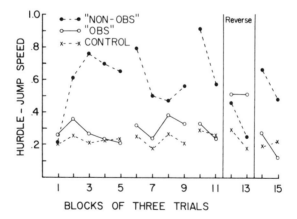

FIG. 5.2. Mean hurdle-jump speeds (1/seconds) to escape from the floor-texture stimuli at the choice-point in an E maze to a neutral box, following E maze training, where one choice resulted in stimuli correlated with reward outcome ("OBS" or discrimination side), and the other choice in stimuli uncorrelated with reward outcome ("NON-OBS" or partial reinforcement side). The control group was never given food reinforcement in any phase of the experiment. During the Reverse phase, subjects were given hurdle-jump training from the floor-texture associated with the other reward condition (reprinted from Daly, 1974).

FIG. 5.3. Percentage of
preference for the predictable
reward side (percent obs.
resp.) in blocks of 2 days (8
trials per day) during E-maze
training, for groups given a
large reward (15 pellets) or a
small reward (1 pellet); 50% is
chance responding (reprinted
from Daly, 1985).

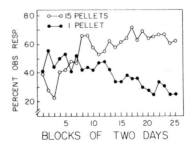

DMOD simulations show any variable that decreases the aversiveness of unpredictable nonreward should not only decrease the preference for predictable rewards, but also result in a preference for unpredictable rewards, due to a blocking phenomenon (see Daly, 1985, in press). Nonreward is not aversive when only a small reward is expected, when under the influence of alcohol, or when few nonrewarded trials are given (lenient reinforcement schedule). DMOD predicted that under these three conditions rats should prefer unpredictable rewards, if rewards are not delayed. No other theory of observing responses makes this prediction (see Daly, 1985, in press). Fig. 5.3 shows the effects of reward magnitude on preference for predictable rewards. Although both groups learned the discrimination on the predictable side, and all other conditions were equal, subjects given a large reward (15 pellets) developed a preference for the predictable reward side (OBS. RESP.), but subjects given a small reward (1 pellet) developed a preference for the unpredictable reward side (50% is chance, and a 25% preference for the predictable reward side is a 75% preference for the unpredictable reward side). The basis for DMOD's predictions is the large Vav value, conditioned by unpredictable nonreward when the large reward conditions a large Vap value. The large Vav value results in a lower Vt value on the unpredictable than the predictable reward side, and the subject chooses the predictable side. When a small reward is given, the Vav value is below threshold and does not counter the Vap value on the unpredictable reward side. The Vap value is small on the predictable side due to blocking (see Daly, 1985). Additional experiments showed that rats preferred unpredictable rewards when they were injected with alcohol, or when a lenient reinforcement schedule was used (Daly, 1989), which supported DMOD's predictions.

All results reviewed in this section have been successfully simulated, using the DMOD computer program. The success of the model in these situations is due to the amount of Vav conditioned when rewards are unexpectedly omitted, and its magnitude is larger the greater the Vap value (see Daly, in press, for a review).

DMOD Simulations

The following simulations were selected to demonstrate the value of computer simulation/mathematical models, and the types of experiments where the different V values are conditioned.

1. Chemicals that Increase Aversiveness of Nonreward

a. Extinction and Trimethyltin (TMT).   Rats given rewards on every trial (CRF schedule) for running down a runway, stop approaching the goal within a few trials when rewards are suddenly omitted (extinction). If rewards were given on only some trials (e.g., 50% of the trials, PRF schedule) prior to extinction, rats continue approaching the goal for many trials. This phenomenon has been called the partial reinforcement extinction effect (PREE). DMOD simulations show that the large Vav value conditioned following CRF training results in the rapid drop in the speed to approach the goal. Simulations show that following PRF training, Vav is large, but Vcc is also conditioned. It is Vcc that keeps the subject approaching the goal. Nation, Bourgeois, Clark, and Elissalde (1984) raised the question whether a drug that increases conditioning of aversive nonreward and results in more rapid extinction following CRF training, would cause less rapid extinction following PRF training. Their prediction was made within the framework of Amsel's Frustration Theory, and they assumed that the drug would not only increase frustration, but would also increase counterconditioning, which would prolong extinction following PRF training. Without having a way of calculating the relative magnitude of frustration and counterconditioning, it was difficult to be sure of this prediction. DMOD simulations show that such a drug should increase Vav following CRF acquisition and result in more rapid extinction. Following PRF training, however, simulations show that the drug should increase Vav more than Vcc, and that the PRF group given the drug should run more slowly during extinction than the PRF group not given the drug, although it should still run more quickly than the CRF group given the drug. The same predictions were made no matter what parameter values for conditioning Vav were used; only the size of the difference between groups differed when the parameter values were changed. These were precisely the results obtained by Nation et al. when they gave rats an injection of TMT: The drug resulted in more rapid extinction in both the CRF and PRF groups, but the PREE occurred.

   This example shows the difficulty of making precise predictions from a verbal model, which can be overcome by taking the major assumptions of a verbal model and translating them into a mathematical model.

b. Ingestion of Toxic Lake Ontario Salmon. Salmon from Lake Ontario (one of the five Great Lakes in the United States) are contaminated with such toxic chemicals as PCBs, dioxin, mirex, mercury, cadmium, and lead. Laboratory rats fed fillets from these salmon acquire a preference for predictable rewards more quickly than the control group fed nontoxic salmon from the Pacific Ocean in an observing response experiment (see previous section) (Daly, Hertzler, & Sargent, 1989). This result was unexpected, because we had thought that the toxins would probably decrease the ability to learn. DMOD has been helpful in not only accounting for the unexpected finding, but also predicting behavioral changes in a number of other experiments. DMOD simulations show that the strength of the preference for predictable reward is determined by the amount of aversiveness aroused by unpredictable nonreward (see earlier section). Since rats fed Lake Ontario salmon showed a larger preference for predictable rewards than control rats fed nontoxic Pacific Ocean salmon, the simplest way to simulate these results was to assume that these rats had a heightened aversive reaction to aversive events. In the preference for predictable reward experiment the aversiveness was aroused by unpredictable nonreward. Simulations then showed that rats fed Lake Ontario salmon should stop approaching a food-reinforced goal more quickly if a shock was introduced, show greater disruption of lever pressing for food if signaled shocks are presented (CER procedure), and show a greater depression of approach to a goal when reward magnitude was shifted from large to small (successive negative contrast or depression effect), than rats fed control Pacific Ocean salmon. All these predictions were subsequently supported by data collected in our laboratory.

Theories, whether they are verbal or mathematical, should not only integrate existing data, but should also point to additional interesting areas of research and make accurate predictions. Our research on the effects of ingestion of Lake Ontario salmon is an example of how DMOD helped us interpret an unexpected finding, and its analysis was then used to determine behavioral situations in which ingestion of these fish should have additional effects.

2. Partial Reinforcement Extinction with Prior Continuous Reinforcement

Amsel developed Frustration Theory in the 1950s and was able to predict many paradoxical reward effects (e.g., large rewards or a large number of acquisition trials lead to less persistence in extinction; Amsel, 1958, 1962, 1972). In 1973, he published two studies that many believed indicated Frustration Theory had to be expanded to include the assumption that when nonreward is unexpected subjects learn to make approach responses to either weak or strong intensities of aversive reactions (rF) and their associated stimuli (sF). It was called the sF intensity hypothesis (e.g., Traupman, Amsel, & Wong, 1973). Computer simulations of DMOD, however, show that the sF intensity assumption is not needed to account for the 1973 data.

Traupman et al. (1973) gave rats 4, 16, or 64 runway acquisition trials on a continuous reinforcement (CRF) schedule, followed by 32 trials on a 50% partial reinforcement (PRF) schedule. During a subsequent extinction phase, a larger number of CRF acquisition trials resulted in greater resistance to extinction early in the session (faster running speeds), but weaker resistance to extinction late in the session (slower running speeds). The data showed a clear-cut crossover effect: Early in the extinction phase the group rankings were 64 > 16 > 4, but late in the extinction phase, the group rankings were 4 > 16 > 64, although all groups were running substantially slower at the end of extinction training. The authors assumed that the larger the number of CRF trials the greater the frustration reaction to nonreward in the partial reinforcement phase. Rewarded trials would therefore countercondition a larger frustration intensity reaction. They assumed that "persistence is determined at any phase of extinction by the similarity of the specific intensity of sF present to the intensity of sF to which $R_{APPROACH}$ was counterconditioned during PR training" (Traupman et al., 1973, p. 220).

DMOD simulations are shown in the upper part of Fig. 5.4, and the same crossover pattern was obtained as was seen in the data (start speeds are presented because Traupman et al. reported only this response measure). This crossover occurred without any assumptions about counterconditioning to specific sF intensities. Fig. 5.4 (lower panels) shows the changes in each of the individual V values. None of the V values show a crossover pattern. Behavior, however, is assumed to be the sum (Vt) of the three V values, and it is their relative values that result in the crossover of the Vt values. Early in extinction the 64–CRF group has large Vap and Vcc values relative to the other groups. Late in training all three groups have small Vap and Vcc values. The Vap and Vcc values for the 64–CRF group are large enough to outweigh the large Vav value early in training, Vt is large, and this group runs quickly. Vav grows larger in all groups early in extinction training, and group differences are maintained for an extended number of trials. Late in training the 64–CRF group still has a relatively large Vav value compared with the other groups. The small Vap and Vcc values cannot outweigh the relatively larger Vav value, and therefore the 64–CRF group has a smaller Vt value and is predicted to run more slowly.

We believe that this is an excellent example of how a mathematical/computer simulation model can help interpret data. It is difficult for a

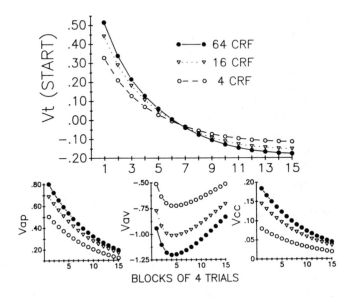

FIG. 5.4.   DMOD simulations of runway speeds during extinction following either 64, 16, or 4 continuously reinforced (CRF), and 16 partially reinforced trials. The upper panel shows the Vt values for the start-speed measure; the lower panels show the Vap, Vav, and Vcc values (see Traupman et al., 1973, Fig. 1, for match between simulations and data).

verbal model to delineate completely the interplay among the different elements of the model. Simulations are also helpful in determining the boundary conditions of phenomena. DMOD simulations show that the predictions are sensitive to the number of trials in each phase, the rate of learning (β_1), and cue salience (α). If too many PRF trials are given, the differences in the V values at the end of CRF training are overcome. In fact, given the typical β_1 value used (.15), we could not use 32 PRF trials, with $\alpha = 0.5$, to obtain the pattern shown (instead the simulation in Fig. 5.4 represents 16 PRF trials). Traupman et al. cited literature that indicated other studies using different procedures did not find the change in resistance to extinction across trials among groups (Traupman et al., 1973).

3. Appetitive Events (Vap*) in Aversive Learning

Pretend you just were given a test for AIDS and to your surprise it was positive. There is no cure and you will die. Vav* is conditioned. A second test is also positive, and Vav* grows. You have a third test: It shows that the first two tests were wrong, you do not have AIDS and you will live. Is there any doubt that the omission of an aversive event is positive? Wouldn't you be in a more positive state than before the first test, when you also thought you did not have AIDS? This is when Vap* is conditioned. Is there any behavioral evidence for Vap*? Yes there is, and we will examine some of this evidence.

a. Tones Paired with Shock Influence Appetitive Discrimination Learning. Fowler (1978) reviewed an impressive series of studies that show counterintuitive transfer effects. In one experiment (e.g., Goodman & Fowler, 1976) a tone was paired with shock (CS+), with the absence of shock (CS−), or the tone and shock were independently presented (random control group, CSo). They then gave food-reinforced T-maze acquisition trials, and presented the tone in one arm of the T-maze. Although one might expect that CS+ would hurt T-maze acquisition if presented in the food arm (CS RIGHT), and help acquisition if presented in the no-food arm (CS WRONG), relative to the CSo control group, Fowler consistently found the opposite results. In addition, CS− helped T-maze acquisition if presented in the no-food arm and hurt if presented in the food arm, an equally counterintuitive result. DMOD can account for the choice data. Since the tone was presented in the T-maze in the absence of shock, simulations show that Vap* will be conditioned to CS+ with repeated tone-alone presentations. Vap* is a positive value and should increase choice of that arm, therefore decreasing errors if presented in the CS RIGHT arm, and increasing errors if presented in the CS WRONG arm. Simulations appear in Fig. 5.5, and show a nice match with the data.

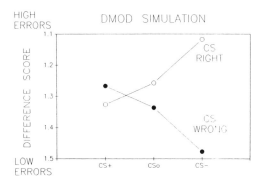

FIG. 5.5. DMOD simulations of errors when a tone (CS), which had been previously paired with the presence (CS+) or absence (CS−) of a shock, was presented in the food arm (CS RIGHT) or in the non-reinforced arm (CS WRONG) during acquisition of a food-reinforced discrimination, compared with a random control group (CSo). Errors are based on the difference in the Vtt values of the reinforced vs. nonreinforced arm: Smaller differences result in more errors (see Goodman & Fowler, 1976, Fig. 1, for match between simulations and data).

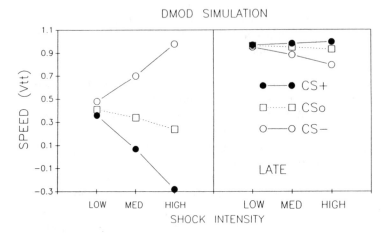

FIG. 5.6. DMOD simulations of speeds (Vtt values) early vs. late in training when a tone (CS), which had been previously paired with the presence (CS +), or absence (CS −), of a high, medium, or low intensity shock, was compared with a random control group (CSo) (see Ghiselli & Fowler, 1976, Fig. 4, for match between simulations and data).

Simulations also show that CS− should have the opposite effect, and is due to complicated changes in the Vav*, Vap*, and Vcc* values.

In another study they tested the effects of the CS in the food arm on speed of running during acquisition of the discrimination (Ghiselli & Fowler, 1976). CS + depressed speeds and CS − increased speeds relative to the CSo control group early in training, but the effects were reversed late in training. The effects were larger the higher the shock intensity. DMOD can also account for the speed data, and simulations appear in Fig. 5.6. In the presence of CS + , Vav* conditioned to the tone initially depresses speeds, but the growth of Vap* results in faster speeds later in training. The effects are larger for more intense shocks. The opposite pattern occurs for the CS − stimulus. All speeds are faster late in training due to Vap conditioned by the food reward, and match the data.

DMOD simulated these counterintuitive results easily. Simple linear models have much difficulty accounting for changes in the ordering of the groups across training trials. The Fowler data are just one example of many where these reversals occur. DMOD has the power to account for these results. In this case it was the growth of Vap* which resulted in the increase in running speeds when the tone was no longer paired with shock.

b. Conditioned Elation with Higher-order Conditioning. Sargent (1986) tested rats in the CER paradigm to determine whether blocking occurs in higher-order conditioning. We simulated his experiment before reading the results, and determined that subjects should *increase* responding in the presence of the "blocked" stimulus. The data and simulations appear in Fig. 5.7 (CS = conditioned stimulus). A conditioned suppression score of .5 indicates no effect of the CS on bar pressing rate, 0 indicates total suppression of responding, and any value above .5 indicates more responding in the presence of the CS than in its absence. Rats were given food rewards on a VI 2-min schedule. They were then given 16 CS1-shock pairings (first-order conditioning), and all rats learned to suppress responding in the presence of CS1. In Phase 2, CS2 was followed by CS1 for 12 trials (higher-order conditioning). Simulations show that Vav* is conditioned to CS2 and subjects should suppress responding in its presence (see Fig. 5.7, Phase 2). Rats suppressed responding faster than the simulation, but Sargent's rats appear to have acquired the higher-order suppression more quickly than usual. CS3 and CS2 were then presented in compound, followed by CS1, for 8 trials in Phase 3. The data and simulation showed suppressed responding in the presence of the compound, but both showed a decrease in suppression on the second block of trials. DMOD predicts this because no shock was presented and Vav* conditioned to CS1 decreases.

In the critical test phase, two CS3 test trials were given to determine if prior conditioning of CS2 blocked conditioning to CS3. The suppression ratio was .57 on the first trial, which indicates that subjects responded more during CS3 than in its absence. The suppression ratio was higher on the

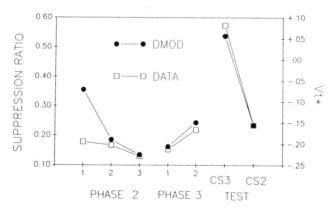

FIG. 5.7. "Blocking" in higher-order conditioning: DMOD simulation (Vt* values) and suppression ratios (from Sargent, 1984) in blocks of four trials for CS2 in Phase 2, CS2 + CS3 in Phase 3, and CS3 and CS2 in the test phase. A suppression ratio greater than .5 and a Vt* value greater than 0.0 indicates more responding in the presence of the stimulus than in its absence.

second test trial (.67 is significantly higher than .5, $p < .02$). Seven of the eight subjects showed suppression ratios of greater than .5 on the second test trial, some showing substantial increases in responding over baseline when CS3 was presented, for example, from 1 to 8, 2 to 5, or 5 to 11 responses. The only subject to show the reverse pattern on the second trial decreased the number of responses from 8 to 6 (data provided by Sargent). The simulation shows a positive Vt^* value, which indicates an increase in responding to CS3, and matches the data. The Vt^* value is positive for two reasons: (1) Vav^* conditioned to CS2 is so high that it almost completely blocks conditioning of Vav^* to CS3, (2) Vap^* is conditioned, because CS1 is presented without a shock. After the 12 trials in Phase 2 and 8 trials in Phase 3, CS1 has a fairly high Vap^* value, but CS2 has not been given enough trials to reach a large Vap^* value and its Vap^* value is still growing. Since the Vap^* value of CS2 is smaller than that of CS1, CS2 does not block conditioning of Vap^* to CS3. The small Vav^* value ($-.037$) and the larger Vap^* value ($+.093$) conditioned to CS3 (see Fig. 5.7, CS3 test) resulted in a positive Vt^* value ($+.056$), and subjects are predicted to press the bar more in the presence of CS3 than in its absence (conditioned elation).

It is the Vap^* value that causes the conditioned elation effect. Based on Vav^* alone, there should have been some suppression. There are no parameter values that would have resulted in conditioned elation based on Vav^* alone.

4. Reintroduction of an Aversive Event

What happens if you have a fourth AIDS test and it is positive? Vap^* is conditioned due to the outcome of the third test, and Vcc^* is conditioned due to the reintroduction of the aversive event. Vcc^* counteracts the effects of Vap^*. Is there any empirical evidence for Vcc^*?

One convincing study was done by McAllister, McAllister, Brooks, and Goldman (1972). They demonstrated the equivalent of a depression or successive negative contrast effect in aversive conditioning. Rats were given 35 light–shock pairings in a white box with a grid floor. On the next day they were given no further light–shock pairings, but were placed into the white box with the grid floor, the light was turned on, and a door was opened so the rats could jump to another box (safe box). This box was either similar to the first box (white, grid floor, and the light came on), or dissimilar (black, solid floor, and no light). Both groups learned to jump to the safe box, but the subjects in the first condition jumped more slowly than the subjects in the second condition. After 12 trials the group that jumped into the dissimilar box was shifted to the condition of the other group, which resulted in a rapid drop in speed of jumping, to a level below the group always run in this condition (similar-looking box).

These results were successfully simulated by DMOD (see Daly & Daly, 1987, Fig. 1). Simulations show that the larger difference between the two boxes in acquisition allowed a greater reduction in Vav*, and therefore Vap* conditioned in the safe box is larger and they jumped more quickly. Since shifting to a "smaller reward" would result in less reduction in Vav* than was expected (Vap*), Vcc* should be conditioned, which should result in a rapid decline in jumping to a level lower than the group always jumped under those conditions. Without Vcc*, there would only have been a slow decline in speed, and the shifted group would not have jumped more slowly than the nonshifted control group. Vcc* is the basis for the "depression" effect obtained by McAllister et al.

CONCLUSIONS

DMOD is probably one of the simplest models possible to account for the large number of diverse phenomena in appetitive and aversive learning it does. It is more complex than the Rescorla and Wagner (1972) model, but it is also able to account for many more phenomena. It is less complex than current computer simulation models in cognitive psychology (PDP, Rumelhart & McClelland, 1986), or the Grossberg model (e.g., 1982).

DMOD is simple because it assumes one basic learning equation with three parameters. The same linear equation is applied to all goal events, including its presence, subsequent omission, and reintroduction. Its success comes from the assumption, based on a large body of data, that there are both positive and negative events in both appetitive and aversive learning, a view previously espoused by Denny (1970). Its ability to account for complex groups × trials interaction effects, as well as reversals in behavior within a group across trials, comes from the interplay among the V values that represent learning about the different goal events. It is this property which gives it some of the power of a nonlinear model.

We do not yet know the boundary conditions of DMOD, and are currently attempting to integrate additional data bases. For example, we have recently simulated all Amsel's (e.g., 1986) work on the ontogeny of paradoxical appetitive reward effects in the rat pup (Daly, 1991). We are also continuing to test novel predictions in the area of preference for predictable appetitive and aversive events, and effects of toxic chemicals on behavior. DMOD is being used as both a research and teaching tool. We believe its success also comes from having integrated successful models and theories into one framework, and written an easy-to-use computer program to simulate predictions of the model. Current learning theories are sufficiently complex to require mathematical modeling and computer simulations.

REFERENCES

Adelman, H. M., & Maatsch, J. L. (1955). Resistance to extinction as a function of the type of responses elicited by frustration. *Journal of Experimental Psychology, 50,* 61–65.

Amsel, A. (1958). The role of frustrative nonreward in continuous reward situations. *Psychological Bulletin, 55,* 102–119.

Amsel, A. (1962). Frustrative nonreward in partial reinforcement and discrimination learning. *Psychological Review, 69,* 306–328.

Amsel, A. (1972). Inhibition and mediation in classical, Pavlovian and instrumental conditioning. In R. A. Boakes & M. S. Halliday (Eds.), *Inhibition and learning* (pp. 275–299). London: Academic Press.

Amsel, A. (1986). Developmental psychobiology and behaviour theory: Reciprocating influences. *Canadian Journal of Psychology, 40,* 311–342.

Amsel, A., & Roussel, J. (1952). Motivational properties of frustration: I. Effect on a running response of the addition of frustration to the motivational complex. *Journal of Experimental Psychology, 43,* 363–368.

Amsel, A., & Surridge, C. T. (1964). The influence of magnitude of reward on the aversive properties of frustration. *Canadian Journal of Psychology, 18,* 321–327.

Atkinson, R. C., Bower, G. H., & Crothers, E. J. (1965). *Introduction to mathematical learning theory.* New York: Wiley.

Brown, J. S. (1948). Gradients of approach and avoidance responses and their relation to level of motivation. *Journal of Comparative and Physiological Psychology, 38,* 450–465.

Bush, R. R., & Mosteller, F. (1951). A mathematical model for simple learning. *Psychological Review, 58,* 313–323.

Bush, R. R., & Mosteller, F. (1955). *Stochastic models for learning.* New York: Wiley.

Daly, H. B. (1968). Excitatory and inhibitory effects of complete and incomplete reward reduction in a double runway. *Journal of Experimental Psychology, 76,* 430–438.

Daly, H. B. (1969a). Aversive properties of partial and varied reinforcement during runway acquisition. *Journal of Experimental Psychology, 81,* 54–60.

Daly, H. B. (1969b). Is responding necessary for nonreward following reward to be frustrating? *Journal of Experimental Psychology, 80,* 186–187.

Daly, H. B. (1969c). Learning of a hurdle-jump response to escape cues paired with reduced reward or frustrative nonreward. *Journal of Experimental Psychology, 79,* 146–157.

Daly, H. B. (1970). Combined effects of fear and frustration on acquisition of a hurdle-jump response. *Journal of Experimental Psychology, 83,* 89–93.

Daly, H.B. (1971). Evidence for frustration during discrimination learning. *Journal of Experimental Psychology, 88,* 205–215.

Daly, H. B. (1972). Hurdle jumping from S+ following discrimination and reversal training: A frustration analysis of the ORE. *Journal of Experimental Psychology, 92,* 332–338.

Daly, H. B. (1974). Reinforcing properties of escape from frustration aroused in various learning situations. In G. H. Bower (Ed.), *The psychology of learning and motivation* (Vol. 8, pp. 187–231). New York: Academic Press.

Daly, H. B. (1985). Observing response acquisition: Preference for unpredictable appetitive rewards obtained under conditions predicted by DMOD. *Journal of Experimental Psychology: Animal Behavior Processes, 11,* 294–316.

Daly, H. B. (1989). Preference for predictable rewards occurs with high proportion of reinforced trials or alcohol injections when rewards are not delayed. *Journal of Experimental Psychology: Animal Behavior Processes, 15*, 3–13.

Daly, H. B. (in press). Preference for unpredictability is reversed when unpredictable non-reward is aversive: A review of data, theory, and DMOD. In I. Gormezano & E. Wasserman (Eds.), *Learning and memory: The behavioral and biological substrates.* New Jersey: Lawrence Erlbaum.

Daly, H. B. (1991, in press). Ontogeny of paradoxical appetitive reward effects in the rat pup: A mathematical model (DMOD) integrates results. *Psychological Bulletin.*

Daly, H. B., & Daly, J. T. (1982). A mathematical model of reward and aversive nonreward: Its application in over 30 appetitive learning situations. *Journal of Experimental Psychology: General, 111*, 441–480.

Daly, H. B., & Daly, J. T. (1984). DMOD—A mathematical model of reward and aversive nonreward in appetitive learning situations. Program and instruction manual. *Behavior Research Methods, Instruments, and Computers, 16*, 38–52.

Daly, H. B., & Daly, J. T. (1987). A computer simulation/mathematical model of learning. Extension of DMOD from appetitive to aversive situations. *Behavior Research Methods, Instruments, & Computers, 19*, 108–112.

Daly, H. B., Hertzler, D. R., & Sargent, D. M. (1989). Ingestion of environmentally contaminated Lake Ontario salmon by laboratory rats increases avoidance of unpredictable aversive nonreward and mild electric shock. *Behavioral Neuroscience, 103*, 1356–1365.

Daly, H. B., & McCroskery, J. H. (1973). Acquisition of a bar-press response to escape frustrative nonreward and reduced reward. *Journal of Experimental Psychology, 98*, 109–112.

Daly, H. B., & Rosenberg, K. M. (1973). Infantile stimulation and its effects on frustration- and fear-motivation behavior in rats. *Learning and Motivation, 4*, 381–396.

Denny, M. R. (1970). A learning model and general effects of aversive stimuli. In M. R. Denny & S. C. Ratner (Eds.), *Comparative psychology: Research in animal behavior* (pp. 630–640, 659–691). Homewood IL: Dorsey Press.

Denny, M. R. (1971). Relaxation theory and experiments. In F. R. Brush (Ed.), *Aversive conditioning and learning* (pp. 235–295). New York: Academic Press.

Fowler, H. (1978). Cognitive associations as evident in the blocking effects of response-contingent CSs. In S. H. Hulse, H. Fowler, & W. K. Honig (Eds.), *Cognitive processes in animal behavior* (pp. 109–153). Hillsdale, NJ: Lawrence Erlbaum Associates.

Ghiselli, W. B., & Fowler, H. (1976). Signaling and affective functions of conditioned aversive stimuli in an appetitive choice discrimination: US intensity effects. *Learning and Motivation, 7*, 1–16.

Gluck, M. A., & Bower, G. H. (1988). From conditioning to category learning: An adaptive network model. *Journal of Experimental Psychology: General, 117*, 227–247.

Gluck, M. A., & Thompson, R. F. (1987). Modeling the neural substrates of associative learning and memory: A computational approach. *Psychological Review, 94*, 176–191.

Goodman, J. H., & Fowler, H. (1976). Transfer of the signalling properties of aversive CSs to an instrumental appetitive discrimination. *Learning and Motivation, 7*, 446–457.

Grossberg, S. (1982). Processing of expected and unexpected events during conditioning and attention: A psychophysiological theory. *Psychological Review, 89*, 529–572.

Hawkins, R. D., & Bower, G. H. (1989). Computational models of learning in simple neural systems. In *The Psychology of learning and motivation* (Vol. 23). New York: Academic Press.

Hearst, E. (1972). Some persistent problems in the analysis of conditioned inhibition. In R. A. Boakes & M. S. Halliday (Eds.), *Inhibition and learning* (pp. 5–39). New York: Academic Press.

Hearst, E., & Franklin, S. R. (1977). Positive and negative relations between a signal and food: Approach-withdrawal behavior to the signal. *Journal of Experiment Psychology: Animal Behavior Processes, 3,* 37–52.

Herrnstein, R. J. (1979). Derivatives of matching. *Psychological Review, 86,* 486–495.

Hilgard, E. R., & Bower, G. H. (1975). *Theories of learning.* Englewood Cliffs, NJ: Prentice–Hall.

Kahneman, D., & Tversky, A. (1982). The psychology of preferences. *Scientific American, 246,* 215–219.

Mandler, G. (1980). The generation of emotion: A psychological theory. In R. Plutchik & H. Kellerman (Eds.), *Theories of emotion* (pp. 219–243). New York: Academic Press.

McAllister, W. R., & McAllister, D. E. (1971). Behavioral measurement of conditioned fear. In F. R. Brush (Ed.), *Aversive conditioning and learning* (pp. 105–179). New York: Academic Press.

McAllister, D. E., McAllister, W. R., Brooks, C. I., & Goldman, J. A. (1972). Magnitude and shift of reward in instrumental aversive learning in rats. *Journal of Comparative and Physiological Psychology, 80,* 490–501.

McAllister, W. R., McAllister, D. E., Douglass, W. K. (1971). The inverse relationship between shock intensity and shuttle-box avoidance learning in rats. *Journal of Comparative and Physiological Psychology, 74,* 426–433.

Nation, J. R., Bourgeois, A. E., Clark, D. E., & Elissalde, M. (1984). Effects of acute trimethyltin exposure on appetitive acquisition and extinction performance in the adult rat. *Behavioral Neuroscience, 98,* 919–924.

Rescorla, R. A. (1969). Pavlovian conditioned inhibition. *Psychological Bulletin, 72,* 77–94.

Rescorla, R. A. (1987). Facilitation and inhibition. *Journal of Experimental Psychology: Animal Behavior Processes, 13,* 250–259.

Rescorla, R. A., & Wagner, A. R. (1972). A theory of Pavlovian conditioning: Variations in the effectiveness of reinforcement and nonreinforcement. In A. H. Black & W. F. Prokasy (Eds.), *Classical conditioning II: Current research and theory* (pp. 64–99). New York: Appleton–Century–Crofts.

Rosen, A. J., Glass, D. H., & Ison, J. R. (1967). Amobarbital sodium and instrumental performance changes following reward reduction. *Psychonomic Science, 9,* 129–130.

Rumelhart, D. E., & McClelland, J. L. (1986). *Parallel distributed processing: Explorations in the microstructure of cognition: Vol. 1. Foundation.* Cambridge, MA: Bradford Books/ MIT Press.

Sargent, D. M. (1986). Blocking in second-order conditioning and sensory preconditioning: An investigation into the generality of the blocking effect. *Dissertation Abstracts International, 42/02,* p. 827-B.

Staddon, J. E. R. (1983). *Adaptive behavior and learning.* Cambridge University Press.

Steinhauer, G. D. (1986). *Artificial behavior.* Englewood Cliffs, NJ: Prentice–Hall.

Sutton, R. S., & Barto, A. G. (1981). Toward a modern theory of adaptive networks: Expectation and prediction. *Psychological Review, 88,* 135–170.

Terrace, H. S. (1972). Conditioned inhibition in successive discrimination learning. In R. A. Boakes & M. S. Halliday (Eds.), *Inhibition and learning* (pp. 99–119). New York: Academic Press.

Tondat, L. M., & Daly, H. B. (1972). The combined effects of frustrative nonreward and shock on aggression between rats. *Psychonomic Science, 28,* 25–28.

Traupman, K. L., Amsel, A., & Wong, P. T. P. (1973). Persistence early and late in extinction as a function of number of continuous reinforcements preceding partial reinforcement training. *Animal Learning and Behavior, 1,* 219–222.

Wagner, A. R. (1959). The role of reinforcement and nonreinforcement in an "apparent frustration effect." *Journal of Experimental Psychology, 57,* 130–136.

Wagner, A. R. (1981). SOP: A model of automatic memory processing in animal behavior.

In N. Spear & R. Miller (Eds.), *Information processing in animals: Memory mechanisms* (pp. 5–47). Hillsdale, NJ: Lawrence Erlbaum Associates.

Wagner, A. R., & Rescorla, R. A. (1972). Inhibition in Pavlovian conditioning: Applications of a theory. In R. A. Boakes & M. S. Halliday (Eds.), *Inhibition and learning* (pp. 301–336). London: Academic Press.

Wyckoff, L. B. (1969). The role of observing responses in discrimination learning. In D. P. Hendry (Ed.), *Conditioned reinforcement* (pp. 237–259). Homewood, IL: Dorsey Press.

Zimmer–Hart, C. L., & Rescorla, R. A. (1974). Extinction of Pavlovian conditioned inhibition. *Journal of Comparative and Physiological Psychology, 86,* 837–845.

APPENDIX: SUCCESSFUL DMOD SIMULATIONS

Appetitive: Discrete trial (see Daly & Daly, 1982)
  Acquisition
    continuous reinforcement (CRF) incremental learning curve
    reward magnitude
    partial reinforcement (PRF) acquisition effect
    varied reinforcement acquisition effect
    blocking and overshadowing
    latent inhibition
    biconditional discrimination and configural learning
    discrimination learning—choice and speeds
  Shifts in reward magnitude
    successive negative contrast effect (depression effect)
    successive positive contrast effect (elation effect)
    simultaneous negative constrast
    gradual reward reduction effects
    extinction following CRF determined by reward magnitude
    partial reinforcement extinction effect
    reacquisition effects
  Escape behavior following reward reductions
    hurdle-jump acquisition
    double runway frustration effect
  Limited vs. extended training
    overlearning extinction effect
    overlearning discrimination reversal effect
    small-trials partial reinforcement extinction effect
    initial nonreward extinction effect
  Delay of reinforcement
    inhibition of delay
    continuous delay
    shifts in delay
  Second-order conditioning and secondary reinforcement effects

Drug influences (alcohol, amobarbital)
   contrast effects
   extinction
   partial reinforcement acquisition and extinction effects
   escape behavior
Toxic chemicals in Lake Ontario salmon
   CRF acquisition (no effect)
   extinction following partial and continuous reinforcement
   successive negative contrast effect
   preference for predictable rewards
Choice behavior
   reward magnitude
   position cues and salience of stimuli
   delay of reinforcement
   one unit of food on CRF vs. two units on PRF
   percentage of reinforcement
Preference for predictable rewards (observing responses) and when a
preference for unpredictable rewards occurs (see Daly, 1985, 1989, in
press)
   reward magnitude
   delay of reinforcement
   percentage of reinforcement
   drive level
   complexity of discrimination
   alcohol
   caffeine (manuscript in preparation)
   ingestion of Lake Ontario salmon (Daly et al., 1989)
   Ontogeny of 13 paradoxical appetitive reward effects in rats (Daly, 1991)
"Atypical" or "intrinsic" reinforcers (manuscript in preparation)
   CRF acquisition
   Successive negative contrast effect
Appetitive: Free operant–acquisition and asymptotic performance (invited
manuscript in preparation)
   CRF
   Fixed Interval–postreinforcement pause
   Fixed Ratio–postreinforcement pause and bursting
   Variable Interval
   Variable Ratio
Aversive: Discrete trial (see Daly & Daly, 1987)
   Escape/avoidance acquisition and extinction
   Escape from Vav*
   Reward magnitude shifts
   Response prevention

Shock during extinction: Vicious circle behavior
Conditioned emotional response (CER)
Punishment
Transfer from aversive to appetitive conditioning
Preference for predictable shocks
  signal duration
  positive, negative, and uncorrelated stimuli
  shock intensity
Ingestion of Lake Ontario salmon (see Daly et al., 1989)
  punishment
  CER

6 Relaxation/Relief: The Effect of Removing, Postponing, or Terminating Aversive Stimuli

M. Ray Denny
Michigan State University

The background for the theoretical position of this chapter is elicitation theory (Denny, 1966, 1967, 1971a, 1971b; Denny & Adelman, 1955) and is clearly in the "connectionist" tradition, which seems to be resurging; the approach is a relatively comprehensive theory of behavior that borrows heavily from Hull, Guthrie, Tolman, and Skinner and attempts, in part, to integrate these neobehavioristic schools.

It emphasizes that a particular response, in contiguity with a particular stimulus, must occur consistently and to the relative exclusion of other responses in order to be learned. Thus many variables that facilitate learning are those that commonly minimize or eliminate competing responses. Response is broadly conceived and includes any implicit activity, for example, imagery and positive and negative affect as well as all overt activity, (Denny, 1971b, 1986). Although it is a contiguity position, the theory differs from Guthrie (1952) in that (a) reinforcers have a central role as consistent elicitors of approach, (b) the removal of an elicitor (UCS) from a learned sequence also consistently elicits a characteristic class of response (also mediates learning, e.g., through frustration instigation), (c) no assumption is made regarding one trial learning, and (d) extinction effects are the result of pitting antagonistic tendencies against the original response tendency (counterconditioning but *no* unhooking of the original response is assumed).

The theory eschews intervening variables (IV), depending instead on a continual, detailed analysis of stimulus (S) and response (R) for the explanation of behavior. Specifically, S and R are the only constructs involved in the statement of S–R laws and thus the only abstract concepts needed in an S–R behavior theory. Thus many referents that ordinarily participate in the definition of IVs are involved in defining S and R. For example, fear, which is an IV for many psychologists, in elicitation theory becomes a response class (R) with specific antecedents and distinctive stimulus accompaniments and after-effects.

The machinery of the theory can be seen in the analysis of instrumental reward learning, which involves the same steps as present in analyzing escape-avoidance behavior. Instrumental learning, traditionally viewed from a reinforcement perspective, is retranslated into a Pavlovian or classical conditioning model: The unconditioned response that mediates instrumental learning is the response of approaching the incentive (food, water, etc.) rather than ingesting it.

The conditioning occurring in instrumental learning can be explicated in detail by describing how a rat learns to turn right in a T-maze. Assume a piece of familiar food is located at the end of the right alley, no food is on the left, and the rat is hungry. Exploratory-approach is sooner or later elicited by the novel stimuli of the alley, and this locomotor behavior eventually brings the rat to the goal area. Fig. 6.1 presents a symbolic representation of the conditioning that occurs; it begins with Step A and proceeds alphabetically, as presented. It is immediately apparent that T-maze learning is not really simple but a complex sequence of learned responses; all responses need to build up gradually in an indirect, backward fashion.

In Fig. 6.1, S^1 is a CS for that part of the goal box that immediately precedes the presentation of food and is the first stimulus to be conditioned to the approach response that is unconditionally elicited by S^R (i.e., the dashed line connection between S^1 and $R_{approach}$ in part A of Fig 6.1). For learning to occur it is critical for the rat to make a definite approach response to the food tray; in fact, it only needs to be hungry on a learning trial (food seeking) while in the goal box (Mendelson, 1966). And with a definite approach to the goal area, there is an increase in the probability of selecting the reinforced side on the succeeding trial, regardless of when the food is eaten after the rat reaches the food tray (Denny & Martindale, 1956). In other words, consistent approach to a goal region, rather than drive reduction, mediates learning. Koob, Fray, and Iversen (1976) argue similarly when they show that tail pinching with a paper clip, which reliably elicits gnawing in a rat, will mediate the learning of a new habit, such as approaching the correct arm of a T-maze to gain access to wood chips, on which the rat can gnaw.

As soon as S^1 has acquired approach value, it serves as a functional US, eliciting approach in close temporal contiguity with S^2. Next, S^2 becomes a functional US and so on throughout the chain. So far the analysis is

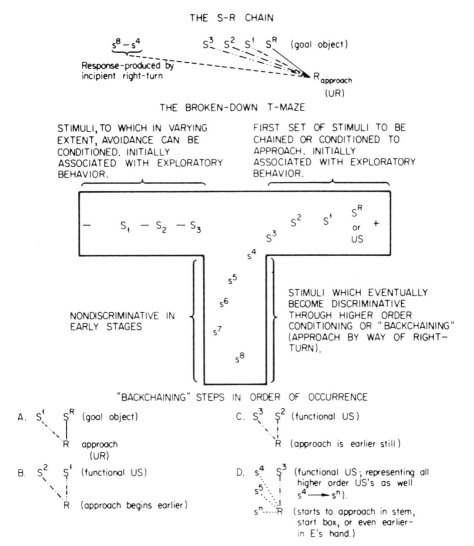

CONDITIONED APPROACH ANALYSIS OF T-MAZE LEARNING

THE S-R CHAIN

$s^8 - s^4$ S^3 S^2 S^1 S^R (goal object)

Response-produced by
incipient right-turn
                                                    $R_{approach}$
                                                    (UR)

THE BROKEN-DOWN T-MAZE

STIMULI, TO WHICH IN VARYING
EXTENT, AVOIDANCE CAN BE
CONDITIONED. INITIALLY
ASSOCIATED WITH EXPLORATORY
BEHAVIOR.

FIRST SET OF STIMULI TO BE
CHAINED OR CONDITIONED TO
APPROACH. INITIALLY
ASSOCIATED WITH EXPLORATORY
BEHAVIOR.

$-$ S_1 $-$ S_2 $-$ S_3 S^3 S^2 S^1 S^R
                                                         or
                                                         US $+$

s^4

s^5

s^6

NONDISCRIMINATIVE IN
EARLY STAGES

s^7

s^8

STIMULI WHICH EVENTUALLY
BECOME DISCRIMINATIVE
THROUGH HIGHER ORDER
CONDITIONING OR "BACKCHAINING"
(APPROACH BY WAY OF RIGHT-
TURN).

"BACKCHAINING" STEPS IN ORDER OF OCCURRENCE

A. S^1 S^R (goal object)

R approach
   (UR)

B. S^2 S^1 (functional US)

R (approach begins earlier)

C. S^3 S^2 (functional US)

R (approach is earlier still)

D. s^4 S^3 (functional US; representing all
   s^5 higher order US's as well
                    $s^4 \longrightarrow s^n$).
   s^n....R (starts to approach in stem,
              start box, or even earlier-
              in E's hand.)

FIG. 6.1. A backchaining, or conditioned, approach analysis of T-maze
learning (elicitation theory).

similar to Tolman's; namely, that the rat learns to go to a particular place. According to the present analysis, Tolman's description is accurate only in the early stages, when approach has only been conditioned to S^1, S^2, or S^3. During this early stage, the rat makes a number of errors and displays considerable vicarious trial-and-error behavior at the choice point (VTE); with continued trials VTE diminishes.

The chain continues to develop, involving kinesthetic stimuli represented here by "little s," and proceeds all the way back to wherever stimuli remain discriminative. Thus when the kinesthetically controlled rat starts to turn almost as soon as it leaves the start box, it becomes legitimate to call the learned response a right turn response. In short, the rat finally learns to approach the food *by way of* a right turn, much as a rat in a Skinner box learns to approach the food tray *by way of* a bar press. In the bar-pressing situation, an early discrimination for the rat to learn is to approach the food tray *after* a bar-press instead of re-approaching the tray *after* eating. One implication of this analysis is that instrumental/operant conditioning differs from Pavlovian conditioning in that the organism, through its own responding, supplies the S^D (CS) in an instrumental situation.

After $R_{approach}$ was fairly well established, it became obvious that new and vigorous responses appeared with the omission of the goal object (frustration-instigated behaviors) and that withdrawal soon tended to come forward in the behavior sequence to replace $R_{approach}$ (Denny, 1946; Denny & Dunham, 1951; Maatsch, 1951). Extinction, therefore, was posited as the backchaining of competing responses (R_c from the goal area to the start region—much like the conditioning of approach). Denny and Adelman (1955) extended this original notion so that the omission of *any* consistent elicitor (US), including the omission of aversive stimuli, such as shock, constituted an eliciting state of affairs for an antagonistic response like relaxation.

THE THEORY AS APPLIED TO ESCAPE-AVOIDANCE BEHAVIOR

According to the present framework, instrumental approach behavior and instrumental escape or avoidance involve a similar or parallel analysis (Denny, 1971a; Denny & Ratner, 1970). Let us examine a prototypical situation in which a rat first learns to escape and then learns to avoid. Just as an organism must be in a special state (hungry, thirsty, etc.) before the positive incentive can be a good elicitor of approach and mediate instrumental reward learning, it must be in a special state before escape-avoidance learning can occur. It must be agitated or emotional, as regularly occurs with the presentation of an aversive stimulus (AS). With further presentations of AS, the associated stimulus situation (CS) comes to elicit a similar state in the organism (conditioned fear).

The importance of this agitated state is that *then* either the removal or omission of AS or the removal of the conditioned aversive stimulus (CAS) has distinct response consequences. These consequences have been identified behaviorally as long-latency relaxation and, more recently, as short-latency relief. Relief starts approximately 3 to 5 sec after the cessation of shock or a strong CAS and is almost all over within the next 10 or 15 sec. The temporal aspects of this response correspond closely with the postshock effects in heart rate as investigated in dogs by Church, LoLordo, Overmeier, Solomon, and Turner (1966), which they also labeled relief.

Like two-factor avoidance theory, the present analysis assumes that fear is soon conditioned to the shock situation, but unlike two-factor theory, the removal of CAS is not supposed to be *immediately* reinforcing. Learning, as always, is mediated by response, and the response in question can have a substantial latency. And since the learning is *instrumental*, as when escape terminates shock or avoidance prevents shock, then the US or UR that mediates the conditioning (backchaining) must be at the very end of the behavior sequence, functioning as a goal.

The crucial UR in escape-avoidance learning is the response that consistently occurs in the safe region or safe period, following the removal of AS or CAS. For example, even bar-press avoidance approaches near-perfect performance when a bar-press opens a door leading to a safe place (Masterson, 1970). Thus the S–R operations in escape-avoidance learning are the reciprocal of instrumental approach: In approach learning, the approach component is elicited by the available incentive, while the withdrawal component—avoiding the wrong choice—is elicited by the omission of the incentive. In avoidance learning the US for the approach component is the absence of AS or CAS, while withdrawal is originally elicited by the presence of AS.

Since relaxation or relief are assumed to be a prerequisite for making $R_{approach}$, the question arises as to why the backchaining of approach takes priority over the backchaining of relaxation (relaxation typically manifests itself later, bringing about extinction effects). Presumably, $R_{approach}$ is compatible with the subject's emotional state while it is still in the shock region, provided it is not freezing extensively, and can therefore come forward in the sequence. Thus a point in the chain is reached where the subject approaches the safe region prior to the onset of shock. At this point it can be asserted that the subject is learning to avoid. Relaxation, on the other hand, would be directly incompatible with the agitated state of S while in the shock region and only gradually "fights" its way back in the chain, to produce extinction effects. Positive affect, of course, may also be directly conditioned to safe places or safety signals.

In sum, escape is reinforced by shock termination plus the removal of CAS, and this conditioning brings about avoidance. But this in no way precludes the learning of avoidance without escape, that is, solely on the basis of the removal of CAS, as found by Marx and Hellwig (1964) and W. R. McAllister and McAllister (1971).

In the theory, initial attempts to escape mainly supply the operant that finally gets the animal away from AS and CAS. When early attempts to escape lack the required operant, learning is impeded; but the escape operant is learned mainly on the basis of what is elicited in the nonshock area or time period rather than on the basis of what is directly elicited by shock. Also, if the operant fails to remove the CAS, avoidance will be seriously hampered. Consistently elicited escape responses doubtless do get conditioned, and these CRs can sometimes be quite independent of a successful avoidance response (Bolles, 1969; Mowrer & Lamoreaux, 1946). As a rule, attempts to escape would tend to come forward in the behavior sequence and are probably best represented by an animal's struggling while being put back into the shock chamber at the start of a trial; alternatively, this conditioning could be viewed as an animal's attempts to avoid the CAS, as is characteristic of phobic humans. This behavior tends to extinguish with the omission of the US, that is, as the subject learns to avoid by making the prescribed operant.

Typically, escape and avoidance are a blend of each other so that the strength of R_{avoid} is often based a great deal on the postshock reinforcement associated with escape. A rat can be readily trained to "avoid" simply by using a solid block of 8 to 10 escape trials in a one-way or jump-out box, with nonshock periods that are about 150 sec long. "Avoidance" is then assessed in a no-shock extinction (test) series (Denny & Dmitruk, 1967). With this technique, the rat is never shocked for failing to respond quickly, yet during the test series the rat typically responds for 25 to 30 trials with a very short latency, well below that needed to avoid. When initial trials are highly massed (ITI of 10 or 15 sec) the rat escapes fairly well but learns to "avoid" very slowly, as observed on interspersed test trials. Massed trials eliminate relaxation-approach in the safe region and thus approach toward the safe place cannot be effectively conditioned to the stimuli of the shock chamber. Only relief is operative. Consequently, the learning of R_{avoid} is impeded.

In the present analysis, the CS does not have to remain a conditioned fear stimulus throughout avoidance conditioning for avoidance to be strengthened and maintained. Fear is not conditioned solely to a specific CS, if there is one, but to the total shock situation, which includes spatial as well as temporal cues. Thus loss of fear to the CS does not mean loss of fear entirely, or even substantially. As soon, however, as relaxation effectively competes with total fear, as soon as the subject begins to approach the cues of the shock region, then R_{avoid} extinguishes.

The theory states that extinction results from the pitting of one or more competing response (R_c) against $S-R_0$ in a stimulus situation that is more or less like the original acquisition situation. When an aversive stimulus is involved in acquisition and is omitted in extinction, R_c is very likely to be relaxation or relief, produced by the omission of the AS or the CAS. In the extinction of avoidance, relaxation/relief typically originate in the safe situation and generalize or backchain to the original shock situation. Even with short nonshock confinements in the safe situation, the subject spends more time there than in the original shock situation. In fact, the back-chaining of relaxation/relief from the safe to the shock situation (extinction effects) will often start during avoidance trials, (data related to this point will be presented later). If, on the other hand, the subject is *forced* to remain in the original shock region well beyond its response latency (Baum, 1970, 1972), then relaxation can originate there and speed up extinction. It also appears that, for some rats, freezing can be the R_c that mediates the extinction of avoidance, even when extinction is designated as a period of shock omission (Bagné, 1968). This notion would seem to handle one of Baum's (1972) main objections to explaining the effects of flooding or response prevention in terms of elicitation theory; namely, for rats that do not relax during flooding.

Both relief and relaxation, as suggested earlier, have dual functions that tend to oppose each other: They both make the nonshock stimuli positive and mediate approach learning to them; they both constitute the R_c that counterconditions fear and fear related responses and thereby produce extinction of escape-avoidance behavior.

EXPERIMENTAL STUDIES

Early Research

Escape-avoidance research stemming from the theory yielded the following results from our laboratory and for the most part was reported in detail in Brush's book (Denny, 1971a):

1. When shock is omitted, extinction effects (relaxation and relief) typically originate in the safe situation rather than in the original shock region and presumably generalize or backchain to the shock area to effect extinction over trials (Denny, Koons, & Mason, 1959; Knapp, 1960, 1965).

2. Dissimilar safe and shock chambers facilitate the acquisition of one-way avoidance (Knapp, 1960, 1965).

3. When the shock and safe areas are dissimilar, the minimax nonshock interval (optimal opportunity to relax) in one-way avoidance learning

is of the order of 150 sec for rats for moderate intensities of shock.[1] In other words, learning that is mediated by relaxation is *not* enhanced by nonshock periods longer than 150 sec. Whereas speed of extinction, when the two areas are similar, is a direct function of length of nonshock confinement; that is, the more the rat relaxes the sooner it extinguishes (Denny & Weisman, 1964).

4. Rats in a two-choice, escape-avoidance situation learn to prefer the distinctive chamber associated with the longer nonshock period; that is, nonshock confinement (relaxation) is an important reinforcing event in avoidance learning (Denny & Weisman, 1964). In both a one-way and shuttle situation, a variety of rodent species prefer or are biased toward the distinctive chamber associated with the longer nonshock confinement interval (Boice, Boice, & Dunham, 1968; Boice, Denny, & Evans, 1967; Reynierse, Weisman, & Denny, 1963; Weisman, Denny, & Zerbolio, 1967).

5. Homogeneous shuttle boxes facilitate the learning of avoidance, compared with shuttle boxes with dissimilar chambers (Denny, Zerbolio, & Weisman, 1969), which is opposite to the results in one-way avoidance (Knapp, 1965). There is only a safe *period* in shuttle avoidance, not a safe *place*. That is, the rat must learn *when* rather than *where* to undergo relaxation/relief in shuttle box avoidance. In the heterogeneous shuttle box, the irrelevant place cues are salient, and salient irrelevant cues can markedly impede learning (Fidura, 1966; Hyman, 1971).

6. Relaxation is most readily conditioned to a flashing light by pairing it with long nonshock periods and by omitting the light during short nonshock periods. The conditioning is indexed by the degree to which the CS subsequently facilitates extinction of an avoidance response (Weisman, Denny, Platt, & Zerbolio, 1966). Relaxation has also been conditioned to the color of a chamber (black or white) by confining a rat there for 150 sec after a 1-sec shock. The conditioning is indexed by the fact that subsequent avoidance learning is facilitated by using the confinement chamber CS as the safe box and impeded by using it

---

[1] The 150-s minimax value for relaxation was determined purposely with a minimum number of acquisition trials (3 to 6) in one-way avoidance, which fortuitously limited the role relief could have played since at least two of these trials were criterial avoidances on which the animal was never shocked. With, say, a 60- or 90-s shock-free period, relief would operate and soon produce two or three avoidances in succession (or a 180-s nonshock period). The resultant relaxation effect could then be conditioned to the safe place, and reinforcement of avoidance (approach to safety) would presumably occur on the next trial and subsequent trials. Thus with a few more trials than needed with 150-s nonshock interval, nonshock intervals of 50 to 100 s, as commonly employed, yield satisfactory avoidance performance.

as the shock box, compared with appropriate controls. For groups *not* confined long enough to relax or undergo relief, neither facilitation nor interference occurs with this procedure (Denny, 1971a; Zerbolio, 1965, 1968).

7. The latency of relaxation onset was discovered to be approximately 30 sec by investigating the optimal placement of a 15-sec buzzer CS when used to condition relaxation to it. That is, a 25–40-sec interval postshock is optimal, but the total nonshock interval has to be at least 150 sec for conditioning to occur to the 15-sec CS. In this research, using a one-way box with dissimilar chambers, we also discovered the phenomenon of short-latency *relief*; namely, that a CS introduced 5–10-sec or 10–15-sec postshock, even during a very short period in the safe chamber, acquires positive approach properties. Conditioned relief was identified after the conditioning trials were over by presenting the CS for the first time in the original shock chamber just prior to the opportunity to "avoid": Such a CS facilitates the extinction of avoidance in much the same way as a CS for conditioned relaxation (Denny, 1971a). Essentially the same sort of conditioning was obtained by Weisman and Litner (1969) when the CS depressed Sidman avoidance.

8. Relief was invoked to help explain self-punitive behavior of rats (increased resistance to extinction) in a runway when they are shocked (punished) in an intermediate section of the alley during extinction. Prior to extinction, all rats learn to escape shock by traveling all the way to the safe goal area. Since relief mainly occurs during postshock confinement (more in a goal dissimilar to shock area) it only functions as a positive reinforcer for the punished experimentals, not for the unpunished controls (Delprato & Denny, 1968; Delprato & Meltzer, 1974). Relief was implicated because a short 2-sec confinement period in the goal area did not mediate increased resistance to extinction, whereas a longer interval for the experimental rats did.

9. Punishing a single failure to avoid markedly increases resistance to extinction of an avoidance response (Baum, 1968; Denny & Dmitruk, 1967). That is, punishing incipient relaxation makes relaxation-produced stimuli become conditioned aversive stimuli. Thus, whenever such relaxation occurs, fear and avoidance are elicited and extinction is prolonged (Denny & Dmitruk, 1967). It may also be true that generalized anxiety in the human is due to the conditioning of fear to relaxation-produced stimuli (Denny, 1971a; 1976), for which some behavior therapists have seemingly found support (e.g., Heide & Borkovec, 1983, 1984).

10. Long confinement periods (e.g., 150 sec or more) in the nonshock

area during acquisition facilitate subsequent extinction (Denny & Weisman, 1964; Weisman et al., 1966). That is, the extinction process (counterconditioning of fear by dual functioning relaxation/relief) can begin while acquisition is also being mediated, even when there are fewer than 10 acquisition trials (see also Delprato, 1974b, #9 in the next section of this chapter).

11. Relief can occur not only with the removal of the AS but with the removal of the CAS if the level of fear conditioned to the CAS is high enough. For example, a shock level of 1.8 ma paired with a CS (Tortora & Denny, 1973) or a sizable number of fear conditioning trials (W. R. McAllister & McAllister, 1971) clearly seem to mediate relief. A strong shock of 1.8 ma or greater may also retard the course of relaxation so that a safe period of 210 sec or greater may be required for complete relaxation (Tortora & Denny, 1973).

More Recent Research

A representative sample of relatively recent findings that are related to relaxation/relief concepts and come from other laboratories or former student associates deserves to be highlighted next:

1. One of the more important findings of late, as I see it, is establishing that a feedback or safety signal is just as positive or inhibitory of fear without a response contingency as with it. A temporal relationship with a shock-free interval is sufficient (Mineka, Cook, & Miller, 1984; Morris, 1975; Rosellini, DeCola, & Warren, 1986; Starr & Mineka, 1977; Weisman & Litner, 1969). This conclusion runs counter to the informational hypothesis of Bolles (1971) and Weiss (1971). Most of the studies show that an escapable response reduces fear of a shock situation more than an inescapable response but not if the yoked inescapable animal is given an exteroceptive feedback stimulus when the master escapes, which is presumably comparable to proprioceptive feedback for the escapable animal.

   Conversely, these studies have established that a short nonshock period following shock has little or no safety or approach value if this period is unaccompanied by stimulus change (a feedback or safety signal or movement to a distinctive place). Presumably response-produced kinesthetic cues, if distinctive enough, can mediate some approach, as probably occurs in Sidman avoidance and some discrete lever-press avoidance.

   These findings are important because all of the experiments in our laboratory which purported to measure relief involved a stimulus change postshock. And nearly all of the research on the conditioning of relief and relaxation involved the rat's escaping or avoiding in a one-way situation prior to experiencing the safety signal (CS for relief or relaxation). If not that, except for Weisman and Litner (1969), the rat was picked up and placed in a completely different environment postshock for the CS. Now we know the escape response was *not* critical.

It also appears from the results of the study by Rosellini, DeCola, and Warren (1986), that mixing short 5-sec shock-free intervals among long shock-free intervals prevents a concomitant safety or feedback signal from acquiring positive, or fear inhibitory, properties. Presumably, the feedback signal with the very short shock-free interval acquires aversive properties and counteracts positive conditioning with the longer intervals. Recall that a nonshock interval of 10 to 15 sec was needed to condition relief in our laboratory.

2. Dillow, Myerson, Slaughter, and Hurwitz (1972) found that a safety signal facilitated the learning of a discriminated avoidance, and though the safety signal did not significantly affect extinction per se it did reduce intertrial responding during extinction of standard bar-pressing. This latter result is actually in keeping with relaxation theory for a single-chamber apparatus because all the relaxing would take place there and continue past the offset of the safety signal (a CS for relaxation) for a sizable part of the ITI, as indicated by measures taken by Weisman and Litner (1969).

3. In 1974, Moot, Nelson, and Bolles replicated our finding that a homogeneous shuttle box is superior to a heterogeneous box and showed that this superiority depended on preventing the occurrence of intertrial responses, which they interpreted cognitively. But their results seem quite consistent with relaxation theorizing. Permitting intertrial responses means that black and white chambers as cues are basically neutral rather than irrelevant. On any particular trial the colors cannot be exclusively associated with relief or relaxation because the rat is moving from one chamber to the other during the critical nonshock period. Nor can black/white for the same reason be readily counterconditioned through punishment. Their salience is hardly important at all.

4. Delprato and Dreilinger (1974) obtained evidence for the proposition that relief or relaxation typically begins in the safe area and backchains to the shock area in the extinction of avoidance. In their experiment, shock-area fear in a passive avoidance test was reduced more following regular extinction trials than following shock-area blocking (flooding) trials that precluded backchaining effects. Thus the backchaining hypothesis was supported. Time spent in the shock area was equated on each of 27 trials for both groups, and overall time spent in safe area was equated as well.

5. Delprato (1974a) found that the facilitation of extinction of discriminated avoidance by delayed termination of the warning signal following extinction responses (Delprato, 1969; Katzev, 1967; Reynierse & Rizley, 1970b) is due to postresponse exposure to the warning signal rather than delayed termination per se. It was found that exposure to the warning signal (buzzer) at postresponse intervals greater than 5 *sec* was the critical variable; at that point in time relief could countercondition fear of the buzzer.

6. Using a differentiated three-chambered box, Delprato and Denny (1970) found that, following termination of a shock, increases in the nonshock confinement (relaxation) period in a passive avoidance task decreases punishment's effectiveness as an inhibitor of the step-down response. Since relaxation is a long-latency response, the longer nonshock period presumably permits more relaxation and more conditioning of approach to the nonshock chamber. All groups were matched on initial step-down latency. And extinction of generalized fear as an alternative interpretation was ruled out by also using a nonshock chamber that was very similar to the rest of the apparatus. The differential nonshock box with long confinement impeded passive avoidance even more rather than less than the similar nonshock box, though not significantly so.

7. Using a one-way box with two distinctive compartments, Reynierse and Rizley (1970a) found that the rat's confinement in the nonshock (safe) box during the ITI facilitates acquisition and increases resistance to extinction over confinement in a neutral box; whereas confinement in the shock box clearly impedes acquisition and markedly facilitates extinction. The handling variable was controlled. In addition to indicating that approach is conditioned to nonshock box cues (presumably relaxation-mediated), such findings are in keeping with our notion that isolating what happens in the shock area from what happens in the safe area prevents fear and relaxation/relief from counterconditioning each other.

   [Note: Denny and Weisman (1964) found fast extinction with long nonshock confinement when, unlike the present study, the shock and safe areas were similar and relaxation/relief could thus generalize to the shock area and directly compete with fear.]

8. In a lever-press avoidance situation, Morris (1974) showed that a long ITI preceding a trial hindered performance, consistent with Pearl (1963) and Pearl and Fitzgerald (1966), while a long ITI after a trial enhanced performance. The total data, as Morris indicated, are broadly consistent with relaxation theory. A within-subject design with short or long ITIs in a Gellerman sequence, made discriminable by preceding

warning signals and counterbalanced across subjects, allowed measures of avoidance of either preceding or predicted ITI to be obtained separately.

The most interesting aspect of the results is that they argue against assuming that the length of the ITI is critical solely for the extinction of fear.

9. Delprato (1974b) trained independent groups of rats to criteria of 1, 3, 9, or 27 consecutive avoidances in a one-way box with distinctive chambers. Fear of shock area was subsequently measured in a passive avoidance test without shock present. Groups 3, 9, and 27 took virtually the same number of shocks to reach criterion and only slightly but nonsignificantly more than Group 1 (so degree of fear conditioning was not a variable). The males showed progressively less fear of the shock area the longer the criterion series; and the females did so when they registered as much fear in the situation as the males (9 and 27 avoidances). Relaxation theory stresses that relaxation/relief has two opposing functions, with the extinction factor operating as soon as it has the opportunity to chain back from the safe box. Thus, as similarly found by Denny and Weisman (1964), Kamin, Brimer, and Black (1963), Mineka (1978), Weisman et al. (1966), and as mentioned earlier, the counterconditioning of fear, or the early stages of extinction, can proceed while avoidance seems intact (See also Bagné, Experiment 2, this chapter).

10. Mackenzie (1974) studied two-choice avoidance learning in which the correct response was followed by the longer nonshock period (90 sec in safe box and 5-sec ITI in shock box with reverse confinements for the incorrect choice). With noncorrection the rats presumably failed to learn the correct choice because the shock-free period (in the shock box) that followed incorrect choices was the same as followed correct choices to the safe box. However, avoidance learning to either box readily occurred; and with a correction method that let the rat leave the incorrect box and go correctly, the correct choice was also readily learned.

Mackenzie also observed that the addition of a safety signal after entering a distinct and effective nonshock area did *not* facilitate avoidance learning. In her other experiments, 20- and 90-sec nonshock confinements were superior to a 10-sec interval and essentially equivalent to each other in mediating avoidance and two-choice learning, which is quite similar to the nonchoice, one-way avoidance data of Denny and Weisman (1964). This is true even though the total ITIs were equivalent for all groups in Denny and Weisman and differed considerably for Mackenzie who left all rats in the shock box for 10 sec during the ITI. Mackenzie did not use nonshock intervals beyond 90 sec so a comparison with Denny and Weisman here, which could have been illuminating, is not possible.

11. Franchina and associates in a series of related studies followed up the research in our lab with similar and complementary results for escape behavior. Franchina, Bush, Kash, Troen, and Young (1973) found, as Knapp (1965) found for avoidance, that similarity of shock and safe compartments impedes escape performance. Franchina and Schindele (1975) replicated this finding and showed, with ITI held constant, that a 20-sec safety confinement is superior to 5-sec even when the shock and safe chambers are similar, that is, when performance conditions are unfavorable (doubtless, there are individual differences for onset of relief, and 20 sec allows more rats to undergo more relief). When the shock and safe chambers are similar and the rats are confined for 20 sec in each one, performance is especially poor; that is, relief presumably counterconditions the fear of the shock box. Franchina, Kash, Reeder, and Sheets (1978) found that an exteroceptive feedback stimulus in the safe box facilitates escape performance, compared with no-feedback controls when safe-box confinement is longer than shock-box confinement (20 vs. 5 sec) but not when the confinements are the same (20 vs. 20 sec, or 5 vs. 5 sec). This result nicely supports relief theorizing rather then Bolles' (1971) feedback hypothesis. Also, feedback during extinction increases responding, distinguishing the shock from the nonshock regions so that the rat approaches only the safe box and continues to fear the shock box. (See also Bagné, this chapter.)

12. A number of studies have demonstrated that the postponement of shock is a critical variable in establishing avoidance. In an operant situation, Hineline (1970) trained rats on a schedule in which each 20-sec cycle began with a retractable bar being inserted into the operant chamber. In the absence of a bar-press, shock occurred after 8 sec, and 2 sec later the bar was removed. If the rat pressed the bar within the first 8 sec, the bar was withdrawn immediately and shock was postponed until 18 sec had elapsed since the beginning of the cycle. Thus bar-pressing did not affect the one for 20-sec shock rate but only postponed shock. All rats learned to bar-press; and subsequent research (Hineline, 1977) showed that learning occurs even if several shocks come later in the cycle. A short latency process, such as relief, is clearly implicated by such data, and its importance highlighted.

13. To test Denny's backchaining hypothesis, Callen, Boyd, and House (1988) examined the temporal course of extinction of fear in a conditioned suppression licking experiment (the relaxation/relief responses presumably originated in the test chamber when free of the

CS). Three distinct measures of fear tapped the temporal order of extinction: Time to first lick upon CS presentation measured the final link in the extinction chain; the traditional suppression ratio measured the middle link (total CS duration); and a recovery latency that measured the time to first lick after CS termination constituted the first link in the chain and the one that should extinguish first.

The results are entirely consistent with the backchaining hypothesis. The maximum decrease in the recovery latency occurred between extinction Trials 2 and 3; the maximum increase in Suppression Ratio (decrease in fear) occurred between Trials 3 and 4; and the maximum decrease in Time to First Lick occurred between Trials 5 and 6. All of these trends are statistically significant, nicely supporting an interference theory of extinction of fear/avoidance by relaxation/relief responses.

Presumably, Baum (1972) also found evidence of backchaining in a repeated flooding experiment when his control group, after 4 days of being repeatedly exposed to an 11-min safe interval between acquisition and extinction, finally extinguished as rapidly as the flooding group that spent that same amount of time in the original shock region.

14. Just as appetitive sign tracking represents a direct derivation from elicitation theory, though never stated in precisely those terms (Denny, 1966, 1967, 1971a, 1971b; Denny & Adelmen, 1955; Denny & Ratner, 1970), sign tracking of a nonshock signal in an aversive situation is a prediction from relaxation/relief theory. The theory explicitly states that an animal learns, in part, to approach the nonshock area (safety cues) during avoidance training; and the sign-tracking study by LeClerc and Reberg (1980) provides clear backing for this assumption. In their study a 2-sec shock preceded a platform CS by 10 sec, and the platform was accompanied by a lengthy shock-free interval. This procedure produced a significant increase in approach to and contact with the platform, compared with appropriate controls.

The authors applied this finding to explaining why one-way avoidance is much easier than shuttle avoidance and why bar-press avoidance is so difficult in much the same way as relaxation/relief theory has done (Denny, 1971a; Denny & Ratner, 1970), but used different terminology in their analysis. It is relevant to note that their CS (platform) started 8 sec after shock cessation (ideal for relief conditioning) and was available for 60 sec at the start of a long nonshock period (1–5 min, mean = 3 min), which was also ideal for conditioning relaxation, at least on most trials.

15. Maier, Rapaport and Wheatley (1976) presented rats with a 10-sec tone CS either 3 or 30 sec after 1.0 mA shock termination. Only the

3-sec UCS–CS interval yielded a conditioning effect, suppressing Sidman avoidance responding by 61%. According to our data (Denny,
1971a), relief should be operative in the 3-sec group but not in the
30-sec group, while relaxation typically requires a longer lasting CS
that begins somewhat sooner than 30 sec to be conditioned effectively.
(The ITI during conditioning was a mean of 3 min and thus sufficiently
long to support the conditioning of relaxation on some trials if other
conditions were right.) Maier et al. (1976) concluded that their results
were consistent with the Solomon–Corbit (1974) opponent-process
model and Denny's relaxation/relief theory, which their study had been
designed to test.

16. Grelle and James (1981) demonstrated that so-called inhibitory con-
    ditioning occurs rapidly postshock in a neutral environment, that is,
    minus the operation of a US expectancy (see chapter by D. E. McAllister
    and McAllister, this volume for details). Thus they point out that the
    rapid conditioning of relief or relaxation found in our lab, for example,
    in 8 or 9 trials (Denny, 1971a, this chapter; Zerbolio, 1968), in contrast
    to the large number of trials required in typical conditioned inhibition
    studies, makes good sense. Postshock, the fear present when an animal
    expects shock (US) would compete with relaxation/relief responses
    and clearly retard the process of conditioning a positive event, or
    inhibition, to the CS.

17. Tortora (1983) extended the relaxation/relief concepts to training dogs
    with behavior problems (specifically, avoidance-motivated aggres-
    sion). He used a safety signal tone in an escape/avoidance learning
    paradigm to train such dogs to master 15 different commands. A series
    of escape trials with command, warning signal, shock, escape, and
    postshock tone in that order preceded a series of avoidance trials.
    During avoidance trials, shock from the this sequence was omitted
    and the safety signal (tone) only followed a correct response with a
    short latency. The ITI during all training was long enough for the tone
    to be associated with relaxation, and learning without the safety signal
    never achieved nearly the level obtained with its use. Dogs learning
    the commands with the safety tone technique had improved carriage
    (posture) and became manageable and prosocial, whereas aggression
    was intractable to other treatment methods.

Some Unpublished Research

The main purpose of this unpublished research (Denny, 1972) was to study
the effects of relaxation and relief in combination, and separately. Are
their combined effects greater than either one separately? We, of course,

expected that this would be the case. And, if so, how do they combine? A number of different groups were used, with $n = 15$ in each group. All groups were shocked (2 mA) for 1 sec, 60 sec after insertion into a black/white diagonally striped shock box (same as used by Zerbolio, 1968, in prior research) for a total of five trials, followed by three such insertions into this box without shock ever being presented. For each of these eight insertions, a rat in an experimental condition was removed from the shock chamber immediately after shock termination (or after 61 sec) and then placed in the smaller all-white box that was subsequently the safe chamber in the one-way avoidance part of the experiment. The 5–3 schedule of shock and nonshock placements was used because the three nonshock placements seemed especially conducive to producing relaxation and no more than five shocks presumably prevented the backchaining of fear to the white-compartment CS that necessarily preceded four shock trials.

The one-way avoidance procedure used to assess the conditioned effects was somewhat unusual. Bagné, in his Ph.D. research (1971), found that excellent stimulus control by the color of a compartment could be attained by using a combined active-passive avoidance procedure so that handling and placement in the apparatus were not cues for running or avoiding. That is, randomly half the time at the beginning of a trial a rat was placed in the shock chamber and half the time in the safe chamber. When placed in the safe chamber, a rat avoided shock by staying there—by a passive-avoidance response. When placed in the shock chamber, the rat avoided by actively running to the safe chamber. The acquisition criterion used here was that four out of five responses were avoidances with at least one avoidance of each type.

If we look at the manipulations used for Group 1 (see Table 6.1), we see that the procedure for this group permitted both relaxation and relief to be conditioned to the white chamber: Postshock, a subject was placed immediately into the white chamber where it could undergo relief, but since it stayed there 150 sec it could also complete the relaxation response. A 5-sec buffer on an open platform or stool preceded the next placement in the striped shock box. Group 2, on the other hand, only spent the first 20 sec in the white chamber and the 135-sec remainder on the stool. Only relief could presumably be conditioned to the white chamber in Group 2. And in Group 3 (Control I) neither relaxation nor relief could be conditioned because all of the postshock period was spent on the stool, with the rat being picked up after the first 20 sec just to control for handling. Group 4 (Control II) is really the same as Group 1 and simply controls for the outside possibility that a total of 155 sec on the stool (Control I procedure) had the effect of inhibiting subsequent one-way avoidance training in the control group rather than that confinement in the safe chamber facilitated subsequent avoidance learning in the experimentals. As can be seen in

TABLE 6.1
Mean Number of Shocks Received to Reach Acquisition Criterion during One-way Avoidance Learning: The Assessment of Prior Conditioning of Relief or Relaxation

Group	Manipulations During Conditioning	Conditioning Trials	Mean	S.D.	t
1. Relaxation and Relief	150 sec. white 5 sec. stool	5 shocks 3 nonshocks	1.53	.99	1 vs. 2 = 1.74 (p = .05)
2. Relief "only"	20 sec. white 135 sec. stool	5 shocks 3 nonshocks	2.26	1.22	2 vs. 3 = 1.81 (p = .05)
3. Control I	20 sec. stool 135 sec. stool	5 shocks 3 nonshocks	3.33	1.83	1 vs. 3 = 3.23 (p = .001)
4. Control II, Relaxation and Relief	150 sec. white 155 sec. stool	5 shocks 3 nonshocks	1.73	.88	4 vs. 1 = .57 (NS)
5. Relaxation only	20 sec. stool 135 sec. white 20 sec. stool	5 shocks 3 nonshocks	2.20	1.52	5 vs. 6 = 2.47 (p = .01)
6. Control	20 sec. stool 135 sec. stool 20 sec stool	5 shocks 3 nonshocks	4.26	2.74	
1 and 4 Combined, (Relaxation and Relief)	—	—	1.63	—	5 vs. 1 + 4 = 1.71 (p = .05)

Table 6.1, the means for Groups 1 and 4 are very close and the t for the difference is only 0.57, so that 155 sec on the stool was not a relevant factor and the manipulations with respect to relief and relaxation presumably did what they were purported to do.

To assess the effects of conditioned relaxation alone required increased handling, as specified for Group 5 in Table 6.1. That is, the rat had to spend the first 20-sec postshock in the neutral area of the stool to eliminate the operation of relief, and after 135 sec in the white chamber, it spent a needed buffer period of 20 sec on the stool—a period that also gave the rat a total of 155 sec of nonshock after the white chamber CS was introduced.

Another control, Group 6, precisely controlled for number of handlings and time spent postshock. This group, as can be seen in the table, learned more slowly and took a mean of 0.93 more shocks than Control I (Group 3). This, as is consistent with the higher S.D. of Group 6, was due to two animals taking one or two shocks more than any other rat in the study. Eliminating these two rats, however, did not change the p value of 0.01 for the Group 5 vs. 6 comparison.

Conditioned relaxation, like conditioned relief, clearly occurred; and conditioned relaxation and conditioned relief combined had, as predicted, a greater effect than either one alone ($p = .05$, one-tailed test). Let us examine how relief and relaxation seem to combine to produce their joint effect (see Table 6.2). In another part of this study, which dealt only with relaxation, there was another group closely comparable to Groups 3 and 6. If we pool the learning scores for all three groups to get the most stable

TABLE 6.2
How Relaxation and Relief Summate

Best estimate of control ($n = 45$) = 3.66 shocks.
Conditioned relaxation = 3.66 − 2.20 = *1.46* (savings score).
Conditioned relief = 3.66 − 2.26 = *1.40* (savings score).

The two savings scores indicate that the amounts of conditioned relaxation and relief were about equal in effect, under the conditions of the present study.

Relaxation + Relief = 3.66 − 1.63 = 2.03 (empirical).
Summated R + R = 1.46 + 1.40 = 2.86 (summation is *not* arithmetic).

Physiological Summation (à la Hull)

$$R + R = 1.46 + 1.40 - \frac{1.46 + 1.40}{3.66 \text{ (Max)}} = 2.86 - .78 = \underline{2.08}$$

Max = 3.66 − zero shocks = 3.66 − 0 = 3.66 (savings).

estimate of learning for the control condition, we arrive at the value of 3.66 shocks, as given in the table. The conditioned effects are best viewed as savings scores, how many fewer shocks are required by the experimental groups than by the controls. Subtracting the number of shocks required by the relaxation only group (2.2) from 3.66 yields a savings of 1.46; for relief only, savings = 1.40. That is, for the conditions of the present study the contributions of relief and relaxation to the conditioning of approach were roughly equivalent.

The best estimate of learning when both relaxation and relief were operative is the mean of Groups 1 and 4, which is 1.63 shocks. This value, subtracted from 3.66, gives a savings score of 2.03. The individual savings scores for relaxation and relief added together yield a total savings of 2.86, which is considerably greater than 2.03. If, however, these two habits are summated according to the formula recommended by Clark–Hull (1943), which he called physiological summation, the result is quite striking. Basically, the formula says that habits summate in the same way increments to a response tendency summate to produce the final habit. To use this formula it is necessary to have a good estimate of what the maximum is to which the total habit can grow. We are uniquely fortunate here in having an excellent estimate of this maximum. The best score possible for any rat in the avoidance learning situation is zero shocks, that is, performing perfectly solely on the basis of the prior conditioning of relief and relaxation, which is what one rat did in Group 1 when both conditioned relief and relaxation were operative. As shown in Table 6.2, this means that the maximum is a savings score of 3.66; and when this value is plugged into Hull's formula it yields a summation savings score of *2.08*, which is remarkably similar to the empirical value of 2.03, as obtained in this study.

THE BAGNÉ STUDY

Method

The apparatus was a shuttle box with compartments separated by a guillotine door. Either compartment could be all black, all white, or black and white stripes and with a grid floor or with a smooth/rough floor. The floors were hinged to measure latencies; shock was scrambled; and the ceiling was a one-way painted screen. Doors on both sides provided access when the shuttle box was rotated 180° on a lazy susan. A wastebasket housed the rat during the intertrial interval (ITI). An habituation box of end-to-end placement of replicas of the stimulus conditions (black, white, and stripes) was available.

Habituation, which began approximately a half-hour before training and after aversiveness to handling had been counterconditioned by feeding, consisted of placing a subject in the habituation box for 20 min, followed by placing the rat for 3 min in the freshly washed shuttle box with shock off and guillotine door up.

A combination of active and passive avoidance trials was used throughout acquisition, extinction, and spontaneous recovery. An active trial began when the rat was placed in the center of the shock area facing the open guillotine door that led to the safe area. The CS–US interval, time between placement in shock area and shock onset, was 5 sec. After an avoidance or an escape, the door between the shock and safe areas was closed. The safe area confinement period (SAC) for all subjects was 30 sec throughout acquisition, extinction, and spontaneous recovery. Then the rat was transferred manually to the ITI basket.

A passive avoidance trial began when the rat was placed in the center of the safe area facing the open door to the shock area. If the rat remained in the safe area for 5 sec, the guillotine door was closed for the remainder of the SAC; it had avoided passively. If the rat made the error of entering the shock area, the door remained open and the procedure was the same as for an active avoidance trial. That is, the rat could avoid shock after making a passive error by returning to the safe area within the 5-sec CS–US interval. After 5 sec, the rat could escape shock by returning to the safe area.

Active and passive trials and box rotation were alternated on a predetermined schedule. Grid shock in acquisition was individually adjusted within a range of 0.3 mA to 0.5 mA to elicit agitated behavior reliably. The safe area was always white with a smooth floor, except for the Color Control group. The acquisition criterion was seven consecutive avoidances, which typically meant at least three active and three passive avoidances.

Extinction began 5 min after the acquisition criterion was met and continued until the rat reached the extinction criterion or for a maximum of 250 massed trials. The extinction criterion consisted of a back-to-back occurrence of one active avoidance trial on which the rat remained in the shock area for 30 sec and 1 passive trial on which the rat entered and stayed in the shock area for 30 sec. The ITI for all extinction trials was 20 sec.

Spontaneous recovery was tested 30 min after the extinction criterion had been reached. Subjects that did not reach criterion within 250 trials were not tested. Spontaneous recovery was always tested with the same shock and safe area stimuli that had been used during acquisition, and trials were conducted as during extinction. Trials were continued until the rat met the same criterion used during extinction or for a maximum of 150 trials.

Six experimental groups ($n = 48$) were formed by the factorial combination of a Short (20-sec) and a Long (150-sec) ITI during acquisition with three extinction conditions: No Change, Change Shock, and Change Safe. From each ITI group 8 subjects were randomly assigned to each of the three extinction conditions. No Change group was extinguished with the same shock and safe area stimuli that had been used during acquisition—namely, the striped shock area with a grid floor and a white safe area with a smooth floor. Change Shock group was extinguished with shock area stimuli changed to black with a rough floor. The safe area for Change Safe group was changed to black with a rough floor.

There was also a Rotation Control group with Long ITI and Change Shock conditions, but the box was never rotated. A Color Control group with Long ITI and Change Safe conditions was also run with the safe area black during acquisition and spontaneous recovery, and white during extinction.

Results and Discussion

The length of the ITI had little effect on performance during acquisition, as both ITI groups reached criterion in approximately 17 trials and produced almost the same number of active and passive avoidances while doing so. The Short and Long ITI groups also received 5.8 and 6.4 shocks, respectively, and were thus equivalent on this measure as well.

The only way in which Short and Long ITI groups differed during acquisition was in the amount of activity exhibited during safe area confinement, with Long ITI rats being more active and presumably more relaxed. Although acquisition ITI had little effect on avoidance during acquisition, the effects of this variable were clearly evident during extinction. Table 6.3 shows the mean number of trials to extinction for all six experimental groups. Both main effects and the interaction were significant.

Five out of eight No Change rats with a long acquisition ITI did not extinguish in 250 extinction trials, while the slowest Short ITI, No Change rat extinguished in 168 trials. As can be seen in Table 6.3, the Long ITI, No Change rats, five of which had an arbitrary score of 250 trials, took twice as many trials to "extinguish" as the Short ITI rats. The higher resistance of the Long ITI condition for both the No Change and Change

TABLE 6.3
Mean Number of Trials to Extinction Criterion

	No Change	*Change Shock*	*Change Safe*
Short ITI	101.8	13.8	68.0
Long ITI	203.3	37.6	68.1

Shock groups is attributed to the superior conditioning of relaxation-mediated approach to a safe area that is followed by a Long ITI.

When the safe area was changed and thereby removed from operation, extinction occurred in only 68 trials for both Short and Long ITI conditions, (i.e., equally for both Change Safe groups). Only the unchanged shock-area stimuli controlled both Change Safe groups' fear-mediated responding, and thus the two groups that performed alike during acquisition extinguished at the same rate. Without the original safe area cues, the ITI variable was inoperative and thus irrelevant. Could data ever be better?

Changing the shock area produced an even larger response decrement than changing the safe area stimuli. Change Shock, Long ITI rats required almost three times as many trials to extinguish as Short ITI rats ($p = .05$), indicating again that a longer period in which to relax increases the approach value of the preceding safe region. But the low level of resistance to extinction in both ITI groups suggests that relaxation-mediated approach is attenuated when fear is minimal, that is, when shock-box cues are absent. Weak approach to the safe area fits the theory; subjects must first be fearful before they can subsequently relax and approach associated stimuli. All of these effects were virtually equivalent across active and passive avoidances.

Long ITI rats were more active in the safe area during extinction than Short ITI animals ($p < .05$), supporting the relaxation-approach interpretation of why Long ITIs mediate greater resistance to extinction. Exploratory activity is assumed to be an observable correlate or manifestation of relaxation (Baum, 1970; Denny, 1971a).

As a final test, all rats that reached the extinction criterion within 250 trials were re-extinguished with the same shock and safe area stimuli used during acquisition. The mean number of spontaneous recovery trials to extinction for each group is presented in Table 6.4.

The effect of the extinction variable is highly significant and quite informative. Both No Change and Change Safe groups required very few trials to reach criterion a second time. When the shock area stimuli were reinstated, *both* Change Shock groups took 60 trials to reach criterion. This finding indicated a high degree of stimulus control by the shock chamber, which contributed only fear to the total learning of avoidance.

TABLE 6.4
Spontaneous Recovery: Mean Number of Trials to
Extinction Criterion

	No Change	Change Shock	Change Safe
Short ITI	7.5	60.4	9.3
Long ITI	6.0	60.0	10.1

When fear was specifically extinguished in the shock area in the Change Safe group, only 9 or 10 spontaneous recovery trials occurred when the safe-area stimuli were reinstated; and this number surpassed the spontaneous recovery score of the No Change group by only 2 to 4 trials, even though the No Change safe area also underwent extinction. Thus, without fear, safety cues do not elicit relaxation-approach to any appreciable degree—just as a rat must be deprived of food to approach it consistently. Such a result is consistent with Feldman's (1977) finding that exposing a stimulus to an animal in the absence of aversive events does not endow it with safety properties. The internal consistency of the data are nicely illustrated in Table 6.4. Note that both Change Shock groups extinguished in about 60 trials after the shock area cues (fear) had been reinstated, which made the conditions for these groups comparable to the Change Safe groups of Table 6.1 that both extinguished in 68 trials. So even though the comparison between Tables 6.3 and 6.4 is for different groups of rats and the two groups that took 60 trials had been extinguished for the second time, all four scores are remarkably similar (note that the extinction criteria for original extinction and test for spontaneous recovery were the same).

No significant differences were found between the Color Control group and its experimental counterpart, ruling out color of box as a relevant variable. On many measures, including a marked increase in variability when the box was not rotated, the Rotation Control group differed significantly from its experimental counterparts, indicating that adequate control of the interior stimuli of the shock and safe chambers would have been impossible without rotation.

A Supplementary Study

Bagné (1971, Experiment 2), using the same experimental situation, found that additional avoidance trials given with the same 150-sec ITI as during precriterial acquisition trials facilitated subsequent extinction with a 20-sec ITI. But facilitation occurred only when relaxation/relief was operative. This meant (a) when all cues remained unchanged during extinction (No Change Group) or (b) when the original shock cues were present during extinction (Change Safe) group *and* when the number of additional avoidance trials were sufficient for relaxation/relief to have backchained from the safe area to the shock area prior to extinction trials (see Table 6.5, Col. 4, Row 3). That this backchaining in fact was occurring is supported by the increase in acquisition errors with additional trials. With 11 extra trials rats made errors 12.6% of the time, and with 28 extra trials they made errors 31.4% of the time over the last 17 trials (no shock occurred on such errors in any group). Changing the shock area cues (Change Shock) minimized fear and thus also minimized the presence of any conditioned

TABLE 6.5
Mean Number of Trials to Extinction Criterion (Exp. 2)

Extra Trials	No Change	Change Shock	Change Safe
0	203.3	37.6	68.1
11	123.5	43.3	62.4
28	42.4	25.4	20.4

relaxation/relief to the "shock" area cues. Therefore with Change Shock conditions, extinction should be relatively rapid and extra avoidances should have little effect on extinction, which is basically what Bagné found (see Table 6.5, Col. 3; the Change Shock group differences here are far from being significant).

A Relevant Consideration

Gray (1975) has strongly suggested that the secondary reinforcing effects (approach value) of stimuli associated with the absence of shock is relatively independent of the degree of fear present in the original shock situation. The results of a study by Lawler (1965) that manipulated fear in the "shock" region in a manner similar to Bagné's were marshaled as evidence in support of this contention. In Lawler's study, rats escaped from a gray start box with a buzzer plus shock by entering a distinctive escape box (either striped or all black) for 20 trials and then were tested without shock for 20 trials with *both* black and striped boxes accessible. On test trials for half the rats, the original start box and buzzer were used; for the other half, a different start box minus grid floor and buzzer was used. Controls were treated the same except for never having been shocked. Confinement in the escape box was 30 sec, the ITI was 60 sec.

All experimental rats chose the original escape box significantly more often than the controls, indicating that this box had approach value. In fact, the rats with the changed start box had the stronger approach response.

As the McAllisters discussed in their chapter, there are several reasons for questioning whether fear was really eliminated in Lawler's changed start-box group (and neither Gray nor Lawler maintained that fear was completely gone). The following points would seem to contradict any such assumption: (a) In the Bagné study handling cues were controlled, because for half the training trials the rat was placed in a safe place and half the time in the shock area. Whereas in Lawler's study the rat, when handled after the ITI, was always placed in the shock box. Thus, in Lawler's study, fear could be conditioned to handling and placement cues (Leonard, Tafeen, & Fey, 1972) irrespective of the interior box cues and be operative during testing. (b) During testing, more than half of Lawler's rats in the unshocked control group with the changed start box failed to leave the startbox within 150 sec; whereas none of the experimental group with the changed start box failed to leave, entering one or the other escape box with a median latency of 5.9 sec. Thus, it would seem that considerable residual fear remained in the experimental rats even though their median response time for a single escape box was 0.9 sec during training. (c) Even the seemingly paradoxical finding by Lawler that the experimental rats with the changed start box showed stronger approach then the unchanged group seems interpretable in terms of his own data. Both of his control groups showed a clear preference for entering the new or different escape box during testing, which is consistent with data on habituation of exploration (e.g., Denny & Leckart, 1965). But considerably more preference was evident in the controls when the start box was unchanged than changed, that is, when nothing else in the stimulus situation was altered. And presumably the unchanged experimental group had the same bias, showing a decreased tendency to approach the original escape box because of the strong tendency to explore the novel box. The probability of such confounding raises the researchable question as to whether the tendency to investigate novel stimuli is generally attenuated when the introductory or starting context is modified.

Thus, the evidence seems quite clear: Without fear there is no avoidance or approach to safety.

CONCLUDING REMARKS

Regardless of how the events described herein are conceptualized, some pair of response-like events with fairly specific temporal parameters is involved in the acquisition and extinction of escape-avoidance responses. Moreover, these events seem implicated in our attempts to understand phenomena such as learned helplessness, self-punitive behavior, implosive therapy (flooding), generalized anxiety, and so on. Whether the events are called relaxation and relief, opponent b processes, fear reduction and extinction, or V_{ap} and V_{cc}, is a minor point. But according to the theory at hand, the events should be conceived of as distinctive response classes in which at least one antecedent condition is the removal/postponement of an aversive stimulus, including CASs. Without fear (emotional state), there is no subsequent relaxation or relief or whatever and no chance for them to operate. We know that any CS paired with these events needs to have a fairly long duration, especially if the long latency event is being conditioned. In addition, the shock-free interval for conditioned relief (the short latency event) must be around 10 sec, and around 150 sec for conditioned relaxation (the long latency event).

According to theory, the extinction of fear and fear-related behavior involves a competing response (e.g., relaxation, relief, or freezing) that typically originates in the presence of safety and ordinarily generalizes or backchains to the CAS. The data from a variety of studies are broadly consistent with the theory.

REFERENCES

Bagné, C. A. (1968). *Escape variables and avoidance conditioning: Two extinction processes.* Unpublished master's thesis, Michigan State University, East Lansing.

Bagné, C. A. (1971). *The role of fear-withdrawal and relaxation-approach in avoidance responding.* Unpublished doctoral dissertation, Michigan State University, East Lansing.

Baum, M. (1968). Efficacy of response prevention (flooding) in facilitating the extinction of an avoidance response in rats. *Behavior Research and Therapy, 6,* 197–203.

Baum, M. (1970). Extinction of avoidance responding through response prevention (flooding). *Psychological Bulletin, 74,* 276–284.

Baum, M. (1972). Repeated acquisition and extinction of avoidance in rats using flooding (response prevention). *Learning and Motivation, 3,* 272–278.

Boice, R., Boice, C., & Dunham, A. E. (1968). Role of docility in avoidance: Gerbils and kangaroo rats in a shuttlebox. *Psychonomic Science, 10,* 381–382.

Boice, R., Denny, M. R., & Evans, T. (1967). A comparison of albino and wild rats in shuttlebox avoidance. *Psychonomic Science, 8,* 271–272.

Bolles, R. C. (1969). Avoidance and escape learning: Simultaneous acquisition of different responses. *Journal of Comparative and Physiological Psychology, 68,* 355–358.

Bolles, R. C. (1971). Species-specific defense reactions. In F. R. Brush (Ed.), *Aversive conditioning and learning* (pp. 183–233). New York: Academic Press.

Callen, E. J., Boyd, T. L., & House, W. J. (1988, March). *The temporal dynamics of fear extinction.* Paper presented at Southeastern Psychological Association meeting, New Orleans.

Church, R. M., LoLordo, V. M., Overmier, J. V. B., Solomon, R. L., & Turner, L. H. (1966). Cardiac responses to shock in curararized dogs: Effects of shock intensity and duration, warning signal, and prior experience with shock. *Journal of Comparative and Physiological Psychology, 62,* 1–7.

Delprato, D. J. (1969). Extinction of one-way avoidance and delayed warning-signal termination. *Journal of Experimental Psychology, 80,* 192–193.

Delprato, D. J. (1974a). Postresponse exposure to warning signal in avoidance extinction. *Animal Learning and Behavior, 21,* 59–62.

Delprato, D. J. (1974b). Fear of the shock side as a function of acquisition criterion in one-way avoidance. *Bulletin of the Psychonomic Society, 3,* 166–168.

Delprato, D. J., & Denny, M. R. (1968). Punishment and the length of nonshock confinement during the extinction of avoidance. *Canadian Journal of Psychology, 22,* 456–464.

Delprato, D. J., & Denny, M. R. (1970). Passive avoidance as a function of the duration of nonshock confinement. *Learning and Motivation, 1,* 44–51.

Delprato, D. J., & Dreilinger, C. (1974). Backchaining of relaxation in the extinction of avoidance. *Behavior Research and Therapy, 12,* 191–197.

Delprato, D. J., Meltzer, R. J. (1974). Type of start box and goal box distinctiveness in self-punitive running of rats. *Journal of Comparative and Physiological Psychology, 87,* 548–554.

Denny, M. R. (1946). The role of secondary reinforcement in a partial reinforcement learning situation. *Journal of Experimental Psychology, 36,* 373–389.

Denny, M. R. (1966). A theoretical analysis and its application to training the mentally retarded. In N. R. Ellis (Ed.), *International review of research in mental retardation* (Vol. 2, pp. 1–27). New York: Academic Press.

Denny, M. R. (1967). A learning model. In W. C. Corning & S. C. Ratner (Eds.), *The chemistry of learning* (Vol. 2, pp. 32–42). New York: Academic Press.

Denny, M. R. (1971a). Relaxation theory and experiments. In F. R. Brush (Ed.), *Aversive conditioning and learning* (pp. 235–295). New York: Academic Press.

Denny, M. R. (1971b). A theory of experimental extinction and its relation to a general theory. In H. Kendler & J. Spence (Eds.), *Essays in neobehaviorism: A memorial volume to Kenneth W. Spence* (pp. 43–67). New York: Appleton–Century–Crofts.

Denny, M. R. (1972, April). *The concept of "relief" in avoidance behavior.* Paper presented at Rocky Mountain Psychological Association meeting, Las Vegas.

Denny, M. R. (1976). Post-aversive relief and relaxation and their implications for behavior therapy. *Journal of Behavior Therapy and Experimental Psychiatry, 7,* 315–321.

Denny, M. R. (1986). "Retention" of S–R in midst of the cognitive invasion. In D. Kendrick, M. Rilling, & M. R. Denny (Eds.), *Theories of animal memory* (pp. 35–50). Hillsdale, NJ: Lawrence Erlbaum Associates.

Denny, M. R., & Adelman, H. M. (1955). Elicitation theory: I. An analysis of two typical learning situations. *Psychological Review, 62,* 290–296.

Denny, M. R., & Dmitruk, V. M. (1967). Effect of punishing a single failure to avoid. *Journal of Comparative and Physiological Psychology, 63,* 277–281.

Denny, M. R., & Dunham, M. D. (1951). The effect of differential nonreinforcement of the incorrect response on the learning of the correct response in the simple T-maze. *Journal of Experimental Psychology, 41,* 382–389.

Denny, M. R., Koons, P. B., & Mason, J. E. (1959). Extinction of avoidance as a function of the escape situation. *Journal of Comparative and Physiological Psychology, 52,* 212–214.

Denny, M. R., & Leckart, B. T. (1965). Alternation behavior: Learning and extinction one trial per day. *Journal of Comparative and Physiological Psychology, 60,* 229–232.

Denny, M. R., & Martindale, R. L. (1956). The effects of the initial reinforcement on response tendency. *Journal of Experimental Psychology, 52,* 95–100.

Denny, M. R., & Ratner, S. C. (1970). *Comparative psychology: Research in animal behavior* (rev. ed.). Homewood, IL: Dorsey Press.

Denny, M. R., & Weisman, R. C. (1964). Avoidance behavior as a function of the length of nonshock confinement. *Journal of Comparative and Physiological Psychology, 58,* 252–257.

Denny, M. R., Zerbolio, D. J., & Weisman, R. G. (1969). Avoidance learning in heterogeneous and homogeneous shuttle boxes. *Journal of Comparative and Physiological Psychology, 68,* 370–372.

Dillow, P. V., Myerson, J., Slaughter, L., & Hurwitz, H. M. B. (1972). Safety signals and the acquisition and extinction of lever-press discriminated avoidance in rats. *British Journal of Psychology, 63,* 583–591.

Feldman, M. A. (1977). The effects of preexposure to a warning or a safety signal on the acquisition of a two-way avoidance response in rats. *Animal Learning and Behavior, 5,* 21–24.

Fidura, F. G. (1966). *The role of selective attention and the distinctiveness of cues in simple and complex discrimination learning.* Unpublished doctoral dissertation, Michigan State University, East Lansing.

Franchina, J. J., Bush, M. E., Kash, J. S., Troen, D. M., & Young, R. L. (1973). Similarity between shock and safe areas during acquisition, transfer, and extinction of escape behavior in rats. *Journal of Comparative and Physiological Psychology, 84,* 216–224.

Franchina, J. J., Kash, J. S., Reeder, J. R., & Sheets, C. T. (1978). Effects of exteroceptive feedback and safe-box confinement durations on escape behavior in rats. *Animal Learning and Behavior, 6,* 423–428.

Franchina, J. J., & Schindele, T. E. (1975). Nonshock confinement duration and shock and safebox similarity during escape training in rats. *Animal Learning and Behavior, 3,* 297–300.

Gray, J. A. (1975). *Elements of a two-process theory of learning.* New York: Academic Press.

Grelle, M. J., & James, J. H. (1981). Conditioned inhibition of fear: Evidence for a competing response mechanism. *Learning and Motivation, 12,* 300–320.

Guthrie, E. R. (1952). *The psychology of learning* (2nd ed.). New York: Harper.

Heide, F. J., & Borkovec, T. D. (1983). Relaxation-induced anxiety: Paradoxical anxiety enhancement due to relaxation training. *Journal of Consulting and Clinical Psychology, 51,* 171–182.

Heide, F. J., & Borkovec, T. D. (1984). Relaxation-induced anxiety: Mechanisms and theoretical implications. *Behaviour Research and Therapy, 22,* 1–12.

Hineline, P. N. (1970). Negative reinforcement without shock reduction. *Journal of Experimental Analysis of Behavior, 14,* 259–268.

Hineline, P. N. (1977). Negative reinforcement and avoidance. In W. K. Honig & J. E. R. Staddon (Eds.), *Handbook of operant behavior* (pp. 364–414). Englewood Cliffs, NJ: Prentice–Hall.

Hull, C. L. (1943). *Principles of behavior.* New York: Appleton–Century–Crofts.

Hyman, L. M. (1971). The effects of irrelevant dimensions and stimuli on two-choice discrimination learning by children. *Psychonomic Science, 22,* 249–250.

Kamin, L. J., Brimer, C. J., & Black, A. H. (1963). Conditioned suppression as a monitor of fear of the CS in the course of avoidance training. *Journal of Comparative and Physiological Psychology, 56,* 497–501.

Katzev, R. (1967). Extinguishing avoidance responses as a function of delayed warning signal termination. *Journal of Experimental Psychology, 75,* 339–344.

Knapp, R. K. (1960). *The acquisition and extinction of instrumental avoidance as a function of the escape situation.* Unpublished doctoral dissertation, Michigan State University, East Lansing.

Knapp, R. K. (1965). Acquisition and extinction of avoidance with similar and different shock and escape situations. *Journal of Comparative and Physiological Psychology, 60,* 272–273.

Koob, G. F., Fray, P. J., & Iversen, S. D. (1976). Tail-pinch stimulation: Sufficient motivation for learning. *Science, 194,* 637–639.

Lawler, E. E. (1965). Secondary reinforcement value of stimuli associated with shock reduction. *Quarterly Journal of Experimental Psychology, 17,* 57–61.

LeClerc, R., & Reberg, D. (1980). Sign-tracking in aversive condition. *Learning and Motivation, 11,* 302–317.

Leonard, D. W., Tafeen, S. O., & Fey, S. G. (1972). The transfer of one-way and handled-shuttle pretraining to standard-shuttle avoidance learning. *Learning and Motivation, 3,* 59–72.

Maatsch, J. L. (1951). *An exploratory study of the possible differential inhibitory effects of frustration and work inhibition.* Unpublished master's thesis, Michigan State College, East Lansing.

Mackenzie, D. L. (1974). *Aversively motivated two-choice discrimination learning.* Unpublished doctoral dissertation, Syracuse University, Syracuse, NY.

McAllister, W. R., & McAllister, D. E. (1971). Behavioral measurement of conditioned fear. In F. R. Brush (Ed.), *Aversive conditioning and learning* (pp. 105–179). New York: Academic Press.

Maier, S. F., Rapaport, P., & Wheatley, K. (1976). Conditioned inhibition and the UCS–CS interval. *Animal Learning and Behavior, 4*, 217–220.

Marx, M. H., & Hellwig, L. R. (1964). Acquisition and extinction of avoidance conditioning without escape responses. *Journal of Comparative and Physiological Psychology, 58*, 451–452.

Masterson, F. A. (1970). Is termination of a warning signal an effective reward for the rat? *Journal of Comparative and Physiological Psychology, 72*, 471–475.

Mendelson, J. (1966). Role of hunger on T-maze learning for food by rats. *Journal of Comparative and Physiological Psychology, 62*, 341–349.

Mineka, S. (1978). The effect of over training on flooding of jump-up and shuttlebox avoidance responses. *Behavior Research and Therapy, 16*, 335–344.

Mineka, S., Cook, M., & Miller, S. (1984). Fear conditioned with escapable and inescapable shock: Effects of a feedback stimulus. *Journal of Experimental Psychology: Animal Behavior Processes, 10*, 307–323.

Moot, S. A., Nelson, K., & Bolles, R. C. (1974). Avoidance learning in a black and white shuttlebox. *Bulletin of Psychonomic Science, 4*, 501–502.

Morris, R. G. M. (1974). Two independent effects of variation in intertrial interval upon leverpress avoidance by rats. *Animal Learning and Behavior, 2*, 189–192.

Morris, R. G. M. (1975). Preconditioning of reinforcing properties of an exteroceptive feedback stimulus. *Learning and Motivation, 6*, 289–298.

Mowrer, O. H., & Lamoreaux, R. R. (1946). Fear as an intervening variable in avoidance conditioning. *Journal of Comparative and Physiological Psychology, 39*, 29–50.

Pearl, J. (1963). Intertrial interval and acquisition of a lever-press avoidance response. *Journal of Comparative and Physiological Psychology, 56*, 710–712.

Pearl, J., & Fitzgerald, J. J. (1966). Better discriminated bar-press avoidance at short intertrial intervals. *Psychonomic Science, 4*, 41–42.

Reynierse, J. H., & Rizley, R. C. (1970a). Relaxation and fear as determinants of maintained avoidance in rats. *Journal of Comparative and Physiological Psychology, 72*, 228–232.

Reynierse, J. H., & Rizley, R. C. (1970b). Stimulus and response contingencies in extinction of avoidance by rats. *Journal of Comparative and Physiological Psychology, 73*, 86–92.

Reynierse, J. H., Weisman, R. G., & Denny, M. R. (1963). Shock compartment confinement during the intertrial interval in avoidance learning. *Psychological Record, 13*, 403–406.

Rosellini, R. A., DeCola, J. P., & Warren, D. A. (1986). The effect of feedback stimuli on contextual fear depends upon the length of the minimum intertrial interval. *Learning and Motivation, 17*, 229–242.

Solomon, R. L., & Corbit, J. D. (1974). An opponent process theory of motivation: I. Temporal dynamics of affect. *Psychological Review, 81*, 119–145.

Starr, M. D., & Mineka, S. (1977). Determinants of fear over the course of avoidance learning. *Learning and Motivation, 8*, 332–350.

Tortora, D. F. (1983). Safety training: The elimination of avoidance-motivated aggression in dogs. *Journal of Experimental Psychology: General, 112*, 176–214.

Tortora, D. F., & Denny, M. R. (1973). Flooding as a function of shock level and length of confinement. *Learning and Motivation, 4*, 276–283.

Weisman, R. G., Denny, M. R., Platt, S. A., & Zerbolio, D. J. (1966). Facilitation of extinction by a stimulus associated with long nonshock confinement periods. *Journal of Comparative and Physiological Psychology, 62*, 26–30.

Weisman, R. G., Denny, M. R., & Zerbolio, D. J. (1967). Discrimination based on differential nonshock confinement in a shuttlebox. *Journal of Comparative and Physiological Psychology, 63*, 34–38.

Weisman, R. G., & Litner, J. S. (1969). Positive conditioned reinforcement of Sidman avoidance behavior in rats. *Journal of Comparative and Physiological Psychology, 68,* 597–603.

Weiss, J. M. (1971). Effects of coping behavior in different warning signal conditions on stress pathology in rats. *Journal of Comparative and Physiological Psychology, 77,* 1–13.

Zerbolio, D. J. (1965). *Relaxation-mediated approach as a necessary component in simple avoidance learning.* Unpublished doctoral dissertation, Michigan State University, East Lansing.

Zerbolio, D. J. (1968). Escape and approach responses in avoidance learning. *Canadian Journal of Psychology, 22,* 60–71.

7 Changes in Memory for Aversively Motivated Learning

David C. Riccio
Kent State University

Norman E. Spear
State University of New York at Binghamton

Unpleasant events often have a potent impact on behavior, and one might expect the learned aspects of such episodes to be highly enduring and resilient in the face of opposing effects. Indeed, several early studies seemed to confirm this surmise. Performance of several types of aversively motivated responses remained strong after retention intervals of weeks or months (Hilgard & Campbell, 1936; Kellogg & Wolf, 1939; Liddell, James, & Anderson, 1935; Wendt, 1937), an outcome emphasized by investigators anxious to demonstrate that conditioned responses were not transient or ephemeral changes (Hilgard & Campbell, 1936). When retention loss over weeks was obtained it tended to come from studies using appetitive reinforcement, such as with the straight runway in rats (Gagné, 1941) or salivary conditioning in humans (Razran, 1939), although Schlosberg's (1934) report that rats failed to retain conditioned response to tail shock for over a 2-month interval is an exception to the picture.

As the early studies suggested, there are many cases of enduring retention of learned behavior for appetitively (e.g., Schwartz & Reilly, 1985; Skinner, 1950) and aversively motivated responses (e.g., Hoffman, Fleshler, & Jensen, 1963). In the Hoffman et al. study, for example, pigeons continued to show conditioned suppression (CER) to a tone (and generalized stimuli) more than 2 years after training. Severe punishment also can produce a suppression of appetitively motivated responding that can be markedly enduring, even when resumption of the response is the only means of obtaining food (Appel, 1961). Furthermore, aversively motivated learning can be highly resistant to changes of other sorts. As is well known, active avoidance behavior can be very difficult to eliminate through ex-

231

tinction (Solomon, Kamin & Wynne, 1953; Solomon & Wynne, 1954). A particularly striking demonstration of the persistence of avoidance responding has been described recently by Stampfl (1987, 1988). In a special treadmill apparatus, rats continued to respond to warning cues for more than a thousand trials following a single shocked episode! Nor is the persistence of avoidance limited to infrahuman subjects. Using a laboratory fear-avoidance conditioning procedure with college students, Malloy and Levis (1988) obtained an average of more than 200 responses in extinction, with a large proportion of subjects failing to extinguish within the upper limit of 500 trials. Indeed, special procedures such as response blocking (flooding) have been devised to hasten the cessation of instrumental responding that had been learned to escape or avoid aversive consequences, because such responding was otherwise so persistent (Baum, 1969; Coulter, Riccio, & Page, 1969; Page & Hall, 1953; Solomon et al., 1953; for review, see Mineka, 1979).

Although response prevention does facilitate the subsequent extinction of avoidance behavior, recent work has begun to focus on ways to increase the efficacy of the blocking manipulation. Guided by the view that the memory of an episode is triggered by certain stimuli (Spear, 1973, 1978) and that reinstatement of these cues can enhance retrieval of target information (e.g., Riccio & Richardson, 1984; Spear, 1976), Richardson, Riccio, and Ress (1988) administered the stress-related hormones epinephrine or ACTH shortly prior to response blocking. During extinction testing, subjects that had been in the condition of memory "reactivation" (or arousal) emitted fewer avoidance responses than a group that had received a saline injection before blocking. This outcome is consistent with the view that the internal stimuli associated with the hormonal state helped re-establish a strong representation of fear during the CS-only exposure, thus permitting more complete extinction. [According to Denny (1976, and this volume), fear and relaxation/relief must be pitted directly against each other to effect extinction, Ed.] Further investigation is needed, but this finding is provocative in suggesting that, in addition to cognitive information about contingencies, elicitation of an affective response may contribute importantly to the elimination of fear-motivated behavior. Although Solomon et al. (1953, p. 299) stated that "the best way to produce extinction of the emotional response would be to arrange the situation in such a way that an extremely intense emotional reaction takes place," and this strategy plays a central role in the "implosive therapy" developed by Stampfl and Levis (e.g., 1967), the notion has received relatively little attention in the experimental literature. However, Richardson and Riccio (in press) have recently suggested that the effectiveness of tranquilizers either in facilitating extinction of avoidance or in accomplishing long-term change in a therapeutic situation may be limited more by their dampening effect on emotional (fear) expression than by their dissociative properties. They also speculated that the value of the old adage about "getting right back on the horse after a fall" may be in arranging extinction to occur under conditions in which the victim is initially in an intense affective state, rather than in preventing the "incubation of fear." In any event, the relationship between the expression of emotion and the effectiveness of treatments to eliminate aversively motivated behavior clearly deserves further examination.

It is the thesis of this chapter, however, that the apparently permanent retention and high resistance to modification are not inevitable consequences of aversively motivated learning. We review a variety of studies which illustrate some circumstances in which aversive memories do undergo marked change. These changes can occur "spontaneously" with the passage of time, or they can be induced by experimental manipulation. In a recent chapter suggesting that substantial continuity exists between stimulus–response (S–R) and contemporary cognitive accounts of memory, Denny (1986) notes that unless interfering learning or stimulus change occurs, little forgetting should be observed with the mere passage of time. Since studies of retention at least nominally hold constant the conditions at training and testing, changes in organismic stimuli are often implicated in memory loss, as this review will demonstrate. It is in any case clear that even for unpleasant events, a case can be made for the biological value of lapses in memory, as B. Heinrich (1987) suggests in his charming description of rearing a great horned owl: "If (the owl's) first experience happened to be with a noxious toad, and his memory were perfect, then he could be shutting himself out of a good food supply. It is better not to remember some things for too long" (p. 139; see also R. Hendersen, 1985, for a similar view).

We will also point to many instances where a memory "loss" is reversible, and suggest that these kinds of fluctuations involve problems with retrieval rather than with degrading of the target information.

'SPONTANEOUS' CHANGES IN MEMORY FOR AVERSIVE EVENTS

A salient example of temporal fluctuations in memory is seen in the nonmonotonic retention curve for avoidance learning known as the "Kamin effect" (Kamin, 1957). Rats receiving 25 active avoidance trials were tested for retention (relearning) after various intervals, ranging from a few minutes to 24 hr, as well as after 19 days. As measured by number of avoidances, retention was very good at the immediate test, as well as after 1 or 19 days. However, retention was impaired at the intermediate intervals in the range of 30 min to 6 hr. Indeed, after 1 hr, the animals made no more avoidances during relearning than during their original acquisition training. (The more recently reported Kamin "blocking effect" in Pavlovian conditioning [Kamin, 1969] is a very different phenomenon, but an occasional source of confusion to the unwary.)

A number of studies soon confirmed the poor performance at intermediate retention intervals and a variety of interpretations were offered, ranging from change in general activity level to incubation of fear (for a review of the early work, see Brush, 1971). Evidence that changes underlying the Kamin effect were an interesting phenomenon of memory rather than a performance artifact, was obtained from experiments employing transfer of training paradigms in which rats trained on either active or passive avoidance tasks were tested on the opposite task after various intervals (Klein & Spear, 1970). The severity of the negative transfer from the reversed contingencies corresponded to an inverted Kamin effect: Impairment was greatest at the short and long intervals, and weak or nonexistent at the intermediate tests. Such an outcome cannot be due to performance artifacts from changes in general activity levels, since the same function was obtained whether the test situation involved "go" (active avoidance) or "no-go" (passive avoidance) requirements. The absence of an impairment on the competing task at intermediate intervals suggested that the memory for the original information was momentarily inaccessible (Klein & Spear, 1970; Spear, 1971).

Why should a memory impairment exist only a few hours after training? Pituitary-adrenal activity is known to correlate with the Kamin effect (e.g., Levine & Brush, 1967); of particular interest is the decreased release of ACTH a few hours after stress such as avoidance training (Brush, 1971). These shifts in motivational cues or, more generally, in the internal context, might impair retrieval. Essentially, "parasympathetic rebound" and other changes characterizing the intermediate intervals will alter the organism's internal context at the time of avoidance retraining. This analysis suggests that the Kamin effect might be analogous to the "state dependent retention" (SDR) obtained with certain drugs. In SDR, organisms trained while under the influence of the drug perform poorly if tested in the absence of the drug (e.g., Overton, 1964; for reviews, see Overton, 1978, 1982); conversely, retention is typically strong if acquisition and testing occur in the same state, whether it is the drug (drug-drug) or normal condition (saline-saline).

Two types of findings support a state dependent interpretation of the Kamin effect. First, if animals are trained an hour or two after being exposed to a stress treatment (i.e., what would be an intermediate interval), they show poor retention when tested a day later (Spear, Klein, & Riley, 1971). Apparently, learning acquired while an organism is in the poststress state several hours later is not retrieved when the subject has recovered.

Second, and more direct, the poor retention at intermediate test intervals seen in the Kamin effect can be eliminated by treatment administered shortly prior to testing. These reminders were designed to reduce the presumed contextual "mismatch" by mimicking many of the internal attributes present at original acquisition. Thus, ACTH injected systemically or implanted into the hypothalamus reduces the impaired performance, as does re-exposure to a strong stressor such as forced swimming or noncontingent foot shock (Denny, 1958; Klein, 1972; Klein & Spear, 1970).

The lack of stability of an aversively established memory is further illustrated in a recent report by Gisquet–Verrier and Alexinsky (1988), who obtained spontaneous enhancement as well as impairment in retention. In one experiment, rats trained to enter the lighted compartment of a Y-maze in order to escape shock were tested at several intervals ranging from 5 min to 28 days after acquisition. A savings measure revealed impaired retention at 1 hour relative to retention after 5 min or 1 day (i.e., the Kamin effect). In addition, retention was better at 8 and 14 days than at 1 day, indicating spontaneous long-term improvement, but performance declined again at the very long intervals. A similar pattern of results was obtained in a second experiment, using a discriminative active avoidance task. The authors interpret these multiphasic fluctuations in memory as reflecting alterations in retrievability, in which different attributes of the training episode change independently and at different rates (see also Gisquet–Verrier, Dekeyne, & Alexinsky, 1985).

Long-term cyclical fluctuations in retention of aversive episodes apparently related to shifts in circadian rhythms have also been found. Holloway and Wansley (1973a) reported that rats trained on a simple passive avoidance showed generally good retention over 3 days when tested at intervals in multiples of 12 hr (12, 24, 36, etc.) after acquisition. Within the same 3-day period, however, performance was substantially poorer if testing occurred in a different phase of the cycle (e.g., 6, 18, 30 hr after training). A similar multiphasic change in retention was obtained with active avoidance (Holloway & Wansley, 1973b). The effect depended on the period of the retention interval, but not on the particular time of day at which training and testing were administered.

As in the case of the Kamin effect, spontaneous retention loss over long intervals is often reversible. For example, Hamberg and Spear (1978) investigated the effects of reminder treatments on retention of choice behavior. In one experiment, rats trained on a brightness discrimination task involving escape from shock in a T-maze were tested 4 weeks later. One day prior to testing, some subjects received a reactivation treatment consisting of a brief, noncontingent exposure to the training foot shock. This reactivation group made significantly fewer errors than retention controls, despite the fact that the noncontingent foot shock afforded no opportunity for further learning about the original task. An important feature of this outcome is in demonstrating that reminder effects are not limited to tasks where level of motor activity indexes retention, but can be observed with choice behavior as well.

One plausible interpretation of these and related findings is that re-exposure to an attribute of the training episode (the motivating and reinforcing stimulus) permits access to, or retrieval of, the target information and thus alleviates the retention deficit. Exactly what attributes are necessary or sufficient to permit recovery of memory is a topic of considerable current interest. One recent direction of investigation involves the use of pharmacological agents. Thus, both Sara (1984) and Quartermain, Judge, and Jung (1988) have reported that amphetamine prior to testing alleviated forgetting of aversively motivated responding. Whether amphetamine enhances retention by reinducing some of the internal attributes associated with stressful learning, or through altering other more general processes, such as attention (see Sara & Deweer, 1982), is not yet known.

ONTOGENETIC MEMORY LOSS

Another type of spontaneous change in memory is linked to development: Aversively motivated learning acquired by immature organisms typically is forgotten more rapidly than similar learning in mature animals (for reviews, see Campbell & Coulter, 1976; Spear, 1978). The phenomenon of rapid forgetting in young animals, often referred to as "infantile amnesia" in recognition of Freud's observations of the striking lack of memory that adults have for early childhood events, is also found with appetitive learning. However, many studies have employed aversive stimuli (generally, electric shock) because performance variables such as motivation (drive) and magnitude of reinforcement can be more readily controlled across a wide age range (Campbell, 1967).

In a seminal paper 25 years ago, Campbell and Campbell (1962) challenged the widely held belief that traumatic experience (aversive conditioning) in an immature organism had a long-term impact (retention) on later behavior. These investigators reported that in rats the retention of Pavlovian fear, assessed in a spatial avoidance task, was directly related to the age at training; the younger the rat (preweanlings in particular) the less effective was the retention. A comparable outcome was obtained with respect to retention of punishment-induced suppression. Care was taken to ensure (as nearly as possible) equal degrees of initial learning, so the inferior retention of immature subjects was not an artifact of weaker response strength.

Campbell and Campbell's (1962) basic finding that long-term retention improves as subjects mature has subsequently been confirmed in a number of other aversively motivated situations, including one-way active avoidance (Feigley & Spear, 1970), passive avoidance (Campbell, Misanin, White, & Lytle, 1974; Feigley & Spear, 1970; Riccio, Rohrbaugh, & Hodges, 1968) and escape learning (Misanin, Nagy, Keiser, & Bowen, 1971; Nagy & Murphy, 1974; Smith & Spear, 1981a, 1981b). Even conditioned taste aversion, which is exceptionally well retained after a single trial in adults and weanlings, is subject to relatively rapid forgetting in young pups (Campbell & Alberts, 1974; Steinert, Infurna, & Spear, 1980).

Further, it is now clear that the more rapid forgetting by immature organisms does not depend on extensive growth over a long retention interval. For instance, retention of conditioned fear resulting from pairing of a black compartment and a mild foot shock decreases more rapidly over a half-hour period for 16-day-old rats than for 21-day-olds or adults (Kucharski, Richter, & Spear, 1985; J. Miller & Spear, 1989). Similarly, substantially greater forgetting of an odor–foot shock pairing occurs within a half-hour of learning in 8-day-old pups than in 12-day-olds, and in 12-day-olds more than in 18-day-olds (J. Miller, Jagielo, & Spear, 1988).

Taken at face value, the evidence indicating an especially rapid rate of forgetting among infants would seem to imply that if early experiences have a long-term consequence, it is not the result of remembering specific instances of these experiences. However, treatments have been established for the alleviation of forgetting in a number of circumstances, and similar processes may operate to maintain early memories.

One way in which forgetting of early learning can be alleviated is through occasional exposure to reminders, that is, a "reinstatement" paradigm (Campbell & Jaynes, 1966). When immature rat pups received a single CS–UCS re-pairing once per week after having undergone Pavlovian fear conditioning, their retention was substantially better than that of trained-only counterparts. Since reminder treatments by themselves were not sufficient to establish learning in untrained animals, the enhanced performance is attributable to maintained memory, rather than "new learning." Other studies have extended the reinstatement paradigm by showing that periodic re-exposure to the conditioned fear cues in conjunction with administration of hormones such as epinephrine or ACTH, which presumably mimic some internal attributes of the fear response (Haroutunian & Riccio, 1977, 1979; Riccio & Haroutunian, 1979), to the UCS (Spear & Parsons, 1976) or even to the CS alone, a nominal extinction procedure, can prevent infantile amnesia (Silvestri, Rohrbaugh, & Riccio, 1970).

A different way in which infantile amnesia can be reduced is by providing the subject with some component of the learning task toward the end of the retention interval. In an early study using this "reactivation" approach, weanling rats (22–24 days) that received Pavlovian fear conditioning were tested after 28 days (Spear & Parsons, 1976). A single noncontingent exposure to the original UCS (in a very different apparatus) 1 day before testing alleviated the retention deficit; various control conditions indicated that the improved performance was not the result of new learning from the reminder itself. (Interestingly, the reactivation treatment was not successful after 28 days in infant pups trained when 16 days old, but it was effective for the younger rats if only 7 days had elapsed.) The reactivation or prior cueing effect has since been demonstrated in other developmental studies as well (e.g., Hinderliter, Lariviere, & Misanin, 1987; Richardson, Ebner, & Riccio, 1981).

A third approach to reducing retention loss for aversive events utilizes distinctive contexts to "override" the sources of long-term forgetting. Richardson, Riccio, and Jonke (1983) trained and tested weanling rats on a conditioned fear task following administration of either saline or a potent state-dependent agent, pentobarbital. In this paradigm the performance of interest is the comparison of the two same-state groups (saline-saline vs. drug-drug). Subjects returned to the drug state at testing showed better memory than when the same state was saline, suggesting that the correspondence of distinctive internal cues at training and testing permits retrieval that otherwise would not occur. Using a rather similar paradigm in much younger pups, Concannon, Smith, Spear, and Scobie (1978) also showed that a distinctive pharmacological context alleviated forgetting in 16-day-old rats, although not in 23-day-old rats. More recent evidence suggests that salient external contexts may also function as an effective source of "contextual matching" (Richardson, Riccio, & Axiotis, 1986).

Collectively, these studies indicate that whereas memories for aversive events are not particularly enduring in an unconditional sense, they might become quite accessible in the right circumstances.

EXPERIMENTALLY INDUCED CHANGES IN MEMORY: AMNESIAS AND THEIR ALLEVIATION

In addition to these "natural" changes in retention, a number of more intrusive treatments administered at (or around) the time of training are known to decrease subsequent retention of aversive events. In this section, we review some of the findings on experimentally induced alterations in retention.

For a brief period of time following aversive learning, memory is susceptible to disruption. In a classic study, Duncan (1949) showed that retention of active avoidance in rats was disrupted when electroconvulsive shock was administered after each trial. The relationship was also time-dependent, with the impairment decreasing as the interval between training and electroconvulsive shock increased. The phenomenon of experimentally induced retrograde amnesia (RA) has been confirmed and extended in subsequent experiments, many of which have used a one-trial punishment or passive avoidance task. This particular type of aversive learning has the advantage of ruling out an alternative interpretation of the impairment in terms of any punishing aspects of the amnestic treatment, as well as providing a clearly definable temporal point at which "learning" occurred. Although a variety of other agents, including carbon dioxide, electrical stimulation of the brain, and thermoregulatory disruptions can induce retrograde amnesia (RA; Spear, 1978), the effect does not appear to be based upon a simple attentional mechanism, such as distraction. For example, no evidence for RA was found in rats exposed to extreme cold for a brief time, although longer exposures which resulted in greater reduction of body temperature were effective (Riccio, Hodges, & Randall, 1968). Also, exposure to a perceptually life-threatening situation (brief submersion in water) failed to disrupt retention (Richardson, Riccio, & Molenda, 1982).

Although treatments given following an aversive episode can alter retention, there is a narrow window of memory vulnerability. This fact has remained an intriguing issue. In a classic review paper, McGaugh (1966) pointed out that such time-dependent changes imply that some type of processing of information (consolidation) occurs following a learning episode. While the temporal gradient of amnesia has often been taken as support for a consolidation model, in which establishment of a long-term trace is disrupted by the more immediate administration of an agent, a strong case can be made for a retrieval failure interpretation (Lewis, 1969; R. Miller & Springer, 1973; Riccio & Richardson, 1984; Spear, 1971, 1973). Quite apart from theoretical issues, the time-dependent characteristic raises an intriguing question, especially for learning based on noxious stimuli. What is the functional value of a system in which such information remains susceptible (for some minutes) to postacquisition events? Shouldn't evolutionary selection pressures have favored organisms whose encoding/storage processes are completed very rapidly, that is, where the target information is quickly locked in? One could suggest that amnestic treatments are "unnatural", but concussive, closed-head injuries seem natural enough, and often have similar consequences for memory.

Forgetting of an unpleasant experience also occurs when an amnestic agent is administered shortly prior to learning; such forgetting is termed anterograde amnesia (AA). For example, Bresnahan and Routtenberg (1980) administered electrical stimulation to the medial forebrain bundle during punishment training in rats. Retention of suppression was poorer than in unstimulated controls, although immediate acquisition was unimpaired. This is important because it indicates that the amnestic agent acted upon retention and forgetting, not merely degree of learning. Similarly, using mild hypothermia rather than brain stimulation during passive avoidance training, Richardson, Riccio, and Morilak (1983) found profound memory loss with a 24-hr retention interval, despite intact performance on an immediate test.

In contrast to the enormous literature on RA, considerably less attention has been paid to experimentally induced AA (with the important exception of drug studies, to be considered shortly). In one sense, this neglect is unfortunate, since in the natural world of traumatic insults, disease episodes, or other acute disturbances of the central nervous system, AA is probably far more common and debilitating than RA. On the other hand, from an analytical perspective, AA poses the very methodological difficulties that retrograde treatments so conveniently avoid. When the insult to the CNS occurs prior to the learning episode, subsequent performance deficits may represent impairment in sensory, motivational, or associative processes, rather than a loss of memory per se. These concerns are no less germane, of course, when the learning involves aversive rather than appetitive reinforcers. The issue is not unique to animal research, as some instances of anterograde forgetting in Korsakoff's patients have been attributed to inadequate perception/registration of information rather than loss of memory (Huppert & Piercy, 1978).

These kinds of considerations led Gold and Zornetzer (1983) to conclude, cogently, albeit pessimistically, that in terms of memory processes the effects of agents given prior to training are generally uninterpretable. The methodological difficulties may be more cumbersome than insurmountable, however. Tests given immediately after training can assess whether acquisition has been successful, although controls for systemic effects of the agent and the UCS are necessary (e.g., Richardson, Riccio, & Morilak, 1983). A more subtle problem is whether the quality and strength of learning in the anterograde paradigm are comparable with those of normals. Some recent work in this area with hypothermia as the anterograde treatment is encouraging. Following induction of mild hypothermia, rats were punished for entering the black compartment of a chamber that was half white and half black. When given immediate forced extinction exposures (prior to onset of AA) to assess strength of learning, these subjects were quite similar to uncooled controls. Further, when subjects were trained under delay of punishment conditions, both normal and hypothermia groups showed delay gradients, although the gradient was somewhat flatter for the former group (Santucci, Kasenow, Riccio, & Richardson, 1987). Finally, the anterograde arrangement does have one methodological advantage: Since the amnestic agent precedes training, performance decrements cannot be due to the agent acting as a punisher for the conditioned response. Thus, discriminative escape training (Boyd

& Caul, 1979; Santucci & Riccio, 1986) and even appetitive tasks are potentially usable.

If memories for aversive events can be suppressed by retrograde or anterograde treatments, they also can often be recovered as well. Although "spontaneous" recovery from experimentally induced amnesias seems uncertain, several types of treatment have been shown to reverse the retention loss. An important series of studies by Lewis, R. Miller, and Misanin (see Lewis, 1979; R. Miller & Springer, 1973) demonstrated that the ECS-induced retrograde amnesia for a punished response could be alleviated simply by administering a "noncontingent foot shock," that is, by presenting the training UCS in an environment markedly different from the conditioning situation. Data from control conditions did not support the important alternative interpretation (Gold & King, 1974) that the recovery was an artifact of generalization of new learning from the reminder to test situations (R. Miller & Springer, 1973; see also DeVietti & Bucy, 1975; Mactutus, Ferek, & Riccio, 1980). Moreover, recovery of memory is dependent on the similarity of the reminder to the training UCS: Amnesia for an appetitive response was reversed by noncontingent presentation of food (UCS), but not by foot shock, while the reverse was true with amnesia for punished responding (Miller, Ott, Berk, & Springer, 1974).

Recovery from RA has also been obtained following brief nonreinforced exposure to the CS (Gordon & Mowrer, 1980), and by re-exposure to the amnestic treatment itself (e.g., Hinderliter, Webster, & Riccio, 1975; Thompson & Neely, 1970), two manipulations unlikely to involve new learning that might strengthen the target response.

One advantage of thermoregulatory disruption over ECS as an amnestic treatment is that graded and conveniently measurable levels of severity are readily induced. With respect to alleviation of hypothermia-induced RA, several studies have shown that a critical level of recooling must be reached before recovery occurs (Mactutus, McCutcheon, & Riccio, 1980; Mactutus & Riccio, 1978), presumably indicative of the matching of internal contextual attributes. Finally, administration of stress released hormones such as ACTH (Mactutus, Smith, & Riccio, 1980; Rigter, van-Riezen, & deWeid, 1974), epinephrine (Concannon & Carr, 1982) or vasopressin (Tinius, Beckwith, Wagner, Tinius, & Traynor, 1986) prior to testing have also been found to alleviate RA.

The forgetting of aversive episodes resulting from acute anterograde treatment is also often reversible. Because the most common recovery manipulation has been re-exposure to the amnestic agent (Ahlers & Riccio, 1987; Gardner, Glick, & Jarvik, 1972; Richardson, Guanowsky, Ahlers, & Riccio, 1984), AA can be conceptualized as a form of state-dependent retention. More specifically, both RA and AA involve training after a specific treatment (e.g., drug; electroconsulsive shock), which elicits unusual or salient internal stimuli; and in both cases retention is poor when testing occurs in the normal (mismatched) state, but is good when the agent is readministered prior to testing. Interestingly, as a consequence of this focus on the "state" aspect of AA, relatively little attention has been paid to other recovery agents, unlike the situation with RA. Indeed, it is of theoretical interest to know if memory for an aversive event can be recovered by manipulations that seem not to involve the experimental "state," such as noncontingent foot shock, in drug-induced, state-dependent retention as well as in AA. In a recent study addressing this issue, Meehan, Gordon, and Riccio (1988) found evidence that a noncontingent foot shock does alleviate the impaired retention of a passive avoidance response when subjects are trained following administration of pentobarbital (state-dependent retention paradigm) or hypothermia (AA) treatment.

MODULATION OF MEMORY

Memory for an aversively motivated episode can be enhanced as well as impaired by posttraining administration of certain drugs or hormones. Because these treatments can affect retention in either direction, the more general term, "modulation" of memory, seems appropriate. As is the case with RA, a central feature of posttrial memory modulation is that the susceptibility of information to change is time-dependent, although it is also recognized that this period may not be identical to the formation of the engram (for reviews, see Gold & McGaugh, 1984; McGaugh, 1983; McGaugh, Liang, Bennett, & Sternberg, 1984).

Enhanced retention of appetitively motivated maze learning by posttraining administration of strychnine was reported some years ago (e.g., McGaugh, 1966). Gordon and Spear (1973) examined this effect with a negative transfer paradigm involving aversively motivated learning. Injection of strychnine following passive avoidance learning increased the subsequent interference in acquiring an opposite, active avoidance response to the same stimuli. This indicated enhanced memory for the passive avoidance learning. The drug-induced enhancement of memory for the first task was time-dependent, since it was obtained with immediate but not with delayed posttrial administration of strychnine. Yet even with an extensive delay, memory was enhanced by strychnine if the drug was immediately preceded by a reminder event from the previous avoidance training.

More recently, attention has focused on whether naturally occurring substances might also modulate memory. Gold and VanBuskirk (1975, 1978) found that administration of epinephrine following passive avoidance conditioning enhanced test performance 24 hr later. The effectiveness of the hormone administered either immediately or 10, 30, or 120 min after training with weak foot shock was an inverse function of the delay interval.

It was suggested that epinephrine mimicked or amplified some of the non-specific internal sequelae of the mildly aversive training experience. That epinephrine was a biological modulator, rather than absolute "enhancer," was revealed by the finding that the same dose levels produced an impairment of retention when a strong foot shock was used in training. The dose of the hormone was also quite critical, interacting with intensity of foot shock to yield either improved or impaired retention of passive avoidance learning.

McGaugh and his colleagues have further elaborated the modulatory role of adrenergic hormones on memory for aversively motivated learning (e.g., Introini–Collison & McGaugh, 1986). They have shown that the enhancing effect of posttraining epinephrine is not limited to a response inhibition task, but occurs in a shock-motivated, Y-maze discrimination, where choice is the measure. Administration of the hormone had an effect much like that of additional training trials, in that the enhancement persisted for a month, for the longest interval sampled. These and other findings (see McGaugh, 1983, for review) suggest that the modifiability of memory following training may represent an adaptive feature of behavior: "The period of susceptibility allows hormones released by experiences to influence memories of the experiences" (McGaugh, Liang, Bennett, & Sternberg, 1985). This is an interesting consideration, although the advantage in the case of impairments (i.e., functional amnesia) is less apparent.

If the modulatory effect of epinephrine is related to the fact that it is an endogenous response to aversive episodes, then other stress-related hormones might be expected to affect memory as well. This proves to be the case for ACTH, the hormone released from the anterior pituitary in response to stressful stimuli discussed earlier with respect to the Kamin effect. Posttrial administration of ACTH modulates retention of a passive avoidance response very much like epinephrine: The degree of enhancement (or impairment) is inversely related to the interval between training and hormone administration, and the dose interacts with intensity of foot shock to determine retention (Gold & VanBuskirk, 1976).

It seems likely that the enhancing and impeding effects of postacquisition hormones are mediated by quite different mechanisms. In particular, the impairment of retention appears to reflect a state-dependent-like effect which differs from the usual paradigm for testing state-dependent retention in that the "state" occurs *subsequent* to training. The existence of a post-training state-dependent retention effect was first demonstrated by Chute and Wright (1973), using pentobarbital after a single, passive avoidance training trial. Subsequently, Richardson, Riccio, and Steele (1986) obtained a clear SDR outcome with posttraining administration of pentobarbital or exposure to severe stress, although the task involved habituation of a neophobic response rather than punishment.

Izquierdo and Diaz (1983) provided direct evidence that posttraining epinephrine and ACTH can have a state-dependent effect. Using parameters in which injection of either epinephrine or ACTH following step-down passive avoidance training resulted in memory impairment, these investigators were able to reverse the deficit by readministering the hormone shortly prior to testing. Further, the two stress-related hormones were partly interchangeable, so that epinephrine would lessen the deficit resulting from posttrial ACTH, and vice versa. These findings indicate that the original storage of memory was not impaired but that the information was processed and encoded in association with the internal hormonally induced context. Re-establishing the internal state at testing permits access to the target memory (see also Izquierdo, 1984, for review). It should be noted, of course, that under naturally occurring conditions the original state will not ordinarily recur to permit reversal of the memory loss. For example, stress-related hormones will not be released if the animal does not remember the aversive event, yet it cannot retrieve the memory without the hormonal state! This "Catch-22" of memory processing might be circumvented in situations where the hormones happen to be released in response to other arousing or stressful stimuli and the organism then is confronted by conditioned fear cues.

Modification of memory for unpleasant events has also been achieved with events that serve as appetitive or aversive reinforcers. In an extensive study by Kesner and Calder (1980), rats received electrical stimulation to the brain immediately following punishment of a consummatory (licking) response. When rewarding stimulation of the brain was used, retention was disrupted (less suppression at testing), whereas aversive stimulation of the brain enhanced memory. These modulatory effects of hedonic stimuli were not obtained when the brain stimulation was delayed for 3 hr after punishment training, nor when the stimulation was immediate but neutral (as measured by level of self-stimulation). Quite different hedonic manipulations, but a similar conceptual framework, are seen in recent work on "counterconditioning" of aversive memory. Presentation of highly palatable fluids (sucrose or maltose solutions) to rats shortly after fear conditioning reduced their retention of fear 24 hr later; no effect on memory was seen when the counterconditioning treatment is delayed by several hours (Richardson, Riccio, & Smoller, 1987). A parallel set of findings was obtained with an "old" (24-hr) memory, but only if the original memory was reactivated by a cueing exposure shortly prior to counterconditioning (Richardson, Riccio, Jamis, Cabosky, & Skoczen, 1982; see also Gordon & Spear, 1973, for an example of modulation of old memory with strychnine).

Stein and Berger (1969) have described an intriguing example of the forgetting of an aversive episode which they interpret as "repression." Their central observation was that conditioned suppression (fear) in rats was increased rather than decreased by the administration of tranquilizing agent. Furthermore, the effect was more pronounced when the intensity of the training UCS was increased. Stein and Berger suggested that memory retrieval could be viewed as an operant response controlled by its consequences. Incipient memories for pain would activate an inhibitory or punishment-like process. However, by blocking this reaction, tranquilizers could permit more complete memory retrieval and thus the intensification of fear.

MEMORY FOR ATTRIBUTES OF AVERSIVE STIMULI

Organisms learn not only what to do, but where to do it. The issues of what is learned about stimuli, how responding transfers to similar stimuli, and how relatively specific stimuli come to control responding have long constituted an important part of research on learning. From the perspective of memory processes, an interesting change in stimulus control typically occurs during a retention interval: There is a loss or reduction in stimulus control, as reflected in the flattening of generalization gradients. In effect then, a broader array of stimuli along the training continuum come to control responding. The loss of differential responding to generalized stimuli over time, originally reported in an appetitive runway task (Perkins & Weyant, 1958) and confirmed in appetitive operant research (e.g., Thomas & Lopez, 1962; see also Thomas, 1981, for review) can be interpreted as the forgetting of stimulus attributes. As Estes (1980) noted with respect to similar changes in human short-term memory, it is as if the memory for particular features of the target stimulus becomes "fuzzier."

Memory for stimuli associated with aversive episodes is not exempt from this form of forgetting. Using an "escape-from-fear" task following Pavlovian conditioning to a light (CS), McAllister and McAllister (1963) tested rats in either the original training apparatus or an identically constructed second chamber. Although this contextual shift was discriminable to the rat, as evidenced by impaired performance to the CS in the second chamber with an immediate test, no effect of the context change was seen after a 24-hr interval; subjects responded equally well to the CS, regardless of the test context. Desiderato, Butler, and Meyer (1966) obtained a similar outcome when a feature of the training stimulus (CS), rather than context, was changed. Hurdle-jump responding to the conditioned fear stimulus itself remained strong across several retention intervals. In contrast, responding to a generalized stimulus was poor at short intervals but improved with longer delays.

Forgetting of stimulus attributes has been obtained in other aversively motivated paradigms as well. D. A. Thomas and Riccio (1979) used the Kamin blocking phenomenon to examine retention of stimulus generalization in a conditioned suppression (CER) task. When the frequency of the tonal stimulus element (CS) was changed during compound conditioning with the added element (light) either 1 or 21 days after initial training, blocking to the light was obtained only after the long retention interval. Presumably, after a delay the generalized CS was no longer distinguishable from the original CS. A more direct assessment of changes in stimulus generalization has been made with respect to conditioned taste aversion (CTA). As the retention interval increased, rats showed increasing aversion to novel (generalized) taste stimuli. Since avoidance of the CS remained essentially constant, the gradient of aversion flattened over time (Richardson, Williams, & Riccio, 1984).

As these cases illustrate, forgetting of stimulus attributes involves enhanced responding to generalized stimuli. As we have noted elsewhere, the implications of this flattening of the generalization gradients are perplexing for interpretations of response decrements in terms of contextual shifts (Riccio, Richardson, & Ebner, 1984; see also Gisquet–Verrier & Alexinsky, 1986). If organisms fail to discriminate a large and explicit change in the stimulus situation after a long interval, how can subtle and implicit shifts in context be invoked to account for the performance decrements referred to as "memory impairment"?

Although the resolution of this apparent paradox is not yet clear, one interesting implication of the analysis is that sources of interference may increase over time. That is, potentially conflicting stimuli that are discriminable from the target situation at a short interval may, through increased generalization, come to compete with the target cues. Consistent with this interpretation, a recent study of Pavlovian fear conditioning found that nonreinforced exposure to the CS in an altered environmental context reduced fear more when given 1 week rather than 1 day after training (Hopkins, Kasenow, MacArdy, & Riccio, 1987). The test for fear was always administered in the original training context 24 hr after the extinction exposure, so the changes in fear level represent the differential effects of the interpolated treatment, not the location of testing. Moreover, no time-related differences were obtained when the extinction exposure occurred in the original context at 1 or 7 days, so age of the memory per se was not the basis for the greater effectiveness of nonreinforced CS exposure in the generalized context after a delay. But since extinction can be seen as a source of conflicting learning (i.e., retroactive interference), this outcome suggests that as the discriminability of stimulus attributes of the two contexts diminished, the degree of interference from an extinction exposure in the novel environment increased.

A second way in which the forgetting of stimulus attributes for aversive events may influence retention phenomena is in terms of "direct reactivation" of the target behavior by re-exposure to the UCS (Spear, 1976).

As mentioned earlier in the chapter, presentation of noncontingent foot shock (NCFS) can alleviate the memory losses resulting from several sources of forgetting (e.g., ontogeny, ECS, thermoregulatory disruption). Our labs, as well as others (e.g., W. C. Gordon, R. R. Miller), are among those that have championed this manipulation as providing evidence of retrieval processes. Extensive and careful studies have, in our judgment, ruled out generalization of new learning or systemic artifacts as the basis for enhanced responding. However, since the noncontingent foot shock does not occur in an environmental vacuum, it remains possible that increased generalization of any partial (residual) memory may interact with the reminder context to modulate the effectiveness of NCFS-induced recovery. Research by MacArdy (MacArdy, Kasenow, Hopkins, & Riccio, 1987; MacArdy & Riccio, 1989) has begun to explore this issue. In one study, rats received Pavlovian fear conditioning, which was then degraded by an extinction treatment. Either 0, 1, or 7 days later, separate groups received the UCS (foot shock) in a chamber distinctly different from training. Although retention controls showed little spontaneous recovery across these intervals, the NCFS was differentially effective in restoring performance: Recovery was substantially less in the immediate (0 days) than the 7-day condition. Presumably, with the shorter interval between extinction and NCFS, subjects discriminated the stimulus feature of the training and reminder contexts and treated them as unrelated events, while at the long interval, the loss of discriminability between the contexts permitted transfer to occur. Manipulating the interval between the NCFS reminder and the test produced a similar effect, in that better performance (recovery) was seen after a long (24-hr) than short (1-hr) delay.

These time-dependent changes in the effectiveness of NCFS reactivation treatment are consistent with the view that stimulus attributes of training and reminder contexts become less discriminable over time. The implications for storage versus retrieval failure interpretations of amnesia are less clear. On the one hand, better recovery after a long delay suggests that under certain conditions a partial or residual memory might summate with new learning from the NCFS treatment, as Gold and King (1974) proposed. Alternatively, the finding that NCFS is more effective with a long delay after a source of performance impairment may be limited to the extinction paradigm. That is, the residual memory following extinction may have quite different characteristics from that produced by retrograde amnesia.

Apart from their theoretical importance, these findings may prove of relevance in understanding occasional failures to obtain reactivation. For example, Callen, McAllister, and McAllister (1984) were unable to obtain the recovery from extinction reported by Rescorla and Heth (1975) when the UCS reminder was administered in a context very different from training. We would simply note that in the MacArdy et al. studies the success of the same type of reminder treatment varied as the retention interval changed.

A quite different issue concerns the nature of the information that gets encoded and retrieved in studies of recovery from experimentally induced amnesia. The concept of memory for stimulus attributes has proven useful here as well. Richardson and Riccio (1986) found that a context shift that produced a performance decrement in normal (control) rats shortly after training, yielded a similar effect in subjects trained while in a mildly hypothermic state and tested immediately, before amnesia occurred (since anterograde amnesia develops over time). Thus, testing prior to the onset of amnesia revealed that the amnestic treatment did not block encoding of information about the external environment. Although such hypothermia produces a severe amnesia for the target behavior after a 24-hr retention interval, reversal of the amnesia for this attribute can be achieved by re-exposure to the amnestic agents (e.g., Riccio & Richardson, 1984). Thus, it is possible to investigate whether information about the environmental context may have been impaired or degraded in "amnesic" subjects. Using this strategy, Richardson and Riccio (1986) observed that amnesic animals that were recooled prior to testing showed the same vulnerability to contextual change as normals—good performance in the original context, poor in the novel context—indicating retention of contextual attributes. Thus, memory for contextual attributes was apparently preserved in the amnesic subjects, and ultimately retrievable given the reactivation treatment of recooling. A similar preservation of information about features of environmental context has been found following induced recovery from retrograde amnesia (Kasenow, Binder, & Riccio, 1988).

These findings provoke a further, intriguing question: Does information in amnesic subjects undergo change during a retention interval? As we have noted, normal animals appear to forget the precise attributes of the context where learning occurred, as seen by the failure to discriminate an altered context after a long interval. Would this same phenomenon be found in animals rendered amnesic, if the reactivation treatment were delayed for a week rather than a day? Or is an amnesic (and generally inaccessible) memory somehow buffered from such changes over time? A preliminary study has suggested that memory for stimulus attributes in an anterograde amnesia condition continues to undergo change; anterograde and normal subjects showed a strikingly similar flattening of the gradient to altered contextual cues between 1 and 7 days (Meehan, Gordon, & Nardecchia, 1989).

On the other hand, in tests with preweanling rats and a relatively long retention interval as the source of forgetting, Richardson, Riccio, and

McKenney (1988) obtained context specific recovery of the learned response when a reactivation was administered after 1 week: Rats given a reminder treatment performed well only if tested in the original (training) environmental context. Thus, information about context apparently was fairly well preserved in developing animals over a relatively long interval. Whether the different outcomes in these two paradigms reflect the differences in source of amnesia, in type of reminder treatment, or in a host of parametric variables is not yet clear.

A third phenomenon related to memory for stimulus attributes is based on a concern with "associative" memory. Revusky (1971) used this term to refer to the memory that permits linkage of a CS with a UCS, as distinguished from the retention of already acquired CS–UCS associations. Conditioned taste aversion, in which learning can occur despite a long interval between the CS and UCS, represents the prototypical example of associative memory. Although conditioning can clearly be obtained under long delay conditions, what is the nature of the CS representation at the time of the association? Estes (1980) has discussed the increased "fuzziness" of human short-term memory as a function of delay of testing, that is, initially discriminable stimuli become increasingly confusable. Does a similar transformation of the stimulus representation take place in animal associative memory? For example, with a long CS–UCS delay, does a rat remember the general characteristics of "sweetness" flavor but not the precise quality of the taste? If so, then a test for generalization (at a constant interval after the UCS) might reveal such a change. Presumably, a less precise representation of the taste at the time of illness (association) with a long interval between the two would be reflected in a tendency to avoid a wider range of related tastes than with a shorter CS–UCS delay. An initial experiment (Payson, Bakner, & Riccio, 1989) has provided data generally consistent with this notion, although several methodological issues remain to be resolved.

The preceding studies have examined aspects of memory for features of the context or CS. Are the attributes of the UCS or reinforcing stimulus forgotten also? For methodological reasons, this issue is more problematical, although within the appetitive domain reward magnitude "contrast effects" have provided a useful tool for assessing reinforcer characteristics. For example, the decline in negative contrast as the retention interval lengthens suggests that subjects have forgotten one particular feature (amount) of the original reinforcing stimulus (Gleitman & Steinman, 1964; Spear, 1967). With respect to memory for aversive stimuli, Hendersen, Patterson, and Jackson (1980) have conducted one of the few studies in the area. Their strategy was to assess the extent to which Pavlovian conditioned stimuli, based on qualitively different UCSs, modulated Sidman avoidance responding. For example, a CS paired extensively with an air blast as the UCS had little influence on shock-motivated Sidman avoidance when introduced after a short retention interval. However, with 45 days between Pavlovian conditioning and the re-presentation of the CS during the free-operant avoidance task, a strong enhancement of response rate was seen. Apparently, at a short interval the particular attributes of the predicted UCS (air blast) are remembered and distinguished from the foot shock, but with a long retention interval the memory for the UCS included a more general expectation of a "bad event" that interacted with the fear-motivated baseline behavior (see also Hendersen, 1985).

CONCLUSIONS

We have reviewed a variety of phenomena in which memories for aversive events undergo substantial change. This modifiability was revealed in the susceptibility of memory to intervention shortly following training, as well as in the spontaneous fluctuations found over longer intervals. From the view that memories for aversive events are persistent or even incessant in their influence on abnormal as well as normal behavior, such malleability of aversively motivated responding would appear surprising. On the other hand, the changes we label as response "deficits" or "impairments" need not be detrimental. From a broader perspective, forgetting can be adaptive: "It keeps one's options open, which is especially valuable in a changing environment" (Heinrich, 1987). As we have seen, it is when the environment (context) returns to its original state that retrieval of target information is most likely to occur, so the organism has the potential to accommodate both stable and changing conditions. In any event, for those of us who suffer the exasperations of unretrieved memories, there is a bit of hope—at least we are keeping lots of options open!

ACKNOWLEDGMENTS

Preparation of this chapter was supported in part by grants from the National Institute of Mental Health (MH37535 to D. C. Riccio and MH35219 to N. E. Spear) and by a Kent State University academic term research leave to D. C. Riccio. The authors wish to thank Dr. Roy S. Lilly for calling their attention to Professor Heinrich's book, *One Man's Owl*. The authors gratefully acknowledge the secretarial assistance of Sally Bowers and Teri Tanenhaus for accurately and speedily deciphering some extremely challenging handwriting.

REFERENCES

Ahlers, S., & Riccio, D. C. (1987). Anterograde amnesia induced by hyperthermia in rats. *Behavioral Neuroscience*, *101*, 333–340.

Appel, J. B. (1961). Punishment in the squirrel monkey. *Science*, *133*, 36.

Baum, M. (1969). Extinction of an avoidance response: Some parametric investigations. *Canadian Journal of Psychology*, *23*, 1–10.

Boyd, S. C., & Caul, W. F. (1979). Evidence of state dependent learning of brightness discrimination in hypothermic mice. *Physiology and Behavior*, *23*, 147–153.

Bresnahan, E. L., & Routtenberg, A. (1980). Medial forebrain stimulation during learning and subsequent retention disruption. *Physiological Psychology*, *8*, 112–119.

Brush, F. R. (1971). Retention of aversively motivated behavior. In F. R. Brush (Ed.), *Aversive conditioning and learning*. New York: Academic Press.

Callen, E. J., McAllister, W. R., & McAllister, D. E. (1984). Investigations of the reinstatement of extinguished fear. *Learning and Motivation*, *15*, 302–320.

Campbell, B. A. (1967). Developmental studies of learning and motivation in infraprimate mammals. In H. W. Stevenson, E. H. Hess, & H. L. Reingold (Eds.), *Early behavior: Comparative and developmental approaches*. New York: Wiley, pp. 43–71.

Campbell, B. A., & Alberts, J. R. (1979). Ontogeny of long-term memory for learned taste aversions. *Behavioral and Neural Biology*, *25*, 139–156.

Campbell, B. A., & Campbell, E. B. (1962). Retention and extinction of learned fear in infant and adult rats. *Journal of Comparative and Physiological Psychology*, *55*, 1–8.

Campbell, B. A., & Coulter, X. (1976). The ontogenesis of learning and memory. In M. R. Rosenzweig & E. L. Bennett (Eds.), *Neural mechanisms of learning and memory*. Cambridge, MA: MIT Press, pp. 209–235.

Campbell, B. A., & Jaynes, J. (1966). Reinstatement. *Psychological Review*, *73*, 478–480.

Campbell, B. A., Misanin, J. P., White, B. C., & Lytle, L. D. (1974). Species differences in ontogeny of memory: Support for neural maturation as a determinant of forgetting. *Journal of Comparative and Physiological Psychology*, *87*, 193–202.

Chute, D. L., & Wright, D. C. (1973). Retrograde state-dependent learning. *Science*, *180*, 878–880.

Concannon, J. T., & Carr, M. (1982). Pre-test epinephrine injections reverse DDC-induced retrograde amnesia. *Physiology and Behavior*, *9*, 443–448.

Concannon, J. T., Smith, G. J., Spear, N. E., & Scobie, S. R. (1978). Drug cues, drug states, and infantile amnesia. In F. C. Colpaert & J. A. Rosencrans (Eds.), *Stimulus properties of drugs: Ten years of progress*. Amsterdam: Elsevier/North-Holland Biomedical Press, pp. 353–396.

Coulter, X., Riccio, D. C., & Page, H. A. (1969). Effects of blocking an instrumental avoidance response: Facilitated extinction but persistence of "fear." *Journal of Comparative and Physiological Psychology*, *68*, 377–381.

Denny, M. R. (1958). The "Kamin Effect" in avoidance conditioning. *American Psychologist*, *13*, 419 (abstract).

Denny, M. R. (1986). "Retention" of S–R in the midst of the cognitive invasion. In D. F. Kendrick, M. E. Rilling, & M. R. Denny (Eds.), *Theories of animal memory*. Hillsdale, NJ: Lawrence Erlbaum Associates, pp. 35–50.

Desiderato, O., Butler, B., & Meyer, C. (1966). Changes in fear generalization gradients as a function of delayed testing. *Journal of Experimental Psychology*, *72*, 678–682.

DeVietti, T. L., & Bucy, C. E. (1975). Recovery of memory after reminder: Evidence for two forms of retrieval deficit induced by ECS. *Physiological Psychology*, *3*, 19–25.

Duncan, C. P. (1949). The retroactive effect of electroshock on learning. *Journal of Comparative and Physiological Psychology*, *42*, 32–44.

Estes, W. K. (1980). Is human memory obsolete? *American Scientist, 68,* 62–69.

Feigley, D. A., & Spear, N. E. (1970). Effect of age and punishment condition on long-term retention by the rat of active- and passive-avoidance learning. *Journal of Comparative and Physiological Psychology, 73,* 515–526.

Gagné, R. M. (1941). The retention of a conditioned operant response. *Journal of Experimental Psychology, 29,* 296–305.

Gardner, E. L., Glick, S. D., & Jarvik, M. E. (1972). ECS dissociation of learning and one-way cross dissociation with physostigmine and scopolamine. *Physiology and Behavior, 8,* 11–15.

Gisquet–Verrier, P., & Alexinsky, T. (1986). Does contextual change determine long term forgetting? *Animal Learning and Behavior, 14,* 349–358.

Gisquet–Verrier, P., & Alexinsky, T. (1988). Time-dependent fluctuations of retention performance in an aversively motivated task. *Animal Learning and Behavior, 16,* 58–66.

Gisquet–Verrier, P., Dekeyne, A., & Alexinsky, T. (1985). Memory reorganization overtime as revealed by interaction between type of pre-test cueing and length of retention interval. In B. E. Will, P. Schmitt, & J. C. Dalrymple–Alford (Eds.), *Brain plasticity, Learning and Memory.* New York and London: Plenum Press.

Gleitman, H., & Steinman, F. (1964). Depression effect as a function of retention interval before and after shift in reward magnitude. *Journal of Comparative and Physiological Psychology, 57,* 158–160.

Gold, P. E., & King, R. A. (1974). Retrograde amnesia: Storage failure versus retrieval failure. *Psychological Review, 81,* 465–469.

Gold, P. E., & McGaugh, J. L. (1984). Endogenous processes in memory consolidation. In H. Weingartner & E. Parker (Eds.), *Memory consolidation.* Hillsdale, NJ: Lawrence Erlbaum Associates.

Gold, P. E., & VanBuskirk, R. B. (1976). Enhancement and impairment of memory processes with post-trial injections of adrenocorticotropic hormone. *Behavioral Biology, 16,* 387–400.

Gold, P. E., & VanBuskirk, R. B. (1975). Facilitation of time dependent memory processes with hormone injections. *Behavioral Biology, 13,* 145–153.

Gold, P. E., & Zornetzer, S. F. (1983). The mnemon and its juices: Neuromodulation of memory processes. *Behavioral and Neural Biology, 38,* 151–189.

Gordon, W. C., & Mowrer, R. R. (1980). The use of an extinction trial as a reminder treatment following ECS. *Animal Learning and Behavior, 8,* 363–367.

Gordon, W. C., & Spear, N. E. (1973). The effects of strychnine on recently acquired and reactivated passive avoidance memories. *Physiology Behavior, 10,* 1071–1075.

Hamberg, J. M., & Spear, N. E. (1978). Alleviation of forgetting of discrimination learning. *Learning and Motivation, 9,* 466–476.

Haroutunian, V., & Riccio, D. C. (1977). Effect of arousal conditions during reinstatement treatment upon learned fear in young rats. *Developmental Psychobiology, 10,* 25–32.

Haroutunian, V., & Riccio, D. C. (1979). Drug-induced "arousal" and the effectiveness of CS exposure in the reinstatement of memory. *Behavioral and Neural Biology, 26,* 115–120.

Heinrich, B. (1987). *One man's owl.* Princeton University Press: Princeton, NJ.

Hendersen, R. W. (1985). Fearful memories: The motivational significance of forgetting. In F. R. Brush & J. B. Overmier (Eds.), *Affect, conditioning and cognition: Essays on the determinators of behavior.* Hillsdale, NJ: Lawrence Erlbaum Associates, pp. 43–53.

Hendersen, R. W., Patterson, J. M., & Jackson, R. L. (1980). Acquisition and retention of control of instrumental behavior by a cue-signaling air blast: How specific are conditioned anticipations? *Learning and Motivation, 11,* 407–426.

Hilgard, E. R., & Campbell, A. A. (1936). The course of acquisition and retention of conditioned eyelid response in man. *Journal of Experimental Psychology, 19,* 227–247.

Hinderliter, C. F., Lariviere, N., & Misanin, J. R. (1987). The differential effects of rein-statement and reactivation on retention of active avoidance in previsual rats. Paper presented at meeting of the Eastern Psychological Association, Arlington, VA.

Hinderliter, C. F., Webster, T., & Riccio, D. C. (1975). Amnesia induced by hypothermia as a function of treatment-test interval and recooling in rats. *Animal Learning and Behavior, 3,* 257–263.

Hoffmann, H. S., Fleshler, M., & Jensen, P. (1963). Stimulus aspects of aversive controls: The retention of conditioned suppression. *Journal of the Experimental Analysis of Behavior, 6,* 575–583.

Holloway, F. A., & Wansley, R. A. (1973a). Multiple retention deficits at periodic intervals after active and passive avoidance learning. *Behavioral Biology, 9,* 1–14.

Holloway, F. A., & Wansley, R. A. (1973b). Multiphasic retention deficits at periodic intervals after passive avoidance learning. *Science, 180,* 208–210.

Hopkins, J., Kasenow, P. M., MacArdy, E., & Riccio, D. C. (1987). *Forgetting of stimulus attributes: Implications for interference as a source of performance deficits.* Paper presented at meetings of the Midwestern Psychological Association, Chicago.

Huppert, F. A., & Piercy, M. (1978). Dissociation between learning and remembering in organic amnesia. *Nature (London), 275,* 317–318.

Introini–Collison, I. B., & McGaugh, J. L. (1986). Epinephrine modulates long-term retention of an aversively-motivated discrimination task. *Behavioral and Neural Biology, 45,* 358–365.

Izquierdo, I. (1984). Endogenous state dependency: Memory depends on the relation between the neurohumoral and hormonal states present after training and at the time of testing. In G. Lynch, J. L. McGaugh, & N. M. Weinberger (Eds.), *Neurobiology of learning and memory.* New York: Guilford.

Izquierdo, I., & Diaz, R. D. (1983). Memory as a state-dependent phenomenon: Role of ACTH and epinephrine. *Behavioral and Neural Biology, 38,* 144–151.

Kamin, L. J. (1957). The retention of an incompletely learned avoidance response. *Journal of Comparative Physiological Psychology, 50,* 475–460.

Kamin, L. J. (1969). Predictability, surprise, attention and conditioning. In B. A. Campbell & R. M. Church (Eds.), *Punishment and aversive behavior* (pp. 279–296). New York: Appleton-Century-Crofts.

Kasenow, P. M., Binder, D., & Riccio, D. C. (1988). *Memory for external contextual attributes prior to, and following recovery from, retrograde amnesia.* Paper presented at meetings of the Eastern Psychological Association, Buffalo, NY.

Kellogg, W. N., & Wolf, I. S. (1939). The nature of the response retained after several varieties of conditioning in the same subjects. *Journal of Experimental Psychology, 24,* 366–383.

Kesner, R. R., & Calder, L. D. (1980). Rewarding periaqueductal gray stimulation disrupts long-term memory for passive avoidance learning. *Behavioral and Neural Biology, 30,* 237–249.

Klein, S. B. (1972). Adrenal-pituitary influence in reactivation of avoidance memory in the rat after intermediate intervals, *Journal of Comparative and Physiological Psychology, 79,* 341–349.

Klein, S. B., & Spear, N. E. (1970). Forgetting by the rat after intermediate intervals ("Kamin effect") as retrieval failure. *Journal of Comparative and Physiological Psychology, 71,* 165–170.

Kucharski, D., Richter, N., & Spear, N. E. (1985). Conditioned aversion is promoted by memory of CS-. *Animal Learning and Behavior, 13,* 143–151.

Levine, S., & Brush, F. R. (1967). Adrenocortical activity and avoidance learning as a function of time after avoidance training. *Physiology and Behavior, 2,* 385–388.

Lewis, D. J. (1969). Sources of experimental amnesia. *Psychological Review, 76,* 461–472.

Lewis, D. J. (1979). Psychobiology of active and inactive memory. *Psychological Bulletin*, *86*, 1054–1083.

Liddell, H. S., James, W. T., & Anderson, O. D. (1935). The comparative psychology of the conditioned motor reflex: Based on experiments with the pig, dog, sheep, goat, and rabbit. *Comparative Psychology Monograph*, *11*, No. 51.

MacArdy, E. A., Kasenow, P. M., Hopkins, J., & Riccio, D. C. (1987). *Changes in the effectiveness of a noncontingent footshock as a function of retention interval.* Paper presented at meetings of the Midwestern Psychological Association, Chicago.

MacArdy, E. A., & Riccio, D. C. (1989). *Effectiveness of noncontingent footshock in producing recovery from extinction or amnesia depends on delay of testing.* Paper presented at meetings of the Midwestern Psychological Association, Chicago.

Mactutus, C. F., Ferek, J. M., & Riccio, D. C. (1980). Amnesia induced by hyperthermia: An unusually profound, yet reversible, memory loss. *Behavioral and Neural Biology*, *30*, 260–277.

Mactutus, C. F., McCutcheon, K., & Riccio, D. C. (1980). Body temperature cues as contextual stimuli: modulation of hypothermia-induced retrograde amnesia. *Physiology and Behavior*, *25*, 875–883.

Mactutus, C. F., & Riccio, D. C. (1978). Hypothermia-induced retrograde amnesia: Role of body temperature in memory retrieval. *Physiological Psychology*, *6*, 18–22.

Mactutus, C. F., Smith, R. L., & Riccio, D. C. (1980). Extending the duration of ACTH-induced memory reactivation in an amnesic paradigm. *Physiology and Behavior*, *24*, 541–546.

Malloy, P., & Levis, D. J. (1988). A laboratory demonstration of persistent human avoidance. *Behavior Therapy*, *19*, 229–241.

McAllister, W. R., & McAllister, D. E. (1963). Increase over time in the stimulus generalization of acquired fear. *Journal of Experimental Psychology*, *65*, 576–582.

McGaugh, J. L. (1966). Time-dependent processes in memory storage. *Science*, *153*, 1351–1358.

McGaugh, J. L. (1983). Hormonal influences on memory. *Annual Review of Psychology*, *34*, 297–323.

McGaugh, J. L., Liang, K. C., Bennett, C., & Sternberg, D. B. (1984). Adrenergic influences on memory storage: Interaction of peripheral and central systems. In G. Lynch, J. L. McGaugh, & N. M. Weinberger (Eds.), *Neurobiology of Learning and Memory.* New York: Guilford, pp. 313–332.

McGaugh, J. L., Liang, K. C., Bennett, C., & Sternberg, D. B. (1985). Hormonal influences on memory: Interaction of central and peripheral systems. In B. E. Will, P. Schmitt, & J. C. Dalrymple-Alford (Eds.), *Brain Plasticity, Learning, and Memory.* New York: Plenum, pp. 313–332.

Meehan, S. M., Gordon, T. L., & Nardecchia, D. (1989). *Memory for stimulus attributes following recovery from amnesia 24 hours or 7 days after training.* Paper presented at meetings of the Midwestern Psychological Association, Chicago.

Meehan, S. M., Gordon, T., & Riccio, D. C. (1988). *Differential effectiveness of footshock in attenuating the memory loss produced by hypothermia-induced anterograde amnesia and pentobarbital state dependent retention.* Paper presented at meetings of the Midwestern Psychological Association, Chicago.

Miller, J. S., Jagielo, J. A., & Spear, N. E. (1988). *Age-related differences in short-term retention of separable elements of an odor aversion.* Presented at meetings of the International Society for Developmental Psychobiology, Toronto.

Miller, J. S. & Spear, N. E. (1989). Ontogenetic differences in short term retention in Pavlovian conditioning. *Developmental Psychobiology*, *22*, 377–387.

Miller, R. R., Ott, C. A., Berk, A. M., & Springer, A. D. (1974). Appetitive memory restoration after electroconvulsive shock in the rat. *Journal of Comparative and Physiological Psychology, 87*, 717–723.

Miller, R. R., & Springer, A. D. (1973). Amnesia, consolidation, and retrieval. *Psychological Review, 80*, 69–79.

Mineka, S. (1979). The role of fear in theories of avoidance learning, flooding, and extinction. *Psychological Bulletin, 86*, 985–1010.

Misanin, J. R., Nagy, Z. M., Keiser, E. F., & Bowen, W. (1971). Emergence of long-term memory in the neonatal rat. *Journal of Comparative and Physiological Psychology, 77*, 188–199.

Nagy, Z. M., & Murphy, J. M. (1974). Learning and retention of a discriminated escape response in infant mice. *Developmental Psychobiology, 7*, 185–192.

Overton, D. A. (1964). State-dependent or "dissociated" learning produced with pentobarbital. *Journal of Comparative and Physiological Psychology, 57*, 3–12.

Overton, D. A. (1978). Major theories of state dependent learning. In B. T. Ho, D. W. Richards III, & D. L. Chute (Eds.), *Drug discrimination and state dependent learning*. New York: Academic Press.

Overton, D. A. (1982). Memory retrieval failures produced by changes in drug states. In R. L. Isaacson & N. E. Spear (Eds.), *The expression of knowledge*. New York: Plenum Press, pp. 113–140.

Page, H. A., & Hall, J. F. (1953). Experimental extinction as a function of prevention of a response. *Journal of Comparative and Physiological Psychology, 46*, 33–44.

Payson, M., Bakner, L. T., & Riccio, D. C. (1989). *Changes in the generalization gradient as a function of delay between CS and UCS*. Paper presented at meetings of the Midwestern Psychological Association, Chicago.

Perkins, C. C., Jr., & Weyant, R. G. (1958). The interval between training and test trials as determiner of the slope of generalization gradients. *Journal of Comparative & Physiological Psychology, 51*, 596–600.

Quartermain, D., Judge, M. E., & Jung, H. (1988). Amphetamine enhances retrieval following diverse sources of forgetting. *Physiology & Behavior, 43*, 239–241.

Razran, G. H. S. (1939). Studies in configural conditioning. VI. Comparative extinction and forgetting of pattern and of single-stimulus conditioning. *Journal of Experimental Psychology, 24*, 432–438.

Rescorla, R. A., & Heth, C. D. (1975). Reinstatement of fear to an extinguished conditioned stimulus. *Journal of Experimental Psychology: Animal Behavior Processes, 104*, 88–96.

Revusky, S. (1971). The role of interference in association over a delay. In W. K. Honig & P. H. R. James (Eds.), *Animal memory*. New York: Academic Press.

Riccio, D. C., & Haroutunian, V. (1979). Some approaches to the alleviation of ontogenetic memory loss. In N. E. Spear & B. A. Campbell (Eds.), *Ontogeny of learning and memory*. Hillsdale, NJ: Lawrence Erlbaum Associates, pp. 289–309.

Riccio, D. C., Hodges, L. A., & Randall, P. K. (1968). Retrograde amnesia produced by hypothermia in rats. *Journal of Comparative and Physiological Psychology, 66*, 618–622.

Riccio, D. C., & Richardson, R. (1984). The status of memory following experimentally induced amnesias: Gone but not forgotten. *Physiological Psychology, 12*, 59–72.

Riccio, D. C., Richardson, R., & Ebner, D. L. (1984). Memory retrieval deficits based upon altered contextual cues: A paradox. *Psychological Bulletin, 96*, 152–165.

Riccio, D. C., Rohrbaugh, M., & Hodges, L. A. (1968). Developmental aspects of passive and active avoidance learning in rats. *Developmental Psychobiology, 1*, 108–111.

Richardson, R., Ebner, D. L., & Riccio, D. C. (1981). Effects of delayed testing on passive avoidance of conditioned fear stimuli in young rats. *Bulletin of the Psychonomic Society, 18*, 211–214.

Richardson, R., Guanowsky, V., Ahlers, S. T., & Riccio, D. C. (1984). Role of body temperature in the onset of, and recovery from, hypothermia-induced anterograde amnesia. *Physiological Psychology, 12,* 125–132.

Richardson, R., & Riccio, D. C. (1986). An examination of a contextual component of memory following recovery from anterograde amnesia in rats. *Physiological Psychology, 14,* 75–81.

Richardson, R., & Riccio, D. C. (in press). Memory processes, ACTH, and extinction phenomena. In C. Flaherty & L. Dachowski (Eds.), *Current topics in animal learning: Brain, emotion, and cognition.* Hillsdale, NJ: Lawrence Erlbaum Associates.

Richardson, R., Riccio, D. C., & Axiotis, R. (1986). Alleviation of infantile amnesia in rats by internal and external contextual cues. *Developmental Psychobiology, 19,* 453–462.

Richardson, R., Riccio, D. C., Jamis, M., Cabosky, J., & Skozcen, T. (1982). Modification of reactivated memory through "counterconditioning." *American Journal of Psychology, 95,* 67–84.

Richardson, R., Riccio, D. C., & Jonke, T. (1983). Alleviation of infantile amnesia in rats by means of a pharmacological contextual state. *Developmental Psychobiology, 16,* 511–518.

Richardson, R., Riccio, D. C., & McKenney, M. (1988). Stimulus attributes of reactivated memory: Alleviations of ontogenetic forgetting in rats is context specific. *Developmental Psychobiology, 21,* 135–143.

Richardson, R., Riccio, D. C., & Molenda, S. (1982). Reducing vulnerability to retrograde amnesia treatments: Can new memory be deactivated? *Physiology and Behavior, 29,* 1117–1123.

Richardson, R., Riccio, D. C., & Morilak, D. (1983). Anterograde memory loss induced by hypothermia in rats. *Behavioral and Neural Biology, 37,* 76–88.

Richardson, R., Riccio, D. C., & Ress, J. (1988). Extinction of avoidance through response prevention: Enhancement by administration of epinephrine or ACTH. *Behavior Research and Therapy, 26,* 23–32.

Richardson, R., Riccio, D. C., & Smoller, D. (1987). Counterconditioning of memory in rats. *Animal Learning and Behavior, 15,* 321–326.

Richardson, R., Riccio, D. C., & Steele, J. H. (1986). State-dependent retention induced by postacquisition exposure to pentobarbital or shock-stress in rats. *Animal Learning and Behavior, 14,* 73–79.

Richardson, R., Williams, C., & Riccio, D. C. (1984). Stimulus generalization of conditioned taste aversion in rats. *Behavioral and Neural Biology, 41,* 41–53.

Rigter, H., van Riezen, H., & de Wied, D. (1974). The effects of ACTH- and vasopressin-analogues on CO_2-induced retrograde amnesia in rats. *Biology and Behavior, 13,* 381–388.

Santucci, A., & Riccio, D. C. (1986). Hypothermia-induced anterograde amnesia and its reversal in rats trained on a T-maze escape task. *Physiology and Behavior, 36,* 1065–1069.

Santucci, A., Kasenow, P., Riccio, D. C., & Richardson, R. (1987). Hypothermia-induced anterograde amnesia: Is memory loss attributable to impaired acquisition? *Behavioral and Neural Biology, 48,* 13–23.

Sara, S. J. (1984). Forgetting of a conditioned emotional response and its alleviation by pretest amphetamine. *Physiological Psychology, 12,* 17–22.

Sara, S. J., & Deweer, B. (1982). Memory retrieval is enhanced by amphetamine after a long retention interval. *Behavioral and Neural Biology, 36,* 146–160.

Schlosberg, H. (1934). Conditioned responses in the white rat. *Journal of Genetic Psychology, 45,* 303–335.

Schwartz, B., & Reilly, M. (1985). Long-term retention of a complex operant in pigeons. *Journal of Experimental Psychology: Animal Behavior Processes, 11,* 337–355.

Silvestri, R., Rohrbaugh, M., & Riccio, D. C. (1970). Conditions influencing the retention of learned fear in young rats. *Developmental Psychology, 2,* 389–395.

Skinner, B. F. (1950). Are theories of learning necessary? *Psychological Review*, *57*, 193–216.

Smith, G. J., & Spear, N. E. (1981a). Role of proactive interference in infantile forgetting. *Animal Learning and Behavior*, *9*, 371–380.

Smith, G. J., & Spear, N. E. (1981b). Home environmental stimuli facilitate learning of shock escape spatial discrimination in rats 7–11 days of age. *Behavioral and Neurobiology*, *31*, 360–365.

Solomon, R. L., Kamin, L. J., & Wynne, L. C. (1953). Traumatic avoidance learning: The outcomes of several extinction procedures with dogs. *Journal of Abnormal and Social Psychology*, *48*, 291–302.

Solomon, R. L., & Wynne, L. C. (1954). Traumatic avoidance learning and the principles of anxiety conservation and partial irreversability. *Psychological Review*, *61*, 353–385.

Spear, N. E. (1967). Retention of reinforcer magnitude. *Psychological Review*, *74*, 216–234.

Spear, N. E. (1971). Forgetting as retrieval failure. W. K. Honig & P. H. R. James (Eds.), *Animal memory*. New York: Academic Press.

Spear, N. E. (1973). Retrieval of memory in animals. *Psychological Review*, *80*, 163–194.

Spear, N. E. (1976). Retrieval of memories. In W. K. Estes (Ed.), *Handbook of learning and cognitive processes*. Hillsdale, NJ: Lawrence Erlbaum Associates.

Spear, N. E. (1978). *The processing of memories: Forgetting and retention*. Hillsdale, NJ: Lawrence Erlbaum Associates.

Spear, N. E., Klein, S. B., & Riley, E. P. (1971). The "Kamin effect" as state dependent learning: Memory retrieval failure in the rat. *Journal of Comparative and Physiological Psychology*, *74*, 416–425.

Spear, N. E., & Parsons, P. (1976). Analysis of a reactivation treatment. Ontogeny and alleviated forgetting. In D. Medin, R. Davis, & W. Roberts, (Eds.), *Coding processes in animal memory*. Hillsdale, NJ: Lawrence Erlbaum Associates.

Stampfl, T. G. (1987). Theoretical implications of the neurotic paradox as a problem in behavior theory: An experimental resolution. *Behavior Analyst*, *10*, 161–173.

Stampfl, T. G. (1988). The relevance of laboratory animal research to theory and practice: One-trial learning and the neurotic paradox. *Behavior Therapist*, *11*, 75–79.

Stampfl, T. G., & Levis, D. J. (1967). Essentials of implosive therapy: A learning-theory-based psychodynamic behavioral therapy. *Journal of Abnormal Psychology*, *72*, 496–503.

Stein, L., & Berger, B. D. (1969). Paradoxical fear-increasing effects of tranquilizers: Evidence of repression of memory in the rat. *Science*, *166*, 253–256.

Steinert, P. A., Infurna, R. N., & Spear, N. E. (1980). Long-term retention of a conditioned taste aversion in preweanling and adult rats. *Animal Learning and Behavior*, *8*, 375–381.

Thomas, D. R. (1981). Studies of long-term memory in the pigeon. In N. E. Spear & R. R. Miller (Eds.), *Information Processing in Animals: Memory mechanisms*. Hillsdale, NJ: Lawrence Erlbaum Associates, pp. 257–290.

Thomas, D. R., & Lopez, L. J. (1962). The effects of delayed testing on generalization slope. *Journal of Comparative and Physiological Psychology*, *55*, 541–544.

Thomas, D. A., & Riccio, D. C. (1979). Forgetting of a CS attribute in a conditioned suppression paradigm. *Animal Learning and Behavior*, *7*, 191–195.

Thompson, C. I., & Neely, J. E. (1970). Dissociated learning in rats produced by electroconvulsive shock. *Physiology and Behavior*, *5*, 783–786.

Tinius, T. P., Beckwith, B. E., Wagner, N., Tinius, K. A., & Traynor, M. M. (1986). Differential actions of arginine vasopressin and alpha-melanocyte-stimulating hormone on reactivation of memory after hypothermia-induced amnesia. *Physiological Psychology*, *14*, 15–22.

Wendt, G. R. (1937). Two and one-half year retention of a conditioned response. *Journal of General Psychology*, *17*, 178–180.

8 Self-punitive Behavior: A Revised Analysis

Sanford J. Dean and Catherine M. Pittman*
Northern Illinois University

In general, when a response is followed by the occurrence of an aversive stimulus, or punishment, the tendency to make that response decreases. Under some conditions, however, punishment has the paradoxical effect of facilitating rather than suppressing the response. Perhaps the most striking example of this paradoxical effect is the phenomenon that has been labeled "Vicious Circle" or "Self-punitive" behavior. This phenomenon was originally observed by Judson S. Brown and first reported by Mowrer (1947). Mowrer suggested a learning theory interpretation of self-punitive behavior that proposed that the behavior was motivated by conditioned fear. In the first systematic study of the effects of punishment on behavior motivated by fear, Gwinn (1949) reported results that were consistent with this interpretation. Brown and his associates, as well as others, subsequently investigated the learning theory interpretation in a number of experiments.

Although there are variations among experiments, in the typical self-punitive experiment rats first are given a number of escape-training trials in a straight alley runway. A drop start is usually employed: The animal is placed in the upper compartment of a two-compartment start box, the platform floor is released, and the animal is dropped onto the electrified grid of the lower start box.[1] The animal learns to run the entire length of

Catherine M. Pittman is now at Saint Mary's College, Notre Dame, IN.

[1]Two variations in the basic paradigm are the use of a guillotine door rather than a drop start box and the use of avoidance training rather than escape training during the fear-acquisition trials. Similar results have been obtained.

259

the electrified alley to escape into a shock-free goal box. Following shock-escape training, subjects are given either "regular" or "punished" extinction trials. Punished-extinction (PE) subjects are dropped into the alley but receive shock only in a midsegment of the runway. Regular-extinction (RE) subjects receive the same treatment except that no shock is present in the runway. For PE subjects, the location of the shock in the runway may vary, but the typical location is the middle segment of a three-segment runway.[2] In this case, the start box and all parts of the runway except the midsegment are shock-free.

If punishment were the only factor involved, the running response would be suppressed by the administration of shock, and PE subjects would stop running sooner than RE subjects. Paradoxically, in the self-punitive paradigm, the aversive stimulus facilitates rather than suppresses the running response. In contrast to RE subjects, PE subjects run faster, persist for many more trials, and sometimes increase their running speeds during extinction. Because of the self-perpetuating nature of the behavior and its apparent similarity to some forms of neurotic behavior, Mowrer (1947) labeled the behavior a "vicious circle." Noting that the animal continues to be shocked as a consequence of its own behavior, Brown introduced the term "self-punitive behavior" (Brown, Martin, & Morrow, 1964) and this term has been most widely used.

Although the learning theory interpretation stressing the central role of conditioned fear has gained wide acceptance, it has not gone unchallenged. Renner and his associates (Dreyer & Renner, 1971; Renner & Tinsley, 1976) proposed an alternative cognitive-discrimination interpretation which asserts that PE animals continue to run as a result of mistaken expectancies that they hold regarding response-outcome contingencies. In the present chapter these theoretical positions will be evaluated in terms of the available research. In addition, several important theoretical and methodological issues will be discussed, and a revised model elaborating the role of conditioned fear will be presented.

THEORETICAL INTERPRETATIONS OF SELF-PUNITIVE BEHAVIOR

The Learning Theory Interpretation

The interpretation of self-punitive behavior that has received the broadest empirical support is the learning theory interpretation. This interpretation, based on principles derived from traditional learning theory, has been

---

[2]Punished extinction with *goal-box* shock will be discussed in a later section of the chapter.

summarized most recently by Brown and Cunningham (1981), who identified several mechanisms assumed to be responsible for the establishment and maintenance of self-punitive behavior. (Interested readers are referred to Brown, 1969, and Brown & Cunningham, 1981, for more thorough summaries of these mechanisms than will be detailed in the present chapter.)

The mechanism of conditioned fear is an essential part of the learning theory interpretation. Mowrer (1947) suggested that fear is classically conditioned to the apparatus cues during shock-escape training. During punished extinction, when shock is absent except in an isolated part of the runway, conditioned fear motivates escape from the shock-free starting area. Furthermore, Mowrer (1947) asserted that the shock that the subject receives in the runway maintains fear of the start area:

> Each time the rat is placed in the experimental apparatus and gets a brief shock on the way to the safety compartment, the part of the alley where the rat is introduced gets "reinforced" as a danger situation (or "conditioned stimulus"), since it continues to be temporally associated with pain. (p. 134)

According to this conditioned-fear hypothesis, the shock in the runway functions as an unconditioned stimulus, reconditioning and maintaining the conditioned fear that motivates the running response. Conditioned fear of the start area was hypothesized to be maintained through generalization of fear from the shock segment to other segments of the homogeneous alley (Brown, 1969). In summary, the Mowrer–Brown theory of the role of fear in self-punitive behavior proposes that fear conditioned to the apparatus cues during shock-escape training provides the motivation for running. During PE trials, the shock encountered by the animal maintains fear conditioned to the shock segment, and this fear generalizes throughout the alley.

Support for the importance of conditioned fear in motivating and maintaining self-punitive behavior has been provided in a variety of studies. Melvin and Stenmark (1968) reasoned that if fear of the starting area motivates self-punitive behavior then it should be possible to demonstrate self-punitive behavior even in the absence of a learned escape response, provided that fear has been conditioned to cues in the starting area. Animals were first dropped into the start box and blocked there while buzzer–shock pairings were administered. When tested, animals crossed the shock in order to escape the buzzer and the start box cues and enter a distinctively marked goal box. In other words, shock-escape training was not necessary for self-punitive behavior to occur if fear was effectively conditioned to the starting area using an alternative procedure.

Evidence that conditioned fear motivates self-punitive running also has been provided by studies that show that self-punitive behavior is responsive to variables known to affect the classical conditioning of fear. For example, the likelihood of self-punitive behavior increases with the number of fear-conditioning trials (Galvani, 1969; Saunders, 1974), and with the intensity of shock administered during conditioning trials (Kruger, 1974; Melvin & Bender, 1968; Saunders, 1974). Furthermore, self-punitive running can be reduced or eliminated by manipulations that are known to reduce conditioned fear, including unreinforced exposure to cues in the start area (Cunningham, Brown, & Roberts, 1976; O'Neil, Skeen, & Ryan, 1970) and the introduction of a safety signal in the start box (Delprato & Carosio, 1976).

The response-potentiating function of shock has been proposed as another mechanism contributing to the maintenance of self-punitive behavior (Brown & Cunningham, 1981). First, the administration of shock facilitates responding by increasing motivation, provided that the level of shock administered does not elicit responses that are incompatible with the running response (Brown, 1969). Second, in the typical self-punitive paradigm, because the animal has learned to run forward in the presence of shock, midsegment shock has a direct facilitative effect on the running response. In support of this hypothesis, Cunningham et al. (1976) demonstrated that running speeds are faster in the segment containing shock than in the other segments. Because some investigators (Bender, 1969; Melvin, Irving, & Prentice–Dunn, 1979; Saunders, 1974) have obtained self-punitive running *without* the use of midsegment shock, Melvin et al. (1979) argued that the response-facilitating effects of shock are not a necessary condition for self-punitive behavior, although these effects probably contribute to the establishment of self-punitive behavior in the typical paradigm.

According to the learning theory interpretation, factors that are responsible for reinforcing the running response are also important in the development and maintenance of self-punitive behaviors. Reinforcement is provided by escape from shock when the animal crosses the shock segment, and also by escape from fear when the animal leaves the alley and enters the goal box (Brown, 1969; Brown & Cunningham, 1981). Two studies have indicated that the reduction of fear is a significant factor in reinforcing self-punitive behavior. Delprato and Denny (1968) demonstrated that if fear reduction (or "relief") is prevented from occurring by reducing the amount of time spent in the goal box, self-punitive behavior is not maintained: PE animals that were removed from the goal box after 2 seconds extinguished as rapidly as RE animals. In addition, Delprato and Meltzer (1974) found that self-punitive running is less likely when the goal box is similar to the alley segments. Because fear reduction should be more complete when the goal box is distinctly different from the alley segments, this finding provides additional support for the hypothesis that escape from fear is an important factor in the reinforcement of self-punitive behavior.

Finally, according to the learning theory interpretation, another important factor in the development of self-punitive behavior is stimulus similarity between acquisition and extinction (Brown & Cunningham, 1981). As Church (1963) observed, when procedures that punish a response reinstate some of the conditions of training, responding may be facilitated. The more similar the stimulus complex during extinction to that which was present during shock-escape training, the more likely that running will continue. Because the presence of shock in the runway enhances the similarity between shock-escape training and extinction, self-punitive running should be facilitated. Conversely, certain changes in apparatus cues during punished extinction should result in a stimulus-generalization decrement that reduces fear and reduces the likelihood of self-punitive behavior. (This prediction will be addressed in more detail later.)

According to the learning theory interpretation, several additional mechanisms affect self-punitive behavior. These include the use of a drop-start procedure, the use of avoidance training rather than escape training, the habit strength of the running response, and postshock emotionality. These mechanisms have all been demonstrated to contribute positively to the establishment and maintenance of self-punitive running (Brown, 1969; Brown & Cunningham, 1981). In summary, the learning theory interpretation emphasizes the central role of conditioned fear in motivating and reinforcing self-punitive behavior, and also recognizes the role of a number of other mechanisms in contributing to the phenomenon.

The Cognitive-discrimination Interpretation

An alternate interpretation of self-punitive behavior proposes a cognitive-discrimination explanation. Mowrer (1960) was the first to propose that self-punitive behavior may result from a failure of discrimination. He suggested that "it is only when they [self-punitive subjects] cannot distinguish between the starting and the shock areas of the runway that they get into and persist in the 'vicious circle' " (Mowrer, 1960, p. 487). Church (1963) also provided a discrimination interpretation when he suggested that punished extinction results in slower extinction because the presence of shock in the alley reduces the likelihood that the conditions of extinction will be discriminated from the conditions of shock-escape training. The most recently advanced cognitive-discrimination interpretation of self-punitive behavior was proposed by Renner and his associates (Dreyer & Renner, 1971; Renner & Tinsley, 1976). Dreyer and Renner (1971) suggested that self-punitive running continues because subjects fail to discriminate a safe from an unsafe start box. Animals do not detect that the start box is safe because they fail to recognize the changed contingencies that are present during punished extinction. According to this interpretation, until the changed contingencies concerning the occurrence and nonoccurrence of shock are discriminated, self-punitive behavior will occur.

In this cognitive-discrimination interpretation, the critical factor that maintains self-punitive behavior is not fear, but the subject's mistaken expectancies about response-outcome contingencies (Renner & Tinsley, 1976). During shock-escape training, the subject learns that running leads to shock termination, and that not running leads to continued shock. During extinction, the contingencies change, however, and the ease with which the new contingencies are learned depends on whether shock is present or absent in the runway. Renner and Tinsley (1976) argue that, for RE subjects, the absence of shock readily leads to disconfirmation of the previous response-outcome contingencies. In contrast, because shock is still present in the runway for PE subjects, these subjects have more difficulty discriminating the new response-outcome contingencies that running leads to shock and that not running leads to no shock. According to Renner and Tinsley, the presence of shock prevents PE animals from discriminating the new contingencies that govern the occurrence of shock, and this failure of discrimination leads to continued running.

To demonstrate that self-punitive responding is due to inaccurate contingency information, Dreyer and Renner (1971) tested *human* subjects in an experiment designed to parallel the self-punitive paradigm employed with rats. Subjects were instructed to press a telegraph key a required number of times to escape shock delivered to the index and ring finger. After acquisition trials during which a buzzer of half-second duration was followed by shock, the shock was turned off for subjects in the RE condition. In the PE condition, the shock was turned on only if the subject made a key press after the buzzer. The data were similar to those obtained with animals in the self-punitive paradigm: Nine of the 11 PE subjects continued to key press, but only 6 of the 11 RE subjects did so. In addition, PE subjects key pressed at a significantly faster rate than did RE subjects. Perhaps the most important finding for the cognitive-discrimination theory is that PE subjects who had continued to respond during extinction trials later reported that they did not know that their own key press turned on the shock. In contrast, the 5 RE subjects who ceased responding reported that key pressing was no longer necessary because there was no shock. Furthermore, when PE subjects were *informed of the contingencies* governing shock occurrence, all but 1 of the subjects stopped key pressing on the next trial.

Although contingency information was readily manipulated through verbal instruction in this human self-punitive experiment, investigating the effects of contingency information on self-punitive behavior in animals is more difficult because there is no generally accepted criterion for determining when discrimination of a new contingency has taken place in animals. Renner and Tinsley (1976) attempted to facilitate discrimination of response-outcome contingencies by temporarily blocking the rat in the shock-free start box on alternate PE trials, and found that the blocking procedure resulted in more rapid extinction than did RE trials or non-blocked PE trials. Renner and Tinsley argued that these results provided evidence for the cognitive-discrimination interpretation because running ceased when the animal was forcibly exposed to the consequences of not running (i.e., when new information about response-outcome contingencies was learned). They acknowledged that the data could also be explained as resulting from the extinction of conditioned fear, but asserted that the effectiveness of the short response-prevention time (5 seconds) argued against this explanation. Nevertheless, because a conditioned-fear explanation predicts that extinction of fear is a function of the amount of un-reinforced exposure to the fear-eliciting cues, the finding that blocked PE subjects extinguished more rapidly than nonblocked PE subjects *and* RE subjects is entirely consistent with the conditioned-fear hypothesis. The conditioned-fear interpretation would predict that blocked PE subjects should extinguish more readily than RE subjects because blocked subjects are exposed to start-box cues longer. Furthermore, fear of the cues in the start box need only be reduced to the level where PE subjects will no longer enter the shock area for these subjects to meet the extinction criterion of failure to enter the goal box. Without the shock barrier, even subjects with relatively low levels of fear may continue to traverse the runway and enter the goal box. In contrast, the cognitive-discrimination interpretation does not specifically predict that blocking will result in faster extinction than will RE trials in which shock is absent. According to the cognitive-discrimination interpretation, the animal's expectancies are strongly affected by the absence of shock: "The old response-outcome contingencies are readily disconfirmed because the shock is no longer present" (Renner & Tinsley, 1976, p. 159). Because shock is present in the runway for blocked PE subjects, the finding that these subjects extinguish most rapidly would not necessarily be predicted by the cognitive-discrimination interpretation.

The focus on expectancies concerning response-outcome contingencies makes it difficult to test the cognitive-discrimination interpretation directly with animal subjects. No method for defining or measuring discrimination of new contingencies *that is independent of the presence or absence of self-punitive responding* has been developed. Nevertheless, data that appear to be inconsistent with the cognitive discrimination interpretation have been reported. For example, when animals are given shock-escape training followed by PE trials with shock in the goal box but not in the alley, they exhibit self-punitive behavior (Babb & Hom, 1971). Because shock is never present in the goal box during escape training and is never present in the start box or runway during extinction, conditions should be even more favorable for the discrimination of new response-outcome contingencies than the RE condition that Renner (Renner & Tinsley, 1976) indicates leads to the ready disconfirmation of the old response-outcome contingencies. Nevertheless, self-punitive behavior is maintained. In addition, Dean, Denny, and Blakemore (1985) found that following shock-escape training, animals given shock in the start box on the first four extinction trials extinguished just as quickly as RE subjects. Subjects given shock in the midsegment on the first four extinction trials took significantly longer to extinguish than either the RE or the start-box-shock group. Of the three groups, the group with shock in the start box should face the most difficult discrimination of changed response-outcome contingencies, but this group extinguished more quickly than the midsegment-shock group and as quickly as the RE group.

Brown and Cunningham (1981) also have suggested that the cognitive-discrimination interpretation ignores some of the contingencies that are available for the subject to learn. For example, although Renner and Tinsley (1976) argue that PE subjects are exposed to contingencies that are similar to those that were present during training (e.g., running leads to shock termination), PE subjects are also exposed to the new contingency that running leads to shock *onset*. This contingency, which should result in cessation of running, is not recognized in the cognitive-discrimination interpretation, and Brown and Cunningham (1981) have argued that it is essential that the interpretation should explain why this new contingency information does not affect responding.

ISSUES AND PROBLEMS IN THE SELF-PUNITIVE PARADIGM

Is the Behavior Self-punitive?

The term "self-punitive," which is typically used to describe the extraordinary resistance to extinction displayed by midsegment-shocked animals, is perhaps an unfortunate one. Some theorists have suggested that it implies that the subject deliberately "chooses" to punish itself (Dreyer & Renner, 1971; Fantino & Logan, 1979; Renner & Tinsley, 1976) and the use of the paradigm as a possible analogue of masochistic behavior (Brown, 1965; Brown & Cunningham, 1981) has probably contributed to this misconception. Whether or not the self-punitive paradigm provides an analogue of masochistic behavior is not the focus of this chapter; rather the focus is on formulating a useful theoretical analysis of the self-punitive phenomenon. What is perhaps most useful about the paradigm is that it illustrates that punishing a behavior may be counterproductive if the goal is to eliminate a fear-motivated behavior. If punishment is paired with cues that elicit fear, then punishment may serve, not to eliminate the fear-motivated behavior, but to strengthen conditioned fear and provide further motivation for behaviors that reduce that fear. Whether this is masochism or not is less important than recognizing that punishment, in this instance, is not effective in eliminating a behavior. The term self-punitive behavior is used here in a simply descriptive sense to signify that the punishment is contingent upon the animal's continued running.

Running Speed as a Measure in the Self-punitive Paradigm

Running Speed as an Indicant of Self-punitive Behavior. Delude (1969, 1973) has suggested that self-punitive behavior may simply be an artifact. If the presence of self-punitive behavior is indexed simply by the presence of faster running speeds in PE animals than in RE animals, then it is possible that differences in running speeds may result from the fact that PE animals cross the shock segment more rapidly and as a result have faster total running times. Indeed, it is not surprising that shocked animals should run more rapidly than nonshocked animals, but this is not the behavior which is the focus of concern. PE animals need not display faster running speeds in order that their continued crossing of the shock be considered self-punitive: The important and paradoxical observation is that *animals that are punished for running continue to run*, a finding that appears to challenge the law of effect. Number of trials to extinction is therefore a more relevant index of self-punitive behavior than is running speed. Because they are being punished, PE animals should stop running sooner, but numerous studies have demonstrated that PE animals typically complete many more trials than do RE animals.

Running Speed as a Measure of Fear. An additional concern about running speeds has been suggested by Renner and Tinsley (1976), who argued that, unless PE animals have faster running speeds in the prepunishment segment of the alley than RE animals, a conditioned-fear explanation of self-punitive behavior is called into question. Their rationale was based on Delude's (1973) assertion that running speed in the prepunishment segments is the most appropriate measure of self-punitive behavior because, when this measure is used, running speed is not affected by the application of shock. Renner and Tinsley reasoned that, if fear of the starting area of the runway is responsible for continued running and is maintained by midsegment shock, PE animals should evidence greater fear and thus run from the starting area more rapidly than RE subjects. This argument is based on the false assumption that running speed is a direct measure of fear and that the relation between running and fear is a symmetrical one.

Running speed is a function of many factors, including the habit strength of the running response; the position, duration, and intensity of shock; the direction and manner in which the animal lands after the drop start; and whether the animal approaches the shock rapidly or pauses before crossing it. Running speed, therefore, is not a reliable index of fear, and its usefulness in assessing the level of fear conditioned to the apparatus cues is limited. An alternate approach to the measurement of fear in the self-punitive paradigm will be addressed later in this chapter.

The Problem of Circularity

Both the learning theory interpretation and the cognitive-discrimination interpretation of self-punitive behavior have been accused of being circular, and these criticisms have been justified. Brown and Cunningham (1981) have pointed out that if conditioned fear is assumed to motivate running, and running serves as the only index of fear, a learning theory interpretation of self-punitive behavior that focuses on conditioned fear is essentially tautological. In order to avoid this difficulty, studies have investigated the effects on self-punitive running of variables known to affect conditioned fear in other situations: The persistence of self-punitive responding is enhanced by increasing the level of shock on fear-conditioning trials (e.g., Kruger, 1974), or by increasing the number of fear-conditioning trials (e.g., Galvani, 1969), and self-punitive responding is decreased by blocking the animal in the presence of start-area cues (e.g., O'Neil et al., 1970). These studies provide noncircular support for the learning theory interpretation and suggest that conditioned fear does indeed provide the motivation for self-punitive behavior. Nevertheless, even stronger evidence for the learning theory interpretation could be provided if a direct and reliable index, independent of the running response, were used to measure fear (Brown & Cunningham, 1981).

The circular nature of the cognitive-discrimination interpretation was pointed out by Brown (1969) and Brown and Cunningham (1981) and acknowledged by Dreyer and Renner (1971) and Renner and Tinsley (1976). Brown (1969) noted that the theory becomes tautological when discrimination of changed contingencies is assumed to result in the cessation of running, and the only evidence for discrimination is that running ceases. Until an independent measure of the discrimination of changed contingencies is developed, or evidence is presented that manipulating contingency information affects self-punitive responding in the expected manner, the explanation relies upon circular evidence. Although Dreyer and Renner (1971) manipulated contingency information with human subjects by informing them that their behavior led to shock, the problem of circularity remains when the cognitive-discrimination explanation is applied to non-human self-punitive behavior.

Problems with the Human Experimental Analogue

Although human studies generally have produced self-punitive effects similar to those produced in animal studies (Rands & Dean, 1975; Dreyer & Renner, 1971; Renner & Tinsley, 1976), generalizing from these results, particularly those results based on informing subjects of changes in response-outcome contingencies, presents a number of problems. The human experimental analogue is a weak one: The shock level that is employed is no more than an annoyance and probably elicits, at most, very mild fear. Furthermore, the situation is artificial and distinctly different from other situations that elicit fear: The human subject knows that the shock is controlled by the experimenter and has no reason to doubt the experimenter's statement that shock will no longer be administered. Complex mediational processes unquestionably play a role in the acquisition, generalization, and extinction of fear in humans. These processes are more limited in the rat, however, and using the results of human studies to support the hypothesis that knowledge of response-outcome contingencies is the important factor determining self-punitive behavior in the animal studies is not justified.

A REVISED ANALYSIS OF THE DEVELOPMENT AND MAINTENANCE OF FEAR IN THE SELF-PUNITIVE PARADIGM

The Measurement of Conditioned Fear

Although a great deal of experimental evidence has provided indirect support for the learning theory interpretation (see Brown & Cunningham, 1981), the conditioned-fear hypothesis has not been directly tested because of the lack of a reliable, independent index of the strength of conditioned fear. The strength of fear sometimes has been inferred from running speed. For a number of reasons, discussed earlier, running speed is not a good index of the strength of fear.

The nature of the self-punitive response must be considered in selecting a useful independent index of fear. Self-punitive behavior frequently has been treated as a simple all-or-none response: The animal either runs or does not run, depending on the strength of fear in the start box. According to this view, an adequate index of fear must provide only evidence, independent of the running response, that fear has been conditioned to the start box and is maintained during punished extinction. Klare (1974) attempted to provide such evidence by measuring activity in the upper start box, but there are a number of interpretational problems with Klare's results, and the index is limited to measuring fear in the upper start box. According to the analysis proposed here, self-punitive running consists of a *sequence* of responses that begins when the animal is placed in the start box and ends when the animal is removed from the goal box. In between these two events, the animal has landed on a grid, traversed a runway with constantly changing cues, experienced shock in one part of the alley and not in others, and perhaps even paused or jumped at one or more points. The proposed analysis requires an independent behavioral index that will permit the measurement of the strength of fear at various alley locations at various times during the development and maintenance of self-punitive behavior. Such an index would permit the testing of a number of hypotheses concerning the conditioning, generalization, and extinction of fear of the cues in various parts of the alley.

Of the several indexes of fear considered by McAllister and McAllister (1971), the escape-from-fear measure seems to have the greatest potential for measuring fear in the self-punitive paradigm. Before the escape-from-fear test procedure is employed, a neutral stimulus is paired with shock for a number of trials. Then the neutral stimulus is presented alone and the subject is permitted to escape from the fear-eliciting conditioned stimulus (CS) by performing a prescribed response. Any learning that occurs can be assumed to be motivated solely by fear and to be reinforced by fear reduction. The escape-from-fear procedure has been shown to be a reliable index of fear which is sensitive to such variables as number of CS–shock pairings and shock intensity (McAllister & McAllister, 1971).

If fear conditioned to the apparatus cues motivates self-punitive behavior, then an escape-from-fear measure can be used as an independent index of the level of conditioned fear. For example, assuming that fear has been conditioned to the lower start-box cues during shock-escape training, the fear of these cues should provide motivation for the subsequent learning of an escape-from-fear response. Dean and Pittman (1988) used the learning of a hurdle-jump response as an independent index of fear of the lower start-box cues following differing numbers of extinction trials. A hurdle with a guillotine door was located in the left wall of the lower start box. Following shock-escape training and a prescribed number of RE or PE trials with the hurdle-jump door closed, subjects were dropped into the lower start box with the hurdle-jump door open and the entrance to the runway blocked. Speed of hurdle jumping over 60 trials provided a measure of learning and an independent index of the strength of the fear conditioned to the lower start-box cues. Subjects in all groups learned the new response, and PE groups evidenced more fear than RE groups. The study provides evidence that the hurdle-jump response can be used as an independent index of fear conditioned to the start box. Subsequent experiments employing a hand placement procedure rather than a drop start have extended the use of the hurdle-jump index to the measurement of fear of the cues in individual runway segments.

The Development and Maintenance of Conditioned Fear

The Previous Analysis. Mowrer (1947) initially proposed that, during escape training, fear is conditioned to the cues throughout the start box and runway but not to the goal box. During punished extinction, fear continues to be conditioned to the cues in the shock area and conditioned fear generalizes from the shock area to the cues throughout the relatively homogeneous runway and start box. The literature, for the most part, has continued to reflect the assumption that during punished extinction fear is conditioned primarily to the shock area and that fear accruing to other areas is primarily a function of generalization. In discussing factors likely to increase the probability of obtaining self-punitive behavior, Brown (1969) states, "Start boxes and punishment zones should probably be similar, however, so as to guarantee the generalization of fear from the punishment region back to the start" (p. 511).

Melvin (1971) proposed an hypothetical gradient of fear based on the assumption that fear is conditioned primarily to the shock segment. With middle-segment shock, the strength of conditioned fear is hypothesized to decrease at the same rate in both directions from the shock segment and to be at the same level at the entrance to the first runway segment and at the entrance to the goal box. In other words, conditioned fear should be strongest in the shock segment and should be at the same level in the prepunishment and postpunishment areas at points which are equidistant from the shock segment. This gradient, in general, conforms with segment running speeds which, during punished extinction, are reported to be faster in the shock segment than in either the preshock or postshock segments with no consistent differences between the latter two (e.g., Cunningham et al., 1976). Running speeds, however, are not a simple function of conditioned fear. In the shock segment, running speeds are faster due to the energizing effect of the shock and the increased speed probably carries over to some extent into the postshock segment.

The Revised Analysis. The expanded conditioned-fear interpretation offered here incorporates hypotheses and interpretations advanced by Beecroft and Bouska (1967), Dean et al. (1985), Dean and Pittman (1988), Perconte, Benson, and Butler (1981), and Pittman and Dean (1989). (The discussion will focus on self-punitive behavior following shock-escape training during which fear has been conditioned to the apparatus cues, but the interpretation can be applied to variations in the paradigm which involve avoidance training or a discrete CS.) Punished extinction is viewed as a period of new learning during which the combined effects of conditioning, generalization, and extinction of fear produce differential changes in the strength of the fear elicited by the cues in various parts of the alley. The maintenance or elimination of self-punitive behavior depends on the balance between the amounts of fear elicited by the cues in successive alley segments.

During shock-escape training, fear is conditioned to the apparatus cues as well as to the internal and external stimuli associated with being dropped in the start box. According to conditioning theory, the strongest conditioning will occur to the stimuli immediately preceding the onset of the unconditioned stimulus. In the self-punitive paradigm, the stimuli immediately preceding shock acquire maximal fear-eliciting properties because of the temporal relationship between these stimuli and the onset of shock. On shock-escape trials, therefore, the strongest fear is associated with the upper start-box cues and the drop stimuli, both of which immediately precede the onset of shock. Because the cues in the alley segments are encountered during ongoing shock as the animal learns to escape to the goal box, relatively less fear is conditioned to these cues. The strength of the fear elicited by runway cues is relatively uniform across runway segments. During shock-escape training, a forward locomotion response is learned to the external stimuli, including the shock, and to the internal stimuli produced by fear.

During regular extinction, the animal never encounters shock and no further fear conditioning occurs. As a result of their temporal relationship to shock during shock-escape training, the start box and the drop stimuli elicit the strongest fear. The cues in the third segment elicit the weakest fear because they are encountered just prior to goal-box entry. With repeated trials, the strength of fear elicited by the cues in all parts of the alley steadily decreases. Because stronger fear initially is elicited by the drop stimuli, fear of these cues will be the last to extinguish, and animals may continue to leave the start area even though they do not traverse the entire runway to the goal box.

When punished-extinction trials are administered, the absence of shock in the lower start box and the first and third runway segments results in a stimulus-generalization decrement in the fear elicited by the cues in these areas. The development of self-punitive behavior depends on the animal learning to run in the presence of these changed cues. On initial PE trials, the strength of fear elicited by the unchanged upper start-box cues and drop stimuli is sufficient to motivate the animal to run forward to the midsegment, where the shock elicits further forward locomotion. A relatively low level of fear of the cues in the third segment is sufficient to maintain the running response until entry into the goal box. Running is reinforced by the reduction of both pain and fear when the animal crosses the shock and enters the goal box.

Because shock is present only in the midsegment of the runway, changes occur in the strength of the fear elicited by the stimuli in different parts of the alley. The strength of fear associated with the cues in any part of the runway at any particular time during punished extinction is a function of the direct conditioning of fear, the generalization of fear, and the extinction of fear. During PE trials, fear is rapidly reconditioned to the modified cues in the preshock area because of the temporal relationship between these cues and the onset of shock. Cues in the midsegment are encountered during shock and little additional fear is conditioned to these cues. Furthermore, fear is not conditioned to runway cues in the postshock segment because these cues are encountered following the offset of shock. Although some fear generalizes to cues in the shock and postshock areas, the fear of these cues is much weaker than the fear elicited by cues in the preshock area and it extinguishes over trials.

The persistence of self-punitive behavior depends on the balance between the amounts of fear elicited by the cues in successive segments of the alley. Fear must be present to motivate the escape response. Moderate increases in fear will facilitate an ongoing escape response. An increase in fear may degrade rather than facilitate performance when the animal moves from one area of the runway to a more feared area if the difference between the amounts of fear elicited by the cues in the two areas is large enough. During punished extinction, a gradient of fear is present in the preshock area and this gradient changes over trials. At the start of extinction, the upper start-box cues and the drop stimuli elicit the strongest fear as a result of having immediately preceded shock onset during shock-escape training. Relatively less fear is elicited by the cues in the lower start box and the first runway segment. Because the cues in the first runway segment and the lower start box are closer to shock onset during punished extinction, more fear is conditioned to these cues than to the upper start-box cues and the drop stimuli. Over trials, the gradient of fear quickly levels off and then is reversed: The first-segment cues that immediately precede shock onset elicit the greatest fear and the lower start-box cues, the drop stimuli, and the upper start-box cues elicit progressively less fear. As long as the slope of the gradient is moderate, performance is maintained. As the gradient becomes increasingly steep, approaching the highly feared cues closest to the shock becomes increasingly aversive until eventually the animal remains in the start box and self-punitive behavior ceases.

A Revised Analysis of Some Previous Findings

The revised conditioned-fear interpretation offered here is entirely consistent with the results of earlier research supporting the learning theory position, and, in some instances, adds clarification to previous findings. Two examples of research findings that are clarified by the application of the revised conditioned-fear interpretation are the effects on response persistence of (1) stimulus change, and (2) goal-box shock. Experiments investigating the effects on self-punitive behavior of changes in the alley stimuli introduced between training and extinction have resulted in some puzzling findings that are not consistent with earlier conditioned-fear interpretations. Experiments investigating the effects of the application, during extinction, of shock in the goal box rather than in the alley have produced inconsistent findings, some of which have been interpreted as challenging the conditioned-fear interpretation. These two sets of findings will be examined briefly and analyzed in terms of the revised conditioned-fear interpretation.

The Effects of Stimulus Change on Response Persistence. Mowrer (1960) proposed that self-punitive behavior is a consequence of the animal's inability to discriminate between the start area and the shock area. If this hypothesis is correct, then when the cues in these two areas are distinctively different from each other, self-punitive behavior should not occur. In an attempt to test Mowrer's discrimination hypothesis, Brown (1970) and Brown, Beier, and Lewis (1971) conducted three experiments in which the visual cues in the shock segment, or the visual and tactual cues in all areas except the shock segment and the upper start box, were changed between shock-escape training and punished or regular extinction. These manipulations were intended to facilitate the discrimination of the shock from the nonshock areas. Self-punitive behavior, as indexed by differences in running speeds between the PE and RE groups, persisted in all three experiments. The authors pointed out that these results are not compatible with the discrimination hypothesis, but failed to indicate in any detail how the results are consistent with the conditioned-fear hypothesis.

Presumably, any change in the apparatus cues should result in some stimulus-generalization decrement in conditioned fear. Marked changes in stimuli, such as the changes employed in the studies conducted by Brown and his colleagues, should have resulted in a decrease in the amount of fear elicited by the changed cues. Less fear should have been elicited by the cues in the midsegment in one experiment and less fear should have been elicited by the cues in the nonshock areas in the other two experiments. It is not clear why the presumed lower level of fear, particularly in the start area and the first segment, did not lead to a decrease in self-punitive behavior. In discussing the running-speed gradients of animals in the typical PE condition, Brown et al. (1971) suggested that fear is reconditioned to the *shock segment* cues and generalizes back to the cues in the start area. The finding that self-punitive behavior occurred despite stimulus change is inconsistent with their interpretation: The marked difference between the cues in the start area and the cues in the shock segment for the punished group with changed stimuli should have markedly reduced the generalization of fear from the shock segment to the preshock area and, therefore, disrupted self-punitive running.

The effects of stimulus change on self-punitive running can be explained within the revised conditioned-fear analysis offered here. The present analysis proposes that during punished extinction the strongest fear is conditioned directly to the cues in the *first segment* immediately preceding shock onset rather than to those in the shock segment. Changing the cues in the shock segment (Brown, 1970, Experiment 1) should have no significant effect on self-punitive behavior. The amount of fear elicited by the cues in the start area at the start of extinction is independent of any stimulus changes in the shock segment. The strong fear elicited by the unchanged drop stimuli initiates running, and running is maintained by fear of the cues in the start box and first runway segment which remain unchanged, except for the absence of shock. During punished extinction, fear is conditioned rapidly to the first-segment cues as a result of their temporal relationship to midsegment shock, and running continues to be reinforced by both pain and fear reduction. Any decrease in the strength of fear elicited by changed cues in the shock segment should not affect self-punitive behavior.

When the stimuli are changed in all areas of the alley except the shock area and the upper start box (Brown, 1970, Experiment 2; Brown et al., 1971), stimulus change should have different consequences than when the change is in the shock area. On the first extinction trial, a marked decrease in the fear elicited by the start box and first-segment cues should occur. Fear of the cues in the shock segment, however, should be unchanged. If, as previous interpretations have assumed, fear is conditioned to the *shock* segment and then generalizes to the other alley segments, generalization of fear to the changed cues in the remaining segments should be minimal, and the incidence of self-punitive behavior should be reduced. An alternative explanation, based on the revised analysis proposed here, predicts continued self-punitive behavior. An initial stimulus-generalization decrement in the strength of the fear elicited by the changed cues in the preshock area is hypothesized to occur. Nevertheless, the fear elicited by the unchanged upper start-box cues and the drop stimuli initiates the strong running response established during shock-escape training, and forward locomotion is further facilitated by the shock administered in the midsegment. On subsequent trials, fear is reconditioned rapidly to the changed stimuli in the preshock area as a result of the temporal relationship of these cues to shock onset and self-punitive running is established.

Perconte et al. (1981) conducted several experiments investigating the effects of stimulus change introduced in the preshock area between shock-escape training and punished extinction. They found that when the stimuli were changed in the segment immediately preceding shock (the first runway segment in the typical paradigm), self-punitive behavior persisted, but when the stimuli were changed in the segment one segment removed from shock (the start box in the typical paradigm), self-punitive behavior was eliminated. The authors explain their results by assuming that during punished extinction fear is reconditioned rapidly to cues that are changed in the segment immediately preceding shock, but not to cues that are changed in the segment one segment removed from shock. Changing cues in the segment immediately preceding shock simply augments the degree of change typically present in all parts of the alley at the start of punished extinction due to the absence of shock. Following this initial stimulus-generalization decrement, fear is reconditioned rapidly to the modified cues because they immediately precede shock, and self-punitive running is maintained. In contrast, when cues are changed in the segment one segment removed from shock (typically the start box), the stimulus-generalization decrement in this segment disrupts the balance between the amounts of fear elicited by the cues in the two segments. The stronger fear elicited by the unchanged cues in the segment immediately preceding shock is augmented by additional conditioning trials. Moving from the modified start box, which elicits minimal fear, to the first segment, which elicits strong fear, results in an increase in fear which punishes the locomotor response and leads to the elimination of self-punitive behavior.

This explanation assumes that during early PE trials, the stimulus-generalization decrement in fear resulting from the changed cues is overcome through reconditioning when the cue change occurs in the segment immediately preceding shock, but not when the cue change occurs in the segment one segment removed from shock. Using hurdle-jumping as an index of fear, Dean and Walker (1988) provided empirical support for this assumption by demonstrating that, following 15 PE trials, fear was reconditioned to changed stimuli in the first runway segment. In contrast, the strength of fear of changed cues in the start box remained significantly lower than the fear of unchanged cues. These findings support the revised conditioned-fear interpretation presented here.

The Effects of Goal Shock on Response Persistence. The term self-punitive behavior has usually been reserved to describe response facilitation when shock is encountered at some intermediate point in the execution of a previously well-learned escape- or avoidance-response sequence. Brown (1969) suggested that a necessary condition for obtaining self-punitive behavior may be that the final element in the response sequence terminate the shock. It seems logical to expect that the application of shock in a previously safe goal box following shock-escape training should result in the conditioning of fear to the goal-box cues and lead to response suppression rather than facilitation relative to a regular-extinction (no-shock) condition. Contrary to this expectation, Babb and his associates have reported obtaining response facilitation with goal shock in a number of experiments (Babb, 1980; Babb & Hom, 1971; Babb, Kostyla, & Bennett, 1980; Hom & Babb, 1975; Matthews & Babb, 1978). Other experiments by the same and other authors have reported response suppression with the use of goal-box shock (Babb, 1963; Babb et al., 1980; Eison & Sawrey, 1967; Kintz & Bruning, 1967; Matthews & Babb, 1985; Meeker, Babb, & Matthews, 1980; Seligman & Campbell, 1965).

In all experiments that have successfully produced response facilitation, Babb and his associates have employed the same basic procedure. Animals are given a series of shock-escape training trials in a straight alley at the rate of one five-trial block per day. During acquisition, animals are placed in the start box, 5 sec later a guillotine door is opened, and a buzzer CS and the shock come on simultaneously. Shock is terminated when the animal enters the goal box, and the buzzer is terminated when a photobeam located 11 cm inside the goal box is broken. Extinction trials are administered in blocks of five trials per day with no shock present in the runway. Five sec after placement of the animal in the start box, the guillotine door is opened simultaneously with buzzer onset. The buzzer is terminated when the photobeam located 11 cm inside the goal box is broken. A 0.5-sec shock of the same intensity as that given during training is administered to PE animals 0.2 sec after termination of the buzzer. RE animals receive the buzzer but no shock. Animals are left in the goal box for 30 sec and then removed to a retaining cage to await the next trial.

A review of the self-punitive studies employing goal shock indicates that response facilitation is *always* found when *both* of the following conditions are present: (a) a discrete CS is used (e.g., a buzzer), and (b) trials are distributed over days. Response facilitation is *never* reported when *either* of these conditions is absent. In the latter case, response suppression is a frequent finding. An adequate theory of self-punitive behavior should account for these findings and any differences found between studies employing goal shock and those employing alley shock.

Babb (Babb, 1980; Babb et al., 1980) has concluded that the conditioned-fear interpretation is unable to account for self-punitive behavior when goal-box shock is used, and has proposed an alternative explanation, referred to as the stimulus-directive view, which purports to eliminate the need for reinforcement (fear reduction). Babb et al. (1980) suggest that in this analysis "fear" should be replaced with "directed movement tendency" or "conditioned aversion." The proponents of this interpretation state that, using their analysis, "The approach is achieved with only one of Mowrer's two factors, and it obtains 'instrumental' performance from what is, conceptually, a classical conditioning event" (Babb et al., 1980, p. 404). It is not apparent from their interpretation why a discrete CS is necessary in order to obtain response facilitation with goal shock but not with alley shock. In addition, the only suggestion they offer as to why distribution of trials is necessary with goal-box shock but not with alley shock is that conditioned aversion may accumulate faster in the goal box under massed trials than under distributed trials.

An alternate analysis of goal-shock response facilitation based on the revised conditioned-fear interpretation is offered by the present authors. The analysis focuses on the Babb paradigm that has been described. During shock-escape training, fear is conditioned to the discrete CS (the buzzer) and, *independently*, to the apparatus cues in the start box and the runway (McAllister & McAllister, 1968; McAllister & McAllister, 1971, p. 146). During shock-escape training, no fear is conditioned to the goal-box cues; in fact, relief conditioned to the goal-box cues (Delprato & Denny, 1968) should inhibit the generalization of fear from the runway. During shock-escape training, a forward locomotion response is learned to the discrete CS, the apparatus cues, and to the internal stimuli produced by fear. At the end of escape training, fear of the CS should be high, whereas fear of the goal-box cues should be minimal.

During RE trials, fear of the start-box cues, the alley cues, and the CS should extinguish, and the animal should stop running. During PE trials, the offset of the discrete CS in the goal box is followed immediately by a very brief shock, which results in additional conditioning of fear to the discrete CS. Although some fear is conditioned to the previously neutral goal-box cues, more fear is conditioned to the apparatus cues at the entrance to the goal box because they immediately precede the shock. During the 30 sec the animal remains in the goal box, goal-box entry is reinforced by the fear reduction which occurs when the animal escapes from the relatively high level of fear elicited by the discrete CS to the relatively low level of fear elicited by the goal-box cues. During the 24-hr interval between blocks of trials, the low level, newly conditioned fear of the apparatus cues in and near the goal box is forgotten more rapidly than is the strong, well-established fear of the discrete CS. This interpretation is based on the McAllister and McAllister (1968) finding that fear is conditioned independently to the apparatus cues and to the discrete CS, and that fear of the apparatus cues is forgotten more rapidly than fear of the CS.

During shock-escape trials, no fear is conditioned to the goal-box-entrance cues prior to the start of punished extinction, and during punished extinction only five brief, half-second shocks followed by a 24-hr forgetting interval are administered each day. On the other hand, the discrete CS has been paired with shock throughout shock-escape trials and can be assumed to elicit a high level of fear at the start of extinction. Furthermore, the CS continues to be followed by shock during punished extinction. Therefore, fear of the discrete CS is maintained at a higher level than fear of the goal box for many trials, and goal-box entry continues to be reinforced by the reduction of pain and fear while the animal is confined in the goal box. As stated earlier, the persistence of self-punitive behavior depends on the amounts of fear elicited by the cues in successive segments of the alley. During punished extinction, fear of the start-box and runway cues should gradually decrease and fear of the goal-box-entrance cues should increase. When fear of the goal-box-entrance cues exceeds that of the runway cues, self-punitive behavior should cease. The presence of grid floors and a uniform gray color throughout the start box, runway, and goal box in the Babb paradigm may serve to retard extinction of fear conditioned to the start box and runway cues and, therefore, to enhance response persistence.

The use of a discrete CS in the runway appears to be a critical element in obtaining goal-shock response facilitation. According to a revised conditioned-fear interpretation, in the absence of a discrete CS, extinction of fear of the start box and runway cues should be similar for both PE and RE subjects. For PE subjects, fear of the goal-box-entrance cues should increase over trials and result in more rapid extinction of the running response for these subjects than for RE subjects. This has been the finding in all instances but one. In one case, Babb (1980) reported facilitatory effects with a no-buzzer group and it is not clear how this group may have differed from no-buzzer groups in other studies. On the other hand, Babb (1963), Babb et al. (1980), and Eison and Sawrey (1967) have all reported response suppression by goal-box shock in the absence of a discrete CS. The Babb studies employ a trace conditioning paradigm, usually with an interval of 0.2 sec between CS offset and goal-box shock onset. Conditioning theory predicts that increasing the length of the interval between CS offset and shock onset should decrease the amount of fear conditioned to the CS. The revised conditioned-fear interpretation would predict that the amount of response facilitation following goal-box shock would be inversely related to the length of the trace interval. Results reported by Babb et al. (1980, Experiment 3) directly support this hypothesis. Without a buzzer, PE subjects extinguished faster than RE subjects. With the CS present only while the subject was in the start box, there were no differences between PE and RE groups in trials to extinction. Response facilitation was obtained both when the CS was continued throughout the runway and when it was continued into the goal box, and the latter condition resulted in the strongest facilitation. These results are directly in line with revised conditioned-fear predictions.[3]

In arguing that reinforcement cannot contribute to an explanation of the self-punitive findings when goal punishment is used, Matthews and Babb (1985) stated, "it is not clear how punishment delivered in the goal box may simultaneously increase and decrease fear" (p. 536). Whether or not shock increases or decreases fear of the goal-box cues is not the critical factor. The critical factor is the level of fear conditioned to the goal box relative to the level of fear conditioned to the discrete CS and the alley cues. Movement from an area eliciting a high level of fear to an area eliciting less fear is reinforcing. As long as the amount of fear elicited by the goal-box cues remains less than the amount of fear elicited by the discrete CS and the runway cues, goal-box entry will be reinforced by fear reduction. The interpretation offered here recognizes the importance of fear reduction in maintaining self-punitive behavior, while also recognizing the importance of changes, over trials, in the amount of conditioned fear elicited by various segments of the alley.

Recent Related Research and Summary

Although the revised conditioned-fear interpretation is based on established conditioning principles, the application of these principles to self-punitive behavior generates a number of hypotheses about levels of fear and changes in levels of fear that require investigation if the explanation is to be more than simply descriptive. The development of an independent index of fear (Dean & Pittman, 1988) has permitted the testing of several specific hypotheses generated by the revised conditioned-fear interpretation. Dean and Pittman (1988) investigated changes in the strength of fear elicited by lower start-box cues after varying numbers of extinction trials. Four groups of subjects were given either 10, 20, 50, or 75 PE trials, and

---

[3]In contrast to the goal-box-shock paradigm, the midsegment-shock paradigm produces response facilitation without requiring the use of a discrete CS. During shock-escape training, fear is conditioned to the apparatus cues in all areas of the alley except the goal box. During punished extinction, the location of the shock in a midsegment maintains fear at a higher level in the preshock area than in the shock or postshock areas and ensures the initiation of the running response. The running response, which has been associated with shock in the punishment zone during shock-escape training, continues to be reinforced by escape to the goal box, where shock has never been experienced.

two groups of subjects were given either 10 or 20 RE trials. All subjects were given 60 hurdle-jump test trials (see description of hurdle-jump procedure, page 270) immediately following the completion of the prescribed number of extinction trials. As predicted by the revised conditioned-fear model, the strength of fear elicited by the start-box cues was significantly greater for subjects that had received PE trials than for subjects that had received RE trials. The results also indicated that fear of the start-box cues was maintained for many trials with a significant decrease in fear finally occurring after 75 PE trials.

The revised conditioned-fear model also predicts, contrary to the previous conditioned-fear interpretation, that, during punished extinction, cues in the preshock area should elicit stronger fear than cues in either the shock or the postshock areas. Pittman and Dean (1989) provided evidence in support of this hypothesis. Following 15 PE trials, four groups of subjects were given hurdle-jump testing in either the start box or one of the three runway segments. An additional group was tested in the first runway segment (the segment immediately preceding shock) after 15 *RE* trials. For the groups receiving PE trials, significantly greater fear was elicited by the cues in both the start box and the first runway segment than by the cues in either the shock segment or the third runway segment. In addition, of the two groups tested in the first runway segment, the group given PE trials showed greater fear than the group given RE trials. The latter finding extends to an additional part of the preshock area (the first runway segment) the Dean and Pittman (1988) finding that greater fear is conditioned to the start box after PE trials than after RE trials. Pittman and Dean (1987) replicated the finding that, following PE trials, stronger fear is elicited by start-box cues than by third-runway-segment cues. In addition, they demonstrated that this difference is not present at the end of shock-escape training, but is significant after as few as five PE trials. Finally, support for the hypothesis that midsegment shock conditions fear most strongly to the cues in the immediately preceding segment is provided by the finding that, early in extinction, fear is reconditioned to changed cues in the first segment but not to changed cues in the start box (Dean & Walker, 1988).

In summary, recent research has supported the revised conditioned-fear interpretation of self-punitive behavior. Punished extinction results in stronger fear of the cues in the start box and in the first runway segment than does regular extinction. In addition, during punished extinction, stronger fear is conditioned to the start-box and first runway-segment cues than to the shock- or the postshock-segment cues. The evidence indicates that fear of the cues in the start box and first-segment is maintained during punished extinction for many trials. The eventual termination of self-punitive behavior is hypothesized to be a function of the incremental development over trials of a difference between the strength of fear elicited by the cues encountered immediately preceding shock onset and the strength of fear elicited by the cues encountered earlier in the preshock area. When fear elicited by the cues immediately preceding shock is sufficiently greater than the fear elicited by cues in the remainder of the preshock area, self-punitive behavior should cease. The finding that PE animals tend to extinguish by remaining in the start box (Delude, 1973; Renner & Tinsley, 1976) and the Dean and Pittman (1988) finding that start-box fear decreased after 75 trials are consistent with this differential fear hypothesis, but direct experimental evidence is not yet available.

As stated earlier, self-punitive behavior depends on the balance between the strength of fear elicited by the cues in successive alley segments and the goal box. Further research investigating factors that affect the strength of fear elicited by the cues in the start box, various runway segments, and the goal box over trials up to and including the terminal extinction trial is necessary to gain a complete understanding of self-punitive behavior.

REFERENCES

Babb, H. (1963). Reinforcement and punishment of an escape response. *Psychological Reports, 13*, 542.

Babb, H. (1980). Facilitation by goal punishment after escape conditioning: CS intensity effects. *Psychological Record, 30*, 229–236.

Babb, H., & Hom, H. L., Jr. (1971). Self-punitive responding by goal-shocked rats. *Journal of Comparative and Physiological Psychology, 77*, 482–488.

Babb, H., Kostyla, S. J., & Bennett, W. R. (1980). Escape conditioning and goal punishment: Effects of acquisition trials, initial punishment trials, and CS extent. *Learning and Motivation, 11*, 386–406.

Beecroft, R. S., & Bouska, S. A. (1967). Learning self-punitive running. *Psychonomic Science, 8*, 107–108.

Bender, L. (1969). Secondary punishment and self-punitive behavior in the rat. *Journal of Comparative and Physiological Psychology, 69*, 261–266.

Brown, J. S. (1965). A behavioral analysis of masochism. *Journal of Experimental Research in Personality, 1*, 65–70.

Brown, J. S. (1969). Factors affecting self-punitive behavior. In B. Campbell & R. M. Church (Eds.), *Punishment and aversive behavior* (pp. 467–514). New York: Appleton–Century–Crofts.

Brown, J. S. (1970). Self-punitive behavior with a distinctively marked punishment zone. *Psychonomic Science, 21*, 161–163.

Brown, J. S., Beier, E. M., & Lewis, R. W. (1971). Punishment-zone distinctiveness and self-punitive locomotor behavior in the rat. *Journal of Comparative and Physiological Psychology, 77*, 513–520.

Brown, J. S., & Cunningham, C. L. (1981). The paradox of persisting self-punitive behavior. *Neuroscience and Biobehavioral Reviews, 5*, 343–354.

Brown, J. S., Martin, R. C., & Morrow, M. W. (1964). Self-punitive behavior in the rat: Facilitative effects of punishment on resistance to extinction. *Journal of Comparative and Physiological Psychology, 57*, 127–133.

Church, R. M. (1963). The varied effects of punishment on behavior. *Psychological Review*, *70*, 369–402.

Cunningham, C. L., Brown, J. S., & Roberts, S. (1976). Startbox-goalbox confinement durations as determinants of self-punitive behavior. *Learning and Motivation*, *7*, 340–355.

Dean, S. J., Denny, M. R., & Blakemore, T. (1985). Vicious-circle behavior involves new learning. *Bulletin of the Psychonomic Society*, *23*, 230–232.

Dean, S. J., & Pittman, C. M. (1988). Self-punitive behavior: An independent measure of fear of the startbox. *Learning and Motivation*, *19*, 442–452.

Dean, S. J., & Walker, L. K. (1988). *Self-punitive behavior: The effects of stimulus change on fear*. Paper presented at the meeting of the Midwestern Psychological Association, Chicago.

Delprato, D. J., & Carosio, L. A. (1976). Elimination of self-punitive behavior with a novel stimulus and safety signal. *Animal Learning & Behavior*, *4*, 210–212.

Delprato, D. J., & Denny, M. R. (1968). Punishment and the length of non-shock confinement during the extinction of avoidance. *Canadian Journal of Psychology*, *22*, 456–464.

Delprato, D. J., & Meltzer, R. J. (1974). Type of start box and goal box distinctiveness in self-punitive running of rats. *Journal of Comparative and Physiological Psychology*, *87*, 548–554.

Delude, L. A. (1969). The vicious circle phenomenon: A result of measurement artifact. *Journal of Comparative and Physiological Psychology*, *69*, 246–252.

Delude, L. A. (1973). Factors affecting the strength of the vicious circle phenomenon. *Psychological Record*, *23*, 467–476.

Dreyer, P., & Renner, K. E. (1971). Self-punitive behavior—Masochism or confusion? *Psychological Review*, *78*, 333–337.

Eison, C. L., & Sawrey, J. M. (1967). Extinction of avoidance behavior: CS presentations with and without punishment. *Psychonomic Science*, *7*, 95–96.

Fantino, E., & Logan, C. A. (1979). *The experimental analysis of behavior: A biological perspective*. San Francisco: W. H. Freeman.

Galvani, P. F. (1969). Self-punitive behavior as a function of number of prior fear-conditioning trials. *Journal of Comparative and Physiological Psychology*, *68*, 359–363.

Gwinn, G. T. (1949). The effects of punishment on acts motivated by fear. *Journal of Experimental Psychology*, *39*, 260–269.

Hom, H. L., Jr., & Babb, H. (1975). Self-punitive responding in rats with goal shock and color change. *Animal Learning & Behavior*, *3*, 152–156.

Kintz, B. L., & Bruning, J. L. (1967). Punishment and compulsive avoidance behavior. *Journal of Comparative and Physiological Psychology*, *63*, 323–326.

Klare, W. F. (1974). Conditioned fear and postshock emotionality in vicious circle behavior of rats. *Journal of Comparative and Physiological Psychology*, *87*, 364–372.

Kruger, B. M. (1974). Self-punitive running in the rat following start box fear conditioning: Shock intensity effects. *Journal of Comparative and Physiological Psychology*, *87*, 555–562.

Matthews, M. D., & Babb, H. (1978). Effects of percentage of goal-punished extinction trials on self-punitive behavior. *Bulletin of the Psychonomic Society*, *12*, 64–66.

Matthews, M. D., & Babb, H. (1985). Self-punitive behavior: Effects of percentage of shocked acquisition trials and percentage of goal-shocked extinction trials. *Psychological Record*, *35*, 535–547.

McAllister, D. E., & McAllister, W. R. (1968). Forgetting of acquired fear. *Journal of Comparative and Physiological Psychology*, *65*, 352–355.

McAllister, W. R., & McAllister, D. E. (1971). Behavioral measurement of conditioned fear. In F. R. Brush (Ed.), *Aversive conditioning and learning* (pp. 105–179). New York: Academic Press.

Meeker, D. J., Babb, H., & Matthews, M. D. (1980). Goal vs. alley punishment after escape training: Massed trials and startbox conditions. *Bulletin of the Psychonomic Society, 16,* 51–54.

Melvin, K. B. (1971). Vicious circle behavior. In H. D. Kimmel (Ed.), *Experimental psychopathology: Recent research and theory* (pp. 95–115). New York: Academic Press.

Melvin, K. B., & Bender, L. (1968). Self-punitive avoidance behavior: Effects of changes in punishment intensity. *Psychological Record, 18,* 29–34.

Melvin, K. B., Irving, T. K., & Prentice–Dunn, S. (1979). Fear-motivated vicious-circle behavior maintained through secondary punishment. *Animal Learning & Behavior, 7,* 185–190.

Melvin, K. B., & Stenmark, D. E. (1968). Facilitative effects of punishment on establishment of a fear motivated response. *Journal of Comparative and Physiological Psychology, 65,* 517–519.

Mowrer, O. H. (1947). On the dual nature of learning—A re-interpretation of "conditioning" and "problem solving." *Harvard Educational Review, 17,* 102–148.

Mowrer, O. H. (1960). *Learning theory and behavior.* New York: Wiley.

O'Neil, H. F., Jr., Skeen, L. C., & Ryan, F. J. (1970). Prevention of vicious circle behavior. *Journal of Comparative and Physiological Psychology, 70,* 281–285.

Perconte, S. T., Benson, B. A., & Butler, D. L. (1981). Effects of stimulus change in prepunishment alley segments on self-punitive behavior. *Animal Learning & Behavior, 9,* 21–27.

Pittman, C. M., & Dean, S. J. (1987). *Self-punitive behavior: Strength of fear of preshock and postshock segment cues during punished extinction.* Paper presented at the meeting of the Midwestern Psychological Association, Chicago.

Pittman, C. M., & Dean, S. J. (1989). Self-punitive behavior: Fear of different alley segments. *Learning and Motivation, 20,* 87–95.

Rands, B. B., & Dean, S. J. (1975). *Choice and vicious circle behavior in human subjects.* Paper presented at the annual meeting of the Psychonomic Society, Denver.

Renner, K. E., & Tinsley, J. B. (1976). Self-punitive behavior. In G. H. Bower (Ed.), *The psychology of learning and motivation* (Vol. 10, pp. 155–198). New York: Academic Press.

Saunders, T. R., Jr. (1974). Effects of US intensity and number of CS–US pairings on maintenance of vicious-circle behavior in rats by secondary punishment. *Journal of Comparative and Physiological Psychology, 86,* 535–542.

Seligman, M. E. P., & Campbell, B. A. (1965). Effect of intensity and duration of punishment on extinction of an avoidance response. *Journal of Comparative and Physiological Psychology, 59,* 295–297.

9 Response Patterns in Shock Avoidance and Illness Aversion

Dennis J. Delprato and Kenneth W. Rusiniak
Eastern Michigan University

I. INTRODUCTION

It is not difficult to convince experimental psychologists that behavior is organized and that experimental manipulations may have many and diverse effects upon such organization. However, the use of measurement procedures that systematically detect more than one or a few behaviors or describe behavioral organization is far from routine. Instead, experimental researchers tend to favor the use of single, familiar, automated response measures, which makes it difficult to describe patterns or organization (Delprato, 1986; Henton & Iversen, 1978). In contrast, animal behaviorists have explicitly incorporated observational techniques that look at several behaviors in describing structural, functional, and hierarchical patterns of behavior in time and space (e.g., see Hinde, 1982; Manning, 1979). Although multibehavioral recording has been fruitful for animal behavior, it is often associated with less rigorous natural observation and is not used regularly in experimental settings. In keeping with the current rapprochement between the fields of ethology and psychology, we feel there is much to be gained by using observational methods in combination with experimental manipulations. The present chapter focuses on illness and shock conditioning studies in which multiple responses have been recorded in an attempt to describe patterns or organization of behavior as conditioning develops. We propose that this methodology makes an important contribution toward understanding reactions in aversive situations, in terms of both a simple structural description of behavior as well as a functional analysis of underlying mechanisms.

II. METHODOLOGICAL CONSIDERATIONS IN INVESTIGATIONS OF RESPONSE PATTERNS

One way to begin looking at behavior in terms of patterns and organization is to abandon linear approaches, such as associationism, and to adopt an integrated field/system approach that emphasizes a kind of ecological approach to behavioral analysis. As field events, behavior encompasses organismic actions, or response functions, stimulating objects, or stimulus functions, media by which organisms come into contact with the environment, and setting factors that are the immediate conditions influencing which particular stimulus and response functions will occur at a particular point in time and space (Kantor & Smith, 1975). Thus, ideally, the investigation of behavioral systems requires multiple-event methodologies that track all relevant components of the behavioral field, not only responses (Ray & Delprato, 1989; Upson & Ray, 1984). However, most of the situations we will discuss in this chapter focus on the response component of the event field.

Following Delprato (1986), we find it convenient to classify response patterns into two groups. Concurrent response patterns are obtained when investigators record more than one behavior, treat the behaviors as mutually exclusive, measure probability, duration, or some other index, and find variation in the scores or codes. Observation may be either point-sample or continuous, and data are usually expressed using some overall index, such as relative frequency or number of subjects showing the response. Concurrent patterns are especially interesting when they vary across experimental conditions. Sequential response patterns are obtained by using multiple, mutually exclusive response codes recorded over time, and then calculating serial dependencies of the behaviors. Data are usually expressed as differential latencies or serial conditional probabilities. Sequential pattern analysis has a much more developed and intricate methodological base, which is known in the literature as sequential analysis and time series analysis (e.g., Bakeman & Gottman, 1986; Gottman, 1981). Sequential patterns are especially interesting when they vary within a subject across treatment conditions.

We should note that there is also temporal pattern, which can be observed by looking at a single response during schedules of reinforcement, presentation of a prolonged CS in classical conditioning or discriminative stimulus in instrumental conditioning. Similarly, response topography analysis, such as investigations of movement differences in sign-tracking studies (Jenkins & Moore, 1973), also constitutes a kind of pattern analysis. Thus, although it may be possible to see some kinds of patterns using a single-response index, it is our contention that multiple-response recording will provide a better description of behavior, particularly in temporal pattern

286

studies. The work of Staddon and Simmelhag (1971) on adjunctive behavior nicely illustrates the advantages of this approach.

Because pattern analysis is relatively new in the area of aversive conditioning and to our knowledge has not been systematically applied to the shock and illness distinction in the literature, a brief review of these techniques may be useful. Most of the patterns described in this work are fairly simple, reflecting the early stage of development in the area. Further, it is implicit that response patterns refer to actions of an individual. One place where pattern analysis is most rudimentary is in shifting between group data (particularly in concurrent response analysis) and individual data (particularly in sequential analysis). In keeping with the current "state of the art," we too will shift and choose between group and individual analysis as suits our purpose in this chapter.

III. REACTIONS IN SHOCK SITUATIONS

A. Defensive Patterns to Shock

Conceptually, there appear to be two separate issues in aversive conditioning. First, is the description or ethogram of the structural pattern and hierarchical organization of defensive behaviors of the species in particular situations. Second, is the question of how these responses change in reaction to stimuli, be they "neutral," warning, species-typical releasers, or inherently painful events, that intrude upon ongoing behavior in time and space. With respect to the first issue, Bolles's (1970) discussion of species-specific defensive reactions and the conditions that encourage freezing, fleeing, or fighting continues to be a standard for describing some major defensive patterns of rodents confronted with painful foot shock. Pinel's recent description of defensive burying and the use of multiple recording provides another example. Specifically, if rats are briefly shocked by one of two identical prods located on opposite walls of an experimental chamber that has a floor covered with bedding material, some rats cover the shock prod with the bedding material (Pinel & Treit, 1978). Several researchers have suggested that burying is but one component of a series of defensive reactions toward aversive stimuli. For example, Peacock and Wong (1982, Experiment 2) measured latency and duration of six responses in addition to burying the shock prod; and Moser and Tait (1983) measured the latency and frequency of freezing, withdrawal from the side of the experimental chamber in which prod-shock occurred, and shock prod burying; they also measured duration of freezing and burying. Results from both experiments suggest that burying is a late component of an extended sequence that starts with freezing and withdrawal. This conclusion is based on the latency measure that implied a sequence: Early responses had short latencies and later responses had longer latencies. However, response sequences were not measured directly. Comparisons of relative latencies is but a weak way of describing sequential response patterns. Future work in this area would be enhanced by more powerful methods such as sequential analytical methods (Bakeman & Gottman, 1986), and behavioral systems methodology (Ray & Delprato, 1989). Be that as it may, research on defensive burying has at least given some indication of the potential value of approaching the area of aversive behavior in terms of behavioral organization.

With respect to the second issue, there is a tendency to assume that the effects of aversive stimuli on behavior vary only as a function of their characteristics and of the subject's past history. However, there is good reason to believe that the effects of aversive stimuli will also be influenced by where a stimulus intrudes in the behavioral stream. In a study involving appetitive stimuli, Ray and Brown (1976) recorded 11 responses made by water-deprived rats during sessions in which filled water dippers were presented irrespective of any particular response. They found that the effectiveness of the dipper in eliciting drinking was greater following certain responses (e.g., head exploration) than it was following other responses (e.g., scratching). These results suggest that the motivationally significant water-filled dipper had effects that were dependent on ongoing behavior. There are analogous results with aversive stimuli.

Geese and game birds, such as ducks and pheasants, display defensive alarm responses (e.g., alarm calls, crouching, mantling) in response to some moving overhead objects under certain conditions (e.g., Delprato, 1980; Tinbergen, 1948, 1951). Other prey species also show defensive reactions. Fentress (1968) evaluated continuously recorded responses of voles to a moving overhead cloth. He found that fleeing was reliably more likely when animals were walking at the onset of the stimulus than when they were not walking; when animals were not walking at stimulus onset, they were likely to freeze upon presentation of the moving cloth. Forrester and Broom (1980) extended Fentress's finding when they observed that domestic chicks' responses to a light varied, depending on what they were doing when the stimulus was presented. For example, chicks that were engaged in stationary responses at stimulus onset were more likely to display immobility than were those that were more active when the light came on. These studies suggest that responses to aversive stimuli are organized in patterns. Therefore, it seems reasonable to expect that sequential and concurrent response organization may be changed by a variety of stimuli intruding in a behavioral field. Thus, it is likely that future research will show that effects of warning stimuli and setting (contextual) events in conditioning experiments may also vary as a function of ongoing response patterns. Indeed, we have not taken systematic data on the matter, but many researchers who observe their subjects have been sensitive to the rather obvious possibility that the direction a rat is facing or whether the animal has been familiarized with the chamber to habituate exploratory sequences will influence subsequent effects of warning signal, shock, or warning signal–shock pairings. Patterning theory provides a framework for such considerations and can serve to drive multiple-response research.

B. Reactions in Pavlovian Conditioning Using Shock as the US

Multiple-response analyses of aversive Pavlovian conditioning indicate that conditioning to signaled response-independent shock is more a matter of response pattern change than of the elicitation of single, isolated defensive twitches. In an early conditioned suppression study, Frick (1953) mechanically recorded sequences of food-deprived rats' lever presses located at one end of the test cage and food-tray approach responses located at the other end of the test cage during CS presentation. He used autocorrelation functions for individual subjects to measure sequential patterning of these two responses. Autocorrelation functions require multiple, time-ordered measures from a single subject. Correlation coefficients are calculated on these scores at various lags, or ordinal positions. The autocorrelation at lag 1 is obtained between the series X_1, X_2, . . . , X_{n-1}, and the series X_2, X_3, . . . , X_n, where each pair of scores consists of X_t and X_{t-1}. Autocorrelations for lags greater than 1 are obtained in a similar way, for example, for lag 2 the pairs of scores are X_t and X_{t-2}. For computational purposes in the case of a two-valued variable such as the response one Frick used, it is possible to assign arbitrarily $+1$ to food-tray approach and -1 to lever press (Frick & Miller, 1951). The result was that after approximately 400 lever presses, the continuous reinforcement schedule that Frick used yielded the autocorrelation functions shown in the left panel of Fig. 9.1. These data are from one 10-min session during which three control (nonshock) rats continued pressing on the 100% reinforcement schedule in the presence of a light stimulus. Not surprisingly, the rats showed a well-organized pattern of alternation between lever pressing and food-tray approach, indicated by significant positive autocorrelations at even-numbered lags (m) and significant negative autocorrelations at odd-numbered lags. Experimental rats were treated identically to the control rats, except prior to any lever press training they received 5 to 10 shocks in the presence of the light. As can be seen in the right panel of Fig. 9.1, the prior light–shock pairings had the effect of disrupting the sequential patterning of lever pressing and food-tray approach. Few autocorrelation coefficients ap-

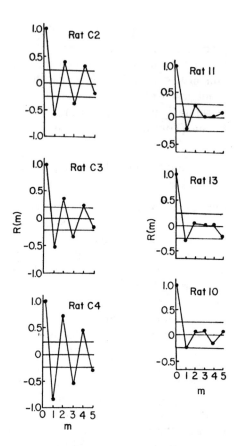

FIG. 9.1. Autocorrelation coefficients (R) at lags (m) 0–5 for series of lever presses and food-tray approach responses of six rats in the presence of a light cue and a continuous reinforcement schedule. Left panel: three rats in baseline condition (no shock). Right panel: three rats previously exposed to light–shock pairings. Horizontal lines above and below R(m) = 0 are limits for p = .05, given null hypothesis of R(m) = 0 (drawn from Frick, 1953, Figs. 1 and 2).

proach significance; the sequence of responses is virtually random. Frick also obtained a similar difference in response patterning under nonshock control and experimental conditions in within-subject comparisons. In addition, these comparisons demonstrated effects of light–shock pairings that were evident in sequential pattern disruptions but not in lever-press response rate measures! In other words, the response pattern measure was more sensitive to experimental effects than was the nonpattern single-response one.

Concurrent response pattern measurement can also be useful. For example, Bouton and Bolles (1980, Experiment 2) monitored freezing and general activity as well as target licking/drinking of rats in either forward (tone-shock) or backward (shock-tone) conditioned suppression conditioning. Fig. 9.2 shows that the greater degree of suppression of licking to the tone CS after forward conditioning relative to backward conditioning is a component of a differential concurrent pattern under the two treatments. In fact, both forward and backward pairings produced response

FIG. 9.2. Concurrent patterns of rats during the first minute of a tone that been paired with foot shock in a forward manner (Forward Conditioning, FC) or a backward manner (Backward Conditioning, BC). Percentages of observations showing freezing (F), activity (A), and licking/drinking (D) (from Bouton & Bolles, Animal Learning and Behavior, 1980, 8, p. 432; reproduced with permission of Psychonomic Society, Inc., and author).

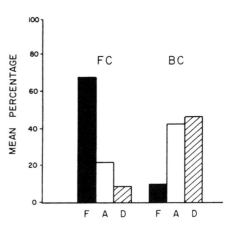

changes, but the effects were upon different patterns. Under somewhat similar training conditions, Ayres, Haddad, and Albert (1987) used response analysis during backward and control conditions with licking as the focal response. These authors reasoned that backward excitatory conditioning could be justifiably demonstrated if there was both decrement in focal licking and increment in defensive responses, such as freezing. In contrast to the results of Bouton and Bolles, their findings indicated that backward conditioning procedures did alter a concurrent pattern of reduction in licking with increment in freezing. Both sets of authors seem to argue that covariations between licking/drinking and other responses, as revealed in these concurrent response patterns, is consistent with competing response theories of aversive conditioning and offer promise for further clarification of the much debated issue of backward conditioning.

Other work also implicates response competition in conditioned suppression and calls for additional multiple-response analyses that yield data on what behaviors fill in for reductions in conventional baseline responses, such as lever pressing, key pecking, and licking. For example, rats (Karpicke, Christoph, Peterson, & Hearst, 1977) and pigeons (Karpicke & Dout, 1980) show withdrawal patterns from localized visual CSs. The work by Bouton and Bolles and Ayres et al. is also indicative, but calls for more data on a broader sample of behavior. Roberts, Cooper, and Richey (1977) reported encouraging results when they used lever pressing as a criterion response and 10 response codes in the context of an unsignaled (Sidman) avoidance study. Much of the success or failure in acquiring an avoidance response could be accounted for by examining response patterns. Thus, a growing number of researchers in the area are adopting the elementary point that no degree of sophistication in interpretation or theory can substitute for descriptions of behavior.

C. Punishment

The punishment procedure is similar to that used in aversive Pavlovian conditioning, except that the aversive stimulation is contingent on occurrence of a specified response. A decrement in the specified, target response is defined as a punishment effect and indeed frequently occurs under these conditions (Azrin & Holz, 1966). Punishment is approached mechanistically if one assumes either that response decrements are caused by the unique property of "aversiveness" of stimuli or that increments in another competing response cause decrements in the target response. The more recently developed field/system approach suggests that punishment, like all effective experimental manipulations, involves intrusions or perturbations into behavioral fields that alter field organization, including patterns of responding. According to this view, punishers are not uniquely different from any other class of functional stimuli such as reinforcers that "select" certain behavioral units at the cost of others to shift the "population" of behavior. And the effects of all field intrusions depend on where they intrude into the behavioral stream and the previous behavioral field at a time just past.

Dunham (1972) provided data that nicely illustrate the field nature of punishment. He concurrently recorded two responses of rats in a confined chamber—either drinking from a tube or running in a wheel. In one experiment, both responses were available; when shock followed occurrences of one, it decreased in probability and the other increased in probability. In a second experiment, both responses were available for the first 24 days; subsequently, one response was eliminated by lack of access to the necessary environmental object (drinking tube or running wheel). Under these conditions, the response that remained available increased in probability as it did in the first experiment when the other response decreased in probability when followed by shock. Thus, a response increased over its baseline rate when another prominent response in the field decreased as a result of either contingent shock (i.e., punishment) or blocking (or restraint). Dunham and Grantmyre (1982) reported similar results with gerbils in that when one of four recorded responses was punished or restricted, the pattern of four responses changed and its change was the same irrespective of how the referent response was decremented.

Dunham and Grantmyre (1982) showed additional descriptive and predictive advantages of field analyses and multiple-response methodology in punishment research with data demonstrating that when electric shock was contingent on a specific response, the alternative response that was most sequentially dependent on the punished response was most likely to be suppressed in subsequent sessions.

The work of Dunham and his collaborators indicates that effective punishment procedures lead organisms to reorganize behavioral fields, and apparently there are some circumstances in which the way a response is eliminated has little bearing on the pattern that emerges. However, as we shall show later, eliminating ingestive behavior with shock or illness has profound effects on the patterns that emerge. Thus, although punishment is commonly thought to be only a decrementing procedure, consistent with response pattern theory, it is also an incrementing procedure (Dunham, 1971, 1972, 1978; Dunham & Grantmyre, 1982). But which behaviors are incremented may depend on the US used to eliminate a response.

D. Reactions in Shock-avoidance Tasks

Mechanistically based descriptions juxtapose fear behavior and avoidance responding, an influential example of which is the two-factor theory of avoidance (Miller, 1951; Mowrer, 1939, 1947). According to two-factor theory, classically conditioned fear serves as a source of motivation for avoidance responses that are in turn reinforced by fear reduction. This theory places great weight on the construct of inhibition. Pavlovian inhibitory factors are assumed to override fear and once fear is inhibited, avoidance responses decrease due to decrements in motivation (i.e., decreased fear).

From the standpoint of field/system and response pattern theory, events frequently referred to as the inhibition of fear and avoidance require descriptions that are quite different from the mechanistic ones. Instead of treating absence of referent responses such as fear as nonactions, all decrements are considered in terms of alternative responding (Denny, this volume; Kantor, 1924). Therefore, it should be possible to describe diminutions in both fear behavior and avoidance responding in terms of reorganized behavioral fields, including altered response patterns.

The flooding procedure for eliminating fear and avoidance responding (Baum, 1970) has produced a few reports of multiple-response research. Flooding, also known as response prevention, involves forcing the subject to confront the cues for fear and avoidance in the absence of shock. The procedure is quite effective in eliminating avoidance responding. Baum (1969) found that over the course of several minutes of response prevention, abortive avoidance responses decreased while other responses, especially general activity, increased. Baum, Pereira, and Leclerc (1985) reported that white noise presented concurrently with flooding treatments enhanced flooding effects and that the effectiveness of the auditory stimulation was monotonically related to its intensity. During flooding, concurrent response patterns, measured on a group-wise basis, systematically varied over several treatment conditions. For example, in the least effective condition (no noise), in comparison with the most effective one, rats were more likely to show abortive avoidance and freezing and less likely to groom and show general activity. When analyzed over all subjects, number of responses on the postflooding, nonshock extinction test correlated positively with abortive avoidance during flooding and correlated negatively with general activity during the same period.

Lapointe and Baum (1987) noted a descriptive shortcoming of the multiple-response observational procedure that Baum and others (e.g., Cook, Mineka, & Trumble, 1987; Miller, Mineka, & Cook, 1982) had used in previous studies. They recognized the limitations of instantaneous time-point sampling and the need for continuous recording in light of the continuity of behavior (Ray & Delprato, 1989). Subsequently, Lapointe and Baum recorded duration of various responses during flooding and examined data for three individual rats. Concurrent response patterns during flooding differed in a way that (a) helps account for the sometimes low and even statistically nonsignificant (Miller et al. 1982) correlations between response patterns during flooding and efficacy of flooding and (b) suggests that time-sampling may not be the most desirable way in which to identify response patterns, that is, describe behavior.

E. Sequential Response Patterns in Unsignaled Avoidance

The potential descriptive/explanatory value of relying on response pattern analysis based on individual subjects is nicely exhibited in Hann and Roberts's (1984) study on free operant avoidance, one of the preparations most notorious for yielding high intersubject variability. Hann and Roberts recorded criterion lever pressing, which postponed shock for 15 sec, as well as nine responses which were not explicitly part of the criterion response. Good avoiders showed identifiable sequential response patterns in the response-shock interval that seemed to incorporate the lever press response into an existing pattern. Although specific sequences varied from rat to rat, one common sequence was walk–no walk with all paws on floor–walk–turn–lever press. Poor avoiders, on the other hand, did not show any regular, identifiable response sequences. It is as though the poor avoiders' behavioral organization, including the target lever press response, was insufficient to permit consistent avoidance responding.

It is interesting that Roberts (1986) did find that when free operant avoidance required a shuttle response of crossing the midline of a box, rats incorporated this response into identifiable sequential response patterns. Again, one prominent pattern was walk–no walk with all paws on floor–turn–walk. These results are similar to those obtained by Bolles in his study of SSDRs and criterion response compatibility. The response pattern framework calls for pattern analyses of subjects' behavior in a variety of learning preparations, for results comparable with those of Hann, Roberts, and Bolles would support the idea that learning involves reorganization (e.g., Koffka, 1935), but reorganization of behavioral fields or systems not of the mental type.

IV. REACTIONS IN ILLNESS SITUATIONS

A. Anecdotal Descriptions of Concurrent Responses During Shock Versus Illness Conditioning

One of the most significant developments in aversive learning has been the study of conditioned flavor aversions that began with the investigations of the aversive effects of X-irradiation (Garcia, Kimeldorf, Hunt, & Davies, 1956; Garcia, Kimeldorf, & Koelling, 1955). In subsequent experiments, Garcia and his collaborators began examining the aversive effects of illness produced by injections of emetic drugs and toxins (e.g., Garcia & Koelling, 1967).

The majority of the work on illness-induced flavor aversions has used some single index of consumption—typically volume or weight consumed, lick rate, or duration of contact with the fluid/food. And the use of consumption measures has served us well, as such studies have had a major impact on learning theory over the last 25 years. For example, Garcia and Koelling (1966) used lick rate in the now-classic study on the relation of cue to consequence. They found that rats were more likely to acquire an aversion, as indicated by reduced licking, to the gustatory component than to the audiovisual component that preceded illness, but were more likely to develop avoidance of audiovisual components than gustatory components when the compound preceded foot shock. Likewise, Garcia, Ervin, and Koelling (1966) used suppression of fluid intake to demonstrate acquisition of flavor aversions over long CS–US delays, when the aversive illness followed exposure to the flavor by several hours.

But in these "early" years, anecdotal observations of other concurrent behaviors were as informative as the response measures, if not more so. Rats confronted with conditioned aversive flavors were observed to smack their lips, to show finicky, hesitant lick patterns, to wipe their muzzles in bouts resembling grooming, to dump aversive mash out of their dishes and push it through the floor of the cage, to bite at the cage or spout without drinking—all in the context of agitated movements. In one case, the use of a single "classic" response measure nearly missed the main effect of the study. Garcia, McGowan, Ervin, and Koelling (1968) gave rats either small or large food pellets coated with either flour or powdered sugar as a taste cue. Using amount consumed as the measure, they reported that toxicosis reduced consumption of flavored pellets regardless of size, whereas shock reduced consumption of large or small pellets, regardless of their taste. But just as important were the observations that poisoned rats often nibbled past the flavored coating and ate the familiar-tasting core of the pellet (just as people eat around bruised or spoiled spots on fruit) and shocked rats picked up large shock-associated pellets and carried them next to or on top of safe pellets. Similarly, Garcia, Kovner, and Green (1970) reported response topography differences toward flavors paired with foot shock or illness. Notably, they reported that unlike poisoned rats, shocked rats stretched out and gingerly licked at spouts containing saccharin water that had been correlated with shock, flinching and squinting as they sampled lick by lick; it was as if they were using the lick response to probe for the presence of shock.

Several years later, Garcia, Rusiniak, and Brett (1977) reviewed conditioned flavor aversion studies conducted on captive predators poisoned for attacking and eating prey. They noted three different classes of reactions. (1) Conditioned illness: Coyotes, cougars, and red-tailed hawks may retch, heave their flanks, or smack their lips/beaks when they encounter aversive prey. (2) Species-typical disgust responses: Coyotes roll on, urinate on, or bury aversive rabbit prey; cougars mouth, then drop deer meat, shaking their paws in rotation; and rats get up on their toes and turn their backs on odorous mice that have been paired with lithium chloride. (3) Conflict responses directed at other stimulus properties of prey: Wolves show social play-bows and dominance-submission responses toward sheep after undergoing aversive conditioning to them; and some coyotes and predatory rats kill aversive prey presented in the home territory, but not elsewhere, as if affective territorial aggression replaced the cool, calculated predatory act. These insightful clinical impressions, though documented in film, represent summaries of unquantified, nonsystematic observations of concurrent patterns.

In 1973, Garcia, Clarke, and Hankins reviewed the laboratory literature on the biological constraints on conditioning. One of their conclusions was that many conditioning studies suggested that experimental stimuli were superimposed on existing behavioral flow, and that conditioning results were due as much to compatibility with biological function, predisposition, and behavioral stream as to novelty, intensity, timing, and information value of stimuli. They exhorted experimenters to observe subjects in Skinner boxes and Pavlovian harnesses, and to "free" response patterns from restrained training and testing situations. Although slow in coming, some have begun to consider the descriptive advantages of formal multiple-response recording. We consider some of this literature here.

B. Reactions to Taste Stimuli Paired with Poison or Pain

Although correlating a distinctive flavor with electrocutaneous shock or with illness-producing lithium chloride can be made to produce equivalent reductions in intake, there is reason to believe that different processes are involved. For example, Garcia et al. (1970) reported that flavor-shock situations produced suppression of intake that is specific to the conditioning context and is therefore probably due to the flavor's signal properties. In contrast, suppression in illness-induced aversions generalizes readily across contexts, and the animal's rejection of a fluid is probably based on its palatability or hedonic value.

Pelchat, Grill, Rozin, and Jacobs (1983) reasoned that a more detailed description of behavior might provide a test of the distinction between fearful avoidance of flavors signaling pain and a disgust-laden aversion for flavors involving a palatability shift. They used a concurrent multiple-response assessment of rats that had received sucrose paired with lithium toxicosis (Experiment 1) or sucrose paired with shock (Experiment 2), employing a coding system and set of conditions dubbed the "taste reactivity test" (Grill & Norgren, 1978). Basically the procedure consisted of videotaping rats during the experiment and coding nine responses. Six of the codes were reactions elicited by bitter quinine, which was rejected without formal training. These aversive responses are shown on the right side of the horizontal axes of Fig. 9.3. In essence, these aversive responses were either functional rejection responses, such as orofacial gaping, chin rubbing, head shaking, and face washing, or functional disgust-arousal discharge patterns, such as forelimb flailing and paw rubbing, perhaps parts of defensive burying mentioned earlier. Another three responses were elicited by a substance such as sucrose when it was ingested under baseline conditions. These consist of rhythmic mouth movements, rhythmic symmetrical tongue protrusions, and lateral tongue protrusions; they are referred to as ingestive responses because they are accompanied by swallowing.

Figs. 9.3 and 9.4 permit within- and between-group comparisons of crude concurrent response patterns elicited by sucrose prior to and following pairing with illness-producing lithium chloride or pain-producing foot shock. (As discussed earlier, recording the number of subjects showing the response is a rudimentary index of concurrent patterns.) Prior to conditioning, the data reveal a pattern dominated by ingestive responses. Subsequent to conditioning that produced equivalent suppression of intake, the sucrose-shock subjects continued to display the ingestion response pattern to sucrose, whereas the lithium chloride-treated subjects showed a high incidence of disgust reactions and a lowered incidence of ingestive responses.

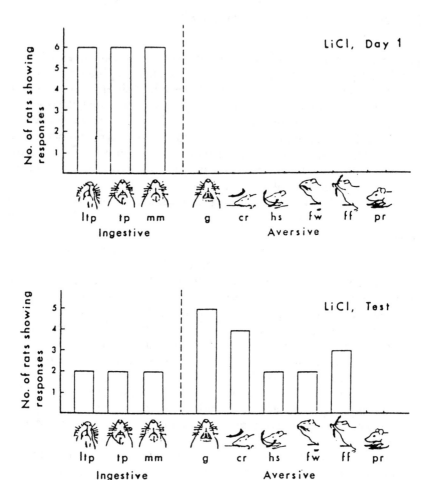

Orofacial responses of poisoned rats to sucrose

FIG. 9.3.   Orofacial/somatic responses of rats to sucrose prior to pairing with lithium chloride (top) and after two pairings with lithium chloride (bottom). Ingestive orofacial responses (left side of the horizontal axis) are lateral tongue protrusions (ltp), tongue protrusions (tp), and mouth movements (mm). Aversive responses are gaping (g), chin rubbing (cr), head shaking (hs), face washing (fw), forelimb flailing (ff), and paw rubbing (pr) (from Pelchat et al., 1983, Fig. 2; copyright, 1983, by the American Psychological Association; reproduced by permission of the publisher and author).

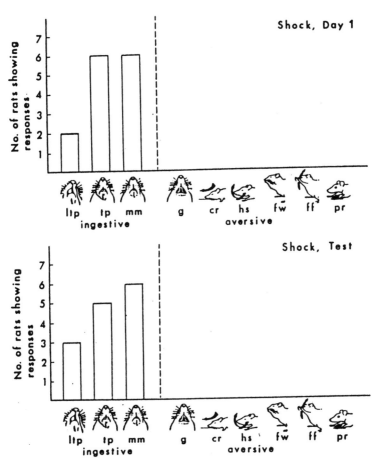

FIG. 9.4. Orofacial/somatic responses of rats to sucrose prior to pairing with shock (top) and after a series of sucrose–shock pairings (bottom). Same response codes as Fig. 9.3 (from Pelchat et al., 1983, Fig. 3; copyright, 1983, by the American Psychological Association; reproduced by permission of the publisher and author).

Thus, although both shock and lithium chloride were effective in producing a suppression of intake, only lithium treatment resulted in a response pattern that was accompanied by disgust responses resembling those elicited by unpalatable, distasteful substances. Furthermore, Pelchat et al. (1983) noted informally that shock was likely to produce a rat that jumped away from the spout containing sucrose and then sat motionless in the back of the chamber until shock was delivered.

In a related study, Miller (1984) re-examined the original Garcia and Koelling (1966) cue-to-consequence study, but also measured concurrent response profiles, including freezing, chin wiping, gaping, and other responses. In support of earlier impressions, he noted that shock-induced patterns included freezing and rearing toward audiovisual stimuli but not toward taste stimuli, whereas illness resulted in chin wiping, gaping, and head shaking elicited by taste but not audiovisual cues. Thus, he replicated the findings related to the consumption index and formally demonstrated that illness and shock induce different response patterns that interact with the type of CS and US.

Findings such as these, in combination with observations of the unconditional response to lithium, bear on the stimulus substitution hypothesis of classical conditioning. As Garcia et al. (1973) noted, "Lithium illness produces an inactive flaccid animal which lies down most of the time" (p. 28). On the other hand, these animals display a very different pattern to the conditioned aversive sucrose. It does not appear that flavor aversion conditioning is a matter of one stimulus substituting for the other. Rather, the conditioning experience is integrated into phylogenetically and ontogenetically established response patterns, calling forth a set of these patterns that is compatible with the testing situation.

C. Reaction to Taste Induced by Different Types of Drug Treatments

Although treatments that produce nausea, such as lithium chloride, X-irradiation, apomorphine, and cyclophosphamide, are the most effective agents in producing conditioned taste aversions (CTAs), drugs that produce no obvious signs of malaise, such as amphetamine, alcohol, or THC, can also induce a suppression of intake of flavored substances. Gamzu, Vincent, and Boff (1985) cataloged a variety of such agents and suggested that "illness" may not be the effective conditioning state in CTA studies. Parker (1982) conducted a series of experiments with multiple-response measurement in order to examine behavioral modifications, in addition to suppression of fluid intake, that occur when a flavor is paired with drug treatment.

Parker (1982, 1984) paired saccharin with either illness-producing lithium or psychoactive amphetamine to produce equivalent suppression of intake and measured multiple concurrent responses. Both lithium and amphetamine induced taste aversions resulting in general locomotion, rearing, stretching, and limb flicking. However, chin rubbing was a component only of the lithium chloride-induced aversion. Given that chin rubbing also occurs to bitter quinine, she argued that suppression following lithium treatment is based on disgust. On the other hand, amphetamine aversion may not be based on unpalatability or hedonic shift so much as rejection based on expectation of some negative sensory-motor consequence.

Subsequent research has extended the multiple-response assessment method to a variety of drugs that induce suppression of intake. When apomorphine, scopolamine, methylscopolamine, physostigmine, and neostigmine were paired with a distinctive flavor, chin rubbing was a prominent response in the conditioned response pattern, suggesting rejection based on hedonic shift or rejection of an unpalatable substance (Smith & Parker, 1985). When amphetamine or nicotine was paired with sucrose, chin rubbing and paw treading (paw rubbing) were absent, suggesting that these drugs did not induce rejection based on palatability shift (Parker & Carvell, 1986). These results imply that there may be more than one kind of CTA.

D. Reactions to Odors and Tastes Paired with Illness

The potentiation effect provides another situation where pattern description and analysis may be useful. In the potentiation effect, food flavor can be considered a compound stimulus with both odor and taste components. Experimental studies have shown that the odor and taste of a compound have different properties. Typically, animals do not quickly acquire an aversion for the odor component unless illness is given immediately and repeatedly. However, if a novel odor is presented in compound with a novel taste before delayed poisoning, animals demonstrate an odor aversion that is much stronger than the aversion acquired to odor conditioned alone. The aversion is manifest even in the absence of the taste component of the odor/taste compound that preceded delayed poisoning and is frequently as large as or larger than the taste aversion itself (Rusiniak, Hankins, Garcia, & Brett, 1979). Empirically, taste during conditioning potentiates odor aversion. That is, potentiation occurs rather than the usual overshadowing by a salient stimulus.

Unlike conditioned taste aversion, odor potentiation is sensitive to many factors, including relative conditionability of the odor and taste components (Bouton & Whiting, 1982; Rusiniak et al., 1979), the developmental history of rats with odor and taste (Rusiniak, Garcia, Palmerino, & Cabral, 1983), and especially the temporal and spatial relationship between the odor and taste (Coburn, Garcia, Kiefer, & Rusiniak, 1984). It is an interesting effect because of the many asymmetries. For example, taste potentiates odor, but odor does not potentiate taste aversion (Rusiniak et al., 1979). Taste potentiates odor when illness is the aversive treatment, but not when shock is the aversive treatment (Rusiniak, Palmerino, Rice, Forthman, & Garcia, 1982). And taste plays a special role as a potentiating agent, as lick-contingent auditory cues may actually disrupt, not potentiate odor illness aversions, whereas the noise may potentiate odor-shock avoidance (Rusiniak, 1984). Finally, taste may potentiate a variety of cues temporally and spatially contiguous with the taste in decreasing hierarchy, including olfactory, visual, and then auditory aspects of the food (Ellins, Cramer, & Whitmore, 1985; Ellins & Von Kluge, 1987; Galef & Osborne, 1978; Rusiniak et al., 1982).

According to the indexing hypothesis of potentiation, novel taste enhances attending to and conditioning toward cues that are temporally and spatially associated with taste. This makes such cues functional food cues and enhances the likelihood they will be associated with illness and that they will suppress consumption (Garcia & Rusiniak, 1980; Rusiniak et al., 1979, 1982). The fact that temporal and spatial contiguity facilitates potentiation is one line of experimental evidence in support of this idea. Informal behavioral observation also provides some support. For example, rats drinking a compound flavored solution for the first time demonstrate a hesitant sampling pattern, repeatedly licking, sniffing, pausing, and spending substantial energy investigating the novel smelly-tasty substance. After conditioning, rats may show disgust reactions toward the odor, and if given the opportunity, will bury paper containing the aversive odor (Garcia, Forthman Quick, & White, 1984). Recently, we have tried to apply concurrent and sequential response pattern analysis in this situation in order to describe formally the changes that occur during the conditioning sequence and to assess the indexing hypothesis, a functional concept, from examining the structure of response sequences.

In these experiments, rats were given either odor alone or odor in compound with taste followed by delayed lithium chloride. They were then tested with the odor and taste components separately. Rats were scored for a variety of sniffing, licking, and disgust behaviors, as well as location in the chamber and some other responses. In one study (Rusiniak, 1986), we measured concurrent behaviors, dividing each test session into twenty 15-sec intervals and simply scoring the incidence of each reaction in each interval. We focused on ingestive and sniffing behaviors, monitoring the number of licks and incidence of licking, orofacial movements/gaping (or lip smacking), and sniffing of the spout, front wall, floor, and the back of the chamber. Fig. 9.5 (upper panel) shows the profiles on the acquisition trial prior to conditioning when neophobia is most prominent. Filled bars indicate changes from baseline values for all subjects in that condition. Note that odor presented around the spout produced increased overall sniffing at all locations, as well as a reduction in both the total number of licks and the number of intervals in which the rats drank. Also note that the odor–taste compound elicited greater unconditioned orofacial lip smacking than odor alone. Thus, the impression of enhanced neophobia was confirmed and also suggests there may be two separate components: an overall activation of gustatory and ingestive reactivity, and odor localization strategies. The odor test profiles (Fig. 9.5, center panel) show that the potentiation effect is reflected in a variety of ways: the Odor–Taste condition

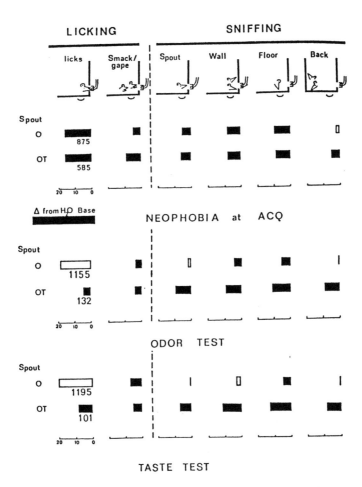

FIG. 9.5. Concurrent licking and sniffing patterns during an odor potentiation study. On one acquisition trial, groups were given odor alone (O) or an odor–taste compound (OT) 30 min before lithium poisoning (top panel) and then tested with odor alone (center panel) or taste alone (bottom panel). Each test session was divided into 20 intervals and the incidence of each licking and sniffing category was recorded. Solid bars indicate changes from baseline. The numbers below each lick incidence bar indicate the conventional intake measure (number of licks); the bar indicates the number of intervals in which an animal licked.

showed (a) reduced number of licks (132 vs. 1,155), (b) reduced incidence of licking, and (c) increased gaping, confirming the hedonic aversion to odor, and (d) increased sniffing of the whole chamber, suggesting continued odor orientation reactions. Oddly enough, although the Odor-Only group showed no reduction in licking or spout sniffing, they did show some gaping and increased sniffing of the wall, floor, and back of the chamber. Comparison of the odor test profiles with those elicited by the aversive taste (Fig. 9.5, bottom panel) indicates similarities between reactions elicited by potentiated odor and aversive taste: reduced licking and increased overall sniffing and orofacial activity (gaping). Probably the most noteworthy feature of the taste test data is that the aversive taste led to as much sniffing as the odor, even though no odor was present. It is also interesting to note that the Odor-Only group, for which the taste cue was novel, showed a slight increase in sniffing as well, as if one function of taste, be it novel or aversive, is to signal investigation of concomitant odors and their sources. These results are certainly compatible with some aspects of the indexing model.

Although the concurrent analysis provides a rough overall profile it does not provide any index of functional grouping or sequences. Therefore, we developed a more extensive behavioral catalog, continuously monitored individual subjects, and then calculated sequential relationships among the observed behavior (LaClaire, 1988). Figs. 9.6, 9.7, and 9.8 show the results

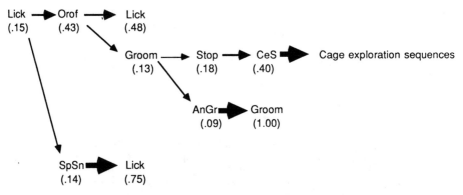

FIG. 9.6. Sequential patterns of a rat drinking an odor–taste compound before poisoning. Numbers below each behavior indicate the conditional probability of that response following the preceding one; however, the unconditional probability is given for the initial response, licking. Codes: Lick (lick the spout); Orof (orofacial lip and jaw movements); SpSn (spout sniffing); Groom (whole body grooming); AnGr (anogenital grooming); Stop (pause in movement of more than 1 sec); CeS (ceiling sniffing); Cage exploration sequence (complex "trees" of sequences that included combinations of floor sniff, side wall sniff, and back wall sniff).

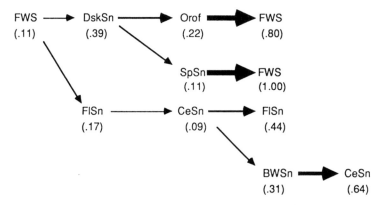

FIG. 9.7. Sequential patterns of a rat tested with a potentiated odor cue. Format and code labels are the same as those of Fig. 9.6. Codes not included in Fig. 9.6 are: FWS (front wall sniff), DskSn (sniffing the odor disc containing the aversive odor), and BWSn (back wall sniffing). The transition FlSn to CeSn occurred with a conditional probability that was significantly less likely ($p < .05$) than chance.

of an individual subject in the potentiation group. The sequential relationships are expressed as flow diagrams of conditional probabilities in which the width of the arrow is roughly proportional to the magnitude of the relationship. Flow diagrams were arbitrarily chosen to start with behaviors of high frequency. Probability values are also given below each sequence. Only statistically reliable sequences are shown.

In general, the sequential data confirm the concurrent analysis. The acquisition trial data suggest several different prevalent sequences. Two different reactions reliably followed the lick response, which had an unconditional probability of .15. If licking occurred, rats either sniffed the spout ($p = .14$) and then licked again ($p = .75$), or they showed orofacial jaw and lip movement ($p = .43$) and then either licked again ($p = .48$) or changed to a new sequence via grooming ($p = .13$). Grooming led either to more grooming (anal groom—groom) or to a pause ($p = .18$) followed by cage exploration, which was initiated by ceiling sniffing ($p = .40$). (The complex cage exploration patterns are not shown for the sake of simplicity.) In another, somewhat independent cluster (not shown in the figure), on the acquisition trial the animal sniffed the front wall ($p = .15$) followed by the odor disc ($p = .34$) then the front wall again, as if trying to localize odor sources. Thus, by looking at the composition of these "probability trees" we note several functional units: (a) spout-directed licking, sniffing, and orofacial movement; (b) systematic cage sniffing toward odor sources, side wall areas, front wall disc areas, or back wall areas; and (c) transitions by either a grooming sequence or movement.

By comparison, the odor test pattern was very simple in terms of reliable

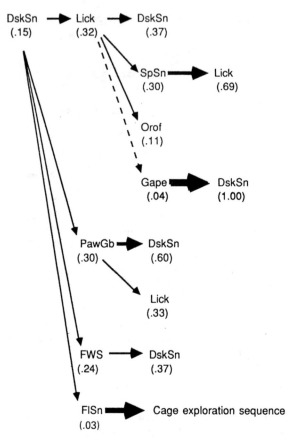

FIG. 9.8. Sequential patterns of a rat tested with the taste component of an illness-conditioned odor-taste cue. Format and codes are the same as those for Figs. 9.6 and 9.7. Additional codes: Gape (gaping), PawGr (grabbing at the spout or odor disc). Data in Figs. 9.6–9.8 are from the same subject.

sequences. Sniffing the front wall ($p = .11$) led either to sniffing the aversive odor on the disc ($p = .39$) followed by either orofacial movements ($p = .22$) or spout sniffing ($p = .11$), or it led to floor sniffing. Also note that floor sniffing was rarely followed ($p = .09$, negative z score) by ceiling—back wall—ceiling investigation, as if the rear of the cage was behaviorally segregated from the front of the cage. Other measures showed that this rat never licked and also showed an overall increase in the probability of ceiling and back wall sniffing. Quite possibly, the avoiding animal was attempting to find an area most distant from the aversive odor.

The taste test data showed four distinct response clusters initiated by sniffing the odor disc ($p = .15$). First, there were spout-directed sniffing and licking responses accompanied by orofacial reactions and gaping, elicited by the aversive saccharin. Second, there were also paw grabbing episodes directed at the spout in conjunction with licking and sniffing, behavior patterns similar to treading and limb flailing. Finally, there were two different sniffing clusters or branches, one directed at the front wall and disc, the other a complex sequence that involved exploration of the cage. It is also noteworthy that there was an overall increase in disc sniffing (recall that no odor was present), suggesting an increased reaction to odors elicited by taste.

The sequential analysis, together with the concurrent analysis, provides some descriptive support for the indexing hypothesis. In addition to support for increased attention toward odor during acquisition trials, we also observed sniffing patterns that might be related to perceptual processes of identifying odors and tastes that are components of food. We also documented increased disgust reactions to both taste and potentiated odor cues and found an unexpected increase in odor reactivity whenever a taste was presented.

V. SOME THEORETICAL CONSIDERATIONS

A. Responses and Approaches to Science

Expanding on the work of Kantor and Smith (1975) and Henton and Iversen (1978), Delprato (1986) has argued that the use of single-response versus multiple-response investigative strategies is tied to assumptions about both science and behavior. A central issue is whether concurrent (simultaneous) responses and sequential (serial) responses are independent of or interdependent on one another. According to an extreme response independence view, each movement always depends on external (from responses) independent variables which serve to organize behavior. The organizing variables may be in the external environment or intraorganismic in the form of biological conditions and cognitive structures. Alternatively, the response interdependence position holds that organization is also imposed by responses themselves, that responses come in structural and functional patterns. This approach maintains that organized responses or response patterns are legitimate constructs in their own right that are necessary for our understanding of the effects of certain experimental manipulations on behavior. For example, the fact that rats show freezing in reaction to a CS is due not only to the presence of the CS in the context where the shock was given, but also to the ongoing behavior when the CS occurs and to other compatible defensive reactions in that setting. Given that patterns are comprised of interrelated components, only multiple-response recording will reveal them.

B. Mechanistic Science and Response Independence

Response independence theory and single-response methodology seem to correspond to one general approach to science and response pattern theory and multiple-response recording are tied to another. The idea that external variables cause responses (effects), and that these external events are independent of responses follows from the classic lineal mechanistic approach to the world and to science. Loeb (1912) and Sherrington (1906) exemplify the application of mechanism in the life sciences with their assumption that organismic activity is reducible to physicochemical causal chains. Mechanistic psychological theories have approached behavioral organization in one of two ways. According to one approach, the external environment and/or response-produced stimulation are causes of subsequent responses; stimulus-response chains organize sequentially related responses that are independent of one another (e.g., Hull, 1930; Keller & Schoenfeld, 1950; Watson, 1907). The other class of mechanistic psychological theory considers that otherwise independent spatially and temporally related responses are caused (chained, organized, constructed) by underlying mental, cognitive, and/or neural (i.e., internal or "central") structure (e.g., Hebb, 1949; G. A. Miller, Galanter, & Pribram, 1960; Tolman, 1932). Relative neglect of multiple-response methodology in favor of single-response recording seems to be supported, in part, by the mechanistic assumption that the source of response organization is external to responses; hence, there is little incentive to measure more than any one response that serves as an indicator of the hypothesized underlying organization.

C. Integrated-fields and Response Patterns

Theorists and researchers are increasingly noting movement from mechanistic science to another view that has enormous implications for how we conceptualize and investigate behavior. Several authoritative historical analyses (Dewey & Bentley, 1949; Einstein & Infeld, 1938; Handy & Harwood, 1973; Kantor, 1946, 1969) as well as behavioral analyses (Altman, 1966; Powers, 1978; Smith, 1972) agree that simple linear chains of causality are inadequate descriptive-explanations of behavior and that the mechanical view is giving way to an integrated-field and system approach. For example, even the physical sciences no longer compare the world with a machine (Frank, 1955; Holton, 1973). According to Einstein and Infeld (1938), the transition from the classic mechanics of Newton's gravitational laws to Maxwell's equations was a critical development in the evolution of field thinking in physics. The mathematical equations "do not connect two widely separated events; they do not connect the happenings *here* with the conditions *there* [instead] the field *here* and *now* depends on the field in the *immediate neighborhood* at a time *just past*" (Einstein & Infeld, 1938, pp. 152–153.) Furthermore, ". . . in the new field language it is the description of the field between the two charges, and not the charges themselves, which is essential for an understanding of their action" (Einstein & Infeld, 1938, p. 157). The field construct has taken physics far away from the mechanistic stage with its bifurcations of nature (e.g., mass and energy, matter and force, gravitational mass and inertial mass) to the inertia-energy concept and the equivalence of mass-energy and gravitational-inertial mass.

Kantor (1959, 1969) and Kantor and Smith (1975) seem to be the theorists who have done the most to develop the field concept per se for behavioral science. According to Kantor (1969), descriptive methodology is important in research based on field thinking, for the psychological field is:

> The entire system of things and conditions operating in any event taken in its available totality. It is only the entire system of factors which will provide proper descriptive and explanatory materials for the handling of events. It is not the reacting organism alone which makes up the event but also the stimulating things and conditions, as well as the setting factors. (p. 371)

Further, just as modern physical scientists no longer approach their science from the cause–effect framework (e.g., Feigl, 1953; Holton, 1973; Russell, 1953), the behavioral sciences may also have to abandon the terms *cause and effect* as used in ordinary language. As Feigl (1953) puts it, "the entire *set* of conditions [event-field]" (p. 410) represents *the* cause of an event. Kantor (1959) further clarifies the field construct:

> All creative agencies, all powers and forces, are rejected. An event is regarded as a field of factors all of which are equally necessary, or, more properly speaking, equal participants in the event. In fact, events are scientifically described by analyzing these participating factors and finding how they are related. (p. 90)

Whether or not one accepts field theory or thinks that theoretical changes in physics have implications for behavior theory, field thinking definitely is found in contemporary behavioral science. Kantor (1941) noted several versions of field theory, including the well-known one of the gestaltists. However, the first attempts to take a field perspective in psychology offered few advantages over earlier mechanical approaches with their internal principles and dualisms (Kantor, 1941, 1969). Add to this deficiency, misguided attempts to draw direct analogies between behavioral events and mathematical and physical fields, and it is understandable that mainstream psychologists were not favorably disposed to field theory.

D. System Theory and Response Patterns

System theory has been a more popular approach in behavioral science. Although relationships between the integrated-field stage of science and system theory perspective rarely have been noted explicitly, it is clear that a system approach is compatible with field theory (Marmor, 1983; Ray & Delprato, 1989; Upson & Ray, 1984). Like integrated-field theorists (e.g., Kantor, 1959, 1971), those advocating a system approach (e.g., Bertalanffy, 1972; Marmor, 1983; Rapoport, 1968) maintain that linear cause–effect mechanisms must be replaced by dynamic systems (or fields) comprised of interdependent components. Rapoport (1968), for example, suggests that in the study of living processes, vitalism (an early attempt to avoid mechanism) and mechanism can be replaced with the concept of a system, that is, "a whole which functions as whole by virtue of the interdependence of its parts" (p. xvii).

From the standpoint of the system view, isolated, independent responses are not to be expected. Instead, like all natural events, behavior is the expression of organized mutually interdependent "chunks" or "action patterns." It is only the methodological blinders of single-response observation that preserves response independence. When we observe a sufficient amount of the behavioral field, we will detect response patterns and multiple effects of experimental manipulations that, when effective, alter the organization of behavioral systems.

E. Systems Theory, Multiple Responses, and Aversive Conditioning

Is multiple-response analysis worth it? After all, observational work is tedious, the data can be complex, and there is no guarantee that these "other" responses are more sensitive to experimental manipulations than the traditional tried and true single-response indexes. Does it tell us anything more than animals fill their time with other behaviors when aversive treatments have restricted or eliminated certain other behaviors.

A review of contributions discussed in this chapter seems to indicate that it is. Behavioral description, which is worthwhile in its own right, has led to the addition of defensive burying into the catalog of aversive behavior. It has led to the recognition that ongoing behavior enhances the predictability of which defensive reactions emerge. It has challenged associative accounts of classical and backward fear conditioning. It provides a reasonable account of the time course and variability in the acquisition and extinction of shock avoidance learning. And it has also provided support for identification of interoceptive and exteroceptive coping systems, each with its own response profiles.

Following Garcia et al. (1977), we propose that multiple-response studies have identified at least three different classes of response patterns during aversive conditioning. First, there are species-typical response patterns released and directed by specific stimuli. For example, tastes paired with nauseating lithium chloride block consumption and elicit a variety of concurrent orofacial disgust reactions as well as paw flicking, treading, shaking, and burying. In contrast, tastes paired with shock produce freezing and other fear responses, but not disgust reactions. Taste stimuli, either novel or aversive, release systematic sequential sniffing reactions directed at localizing concomitant odors, a process that seems related to associative potentiation. Second, there are opportune response patterns structured by compatibility with the ongoing species-typical patterns and available alternatives. For example, defensive burying may be part of the somatic motor discharge patterns elicited by aversive stimuli in the context of available material. And restricting responses by either punishment or by simple response blocking may both produce increases in any available alternative, such as wheel running. The "conflict" responses directed toward aversive prey described by Garcia et al. (1977) probably also fit into this category. And in fact, opportune running or jumping may be the origins of many "conditioned responses" in shock studies. Finally, there are filler or transition patterns, such as moving, grooming, or pausing, whose frequency and location is determined by the temporal and spatial distribution of the first two categories. These patterns and the field/system approach blend with ethological approaches that view aversive conditioning episodes as events that intrude upon an animal in the phylogenetic and ontogenetic flow of time and space.

REFERENCES

Altman, J. (1966). *Organic foundations of animal behavior.* New York: Holt, Rinehart, & Winston.

Ayres, J. J. B., Haddad, C., & Albert, M. (1987). One-trial excitatory backward conditioning as assessed by conditioned suppression of licking in rats: Concurrent observations of lick suppression and defensive behaviors. *Animal Learning and Behavior, 15,* 212–217.

Azrin, N. H., & Holz, W. C. (1966). Punishment. In W. K. Honig (Ed.), *Operant behavior: Areas of research and Application* (pp. 380–447). New York: Appleton–Century–Crofts.

Bakeman, R., & Gottman, J. M. (1986). *Observing interaction: An introduction to sequential analysis.* Cambridge, England: Cambridge University Press.

Baum, M. (1969). Extinction of an avoidance response following response prevention: Some parametric investigations. *Canadian Journal of Psychology, 23,* 1–10.

Baum, M. (1970). Extinction of avoidance responding through response prevention (flooding). *Psychological Bulletin, 74,* 276–284.

Baum, M., Pereira, J., & Leclerc, R. (1985). Extinction of avoidance responding in rats:

The noise-intensity parameter in noise-facilitation of flooding. *Canadian Journal of Psychology, 39,* 529–535.

Bertalanffy, L. (1972). The history and status of general systems theory. In G. J. Klir (Ed.), *Trends in general systems theory* (pp. 21–41). New York: Wiley.

Bolles, R. C. (1970). Species-specific defense reactions and avoidance learning. *Psychological Review, 71,* 32–48.

Bouton, M. E., & Bolles, R. C. (1980). Conditioned fear assessed by freezing and by the suppression of three different baselines. *Animal Learning and Behavior, 8,* 429–434.

Bouton, M. E., & Whiting, M. R. (1982). Simultaneous odor-taste and taste-taste compounds in poison avoidance learning. *Learning and Motivation, 13,* 472–494.

Coburn, K. L., Garcia, J., Kiefer, S. W., & Rusiniak, K. W. (1984). Taste potentiation of poisoned odor by temporal contiguity, *Behavioral Neuroscience, 98,* 813–819.

Cook, M., Mineka, S., & Trumble, D. (1987). The role of response-produced and exteroceptive feedback in the attenuation of fear over the course of avoidance learning. *Journal of Experimental Psychology: Animal Behavior Processes, 13,* 239–249.

Delprato, D. J. (1980). Hereditary determinants of fears and phobias: A critical review. *Behavior Therapy, 11,* 79–103.

Delprato, D. J. (1986). Response patterns. In H. W. Reese & L. J. Parrott (Eds.), *Behavior science: Philosophical, methodological, and empirical advances* (pp. 61–113). Hillsdale, NJ: Lawrence Erlbaum Associates.

Dewey, J., & Bentley, A. F. (1949). *Knowing and the known.* Boston: Beacon Press.

Dunham, P. J. (1971). Punishment: Method and theory. *Psychological Review, 78,* 58–70.

Dunham, P. J. (1972). Some effects of punishment upon unpunished responding. *Journal of the Experimental Analysis of Behavior, 17,* 443–450.

Dunham, P. J. (1978). Changes in unpunished responding during response-contingent punishment. *Animal Learning and Behavior, 6,* 174–180.

Dunham, P. J., & Grantmyre, J. (1982). Changes in a multiple-response repertoire during response-contingent punishment and response restriction: Sequential relationships. *Journal of the Experimental Analysis of Behavior, 37,* 123–133.

Einstein, A., & Infeld, L. (1938). *The evolution of physics.* New York: Simon & Schuster.

Ellins, S. R., Cramer, R. E., & Whitmore, C. (1985). Taste potentiation of auditory aversions in rats: A case for spatial contiguity. *Journal of Comparative Psychology, 99,* 108–111.

Ellins, S. R., & Von Kluge, S. (1987). Preexposure and extinction effects of lithium chloride induced taste-potentiated aversions for spatially contiguous auditory food cues in rats. *Behavioral Neuroscience, 101,* 164–169.

Feigl, H. (1953). Notes on causality. In H. Feigl & M. Brodbeck (Eds.), *Readings in the philosophy of science* (pp. 408–418). New York: Appleton–Century–Crofts.

Fentress, J. C. (1968). Interrupted ongoing behaviour in two species of vole (*Microtus agrestis*) and (*Clethrionomys britannicus*). I. Response as a function of preceding activity and the context of an apparently "irrelevant" motor pattern. *Animal Behaviour, 16,* 135–153.

Forrester, R. C., & Broom, D. M. (1980). Ongoing behaviour and startle responses of chicks. *Behaviour, 73,* 51–63.

Frank, P. (1955). Foundation of physics. In O. Neurath, R. Carnap, & C. Morris (Eds.), *Foundations of the unity of science* (Vol. 1, pp. 423–504). Chicago: University of Chicago Press.

Frick, F. C. (1953). The effect of anxiety—A problem in measurement. *Journal of Comparative and Physiological Psychology, 46,* 120–123.

Frick, F. C., & Miller, G. A. (1951). A statistical description of operant conditioning. *American Journal of Psychology, 64,* 20–36.

Galef, B. G., & Osborne, B. (1978). Novel taste facilitation of the association of visual cues with toxicosis in rats. *Journal of Comparative and Physiological Psychology, 92,* 907–916.

Gamzu, E., Vincent, G., & Boff, E. (1985). A pharmacological perspective of drugs used in establishing conditioned food aversions. In N. S. Braveman & P. Bronstein (Eds.), *Experimental assessments and clinical applications of conditioned food aversions.* Annals of the New York Academy of Sciences (Vol. 443, pp. 231–249). New York: New York Academy of Sciences.

Garcia, J., Clarke, J. C., & Hankins, W. G. (1973). Natural responses to scheduled rewards. In P. P. G. Bateson & P. H. Klopfer (Eds.), *Perspectives in ethology* (pp. 1–41). New York: Plenum Press.

Garcia, J., Ervin, F. R., & Koelling, R. A. (1966). Learning with prolonged delay of reinforcement. *Psychonomic Science, 5,* 121–122.

Garcia, J., Forthman Quick, D., & White, B. (1984). Conditioned disgust and fear from mollusk to monkey. In D. L. Alkon & J. Farley (Eds.), *Primary neural substrates of learning and behavioral change* (pp. 47–61). Cambridge, MA: Cambridge University Press.

Garcia, J., Kimeldorf, D. J., Hunt, E. L., & Davies, B. P. (1956). Food and water consumption of rats during exposure to gamma radiation. *Radiation Research, 4,* 33–41.

Garcia, J., Kimeldorf, D. J., & Koelling, R. A. (1955). A conditioned aversion towards saccharin resulting from exposure to gamma radiation. *Science, 122,* 157–159.

Garcia, J., & Koelling, R. A. (1966). Relation of cue to consequence in avoidance learning. *Psychonomic Science, 4,* 123–124.

Garcia, J., & Koelling, R. A. (1967). A comparison of aversions induced by x-rays, drugs and toxins. *Radiation Research, 7*(Suppl.), 439–450.

Garcia, J., Kovner, R., & Green, K. F. (1970). Cue properties *vs.* palatability of flavors in avoidance learning. *Psychonomic Science, 20,* 313–314.

Garcia, J., McGowan, B. K., Ervin, F. R., & Koelling, R. A. (1968). Cues: Their relative effectiveness as a function of the reinforcer, *Science, 160,* 794–795.

Garcia, J., & Rusiniak, K. W. (1980). What the nose learns from the mouth. In D. Muller-Schwarze & R. M. Silverstein (Eds.), *Chemical signals* (pp. 141–156). New York: Plenum Press.

Garcia, J., Rusiniak, K. W., & Brett, L. P. (1977). Conditioning food-illness aversions in wild animals: *Caveant Canonici.* In H. Davis & H. M. B. Hurwitz (Eds.), *Operant-Pavlovian interactions* (pp. 273–311). Hillsdale, NJ: Lawrence Erlbaum Associates.

Gottman, J. M. (1981). *Time-series analysis: A comprehensive introduction for social scientists.* Cambridge, England: Cambridge University Press.

Grill, H. J., & Norgren, R. (1978). The taste reactivity test. I. Mimetic responses to gustatory stimuli in neurologically normal rats. *Brain Research, 143,* 263–269.

Handy, R., & Harwood, E. C. (1973). *A current appraisal of the behavioral sciences* (rev. ed.). Great Barrington, MA: Behavioral Research Council.

Hann, D. M., & Roberts, A. E. (1984). Free operant avoidance behavior in hooded rats: IRTs and response chains. *Animal Learning and Behavior, 12,* 175–183.

Hebb, D. O. (1949). *The organization of behavior.* New York: Wiley.

Henton, W. W., & Iversen, I. H. (1978). *Classical conditioning and operant conditioning: A response pattern analysis.* New York: Springer–Verlag.

Hinde, R. A. (1982). *Ethology.* New York: Oxford University Press.

Holton, G. (1973). *Introduction to concepts and theories in physical science* (2nd ed.). Reading, MA: Addison–Wesley.

Hull, C. L. (1930). Knowledge and purpose as habit mechanisms. *Psychological Review, 37,* 511–525.

Jenkins, H. M., & Moore, B. R. (1973). The form of the autoshaped response with food or water reinforcers. *Journal of the Experimental Analysis of Behavior, 20,* 163–181.

Kantor, J. R. (1924). *Principles of psychology* (Vol. 1). Chicago: Principia Press.

Kantor, J. R. (1941). Current trends in psychological theory. *Psychological Bulletin, 38,* 29–65.

Kantor, J. R. (1946). The aim and progress of psychology. *American Scientist, 34,* 251–263.

Kantor, J. R. (1959). *Interbehavioral psychology.* Granville, OH: Principia Press.

Kantor, J. R. (1969). *The scientific evolution of psychology* (Vol. 2). Chicago: Principia Press.

Kantor, J. R., & Smith, N. W. (1975). *The science of psychology: An interbehavioral survey.* Chicago: Principia Press.

Karpicke, J., Christoph, G., Peterson, G., & Hearst, E. (1977). Signal location and positive versus negative conditioned suppression in the rat. *Journal of Experimental Psychology: Animal Behavior Processes, 3,* 105–118.

Karpicke, J., & Dout, D. (1980). Withdrawal from signals for imminent inescapable electric shock. *Psychological Record, 30,* 511–523.

Keller, F. S., & Schoenfeld, W. N. (1950). *Principles of psychology: A systematic text in the science of behavior.* New York: Appleton–Century–Crofts.

Koffka, K. (1935). *Principles of gestalt psychology.* New York: Harcourt, Brace, & World.

LaClaire, T. L. (1988). *Effects of odor location on taste potentiated odor aversions: Analysis of sequential sniffing patterns.* Unpublished master's thesis, Eastern Michigan University, Ypsilanti.

Lapointe, A., & Baum, M. (1987). Description of spontaneous behavior of individual rats undergoing avoidance-response-prevention (flooding). *Psychological Reports, 61,* 879–885.

Loeb, J. (1912). *The mechanistic conception of life.* Chicago: University of Chicago Press.

Manning, A. (1979). *An introduction to animal behavior.* Menlo Park, CA: Addison–Wesley.

Marmor, J. (1983). Systems thinking in psychiatry: Some theoretical and clinical implications. *American Journal of Psychiatry, 140,* 833–838.

Miller, G. A., Galanter, E., & Pribram, K. H. (1960). *Plans and the structure of behavior.* New York: Holt, Rinehart & Winston.

Miller, N. E. (1951). Learnable drives and rewards. In S. S. Stevens (Ed.), *Handbook of experimental psychology* (pp. 435–472). New York: Wiley.

Miller, S., Mineka, S., & Cook, M. (1982). Comparison of various flooding procedures in reducing fear and in extinguishing jump-up avoidance responding. *Animal Learning and Behavior, 10,* 390–400.

Miller, V. (1984). Selective association learning in the rat: Generality of response system. *Learning and Motivation, 15,* 58–84.

Moser, C. G., & Tait, R. W. (1983). Environmental control of multiple defensive responses in a conditioned burying paradigm. *Journal of Comparative Psychology, 97,* 338–352.

Mowrer, O. H. (1939). A stimulus-response analysis of anxiety and its role as a reinforcing agent. *Psychological Review, 46,* 553–565.

Mowrer, O. H. (1947). On the dual nature of learning—a re-interpretation of "conditioning" and "problem-solving." *Harvard Educational Review, 17,* 102–148.

Parker, L. A. (1982). Nonconsummatory and consummatory behavioral CRs elicited by lithium- and amphetamine-paired flavors. *Learning and Motivation, 13,* 281–303.

Parker, L. A. (1984). Behavioral conditioned responses across multiple conditioning/testing trials elicited by lithium- and amphetamine-paired flavors. *Behavioral and Neural Biology, 41,* 190–199.

Parker, L. A., & Carvell, T. (1986). Orofacial and somatic responses elicited by lithium-, nicotine- and amphetamine-paired sucrose solution. *Pharmacology Biochemistry and Behavior, 24,* 883–887.

Peacock, E. J., & Wong, P. T. P. (1982). Defensive burying in the rat: A behavioral field analysis. *Animal Learning and Behavior, 10,* 103–107.

Pelchat, M. L., Grill, H. J., Rozin, P., & Jacobs, J. (1983). Quality of acquired responses to tastes by *Rattus norvegicus* depends on type of associated discomfort. *Journal of Comparative Psychology, 97,* 140–153.

Pinel, J. P. J., & Treit, D. (1978). Burying as a defensive response in rats. *Journal of Comparative and Physiological Psychology*, *92*, 708–712.

Powers, W. T. (1978). Quantitative analysis of purposive systems: Some spadework at the foundations of scientific psychology. *Psychological Review*, *85*, 417–435.

Rapoport, A. (1968). *Forward*. In W. Buckley (Ed.), *Modern systems research for the behavioral scientist*. Chicago: Aldine.

Ray, R. D., & Brown, D. A. (1976). The behavioral specificity of stimulation: A systems approach to procedural distinctions of classical and instrumental conditioning. *Pavlovian Journal of Biological Science*, *11*, 3–23.

Ray, R. D., & Delprato, D. J. (1989). Behavioral systems analysis: Methodological strategies and tactics. *Behavioral Science*, *34*, 81–127.

Roberts, A. E. (1986). The shuttle-avoidance response chains of rats. *Bulletin of the Psychonomic Society*, *24*, 163–165.

Roberts, A. E., Cooper, K. G., & Richey, T. L. (1977). Rat behaviors during unsignaled avoidance and conditioned suppression training. *Bulletin of the Psychonomic Society*, *9*, 373–376.

Rusiniak, K. W. (1984, May). *Potentiation of odor-shock and disruption of odor-illness conditioning by auditory cues*. Paper presented at the meeting of the Midwestern Psychological Association, Chicago.

Rusiniak, K. W. (1986). Differential sniffing and licking during odor potentiation. *Ninth International Conference on the Physiology of Food and Fluid Intake*, *9*, 67.

Rusiniak, K. W., Garcia, J., Palmerino, C. C., & Cabral, R. J. (1983). Developmental flavor experience affects utilization of odor, but not taste in toxiphobic conditioning. *Behavioral and Neural Biology*, *39*, 160–180.

Rusiniak, K. W., Hankins, W. G., Garcia, J., & Brett, L. P. (1979). Flavor-illness aversions: Potentiation of odor by taste. *Behavioral and Neural Biology*, *25*, 1–17.

Rusiniak, K. W., Palmerino, C. C., Rice, A. G., Forthman, D. L., & Garcia, J. (1982). Flavor-illness aversions: Potentiation of odor by taste with toxin but not shock in rats. *Journal of Comparative and Physiological Psychology*, *96*, 527–539.

Russell, B. (1953). On the notion of cause, with applications to the free-will problem. In H. Feigl & M. Brodbeck (Eds.), *Readings in the philosophy of science* (pp. 387–407). New York: Appleton–Century–Crofts.

Sherrington, C. (1906). *The integrative action of the nervous system*. New Haven, CT: Yale University Press.

Smith, K. U. (1972). Cybernetic psychology. In R. N. Singer (Ed.), *The psychomotor domain: Movement behavior* (pp. 285–347). Philadelphia: Lea & Febiger.

Smith, R. J., & Parker, L. A. (1985). Chin rub CRs are elicited by flavors associated with apomorphine, scopolamine, methscopolamine, physostigmine and neostigmine. *Pharmacology Biochemistry and Behavior*, *23*, 583–589.

Staddon, J. R., & Simmelhag, V. L. (1971). The "superstition" experiment: A reexamination of its implications for the principles of adaptive behavior. *Psychological Review*, *78*, 3–43.

Tinbergen, N. (1948). Social releasers and the experimental method required for their study. *Wilson Bulletin*, *60*, 6–51.

Tinbergen, N. (1951). *The study of instinct*. London: Oxford University Press.

Tolman, E. C. (1932). *Purposive behavior in animals and men*. New York: Appleton–Century–Crofts.

Upson, J. D., & Ray, R. D. (1984). An interbehavioral system model for empirical investigation in psychology. *Psychological Record*, *34*, 497–524.

Watson, J. B. (1907). Kinesthetic and organic sensations: Their role in the reactions of the white rat to the maze. *Psychological Monographs*, *8* (2, Whole No. 33).

10 Conditioned Excitation and Conditioned Inhibition of Fear: Asymmetrical Processes as Evident in Extinction

Harry Fowler and Donald T. Lysle
University of Pittsburgh

Paul L. DeVito
Saint Joseph's University

The twenty or so years spanning publication of the present text and its parent volume (Brush, 1971) have witnessed a number of significant developments in the study of aversive conditioning and learning. Perhaps foremost among those developments was the resurgence of interest in and the emergence of new perspectives on the nature of the Pavlovian conditioning process. Although traditionally viewed by Western psychologists as involving a simple associative mechanism by which an "excitatory" reaction could be attached to a neutral cue, Pavlovian conditioning came to be recast in the late 1960s as a dual-learning process: In addition to its excitatory component, it contained an inhibitory counterpart which could oppose and completely offset the former. The apparent symmetry of those two processes was attested to by both their establishing operations and behavioral effects. To engage the inhibitory process, all that one had to do was to employ an operation opposite to that used to condition an excitatory response and, as a result, the behavioral outcome would be opposite as well. This symmetrical-process view was quite appealing to conditioning theorists for such a view was sustained throughout the 1970s and most of the 1980s, despite some early evidence to the contrary (Baker, 1974; Zimmer–Hart & Rescorla, 1974). However, within the past several years, another body of data has emerged to challenge seriously that view and to promote the alternative conception that inhibition is not a primary process, opposite in kind to excitation, but a subsidiary process that merely moderates the excitatory process.

   The present chapter seeks to document the asymmetrical relationship between conditioned excitation (CE) and conditioned inhibition (CI) by

317

selectively reviewing findings in the area of aversive conditioning on the extinction of CI. Such findings become pertinent when one considers that a symmetrical-process view calls for opposite operations and effects in both the conditioning and extinction of excitatory and inhibitory reactions. To elucidate these theoretical symmetries, we need to take stock of the conceptual developments that occurred during the late 1960s and early 1970s. With those perspectives at hand, we will have a better basis for interpreting the findings to be reviewed.

CONTEMPORARY VIEWS ON THE CONDITIONING AND EXTINCTION OF EXCITATION AND INHIBITION

Although Pavlov (1927) had early suggested that the temporal relationship between a neutral or a conditional stimulus (CS) and an unconditional stimulus (US) was crucial in determining whether the CS would acquire the ability either to "excite" (elicit) or inhibit a conditional response (CR), many Western psychologists were reluctant to acknowledge the process of conditioned inhibition. Their reserve was prompted by questions concerning the empirical validity of an inhibitory-conditioning effect (e.g., Skinner, 1938) and also by the altered and idiosyncratic way in which the concept had been used by certain theorists (e.g., Hull, 1943, 1952). However, in the late 1960s, there was a dramatic change in the recognition afforded CI. Undoubtedly, the most influential factor in altering the disposition of Western psychologists was the reinterpretation of the conditioning process proposed by Rescorla (1967).

The Contingency Perspective

According to Rescorla, excitatory conditioning was not accomplished merely by pairing a CS and a US, but by arranging a positive contingency or correlation between them. By that account, the US had to occur contiguously with the CS *and also* be less likely in the absence than in the presence of the CS. Support for this contingency view of conditioning was obtained in several impressive experiments (e.g., Rescorla, 1966, 1968b) showing that there was little, if any, conditioning when the US was presented randomly with the CS, even though such a schedule allowed occasional chance pairings of the CS and the US. Those findings were important in another respect because, at the time, the commonly employed control procedure for Pavlovian conditioning involved explicitly unpairing the CS and the US. However, by Rescorla's contingency interpretation, that procedure generated a negative CS–US correlation by which the CS could become a signal for the absence of the US and function in an inhibitory capacity.

In effect, it would promote a response tendency opposite to the excitatory tendency generated by a CS that was positively correlated with the US.

From a contingency standpoint, explicitly unpairing a CS and a US was not the only procedure by which one could empower a CS with an inhibitory property. In a review of the literature on CI, Rescorla (1969b) argued that reliable inhibitory conditioning could also be accomplished via at least two other procedures that had been in vogue since Pavlov (1927). These included discriminative or differential conditioning, in which the US is contingent upon one CS but not upon another, the putative inhibitor, and delay or trace conditioning, in which the US is contingent upon the CS but occurs only after an extended delay or trace interval following onset of that CS. Like the explicitly unpaired procedure, these two procedures also allowed a negative correlation of the designated CS and the US because, in each, onset of that CS occurs in and is followed for an extended duration by the absence of the US.

In line with this analysis, research by Rescorla and others (e.g., Rescorla, 1968a, 1968b, 1969a; Weisman & Litner, 1969, 1971) showed that all three procedures generated a target CS that would satisfy certain criteria for an inhibitory-conditioning effect. Those criteria included: (1) a summation test, in which the purported inhibitor is presented in compound with an excitatory CS and is shown to inhibit the effect of the latter appreciably more so than a novel CS similarly compounded; and (2) a retardation test, in which the purported inhibitor is reinforced by (i.e., is positively correlated with) the US and is shown to be retarded in its development as an excitatory CS by comparison with a novel CS similarly reinforced. The findings from these tests of a negative contingency were especially important because, in documenting the phenomenon of CI, they indicated that an inhibitory CS was symmetrical to an excitatory CS in its establishing operation, associative property, and behavioral effect. Indeed, excitatory and inhibitory CSs soon came to be respectively designated as a CS+ and a CS−, a convenient notation in which the algebraic sign indicates that the CS (a) is either positively or negatively correlated with the US, (b) acquires either a positive or negative associative value by which it signals the presence or absence of the US, and thus (c) produces either a positive (excitatory) or a negative (inhibitory) CR that is directly opposed to the other.

Rescorla's (1967) contingency interpretation enjoyed considerable success in assimilating the extant conditioning literature, but it soon became apparent that the analysis suffered two major limitations. For one, the analysis could not describe the rate at which the associative value of a CS would change over the course of conditioning, nor the asymptote to which the value of the CS would grow, as when different magnitudes or intensities of a US were employed. All that the interpretation described was whether the CS would end up being a CS+, a CS−, or, in the case where the CS and US were uncorrelated, a nonfunctional CS, designated a CSo. Equally, if not more, disconcerting was the fact that the analysis could not address certain conditioning phenomena that were uncovered at the time, notably Kamin's (1968, 1969) demonstration of "blocking." Kamin's research indicated that little, if any, excitatory conditioning would occur to a novel CS when that CS was placed in compound with a pretrained CS+ and the two were positively correlated with the US predicted by the CS+. Thus, it was obvious that something more than a contingency analysis was needed to account for the presence or absence of a conditioning effect.

Given its limitations, Rescorla's (1967) contingency interpretation was shortly supplanted by a far more encompassing theory of conditioning that was jointly developed by Rescorla and Wagner (1972; Wagner & Rescorla, 1972). At first sight, this new theory appeared to contrast markedly with the former interpretation because it contended that conditioning was based on the contiguous, and not the contingent, relationship between a CS and a US. However, the theory ingeniously incorporated the contingency principle within its structure.

The Discrepancy Perspective

The Rescorla–Wagner (1972) theory of conditioning postulated that changes in the associative value of a CS resulted from positive and negative discrepancies between a CS and its US consequence. In particular, the theory posited that whenever the associative value of a CS or CS compound was less than that which a contiguous US outcome could support, a positive discrepancy resulted and the value of the CS or CSs was increased. Conversely, whenever the associative value of a CS or CS compound was greater than that which a contiguous US outcome could support, a negative discrepancy resulted and the value of the CS or CSs was decreased. Those relationships were formally expressed in the equation, $\Delta Vcs = \alpha\beta(\lambda - \overline{V})$. In this equation, ΔVcs represents the change in the associative value of the CS on a particular trial, α and β are learning-rate parameters corresponding to the salience of the CS and US, respectively, λ is the limit of conditioning supported by the particular magnitude of the US on that trial, and $\overline{V}$ is the net associative value of all the CSs present on that trial. Note that the α and β learning-rate parameters and the λ asymptote parameter of the equation addressed one of the major limitations of the contingency analysis. However, far more important theoretically was the quotient describing the discrepancy between what the net associative value of the CSs on a trial $(\overline{V})$ predicted would happen and what actually did happen on that trial; that is, whether λ assumed some positive value, corresponding to the particular magnitude of the US that was present, or a zero value, reflecting an absence of the US.

For ease of exposition in applying the Rescorla–Wagner (1972) equation, we shall ignore possible variations in the magnitude of the US and simply designate the US's presence or absence on a trial as 1 and 0, respectively. With that simplification, excitatory conditioning to a novel CS is typified by the case in which the discrepancy quotient, $(\lambda - \overline{V})$, reads $(1 - 0) = +1$. That signifies that, at the start of conditioning, the CS will be incremented in strength as a result of the positive discrepancy between its zero value and the unitary value of its contiguous US. By the theory, such associative increments would continue over the course of additional CS–US pairings until the value of the CS equaled that of the US and yielded no discrepancy, that is, $(1 - 1) = 0$. At that point, the limit of conditioning with the particular US would be reached. This interpretation of excitatory conditioning easily overcame the other, major limitation of the contingency analysis; that is, in accounting for phenomena such as blocking (e.g., Kamin, 1969). Because the associative value of a pretrained CS+ could equal that of its contiguous US, there would then be no discrepancy between the value of the CS and that of the US, and hence no further conditioning to that CS or to a novel CS that was reinforced in compound with the CS+.

The elegance and facileness of the Rescorla–Wagner (1972) theory were also evident in its treatment of excitatory extinction as a process symmetrical to excitatory conditioning. In fact, that symmetry provided the means by which the theory was able to incorporate the contingency principle within its structure and also account for the phenomenon of CI. In line with our simplified notation for the theory, the extinction of a CS+ is typified by the case where the discrepancy quotient reads $(0 - 1) = -1$. That signifies that an established CS+ is presented in the absence of the US and generates a negative discrepancy. By the theory, such nonreinforced training would decrement the associative value of the CS+ until that CS approached a zero value and yielded no discrepancy, that is, $(0 - 0) = 0$. At that point, the limit of extinction training would be reached.

The way in which the theory used the negative discrepancy generated by excitatory extinction to incorporate a contingency principle can be illustrated in the case where the CS and US are negatively correlated, as in explicitly unpaired training. Because that training allows the US to occur in the presence of apparatus or contextual cues (designated X), those cues will initially accrue positive associative value. Accordingly, on occasions when the US is not presented and X occurs either by itself or in conjunction with a novel CS, a negative discrepancy will result, that is, $(0 - 1) = -1$, and therefore X, as well as the CS, will be decremented in value. However, whereas X will recover the partial loss of its positive associative value through additional occurrences of the US for X alone, the CS will be continuously decremented and thus driven from its initial zero value to a negative associative value. In short, the CS will become a CS−.

Rescorla and Wagner's (1972) derivation of inhibitory conditioning was enlightening because it indicated that the inhibitory value of an explicitly unpaired CS depended on the extent to which the X contextual cues had accrued excitatory value. However, because contextual cues are present throughout an experimental session and are only intermittently reinforced by presentations of the US during that session, their development of excitatory value would only be modest. Consequently, the negative discrepancy and inhibitory conditioning that resulted from nonreinforcing a novel CS in X would also be modest. By the theory, a far better procedure for producing CI would be to use a discrete event (stimulus A), instead of the X contextual cues, to mediate the excitatory conditioning effect. In that way, A could be consistently reinforced by the US when presented by itself and only nonreinforced when presented in compound with another discrete event (stimulus B) intended as the inhibitor. That arrangement would allow robust excitatory conditioning to A, a large negative discrepancy for the AB compound, and hence robust inhibitory conditioning for B. This procedure, which came to be labeled the "Pavlovian" CI procedure, had earlier been described by Pavlov (1927) as his "method of contrasts." In fact, the procedure was advocated by Pavlov as his preferred means for producing CI.

The Rescorla–Wagner (1972) theory was quite provocative in its treatment of inhibitory conditioning as a process identical to excitatory extinction. As noted, both processes derived from the negative discrepancy that was generated by presenting a CS+ (with or without a novel CS) in the absence of the US, that is, $(0 - 1) = -1$. Indeed, the only difference between the two processes was whether the target CS subject to that discrepancy initially had a positive associative value and was then decremented to a zero value (as in excitatory extinction) or initially had a zero value and was then decremented to a negative associative value (as in inhibitory conditioning). Given the equivalence of the two processes and hence the symmetry of both to excitatory conditioning, it followed that the extinction of inhibition would be identical in principle to the conditioning of excitation. Accordingly, inhibitory extinction would result from a positive discrepancy between the CS− and its US consequence.

By the theory, all that one had to do to extinguish a CS− was to omit both its previously associated CS+ and negatively correlated US and simply present the CS− by itself. With that arrangement, the discrepancy quotient for the CS− would read $(0 - (-1)) = +1$, signifying a positive discrepancy by which it would be incremented from a negative associative value to zero. It is noteworthy that the theory also made the counterintuitive prediction that such an arrangement could be used to condition excitation to a novel CS that was presented concomitantly with the CS− during the extinction operation. Like the CS−, that novel CS would also be subject to a positive discrepancy and hence it, too, would be incremented in value. Although some preliminary evidence was obtained in support of such an outcome (Rescorla, 1971), more stringent tests by Baker (1974), using a strongly-developed and well-maintained inhibitor, failed to detect any CE to a novel CS that was nonreinforced in compound with a CS −. Furthermore, in a series of between- and within-subject experiments which attempted to extinguish a CS − by presenting it alone, Zimmer–Hart and Rescorla (1974) failed to gain any evidence supporting a loss in the inhibitory value of that CS. Given those findings on inhibitory extinction, the theory and/or its treatment of inhibition as symmetrical to excitation lay in question.

SUBSEQUENT RESEARCH ADDRESSING THE EXTINCTION OF INHIBITION

Because of the success of the Rescorla–Wagner (1972) theory in assimilating most of the known facts on excitatory and inhibitory conditioning, a number of investigators were motivated during the late 1970s and early 1980s to readdress the problem of inhibitory extinction (e.g., Owren & Kaplan, 1981; Pearce, Nicholas, & Dickinson, 1982; Rescorla 1981, 1982; Witcher, 1978; Witcher & Ayres, 1984). However, the findings of their investigations uniformly showed that a CS −, unlike a CS +, could not be extinguished by presenting the CS by itself. In fact, it was reported that, if anything, presentations of a CS − by itself enhanced its inhibitory effect, at least when assessed in a summation transfer test involving an independently trained excitor (e.g., Rescorla, 1982). We also took up the problem of inhibitory extinction at about the same time, but our approach differed from the other studies in two, distinct ways. In one line of research (Lysle & Fowler, 1985), we entertained the possibility that the previous investigations had inadvertently failed to satisfy the conditions specified by the Rescorla–Wagner (1972) theory as necessary for the extinction of a CS −. In the other line of research (DeVito & Fowler, 1986), we asked whether the extinction of a CS − required an operation symmetrical to that used to extinguish a CS +. Although these two lines of investigation were conducted virtually concomitantly, we shall treat them in their stated order because they bear on the nonassociative and associative extinction of CI, respectively.

Evidence for the Nonassociative Extinction of Inhibition

By Rescorla and Wagner's (1972) account, the effectiveness of a CS-alone procedure in extinguishing a CS − depended on a positive discrepancy between the negative associative value of the CS− and its zero US consequence, that is, $(0 - (-1)) = +1$. However, to the extent that any excitatory cues were present with the CS− during its extinction trials, that positive discrepancy and hence the basis for extinction of the CS− would be reduced, if not eliminated. That suggested that the prior investigations of inhibitory extinction might have been inadequate because, in all of those studies, the experimental chambers which were used for excitatory and inhibitory conditioning, and which themselves may have been excitatory, were also employed during the inhibitory-extinction phase. Equally important in this regard were the findings of several studies in the early 1980s which examined the interstimulus relationships of Pavovian CI training (e.g., Cunningham, 1981; Rescorla, 1981). Those studies showed that a strong association developed between the CS− and the CS+ with which the CS− had been nonreinforced in compound. That being the case, presentations of a CS− by itself could evoke a memorial representation of its previously associated CS+, with the result that the net associative value of the CS− and its *retrieved* CS+ (and any excitatory contextual cues) effectively approached zero. Thus, there would be little, if any, positive discrepancy and extinction of the CS− would be blocked. In light of those considerations, our first line of research (Lysle & Fowler, 1985) investigated whether a CS− would extinguish its inhibitory property if both the training context and a memorial representation of the CS+ previously associated with the CS− were neutralized prior to presentations of the CS− by itself.

Experiment 1: Neutralization of Excitation Prior to Inhibitory-extinction Training

Our first experiment (Lysle & Fowler, 1985, Experiment 1), as well as the others in this series, employed a conditioned-suppression methodology in which male rats of the Sprague–Dawley strain (80–90 days old, 300–350 g) were trained to lick for water, as an evaluative baseline response. Initially, the subjects were acclimated to a home-cage deprivation schedule which provided water for 8 min per day and food ad libitum. Then, on succeeding days, the subjects were given a daily 8-min session in one of a set of four conditioning chambers (X) where they were permitted to lick at a contact-sensitive drinking tube. That provided their total water intake for the day and maintained the 24-hr deprivation cycle. After stable licking rates had been achieved, the subjects received several on-baseline habituation trials to each of the intended CSs (a 10-sec clicker, white noise, and flashing light), so as to reduce unconditioned suppression to those events. By the end of those trials, mean suppression to the CSs had stabilized at .40–.45, in evidence of their relative neutrality. Suppression scores were based on the ratio, CS/(CS + PreCS), where CS refers to the number of licks during the 10-sec CS and preCS refers to the number of licks during the 10-sec period immediately prior to the CS. Hence, a ratio of .5 indicates absolutely no suppression and a ratio of zero, complete suppression to the CS.

After the habituation trials, the subjects were given on-baseline excitatory conditioning in X in which a single daily presentation of the 10-sec clicker (stimulus A) always terminated with the onset of a .5-sec, 1.2-mA, grid-shock US. At the end of five such reinforced trials, mean suppression to A was .02, indicating that A had been established as a robust CS +. On-baseline inhibitory conditioning in X commenced thereafter and involved a Pavlovian CI procedure: For all subjects, there were two daily reinforced presentations of A (as described earlier) and, for counterbalanced subjects within each group, six daily nonreinforced presentations of A in simultaneous compound with either the 10-sec flashing-light or white-noise CS, the intended inhibitor (stimulus B). That training was highly effective in empowering B with the ability to inhibit suppression to A. By the end of 20 such sessions, the overall mean suppression ratio for A was .04, whereas that for the AB compound was .38.

To extinguish CE to A and thereby neutralize a memory representation of A prior to extinction training on the B inhibitor, all subjects were given 96 nonreinforced presentations of A in X for the next 12 days. By the end of that training, CE to A had appreciably extinguished, as the overall mean suppression ratio for A was .38. For 6 days thereafter, two sets of three groups each were given just baseline training in either the original X chambers or a different set of neutral chambers (Y), where no CS or US presentations had ever been administered. (The X and Y chambers were of different construction, with different dimensions, grid floors, and internal features, such as vertically stripped black and white walls and an air freshener in Y but not in X.) That training was intended to further extinguish any CE to X, as well as provide a neutral Y context, in either of which the inhibitory B stimulus could be presented by itself and presumably extinguished.

For the inhibitory-extinction phase, which lasted 8 days, a pair of experimental groups from the two sets were given a total of 64 presentations of B alone while they were drinking in that context, X or Y, to which they had been exposed in the baseline sessions following their excitatory extinction on A. Those two groups are designated B(X) and B(Y) to indicate extinction training on B in either X or Y. To evaluate whether that training would reduce inhibition to B, a pair of control groups from the two sets was given continued baseline training in their respective X and Y contexts without any presentations of B. Accordingly, those two groups are designated (X) and (Y). Finally, to evaluate whether inhibition to B for the experimental groups would extinguish completely, a second pair of control groups from the two sets was trained and extinguished exactly like the experimental groups but with a different stimulus, C (a counterbalanced noise or light), used in place of the particular B stimulus for the experimental subjects. Hence, those two control groups, which are designated C(X) and C(Y), received a novel B stimulus in a subsequent test of B's inhibitory effect. Because there was no viable excitatory CS with which the B stimulus could be summated, all subjects were given an excitatory retardation test on B. In preparation for that test, the subjects received 2 days of baseline training in X and then a single pretest session in X, involving four nonreinforced presentations of B alone. For the retardation test in X which followed and lasted 6 days, all subjects received two daily presentations of B, reinforced on a random 50% basis.

Fig. 10.1 presents the results of both the pretest (PRE) and the retardation test on B. As shown, there were no group differences during the pretest. However, during the retardation test, the B(X) and B(Y) groups developed suppression to B at a significantly slower rate than the C(X) and C(Y) controls, which had been given a novel B stimulus in that test. That difference suggested that B was still a viable inhibitor for the B(X) and B(Y) groups and had not been extinguished. However, there was a perplexing aspect of the results in that the (X) and (Y) controls developed

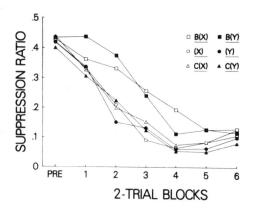

FIG. 10.1.   Group mean suppression to the B stimulus during the pretest (PRE) and the retardation test of Experiment 1. Following extinction on their excitatory A stimulus in the X training context, the B(X) and B(Y) groups and, likewise, the C(X) and C(Y) groups were given nonreinforced presentations of their inhibitory B or C stimulus in either X or a novel Y context; the (X) and (Y) groups were given exposures to those contexts without any presentations of their inhibitory B stimulus (from Lysle & Fowler, 1985; copyright by the *American Psychological Association;* reprinted by permission).

suppression to their inhibitory B stimulus just as rapidly as the C(X) and C(Y) controls did to their novel B stimulus. In other words, even though B had been established as a robust inhibitor for the (X) and (Y) subjects and had never been presented to those subjects during the inhibitory-extinction phase, it had somehow lost its inhibitory property!

In an effort to make some sense of our findings, we subsequently gave all subjects several baseline sessions in X and then reconditioned them to their extinguished A excitor by reinforcing four presentations of A in X on a random 50% basis. Following that, the subjects were given a 2-day summation test in X in which there were four nonreinforced presentations per day: one of A alone, two of A in simultaneous compound with C, and one of C alone. From that test, we hoped to determine whether C was still an inhibitory CS for the C(X) and C(Y) subjects because they had been given extinction training on C identical to the extinction training on B administered to the B(X) and B(Y) subjects.

The results of the summation test on C are shown in Fig. 10.2, with the data for the X and Y subgroups of each treatment pooled because there were no differences between them. As Fig. 10.2 indicates, suppression to both the AC compound and C itself was significantly reduced for the C(X,Y) subjects, that is, the pooled C(X) and C(Y) groups, by comparison with the other groups which had received a novel C stimulus in the sum-

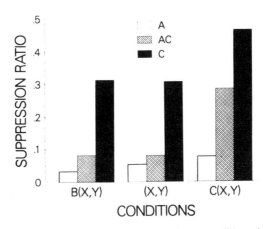

FIG. 10.2. Group mean suppression to the reconditioned A excitor, the AC compound, and the C stimulus during the summation test of Experiment 1. The B(X,Y) and C(X,Y) conditions involved prior non-reinforced presentations of either an inhibitory B or C stimulus in the X training context or a novel Y context; the (X,Y) condition involved prior exposure to those contexts without any presentations of the in-hibitorily trained B stimulus (from Lysle & Fowler, 1985; copyright by the *American Psychological Association;* reprinted by permission).

mation test. These group differences were consistent in indicating that C had retained its inhibitory property for the C(X,Y) subjects because it not only inhibited the conditioned suppression elicited by A but it also eliminated the apparent unconditioned suppression that was generated when C was a neutral stimulus and not a CS −, as in the case of the B(X,Y) and (X,Y) subjects.

The findings of this first experiment made it clear that presentations of a CS − by itself would not extinguish its inhibitory property even when a concerted effort was made to neutralize all possible sources of excitation prior to the inhibitory-extinction phase. Although all subjects were given extensive extinction training on A in X, followed by nonreinforced exposure to X or Y, so as to extinguish further any excitatory contextual cues or replace them with a neutral context, the B(X,Y) subjects, which had received extinction training on B, still showed an inhibitory effect of that stimulus in the retardation test, and the C(X,Y) subjects, which had received extinction training on C, still showed an inhibitory effect of that stimulus in the summation test. Nonetheless, it was evident that some other factor was at play because the results of the B retardation test also indicated that the inhibitory effect of B for the (X,Y) subjects had been eliminated, despite the fact that those subjects had not received any extinction training on B.

We considered two interpretations of our findings. One was that CI is a labile process which decays with the passage of time between training and testing (e.g., Henderson, 1978; but see Thomas, 1979). A similar interpretation had earlier been used by Pavlov (1927) to account for the "spontaneous recovery" of conditioned excitation. He assumed that a delay between excitatory extinction and testing dissipated the inhibition that presumably developed to a CS + during its extinction training. Other, contemporary theorists had also viewed inhibition as a relatively unstable process. For example, Solomon and Corbit (1974; Solomon, 1980) posited that both the inherent and conditionable opponent (or inhibitory) reactions to a US were strengthened by their evocation and weakened by their nonevocation or disuse over time. Thus, it may have been the case that CI to B for our (X,Y) subjects was appreciably weakened by the 28-day period that intervened between inhibitory conditioning and retardation testing. In contrast, the B(X,Y) and C(X,Y) subjects would not have been affected as much by that delay because they received numerous presentations of their respective inhibitors toward the end of that period.

The second interpretation which we entertained was that inhibition is not a primary process, like excitation, but a subsidiary and subservient process which merely tempers excitation. As such, inhibition would be dependent on excitation for its operation and expression and thus it would not be functional when the excitatory process itself was not viable. By this "slave" interpretation, the absence of an inhibitory effect of B for the (X,Y) subjects was due merely to extinction of the A excitor and any excitatory contextual cues. That being the case, the inhibitory stimulus for the B(X,Y) subjects would also have been neutralized but, as a neutral stimulus, it would have been subject to a learned-inattention or "latent-inhibition" effect (e.g., Lubow, 1973; Reiss & Wagner, 1972) because of the numerous presentations of B by itself that were administered prior to the retardation test. Neutralization of the inhibitory C stimulus for the C(X,Y) subjects should also have resulted from A's extinction, but due to the excitatory conditioning of B in the retardation test and the reconditioning of A following that test, C could have been reactivated as an inhibitory CS and rendered functional in the summation test. It is important to recognize that this slave interpretation did not imply that the neutralized B stimulus for the (X,Y) subjects would be reactivated by the shock US that was presented in the retardation test. This US was contingent upon B and therefore B, as a neutralized stimulus, would acquire an excitatory bias which would oppose, if not offset, its function as a signal for the absence of the US.

Experiment 2: Neutralization of Excitation Without Inhibitory-extinction Training

Our second experiment in this series (Lysle & Fowler, 1985, Experiment 2) was designed to evaluate the decay and slave interpretations suggested by the first experiment. For that purpose, the present subjects were given the same Pavlovian CI training as before (i.e., A+ and either AB− or AC−) and then, pairs of groups trained with B and C received one of the following treatments prior to a retardation test on B and a subsequent retardation test on C: (1) extensive extinction training on the A excitor in the X training context; (2) comparable extinction training but just to the X context; and (3) no extinction training to either the A excitor or the X context. For those subjects trained with B, a slave interpretation predicted that inhibition in the B retardation test would be maintained without loss for the no-extinction subjects but appreciably decremented (i.e., deactivated) for those subjects given extinction training on A in X and, to a lesser extent, for those subjects given extinction training on just X. The latter prediction derived from the fact that nonreinforced exposure to a training context partly reduces excitation to a CS+ trained in that context (e.g., Marlin, 1982). On the other hand, the same interpretation predicted that inhibition to C in the subsequent retardation test would be fully reactivated for all groups trained with that stimulus. This prediction follows because all groups would have a fully viable excitatory process as a result of their reinforced training in the retardation test on B. In contrast, a decay interpretation predicted that inhibition in both the B and C retardation tests would be comparably diminished (i.e., decayed) for all subjects that had earlier been trained with the particular inhibitor used in that test.

The procedure for the present experiment was similar to that used in the first experiment, except that all sessions were conducted in the X context. After baseline training and several habituation trials to the intended CSs, all subjects received on-baseline conditioned-suppression training to A (the 10-sec clicker) and then Pavlovian CI training involving reinforced presentations of A and, for different groups, nonreinforced presentations of A in simultaneous compound with either B or C (the white noise and flashing light, counterbalanced within and across groups). Following 20 such sessions, one pair of groups trained with B and C was given 96 non-reinforced presentations of A over a period of 12 days. Those two groups are designated A(B) and A(C) to indicate excitatory extinction on A after inhibitory conditioning to either B or C. A second pair of groups trained with B and C was given the same number of extinction sessions in X but without any presentations of A. Those two groups are designated X(B) and X(C). A third pair of groups trained with B and C did not receive any extinction training on A or X; instead, those two no-extinction groups, designated N(B) and N(C), were merely transported to the experimental room during the extinction phase and given their daily 8-min drinking sessions in detention cages identical to their home cages. Following the excitatory-extinction phase, all subjects received both a pretest and a retardation test on B identical to those administered in Experiment 1. Subsequent to that, all subjects were given a nonreinforced posttest on A, to assess whether the differences in extinction to A had been maintained, and then both a pretest and a retardation test on C, identical to those administered for B.

Fig. 10.3 presents the results of both the pretest (PRE) and the retardation test on B. As shown, conditioned suppression to B developed at comparably rapid rates for the three control groups that were trained with C but were tested on a novel B stimulus. In contrast, the three groups that were both trained and tested on B developed suppression to B at generally slower but markedly different rates. In particular, the N(B) group developed suppression least rapidly, the X(B) group, at an intermediate rate, and the A(B) group, most rapidly—in fact, virtually as rapidly as the three control groups that were tested with a novel B stimulus. Those differences among the three B-trained groups were highly significant and represented reliably ordered effects, that is, suppression to B developed significantly faster with the A than X extinction treatment, and significantly faster with the X than N extinction treatment.

Clearly, the findings of the B retardation test were not in agreement with an interpretation which merely posited that CI decays with disuse.

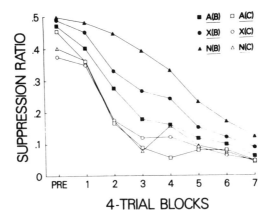

FIG. 10.3. Group mean suppression to the B stimulus during the pre-test (PRE) and initial retardation test of Experiment 2. After excitatory conditioning to stimulus A and inhibitory conditioning to either stimulus B or C, the A(B) and A(C) groups were given excitatory extinction to A in the X training context, the X(B) and X(C) groups, extinction to only the X context, and the N(B) and N(C) groups, no extinction to either A or X (from Lysle & Fowler, 1985; copyright by the *American Psychological Association*; reprinted by permission).

That interpretation predicted an equal loss of inhibition between inhibitory conditioning and testing for all of the B-trained groups, regardless of the type of excitatory extinction that they received. On the other hand, the findings were fully amenable to a slave interpretation positing that CI is functionally dependent on excitation and operates only to the extent that the excitatory process is viable. Accordingly, when CE to A and the X context was maintained, as in the N(B) treatment, inhibition to B was maintained seemingly at full strength. But when CE to both A and the X context was extinguished, as in the A(B) treatment, inhibition to B was reduced virtually completely. The fact that the development of suppression to B for the A(B) group was slightly less pronounced than that for the three control groups suggests that there may have been some additional, *unconditioned* suppression to the novel B stimulus for the three controls, as the same difference was also apparent in the pretest, when B was not reinforced. However, it may also have been the case that there was some residual inhibition to B for the A(B) group. But that, too, would be amenable to a slave interpretation because it is known that a CS+ retains some of its excitation even after prolonged extinction training (e.g., Reberg, 1972). By a slave interpretation, that residual excitation would allow residual inhibition.

The partial loss of inhibition to B for the X(B) group, which had received extinction training on only the X contextual cues, was also in line with a slave interpretation. As noted earlier, mere exposure to a training context can partly reduce excitation to a CS + trained in that context (e.g., Marlin, 1982). In addition, a number of theorists (e.g., Rescorla, 1980; Wagner, 1978) have argued that contextual cues acquire second-order CE as a result of their association with a first-order CS +. In fact, some theorists (e.g., Nadel & Willner, 1980) have suggested that a hierarchical relationship is established in which the training context becomes excitatory by signaling the occurrence of a discrete CS + which, in turn, predicts the occurrence of the US. The common implication of these interpretations is that, even when a discrete CS + is selectively reinforced by an aversive US, some fear will develop to and be potentiated by the context. Consequently, exposure to the context alone should reduce that fear by disassociating the context from its predicted CS + and the US. According to a slave interpretation, the reduction of that fear would also reduce the inhibitory effect of a CS −.

Confirmation of a slave interpretation rested, though, on the outcome of the C retardation test because the interpretation predicted equally strong inhibitory effects for all of the C-trained groups, despite the different excitatory-extinction treatments that they had received. To ensure that those treatments were still effective, at least insofar as CE to A was concerned, all subjects were given four nonreinforced test presentations of A in X on each of 3 days prior to their pretest and retardation test on C. The left panel of Fig. 10.4 shows the results of the posttest on A and the right panel, the results of both the pretest (PRE) and the retardation test on C. As indicated in the left panel, fear of A was appreciably reinstated for the A(B) and A(C) groups, presumably as a result of the US presentations in the prior retardation test. Nonetheless, the difference between those two groups and the rest was reliable throughout and was even amplified over the A test sessions. The right panel of Fig. 10.4 shows that, in spite of those differences in suppression to A, conditioned suppression to C developed at comparably slow rates for the A, X, and N groups that were trained and tested on C, and at comparably fast rates for the A, X, and N groups that were trained on B but were tested with a novel C stimulus.

The findings of the C retardation test accorded well with a slave interpretation because that interpretation posits that the effective strength of an inhibitory reaction to a CS − depends on the viability of the excitatory process. Thus, even though the A excitor had been differentially extinguished for the A, X, and N groups immediately prior to their retardation test on C, there still was a fully viable excitatory process by which C could function as as inhibitor for the groups trained on that stimulus because B had been established as a strong conditioned excitor for all groups in the prior retardation test. The findings of the C retardation test indicated, therefore, that the maintenance (or reactivation) of a conditioned inhibitor

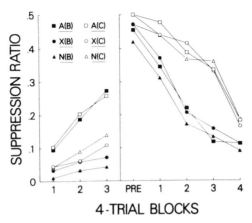

FIG. 10.4. Group mean suppression in Experiment 2 to the A stimulus following the B retardation test (left panel) and to the C stimulus during the subsequent pretest (PRE) and retardation test (right panel). After excitatory conditioning to stimulus A and inhibitory conditioning to either stimulus B or C, the A(B) and A(C) groups were given excitatory extinction to A in the X training context, the X(B) and X(C) groups, extinction to only the X context, and the N(B) and N(C) groups, no extinction to either A or X (from Lysle & Fowler, 1985; copyright by the *American Psychological Association*; reprinted by permission).

is dependent, not merely on the viability of the excitor used to develop that inhibitor, but also on the viability of other excitors that are independently trained in the same context. That conclusion is consonant with the results of other investigations (e.g., Rescorla, 1982; Rescorla & Holland, 1977) showing that a CS − can function in an inhibitory capacity with an independently trained excitor (as in a summation transfer test), even though the CS +, by which the CS − was initially established, has been extinguished.

Experiments 3 and 4: Neutralization of Excitation Within but not Outside of the Test Context

The findings of our first two experiments showed that CI was deactivated when all forms of CE associated with the training context were eliminated. However, they also showed that CI was fully reactivated when the extinguished CS +, by which the CS − had earlier been developed, was reconditioned (Experiment 1) or when another CS was developed as a conditional excitor in place of the extinguished CS + (Experiment 2). In turn, those findings indicated that as long as there was some viable form of CE associated with the test context, the CS − would retain its inhibitory effect. To our knowledge, though, no one had ever evaluated whether a CS −

would continue to function as an inhibitor when CE was extinguished in the test context but was concomitantly established in a distinctively different context. Apparently, that assessment had not been made because the common procedure for testing CI was to summate the CS– with a CS+, and that arrangement guaranteed the presence of CE in the test context. We felt that the considered assessment was important because it could provide information on the conditions under and, possibly, the mechanisms by which CI operated. Thus, our third experiment in the series (Lysle & Fowler, 1985, Experiment 3) investigated whether CI would be maintained when CE was extinguished in the original context (the X chambers) but was concomitantly developed in a distinctively different context (the Y chambers).

In the present experiment, the subjects were given baseline training and several CS habituation trials in both the X and Y chambers but on separate days. Then, on-baseline in X, they received conditioned-suppression training to A (the 10-sec clicker), followed by Pavlovian CI training in which, as before, there were reinforced presentations of A alone and, for different groups, nonreinforced presentations of A in simultaneous compound with either B or C (the white noise and flashing light, counterbalanced within and across groups). Following that training, the subjects received 16 days of conditional-discrimination training in which there were two 8-min sessions per day, one each in X and Y, but with water available in only one context on any day. During this conditional phase, one pair of B and C groups received an average of two daily reinforced presentations of A in X, together with six daily nonreinforced presentations of A in Y. Those two groups are designated B:A+/A and C:A+/A to indicate inhibitory training with either B or C and then conditional training in which presentations of A were reinforced (A+) and nonreinforced (A) in X and Y, respectively. A second pair of groups trained with B and C received just the opposite: six daily nonreinforced presentations of A in X and an average of two daily reinforced presentations of A in Y. These two groups are designated B:A/A+ and C:A/A+. This conditional training was highly effective in allowing the context to control the subjects' fear of A. By the end of this phase, conditioned suppression to A in X for the pair of A+/A groups was .07, whereas for the pair of A/A+ groups it was .47 (responding in Y was not recorded).

A fifth group, also trained with B as the inhibitor, was included to evaluate any general influence which the conditional training might exert on B's inhibitory effect in a subsequent retardation test in X. This fifth group was not given any presentations of A or the US during the conditional phase; instead, it received daily placements in the detention cages instead of X (i.e., a no-extinction treatment), together with daily exposures to Y that matched the sequence of exposures given the conditional subjects.

This fifth group is designated B:N/—, to indicate no extinction of any kind in X and just exposure to Y.

Fig. 10.5 presents the results of both the pretest (PRE) and the retardation test on B that were administered to all groups after they had received a single baseline-recovery session in X. As shown, suppression to B developed at comparably rapid rates for the two control groups that were trained on C but were tested with a novel B stimulus. In contrast, suppression to B developed at comparably slow rates for the three groups that were both trained and tested with their inhibitory B stimulus. In that the effects of B were virtually identical for the B:A+/A and B:A/A+ groups, despite their differential training on A in X and Y, the present results established that B's inhibitory effect depended, not on the animal's fear of A in X, but rather on its fear of A in *some* context (either X or Y). Thus, the findings suggested that inhibition was maintained by some general, presumably memorially stored form of excitation which the animal "carried with it" into the X context.

Our purpose in using a conditional discrimination in the prior experiment

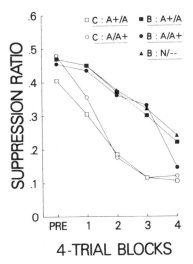

FIG. 10.5. Group mean suppression to the B stimulus during the pretest (PRE) and the retardation test of Experiment 3. After excitatory conditioning to stimulus A and inhibitory conditioning to either stimulus B or C in the X training context, the B:A+/A and C:A+/A groups received A reinforced in X but nonreinforced in a neutral Y context; the B:A/A+ and C:A/A+ groups received A nonreinforced in X but reinforced in Y; the B:N/—group received no exposure to either A or X and only nonreinforced exposure to Y (from Lysle & Fowler, 1985; copyright by the *American Psychological Association;* reprinted by permission).

was to enable us to measure conditioned suppression to A in X and thereby determine whether fear of A in that context had been differentially extinguished for the A+/A and the A/A+ groups. However, once it became apparent that the animals easily discriminated the X and Y contexts in determining their response to A, we replicated the foregoing experiment with a procedure that essentially involved differential conditioning of just the X and Y contexts (Lysle & Fowler, 1985, Experiment 4). Accordingly, after receiving the usual preliminary training in X, including Pavlovian CI training that established A as an excitor and only B as an inhibitor, the present subjects were given extensive excitatory extinction on A in X, along with concomitant training in Y that involved one of the following treatments: (a) just US presentations in Y; (b) US presentations contingent upon a novel C stimulus in Y; (c) US presentations explicitly unpaired with presentations of A in Y; and (d) just exposure to Y. Thereafter, all subjects received both a pretest and a retardation test on B in X, identical to those previously described.

Like the results of the prior experiment, those of the present study showed that conditioned suppression to B in X developed at comparably slow rates for all of the groups that had received excitatory extinction on A in X, along with US presentation in Y. Indeed, it did not matter whether those US presentations in Y occurred alone, positively correlated with a novel CS, or even negatively correlated with A. All that was necessary to maintain B's inhibitory effect in X was some form of excitatory conditioning in Y. In contrast, the group which had received excitatory extinction on A in X and mere exposure to Y showed a very rapid development of suppression to B, in evidence of a loss of the inhibitory property of that CS. Those effects, of course, replicated and extended our earlier findings for they indicated that CI was deactivated when CE was completely eliminated from the test context, and was not established in a discriminably different context.

The foregoing results were in line with the conclusion drawn from our conditional discrimination experiment: The maintenance and functional expression of CI depends not merely on the viability of a discrete CS+ in the test context but upon some general excitatory representation—or disposition—which the animal carries with it into that context. Our use of that description is not meant to imply that once an animal has been subjected to excitatory conditioning anywhere in its environ (say, the colony room or some other room), it will necessarily exhibit CI in a test context where CE has been extinguished. Rather, we would argue that the potentiation of CE and hence the expression of CI in the test context has a hierarchical basis, analogous to that earlier described for excitatory contextual cues. In other words, just as an experimental chamber, such as the X or Y context, can promote fear by signaling the occurrence of a CS for shock in that context, so likewise should the experimental room (or cart by which the animal is transported to that room) potentiate fear by signaling the X and Y contexts. We believe that these general "antedating" cues make the animal wary of its circumstance and thereby afford the excitatory basis by which a CS − will function as an inhibitor in the test context, even though the CS + previously associated with the CS − in that context has been neutralized.

Generality and Implications of the Findings

The generality of our findings on the nonassociative extinction of CI was not restricted by our use of a conditioned-suppression paradigm. Shortly after publication of our results, Best and colleagues (Best, Dunn, Batson, Meachum, & Nash, 1985) reported similar effects with an aversive-conditioning procedure that involved a lithium-mediated toxicosis as the US. In their research, which also used a Pavlovian CI procedure, water-deprived rats were given an injection of lithium chloride immediately after their exposure to a distinctive context in an experimental room (A +), but not after their exposure to a vinegar-tasting solution in that context (AB −). Best et al. showed that those experimental subjects consumed more vinegar than water in a subsequent preference test in that context, compared with controls that had received the same exposures but with the lithium-chloride injections administered in the colony room 6 hours after their exposure to the experimental context. That outcome documented the inhibitory effect of vinegar for the experimental subjects. However, the more important finding for our purpose was that obtained for other experimental subjects which had been given CI training and then excitatory extinction to the experimental context. In evidence that CI was fully deactivated by the extinction of CE, Best and colleagues found that the consumption of vinegar by those subjects was not significantly different from that of the controls.

Best et al. (1985) replicated their deactivation effect in a subsequent experiment and also showed that when the experimental context was reconditioned for CI-trained subjects that had earlier been given excitatory extinction to that context, their consumption of vinegar was significantly enhanced, compared with the controls, and was comparable to that of other experimental subjects which had not been given any excitatory extinction. Hence, the findings of Best et al., like our own, established that inhibition is functionally dependent on and thus is subservient to the primary process of excitation. Both sets of results showed that when CE is eliminated from an experimental context (and is not developed in an associated context), CI is fully deactivated; and, yet, when CE is reinstated in that context (or in an associated context), CI is fully restored (both of which Bagné also found, see Chapter 7, Ed.).

CI's dependence on CE is not restricted to its maintenance and expression but involves its conditioning, as well. Such a relationship is acknowledged by every extant theory of conditioning (e.g., Denny, 1971; Konorski, 1948, 1967; Mackintosh, 1975; Pearce & Hall, 1980; Rescorla & Wagner, 1972; Schull, 1979; Solomon, 1980) because each implicitly, if not explicitly, posits that excitation is necessary to develop a CS −. For example, within the framework of Rescorla and Wagner's theory, CI develops only via the negative discrepancy which is typically generated by nonreinforcing a novel CS in the presence of a discrete CS + or an excitatory context. That dependence of inhibitory conditioning on CE is substantiated by the fact that, in the absence of CE, nonreinforcement of a novel CS does not empower the CS with a conditioned-inhibitory effect (e.g., Reiss & Wagner, 1972). Furthermore, when CI does develop to a novel CS, its strength is found to be positively related to the strength of the excitatory cues that are nonreinforced in compound with the CS (see Fowler, Kleiman, & Lysle, 1985, Experiments 1–3). That positive relationship is also the basis by which a Pavlovian CI procedure is claimed to generate stronger CI than an explicitly unpaired procedure. In the former, strong excitation is mediated by a discrete CS + that is consistently reinforced on its own, whereas in the latter, relatively weak excitation is mediated by contextual cues that are only intermittently reinforced on their own. Although these two procedures have not been extensively compared, it is noteworthy that no one, to our knowledge, has ever reported any difficulty in producing CI with a Pavlovian procedure; however, the same does not hold true for an explicitly unpaired procedure (see Kleiman & Fowler, 1984; Maier, Rapaport, & Wheatley, 1976; Plotkin & Oakley, 1975).

Viewed in conjunction with our findings and those of Best et al. (1985), the foregoing considerations on the development of CI argue that inhibition is a process fundamentally different from excitation. That difference is made clear when one considers that both the conditioning and extinction of excitation are not in any way dependent on the presence or absence of CI; and yet, in the case of inhibition, its acquisition and nonassociative extinction are dependent, respectively, on the presence and absence of CE. The different nature of the two processes also seems evident in their behavioral manifestations. While it is commonly accepted that a CS + can evoke a CR entirely on its own, we know of no evidence which convincingly documents that a CS − will autonomously generate a CR rather that moderate some excitatory baseline. In this respect, the findings of our conditional and differential-conditioning studies (Experiments 3 and 4) are important because they indicate that the excitatory basis by which a CS − operates and gains functional expression is mediated by an assortment of cues: not merely by a discrete CS + for the US, but also by "high-order" contextual cues that are associated with the CS + , and even by more general cues that antedate those contexts, for example, a transportation cart or the experimental room in which the experimental chambers are housed. It is perhaps difficult to conceive of these general, antedating cues as sufficient to potentiate the excitatory process and provide the basis by which a CS − will be fully operative. However, their role is made patently clear by the fact that when all forms of CE are eliminated from an experimental context and are not established in an associated context, the CS − is fully deactivated and functions essentially as a neutral stimulus.

Given that a CS − does not operate autonomously and yet exerts an inhibitory effect in the presence of a CS +, one is left with the view that CI is a subsidiary and subservient process which merely moderates excitation, for example, by raising the threshold of excitation required for a CR (see Konorski, 1948; Rescorla, 1979). That subservient function of CI implies, in turn, that a CS − is not on a common dimension with a CS + in the sense of occupying the opposite (i.e., negative) end of an associative continuum; rather, the CS − is located on a dimension that is orthogonal to the associative continuum. Where that orthogonal dimension interacts with or intersects the associative continuum of excitation will undoubtedly be determined by the conditions that are used to develop the CS −. However, in the typical case, where a CS − is developed by nonreinforcing it in the presence of a CS +, that intersection should occur at the zero point on the associative continuum. Accordingly, the CS − will acquire a zero associative value as a result of its association with a zero US outcome.

Accepting the view that a CS − has an associative value of zero (which should not be confused with *no* associative value, as in the case of a novel or randomly presented CS), one can readily comprehend the null effects of those earlier studies which attempted to extinguish a CS − by presenting it alone: In predicting a zero US outcome, the CS − could not possibly be extinguished by that consequence. To use the language of Rescorla and Wagner's (1972) theory, nonreinforcement of a CS − would generate a zero discrepancy, that is, $(0 − 0) = 0$, and not the positive discrepancy by which its presumed negative associative value would be incremented to zero. Indeed, if the associative value of the CS − were to deviate at all from zero, as might well happen via an evoked representation of its previously associated CS + (see Cunningham, 1981; Rescorla, 1981), then presentations of the CS − by itself would produce a negative discrepancy, that is, $(0 − 1) = −1$, and afford the basis by which its inhibitory effect could be enhanced. Consistent with this analysis, several studies have now documented that such enhancement does occur and is evident when the CS − is summated either with an independently trained excitor (e.g., Rescorla, 1982; Williams, Travis & Overmier, 1986) or with its previously associated CS + (e.g., DeVito & Fowler, 1987; Holland, 1985). The latter findings are particularly important because they rule out the possibility that the enhancement results merely from extinction of the excitatory representation which the CS− evokes (see DeVito & Fowler, 1987).

Evidence for the Associative Extinction of Inhibition

The rationale for our second line of research (DeVito & Fowler, 1986) was not couched in the language and terms of the preceding argument, but it took basically the same form. We argued that the procedure of presenting a CS by itself is not an extinction operation that is applicable to all CSs. In the case of a CS+, the CS-alone procedure extinguishes excitation to that CS because it omits the contingent US that is used to develop the CS+ and therefore it disconfirms that US outcome predicted by the CS+. However, in the case of a CS−, the same procedure does not omit the contingent nonreinforcement, that is, the zero US outcome, that is used to develop the CS−. Instead, it confirms that outcome and, as a result, it maintains and can even strengthen the CS−, as previously documented. By this line of reasoning, as well as by our previous argument ascribing a zero associative value to a CS−, it followed that the only means of extinguishing a CS− was to have the US occur contiguously with that CS, so as to disconfirm its predicted outcome of nonreinforcement. However, the US could not be selectively administered after the CS− because that would merely transform the CS− into a CS+, as in a retardation test. What was needed to neutralize a CS− associatively was a procedure in which the US was occasionally contiguous but generally uncorrelated with the CS−.

Such a procedure had earlier been used by Zimmer–Hart and Rescorla (1974). After failing to detect any loss of CI in several between- and within-subject experiments which attempted to extinguish a CS− by presenting it alone, those investigators evaluated whether inhibition could be extinguished by employing a zero CS−US correlation in place of the negative correlation used to develop the CS−. To allow a comparison with their prior findings with a CS-alone procedure and also to evaluate the role of noncontingent US presentations, Zimmer–Hart and Rescorla (Experiment 4) used two variations of a zero-contingency procedure. After Pavlovian CI training in which there were reinforced presentations of stimulus A and nonreinforced presentations of A in compound with the intended inhibitor, stimulus B, one experimental group was given an equal number of A and AB compound trials that were *never* reinforced, whereas a second experimental group was given an equal number of A and AB compound trials that were *always* reinforced. Note that, in contrast to the latter US-always procedure, the former US-never procedure represents a variation of the CS-alone procedure in that both A and AB are presented by themselves, in the absence of any US. Note also that, despite the presence or absence of the US in the two procedures, both constitute a zero-contingency manipulation because, in both, the percentage of reinforcement (0 or 100), and thus the probability of the US, is equated for the presence and absence of B in the context of the A stimulus event, that is, $p(US/B$ in $A) = p(US/$ no B in A). Hence, by a contingency interpretation, neither procedure would condition excitation to B.

After the extinction phase, the two experimental groups, as well as a control group that had not received any extinction training, were given reinforced presentations of A alone. That was designed to equate conditioned suppression to A for all groups prior to a test in which B was summated with A. Like Zimmer–Hart and Rescorla's (1974) earlier findings, the results of the summation test in Experiment 4 showed that there was no loss in B's inhibitory effect for the experimental group given the CS-alone (or US-never) treatment. In fact, for that group, B's inhibition of the suppression produced by A was greater, although not reliably so, than that for the control group. In contrast, there was no difference in suppression between A and AB for the experimental group given the US-always treatment, as that group showed complete suppression to both. On the surface, that outcome indicated that the US-always treatment had eliminated inhibition and had not conditioned any excitation to B since there was no greater suppression to AB than to A. However, that conclusion could not be drawn for several reasons. First, because of the "floor" effect, that is, the physical limit to performance, that was manifest in the complete suppression shown to A and AB, it was impossible to determine whether there was any difference in the underlying associative values for those events. Thus, it was conceivable that the complete suppression shown to AB by the US-always group was due, not to the extinction of CI to B, but to increased CE to A. That was reasonable because the consistent reinforcement for both A and AB during US-always training might have allowed A to become a more reliable predictor of the US (compared with its value in the prior $A+/AB-$ phase) and, as a stronger excitor, to overcome the inhibitory effect of B. In addition, it was conceivable that US-always training had allowed excitation to be conditioned to the AB *configuration* and that CI to B had been maintained but was obscured by CE to the AB configural cue.

What was needed to eliminate the possible confounds of Zimmer–Hart and Rescorla's (1974) zero-contingency study, and thus properly evaluate US-always training as a means of extinguishing CI to B, was a final summation test of B with A but after US-always extinction training that involved B and a novel stimulus, C, in place of A, that is, $C+/BC+$ training. With that arrangement, any CE which developed during US-always training would be restricted to the novel C stimulus and the BC compound and therefore it would not confound a subsequent test in which B was summated with A. In addition, that arrangement would allow the A excitor to be independently maintained at a comparable but less than complete level of suppression for all groups. That was important because it could permit an assessment of whether B had acquired any CE during US-always training, as would be evident in a summation test if there were greater suppression to AB than to A. Utilizing these procedural modifications, our second line of research (DeVito & Fowler, 1986) investigated whether various zero-contingency treatments that involved different percentages of reinforcement ranging from 0 to 100 would extinguish inhibition without conditioning excitation to a CS−.

Experiment 1: Equal US Probabilities For the Presence and Absence of an Inhibitory CS

The subjects, apparatus, and general procedure for our first experiment (DeVito & Fowler, 1986, Experiment 1), as well as for the others of this series, were similar to those used in the prior set of experiments (Lysle & Fowler, 1985). Initially, male Sprague–Dawley rats (90–100 days old, 350–400 g) were acclimated to a home-cage deprivation schedule which provided water for 8 min per day and food ad libitum. Then the subjects were given daily 8-min sessions in the conditioning chambers (X) where they were permitted to lick at a contact-sensitive drinking tube for their daily water intake. After stable licking rates had been achieved, the subjects received several on-baseline habituation trials to the intended CSs: a 20-sec clicker, tone, and flashing light. (In this, as well as a subsequent, experiment using 20-sec CSs, suppression ratios were based on the number of licks during the CS and during the 20-sec preCS period.) For excitatory conditioning, the subjects were given 5 days of on-baseline training in which a single daily presentation of stimulus A (the tone or clicker, balanced across subjects within each group) always terminated with the onset of a .5-sec, 1.3-mA, grid-shock US. For inhibitory conditioning, the subjects received 20 days of on-baseline training in which there was one daily reinforced presentation of A, as indicated, and three daily nonreinforced presentations of A in simultaneous compound with stimulus B (the flashing light). Following that, all subjects received 2 days of on-baseline training in which there were four daily nonreinforced presentations of B alone. That training was intended to enhance B's inhibitory effect, as well as attenuate any conditioned suppression that might have developed to B from its prior association with A (see Cunningham, 1981; Rescorla, 1981).

For the inhibitory-extinction phase, which lasted 6 days, three groups were given daily on-baseline sessions in which there were four stimulus presentations per day: two of B in simultaneous compound with a novel stimulus, C (the clicker or tone, counterbalanced with A), and two of C alone. To generate various zero-contingency treatments, both the C and BC compound trials were subjected to equal percentages of reinforcement that varied across the three groups at 0 (CS alone), 50, and 100 (US always). Hence, for the CS-alone group (designated CSa), none of the C and BC trials were reinforced, whereas for the US-always group (designated USal), all of the C and BC trials were reinforced. In comparison, the group given the 50% treatment (designated CSo) had one each of its two daily C and BC trials randomly reinforced. That treatment was included because it represented a midpoint on the continuum of reinforcement percentage and simulated the occasional CS–US pairings that characterize a "truly random" procedure, that is, where US presentations are scheduled without regard to occurrences of the CS.

Based on our analysis of inhibitory extinction, we expected the CSo and USal treatments, but not the CSa treatment, to extinguish CI to B. However, this expectation was not based on the elimination of B's negative correlation with the US because all three procedures preclude any correlation of B and the US in the context of C, that is, $p(US/B$ in $C) = p(US/$ no B in $C)$. Rather, we expected the CSo and USal treatments to extinguish CI to B because those treatments, unlike the CSa treatment, violate the nonreinforcement outcome predicted by B. That rationale implied that only reinforcement in the presence of B is needed to extinguish B's inhibitory effect; reinforcement in the absence of B (i.e., for C itself) should merely allow the C stimulus common to the C and BC trials to become the more reliable predictor of the US and thereby block CE to B. However, it was conceivable that such a blocking effect could also be accomplished by reinforcing just the BC compound, that is, without presenting and reinforcing C itself. That possibility stemmed from the fact that a novel stimulus which is reinforced in compound with a CS− is supranormally conditioned as an excitor (e.g., Rescorla, 1971; Wagner, 1969). Consequently, its rapid and robust conditioning might also block CE to B (see Rescorla & Wagner, 1972). To evaluate that possibility, we included a fourth group (designated CS+), which was given inhibitory-extinction sessions involving two daily reinforced presentations of BC but no presentations of C alone.

Fig. 10.6 shows the effects of the group treatments during the inhibitory-extinction phase; the left panel presents group mean suppression ratios for the BC compound and the right panel, those for C alone. As shown in the right panel, the CSo and USal groups developed substantial suppression to C during the first block of three C trials. In comparison, the left panel shows that the same groups (as well as the CS+ group) exhibited less suppression to the BC compound during the first block of three BC trials. That difference attested to B's initial effect in inhibiting the suppression that was conditioned to C. However, on all succeeding trial blocks, there

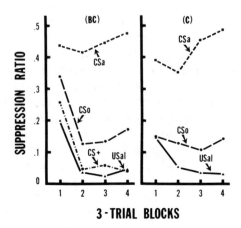

FIG. 10.6. Group mean suppression during the extinction phase of Experiment 1 to the inhibitory B stimulus in compound with a novel C stimulus (BC, left panel) and to the C stimulus alone (right panel). The CSa, CSo, and USal groups were given 0%, 50%, and 100% reinforcement, respectively, for both BC and C alone; the CS+ group was given 100% reinforcement for BC but no presentations of C alone (from DeVito & Fowler, 1986; copyright by the *American Psychological Association;* reprinted by permission).

was no difference in suppression to BC and C for either the CSo or the USal group, indicating that, with continued training, B rapidly lost its inhibitory effect for these groups.

With one exception, the CSa group showed the same effects. That group also exhibited less suppression to BC than to C early in extinction training, presumably reflecting B's effect in inhibiting *unconditioned* suppression to the novel C stimulus for that group. Likewise, the CSa group showed equivalent performance to BC and C by the end of the extinction phase. However, that outcome could not reflect a loss of B's inhibitory effect for the CSa group because there was no suppression to C for B to inhibit. What was needed, of course, to evaluate B's effect for the CSa group, as well as for the other groups, was a summation test of B with the original A excitor.

In preparation for the summation test, all groups were given a baseline session in X after the inhibitory-extinction phase and then 2 days of on-baseline training in which there were four daily nonreinforced presentations of A. That training was designed to attenuate complete suppression to A and allow a test which could detect either more or less suppression to the AB compound than to A itself. B-alone trials were also included in the test, so as to check further on whether B had maintained its inhibitory effect or had been converted into either a neutral or an excitatory CS. To ensure consistent effects, the summation test was conducted for 4 days and included four nonreinforced stimulus presentations per day: two of the AB compound and one each of A and B.

Fig. 10.7 shows the results of the summation test, with the data for the 4 test days pooled because there were no group interactions across those days. As indicated, all groups exhibited substantial (but not complete) suppression to the A excitor. However, the CSa group showed little suppression to the AB compound, whereas the CSo, USal, and CS + groups showed suppression to AB that was not significantly different from that shown to A itself. Those group differences in suppression to AB indicated that B had maintained, if not increased, its inhibitory effect for the CSa subjects (since their suppression to AB was reliably less than that exhibited at the end of CI training) and that B had lost its inhibitory effect for the CSo, USal, and CS + groups and yet had not been converted into an excitatory CS for those groups. Otherwise, their suppression to AB would have been greater than that shown to A itself. Similar effects were evident with the B-alone measure. Although the CSa group exhibited virtually no suppression to B, the CSo, USal, and CS + groups showed moderate suppression to B. That moderate suppression to B did not necessarily reflect any CE to B for those groups. Rather, it suggested a lack of CE because it matched the level of unconditioned suppression shown to B at the end

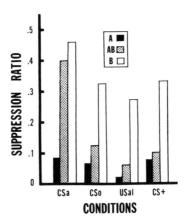

FIG. 10.7. Group mean suppression in the summation test of Experiment 1 to the original A excitor, the AB compound, and the B inhibitor. In prior inhibitory-extinction training, the CSa, CSo, and USal groups were given 0%, 50%, and 100% reinforcement, respectively, for both B in compound with a novel C stimulus and C alone; the CS + group was given 100% reinforcement for B in compound with C but no presentations of C alone (from DeVito & Fowler, 1986; copyright by the *American Psychological Association;* reprinted by permission).

of habituation training, that is, when B, as a relatively neutral stimulus, produced a suppression ratio of .30.

Consistent with our expectations, the results of this first experiment indicated that a CS− would extinguish its inhibitory property if its predicted outcome of nonreinforcement were violated by contiguous occurrences of the US. Furthermore, those reinforcements for the CS− did not condition any excitation to that CS, providing it was reinforced in compound with a novel CS which, as in the case of the CSo and USal groups, was comparably reinforced on its own. Under those circumstances, the animal apparently "lost faith" in the CS− as a signal for nonreinforcement but did not attribute the occurrence of the US to that CS; instead, it attributed the occurrence of the US to the novel C stimulus. That account of our findings accorded well with the fact that supranormal excitation is conditioned to a novel CS which is reinforced in compound with a CS− (e.g., Rescorla, 1971; Wagner, 1969); and that effect spoke to the comparable outcome obtained for the CS+ group. That group had received reinforced BC compound trials but no presentations of C alone and yet it, too, showed a loss of inhibition without any detectable excitation being conditioned to B.

Experiment 2: Equal but Reduced US Probabilities for the Presence and Absence of a Less Salient Inhibitor

To extend the findings of the prior experiment, our second experiment in this series (DeVito & Fowler, 1986, Experiment 2) investigated whether considerably reduced percentages of uncorrelated reinforcement would also extinguish inhibition to B. The fact that CI to B in the prior experiment was comparably extinguished by CSo and USal treatments involving 50% or 100% reinforcement for both BC and C suggested that, with sufficient training, any percentage of uncorrelated reinforcement *greater than zero* would violate B's predicted outcome of nonreinforcement and extinguish its inhibitory effect. To assess that possibility, we gave the present subjects the same inhibitory conditioning as before, that is, A+/AB− training, and then inhibitory-extinction training in which the percentage of reinforcement for both a novel C stimulus itself and for the B inhibitor in compound with C was set at 12.5, 25, or 50 for three experimental groups. In addition, because the prior experiment had shown markedly different outcomes for extinction treatments that either omitted the US (i.e., CSa) or included it (i.e., CSo, USal, and CS+), we added a fourth group to control for the possibility that B's inhibitory effect was eliminated merely by the occurrence of the US for some stimulus, for example, C, other than the A excitor upon which the B inhibitor had been based. Accordingly, this control group was given the same extinction training as the experimental groups but with reinforcement set at 50% for C and at 0% for BC.

The procedure for the present experiment was identical to that described for Experiment 1 of this series, except for the following: Instead of the flashing light, the less salient tone stimulus was used as the B inhibitor, so that there would be little, if any, unconditioned suppression to B at the end of habituation training. In that way, there would be little, if any, suppression to B in the final summation test, apart from that possibly conditioned to B during the inhibitory-extinction phase. Also, the duration of each CS was reduced to 10 sec to provide a short-delay conditioning arrangement and allow substantial conditioned suppression to the novel C stimulus (the flashing light) in the extinction phase, when relatively small percentages of uncorrelated reinforcement would be used. In addition, excitatory conditioning to stimulus A (the clicker) was restricted to 4 days but involved a total of seven reinforced A trials, one the first day and two per day thereafter. Likewise, inhibitory conditioning to stimulus B was restricted to 18 days but involved a daily 2:6 ratio of reinforced A trials and nonreinforced AB compound trials. Because of the reduced percentages of reinforcement used in the inhibitory-extinction phase, that phase was extended to 12 days, for a total of 24 C and 24 BC compound trials, two each per day. As noted, the three experimental groups were given 12.5%, 25%, or 50% reinforcement for both C and BC (the percentages designate those groups), whereas the control group (designated CTL) received 50% reinforcement for C and 0% reinforcement for BC. Following the extinction phase, all groups received 2 days of baseline training and then a single on-baseline session involving four nonreinforced presentations of A. Summation testing followed for 4 days and was identical to that described for the prior experiment.

Fig. 10.8 shows the effects of the group treatments during the inhibitory-extinction phase; the left panel presents group mean suppression ratios for BC and the right panel, those for C. A comparison of the panels indicates that, over the course of extinction training, comparable suppression developed to BC and C for each experimental group but with the rate and amount of conditioning being faster and larger, the greater the percentage of reinforcement received. In contrast, the CTL group exhibited relatively little suppression to BC but, like the 50% experimental group, it showed rapid and substantial conditioning to C. Those results indicated that inhibition to B had been maintained for the CTL group, but had been appreciably decremented, if not eliminated, for all of the experimental groups, despite the different percentages of reinforcement that they received. Confirmation of those effects rested, of course, on the outcome of the summation test, in which there were nonreinforced presentations of the original A excitor, the AB compound, and B.

Fig. 10.9 presents the results of the summation test, with the data for the 4 test days pooled because there were no group interactions across those days. As indicated, all groups showed substantial and comparable

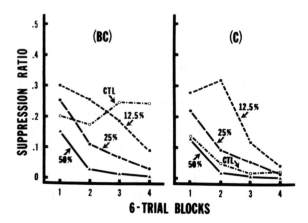

FIG. 10.8. Group mean suppression during the extinction phase of Experiment 2 to the inhibitory B stimulus in compound with a novel C stimulus (BC, left panel) and to the C stimulus alone (right panel). As designated, experimental groups were given 12.5%, 25%, or 50% reinforcement for both BC and C; a control (CTL) group was given 0% reinforcement for BC and 50% reinforcement for C (from DeVito & Fowler, 1986; copyright by the *American Psychological Association*; reprinted by permission.

suppression to the A excitor. However, whereas the CTL group exhibited little suppression to the AB compound, the three experimental groups showed pronounced suppression to AB which, in the case of the 25% and 50% groups, was virtually as great as that shown to A itself. In line with those group differences in suppression to AB, separate comparisons indicated that the difference in suppression to A and AB was highly reliable for the CTL group ($p < .001$), marginally reliable for the 12.5% group ($p < .05$), and unreliable for the 25% and 50% groups. Collectively, these results established that, whereas inhibition to B had been maintained for the CTL group, it had been appreciably decremented for the 12.5% group and completely eliminated for the 25% and 50% groups. Furthermore, there was no evidence that the 25% and 50% groups had acquired any excitation to B because their suppression to AB was not greater than that shown to A itself. In addition, their suppression to B alone was not different from that exhibited by the 12.5% group and/or the CTL group. In fact, the minimal suppression shown to B by all four groups was not different from that shown to B at the end of habituation training, when B, as a relatively neutral stimulus, produced a suppression ratio of .44.

The findings of the present experiment were important in three respects. First, they indicated that the observed loss of inhibition to B for the three experimental groups (as well as for their CSo and USal counterparts of the prior experiment) was not due merely to the occurrence of the US in conjunction with some stimulus other than the A excitor upon which the

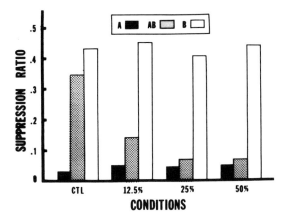

FIG. 10.9. Group mean suppression in the summation test of Experiment 2 to the original A excitor, the AB compound, and the B inhibitor. In prior inhibitory-extinction training, the experimental conditions had involved 12.5%, 25%, or 50% reinforcement for both B in compound with a novel C stimulus and C alone; the control (CTL) condition had involved 0% reinforcement for B in compound with C and 50% reinforcement for C alone (from DeVito & Fowler, 1986; copyright by the *American Psychological Association;* reprinted by permission).

B inhibitor had been based, that is, C. Like the experimental groups, the CTL group of the present study also received presentations of the US in conjunction with C. However, unlike the experimental groups, the CTL group continued to show an inhibitory effect from B when that CS was compounded either with the reinforced C stimulus in the extinction phase or with the original A excitor in the summation test. Those results for the CTL group argued that the loss of inhibition to B for the three experimental groups was due specifically to occurrences of the US that, although generally uncorrelated, were occasionally contiguous with B.

Secondly, the present findings complement those of the prior experiment by showing that inhibition to B can be extinguished even when there are considerably reduced percentages of uncorrelated reinforcement for B. In fact, the substantial, albeit incomplete, loss of inhibition shown to B by the 12.5% group is impressive because that group had received 21 nonreinforcements, as opposed to only 3 reinforcements, for both BC and C. Thus, in spite of any strengthening of B's inhibitory effect that might have resulted for that group from the many nonreinforced BC compound trials, a few contiguous US presentations for B were sufficient to violate that CS's predicted outcome of nonreinforcement and substantially extinguish its inhibitory effect. That suggested that the complete loss of inhibition shown to B by the 25% and 50% groups might also have occurred for the 12.5% group, had extinction training been extended.

The third and perhaps most important aspect of the present findings is that they provide strong evidence that the experimental treatments did not extinguish inhibition to B by conditioning excitation to that CS. In the present study, the less salient tone CS was used as the B inhibitor, so as to reduce unconditioned suppression to B and allow a more sensitive assessment in the summation test of any excitation that might have been conditioned to B in the preceding extinction phase. However, there was no evidence of any conditioned suppression to B in the summation test when B was presented in compound with the original A excitor or by itself. Indeed, the minimal suppression shown to B itself by the three experimental groups was comparable to that exhibited by the CTL group, for which B had been maintained as a robust inhibitor. In the case of the 25% and 50% groups, that outcome could not be ascribed to residual CI for B because both of those groups showed a complete loss of inhibition to B when it was assessed in compound with A. Furthermore, one is hard pressed to argue that the frequency of reinforcement for B in the extinction phase was insufficient to allow B's associative property to aquire some positive, that is, excitatory, value because the 50% group received twice as many reinforcements for B as the 25% group and yet both showed a complete loss of CI and no CE to B. (This conclusion is supported, as well, by the comparable performances of the 50% and 100%, i.e., CSo and USal, groups of the prior experiment.)

The present results also complemented some earlier findings by Witcher and Ayres (1984). As in the outcome observed for the 12.5% group of the present study, Witcher and Ayres found that CI was appreciably but not completely extinguished when there were truly random presentations of a shock US that resulted in a US probability of .083 for both the CS− and the context in which that CS was presented. By itself, that outcome might suggest that a CS− is extinguished merely by subjecting it to a sufficiently long period of zero-contingency training, that is, so that its correlation with the US is reset to zero. However, that conclusion is not correct for, at least, two reasons. First, a CS-alone procedure also equates US probability, albeit at zero, for both the CS− and the stimulus context (e.g., C or X) in which it is presented, but that procedure does not extinguish CI; instead, it maintains or even enhances CI, as previously documented. Secondly, the findings of the present and prior experiment show that a CS− is associatively neutralized not only by a zero contingency in which there is a US probability greater than zero (as in the case of the experimental groups of the present study), but also by a positive contingency in which the US is presented for just the compound of the CS− and a novel CS (as in the case of the CS+ group of the prior experiment). Taken in conjunction with the fact that the CTL treatment of the present study did not extinguish CI, those considerations argue strongly that inhibition is extinguished only when the US occurs contiguously with the CS− and violates its prediction of nonreinforcement. (Or safety, see chapter by Denny, this volume, Ed.). That is the particular feature of a zero-contingency procedure involving the US that enables it to extinguish a CS −.

Experiment 3: Equal US Probabilities for the Presence and Absence of a Novel Stimulus

The purpose of our third experiment in this series (DeVito & Fowler, 1986, Experiment 3) was to evaluate the basis by which treatments involving contiguous US presentations for a CS − in the prior two experiments could extinguish inhibition and yet fail to condition excitation to that CS. As previously noted, there were two possible mechanisms for such a blocking effect, one that applies to any CS and the other, only to a CS −. The former, or general, mechanism relates to our prior use of a zero-contingency procedure in which a US probability greater than zero is equated for the presence and absence of the CS − in the context of a novel stimulus, that is, BC+/C+ training. With that arrangement, CE to the B inhibitor was presumably blocked because the US occurred equally often in the absence and presence of B but never in the absence of the novel C stimulus. Consequently, the C stimulus became the more reliable, if not the only, predictor of the US and "captured" the excitatory-conditioning effect (see Rescorla & Wagner, 1972). With this mechanism of blocking, it did not matter that B was an inhibitory CS. What mattered was that C, and not B, was positively correlated with the US.

The other possible mechanism of blocking pertains specifically to a CS −, in particular, to the fact that reinforcement of a CS − in compound with a novel CS supraconditions excitation to the novel CS (e.g., Rescorla, 1971; Wagner, 1969). By a discrepancy interpretation (Rescorla & Wagner, 1972), such supraconditioning to the novel CS would equal, if not exceed, the limit of conditioning supported by the US and therefore it would oppose excitatory conditioning to the CS −. This interpretation was supported by our findings for the CS + group of Experiment 1 of this series. That group showed a loss of inhibition without any excitatory conditioning to the CS − even though it received only reinforced compound presentations of the CS − and the novel CS, that is, just BC+ training. However, this finding did not preclude the possibility that comparable reinforcement of the novel CS itself, that is, added C+ training, would also block CE to B because, even in the absence of any supraconditioning effect, the novel C stimulus should still become the only reliable predictor of the US.

To assess the latter possibility, and thus test the general mechanism of blocking, we gave three groups of experimental subjects conditioned-suppression training in which a US probability greater than zero was equated for the presence and absence of one novel stimulus (A) in the context of a second novel stimulus (B), that is, AB+/B+ training. As a novel and not an inhibitory stimulus, A could not supercondition excitation to stimulus B and therefore B could only block CE to A by becoming the more reliable predictor of the US. To duplicate the zero-contingency treatments that had eliminated inhibition without conditioning excitation to a CS− in the prior research, the three experimental groups were given 25%, 50%, or 100% reinforcement for an equal number of presentations of the AB compound and B itself. Matching control groups received the same number of trials and the same percentages of reinforcement but without presentations of A. To assess whether any CE developed to A, suppression to AB for the experimental groups was compared with that to B for both those groups and their corresponding control groups. In addition, all groups were given nonreinforced probe tests of A alone after successive thirds of training that duplicated, as well as exceeded, the different amounts of inhibitory-extinction training that had been administered in the prior two experiments. Furthermore, after the last probe test, all groups received a retardation (savings) test in which A alone was reinforced. That test was used to detect any weak excitation that might have been conditioned to A but been obscured in both the initial conditioning phase and the probe testing.

The general procedure for the present experiment was identical to that used in the prior two experiments, except for the following: Only the tone and flashing light stimuli were employed as CSs, with the duration of each being set at 20 sec throughout training and testing. During the initial conditioning phase, which lasted 12 days, all subjects were given a daily 8-min, on-baseline session in X that involved four presentations of stimulus B (the tone or light, balanced across subjects within each group). The three experimental groups (designated E) received stimulus A (the light or tone, counterbalanced with B) on a random half of the B trials, with the percentage of reinforcement for both AB and B set at 25%, 50%, or 100%. The three control groups (designated C) received the same percentages of reinforcement but no presentations of A. Thus, there were a total of 36 AB and 36 B trials for the three E groups and a total of 72 B trials for the three C groups. After 24, 48, and 72 trials involving B, all groups were given a nonreinforced probe test on A alone. Each probe test consisted of two A-alone presentations, one at the end of each session concluding each third of training and the other at the beginning of the session on the next day. After the last probe test, all subjects received a baseline session in X and, for 8 days thereafter, a retardation test in X, during which A was presented twice per day and was reinforced on a random 50% basis.

Fig. 10.10 shows the effects of the group treatments during the initial conditioning phase; the left panel presents mean suppression ratios for the three E groups on corresponding blocks of AB and B trials, and the right

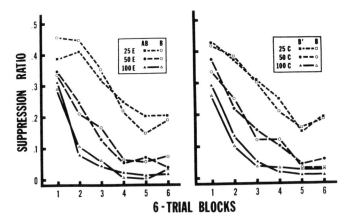

FIG. 10.10. Mean suppression during the initial conditioning phase of Experiment 3 for experimental (E) groups that were given 25%, 50%, or 100% reinforcement for both the compound of a novel A and B stimulus (AB) and B alone (left panel); and for control (C) groups that were given comparable percentages of reinforcement for the novel B stimulus without any presentations of A (right panel). Trials designated B' for the C groups correspond to the AB trials for the E groups (from DeVito & Fowler, 1986; copyright by the *American Psychological Association*; reprinted by permission).

panel presents those for the three C groups on their B-alone trials. (Trials designated B' for the C groups correspond to the AB trials for the E groups; the numerical values indicate the percentage of reinforcement that the groups received.) As indicated, conditioned suppression to stimulus B for both the E and C groups developed more rapidly and strongly, the greater the percentage of reinforcement that they received. However, throughout training, there was no difference in suppression between AB and B for any of the E groups, nor between B' and B for any of the C groups, nor between AB and B' for any pair of E and C groups given the same percentage of reinforcement. Hence, these findings indicate that the conditioned suppression shown to AB by the three E groups was mediated entirely by B and that A had not acquired any CE.

This conclusion was strengthened by the results of the A probe tests which showed that, overall, there were no reliable differences in suppression to A among any of the E and C groups, despite the different percentages of reinforcement that they received. This result was not due to an insensitivity of the probe tests because they showed that there was significantly more suppression to A at the end than at the beginning of a session (.39 and .42, respectively) and more on the last than on the first set of probe tests (.38 and .43, respectively). Incidentally, these effects were common to both E and C groups and presumably reflected general

FIG. 10.11. Group mean suppression during the retardation test of Experiment 3 to the 50% reinforced A stimulus. In the prior conditioning phase, the experimental (E) groups were given 25%, 50%, or 100% reinforcement for both the compound of a novel A and B stimulus and B alone; the control (C) groups were given comparable percentages of reinforcement for B without any presentations of A (from DeVito & Fowler, 1986; copyright by the *American Psychological Association*; reprinted by permission).

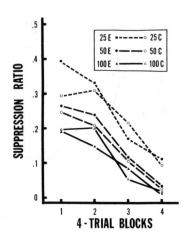

effects of the conditioning phase: for example, greater satiation and thus a more easily disrupted rate of licking at the end than at the beginning of a session; and also a greater inclination to suppress to any discrete event, such as A, after greater amounts of conditioned-suppression training with another discrete event, namely, B.

The results of the subsequent retardation test on A were equally revealing. Fig. 10.11, which presents the results of that test, shows that, despite the 50% reinforcement for A for all subjects, conditioned suppression to A developed at a faster rate for those groups that had received a greater percentage of reinforcement in the conditioning phase. But that, too, was a general effect because, with one exception, there were no reliable differences in suppression to A between those E and C groups given the same percentage of reinforcement in the conditioning phase. The single exception was the difference in suppression shown to A by the 25% E and 25% C groups on the first block of test trials. However, that difference, which indicated greater suppression to A for the C than E group, was apparently a spurious effect because it did not appear on any subsequent block of test trials.

Collectively, the findings of this experiment indicate that CE to even a novel CS is blocked when that CS is reinforced in compound with another novel CS that is comparably reinforced on its own. That blocking effect could not be ascribed to an ineffectiveness of the conditioning treatments that were imposed on the E and C groups. Those treatments resulted in substantial conditioned suppression to B and to A in compound with B, and yet there was no greater suppression to AB than to B (or to B′) with any of the reinforcement percentages that were used. Nor could the blocking effect be attributed to an insensitivity of the tests of conditioned suppression that were employed. The probe tests detected greater suppression to A over successive tests and when the probe constituted the last, rather than the first, trial of a session; however, those effects were common to the E and C groups. Likewise, the retardation test detected greater suppression to A for those subjects which had received a greater percentage of reinforcement in the conditioning phase. But that effect was not due to any prior conditioning of A for the E groups because it was equally present for the C groups, for which A had never been associated with B or the US in the conditioning phase. Evidently, that outcome reflected a sensitization effect or a general learning set whereby the more consistently one event, B, is reinforced, the more predisposed is the animal to learning that a second event, A, will also be reinforced. Whatever the basis for that outcome, it was apparent from its presence that the lack of a difference in suppression to A between the E and C groups was not due to the inoperation of the conditioning process but to B's role in blocking its effect on A.

Given that the A and B events had no history of conditioning prior to the initial conditioning phase, it was equally apparent from the present findings that the blocking of CE to A resulted from B's development as the more reliable predictor of the US, rather than from any effect which A could have exerted upon B. Hence, with regard to the inhibitory-extinction effects of the zero-contingency treatments that were used in Experiments 1 and 2 of this series, the present findings indicated that the absence of CE to the extinguished CS− was not due merely to the role of the CS− in supraconditioning excitation to the novel CS which accompanied it. That is not to say that a CS− can not supracondition excitation to a novel CS (however, see Navarro, Hallam, Matzel, & Miller, 1989). Rather, the present findings argue that a zero-contingency procedure involving comparable reinforcement for the presence and absence of a CS− in the context of a novel CS constitutes an effective means of disassociating the CS− from contiguous US occurrences, and thereby extinguishing inhibition without conditioning excitation to that CS. Evidently, the animal learned two relationships with that zero-contingency training: (1) that the novel CS is the only reliable predictor of the US, and (2) that the CS− no longer signals the absence of the US but does not itself predict the presence of the US because the US also occurs when the CS− is absent.

SUMMARY AND CONCLUSIONS

Taken as a whole, the findings of our two series of studies are important in addressing, not only the nature of CI and its relation to CE, but also the nature of extinction as it applies to any CS. With regard to the extinction of an inhibitory CS that is developed through nonreinforcement, the results of our second series of experiments (DeVito & Fowler, 1986) show that the CS − can be associatively neutralized by employing a zero-contingency procedure in which a US probability greater than zero is equated for the presence and absence of that CS in the context of a novel CS. This extinction effect is not restricted to the use of consistent reinforcement, as in a US-always treatment, because it occurs as well with sparse schedules of uncorrelated reinforcement as low as 12.5%. However, the effect does not occur with a zero-contingency procedure in which the US is omitted and only the novel CS and the compound of that CS and the CS − are presented. The failure of this CS-alone treatment to extinguish CI is not due solely to the absence of the US, though, because a control treatment is which the US is presented after the novel CS, but not after the compound of that CS and the CS −, also prevents extinction of CI to the CS −. On the other hand, a treatment in which the US occurs only after a compound of the novel CS and the CS − is quite effective in extinguishing inhibition to the CS −, without conditioning excitation to that CS. Collectively, these findings establish that the necessary and critical condition for extinguishing a CS − is the occurrence of the US in a contiguous relationship with that CS.

The foregoing conclusion is fully in line with the findings of our first series of experiments on the nonassociative extinction of CI (Lysle & Fowler, 1985). That research documented that a CS − does not operate autonomously because it is deactivated and made functionally inoperative when all forms of CE are eliminated from the training context and are not established in an associated context. On the basis of these and other findings highlighting the subservient and yet modulatory function of a CS −, we argued that CI is not on a common dimension with CE in the sense of occupying the opposite (i.e., negative) end of an associative continuum. Rather, it occupies an orthogonal dimension whose intersection with the associative continuum of excitation is dependent on the specific conditions of training that are used to develop the CS −. In the typical case, where the CS − is established by nonreinforcing it in the presence of a CS +, that intersection will occur at the zero point on the associative continuum and therefore the CS − will acquire a zero associative value by virtue of its association with a zero US outcome. By that interpretation, CI will be extinguished, as observed in our second series of experiments, by any treatment which allows the US to occur contiguously with the CS − and violate its prediction of nonreinforcement, but not by treatments that maintain that consequence.

The fact that contiguous US presentations are needed to extinguish a CS − should not be viewed as opposed to a contingency interpretation of conditioning. Some investigators have apparently fallen trap to the idea that if a positive or negative CS–US correlation is required to develop an excitatory or an inhibitory CS, then the resulting conditioning will only be undone by resetting the CS–US correlation to zero. However, that does not follow. To acquire an inhibitory response to a CS, the organism must process an inverse relationship between the presence of that CS and the occurrence of the US because that, in essence, is the only way in which it can learn that the CS signals the absence of the US. However, once acquired, that relationship can be altered by any one or more experiences which disconfirm the zero US outcome predicted by the CS−. Consequently, just a few contiguous occurrences of an uncorrelated US, such as those provided by the 12.5% reinforcement schedule of our research or the 8.3% schedule of Witcher and Ayres's (1984) research, will suffice to degrade the predictive value of the CS− and substantialy reduce its inhibitory effect. On the other hand, completely omitting the US, as in a CS-alone treatment, will only confirm the outcome predicted by the CS− and thereby sustain or enhance its inhibitory effect.

A similar argument can be made with reference to the extinction of an excitatory CS. Even though such a CS is readily devalued by a zero-contingency treatment in which there is zero reinforcement for both the presence and absence of the CS+, as in a CS-alone treatment, that outcome does not warrant the conclusion that a CS+ is extinguished merely by resetting its positive correlation with the US to zero. That reasoning is faulty because presenting the CS+ by itself has two effects: It generates a zero US-contingency and it also violates the US outcome predicted by the CS+. To distinguish between those two effects, one needs a procedure in which the positive correlation between the CS+ and the US is reset to zero but without altering the US outcome predicted by the CS+. That can be arranged by employing a US-always treatment in which consistent re-

---

Editor's note: Another, and not necessarily conflicting, interpretation according to relaxation theory is that the shock-elicited responses during extinction interfere with the occurrence of relief/relaxation in the presence of CS− to such an extent that CI is neutralized or extinguished. Fear (excitation), however, would be conditioned primarily to the common, or more consistently predictive, stimulus, as found by Fowler and associates. According to Denny, the US for the conditioning of inhibition or relief/relaxation (the UR) to CS− is the omission of the conventional US (shock). [See Chapter 6]. So the removal of this US (shock omission) in order to effect extinction means reintroducing the shock-US, if only occasionally, as convincingly demonstrated in this chapter. In a way, this is a more traditional analysis of extinction and is similar to one we made for the extinction of conditioned inhibition in rotary pursuit performance in which the US was massing of trials and its removal, the introduction of spaced trials, produced extinction of CI. [See Denny, Frisbey, & Weaver (1955), *J. Exp. Psychol.*, pp. 48–54.]

inforcement is administered for both the presence and absence of the CS +
in the context of a novel stimulis, that is, AB +/B + training. When that
is done, the preconditioned A stimulus does not show any loss of its excitatory effect when it is subsequently assessed alone, even though the
novel B stimulus, as a result of its positive correlation with the US, has
become the only reliable predictor of the US (see DeVito & Fowler, 1986,
Experiment 4). That outcome complements our findings for a CS − and
argues that a CS + is extinguished, not by resetting its positive correlation
with the US to zero, but by violating the US outcome predicted by that
CS.

In demonstrating that markedly different treatments are needed to extinguish a CS + and a CS − , the present findings encourage us to broaden
our description of the extinction process because, clearly, one cannot refer
to the procedure of presenting a CS by itself as a general extinction operation. That is evident not only with conditioned inhibition, but also with
other phenomena, such as latent inhibition, where the animal seemingly
learns to ignore a novel CS that is repeatedly presented by itself (e.g.,
Lubow, 1973; Reiss & Wagner, 1972). Quite obviously, that effect, like
conditioned inhibition, will not be extinguished by allowing the CS to occur
on its own because that operation is the very means by which the phenomenon is established. To address these kinds of problems and, at least,
describe the basis by which both a CS − and a CS + are extinguished, one
needs to acknowledge the respective roles that are played in the extinction
of those CSs by the presence and absence of the US. That can be conveniently done by redefining extinction as an operation in which one alters
the associative relationship between a CS and its contingent outcome or
"effective reinforcer." Accordingly, in the case of a CS + , where the reinforcer is the occurrence of the US, extinction is accomplished merely by
omitting the US. However, in the case of a CS − , where the effective
reinforcer for the CS is the omission of an anticipated US, extinction is
accomplished only by allowing the US to occur contiguously with that CS.
This description of extinction operations has an additional advantage because it acknowledges that the associative relationships for a CS + and a
CS − are not only extinguished but are also established on the basis of the
occurrence or the omission of a US, thus extending to the Pavlovian process
the concepts of positive and negative reinforcement as used in instrumental
learning.

The present findings are also instructive for theories of conditioning,
like Rescorla and Wagner's (1972), which speak to the associative nature
and the interrelation of CI and CE. As described earlier, the Rescorla–
Wagner treatment of inhibition as a process symmetrical to excitation was
brought into question by its account of inhibitory extinction. Because the
theory ascribed a negative associative value to a CS − , its description of

inhibitory extinction required a positive discrepancy in which the component values of the discrepancy quotient read $(0 - (-1)) = +1$. The shortcoming of that description, of course, was that it wrongly predicted that a CS-alone procedure would extinguish a CS $-$. That failure, however, does not necessarily undermine the theory or the discrepancy principle by which it operates. By our earlier argument assigning a zero associative value to a CS $-$ and by our findings showing that a CS $-$ is extinguished by contiguous occurrences of the US, it follows that the discrepancy quotient for inhibitory extinction should be altered to read $(1 - 0) = +1$. That account of inhibitory extinction has the same component values as the positive discrepancy specified for excitatory conditioning; and therefore the establishing operations for those phenomena are symmetrical to the operations constituting the negative discrepancy that is required for both excitatory extinction and inhibitory conditioning, that is, where the discrepancy quotient reads $(0 - 1) = -1$. This resolution is instructive because it indicates that the symmetrical operations underlying the action of positive and negative discrepancies in generating opposite effects for a CS $+$ and a CS $-$, namely, their conditioning or extinction, do not necessarily imply that the associative values for those CSs are symmetrical. Indeed, by the present account, the integrity of the theory is maintained only by assuming that the associative values, and hence the processes, for a CS $+$ and a CS $-$ are asymmetrical.

ACKNOWLEDGMENTS

The research reported in this chapter was supported in part by a National Institute of Health grant (MH24115) and a University of Pittsburgh Research Development Award to Harry Fowler and by a St. Joseph's University faculty research grant to Paul L. DeVito.

REFERENCES

Baker, A. G. (1974). Conditioned inhibition is not the symmetrical opposite of conditioned excitation: A test of the Rescorla–Wagner model. *Learning and Motivation, 5*, 369–379.

Best, M. R., Dunn, D. P., Batson, J. D., Meachum, C. L., & Nash, S. M. (1985). Extinguishing conditioned inhibition in flavour-aversion learning: Effects of repeated testing and extinction of the excitatory element. *Quarterly Journal of Experimental Psychology, 37B*, 359–378.

Brush, F. R. (1971). *Aversive conditioning and learning.* New York: Academic Press.

Cunningham, C. L. (1981). Association between the elements of a bivalent stimulus. *Journal of Experimental Psychology: Animal Behavior Processes, 7*, 425–436.

Denny, M. R. (1971). Relaxation theory and experiments. In F. R. Brush (Ed.), *Aversive conditioning and learning* (pp. 235–295). New York: Academic Press.

DeVito, P. L., & Fowler, H. (1986). Effects of contingency violations on the extinction of a conditioned fear inhibitor and a conditioned fear excitor. *Journal of Experimental Psychology: Animal Behavior Processes, 12,* 99–115.

DeVito, P. L., & Fowler, H. (1987). Enhancement of conditioned inhibition via an extinction treatment. *Animal Learning and Behavior, 15,* 448–454.

Fowler, H., Kleiman, M. C., & Lysle, D. T. (1985). Factors affecting the acquisition and extinction of conditioned inhibition suggest a "slave" process. In R. R. Miller & N. E. Spear (Eds.), *Information processing in animals: Conditioned Inhibition* (pp. 113–150). Hillsdale, NJ: Lawrence Erlbaum Associates.

Henderson, R. W. (1978). Forgetting of conditioned fear inhibition. *Learning and Motivation, 9,* 16–30.

Holland, P. C. (1985). The nature of conditioned inhibition in serial and simultaneous feature negative discriminations. In R. R. Miller & N. E. Spear (Eds.), *Information processing in animals: Conditioned inhibition* (pp. 267–297). Hillsdale, NJ: Lawrence Erlbaum Associates.

Hull, C. L. (1943). *Principles of behavior.* New York: Appleton–Century–Crofts.

Hull, C. L. (1952). *A behavior system.* New Haven, CT: Yale University Press.

Kamin, L. J. (1968). "Attention-like" processes in classical conditioning. In M. R. Jones (Ed.), *Miami symposium on the prediction of behavior: Aversive stimulation* (pp. 9–31). Miami, FL: University of Miami Press.

Kamin, L. J. (1969). Predictability, surprise, attention, and conditioning. In B. A. Campbell & R. M. Church (Eds.), *Punishment and aversive behavior* (pp. 279–296). New York: Appelton–Century–Crofts.

Kleiman, M. C., & Fowler, H. (1984). Variations in explicitly unpaired training are differentially effective in producing conditioned inhibition. *Learning and Motivation, 15,* 127–155.

Konorski, J. (1948). *Conditioned reflexes and neuron organization.* Cambridge, England: Cambridge University Press.

Konorski, J. (1967). *Integrative activity of the brain.* Chicago: University of Chicago Press.

Lubow, R. E. (1973). Latent inhibition. *Psychological Bulletin, 79,* 398–407.

Lysle, D. T., & Fowler, H. (1985). Inhibition as a "slave" process: Deactivation of conditioned inhibition through extinction of conditioned excitation. *Journal of Experimental Psychology: Animal Behavior Processes, 11,* 71–93.

Mackintosh, N. J. (1975). A theory of attention: Variation in the associability of stimuli with reinforcement. *Psychological Review, 82,* 276–298.

Maier, S. F., Rapaport, P., & Wheatley, K. L. (1976). Conditioned inhibition and the UCS–CS interval. *Animal Learning and Behavior, 4,* 217–220.

Marlin, N. A. (1982). Within-compound associations between the context and the conditioned stimulus. *Learning and Motivation, 13,* 526–541.

Nadel, L., & Willner, J. (1980). Context and conditioning: A place for space. *Physiological Psychology, 8,* 218–228.

Navarro, J. I., Hallam, S. C., Matzel, L. D., & Miller, R. R. (1989). Superconditioning and overshadowing. *Learning and Motivation, 20,* 130–152.

Owren, M. J., & Kaplan, P. S. (1981, April). *On the failure to extinguish Pavlovian conditioned inhibition: A test of a reinstatement hypothesis.* Paper presented at the meeting of the Midwestern Psychological Association, Detroit.

Pavlov, I. P. (1927). *Conditioned reflexes.* Oxford, England: Oxford University Press.

Pearce, J. M., & Hall, G. (1980). A model for Pavlovian learning: Variations in the effectiveness of conditioned but not of unconditioned stimuli. *Psychological Review, 87,* 532–552.

Pearce, J. M., Nicholas, D. J., & Dickinson, A. (1982). Loss of associability by a conditioned inhibitor. *Quarterly Journal of Psychology, 34,* 149–162.

Plotkin, H. C., & Oakley, A. D. (1975). Backward conditioning in the rabbit (*Oryctolagus cuniculus*). *Journal of Comparative and Physiological Psychology, 66*, 673–678.

Reberg, D. (1972). Compound tests for excitation in early acquisition and after prolonged extinction of conditioned suppression. *Learning and Motivation, 3*, 246–258.

Reiss, S., & Wagner, A. R. (1972). CS habituation produces a "latent inhibition effect" but no active "conditioned inhibition." *Learning and Motivation, 3*, 237–245.

Rescorla, R. A. (1966). Predictability and number of pairings in Pavlovian fear conditioning. *Psychonomic Science, 4*, 383–384.

Rescorla, R. A. (1967). Pavlovian conditioning and its proper control procedures. *Psychological Review, 74*, 71–80.

Rescorla, R. A. (1968a). Pavlovian conditioned fear in Sidman avoidance learning. *Journal of Comparative and Physiological Psychology, 65*, 55–60.

Rescorla, R. A. (1968b). Probability of shock in the presence and absence of CS in fear conditioning. *Journal of Comparative and Physiological Psychology, 66*, 1–5.

Rescorla, R. A. (1969a). Conditioned inhibition of fear resulting from negative CS–US contingencies. *Journal of Comparative and Physiological Psychology, 67*, 504–509.

Rescorla, R. A. (1969b). Pavlovian conditioned inhibition. *Psychological Bulletin, 72*, 77–94.

Rescorla, R. A. (1971). Variations in the effectiveness of reinforcement and nonreinforcement following prior inhibitory conditioning. *Learning and Motivation, 2*, 113–123.

Rescorla, R. A. (1979). Conditioned inhibition and excitation. In A. Dickinson & R. A. Boakes (Eds.), *Mechanisms of learning and motivation: A memorial volume to Jerzy Konorski* (pp. 83–110). Hillsdale, NJ: Lawrence Erlbaum Associates.

Rescorla, R. A. (1980). *Pavlovian second-order conditioning: Studies in associative learning.* Hillsdale, NJ: Lawrence Erlbaum Associates.

Rescorla, R. A. (1981). Within-signal learning in autoshaping. *Animal Learning and Behavior, 9*, 245–252.

Rescorla, R. A. (1982). Some consequences of associations between the excitor and the inhibitor in a conditioned inhibition paradigm. *Journal of Experimental Psychology; Animal Behavior Processes, 8*, 288–298.

Rescorla, R. A., & Holland, P. C. (1977). Associations in Pavlovian conditioned inhibition. *Learning and Motivation, 8*, 429–447.

Rescorla, R. A., & Wagner, A. R. (1972). A theory of Pavlovian conditioning: Variations in the effectiveness of reinforcement and nonreinforcement. In A. H. Black & W. H. Prokasy (Eds.), *Classical conditioning. II: Current research and theory* (pp. 64–99). New York: Appleton–Century–Crofts.

Schull, J. (1979). A conditioned opponent theory of Pavlovian conditioning and habituation. In G. H. Bower (Ed.), *The psychology of learning and motivation* (Vol. 13, pp. 57–90). New York: Academic Press.

Skinner, B. F. (1938). *The behavior of organisms.* New York: Appleton–Century.

Solomon, R. L. (1980). The opponent-process theory of motivation: The costs of pleasure and the benefits of pain. *American Psychologist, 35*, 691–712.

Solomon, R. L., & Corbit, J. D. (1974). An opponent-process theory of motivation. *Psychological Review, 81*, 119–145.

Thomas, D. A. (1979). Retention of conditioned inhibition in a bar-press suppression paradigm. *Learning and Motivation, 10*, 161–177.

Wagner, A. R. (1969). Stimulus validity and stimulus selection. In W. K. Honig & N. J. Mackintosh (Eds.), *Fundamental issues in associative learning* (pp. 90–122). Halifax, Canada: Dalhousie University Press.

Wagner, A. R. (1978). Expectancies and the priming of STM. In S. H. Hulse, H. Fowler, & W. K. Honig (Eds.), *Cognitive processes in animal behavior* (pp. 177–209). Hillsdale, NJ: Lawrence Erlbaum Associates.

Wagner, A. R., & Rescorla, R. A. (1972). Inhibition in Pavlovian conditioning: Applications of a theory. In R. A. Boakes & M. A. Halliday (Eds.), *Inhibition and learning* (pp. 301–336). London: Academic Press.

Weisman, R. G., & Litner, J. S. (1969). The course of Pavlovian excitation and inhibition of fear in rats. *Journal of Comparative and Physiological Psychology, 69,* 667–672.

Weisman, R. G., & Litner, J. S. (1971). Role of the intertrial interval in Pavlovian differential conditioning of fear in rats. *Journal of Comparative and Physiological Psychology, 74,* 211–218.

Williams, D. A., Travis, G. M., & Overmier, J. B. (1986). Within-compound associations modulate the relative effectiveness of differential and Pavlovian conditioned inhibition procedures. *Journal of Experimental Psychology: Animal Behavior Processes, 12,* 351–362.

Witcher, E. S. (1978). *Extinction of Pavlovian conditioned inhibition.* Unpublished doctoral dissertation, University of Massachusetts.

Witcher, E. S., & Ayres, J. J. B. (1984). A test of two methods for extinguishing Pavlovian conditioned inhibition. *Animal Learning and Behavior, 12,* 149–156.

Zimmer–Hart, C. L., & Rescorla, R. A. (1974). Extinction of Pavlovian conditioned inhibition. *Journal of Comparative and Physiological Psychology, 86,* 837–845.

11

Analysis of Aversive Events in Human Psychopathology: Fear and Avoidance

Thomas G. Stampfl
University of Wisconsin at Milwaukee

> *He's never killed anyone, but he might. He gets behind another patient and chokes him, and we know about it because the guy's feet are waving in the air. He always lets the guy go when he's unconscious, but some day he might not let go in time.*
> —(Karon & Vandenbos, 1981, p. 35)

The behavior of this hospitalized patient fits Skinner's (1953) statement, "We frequently observe strong behavior without knowing much about the circumstances which account for its strength" (p. 271). In fact, Karon and Vandenbos (1981) report that the patient had a long history of assaultive behavior. Although he had been treated for many years, there was nothing in his case history (voluminous psychiatric and social work records existed) to account for the assaultive behavior. Skinner (1953, 1954) might well postulate aversive events as representing the circumstances under which such strong behavior was acquired. But what might the aversive events be? If aversive events are implicated in the assaultive behavior, what direction would a learning-conditioning analysis suggest in understanding (and treating) this patient? How might the analysis be tested further in the animal laboratory?

A question of pressing importance for contemporary theoreticians interested in forging links between the animal laboratory and human psychopathology is the extent to which the principles, empirical findings, and other observations from laboratory research may be usefully directed to the human condition as seen in clinical practice. In research with nonhuman animals, aversive events play a major role as central causal factors in

363

phenomena similar to those observed in humans. Aversive events are likewise considered to be of major causal significance in virtually all major therapies, behavioral and psychodynamic, in understanding the complex manifestations of human psychopathological behavior (Hunt & Dyrud, 1968).

A major advantage of laboratory research is that aversive events are examined in greater detail with far more rigorous control than is possible in clinical experimentation. Moreover, exciting advances in the animal laboratory over the past two decades now offer a more complete picture of many facets of behavioral phenomena than was formerly possible (Domjan, 1987). The value of replicable specific behavioral effects (blocking, retardation, summation, preexposure, contrast, partial reinforcement, extinction, etc.) as the expression of recent systematic research in learning can hardly be overestimated. Such phenomena enable analyses of experimental events to be made in a way that was previously unattainable and perhaps unimaginable to early investigators in the field. Of primary significance is that the behavioral principles and phenomena appear to have wide generality over species, even extending from vertebrates to invertebrates (Bitterman, 1988; Couvillon & Bitterman, 1980). An obvious conclusion is that use of firmly grounded basic behavioral principles will lead to new and powerful applications to diverse social and economic problems. Practical applications of great scope and power now seem within the realm of possibility.

For the area of human psychopathology, it is of special significance that the discoveries made in the animal laboratory have been accompanied by remarkable progress in methodological sophistication. The relative certainty of the principles of behavior thus established creates the means of providing a solid scientific basis for many theories and models that shape contemporary clinical formulations—views that are presently chaotic, steeped in uncertainty, and whose proponents tend not to undertake research that would place their models on a scientific basis. Further evidence that the empirical findings of the laboratory are closely linked to those operative in humans can only increase the confidence of those theorists interested in linking the two areas of endeavor.

The main goal of this chapter is to provide a learning analysis of aversive events as they occur in natural environments for humans as this bears on the development, maintenance, and treatment of psychopathological disorders. A central limitation of laboratory animal research, in the study of basic behavioral principles, is the necessary requirement that the experimental situation be greatly simplified. The simplification required obscures relationships existing between basic principles of behavior and known features of human mental disorder (Stampfl, 1987). Furthermore, much of the experimental research with animals is directed at important problems not immediately related to human psychopathology. Under these circumstances, it is not surprising that difficulties exist in trying to convince critics who question the validity of extrapolations from animal research to human mental disorders that the two sets of phenomena are quite similar.

A careful consideration of properties of aversive events in natural settings clearly reveals characteristics that reflect principles obtained in basic laboratory research. At the same time, analysis of natural settings reveals information not readily obtainable in the simplified laboratory situation. This is especially so in specifying how laboratory principles may be combined to understand apparent paradoxes and other puzzles existing in the relationship between human and animal data. The analysis of natural settings permits the identification of laboratory principles critical to the bridge between the two sources of information. Skinner (1953) explicitly recognized the problem:

> It is true that the simplicity is to some extent artificial. We do not often find anything like it outside the laboratory—especially in the field of human behavior, which is of primary interest. . . . A common source of misunderstanding is the neglect of what happens when variables are combined in different ways. (pp. 204–205)

Finally, since many of the analyses delineated in this chapter are testable in the animal laboratory, the analysis itself may throw light on some difficult problems in the simplified laboratory situation.

AVERSIVE EVENTS AND AVOIDANCE BEHAVIOR

Fear-avoidance Model

One of the most common behaviors associated with aversive events is the strong tendency of organisms to escape from stimuli correlated with the aversive event. Escape from some aversive stimuli permits avoidance of other, or later, aversive stimuli. Avoidance models of learning developed from a vast research literature with nonhuman animals was early perceived as possessing theoretical generality to human psychopathology (Brown, 1961; Dollard & Miller, 1950; Mowrer, 1939; Shaw, 1946; Shoben, 1949; Skinner, 1953, 1954; Stampfl, 1961; Wolpe, 1958).

It was seen that avoidance behavior generated by aversive events in the laboratory provided a systematic data base for understanding the development and maintenance of human symptomatic behavior, the generation and use of defense mechanisms, and many other clinical phenomena observed with humans (e.g., Dollard & Miller, 1950; Shoben, 1949; Skinner, 1953, 1954). The opportunity to place clinical phenomena within the realm of thorough scientific analysis as Hull (1945) had once suggested now seemed possible.

Today, notable successes in therapies directed along lines suggested by the fear-avoidance model have occurred. Phobic disorders and especially the previously resistant to treatment obsessive-compulsive disorders are now considered the "treatment of choice" by "exposure" therapies. A degree of validation and consensus never attained for any treatment now exists for exposure procedures (Barlow & Wolfe, 1981). Numerous experimental studies suggest that the fear-avoidance model is useful for understanding many other mental disorders (see Levis & Hare, 1977, for a review).

Major investigators of animal learning have commented from time to time as to the relevance of their interpretations of various human mental disorders in terms of the learning process. Hull (1929) considered some "dilemmas" of Pavlovian extinction relevant to human phobias. He also presented a translation of psychoanalytic concepts into learning theory terms (Hull, 1939). Hull (1945) also reported similarities between his theorizing and the "flight of ideas" in "mania," and suggested that all practitioners of mental disorders might one day study animal learning to help determine causal factors in etiology and treatment "at least where research and creative scholarship are contemplated" (p. 60).

In 1938, Guthrie interpreted a variety of human mental disorders in a book solely concerned with this topic. Guthrie described his own "loss of voice" as an example of the process:

> Two of the three occasions on which I myself have suffered from a loss of voice and have been compelled to speak in a whisper were during the day preceding speeches which I had engaged myself to make without realizing that they were on subjects quite outside my own interests and range of information. This could not have been a coincidence. In my anxious state . . . it is impossible to produce anything but a whisper. But the voice does not return until the speech has been made by my obliging substitute. (p. 264)

Mowrer (1939) developed an avoidance model based on classical conditioning of fear, and instrumental responding seen as an escape from fear. Mowrer directly linked his fear-avoidance model with Freud's (1926/1936) signal theory of anxiety—a theory still widely maintained by many clinical practitioners (Michels, Frances, & Shear, 1985). Earlier, Hollingworth (1928) captured the essence of much of what is to be discussed in this chapter when he analyzed the behavior and treatment of a soldier suffering from a "traumatic neurosis." Even earlier, Rivers (1920) insightfully examined his treatment of World War I battle casualties and other cases. In contrast to all other medical practitioners of the World War I period, Rivers successfully utilized treatment techniques surprisingly consistent with a fear-avoidance-extinction model.

Objections to the Avoidance Model

Despite the demonstrated efficacy of the fear-avoidance model for therapeutic purposes as well as other striking successes of learning-conditioning analyses (e.g., Siegel, 1979, see Kalish, 1981, for an extensive review), the study of relevant phenomena in the animal laboratory progressively became less favorably viewed by clinical theorists and even by theorists identified with the behavior therapy movement (Barlow, 1982; Rachman, 1976, 1977; Wilson, 1982). Domjan (1987) commented on the extrapolation from animals to humans, "Such enthusiastic embrace of animal research has been discouraged by increasing evidence of the complexity of various forms of human behavior" (pp. 558–559).

Tuma and Maser (1985), editors of the influential National Institute of Mental Health-sponsored volume concerning anxiety and human mental disorders, expressed their evaluation of several chapters dealing with animal research when they said: "The laboratory seldom closely approximates the complexities of living with which organisms in the natural environment must cope. One goal for the next generation of researchers is to facilitate making laboratory settings more representative of human experience" (p. xxii).

This statement is consistent with the main theme of the present chapter. The limitations advanced by informed critics (e.g., Mineka, 1985) rest heavily on the assumption that since laboratory animal research fails to manifest phenomena related to human psychopathology, it therefore reflects intrinsic deficiencies in the generality of principles such research has disclosed. This assumption is questioned in this chapter. It is replaced by the assumption that a detailed analysis of the complex natural setting helps resolve limitations, and makes the human situation quite interpretable in terms of principles from the research laboratory.

The Treatment Model

Observations of natural avoidance phenomena were prompted by the development of a therapeutic method (implosive therapy) for use with humans undergoing treatment for a wide range of mental disorders (Stampfl, 1961, 1966, 1970; Stampfl & Levis, 1967, 1969, 1973, 1976). The model depended heavily on a two-factor, fear-avoidance model of learning. The main therapeutic change agent was that of exposure to conditioned aversive stimuli—an extinction paradigm.

Initially, experience gained while doing "play" therapy with emotionally disturbed children had suggested that virtually all of the effects of the therapy could be accounted for by exposure to stimulus features of the play material that reactivated aversive events in the child's history. No verbal interpretations were made to the child at any time in reference to the "meaning" of the play activity, but the aversive events were typically repeated in the play activity of the child. Repetition of the aversive events progressively led to more intense aversive events that were replayed in the therapy. Some stimulus feature of the play material appeared to activate the replay of an actual past aversive event. Repetition of this event led to a reduction of emotionality followed by the playing of a new aversive event. Replaying an aversive event thus seemed to be an excellent reactivator for the elicitation of other aversive events. An extinction model based on repeated exposure to stimulus features of the play material and the child's behavior (seen as response-produced stimuli) was interpreted (eventually) as a viable explanation for the effects of the treatment. Clinical improvement in the child correlated with progressive reduction in the emotionality that resulted from the procedure. Thus, the principle of extinction of emotionality conditioned to stimuli related to aversive events seemed sufficient to account for the behavioral changes that occurred.

Early use of this model in the late 1950s with adult patients employing imagery, fantasy enactment, and *in vivo* reproductions of the stimulus features of aversive events appeared highly successful. Clinical improvement in the symptomatic behavior of a wide range of patients followed use of the procedure (implosive therapy). Substantial changes in personality functioning also seemed to be a correlate of the treatment. Many controlled studies of the effectiveness of the therapy including some with psychotic patients were conducted (see Boudewyns & Shipley, 1983; Levis & Hare, 1977, for reviews).

Aversive Events in Natural Settings

The rigorous use of an animal model permitted observations of naturally occurring phenomena within a learning-conditioning framework that are unlikely when other theoretical models guide treatment strategy. It was early recognized that many of these observations were testable in the animal laboratory. The underlying assumption is that a close parallel, in principle, exists between animal and human behavior. If principles of animal behavior can be generalized to humans then observations of human behavior may highlight principles and features that are generalizable to animals. This view is consistent with Brown (1961) when he commented: "But most research workers wish to know whether functional relations obtained with one organism can be generalized to other organisms including man. Actually, the process is a two-way one. *We can learn important things about rats' fears from human beings and vice versa* [italics added]" (p. 169).

The use of a two-factor avoidance model, with therapy based mainly on the principle of extinction, offered a unique opportunity to study the properties of aversive events and avoidance behavior as they occur in natural settings.

As early as 1959, it was evident that stimuli comprising aversive events were multiple, complex, and sequentially organized, and that contextual stimuli played an important role in the expression and extinction of the effects of aversive stimuli. Further analysis of aversive events over a period of many years of using implosive therapy revealed other features of aversive events and avoidance behavior that called into question any important differences between behavior in the animal laboratory and human behavior as seen in clinical practice. Learning theorists had noted some of these features (e.g., Hull, 1943, pp. 204–206) but with rare exception they were ignored in avoidance research with animals. Randich and Ross (1985) discussed some of the reasons why context, though well known by early workers, received little systematic research in the laboratory (but see McAllister & McAllister, 1965, 1971).

Exciting to me at the time, aside from the development of the therapy itself, was the possibility of direct tests in the animal laboratory of the features and principles that seemed operative in human psychopathology (Krasner, 1970, p. 205).

A summary of behavioral features that appear to play a key role in human psychopathology includes the sequential order of CSs and complexity of CSs; the role of context (external and internal); the role of multiple CSs, multiple USs, and multiple contexts; moving as contrasted to static CSs; CSs as correlates or sources of USs; components of the US as CS; pain and fear as CSs; CSs as representations of USs; and unique forms of pain as a consequence of strong USs. Some of the principles of behavior that play a key role involve secondary intermittent reinforcement, work requirement or response cost, time out from avoidance, alternative responding, associative cue reactivation, and overlapping generalization of extinction gradients for both CSs and contexts. Other standard principles of learning-conditioning, such as higher-order conditioning, generalization, and intermittent primary reinforcement, are also involved in the analysis.

Finally, some general observations should be made. The sheer number and variety of aversive events is far greater in the human case than in the laboratory. The features and principles listed earlier are embedded in a set of natural aversive events, and their unique combination generates the particular psychopathological phenomena observed. The effects of such unique organizations are directly testable in the animal laboratory. Intuitively plausible explanations from learning principles to disorders in humans, though valuable, are not sufficient alone to demonstrate the relationship. Direct tests in the laboratory fulfill the Tuma and Maser (1985) requirement for defining the relevance of animal research to human mental disorder.

At first blush, the enormous complexity of aversive events in the human case appear to doom the investigator to precisely the chaos Pavlov feared. Progress in the animal laboratory over the past years, however, now makes the study of complex cases feasible though, of course, still exceedingly difficult. Nevertheless, Pavlov's caution remains valid in one respect. Conventional laboratory research demands that the effects of independent variables be isolated in order to permit quantitative evaluation. In order to evaluate the contribution of stimuli in complex situations, that is, to tease out the relative contributions of controlling stimuli among the multiple variables and principles involved, would require an extensive paradigmatic experimental program. Programs of this magnitude would entail prohibitive laboratory expenditures of time, animals, and equipment. Nor would there be any guarantee of success. Something of the same problem was reported by D'Amato and Van Sant (1988) in their study of human concept formation in monkeys.

Plan of the Exposition

The plan is to analyze a relatively simple case to illustrate some general features that must be considered. The second step is to describe some common childhood aversive events in the history of adult clinical cases. A third step identifies the critical properties of the events seen from a learning-conditioning analysis. A final step briefly illustrates use of the analysis to make unique predictions for rats relevant to human phobias (Stampfl, 1987). These predictions help resolve the long-standing neurotic paradox (Eglash, 1952; Freud, 1926/1936; Mowrer, 1948, 1950, 1952) frequently advanced as the major challenge for any learning-based model of human psychopathology (Eysenck, 1976, p. 252).

PROPERTIES OF AVERSIVE EVENTS
IN THE NATURAL SETTING

Owner–Dog–Newspaper Example

Since a learning analysis of human aversive events becomes extraordinarily complex, a less complex example helps illustrate the form of the analysis to follow. Consider the situation where a dog is punished for some behavior by being struck with a rolled-up newspaper.

The newspaper is picked up, rolled up, and the dog is swatted on some part of its anatomy (e.g., the nose). Usually, a stern tone of voice precedes and accompanies the punishment. Following the "swat," the dog may run behind a chair or couch or into another room. Escape behavior of this kind may precede or follow being hit by the newspaper.

Assuming that the foregoing segments are "attended to" or "sampled" by the dog, one can identify separate segments that are potentially conditionable: tone of voice, picking up the newspaper, rolling up newspaper, approaching, raising newspaper, hitting the animal on nose or other parts of the anatomy.

It will be noted that stimulus segments are sequentially organized in a spatial-temporal order. One may designate the tone of voice as CS1, picking up the newspaper (CS2), approaching the animal (CS3), raising the newspaper (CS4), sight of the newspaper descending on the nose (CS5). Contextual stimuli may change throughout the sequence; the dog may run behind a chair or couch, into another room or even escape to the outside. The dog may have to be caught and held in order to swat the nose. "Holding the dog" stimuli then become relevant. When some specific behavior precedes the sequence, the response-produced stimuli of this behavior may be regarded as CS1. In this respect, however, behavior preceding the sequence is itself usually organized into a series of CSs within the behavior. In other words, the dog's behavior preceding "tone of voice" stimulus may be separated into a CS1, CS2, CS3, . . . n series. These response-produced stimuli may also correlate with contextual changes.

Later, the dog's behavior is modified by earlier stimulus segments such as tone of voice, and finally by initial segments of the response-produced behavior. What actually function as CSs in a particular organism must be determined on a case-by-case basis. The dog may be swatted on its nose and then on its rear. Different behaviors may be punished on different occasions in different rooms of the house or outside of the house.

It is important to note that the newspaper is the source of the US, the impact of the newspaper on the nose disturbing the receptors ultimately generating "painful" sensations (UCR), and both the newspaper and the dog's owner are moving in the sequence. The assumption made here is that CS sequences, including the movement components, enter the associative network. They may be reactivated by a component of the original event.

Conditioned stimuli in the animal laboratory are typically discrete and frequently only a single CS is used. Contextual stimuli are relatively constant. The predominant US is footshock. In contrast, in the natural setting the CS is complex, is constantly changing (the CS moves), and multiple CSs are involved. The multiple CSs are sequentially organized (one CS or cue precedes another), and pronounced contextual changes are present.

Aversive Events for Children

A limited number of aversive events as they occur in childhood for many persons experiencing mental disorder is listed below. The events may follow "transgressive" behaviors or may occur in the absence of any consistent specific behavior.

Children may be slapped, punched, shaken, thrown, choked, pinched, kicked, bitten, burned, locked up or tied up, and deprived in various ways. They may be struck with a variety of objects (sticks, brooms, coat hangers, ironing cords, switches, whips, etc.). Numerous objects may be thrown at them. They may be made to sit on a shelf in a clothes closet for hours and even days or tickled in a manner that borders on torture. Soap, handkerchiefs, and other material may be forced into their mouths. They may be ducked in water, bags may be placed over their heads, blankets may pin them to the floor. Humiliating actions may be imposed such as dressing them in ludicrous costumes or placing them in play pens to be treated like babies. Extreme verbal abuse is common. Sexual abuse is common. They may be deliberately frightened when threats of bodily injury or worse are directed at them. Screaming and yelling frequently accompany the punishing events.

The list can easily be extended. One patient, for example, reported hundreds of painful enemas given over a period of many years. By the patient's own calculation, the number exceeded 2,000, and this was just one of a great number of other punishments he experienced some of which were truly extraordinary. The symptomatic behavior experienced by this patient was also truly extraordinary.

Clearly, the events for humans might be applied to the dog. The dog might be repeatedly struck with a stick, broom, coat hanger, and so on. It could be thrown, punched, kicked, or tied up. Nearly all of the events described for humans might apply. Objects could be thrown at the dog, material could be forced into its mouth, etc. The stimuli aversively conditioned would then differ sharply from the newspaper example. Although the aversive events commonly follow specific "transgressive" (forbidden) behaviors this is not always the case in either humans or dogs. In some cases, the delivery of aversive events occurs because of propensities in the deliverer, irrespective of any specific acts on the part of the subject to whom the event is delivered. Parents or parent surrogates, siblings, and peers readily engage in delivering unpredictable punishments, on occasion, for no particular behavior of the recipient. Naturally occurring aversive events frequently reflect this form of unpredictability.

Despite the obvious nature of the multiplicity of stimuli involved in such aversive sequences, analyses by learning theorists tend to omit such complexities in favor of assuming a single CS controls the symptomatic expressions of humans. Limitations on application from the research laboratory are then advanced because of disparities existing between fear-avoidance responding in the simplified laboratory situation and the far more complex human situation. The systematic differences alleged to exist between the two situations ignore actual differences in the original conditioning events that constitute the history of the organisms' behavior.

As previously mentioned, the CS sequence is assumed to include the movement components that enter the associative network and can be reactivated at a later time when appropriate reactivation cues are present. A further assumption is that they tend to be reactivated in the sequential order experienced at the time of the original conditioning. Clinical practice reveals the successive emergence of stimuli in sequential order.

The question of the potential range of stimuli conditionable must be considered. Pavlov (1927) voiced his concern in relation to what is conditionable:

> We must now take some account of the agencies which can be transferred into conditioned stimuli. This is not so easy a problem as appears at first sight. Of course to give a general answer is very simple; any agent in nature which acts on any adequate receptor apparatus of an organism can be made into a conditioned stimulus for that organism. *This general statement, however, needs both amplification and restriction* [italics added]. (p. 38)

It is beyond the scope of this chapter to consider the exceptions alluded to by Pavlov. Of interest, however, is that some of them relate to complex natural settings. The simple assumption made here is that a very wide range of stimuli are potentially conditionable. In the human treatment situation there are some subtle cues that play a critical role when extinction trials are used for treatment.

Identifying the Original Conditioning Event

There are some major difficulties associated with the straightforward use of a laboratory-based extinction model when applied to behavior change in human patients. For example, laboratory research typically is concerned with original conditioning events. Extinction is conducted under the original stimulus conditions known to be present when the aversive event occurred. Identification of early aversive events in humans hypothesized to account for symptomatic behavior is quite another matter. As Skinner (1954) remarked, "Early punishment of sexual behavior is an observable fact that undoubtedly leaves behind a changed organism" (p. 231). Huschka

(1943) reported some descriptions of mothers' reports of punishment for their children's sexual behavior:

> Deprived him of comic strips and his favorite food, eggs. Shamed him saying the masturbation was due "to the animal in him." Later threatened, "You're going to get softening of the brain; you're going to be like Gerald" (a "silly" boy whom the children called "Crazy"). Later threatened reform school and put him on a reform school regime. (p. 59)

> Mother slaps his hands and whips him for it. Tells him "everyone will be talking about him" and that "he'll have to go to the hospital where the doctor will cut his penis off and he won't be able to urinate." (p. 58)

Another mother said, "I spanked him terribly and told him if he ever did it again I was going to cut his hands off" (p. 59).

Children punished for sexual behavior may well display symptomatic behavior later in life as Skinner (1954) suggested. When events of this nature are not accessible to memory the problem of reproducing the original events appears. Fortunately, answers to this problem are provided from the animal laboratory, and from clinical practice (e.g., implosive therapy, Stampfl, 1970; Stampfl & Levis, 1967, 1969, 1973, 1976).

Hollingworth

The work of Hollingworth (1928) helps to clarify the exposition. On the basis of his treatment of a World War I soldier suffering from a traumatic event, Hollingworth offered some insightful observations that are relevant today. In presenting his laws of redintegration, Hollingworth recognized the importance of stimulus complexity, complexity of the fear response, summation of fear stimuli, initial context, varied contexts in extinction procedures, and subjective events as well as objective events functioning as stimuli in the redintegrative sequence.

It is noteworthy that Hollingworth, a past president of the American Psychological Association, chose to illustrate his general laws of redintegration with a clinical example:

> For this we need not a careful and quantitatively determined picture, but a genuine one, which is familiar and intelligible. We choose, as the general field for our example, certain of the activities of a neurotic soldier, especially those events which we call his trembling, stammering and running away. The particular soldier we here have in mind was named S. (pp. 80–81)

Number and Variety of Aversive Events

Many human patients, especially the more severe cases, experience a very large number and variety of aversive events in many different contexts. The sheer number experienced over long periods of time "fill" the associative network with numerous sequential stimulus constellations. The anxiety (fear/aversiveness) conditioned to some of the early stimuli in the sequential set of stimulus segments is thus cued off by numerous potential reactivators leading to an extensive set of "defensive" or symptomatic behaviors. Escape responses to early reactivated aversive stimuli permit complete avoidance of later ones. Skinner (1953) refers to the difference in number of aversive events as having powerful effects for difficult cases: "When many different kinds of responses have been punished under many different circumstances, conditioned aversive stimuli may be widely distributed in the environment" (p. 367). Dollard and Miller (1950) also seem to be saying something similar:

> Although there is no direct experimental evidence on the point, we have every reason to expect fears to be more resistant to extinction when they are attached to a greater number of variable cues (that are sometimes present and sometimes absent) in complex stimulus situations. (p. 73)

Complexity of CS, Moving vs. Static Stimuli, Context

Hollingworth (1928, p. 79) captures complexity, movement, and context in his description of a snake as a stimulus for fear:

> In the first place the "appearance of the snake" is complex. The snake itself is an elaborate pattern of occurrences—color, shape, size, movements. Moreover, the "appearance" implies the presence of a further background from which this pattern emerges. And there are adjacent objects, the time, place, and other attendant circumstances. The fear is not of the snake but of the total situation and circumstances.

It is this conception of the stimulus (CSs) that Hollingworth uses in understanding and treating the traumatized soldier. Hollingworth, however, doesn't consider what the stimulus might be if, in fact, the snake inflicted injury. What stimuli would then enter the associative network?

In the human situation where punishment is inflicted, the stimulus (parent, sibling, peer) moves toward the recipient and is followed by aversive USs. There are facial contortions, mouth movements, and eye movements that function in compound with larger movements prior to any of the punishments as previously described. In fact, the stimulus represents "movement within movement" in compound with visual, auditory, tactile, and other stimuli. Moving CSs are especially potent when they serve as the source of the US. The sight of the leg that delivers the kick, the arm that delivers the punch, the hands that pull the hair or ears generate intense emotional responses in the human when combined with the aversive stimuli that have been described. Threats may be pantomimed. Extinction trials with humans during therapy reveal an extensive set of stimuli that produce emotional reactions of great intensity when activated.

Conditioning almost always takes place in specific contexts. Contextual stimuli may be organized sequentially. That is, a series of contexts may immediately precede the context where the aversive event occurs. A further complication is that an operant response frequently terminates contextual stimuli as well as the set of CSs by a person's escaping to another context before or after the US is delivered. For example, a boy enters his house and is immediately threatened. He moves through the kitchen into the basement where he is beaten. He escapes and runs into the backyard. Outdoor stimuli precede kitchen stimuli that are followed by basement stimuli that are followed by USs terminated by escape to backyard stimuli.

In summary, when complex CSs are conditioned, many more stimuli (external and internal) serve as potential reactivators in the environment. Complex stimuli are easily "discriminated," and stimulus movement accentuates the sampling or attending that facilitates conditioning (see Freyd, 1987; Pavlov, 1927, p. 20).

Fear as CS and Pain as US and CS

Hollingworth describes the complexity of the sensory effects of fear:

> The fear which ensues is also a complex pattern of events. For one thing there is a unique set of sensory qualities,—tension, chill, palpitation, dizziness, and varied quivers. There is an abrupt halt in current activities. Excitement, confusion, panic may occur, and such actions as screaming, blanching, trembling, fleeing or fainting. The situation is colored by disagreeableness, and perhaps also by such feelings as shame and despair. Some of these events are reported in common by the actor and by other observers,—as screaming, trembling, running. Other features can be directly observed and reported only by the fearful,—as the dizziness, the shame, the chill, tension and unpleasantness. (1928, pp. 79–80)

The import of the quotation is clear. Once fear is conditioned to sequential constellations of stimuli, the sensory effects of the fear itself, when followed by aversive USs, become CSs for further fear responses. If mild fear responses could be induced quickly by artificial means (e.g., electrical cortical stimulation), one could arrange a US (footshock) to follow that would evoke intense fear. The sensory effects of low fear (cortical stimulation) then would function as a CS for high fear (see Mowrer, 1960, pp. 131–132). One would observe intense fear evoked by stimuli that ordinarily evoke only mild fear.

Many sensory effects of fear (anxiety) are observed in human patients during extinction. Conditioning as described herein mandates that sensory effects of fear be identified for their possible role as CSs. Sensory effects of the kind described by Hollingworth (e.g., tingling) are commonplace.

Another phenomenon emerges when a patient focuses on the fear response. Many patients report internal stimuli such as a balloon expanding in their chest or icicles creeping up their legs or rusty nails pressing inside their necks. The list is extensive. Patients use such metaphors to describe their sensations, but the metaphors frequently relate to key features of aversive events later recovered. However, a few patients report that they experience the balloon, icicle, or nail as something real existing within them. Of course, patients are aware (with rare exceptions) that this is impossible. The "phantom limb" experience is perhaps the best analogy. The amputated limb is not there, but sensations experienced make it feel as if it actually exists. The sensory effect itself (balloon expanding) is embedded in many other stimuli. Extinction trials with "balloons" and "nails" considered as response-produced components of the fear reaction frequently reactivate other aversive events. It is surprising how often reified sensory effects (balloons, ropes, nails, clock gear, fish line, etc.) are present in newly recovered aversive events. Such internalized objects disappear from the record with repeated extinction trials. When the object is related to a new aversive event, perhaps as a contextual detail, it is given special emphasis during extinction trials.

Strong fear reactions as well as weak ones commonly precede unconditioned aversive stimulation. A father uses a belt to whip his child. Taking off the belt becomes one of the CSs for strong fear reactions. The sensory effects of the fear then precede aversive USs. Sensory effects of intense fear function like a CS for strong fear. Sight of the belt taken off induces a chain reaction in which intense fear generates more fear. The child may experience fear for a long time following sight of the belt taken off, even when not punished on that occasion, as a function of the chain reaction. The process, however, is more complex than described here.

Aversive USs producing physical pain function in a similar manner. Mild pain when followed by USs that generate severe pain conditions the mild pain to act as a CS for intense fear. That the fear response in such situations may include internalized (synthetic) pain sensations that function like internalized objects (e.g., balloons) seems quite possible. Conditioned "pain" sensations then would mimic "real" pain. Little experience with "pain" patients is available with extinction procedures (but see Horowitz, 1985).

Role of Multiple CSs, Multiple Contexts, and Multiple USs

The wide range of stimulus compounds organized sequentially leads to conditions that maximize resistance to extinction. Contexts that are escaped from function like supercomplex CSs. Escape (avoidance) behavior receives maximal reinforcement under such circumstance. A drunken father takes off his belt when child enters house from outside. Child runs into the kitchen and out into the backyard, successfully escaping a beating by the pursuing father. The father sobers up and the child eventually returns to the house where no beating occurs. Powerful tendencies to avoid are reinforced in such sequences. A very large number of stimuli may then elicit avoidance responses characterized by "flight."

A child may be punished in each of the contexts, with different aversive USs occurring in each context. The child may be kicked and thrown about in one context, slapped in another context, and beaten by a belt in another. Note that crying, pleading, and other behaviors may reduce the severity of the beating or perhaps prevent it completely. Operant crying, and pleading may then be reinforced as escape-avoidance behaviors. There are endless variations on such themes. The symptomatic behavior of patients frequently relates to the nature of the escape-avoidance responses that are effective in reducing or preventing the punishment. Solomon and Wynne (1953, p. 14) reported "perceptual" defense in some of their dogs, that is, a dog shied away from the gate and hid its head in a corner so as not to see an open gate (CS). If reinforced, instead of the experimenter-designated jumping response, this avoidance of CS response would be strengthened.

Secondary Intermittent Reinforcement

Secondary intermittent reinforcement slows the extinction process. Whenever aversive stimuli early in the sequence (CS1) are activated a sufficient number of times, CS1 undergoes extinction. Ordinarily, the instrumental response made to CS1 precludes exposure to subsequent aversive stimuli (avoidance). When escape responses fail to be made to CS1, exposure to subsequent aversive stimuli (CS2) occurs. Since CS2 has retained its aversiveness, the instrumental response (symptomatic behavior or defense mechanisms) is made to CS2. However, the aversiveness of CS1 is reconditioned to fear based on its pairing with CS2 in a manner similar to higher-order conditioning. CS2 also extinguishes since each time it reconditions CS1 an extinction trial occurs for CS2. When CS2 no longer is sufficiently aversive to initiate instrumental symptomatic behavior (avoidance) the activation of CS3 renews aversiveness to CS2. The process is repeated for the entire chain. Secondary intermittent reinforcement is an important factor in the high resistance to extinction of human symptomatic behavior. Responses to early stimulus segments preclude exposure to subsequent segments in the sequence. Research in my laboratory in 1959 indicated that the principle of secondary intermittent reinforcement is an important factor in generating high resistance to extinction in rats (see London, 1964). Subsequent laboratory research with rats prompted by this interpretation (Boyd & Levis, 1976; Kostanek & Sawrey, 1965; Levis, 1979; Levis & Boyd, 1979) supported the principle of intermittent secondary reinforcement which was derived from an analysis of symptomatic behavior in humans.

Work Requirement or Response Cost, Timeout from Avoidance

Secondary intermittent reinforcement is not sufficient to account for the extraordinary resistance to extinction of human symptomatic behavior. Such behaviors (e.g., phobias) last for years (Stampfl, 1987). Specifically, the work requirement or response cost is minimized the earlier the response is made to the CS sequence and can thus contribute to the strength of symptoms (Stampfl, 1987). This factor is seen most easily in phobic behaviors, but is also present in other disorders. Timeout from avoidance is an additional factor providing further reinforcement for responses that occur early in the sequence. A study by Baron, DeWaard, and Lipson, (1977) is especially instructive here. Timeout from avoidance could occur in a context (staying on a shelf inserted in the Skinner box) different from the one in which avoidance training was conducted. Such a timeout had a strong effect on avoidance. In the Sidman avoidance schedule used, timeout on the "shelf" resulted in a marked reduction in number of shocks received, compared with rats in various control conditions.

Alternative Responding

A further principle accounting for high resistance to extinction of human symptomatic behavior is that organisms can respond in ways that bypass aversive stimuli while minimizing the loss of positive reinforcers (e.g., food). Such behavior may be considered maladaptive if the alternative set of responses results in the postponement of reinforcers or reflects loss of highly preferred behaviors. A simple example of alternative responding is traveling by train or automobile by a person who has a phobia of traveling by air. Alternative responding differs from typical laboratory avoidance in that primary reinforcers typically follow the alternative response.

Whiting and Mowrer (1943) showed that hungry rats would go to a goal box for food by way of an alternate runway as long as 40 feet if they were shocked on the way to the goal box in the preferred 5-foot runway. Azrin and Holz (1966) found that pigeons given very mild tail shock (50 volts) continued key pecking when a single response manipulandum was available; response rate was reduced by only 10%, compared with a nonshock condition. When two response keys were available, the same shock intensity when delivered to the preferred key resulted in a 100% shift to the alternate nonpreferred key. Azrin and Holz point out that even a 60-volt tail shock delivered when only one key is present reduces rate of responding by only 30%.

As with tail shock, essentially the same effect could doubtless be produced by pairing strong aversive CSs with the preferred key. Pecking on the alternative key would preclude exposure to aversive CSs paired with the preferred key. Resistance to extinction would increase because the organism would not receive extinction trials for the aversive CSs when pecking on the alternate key. Alternative responding can be maladaptive in a variety of ways, for example, in presenting a reduced number of positive reinforcers for the alternative response. Alternative responding, however, is a robust phenomenon. In both the Whiting and Mowrer (1943), and Azrin and Holz (1966) studies, the shift to alternative responding is virtually 100%. Alternative responding is sensitive to small degrees of aversiveness. It is hypothesized to account for the avoidance of reactivating cues with very low degrees of aversiveness.

Humans sometimes employ alternative responding with little loss of reinforcement. Reactivating cues are aversive, and it is possible to bypass reactivating cues by alternative responding. People, situations, and activities with a relatively high density of reactivating cues are bypassed with behavior that results in little, if any, loss of positive reinforcers. Unique characteristics of personality functioning are presumably "guided" by differential densities of reactivating cues present in the environment.

Duration and Severity of US-produced Physical Pain

In the natural setting, the painful consequences of aversive events may last for hours, days, or weeks. Sustained tissue injury (welts, bruises) and worse (broken bones) may result from childhood discipline or natural events. Electric shock, the US typically used in the animal laboratory, on the other hand has transient painful effects. When pain persists following aversive events, additional effects may be generated. The degree of avoidance to stimuli correlated with sustained severe physical injury is not available in the animal laboratory (see Pavlov, 1927, pp. 29–31, for discussion of physical injury in classical conditioning).

Associative Cue Network: Reactivating Stimuli

Hollingworth described the behavior of his soldier as quite ordinary. However, if reactivating cues were present appreciable changes were observed:

> But certain events would, if he were in their proximity, speedily touch off a characteristic pattern of activity, including either stammering, trembling or running aimlessly away, or some combination of these. A sudden sound, a slap on the back, the passing of an officer in uniform, a dog fight, or the handling of weapons or knives,—any one of these was commonly followed by a mild panic in which trembling, stammering or running might appear. (1928, p. 81)

Hollingworth acknowledged that the case of the soldier illustrates in exaggerated form the functioning of redintegrative (reactivating cues) in the general environment.

Numerous additional reactivators are described. Some are relatively weak, others are strong. They obey summation, temporal sequence, and context influence. The function of stimuli that evoke other associations through various "reminder" or "retrieval" cues is universally acknowledged by virtually all clinical practitioners and learning theorists. However, systematic investigation of "memory reactivation" is relatively recent (e.g., Riccio & Ebner, 1981; Spear & Miller, 1981).

Associative Cue Network: What is Reactivated?

Hollingworth (1928, p. 87) emphasizes that *"subjective as well as objective events participate in redintegrative sequences."* He states:

> But S reports that other events, not accessible to our general inspection, also occurred. Not only did he see his own trembling and hear his own stammering voice. Sudden stimuli, he says, were followed also by feelings of confusion, dread, excitement. There were 'prickling' sensations, wide-spread strains and tensions, 'numbness' in parts of his body, and sometimes what he called 'pictures of the battle' and 'gloomy thoughts about the war.' (1928, p. 88)

Unfortunately, Hollingworth focused his attention exclusively on the redintegrative cues and did not directly examine details of the actual traumatic event. The approach advocated here is that aversive events in the history of this particular soldier contributed to the long-lasting symptoms he expressed. As previously noted, aversive events are linked by commonalities that exist between them. Not only are stimuli linked in a single aversive event, but multiple aversive events are linked. Exposure to stimuli representing one aversive event tends to reactivate initial stimulus segments for other aversive events.

THE CS–US DISTINCTION

CS as Representation of the US

The drawing of a parallel between classical conditioning of fear/aversiveness with nonhuman animals and the human condition encounters a major difficulty. When Pavlovian extinction is used as a treatment manipulation it is imperative that CSs be differentiated from USs. Although this is easy to accomplish in the animal laboratory, it is far more difficult to do in naturally occurring human situations. The difficulty arises because reactivated stimuli in humans frequently include many of the original US components. The question is whether or not to provide repeated extinction trials that include the reactivated US components. The belief is present, though seldom explicitly stated, that some reactivated stimuli function as "true" USs (the term "US" is sometimes used to describe a "first-order" CS that conditions a "second-order" CS). Even conservative workers in the animal area sometimes seem to suggest that humans may differ from animals in key features of conditioning. McAllister and McAllister (1979) explicitly commented on this issue when they discussed Eysenck's (1979) theory that strong CSs (under certain conditions) may enhance fear and are immune from the effects of extinction (function like true USs).

> It may turn out to be the case that enhancement can be demonstrated with humans but not with animals. . . . it seems possible that the reported increases in neurotic symptoms . . . are explicable in terms of symbolic processes. That is, the UCS and hence, the UCR may be supplied through imaginal processes. If so, of course, "enhancement" would be simply the result of further self-administered conditioning trials. (1979, p. 177)

In effect, imagining a US event might function as a true US, that is, would strengthen fear and maintain avoidance responding indefinitely.

There is little doubt that this view permeated clinical practice in the past. Even Dollard and Miller (1950) seemed to agree. They described the effects of too deep interpretations as equivalent to the client sitting on a chair where electric shock is delivered. Their comments were made before laboratory "response prevention" studies of avoidance were undertaken.

Strong emotionality is observed during initial response prevention trials followed by extinction effects with more trials.

The necessity of "dosing anxiety" in therapy was axiomatic in clinical practice several decades ago. Many contemporary clinicians still adhere to this belief, but it is no longer an axiomatic principle of therapy. Although seldom stated explicitly, the view of the equivalence of CS and US permeates contemporary clinical practice even for many who adhere to a signal theory of anxiety. Of course, few clinicians think in terms of what is CS and what is US.

There is a complication that makes understandable the confusion concerning this problem. When, for example, strong fear responses generate behaviors that are followed by true USs (or strong CSs) there is reason to believe that CSs that evoke such fear-CRs will not readily undergo extinction. For example, panic reactions of humans in natural settings may be followed by painful injuries. In the frantic behavior that correlates with panic, persons may injure themselves by falling, bumping objects, and so on. Skin lacerations or even broken bones may result from such behavior. More commonly, other aversive events follow panic behavior, such as embarrassing social consequences.

An example from the animal laboratory illustrates the principle. When "forced exposure" to the CS was originally used in the Solomon, Kamin, and Wynne study (1953, p. 292) one dog "smashed its head against the glass" barrier that prevented the instrumental jumping-the-hurdle-response. Fear to the CS might be strengthened on that trial since crashing into the glass barrier may well be regarded as an aversive US. If the experimenter had delivered shock on a response-prevention trial following "frantic behavior" this would simply have represented another conditioning trial for the CS. When the animal's behavior during response-prevention generates a US other than that used in training, a similar interpretation is possible. A parallel may be drawn to the self-punitive paradigm that Brown (1969) and others have extensively studied.

A second reason for the "dosing anxiety" assumption is the observation that clients in therapy appear to get "worse" when strong emotionality is evoked in the therapy session. In response prevention studies, animals in the initial stage certainly appear to be far more "upset" than animals not given such trials. The counterintuitive conclusion is that higher levels of fear during extinction lead to better terminal behaviors reflecting less fear (see Bouton, 1988; Denny, 1976; Richardson, Riccio, & Ress, 1988, for similar interpretations of the role of increased fear in extinction).

A third complication is that some of the original conditioning events in the history of adults suffering from mental disorder are so aversive that therapists have difficulty in even discussing such events. Reproducing strong original CSs and USs symbolically (in imagery or fantasy) is extremely aversive to therapists as well as to clients. Yet the failure to incorporate critical aversive stimuli in the extinction-therapy leaves them untouched in the associative network. Later, if reactivated, such stimuli renew the symptomatic behavior. Therapy may appear successful but if stimulus components of the original conditioning events are not subjected to extinction "relapse" may result. Pavlov (1927, pp. 313–315) described the "relapse" of a dog exposed to the Petrograd flood of 1924. Following successful "treatment" to laboratory stimuli (as indexed by recovery of conditioned reflexes disrupted following the flood) the dog's behavior reverted to the original "pathological" behavior. The critical stimulus, introduced by Pavlov for the first time, was a small pool of water on the floor of the experimental room. It should be noted that the "pathological" behavior of this dog went well beyond the simple disruption of conditioned reflexes.

Rivers (1920) treated many World War I soldiers by having them discuss, think about, and relive original aversive events of the battlefield. They were taught not to avoid memories of the events in direct opposition to medical practice of the time. Rivers described one case that was so aversive he considered it untreatable:

> Sometimes the experience which a patient is striving to forget is so utterly horrible or disgusting, so wholly free from any redeeming feature which can be used as a means of readjusting the attention, that it is difficult or impossible to find an aspect which will make its contemplation endurable. Such a case is that of a young officer who was flung down by the explosion of a shell so that his face struck the distended abdomen of a German several days dead, the impact of his fall rupturing the swollen corpse. Before he lost consciousness the patient had clearly realized his situation, and knew that the substance which filled his mouth and produced the most horrible sensations of taste and smell was derived from the decomposed entrails of an enemy. When he came to himself he vomited profusely, and was much shaken but "carried on" for several days, vomiting frequently, and haunted by persistent images of taste and smell. When he came under my care, several months later, suffering from horrible dreams, in which the events I have narrated were faithfully reproduced, he was striving by every means in his power to keep the disgusting and painful memory from his mind. (1920, p. 192)

Fussell (1989) has argued that even historians are influenced by aversive events of an extreme nature. Historical records, periods, and events become distorted as a consequence of the repulsive and abhorrent quality of incidents occurring during particular periods of time (e.g., World War II).

Clinical practice requires deep empathy for the client being treated. The repeated elicitation of stimuli that produces intense emotional reactions in a client and concurrently in the therapist make it improbable for therapists to employ such a model of treatment easily.

The view taken here is that "imaginal USs" function as CSs and not as true USs provided the CSs occur in settings that preclude US consequences (injury-provoking behavior). Such a procedure is fully feasible under treatment conditions. A further argument may be made. Clinical experience suggests that extinction of "imaginal USs" functioning as reactivated CSs has profound therapeutic consequences for otherwise difficult human cases. When combined with cue categories derived from a learning-conditioning model, such CSs appear to generate symptom-free behavior with longer durations and fewer relapses. Clinical observation also suggests that even very severe types of human mental disorders seem treatable when the learning-conditioning analysis is rigorously applied.

Components of the US as CS

Many aversive USs have some neutral or minimally aversive sensory effects beyond those of pain or fear. A child may be tied and scrubbed with cleanser. The sensation of pain from the abrasive is correlated with tactile sensations of rubbing on the skin that may be considered as independent stimuli. Or gagging may result from cloth stuffed into a child's mouth. When a child is choked, tactile sensations in the throat or on the neck and temporary loss of breath correlate with the original aversive event. Any stimulus directly related to the sensory effects of the US without any appreciable UCR effects tends to generate extremely intense emotional responses. Numerous escape-avoidance responses that represent symptomatic behaviors result from such stimuli. A rubbing motion on the skin, a slight gagging resulting from swallowing food, a tight collar around the neck combined with some temporary loss of breath may initiate the symptomatic (escape-avoidance) behavior.

It is revealing to find that characteristics of the symptomatic behaviors expressed in humans frequently refer to the nature of the original aversive events. For example, the hospitalized patient with the assaultive "choking" behavior as described at the beginning of this chapter had been choked by his mother as a child: "What was reconstructed with him was that as a young child his mother would place a cloth around his neck and choke him briefly for minor offenses" (Karon & Vandenbos, 1981, p. 37). Rarely, however, do contemporary therapeutic strategies identify early aversive events of this nature. On the other hand, the frequency with which early aversive events relate to current symptomatic behavior is striking when an animal fear-avoidance-extinction model is rigorously followed in treatment.

Many terms used to describe problem behavior in humans, such as loss of self-esteem, overly independent or dependent, fear of abandonment, loss of love, and castration anxiety, may be reduced to their stimulus antecedents and traced to aversive events that appear to relate directly to the etiology of the disturbance.

COMBINING PRINCIPLES TO RESOLVE LIMITATIONS

It is a near-impossibility to verify the causal linkages between the vast number of controlling stimuli for the symptomatic behaviors of human patients. However, certain principles of learning/conditioning do emerge from treatment experience. Most importantly, perhaps, is that experience reveals how principles may be combined to account for behavior that has been cited as presenting limitations to the animal model. Direct tests of such combining of principles are possible and available in the animal laboratory. The main thesis, then, is that limitations to the animal model are resolvable when tests are conducted that involve principles and features of the human situation. An example from Stampfl (1987) is described later to document this point.

Three "limitations" to the fear-avoidance model that have been cited in the literature are the following: (1) the neurotic paradox, (2) one-trial acquisition of the active avoidance response, and (3) avoidance of the CS. They are described in greater detail herein.

The Neurotic Paradox

A long-standing paradox (Freud, 1926/1936; Eglash, 1952; Mowrer, 1948, 1950, 1952) is frequently advanced as the major challenge for any learning-based model of human psychopathology (Eysenck, 1976, p. 252). The neurotic paradox as stated by Mowrer is that laboratory animal studies repeatedly demonstrate that conditioned fears extinguish with repetition in the absence of the unconditioned aversive stimulus. If this is so Mowrer asks, "Why is it, then, that in neurosis we have fears which appear to have long outlived any real justification but which stubbornly persist or which may even augment to the point of seriously incapacitating the individual" (1952, p. 679). Human phobias conform to the requirements of the paradox since phobic behavior lasts for months and years with little or no signs of abatement over time. For Mowrer, "It is the question as to why so-called neurotic behavior is at one and the same time *self-defeating and yet self-perpetuating*, instead of self-eliminating" (1950, p. 351).

1-Trial Learning

Some additional limitations of laboratory evidence as it relates to human phobias were reviewed by Mineka (1985). Mineka stated "that most phobias acquired through traumatic conditioning are acquired in one trial, whereas only a very few laboratory studies have ever demonstrated one trial fear conditioning" (p. 206). Many writers have referred to single-event acquisition in the human case (e.g., Allport, 1937; Skinner, 1953).

386

Although substantial resistance to extinction of avoidance responding has been found in special instances (Boyd & Levis, 1976; Denny & Dmitruk, 1967; McAllister, McAllister, Scoles, & Hampton, 1986), all of these studies employed multiple-shock trials and the mean number of trials to extinction was fewer than 500. Also a number of shock trials (range 4–13) were used in the studies of Solomon and his colleagues (Solomon & Wynne, 1953) that showed high resistance to extinction of avoidance.

Avoidance of the CS

Another limitation of the animal laboratory model as emphasized by Mineka (1985) is that human phobics:

> Generally go to great lengths to avoid their phobic stimulus (the presumed CS in an avoidance paradigm) whereas animals trained to avoid aversive stimulation in the laboratory are trained to avoid the US, not the CS. . . . We see here a significant and important difference in a crucial feature of avoidance learning as studied in the laboratory and in naturally occurring phobias (p. 204)

Williams and Watson (1985) describe the human phobic's strong tendency to avoid the CS(s):

> Height phobics typically refrain from taking part in skiing long before they are standing in line for the chair lift; social phobics decline invitations to future social events from the safety of their living rooms; and bridge phobics plan vacation routes precisely to insure that they will not be confronted with an intimidating span. (pp. 138–139)

One may note that behavior that avoids the "phobic" CS helps resolve the neurotic paradox. Avoidance behavior early in the sequence precludes exposure to aversive stimuli later in the sequence. The conditions for extinction are absent and are reminiscent of Guthrie's (1938) explanation for the persistence of neurotic behavior. As summarized by Hilgard and Marquis (1940): "Guthrie's (1938) theory of neurotic symptoms is based largely on the proposition that neurotic behavior never gets extinguished because the neurotic individual avoids the stimuli in the presence of which extinction might take place" (p. 293).

The typical explanation of the presumed differences between humans and nonhumans simply assert that the differences are qualitative. But such an explanation overlooks the many situational differences that exist in the two avoidance conditions: Human phobics make responses not only to a sequential series of CSs (many stimuli set in many different contexts) but their avoidance responses are also highly variable, and response variability can reduce the work requirement for the human. In contrast, the response requirement in laboratory avoidance is relatively constant. When the human avoids stimuli early in the sequence, both the work requirement and exposure to aversive stimuli are minimized. Also, timeout from avoidance is maximized with early responses. Other differences exist as well. The "phobic" CS in the human situation is complex in contrast to the discrete CSs typically used in the animal laboratory. Contextual stimuli ordered on a spatial-temporal continuum commonly precede the "phobic" CS in the human situation, and the sequential nature of CSs and contexts maximizes secondary intermittent reinforcement effects.

The question is simply one of asking whether the incorporation of the features of the human situation will generate similar effects in animals. This can be determined by exploring the alleged limitations of the animal model as previously described. A major problem is one of devising an appropriate experimental apparatus that includes the features that simulate the human situation.

Stampfl (1987) used a small, commercial remote-controlled conveyor belt to permit variability of the avoidance response. The belt formed the top of a 5-foot straight alley. Rats were shocked in a very distinctive black compartment located at one end of the alley. The alley had white side panels, except for a black 16 inch section immediately preceding the shock compartment. This section represented imminent proximity of the phobic stimulus as it occurs in human phobics (e.g., approaching the bridge or social situation or getting on the chair lift). Breaking the photocell located at the far end of the smooth floor straight alley defined the active avoidance response. Following an initial single shock trial, rats reliably ran to the far end of the white alley breaking the photocell. A 3-minute safety interval followed each response. The interval of 3 minutes following responding helped facilitate acquisition of the response in one trial (see Denny, 1971 or his chapter in this volume). A trial was defined by moving the floor in the direction of the "phobic" shock compartment. In effect, the floor carried the rat toward the "phobic" CS black compartment until it turned and ran to the far end of the white straight alley, breaking the photocell and stopping the floor. Thereafter, rats quickly learn (like human phobics) to respond early in the sequence. Such early responding minimizes exposure to aversive stimuli and amount of work involved. The active avoidance response is typically made within a few inches of movement rather than several feet.

Secondary intermittent reinforcement effects are maximized by the experimental arrangement. Contextual changes rather than discrete CSs form the sequential continuum (human phobics respond similarly to contextual changes). Being carried toward the black "phobic" compartment is a perceptual analogue of a "moving CS." Perceptually, the CS "phobic" stimulus (black compartment) may be viewed as one that is moving toward the rat. Timeout from avoidance is maximized per unit of time by early responding.

The experimental arrangement is still a fairly weak analogue of the human phobic situation. Response cost in humans goes well beyond that of the work requirement for the rat, and stimuli in the human situation are far more complex. Many improvements in the experimental arrangement are possible. Nevertheless, rats made more than 1,000 consecutive avoidance responses with little indication of the beginning of extinction (vitiating the neurotic paradox). The rat completely avoided the "phobic" CS complex (failed to enter the black compartment over the 1,000 trials) thus answering the "avoidance of the CS" limitation. The presumed limitation of one-trial acquisition was also met by the procedure used (see Stampfl, 1987, for a more extensive discussion of the conceptual issues involved).

Basic principles described in this chapter are directly testable in the laboratory (e.g., multiple USs, variable contexts, "moving CSs," etc.). Combining principles derived from observation of humans also leads to unique predictions in the animal laboratory. Additionally, many variants of human mental disorders can be modeled with animals, though special apparatus may be required to accomplish research programs of this type. The link between basic learning-conditioning principles and the human situation is firmly confirmed or disconfirmed by such research, and new implications for contemporary models of avoidance learning are likely to surface. Finally, new and powerful treatments for human patients are likely if analysis proceeds along lines generated by basic research in the animal laboratory.

REFERENCES

Allport, G. W. (1937). The functional autonomy of motives. *American Journal of Psychology*, *50*, 141–156.

Azrin, N. H., & Holz, W. C. (1966). Punishment. In W. K. Honig (Ed.), *Operant behavior* (pp. 380–447). New York: Appleton.

Barlow, D. (1982). The context of learning in behavior therapy. In J. C. Boulougouris (Ed.), *Learning theory approaches to psychiatry* (pp. 75–84). New York: Wiley.

Barlow, D. H., & Wolfe, B. E. (1981). Behavioral approaches to anxiety disorders: A report on the NIMH–SUNY, Albany, research conference. *Journal of Consulting and Clinical Psychology*, *49*, 448–454.

Baron, A., DeWaard, R. J., & Lipson, J. (1977). Increased reinforcement when timeout from avoidance includes access to a safe place. *Journal of the Experimental Analysis of Behavior*, *27*, 479–494.

Bitterman, M. E. (1988). Vertebrate–invertebrate comparisons. In H. J. Jerison & I. Jerison (Eds.), *Intelligence and evolutionary biology* (pp. 251–275). NATO ASI Series, Vol. G17, Berlin: C. Springer–Verlag.

Boudewyns, P. A., & Shipley, R. H. (1983). *Flooding and implosive therapy.* New York: Plenum Press.

Bouton, M. E. (1988). Context and ambiguity in the extinction of emotional learning: Implications for exposure therapy. *Behaviour Research and Therapy, 26,* 137–149.

Boyd, T. L., & Levis, D. J. (1976). The effects of single component extinction of a three-component serial CS on resistance to extinction of the conditioned avoidance response. *Learning and Motivation, 7,* 517–531.

Brown, J. S. (1961). *The motivation of behavior.* New York: McGraw–Hill.

Brown, J. S. (1969). Factors affecting self-punitive locomotor behavior. In B. A. Campbell & R. M. Church (Eds.), *Punishment and aversive behavior* (pp. 467–514). New York: Appleton.

Couvillon, P. A. & Bitternman, M. E. (1980). Some phenomena of associative learning in honeybees. *Journal of Comparative and Physiological Psychology, 94,* 878–885.

D'Amato, M. R., & Van Sant, P. (1988). The person concept in monkeys (*Cebus apella*). *Journal of Experimental Psychology: Animal Behavior Processes, 14,* 43–55.

Denny, M. R. (1971). Relaxation theory and experiments. In F. R. Brush (Ed.), *Aversive conditioning and learning* (pp. 235–295), New York: Academic Press.

Denny, M. R. (1976). Post-aversive relief and relaxation and their implications for behavior therapy. *Journal of Behavior Therapy and Experimental Psychiatry, 1,* 325–341.

Denny, M. R., & Dmitruk, V. M. (1967). Effect of punishing a single failure to avoid. *Journal of Comparative and Physiological Psychology, 63,* 277–281.

Dollard, J., & Miller, N. E. (1950). *Personality and psychotherapy.* New York: McGraw–Hill.

Domjan, M. (1987). Animal learning comes of age. *American Psychologist, 42,* 556–564.

Eglash, A. (1952). The dilemma of fear as a motivating force. *Psychological Review, 59,* 376–379.

Eysenck, H. J. (1976). The learning theory model of neurosis—A new approach. *Behaviour Research and Therapy, 14,* 251–267.

Eysenck, H. J. (1979). The conditioning model of neurosis. *Behavioral and Brain Sciences, 2,* 155–199.

Freud, S. (1926/1936). *The problem of anxiety* (H. A. Bunker, Trans.) New York: Norton. (Original work published 1926)

Freyd, J. J. (1987). Dynamic mental representations. *Psychological Review, 94,* 427–438.

Fussell, P. (1989, August). The real war 1939–1945. *Atlantic Monthly,* 32–48.

Guthrie, E. R. (1938). *The psychology of human conflict.* New York; Harper.

Hilgard, E. R., & Marquis, D. G. (1940). *Conditioning and learning.* New York: Appleton–Century–Crofts.

Hollingworth, H. L. (1928). General laws of redintegration. *Journal of General Psychology, 1,* 79–90.

Horowitz, L. G. (1985). Progressive relaxation and implosion therapy for dental phobias. *Clinical Preventive Dentistry, 7,* 11–17.

Hull, C. L. (1929). A functional interpretation of the conditioned reflex. *Psychological Review, 36,* 498–511.

Hull, C. L. (1939). Modern behaviorism and psychoanalysis. *Transactions of the New York Academy of Sciences, 1,* 78–82.

Hull, C. L. (1943). *Principles of behavior.* New York: Appleton.

Hull, C. L. (1945). The place of innate individual and species differences in a natural-science theory of behavior. *Psychological Review, 52,* 55–60.

Hunt, H. F., & Dyrud, J. E. (1968). Commentary: Perspective in behavior therapy. In J. M. Schlien (Ed.), *Research in psychotherapy,* (Vol. 3, pp. 140–152). Washington, DC: American Psychological Association.

Huschka, M. (1943). The incidence and character of masturbation threats in a group of problem children. In S. S. Tomkins (Ed.), *Contemporary psychopathology* (pp. 49–62). Cambridge, MA: Harvard University Press.

Kalish, H. I. (1981). *From behavioral science to behavior modification*. New York: McGraw–Hill.

Karon, B. P., & Vandenbos, G. R. (1981). *Psychotherapy of schizophrenia: The treatment of choice*. New York: Aronson.

Kostanek, D. J., & Sawrey, J. M. (1965). Acquisition and extinction of shuttlebox avoidance with complex stimuli. *Psychonomic Science, 3*, 369–370.

Krasner, L. (1970). Comment. In D. J. Levis (Ed.), *Learning approaches to therapeutic behavior change* (pp. 205–207). Chicago: Aldine.

Levis, D. J. (1979). The infrahuman avoidance model of sympton maintenance and implosive therapy. In J. D. Keehn (Ed.), *Psychopathology in animals: Research and clinical implications* (pp. 257–277). New York: Academic Press.

Levis, D. J., & Boyd, T. L. (1979). Symptom maintenance: An infrahuman analysis and extension of the conservation of anxiety principle. *Journal of Abnormal Psychology, 88*, 107–120.

Levis, D. J., & Hare, N. (1977). A review of the theoretical rationale and empirical support for the extinction approach of implosive (flooding) therapy. In M. Hersen, R. Eisler, & P. Miller (Eds.), *Progress in behavior modification* (Vol. 4). New York: Academic Press.

London, P. (1964). *The modes and morals of psychotherapy*. New York: Holt.

McAllister, W. R., & McAllister, D. E. (1965). Variables influencing the conditioning and the measurement of acquired fear. In W. F. Prokasy (Ed.), *Classical conditioning* (pp. 172–191). New York: Appleton.

McAllister, W. R., & McAllister, D. E. (1971). Behavioral measurement of conditioned fear. In F. R. Brush (Ed.), *Aversive conditioning and learning* (pp. 105–179). New York: Academic Press

McAllister, W. R., & McAllister, D. E. (1979). Are the concepts of enhancement and preparedness necessary? *Behavioral and Brain Sciences, 2*, 177–178.

McAllister, W. R., McAllister, D. E., Scoles, M. T., & Hampton, S. R. (1986). Persistence of fear-reducing behavior: Relevance for the conditioning theory of neurosis. *Journal of Abnormal Psychology, 95*, 365–372.

Michels, R., Frances, A., & Shear, M. K. (1985). Psychodynamic models of anxiety. In A. H. Tuma & J. Maser (Eds.), *Anxiety and the anxiety disorders* (pp. 595–618). Hillsdale, NJ: Lawrence Erlbaum Associates.

Mineka, S. (1985). Animal models of anxiety-based disorders: Their usefulness and limitations. In A. H. Tuma & J. Maser (Eds.), *Anxiety and the anxiety disorders* (pp. 199–244). Hillsdale, NJ: Lawrence Erlbaum Associates.

Mowrer, O. H. (1939). A stimulus–response analysis of anxiety and its role as a reinforcing agent. *Psychological Review, 46*, 553–565.

Mowrer, O. H. (1948). Learning theory and the neurotic paradox. *American Journal of Orthopsychiatry, 18*, 571–610.

Mowrer, O. H. (1950). *Learning theory and personality dynamics: Selected papers*. New York: Ronald Press.

Mowrer, O. H. (1952). Learning theory and the neurotic fallacy. *American Journal of Orthopsychiatry, 22*, 679–689.

Mowrer, O. H. (1960). *Learning theory and behavior*. New York: Wiley.

Pavlov, I. P. (1927). *Conditioned reflexes* (G.V. Anrep, Trans.). London: Oxford University Press.

Rachman, S. (1976). The passing of the two-stage theory of fear and avoidance: Fresh possibilities. *Behaviour Research and Therapy, 14*, 125–131.

Rachman, S. (1977). The conditioning theory of fear-acquisition: A critical examination. *Behaviour Research and Therapy, 15*, 375–387.

Randich, A., & Ross, R. T. (1985). Contextual stimuli mediate the effects of pre- and postexposure to the unconditioned stimulus on conditioned suppression. In P. D. Balsam & A. Tomie (Eds.), *Context and learning* (pp. 105–132). Hillsdale, NJ: Lawrence Erlbaum Associates.

Riccio, D. C., & Ebner, D. L. (1981). In N. E. Spear & R. R. Miller (Eds.), *Information processing in animals: Memory mechanisms*. Hillsdale, NJ: Lawrence Erlbaum Associates.

Richardson, R., Riccio, D. C., & Ress, J. (1988). Extinction of avoidance through response prevention; Enhancement by administration of epinephrine or ACTH. *Behaviour Research and Therapy, 26*, 23–32.

Rivers, W. H. R. (1920). *Instinct and the unconscious*. London: Cambridge University Press.

Shaw, F. J. (1946). A stimulus–response analysis of repression and insight in psychotherapy. *Psychological Review, 53*, 36–42.

Shoben, E. J. (1949). Psychotherapy as a problem in learning theory. *Psychological Bulletin, 46*, 366–392.

Siegel, S. (1979). The role of conditioning in drug tolerance and addiction. In J. D. Keehn (Ed.), *Psychopathology in animals: Research and clinical implications* (pp. 143–168). New York: Academic Press.

Skinner, B. F. (1953). *Science and human behavior*. New York: Macmillan.

Skinner, B. F. (1954). Critique of psychoanalytic concepts and theories. In T. Millon (Ed.), (1967), *Theories of psychopathology* (pp. 228–235). Philadelphia: Saunders. (Reprinted from *Scientific Monthly, 79*, 300–305)

Solomon, R. L., Kamin, L. J., & Wynne, L. C. (1953). Traumatic avoidance learning: The outcomes of several extinction procedures with dogs. *Journal of Abnormal and Social Psychology, 48*, 291–302.

Solomon, R. L., & Wynne, L. C. (1953). Traumatic avoidance learning: Acquisition in normal dogs. *Psychological Monographs, 67*(4, Whole No. 354).

Spear, N. E., & Miller, R. R. (Eds.). (1981). *Information processing in animals: Memory mechanisms*. Hillsdale, NJ: Lawrence Erlbaum Associates.

Stampfl, T. G. (1961, May). *Implosive therapy: A learning theory derived psychodynamic therapeutic technique*. Paper presented at the University of Illinois, Champaign.

Stampfl, T. G. (1966). Implosive therapy: The theory, the subhuman analogue, the strategy, and the technique. Part I: The theory. In S. G. Armitage (Ed.), *Behavior modification techniques in the treatment of emotional disorders* (pp. 12–21). Battle Creek, MI: Veterans Administration Publications.

Stampfl, T. G. (1970). Implosive therapy: An emphasis on convert stimulation. In D. J. Levis (Ed.), *Learning approaches to therapeutic behavior change* (pp. 182–204). Chicago: Aldine.

Stampfl, T. G. (1987). Theoretical implications of the neurotic paradox as a problem in behavior theory: An experimental resolution. (*Behavior Analyst, 10*, 161–173.

Stampfl, T. G., & Levis, D. J. (1967). Essentials of implosive therapy: A learning-theory-based psychodynamic behavioral therapy. *Journal of Abnormal Psychology, 72*, 496–503.

Stampfl, T. G., & Levis, D. J. (1969). Learning theory: An aid to dynamic therapeutic practice. In L. D. Eron & R. Callahan (Eds.), *Relationship of theory to practice in psychotherapy* (85–114). Chicago: Aldine.

Stampfl, T. G., & Levis, D. J. (1973). *Implosive therapy: Theory and technique*. Morristown, NJ: General Learning Press.

Stampfl, T. G., & Levis, D. J. (1976). Implosive therapy: A behavioral therapy? In J. T. Spence, R. C. Carson, & J. W. Thibaut (Eds.), *Behavioral approaches to therapy* (pp. 189–110). Morristown, NJ: General Learning Press.

Tuma, A. H., & Maser, J. (Eds.). (1985). *Anxiety and the anxiety disorders*. Hillsdale, NJ: Lawrence Erlbaum Associates.

Whiting, J. W. M., & Mowrer, O. H. (1943). Habit progression and regression—A laboratory study of some factors relevant to human socialization. *Journal of Comparative Psychology*, *36*, 229–253.

Williams, S. L., & Watson, N. (1985). Perceived danger and perceived self-efficacy as cognitive determinants of acrophobic behavior. *Behavior Therapy*, *16*, 136–146.

Wilson, G. T. (1982). The relationship of learning theories to the behavioral therapies: Problems, prospects, and preferences. In J. C. Boulougouris (Ed.), *Learning approaches to psychiatry* (pp. 33–56). New York: Wiley.

Wolpe, J. (1958). *Psychotherapy by reciprocal inhibition*. Palo Alto CA: Stanford University Press.

12 A Clinician's Plea for a Return to the Development of Nonhuman Models of Psychopathology: New Clinical Observations in Need of Laboratory Study

Donald J. Levis
State University of New York at Binghamton

The chapters in this volume attest to the fact that establishing the basic laws of behavior through nonhuman research is still considered important. But it cannot be denied that the field as a whole has lost the sense of the significance of such research, and the belief that this research will increase our understanding of human behavior is no longer widely held. With the experience of more than 25 years of treating a wide range of human psychopathology, I have become strongly convinced that laboratory work with nonhumans, whose application has been largely ignored, is essential to our understanding and resolution of human problems. The primary purpose of the present chapter is to generate greater interest in the issues confronting the clinician by investigators of nonhuman basic research.

To achieve this objective, the chapter outlines the learning approach of Implosive Therapy, which is based on an extension of Mowrer's (1947) two-factor theory of avoidance. This theory has proved to be unusually powerful for both understanding and treating human psychopathology; and, in a clinical setting, has led to a number of new discoveries about the origin and maintenance of such behavior (Levis, 1988). To bolster my attempt at seduction, a brief historical perspective is presented first as an appetizer and critical case material is offered last as a dessert.

EXTENSION OF BEHAVIORAL PRINCIPLES TO PSYCHOPATHOLOGY

From the beginning, principles derived mainly from nonhuman animal research were seen as providing the foundation for the building of behavioral laws designed not only to predict and explain complex human behavior but to aid in the removal of human suffering especially in the area of psychopathology. The writings and research of Pavlov (1927), Watson (1924), Guthrie (1938), Skinner (1953, 1954), Dollard and Miller (1950), Brown (1961), Mowrer (1960a, 1960b) and many others pointed the direction in which an orderly science of behavior may proceed in understanding and treating clinical psychological phenomena. Behavioral analysis provided interpretations of various psychodynamic concepts such as repression and other defense mechanisms, as well as providing explanations for a host of clinical symptoms and interpersonal conflicts. These efforts did not go unnoticed and paved the way for the development of the behavior therapy movement that started in the late 1950s and continues today.

The behavior therapy movement nurtured the seeds sowed by basic science researchers and set the stage for the possible development of a revolutionary movement of great potential and historical importance (Levis, 1970). It appeared that the field was at the threshold of a new development, the uniting of two important fields of psychology: clinical and learning. The promise this movement held was that such a marriage would remove the existing schizophrenia between the applied and experimental fields of psychology providing each partner with a sense of direction and purpose.

Although the accomplishments of the behavior therapy movement over the last 25 years have been extensive (see Kalish, 1981), the goal to produce a new breed of scientifically trained clinicians has not been fully realized. The objective was to produce an expert in the fields of learning and clinical who was capable of extrapolating from the learning laboratory to the clinical situation and from the clincial setting back to the laboratory.

As the years progressed, it became clear that the vision of what the behavioral therapy movement might have achieved never really materialized. The powerful, well-conceptualized learning models of clinical importance derived from the decades of laboratory research efforts were either arbitrarily dismissed or never systematically explored. In place of superscientifically trained behavior therapists, there emerged individuals who exhibited limited knowledge of both the field of learning and the intricacies of psychopathology. The end result was a movement in disarray, moving away from a basic learning orientation toward a cognitive and traditional clinical viewpoint (Levis, 1988). As Stampfl (1983) observed:

> Learning-based behavioral treatment techniques received most of their impetus and development from experimental research with lower animals. The major theories of learning and conditioning were products of decades of research effort that generated a wealth of empirical generalizations, principles, and various formulations that explicated central phenomena of the learning laboratory. As Teasdale aptly remarks, "the single most important

theoretical exercise in the development of the behavioral treatments was the imaginative leap of regarding aspects of clinical problems as similar to behaviors studied within these established paradigms" (p. 59). The "imaginative leaps"of the pioneers of behavior therapy were made by individuals thoroughly familiar with the animal learning and conditioning literature available at that time. The "growing dissatisfaction" (and lack of imagination) is more likely a consequence of the growing neglect of general-experimental courses in learning and conditioning in our clinical training programs combined with expanding economic opportunities for purely clinical skills. It is ironic that this state of affairs should exist precisely at a time when marvelous opportunities for solidly based theoretical innovations to the human condition may readily be inferred from the contemporary learning and conditioning literature. (p. 528)

The Case for the Return of Laboratory Models

If nonhuman learning research is to regain its leadership role and remove its current "third-world" status, it must reassert the philosophy of science upon which it is based and reject the premise that the complexity of various forms of human behavior diminishes the importance of laboratory animal research. Clinical experience gained over many years by this writer reveals that the complexity of human behavior is vastly overrated; regardless of complexity, behavior appears to be governed by the interaction of basic behavioral principles (also see Stampfl, 1987). As Dinsmoor (1983) warned:

> There is a strong tendency in contemporary writings, from the research report to the undergraduate text, to follow the fashion of the moment, to abandon— almost frivolously—well-established principles in favor of whatever fits the spirit of the time. This, however, is not the way to construct a strong and orderly science, one capable of bending nature to its will. (p. 704)

The power of nonhuman research resides in the methodological rigor allowing for the establishment of a functional relationship among variables. The use of nonhumans such as the rat not only provides a less complex organism which may be more advantageous for deciphering basic laws but provides an emotional system not unlike that of the human. If, as experience indicates, maladaptive behavior is motivated by the conditioning of emotional or autonomic responses, and if, as experience indicates, mediated internal cues such as words, thoughts, images, and memories in the human turn out to follow essentially the same conditioning laws as extroceptive stimuli, the argument for nonhuman animal research becomes much stronger. Animals are also subject to experimentation that for ethical reasons cannot be conducted with humans. Even if such experimentation only provides a vehicle for illustration and confirmation of suspected hypotheses about human behavior, the effort is more than worthwhile (Levis, 1970).

Critics such as Hunt (1964, p. 28), in commenting on the contributions of nonhuman "experimental neurosis" studies reflected in the work of Liddell (1965), Maier (1939), Miller (1964), Masserman (1943), and Pavlov (1927), argue that although such illustrations and confirmation are not trivial, they only illustrate, duplicate, or confirm things already known about the human case. Hunt goes on to ask why this comparative sterility exists. This issue of comparative sterility of animal experimentation in providing insight into human psychopathology, say, compared with cognitive or psychoanalytical theory, may well be argued. But the existing contributions of nonhuman animal research in our quest to understand psychopathology have been far greater than that offered by those who dismiss on philosophical grounds any relevance of nonhuman experimentation and provide alternative interpretations which are too often nontestable and devoid of predictive power. The sterility of nonhuman animal research, if it exists, is perhaps more a function of experimental psychologists' lack of clinical experience, which can be critical for generating stimulating research, than the inherent problem of generalizing from one organism to another. As Eysenck (1960) reasoned:

> If the laws which have been formulated are not necessarily true, but at least partially correct, then it must follow that we can make deductions from them to cover the type of behavior represented by neurotic patients, construct a model which will duplicate the important and relevant features of the patient and suggest new and possible helpful methods of treatment along lines laid down by learning theory. (p. 5)

A major advance made in the direction suggested by Eysenck was conceptualized in the late 1950s by Thomas G. Stampfl. His extensive clinical experience with both severe child and adult psychopathology, coupled with his knowledge of the nonhuman avoidance literature, led to the development of Implosive Theory and Therapy (Levis, 1985; Stampfl, 1966; Stampfl & Levis, 1967). Stampfl's approach represents a CS exposure, extinction approach to treatment, based primarily on a revision of Mowrer's (1947, 1960a, 1960b) two-factor theory of avoidance. His thinking has been influenced by the nonhuman research of a number of contributors, including that of Abraham Amsel, Judson S. Brown, M. Ray Denny, and Dorothy and Wallace McAllister. From the start, Stampfl (1988) believed that strong support for the value of nonhuman animal research could be obtained by making genuine predictions in this area based on clinical observations obtained from the treatment of human patients. For example, his clinical experience supported the observation that stimuli eliciting anxiety in the human client were multiple, complex, and characteristically organized sequentially. That is to say, the exposure of one set of stimuli is followed by another, with each new set being more aversive than the former. It was also clear to him that context stimuli were important contributors to the total amount of fear experienced by the human patient. These previously conditioned aversive stimuli frequently were embedded in a compound, and the avoidance behavior (the patient's symptom) typically occurred at the start of therapy to generalized sets of feared stimuli. The successful avoidance of these generalized stimuli, in turn, prevented exposure to the more aversive stimulus subsets that were more closely associated with the UCS. This process presumably retarded extinction and aided in the maintenance of the symptom. Observations were also made concerning the nature of stimuli present in the conditioning history, such as frequency of stimulus movement and what was historically referred to as "redintegration" or the tendency of an association or stimulus unit to reactivate or reinstate another association.

At the time of the development of implosive therapy, relatively little research existed in the foregoing areas to support the underlying principles believed responsible for the clinical phenomena observed. Since that time considerable research has been conducted at the animal level to aid in validating the theory and to reproduce some of the clinical phenomena observed (see Balsam & Tomie, 1985; Levis, 1985, 1989; Stampfl, 1970). Although a number of other very important advances have been made by animal researchers in the last 20 years, most of those contributions, do not directly address issues of concern to students of human psychopathology. As Stampfl (1988) noted, laboratory research is ordinarily greatly simplified for its own purposes which, in turn, leads to the omission of requirements needed to demonstrate adequately phenomena which critics have asserted are necessary to validate an animal model of human psychopathology. As Stampfl reasoned and suggested earlier, it follows that the validation of animal research could be enhanced if the latter led to the successful solution of problems based on principles observed with humans. This would be true expecially if predictions were made for heretofore undiscovered relationships. That is to say, the predictions would confer even greater validity to the extent to which they were made in the nature of a genuine theoretical prediction. Such support would generate considerable more confidence in applying the clinical technique to the treatment of human psychopathological problems.

Unfortunately, numerous problems arise in any attempt to encourage more basic researchers to focus their efforts on theoretical paradoxes confronting the clinical field. For one thing, a kind of schizophrenic state still exists between those interested in animal research and those attempting to deal with psychopathology. For another, the observation of greatest interest are observed mostly by those clinicians unfamiliar with the learning literature and scientific language system. Unfortunately, few nonhuman researchers have sufficient experience with human psychopathology to restructure the critical clinical phenomena into testable hypothesis. The marriage between the basic researcher and the applied clinical observer, which often has been suggested, has yet to materialize. Given the recent trend against the value of animal research and the recent economic inroads by clinicians to be self-sustaining, the possibility of such a marriage seems even more remote today. Yet the human suffering persists, as does the need for a systematic scientific analysis and treatment rationale.

The clinical model of implosive therapy under consideration makes a serious attempt to bridge the gap between the basic animal researcher and the applied scientist. A refinement of the memory-reactivating component of this technique has resulted in a series of observations over the last 5 years by this writer that not only appear to be systematic across patients and nosologies but if accurate, will require a major rethinking of what factors are responsible for motivating human pathology as well as how best to treat them. These clinical observations appear not only to support the power of existing principles of learning developed in the animal laboratory but represent a rich source of hypotheses that for ethical and practical concerns may only be testable at the nonhuman level. But before this clincial material and related hypotheses are shared, a brief overview of the theory and technique which generated them is needed to comprehend their predictive importance.

IMPLOSIVE THEORY—AN OVERVIEW

Implosive theory involves an extension of Mowrer's (1947) two-factor theory of avoidance to the area of psychopathology. Mowrer (1950), who was also interested in providing a working model of psychopathology, retranslated Freud's (1936) analysis of symptom formation into learning terminology (Mowrer, 1939). His two-factor position, with its emphasis on the construct of fear, initially gained considerable acceptance and attention. Basic researchers were becoming sensitive to unresolved theoretical issues posed by avoidance learning. The commonsense explanation (Hilgard & Marquis, 1940) that the organism responded in order to avoid the occurrence of painful stimulation, a teleological interpretation, did not sit well with the growing behavior movement. As Schoenfeld (1950) put it, how could learned avoidance be maintained in the absence of the UCS, which is the established condition for extinction? This paradox was resolved by the introduction of the theoretical construct of fear (Miller, 1948; Mowrer, 1939, 1947).

Early fear theory and its subsequent modifications (Brown & Farber, 1958; Dollard & Miller, 1950; Levis, 1989; McAllister & McAllister, 1965; Rescorla & Solomon, 1967; Solomon & Wynne, 1954; Stampfl, 1987; Stampfl & Levis, 1969) provided a cogent explanation for the development, maintenance, and extinction of both laboratory avoidance behavior and human avoidance behavior associated with psychopathology. Although ingenious attempts were made by behaviorists to offer nonfear, nonteleological alternative explantions of avoidance behavior (Dinsmoor, 1950; Herrnstein, 1969; Schoenfeld, 1950), or a biological-genetic modification (Bolles, 1970; Seligman, 1971), these explanations fell short in resolving critical paradoxes (Levis, 1989; Mackintosh, 1974). Fear theory's power resides in its ability to generate numerous supported differential predictions (Brown & Farber, 1958; Levis, 1989; McAllister & McAllister, 1965, 1971; Mowrer, 1960a, 1960b) and the failure of alternative positions to replace the theory with an equally comprehensive and predictive model. Thus, it is surprising and somewhat puzzling as to why the theory has met with considerable disfavor in the last 20 years. A review of the criticisms offered (Levis, 1989) suggests that this trend is primarily motivated by a desire to move psychology away from an S–R viewpoint rather than by the availability of any damaging empirical data. In fact, most of the criticism offered is based on a misrepresentation of fear theory and questionable empirical support (see Levis, 1989).

The power of conditioning interpretations to explain clinical phenomena has also been ignored by a clinical field largely unconcerned with the importance of learning theory and comfortable in the belief that cognitive factors such as insight, self-understanding, and corrective rational thinking are the means by which psychopathology can be eradicated. The role of emotional factors in maintaining psychopathology is again taking a back seat to those who hold the view that "irrational" thoughts can be corrected through a process of "rational" re-education.

The model, here presented, reaffirms the historically accepted position that psychopathology is an emotional, not a cognitive, disorder that can best be understood and analyzed within a learning-conditioning framework (Alexander, 1965). The implosive model attempts to extrapolate established laboratory principles of conditioning to explain and treat clinical symptoms. The theory is unique, in that it addresses the issue of symptom maintenance, provides a detailed analysis of the CS complex motivating human symptoms, and stresses the important role that memory encoding and reactivation play in both maintaining and removing pathology. Besides adapting the avoidance theory of Mowrer (1947, 1960a, 1960b), the theory incorporates the contribution of Miller's (1951) and Brown's (1961) theory of conflict, Solomon and Wynne's (1954) conservation of anxiety hypothesis, Amsel's (1958; 1962) theory of frustration, and the learning conceptualization of psychopathology offered by Dollard and Miller (1950).

Symptom Acquisition

Both the theory and treatment technique of implosive therapy have been described in detail elsewhere (Levis, 1980a, 1985; Stampfl & Levis, 1967, 1969, 1976). Only a cursory review will be provided here. The position is taken that psychopathology is learned avoidance behavior resulting from the organism's exposure to past, specific aversive conditioning experiences of considerable intensity. The conditioning of aversive stimulation in the human, as is the case with nonhumans, results from the simple contiguity of this stimulation in time or space with primary (unconditioned) or other previously conditioned aversive stimuli. The primary drive (emotional) states produced by the unconditioned stimulus (UCS) involve pain, fear, frustration, or severe deprivation. Most importantly, the conditioning events are multiple, involve a complex set of stimuli comprising both external and internal conditioned stimulus (CS) complexes, and are encoded in long-term memory. From this analysis it is possible for central state constructs such as images, thoughts, and memories to function as conditioned cues and in many cases represent the major part of the stimulus complex maintaining human psychopathology. Although the traumatic conditioning always involves the presence of a primary UCS, a great deal of human aversive emotional learning becomes conditioned through association or pairings with other aversive CSs. The learning principles involved in this transfer include the process of secondary conditioning, higher-order conditioning, primary stimulus generalization, response-mediated generalization, semantic and symbolic-mediated conditioning, and memory reactivation or reintegration of past aversive events. These principles are needed to explain, for example, why children fear ghosts and skeletons, when they have not been directly hurt by them, or why many adults fear riding in an airplane, or being exposed to a spider, rat, or snake, when such stimuli have never been directly paired with bodily injury or physical pain.

The foregoing established learning principles also provide an explanation for the development of symbolism and displacement (Miller & Kraeling, 1952). For example, if the sight of a knife has been conditioned to elicit a strong fear reaction, the fear may generalize to all shaped objects or to objects that can potentially produce bodily injury, such as cars, guns, unprotected high places, and so on. Or if the sight of feces is associatively chained to the fear of disease, the cue transference may include such items as dirt, money, water fountains, and public toilets. Similarly, the fear of a penis may generalize or be displaced to other objects, such as, snakes, telephone poles, and knives, which have some stimulus characteristics similar to those involved in the original feared object (Dollard & Miller, 1950; Kimble, 1961; Levis, 1985; Levis & Hare, 1977; Stampfl & Levis, 1969).

Most of the conditioning events uncovered in clinical patients represent a conflict situation involving the pitting of more than one primary and secondary drive states (Levis, 1985; Levis & Hare, 1977). Any behavior that reduces the level of aversive stimulation generated by the traumatic conditioning sets the stage for learning the secondary class of responses correlated with psychopathology, referred to as avoidance or symptomatic behavior. These behaviors, in turn, are reinforced by the resulting reduction in aversive stimulation. The learning associated with the conditioning of emotional states are governed by the laws of classical conditioning while symptomatic behavior is believed to be under the control of the laws of instrumental conditioning.

It is postulated that human psychological symptoms (maladaptive behavior) comprise response topographies that involve the skeletal nervous system and can be classified as external, overt, or behavioral; the higher mental processes of the central nervous system (cognitive processes) that can be classified as internal or convert; and the autonomic nervous system. Overt avoidance behaviors involving the skeletal nervous system can be seen in flight responses, aggressive acts, compulsive rituals and passive avoidance behavior. Covert avoidance behavior mainly involves the classic cognitive defenses, such as repression (not thinking or remembering), denial, rationalization, intellectualization, suppression, and projection. Clinical experience also suggests that by focusing on the emotional consequence of autonomic reactivity (e.g., stimulus consequences of emotions labeled anxiety, guilt, or anger), the patient can avoid exposure to the stimulus situation eliciting the emotion and thereby reduce the overall fear level. In the same vein, by focusing on one's emotion and maintaining it, one can avoid exposure to cues eliciting more aversive emotion. For example, feeling guilty can help avoid feelings of anger or fear or feeling angry can help avoid feeling fear or guilt.

Although the conditioning sequences of the human involve multiple CS complexes comprising both external and internal stimuli and usually including the presence of more than one primary drive, the complexity observed can be reduced to a few basic, established learning principles operating independently or in combination with each other. These laws have been the subject of considerable controlled laboratory research with nonhumans, and with some forethought the interaction effects of these established principles noted with patients are amenable to test at the nonhuman level. The assumption that the emotional conditioning of internal states follows the same laws as those established with external stimuli, helps reduce the complexity issue and appears to be supported at the clinical level.

Symptom Maintenance

As previously noted, the strength of fear theory is the ability of the model to resolve the avoidance acquisition paradox. By adding the construct of fear, the theory is able to explain why the strength of the avoidance response initially increases in the presence of a CS-alone condition. The fear construct not only sets the stage for motivating and strengthening avoidance behavior, but the extinction of fear also explains the orderly weakening of this response system with CS exposure. Thus, the theory keeps intact the time-honored principle of experimental extinction: The presentation of the CS in the absence of the UCS leads to weakening of conditioned responses to the CS.

It is ironic that the established empirical principle for extinguishing fear and avoidance behavior, CS exposure, became the Achilles heel of two-factor theory's attempt to explain psychopathology. Symptomatic behavior in humans can last a long time without any apparent significant signs of extinction. Freud (1936, pp. 89–92), after years of theoretical analysis, raised the critical question as to what is the source of neurosis, what is its ultimate, and what is its specific, underlying principle? In his words: "After decades of analytic effort this problem rises up before us, as untouched as at the beginning" (p. 92). Mowrer (1950, p. 351), who labeled the phenomenon described by Freud, the "neurotic paradox," asked the question as to why so-called neurotic behavior is at one and the same time self-defeating and yet self-perpetuating, instead of self-eliminating." Not only did Mowrer regard this paradox as central for clinical theory and practice but he correctly noted that the issue of sustained avoidance or persistent symptomatic behavior posed severe difficulties for two-factor explanations of neurotic behavior.

The problem confronting fear theory is the empirical finding that in the vast majority of nonhuman studies in the avoidance area both fear and avoidance fail to show great resistance to extinction in the presence of a CS alone extinction condition (Mackintosh, 1974). This also appears to be the case for human avoidance laboratory conditioning (Levis, 1971). Although exceptions to this observation exists (e.g., Solomon, Kamin, & Wynne, 1953), and are becoming more frequent at the nonhuman level (Levis, 1966a, 1966b; Levis, Bouska, Eron, & McIlhon, 1970; Levis & Boyd, 1979; McAllister, McAllister, Scoles, & Hampton, 1986) and with humans (Levis, 1971; Malloy & Levis, 1988), this pivotal issue has resulted in the abondonment of traditional fear theory by many psychologists. The addition of such theoretical concepts as partial irreversibility (Solomon & Wynne, 1954), automatization (Kimble & Perlmuter, 1970), CS incubation (Eysenck, 1976), uncontrollability (Seligman, 1975), and cognitive expectancy (Seligman & Johnston, 1973) offer such a departure. Each of these new positions represent an attempt to provide an exception to the Pavlovian law of extinction, a state of affairs theoretically unnecessary and empirically unsupported (see Levis, 1985, 1989).

For fear theory to remain a powerful theoretical model in our quest to understand human psychopathology, a principle is needed to resolve the issue of sustained symptom maintenance, and, ideally, a principle that is faithful to the established laws of extinction. Such a principle has been offered by Stampfl (1966; Stampfl & Levis, 1967, 1969) and was in large part based on clinical observations of how human symptoms undergo an extinction effect. Observations regularly reveal that although some clinical symptoms do appear to last for long periods of time, the cues initially reported for eliciting symptom onset change over time with the earlier fear-eliciting cues frequently failing to trigger the symptom. It would theoretically follow that because of regular CS exposure, the fear-eliciting properties associated with these cues extinguish and are replaced with a new set of cues with fear-motivating properties which have not previously received much CS exposure. These new cues can be regularly observed when symptom occurrence is prevented. This observation led Stampfl to conclude that a network of cues were involved in motivating a given symptom and that these cues which represent past association to conditioning events involving pain or severe states of deprivation were stored in memory and ordered in a sequential or serial arrangement in terms of their accessibility. It also appears that these cue patterns are ordered along a dimension of stimulus intensity with the more aversive cue patterns being least accessible. It appears that these memorial encoded cues are activated by a stimulus situation in the patient's current life which is similar on a generalization dimension to those cues associated to the previous traumatic conditioning event. The patient's symptom is designed to block the release of such cues and to avoid the intense emotional properties attached to them. However, because these generalized cues are exposed, the fear attached to them undergoes an extinction effect, which, in turn, reactivates that next set of cues in the serial chain. Stampfl ingeniously translated this observation into S–R terminology by extending and modifying the now-classic conservation of anxiety hypothesis suggested by Solomon and Wynne (1954).

Solomon and Wynne introduced the conservation hypothesis, based on previous empirical work (Solomon et al., 1953; Solomon & Wynne, 1953). They used a standard discrete-trial shuttle-box avoidance situation with a 10-second CS–UCS interval. Dogs served as subjects and the UCS was a very intense shock. They found that the dogs continued to avoid with short latency responses some 200 trials later, without showing appreciable signs of extinction. Except for one animal that made 490 avoidance responses during extinction before a punishment procedure was introduced, all animals in these studies were removed from the experiment at trial 200 if they had not met the extinction criterion. The importance of these findings reside in the demonstration of extreme resistance to extinction of laboratory-conditioned avoidance behavior.

From their empirical work, four important observations emerged which Solomon and Wynne (1954) believed required explanation: (1) The avoidance latencies of the dogs shortened considerably with training, with response latencies of 2 to 4 sec becoming common; (2) Overt signs of anxiety appeared to diminish with training and at times appeared nonexistent in extinction; (3) Upon the occurrence of a long-latency response in extinction, behavioral signs of anxiety reappeared followed by the return to short latency responses and subsequent trials; and (4) The apparent failure of extinction to occur after 200 trials. Point (1) required no new explanation and simply reflected the empirical finding that fear conditioned to the CS backs up to the onset of the CS and mediates the avoidance response. To handle point (2), the apparent absence of overt signs of fear following sustained responding to the onset segment of the CS–UCS interval, Solomon and Wynne concluded that overt signs of anxiety rapidly disappeared because the short exposure to the CS resulting from a quick avoidance response did not permit the time required for the full elicitation of the classical conditioned fear reaction. Point (3), the occurrence of long-latency responses and the subsequent return to short-latency avoidance, follow the re-emergent of behavioral signs of fear, set the stage for the conservation hypothesis. Longer latency responses periodically occurred because of subsequent fear extinction to the first part of the CS–UCS interval. The longer response latency permitted sufficient time for the full elicitation of the fear response, resulting in the behavioral observation of the fear response. The return to a short latency response was explained by the resulting strengthening of the avoidance response by the increased fear reduction following the longer latency avoidance response. To account for the final point, the apparent failure of extinction to the CS–UCS interval, Solomon and Wynne introduced yet another principle, that of partial-irreversibility. This principle was predicated on the assumption that the very intense pain-fear reaction produced by the use of traumatic shock became associated to the CS resulting in a permanent fear-reaction.

Although Solomon and Wynne (1954) attempted to extend two-factor theory to account for the varying avoidance response latencies noted during extinction for the maintenance of avoidance responding, their combined principles of conservation of anxiety and partial irreversibility, as stated, raised some critical concerns. For one thing, if a short CS exposure does not provide sufficient time for the fear response to occur, how can the avoidance response be elicited (Seligman & Johnston, 1973)? Fear stimuli must be present in sufficient strength to elicit avoidance behavior. For another, the principle of partial irreversibility suggests a kind of functional autonomy for avoidance responding which is contrary to the laws of Pavlovian extinction. Solomon and Wynne used traumatic shock in their attempt to assimilate human symptom maintenance. But if the avoidance maintenance is irreversible, how can therapy work?

Fear theory must maintain that fear is present in the short CS exposure period, if such exposure elicits avoidance responding. Behavioral sign of fear to short CS exposures are noted early in training and only appear to dissipate over trials. Levis and Boyd (1979) argued that the avoidance response when rapidly learned reaches asymptote quickly. Once at asymptote only a fractional level of fear activation is needed to elicit the avoidance response and such small levels of fear may not be visually observable. They tested this hypothesis by training animals to make 50 consecutive short-latency avoidance responses. Fear to the short CS exposure was still present as indexed by CER testing following the 50th consecutive avoidance response. Fear theory also maintains that the laws of Pavlovian extinction work. Repeated exposure to the CS or a CS segment in the absence of any further UCS presentation eventually leads to the extinction of the fear response. Thus, the partial irreversibility hypothesis must be rejected in favor of the position that Solomon's dogs would have extinguished if a sufficient number of trials had been administered, a point empirically supported by Levis and Boyd (1979, Experiment 1). Before introducing the partial irreversibility hypothesis, Solomon never compared the effects of a moderate UCS with his traumatic shock level. Brush (1957) conducted the appropriate study in Solomon's laboratory. Shock intensity was found not to be the key variable responsible for the extreme avoidance maintenance. Rather, the key variable appears to be related to the use of a very noisy drop gate which both added to the CS complex and blocked intertrial response. When the drop gate wasn't used, animals extinguished even with the use of traumatic shock (see Brush, 1957; Church, Brush & Solomon, 1956).

Stampfl's Extension of the Conservation of Anxiety Hypotheses

The conservation part of Solomon and Wynne's hypotheses refers to the notion that the avoidance response prevents full exposure to the CS and that the part of the CS that is unexposed is thus protected from fear extinction. Stampfl reasoned from his observations of human symptom maintenance that the neurotic paradox could be conceptually understood by developing the conservation of anxiety hypothesis. The traumatic conditioning events maintaining human symptomology are assumed to occur to a complex set of cues that are presumably ordered sequentially in order of their aversive loading and in terms of their accessibility to reactivation. It would follow that if short-latency avoidance responses conserved the fear to longer CS segments by preventing their exposure, then the process of conservation could be maximized even further by dividing the CS–UCS interval into distinctive stimulus components. This procedure should, in turn, enhance the conservation of anxiety effects by reducing the generalization of extinction effects from a short CS exposure to a long CS exposure. For example, consider the presentation of a 18-sec CS–UCS interval in which the first 6 sec of the CS involve the presentation of a buzzer (S1), the next 6 sec involve the presentation of flashing lights (S2) and the last segment, the presentation of a tone (S3). Once avoidance responding is firmly established to the S1 component, S2 and S3 are prevented from exposure. The conservation of anxiety to the S2 and S3 components should be maximized because any extinction effects from exposure to the S1 component would be unlikely to produce generalization of extinction effects to the remaining unexposed segment of the CS–UCS interval when the remaining cues in the segment are highly dissimilar to the exposed part of the interval. The greater the reduction in generalization of extinction from the early exposed part of the CS–UCS interval to the unexposed parts, the greater the degree of anxiety conservation to the components closer to UCS onset.

In principle, the use of a serial CS presentation should maximize the conservation effect and retard extinction in the following manner. Eventually exposure to the S1 component will result in sufficient extinction to produce long avoidance latencies, thus exposing the S2 component. When this occurs the level of fear activation will change from a relatively low level as elicited by the S1 component to a high state as elicited by the S2 component. The S2 component is more fear-provoking because much of the original fear level has been conserved and because the initial conditioning effects were stronger due to closer proximity to the UCS. Upon exposure of the S2 component, behavioral signs of fear should be observed. Once exposed, the S2 component is now capable of functioning as a second-order conditioning stimulus capable of reconditioning fear to the S1 component (see Rescorla, 1980). The reconditioning effect (S1–S2) should result in a return of short-latency responses to the S1 component, which in turn should preserve any further extinction of the S2 component. The reconditioning of S1 via S2 exposure should continue to occur until the S2 component's fear level has undergone a sufficient extinction effect. Responding should then be mainly under the control of S2. When fear to S2 extinguishes, S3 will be exposed and the process of reconditioning fear to S2 and S1 recurs. Thus by adding components in a serial fashion one both maximizes the conservation of anxiety hypotheses and the process of second-order conditioning, which should produce extreme resistance to extinction. The overall effect is a distribution of avoidance latencies in extinction that has a seesaw appearance (see Levis, 1979, 1989). The assumption is made that the foregoing principles are also operating at the human level.

There is support for the principle of anxiety conservation using a non-serial procedure (Delude & Carlson, 1964; Weinburger, 1965), as well as support for the enhancement of this principle through the use of a serial CS in nonhumans (Levis & Boyd, 1979; Levis & Stampfl, 1972) and in humans (Malloy & Levis, 1988). The serial CS procedure has also been shown to increase resistance to extinction (Boyd & Levis, 1976; Kostanek & Sawrey, 1965; Levis & Dubin, 1973; Levis & Stampfl, 1972; Oliverio, 1967) as well as extreme resistance to extinction (Levis, 1966a, 1966b; Levis et al., 1970; Levis & Boyd, 1979; Malloy and Levis, 1988). A serial compound procedure (S1/S1S2) has been shown to enhance the effects over a straight serial procedure (S1/S2) as has the addition of a third component (Levis, 1970; Levis et al., 1970; Levis & Stampfl, 1972). The effect is not dependent on the duration of a given component (Levis & Dubin, 1973; Levis & Stampfl, 1972) or on the increased number of stimulus onsets or offsets resulting from the use of the procedure (Levis & Boyd, 1979; Levis & Stampfl, 1972; Malloy & Levis, 1988). Thus, empirical support exists for a fear interpretation of extended maintenance of avoidance, keeping intact fear theory and the law of Pavlovian extinction (see Levis, 1989).

The Extinction of Avoidance or Symptoms

As previously discussed, the extinction of fear as the result of exposure to the CS in the absence of the UCS is retarded by the occurrence of an instrumental response that prevents full CS exposure. It follows logically that the extinction of both fear and the instrumental avoidance response would be facilitated by exposing the subject to the total CS complex. In the laboratory this can be achieved by directly preventing or blocking the occurrence of the avoidance response, by permitting the response to occur without CS termination, or by delaying the occurrence of the response until after full per-trial CS exposure. Each of these procedural manipulations has been shown to facilitate the extinction both of fear and avoidance (Baum, 1970; Shipley, 1974; Shipley, Mock, & Levis, 1971).

Despite strong empirical support for the CS exposure hypothesis, the position has been challenged. For example, it has been suggested that the use of a response prevention procedure does not lead to the extinction of fear but only to the development of "freezing" responses which are directly incompatible to the avoidance response (Coulter, Riccio, & Page, 1969). However, when direct measurement of incompatible responses is made with concurrent measures of fear both processes have been shown to be operating. Further work indicates that the extinction of fear is the more important factor (e.g., Levis, 1989; Shipley et al., 1971).

Other investigators have also questioned the relationship between extinction of fear and avoidance as viewed from two-factor theory (e.g., Kamin, Brimer & Black, 1963; Seligman & Johnston, 1973); but, as illustrated herein, a careful analysis raises more concerns about the validity of the criticisms than about fear theory. For example, Seligman and Johnston (1973) noted that one of Solomon's dogs responded for 490 extinction trials without showing any signs of extinction, and some other dogs were still making short-latency responses when stopped after 200 extinction trials. After making the point that avoidance responses are highly resistant to extinction, Seligman and Johnston argued that the extinction of fear, on the other hand, is rapid. To support this latter point, they quoted Annau and Kamin's (1961) study which reported that rats exposed to a classical fear-conditioning procedure showed signs of fear extinction within 40 CS alone trials following acquisition with high levels of shock. Based on this disparity between studies, Seligman and Johnston concluded that fear to the CS had extinguished in the Solomon studies long before the avoidance responding was terminated. This conclusion provided the basic rationale for the dismissal of fear-theory and the development of their cognitive "expectancy" theory.

Unfortunately, Seligman and Johnston failed to consider in their comparison the issue of total CS exposure. CS exposure varies considerably between an avoidance paradigm where full per trial CS exposure is prevented on each response trial and a classical conditioning extinction procedure in which full CS exposure is given on each trial. Assuming the average response latency for Solomon's dogs was around 2 sec, total CS exposure for an animal that responded to 500 trials would be 1,000 sec. Total CS exposure for complete extinction in the Annau and Kamin study was 40 trials times a 60-sec exposure period per trial, equaling 2,400 sec. Thus, when total CS exposure is considered a different picture emerges, leading one to conclude that fear was present throughout avoidance responding in the Solomon studies and that for extinction of avoidance to occur more CS exposure was needed (see Levis & Boyd, 1979). Other attempts to modify or make exceptions to the principle of experimental extinction, such as partial irreversibility, automatization, and CS incubation, have yet to generate the empirical support necessary to be considered a serious challenge (see Levis, 1985; Levis & Boyd, 1979).

If the extinction of fear is a function of repeated CS exposure, then it follows that the established laboratory procedures for facilitating this effect may be effective in the treatment of human psychopathology. CS exposure is a common link binding all psychotherapeutic procedures. What makes implosive therapy unique is the theoretical assumption that CS exposure and subsequent emotional extinction is the key variable in producing symptom removal. It follows from this orientation that with each occurrence of a patient's symptom some extinction is taking place due to partial CS exposure. This leads to the prediction that remission of symptoms is especially noted in those cases in which the patient's avoidance is only partly effective in preventing CS exposure, which appears to be the case for depression and pervasive anxiety (see Boyd & Levis, 1980; Hare & Levis, 1981; Levis, 1980b, 1987). A change in the stimuli that elicit symptom onset should also occur over time and reflect the process of CS extinction. Similarly, changes in the patient's response pattern should occur when new conflicts emerge and when the existing symptom ceases to function as an effective CS terminator.

To obtain a complete extinction effect, repeated exposure is needed not only to the CS cues directly correlated with symptom onset but also to all the cues reactivated by the exposure procedure and associated with the traumatic conditioning events. However, for symptom reduction or removal to occur it is not essential that all the conditioned stimuli comprising the total CS complex motivating a given symptom be presented by the therapist or that their presentation be completely accurate. Extinction effects occurring from exposure to a given set of cues should generalize to other CS cues not exposed, as a function of stimulus similarity. This is the reverse process to that taking place during fear acquisition. However, it is important that extinction effects are obtained to those cues with the greatest affective loading. Finally, it follows that the speed of extinction is enhanced when stronger per-trial emotional responses are obtained to the exposed CS complex (see Levis, 1980a, 1985).

The technique of implosive therapy is based primarily on a single principle, that of direct experimental extinction. The task of the therapist is to extinguish fear to the conditioned aversive CS complexes that provide the motivation for symptom occurrence and maintenance. This can be achieved by representing, reinstating, or symbolically reproducing in the absence of physical pain (UCS) the previously conditioned cues motivating the patient's symptomatology. In those cases in which the CS patterns being avoided involve discrete external stimuli, *in vivo* exposure to these cues has been found to be very effective (Levis & Boyd, 1985; Levis & Hare, 1977). Such *in vivo* CS exposure should function as an activator of other internally coded cues. If pathology is not severe, sufficient generalization of extinction effects from exposure to the *in vivo* cue may be sufficient to reduce symptom behavior. However, in those cases in which the conditioning history is severe or the symptom-eliciting cues are primarily internal, the therapist can introduce these avoided cues by using an imagery technique.

The use of an imagery procedure is especially needed for the presentation of those internal cues associated with the neural representation of specific past conditioning events involving pain and punishment. Through verbal instruction to imagine, scenes incorporating various stimuli (visual, auditory, tactual) hypothesized to be linked to the original conditioning events are represented to the patient. The technique is an operational procedure in that confirmation of a suspected cue area is determined by whether the presentation of the material elicits a strong emotional response. According to theory, cues that elicit negative affect in imagery do so because of previous learning and thus are extinguishable through repetition. Images function solely as CSs; the same is true for all thoughts or memories.

The technique used is a feedback approach and analogous to the situation in which an experimenter is given the task of extinguishing a rat's avoidance behavior but is not told what CS the rat was conditioned to (e.g., a 4-KHz tone). Although there is an indefinite number of possible CSs that could have been used to condition the rat, knowledge of the avoidance literature should increase the probability of finding the right CS. A smart experimenter would start to introduce in a systematic way a variety of stimuli known to be used with rats, such as lights, buzzers, and tones. If signs of fear or avoidance behavior occur when the probe stimulus is introduced, support for the preconditioning of this stimulus is obtained. The stronger the overt response the greater the support. Let us assume by a process of elimination, the experimenter determines that a 8-KHz tone is the CS, since its presentation elicits a strong emotional response. By presenting the tone selected over and over, the experimenter is now able to extinguish the emotional response to the tone. Note that because of the generalization of extinction effects precise accuracy is not necessary. Repeated presentation of an 8-KHz tone should effectively weaken the eliciting tendencies of a 4-KHz tone. This is basically the strategy employed by the implosive therapy (Stampfl, 1970).

The foregoing description represents only a cursory overview of the Implosive procedure (see Levis, 1980a, for a more detailed presentation). The intent of this brief description is not to make converts but to provide an outline of the method that produced the clinical material to be discussed. By paying close attention to the patient's reported associations to the scenes presented and incorporating these associations into additional scenes, a chain of associations is produced that appear to reflect an actual memory. The activation of one memory appears to elicit associations with another memorial event. Presenting new cues from the last set of associations elicits a second memory and more associations and so on, until exposure of the conditioning history is complete.

CLINICAL OBSERVATIONS

The clinical observations to be described and the conclusions reached are based on 25 years of therapeutic experience by this writer in dealing with a wide range of psychopathological behaviors. My most startling discoveries have come within the last 5 years following a refinement of the memory-reactivating component of the implosive procedure. Many of these findings have yet to be reported and, if borne out by others, should result in a major rethinking of current conceptualization and treatment strategies. At first, these observations were difficult to believe but when they repeatedly occurred within and across a variety of different cases, even in cases where such material was not suspected, they could not be dismissed as fantasy. The implosive technique, which elicited these associations and the accompanying intense emotional reactions, is based on principles of memory reactivation established by experimental psychologists (e.g., Spear, 1978). The reactivation process appears lawful in that the decoding process seems similar across patients. Despite the independent confirmation of the validity of some of these reported traumatic memories, it should be clearly understood from the start that the intent is not to convince anyone of the scientific validity of these observations and resulting conclusions. Case material does not represent, nor can it be a substitute for, experimental validation or controlled observation. Rather, the intent is to focus the reader on the importance of such observations in advancing theory, developing new hypotheses, and facilitating new discoveries.

Origins of Psychopathology

As I gained experience with the direct extinction approach of implosive therapy, it became apparent that the scenes presented to the patient resulted in their reporting strange and puzzling associations. These associations appeared disjointed and unconnected to the material presented. When these associations were reintroduced into the scene being described or when simply represented by themselves, they elicited other more puzzling associations. By repeating this process, these disjointed associations eventually came together in what appeared to be a stored memory of a traumatic conditioning event. As each new component of the memory was reactivated, an increase in affect was exhibited, which at times reached a very high level of responding when the key components of the memory were recovered. Although the level of emotional responding could become unbelievably strong, completion of the memory produced considerable relief and repetition of the material led to an orderly extinction of affect and to the reporting of greater detail. As the apparent memory was reconstructed and repeated, new associations occurred which appeared not to be a part of the memory being decoded. Continual exposure to these new associations led to the reactivation of another, even more anxiety-eliciting memory, and so on. It appears in case after case that the key factor in linking associations is the principle of stimulus similarity.

For example, a patient reported seeing a white field in imagery whenever she closed her eyes. When asked to focus on the white field she reported seeing a white table. Continued focus led to seeing a bottle on the table and hearing a background noise which sounded like people talking. She also smelled alcohol. With each new association, the patient manifested more intense signs of emotional responding, reporting that she was very frightened. By repeating this process and encouraging the patient to confront the feared stimuli, the memory was fully recovered. According to the patient, she was around 4 or 5 years of age, a factor determined by having her focus on the height of the table in relationship to her size (eye-level of table). The white field represented the color of the wall, table, and flooring. When the visual image appeared in focus, she described herself as being in a hallway. She was puzzled at first because her childhood home did not have a white hallway. With repeated focus, she recalled that her parents had a summer cottage with such a white hallway. She appeared very surprised, she had forgotten about this cottage which she had visited each summer for many years. The noise she heard turned out to be a party her parents were having in an adjoining room. Both parents were alcoholics and would take great delight in forcing the child to drink some of their beer. This memory was activated when in the middle of the scene the patient started to gag and reported smelling a heavy odor of alcohol. The hallway memory involved an uncle who inserted a beer bottle into her vagina. This memory, which is one of the least aversive memories recovered, represents only 1 of more than 50 different traumatic events the patient has recovered from memory. She was sexually and physically abused by her uncle as well as by both her mother and father. Twice, when she became pregnant, her parents aborted the fetus. She was subjected to unbelievable punishment on a regular basis, including slashed and having various objects such as a knife inserted into her vagina. Her father would subject the patient to ritualistic sadistic sexual encounters, sometimes accompanied by the uncle, and at other times in the presence of siblings. Her mother would burn and punish her regularly, and on more than one occasion the patient was so severely beaten she almost died. Memories of being treated in a hospital for these injuries also were recovered. Her brother has been hospitalized a number of times for self-inflicted cutting behavior.

Although severe traumatic conditioning cases such as the foregoing have been reported in the literature, what has been discovered with the implosive procedure is that *such cases are the rule, not the exception.* I am finding this type of severe sadistic physical and sexual abuse to have occurred in a vast majority of patients I see independent of their presenting problems. These events, in a large number of cases, have been completely "blocked out" or disassociated.

Such traumatic memories do not come back in a descriptive sequence but rather in a fragmented and disjointed manner. Repetition of the disjointed fragments is the key to bringing the complete memory into focus. The various sensory components of the memory seem to return in an orderly, lawful sequence with physical sensation (e.g., a sensation of pain in the genital area) occurring first followed by visual flashes, auditory or odor stimuli involving contextual cues or a key component of the memory such as the visualization of a knife or a clothes hanger. The patient appears to be reliving the event as if it were happening. Voice and language changes are common and appear to reflect the childhood period of the memory. The reporting of physical pain in the body area which was injured almost always occurs during the memory. Full visualization is only achieved after the affect being experienced undergoes extinction. A component of the memory, usually a contextual cue, is also correlated with a similar cue in the patient's life that is associated with a presenting symptom. With affective deconditioning of the memory, the symptom drops out. Therapeutic experience clearly supports the contention that the recovery of the memory does not necessarily change symptom behavior. Self-understanding and insight, which are partly correlated with emotional extinction and memory recovery, are not sufficient for removing symptomatology. Support from the therapist, although important in helping motivate the patient to continue the process of memory recovery, is also not directly tied to symptom reduction. Rather, it is clear clinically that symptom reduction occurs only when the intense affect associated with memorial cues undergoes extinction through the innocuous repetition of these cues. That is to say, Pavlovian extinction appears to be the corrective therapeutic change agent.

Since the patient recovers these traumatic memories in fine detail, it seems that memory loss is minimal. Furthermore, there appears to be a direct relationship between the strength of the conditioning sequence and the ability of the biological system to defend against a reactivation of the memorial event. Defense mechanisms, especially the mechanism of disassociation, seem to play a major role in preventing the deconditioning and reactivation of these traumatic memories. It appears that this disassociative reaction can produce complete amnesia, similar to that frequently reported following the physical trauma associated with a severe car accident.

Memorially Reactivated Physical Symptoms

One of the most interesting discoveries with the implosive technique is the finding that, as the decoding process is unfolding, the patient will often report experiencing a physical symptom. Examples of such symptoms include a heavy weight on the chest, a sore arm, bumps on the genital area, severe pain in the lower abdomen, a burning sensation in the vagina or anal area, vomiting, severe stomach cramps, difficulty in breathing, blood discharge from the vagina, and involuntary body spasms. At first, the patient sees no connection between the occurrence of the physical symptom and the therapy. By having the patient focus on these symptoms a memory is reactivated in which the contents reveal the prior administration of pain to the body area currently experiencing pain. For example, a patient reported the appearance of bumps or sores on the outside and inside of her genital area. Medical examination could not determine what these marks were and futher laboratory tests were ordered. Upon reporting this occurrence to the therapist, a scene was developed in which the patient was asked to visualize these sores and focus on the pain. A number of associations were produced and incorporated into the scene as the memory was fully decoded. The elicited memory revealed that the mother discovered her daughter (patient) had had sex with her husband, stripped her naked, and then forced her to sit in a chair for a very long period. The mother periodically came into the room where the patient was being punished and grabbed and pulled her skin both around and inside the vaginal area. She repeated this process over and over again, screaming at the patient for loving her father and not her and for enjoying his penis. Photographs of the patient's bumps on her body were consistent with the type of marks reportedly produced by the mother's sadistic activities. Once the full memory was recovered and the accompanying emotional affect extinguished by repeating the memory, the physical symptoms disappeared as quickly as they materialized. This finding was true for each of the other symptoms noted above.

Physical symptoms also occur during the therapeutic process itself and usually precede the visual image of a recovered event. For example, patients will start choking and coughing, reporting that they can't breathe during a scene which is followed by a memory of having been choked. Or a patient will double up with stomach pains when they are close to remembering being kicked or struck in this area. It appears that the encoded trauma includes a memory of the pain inflicted and is a critical part of the CS complex that is in need of extinction. Dramatic therapeutic changes always occur once the affect to all the cues associated with the memory, including the memory of pain, are extinguished.

The Hidden Cue

Once the memory reactivation process starts, the activation of one memory leads to the next and so on. But what was not realized until considerable experience was gained with this technique was that the patient's associative movement from one memory to another was also, in a sense, avoidance behavior. What initially appeared to be a completed memory rarely was. Imbedded within each memory were "hidden" cues encapsulating extremely intense levels of conditioned affect. For example, one patient reported feeling very guilty about her seductive sexual behavior. This feeling was triggered by a partial memory being reactivated. The memory, which took a number of repetitions to complete, occurred around age 5. The patient's father had her dress up in one of her best outfits, including a pair of patent-leather shoes. Interestingly, prior to starting this particular scene the patient reported having visual flashes of these shoes. After she was properly dressed, the father took her to a restaurant where he was employed. After closing the restaurant, one customer remained (this individual turned out to be her father's father). Her father than asked her to dance on the counter top for her grandfather, and at one point he told her to kiss him. This memory elicited feelings of seductiveness, shame, and humiliation. The patient reported remembering she intentionally tried to make her father jealous by paying attention to the grandfather. The scene was repeated a number of times until the strong emotional conflicts elicited by the scene started to extinguish.

　　Throughout the memory recovery, the patient displayed a high level of emotional reactivation which did not seem commensurate with the material elicited. Further, the patient could not get the patent-leather shoes out of her thoughts; the image of these shoes seemed to elicit a strong emotional reaction. Since we had already uncovered a large number of other traumatic memories of severe physical and sexual abuse by both parents, the strong reactions to this scene seemed puzzling. Scene repetition added important details but nothing of a serious traumatic nature. Then the patient reported that she was having severe cramps in the lower abdomen, which forced her to seek medical attention. She also reported other new symptoms, such as periodic bleeding from the vagina and severe rectal pain. The scene was again repeated with stomach cramps as an added cue. A stairwell appeared in the patient's image and a new memory emerged. Apparently she had been taken down to the basement of the restaurant, stripped of her clothes except for her shoes, and placed on a wooden cutting block. After money passed from the grandfather to the father, the patient was exposed to a variety of sexual abuses. At one point, the father inserted a large beef bone into her vagina, causing great pain. Both men were laughing at this. Her legs were spread and held up in the air. Apparently to reduce the physical pain she concentrated on her patent-leather shoes. The patient reported seeing and feeling her father alternating the insertion of the bone and his penis, while the other man forced his penis into her mouth. In the middle of the scene, the patient appeared to be shivering violently which at first appeared to be the effects of anxiety. However, as the memory unfolded, the patient saw herself fighting back. She kicked her father and bit the man's penis. This led to her being severely punished, which resulted in unbearable pain, including being forced to have both oral and anal sex. Her arms were twisted until she verbalized to both men how much she loved them. After they had violently attacked her, they threw her into a freezer where they told her they were going to leave her to die. Thus, the shivering noted earlier appears to have been an anticipatory response to the freezer memory. During the same memory, the patient reported that her left hand was cold (it was, and measured a 10-degree difference in temperature from her right hand). She later remembered her left hand got frozen to the floor of the refrigerator. It is not uncommon for physical sensations such as these to precede the memory of the traumatic event.

This memory was followed by yet another memory involving additional pain administered by the patient's mother when the child was returned home and found to be bleeding from the vagina. In the process of cleaning the patient's wounds, the mother intentionally inflicted more pain, blaming the child for not calling her and telling her what was happening.

Clearly this type of material is difficult to comprehend and believe. Yet, for this patient, and for most patients, other events just as traumatic occur throughout the many years of "hell" with the parents, as recovered memories during therapy indicate. Remember, these memories do not at first come back in a descriptive order but in fragments and pieces. The patient eventually puts them together in sequence once sufficient affect is extinguished. During this process critical cues will flash in like a bone, a knife, or a pair of shoes. Focusing on these cues leads to the recovery of new segments. Finally, it should be noted that at the point of intense pain, patients frequently report either a visual or auditory hallucination or that their mind has separated from their body. I believe these sensations occurred at the time of original trauma and represent a natural defense against the intense pain.

A careful analysis of the patient's current symptoms often provides excellent leads to what might have happened historically. For example, consider the case of a patient who periodically cut her shoulder with a razor blade. A memory was eventually reactivated in which the patient, following a rape experience with her father, threatened him by saying she would tell her mother. The father, upon hearing this threat, went into the bathroom, got a razor blade, came back and told the patient if she ever said a word about this to anyone he would cut out her tongue. To prove that his threat was serious, he cut the patient on the right shoulder. Following the recovery of this memory, the patient opened her eyes and said in surprise "Oh my God, I could never understand why, since I am right handed, I used my left hand to cut my right shoulder." It should be noted at this point that such "emotional insights," drawing a connection between a recovered memory and a symptom, frequently occur but that such "insights" appear to have little effect on modifying the symptoms. Rather, the key to symptom removal is the complete extinction of the affect associated with the memories driving the symptom. Further, once the process of memory recovery has occurred, any attempt by the therapist to alter scene content either through suggestion or false hypotheses has no effect. Patients regularly correct you if the cues suggested were not part of their memory. It appears the process of recovery has a life of its own.

To date, I have collected detailed verbatim notes and tape recordings of a variety of reactivated traumatic material similar to what has been reported. This material could fill volumes. These traumatic experiences are not only common but are believed to be the main reason people develop clinical symptoms. They appear across nosologies, and in many cases the patient upon entering therapy reports having no memory of such events. Further, in a number of cases, the patient's clinical picture does not suggest the occurrence of such a traumatic history. This may help explain why the clinical field has generated so many different theories and techniques to explain and treat psychopathology.

If the observations obtained from the memory reactivation component of the implosive procedure are correct, and a growing body of data within the sexual abuse field suggest this may be the case, then the implications for theory and treatment are clear-cut. Psychopathology is a direct result of a large number of severe traumatic conditioning events, the memories of which are avoided. Symptoms develop to avoid being exposed to the affective component of these memories or other parts of the avoided CS complex. The process of emotional responding is under the control of the autonomic nervous system; cognitive factors only play a role when functioning as protective defenses or as representing cues in the CS complex. Thus, according to this analysis, cognitive and "insight" approaches that fail to deal with the patient's emotional history represent little more than mental exercises. Rather, the solution to understanding and treating human suffering of this type requires a conditioning interpretation and a corresponding expansion of knowledge in the area of emotional learning.

IMPLICATIONS FOR LABORATORY RESEARCH

It should be clear from this analysis that previous attempts to establish a model of experimental neurosis in the laboratory represent merely a starting point. It also seems that critics of a conditioning interpretation have insufficient appreciation of the factors responsible for developing and maintaining psychopathology. For example, Mineka (1985) argues that most phobias are acquired through one-trial traumatic conditioning and that only a few laboratory studies have ever demonstrated one-trial fear conditioning. My clinical experience, and for that matter that of many others, suggests that hundreds of conditioning trials are involved in the development of psychopathology. I have yet to find a single clinical case where only one-trial learning occurred. This is not to suggest that one-trial learning cannot occur. In fact, I believe it regularly does occur and can easily be shown in the nonhuman laboratory. Analysis of our own one-way avoidance learning data suggest about a third of the animals learned to avoid in one trial. The point being made, however, is that patients who show signs of clinical psychopathology have typically been subjected to more than one traumatic conditioning trial involving more than one emotional drive state. If only one trial were involved, symptom maintenance would most likely show clear signs of weakening over time from repeated CS exposure, just as our nonhuman subjects do (Levis & Boyd, 1979). Symptom maintenance occurs and is highly resistant to extinction precisely because there were numerous conditioning trials involving a host of different emotional states and CS complexes. *It is the avoidance of a large number of CS complexes that maintain symptomatology over time.*

In the same article, Mineka (1985) states that patients go to great lengths to avoid the phobic stimulus whereas attempts in the laboratory to train animals to avoid the CS have failed. One can take issue with the latter point on a number of grounds, such as referring to the passive avoidance literature, but arguments about the differences between the human and nonhuman literature will continue until more creative research is conducted. For example, Stampfl (1987) achieved this objective in an ingenious nonhuman experiment in which he combined the principle of secondary intermittent reinforcement which was maximized by the sequential ordering of conditioning stimuli with the law of least effort by using a work requirement and a time-out manipulation. This combination of variables yielded evidence for one-trial fear and avoidance learning, the complete avoidance of the "phobic" CS, and truly persistent avoidance responding (thousands of trials). Stampfl's work represents an excellent start on developing a working model of agoraphobia.

By combining the principle of secondary intermittent reinforcement (Levis & Boyd, 1979) with the principle of primary intermittent reinforcement (McAllister et al., 1986) and adding the escape from work principle (Stampfl, 1987), an even more powerful avoidance paradigm should be attainable. The addition of a more aversive UCS and the conditioning of drive states in conflict could approach even closer what is observed at the human level. The content of a human patient's memories typically involves severe physical and sexual abuse, combined with a variety of emotional conflicts, including feelings of intense fear, rage, loss of control, guilt, humiliation, abandonment, and isolation. I contend that each of these emotional states can be analyzed in terms of an S–R paradigm and can be reproduced with nonhuman subjects. Most of these emotions involve a conflict paradigm, an area of nonhuman research that has stimulated little recent interest. Amsel's work (1967, 1972) on frustration and persistence made an excellent start in establishing the principles of understanding this emotion in humans. But for the most part, the study of various drive states in conflict, especially combining the sexual drive with fear and punishment, still represents a largely untapped, yet potentially fruitful area.

The central point being made is that, in the laboratory, we have only just begun to study the combination of principles responsible for creating and maintaining human psychopathology; numerous creative new paradigms could be developed. The main purpose would be to provide a working model of nonhuman psychopathology in order to isolate the basic principles involved and determine effective treatment strategies. The attainment of this goal is critical because manipulations made at the nonhuman level are often not possible or easily assessed at the human level.

The potential for such extrapolation, can be illustrated by reference to the clinical literature that shows that physically abused children tend to abuse their children. My experience suggests that this repeated cycle is due to the abuser's blocking out painful memories of his or her past by engaging in abuse. To be more specific, the abused child's behavior is frequently similar to behavior the abuser was punished for. In theory, this similarity could reactivate part of the avoided memory of the abuser's past which involves cues associated with fear, pain, frustration, anger, and rejection. To avoid any further reactivation, the abuser attempts to stop the child's behavior in order to suppress his or her own traumatic memories. In addition, the child's objectionable behavior can function as a cue for the abuser's pent-up anger (frustration analysis), which in turn reactivates feelings of out of control rage that are vented on the child.

From such an analysis it would seem possible to develop a paradigm in which a young rat is severely punished by an older rat for engaging in an instrumental act. After the abused rat reached adulthood, it could be tested by being exposed to a young rat engaged in the same behavior for which the adult had been previously punished. If it can be shown that the previously abused rat will differentially punish the younger rat's behavior over a controlled adult rat, we may be able to develop a paradigm to study child abuse. Whether or not this example is obtainable, efforts in this area as well as others, should lead to the development of important contributions. By analyzing complex human behavior into an S–R framework, the seed has been sown for developing creative laboratory models.

Whether one's interest is in the area of avoidance learning, punishment, conflict, memory reactivation, or autonomic conditioning, the potential for creating functional paradigms in these areas to help solve the riddles of human psychopathology is immense. But the time is short. In the age of specialization, only a handful of psychologists are left who have both clinical experience and knowledge of the learning literature. The belief that psychopathology is an emotional disorder that can be more fully understood by controlled laboratory research is in need of your support. Collaborate with us and return the area of animal learning to its proper place—the scientific forefront in the quest to understand and help the most destructive and the most suffering animal of all, the Homo sapiens.

REFERENCES

Alexander, F. (1965). The dynamics of psychotherapy in the light of learning theory. *International Journal of Psychiatry, 1,* 189–197.

Amsel, A. (1958). The role of frustration nonreward in noncontinuous reward situations. *Psychological Bulletin, 55,* 102–119.

Amsel, A. (1962). Frustrative nonreward in partial-reinforcement and discrimination learning: Some recent history and a theoretical extension. *Psychological Review, 69,* 306–328.

Amsel, A. (1967). Partial reinforcement effects on vigor and persistance: Advances in frustration theory derived from a variety of within-subject experiments. In K. W. Spence & J. T. Spence (Eds.), *The psychology of learning and motivation, (Vol. 1).* New York: Academic Press.

Amsel, A. (1972). A behavioral habituation, counter-conditioning and a general theory of persistence. In A. H. Black & W. F. Prokasy (Eds.), *Classical conditioning II.* New York: Appleton–Century–Crofts.

Amsel, A., & Rashotte, M. E. (1984). *Mechanisms of adaptive behavior: Clark L. Hull's theoretical papers with commentary.* New York: Columbia University Press.

Annau, Z., & Kamin, L. J. (1961). The conditioned emotional response as a function of intensity of the US. *Journal of Comparative and Physiological Psychology, 54,* 428–430.

Balsam, P. D., & Tomie, A. (Eds.) (1985). *Context and learning.* Hillsdale, N.J.; Erlbaum.

Baum, M. (1970). Extinction of avoidance responding through response prevention (flooding). *Psychological Bulletin, 74,* 276–284.

Bolles, R. C. (1970). Species-specific defense reactions and avoidance learning. *Psychological Review, 77,* 32–48.

Boyd, T. L., & Levis, D. J. (1976). The effects of single-component extinction of a three-component serial CS on resistance to extinction of the conditioned avoidance response. *Learning and Motivation, 7,* 517–531.

Boyd, T. L., & Levis, D. J. (1979). The interactive effects of shuttlebox situational cues and shock intensity. *The American Journal of Psychology, 92,* 120–123.

Boyd, T. L., & Levis, D. J. (1980). Depression. In R. J. Dartzman (Ed.), *Clinical behavior therapy and behavior modification, Volume 1.* New York: Garland STPM Press.

Brown, J. S. (1961). *The motivation of behavior.* New York: McGraw-Hill.

Brown, J. S. (1965). A behavioral analysis of masochism. *Journal of Experimental Research in Personality, 1,* 65–70.

Brown, J. S., & Farber, I. E. (1951). Emotions conceptualized as intervening variables—with suggestions toward a theory of frustration. *Psychological Bulletin, 48,* 465–495.

Brown, J. S., & Farber, I. E. (1958). Secondary motivational systems. *Annual Review of Psychology, 19,* 99–134.

Brush, F. R. (1957). The effect of shock intensity on the acquisition and extinction of an avoidance response in dogs. *Journal of Comparative and Physiological Psychology, 50,* 547–552.

Church, R. M., Brush, F. R., & Solomon, R. L. (1956). Traumatic avoidance learning: The effects of CS-US interval with a delayed-conditioning procedure in a free responding situation. *Journal of Comparative and Physiological Psychology, 49,* 301–308.

Coulter, X., Riccio, D. C., & Page, H. A. (1969). Effects of blocking an instrumental avoidance response: Facilitated extinction but persistence of "fear". *Journal of Comparative and Physiological Psychology, 68,* 377–381.

Delude, L. A., & Carlson, N. J. (1964). A test of the conservation of anxiety and partial irreversibility hypothesis. *Canadian Journal of Psychology, 18,* 15–22.

Dinsmoor, J. A. (1950). A quantitative comparison of the discriminative and reinforcing functions of a stimulus. *Journal of Experimental Psychology, 41,* 458–472.

Dinsmoor, J. A. (1983). Observing and conditioned reinforcement. *Behavioral and Brain Sciences, 6,* 693–72.

Dollard, J., & Miller, N. E. (1950). *Personality and psychotherapy.* New York: McGraw-Hill.

Eysenck, H. J. (Ed.). (1960). *Behaviour therapy and the neuroses.* New York: Pergamon Press.

Eysenck, H. J. (1968). A theory of the incubation of anxiety/fear responses. *Behaviour Research and Therapy, 6,* 309–322.

Eysenck, H. J. (1976). The learning theory model of neurosis—a new approach. *Behaviour Research and Therapy, 14,* 251–267.

Freud, S. (1936). The problem of anxiety. (H. A. Bunker, Trans.), New York: Norton.

Freud, S. (1938). The psychopathology of everday life. In *The basic writings of Sigmund Freud.* New York: Random House.

Gray, J. A. (1975). *Elements of a two-process theory of learning.* New York: Academic Press.

Guthrie, E. R. (1938). *The psychology of human conflict.* New York: Harper & Row.

Hare, N., & Levis, D. J. (1981). Pervasive ("Free-Floating") anxiety: A search for a cause and treatment approach. In S. Turner, K. Calhoun and H. Adams (Eds.), *Handbook of clinical behavior therapy.* New York: John Wiley and Sons, Inc.

Herrnstein, R. (1969). Method and theory in the study of avoidance. *Psychological Review, 76,* 49–69.

Hilgard, E. R., & Marquis, P. G. (1940). *Conditioning and learning.* New York: Appleton-Century.

Hull, C. L. (1930). Simple trial and error learning: A study in psychological theory. *Psychological Review, 37,* 241–256.

Hull, C. L. (1931). Goal attraction and directing ideas conceived as habit phenomena. *Psychological Review, 38,* 487–506.

Hunt, H. F. (1964). Problems in the interpretation of experimental neurosis. *Psychological Reports, 15*, 27–35.

Kalish, H. I. (1981). *From behavioral science to behavior modification*. New York: McGraw Hill.

Kamin, L. J., Brimer, C. J., & Black, A. H. (1963). Conditioned suppression as a monitor of fear of the CS in the course of avoidance training. *Journal of Comparative and Physiological Psychology, 56*, 497–501.

Kimble, G. A. (1961). *Hilgard & Marques' Conditioning and learning*. New York: Appleton–Century–Crofts, Inc.

Kimble, G. A., & Perlmuter, L. C. (1970). The problem of volition. *Psychological Review, 77*, 361–384.

Kostanek, D. J., & Sawrey, J. M. (1965). Acquisition and extinction of shuttlebox avoidance with complex stimuli. *Psychonomic Science, 3*, 369–370.

Levis, D. J. (1966a). Effects of serial CS presentation and other characteristics of the CS on the conditioned avoidance response. *Psychological Reports, 18*, 755–766.

Levis, D. J. (1966b). Implosive therapy, Part II: The subhuman analogue, the strategy, and the technique. In S. G. Armitage's (Ed.), *Behavioral modification techniques in the treatment of emotional disorders*. Battle Creek, MI: V. A. Hospital Publications, pp. 22–37.

Levis, D. J. (1970). Behavioral therapy: The fourth therapeutic revolution? In D. J. Levis (Ed.), *Learning approaches to therapeutic behavior change*. Chicago: Aldine.

Levis, D. J. (1971). Short- and long-term auditory history and stimulus control in the rat. *Journal of Comparative and Physiological Psychology, 74*, 298–314.

Levis, D. J. (1980a). Implementing the technique of implosive therapy. In A. Goldstein & E. B. Foa (Eds.), *Handbook of behavioral interventions. A clinical guide*. New York: Wiley, pp. 92–151.

Levis, D. J. (1980b). The learned helplessness effect: An expectancy, discrimination deficit and motivational induced persistence? *Journal of Research in Personality, 14*, 158–169.

Levis, D. J. (1985). Implosive theory: A comprehensive extension of conditioning theory of fear/anxiety to psychopathology. In S. Reiss & R. R. Bootzin's (Eds.), *Theoretical issues in behavior therapy*. New York: Academic Press, pp. 49–82.

Levis, D. J. (1987). Treating anxiety and panic attacks: The conflict model of implosive therapy. *Journal of Integrative and Eclectic Psychotherapy, 6(4)*, 450–461.

Levis, D. J. (1988). Observation and experience from clinical practice: A critical ingredient for advancing behavior theory and therapy. *Behavior Therapist, 11(5)*, 95–99.

Levis, D. J. (1989). The case for a return to a two-factor theory of avoidance: The failure of non-fear interpretations. In S. B. Klein & R. R. Mowrer (Eds.), *Contemporary learning theories: Vol. 1. Pavlovian conditioning and the status of tradition*. Hillsdale, NJ: Lawrence Erlbaum Associates.

Levis, D. J., Bouska, S., Eron, J., & McIlhon, M. (1970). Serial CS presentation and one-way avoidance conditioning: A noticeable lack of delayed responding. *Psychonomic Science, 20*, 147–149.

Levis, D. J., & Boyd, T. L. (1979). Symptom maintenance: An infrahuman analysis and extension of the conservation of anxiety principle. *Journal of Abnormal Psychology, 88*, 107–120.

Levis, D. J., & Boyd, T. L. (1985). The CS exposure approach of Implosive Therapy. In R. McMillian Turner & L. M. Ascher (Eds.), *Evaluation of behavior therapy outcome*. New York: Springer, pp. 56–94.

Levis, D. J., & Dubin, W. J. (1973). Some parameters affecting shuttle-box avoidance responding with rats receiving serially presented conditioned stimuli. *Journal of Comparative and Physiological Psychology, 82*, 328–344.

Levis, D. J., & Hare, N. (1977). A review of the theoretical rationale and empirical support for the extinction approach of implosive (flooding) therapy. In M. Hersen, R. M. Eisler,

& P. M. Miller (Eds.). *Progress in behavior modification (Vol. 4)*. New York: Academic Press, pp. 300–376.

Levis, D. J., & Stampfl, T. G. (1972). Effects of serial CS presentation on shuttlebox avoidance responding. *Learning and Motivation, 3*, 73–90.

Liddell, H. S. (1965). The challenge of Pavlovian conditioning and experimental neuroses in animals. In J. Wolpe, A. Sulter, & L. J. Reyne (Eds.), *The conditioning therapies*. New York: Holt, Rinehart, & Winston.

McAllister, W. R., & McAllister, D. E. (1965). Variables influencing the conditioning and the measurement of acquired fear. In W. F. Prokasy (Ed.), *Classical conditioning: A symposium*. New York: Appleton–Century–Crofts.

McAllister, W. R., & McAllister, D. E. (1971). Behavioral measurement of conditioned fear. In F. R. Brush (Ed.), *Aversive conditioning and learning*. New York: Academic Press.

McAllister, W. R., McAllister, D. E., Scoles, M. T., & Hampton, S. R. (1986). Persistence of fear-reducing behavior: Relevance for conditioning theory of neurosis. *Journal of Abnormal Psychology, 93*, 365–372.

Mackintosh, N. J. (1974) *The psychology of animal learning*. New York: Academic Press.

Maier, N. R. F. (1939). *Studies of abnormal behavior in the rat*. New York: Harper.

Malloy, P., & Levis, D. J. (1988). A laboratory demonstration of persistent human avoidance. *Behavior Therapy, 19*, 229–241.

Masserman, J. H. (1943). *Behavior and neurosis*. Chicago: University of Chicago Press.

Miller, N. E. (1948). Studies of fear as an acquirable drive: I. Fear as motivation and fear-reduction as reinforcement in the learning of a new response. *Journal of Experimental Psychology, 38*, 89–101.

Miller, N. E. (1951). Learnable drives and rewards. In S. S. Stevens (Ed.), *Handbook of experimental psychology*. New York: Wiley.

Miller, N. E. (1959). Liberalization of the basic S–R concepts: Extensions to conflict behavior, motivation and social learning. In S. Koch (Ed.), *Psychology: A study of a science (Vol. 2)*. New York: McGraw–Hill.

Miller, N. E. (1964). Some implications of modern behavior theory for personality change and psychotherapy. In P. Worchel & D. Byrne's (Eds.), *Personality change*. New York: Wiley.

Miller, N. E., & Kraeling, D. (1952). Displacement: Greater generalization of approach than avoidance in generalized approach-avoidance conflicts. *Journal of Experimental Psychology, 43*, 217–221.

Mineka, S. (1985). Animal models of anxiety based disorders: The usefulness and limitations. In A. Tuma & J. Maser (Eds.), *Anxiety and anxiety disorders*. Hillsdale, NJ: Lawrence Erlbaum Associates.

Mowrer, O. H. (1939). A stimulus response analysis and its role as a reinforcing agent. *Psychological Review, 46*, 553–565.

Mowrer, O. H. (1947). On the dual nature of learning—A re-interpretation of "conditioning" and "problem-solving." *Harvard Educational Review, 17*, 102–148.

Mowrer, O. H. (1950). *Pain, punishment, guilt, and anxiety*. (pp. 27–40). New York: Grune & Stratton.

Mowrer, O. H. (1960a). *Learning theory and behavior*. New York: Wiley.

Mowrer, O. H. (1960b). *Learning theory and the symbolic processes*. New York: Wiley.

Oliverio, A. (1967). Effects of different conditioning schedules based on visual and acoustic conditioned stimulus on avoidance learning of two strains of mice. *Journal of Psychology, 65*, 131–139.

Pavlov, I. P. (1927). *Conditioned reflexes*. London: Oxford University Press.

Rescorla, R. A. (1980). Pavlovian second-order conditioning: Studies in associative learning. Hillsdale, N.J.: Lawrence Erlbaum Associates.

Rescorla, R. A., & Solomon, R. L. (1967). Two-process learning theory: Relationships between Pavlovian conditioning and instrumental learning. *Psychological Review, 74*, 151–182.

Schoenfeld, W. N. (1950). An experimental approach to anxiety, escape and avoidance behavior. In P. H. Hock & J. Zubin (Eds.), *Anxiety*. New York: Grune & Stratton.

Seligman, M. E. P. (1971). Phobias and preparedness. *Behavior Therapy, 2*, 307–321.

Seligman, M. E. P. (1975). *Helplessness: On depression, development and death*. San Francisco: W. H. Freeman.

Seligman, M. E. P., & Johnston, J. C. (1973). A cognitive theory of avoidance learning. In F. J. McGuigan & D. B. Lumsden (Eds.), *Contemporary prospectives in learning and conditioning*. Washington, DC: Scripta Press.

Shipley, R. H. (1974). Extinction of conditioned fear in rats as a function of several parameters of CS exposure. *Journal of Comparative and Physiological Psychology, 87*, 699–707.

Shipley, R. H., Mock, L. A., & Levis, D. J. (1971). Effects of several response prevention procedures on activity, avoidance responding, and conditioned fear in rats. *Journal of Comparative and Physiological Psychology, 77*, 256–270.

Skinner, B. F. (1950). Are theories of learning necessary? *Psychological Review, 57*, 193–216.

Skinner, B. F. (1953). *Science and human behavior*. New York: Macmillan.

Skinner, B. F. (1954). Critique of psychoanalytic concepts and theories. In T. Millon (Ed.), (1967), *Theories of psychopathology*. (pp 228–235). Philadelphia: Saunders. (Reprinted from *Scientific Monthly, 79*, 300–305).

Skinner, B. F. (1984). The shame of American education. *American Psychologist, 39*, 947–954.

Solomon, R. L., Kamin, L. J., & Wynne, L. C. (1953). Traumatic avoidance learning: The outcome of several extinction procedures with dogs. *Journal of Abnormal and Social Psychology, 48*, 291–302.

Solomon, R. J., & Wynne, L. C. (1953). Traumatic avoidance learning: Acquisition in normal dogs. *Psychological Monographs, 67*, No. 354, 1–19.

Solomon, R. L., & Wynne, L. C. (1954). Traumatic avoidance learning: The principle of anxiety conservation and partial irreversibility. *Psychological Review, 61*, 353–385.

Spear, N. E. (1978). *The processing of memories, forgetting and retention*. Hillsdale, NJ: Lawrence Erlbaum Associates.

Spence, K. W. (1966). Cognitive and drive factors in the extinction of the conditioned eyeblink in human subjects. *Psychological Review, 73*, 445–458.

Stampfl, T. G. (1966). Implosive therapy, Part I: The theory. In S. G. Armitage (Ed.), *Behavioral modification techniques in the treatment of emotional disorders*. Battle Creek, MI: V. A. Hospital Publications, pp. 12–21.

Stampfl, T. G. (1970). Implosive therapy: An emphasis on convert stimulation. In D. J. Levis (Ed.), *Learning approaches to therapeutic behavior change*. Chicago: Aldine.

Stampfl, T. G. (1983). Exposure treatment for psychiatrists? [Review of learning approaches to psychiatry]. *Contemporary Psychology, 28*, 527–529.

Stampfl, T. G. (1987). Theoretical implications of the neurotic paradox as a problem in behavior theory: An experimental resolution. *Behavior Analyst, 10*, 161–173.

Stampfl, T. G. (1988). The relevance of laboratory animal research to theory and practice: One-trial learning and the neurotic paradox. *Behavior Therapist, 11(4)*, 75–79.

Stampfl, T. G., & Levis, D. J. (1967). The essentials of implosive therapy: A learning-theory based psychodynamic behavioral therapy. *Journal of Abnormal Psychology, 72*, 496–503.

Stampfl, T. G., & Levis, D. J. (1969). Learning theory: An aid to dynamic therapeutic practice. In L. D. Eron & R. Callahan (Eds.), *Relationship of theory to practice in psychotherapy*. Chicago: Aldine.

Stampfl, T. G., & Levis, D. J. (1976). Implosive therapy: A behavioral therapy. In J. T. Spence, R. C. Carson, & J. W. Thibaut (Eds.), *Behavioral approaches to therapy*. Morristown, NJ: General Learning Press.

Watson, J. B. (1924). *Behaviorism*. New York: Horton.

Weinberger, N. M. (1965). Effects of detainment on extinction of avoidance responses. *Journal of Comparative and Physiological Psychology, 60*, 135–138.

Wolpe, J. (1958). *Psychotherapy by reciprocal inhibition*. Stanford, CA: Stanford University Press.

Author Index

Italics denote pages with bibliographic information.

Subject Index